Architecting ASP.NE Applications

Third Edition

An atypical design patterns guide for .NET 8, C# 12, and beyond

Carl-Hugo Marcotte

BIRMINGHAM—MUMBAI

Architecting ASP.NET Core Applications

Third Edition

Publishing Product Manager: Lucy Wan
Acquisition Editor – Peer Reviews: Gaurav Gavas
Project Editor: Rianna Rodrigues
Content Development Editor: Rebecca Youé
Copy Editor: Safis Editor
Technical Editor: Srishty Bhardwaj
Proofreader: Safis Editor
Indexer: Rekha Nair
Presentation Designer: Rajesh Shirsath
Senior Developer Relations Marketing Executive: Priyadarshini Sharma

First published: December 2020
Second published: March 2022
Third edition: March 2024

Production reference: 1150324

Published by Packt Publishing Ltd.
Grosvenor House
11 St Paul's Square
Birmingham
B3 1RB, UK.

ISBN 978-1-80512-338-5

`www.packt.com`

Foreword

I've been programming for over 20 years now. Some of those years were spent as a kid trying to build stuff for fun, but for the majority of that time I've been building software professionally. C# has been my go-to when building software systems, and I've been fortunate to work in organizations that fully embrace it (including Microsoft!).

Early on in my professional career I became a software engineering manager, and I was able to shift my efforts toward helping other software engineers become better at their craft. I've spent years working with software developers, helping to keep them engaged in their work and their learning. It's my personal mission to ensure the barrier to becoming an awesome software engineer is brought down, and C# and .NET have been excellent programming tools to assist in that journey.

Carl-Hugo Marcotte's *Architecting ASP.NET Core Applications* is fully in line with my preferred way to teach others software engineering concepts. The content in the book is organized in a way that gradually builds on programming principles as demonstrated in C#, giving readers some theory that is quickly followed by code examples. From there, learning is solidified with mini projects where readers can apply their theory immediately to something practical.

Readers that work through the content in this book should expect to build confidence in design and architectural patterns in ASP.NET Core. This will allow for building more robust and scalable systems. Having tangible and concrete code examples to refer back to every step of the way through this book is one of its greatest strengths.

The design patterns are gradually introduced with explanations regarding their purpose and guidelines for implementations. From there, they're given a practical application in ASP.NET Core. The visuals coupled with hands-on code examples and projects all play together to reinforce learning from different angles. Seeing concepts directly applied in realistic scenarios helps reinforce the pros and cons of each.

Additionally, testing approaches are built into the content of this book at every opportunity. This is a refreshing take on software engineering material where there's typically a hyper-focus on design, performance, and computer science. However, Carl-Hugo Marcotte's examples are backed by excellent testing examples that highlight how to validate the different concepts being implemented.

For software developers reading this book who are newer to developing ASP.NET Core applications, I hope that you feel more confident in your skillset by the end. For those readers that have more experience developing web applications in C#, I believe that this book will help to reinforce good design decisions and offer you some alternative perspectives on things you are already familiar with. Regardless of your prior skill level, by the end of this book, you will be positioned to build better applications.

Nick Cosentino, Principal Software Engineering Manager at Microsoft

Contributors

About the author

Carl-Hugo Marcotte is a software craftsman who has developed digital products professionally since 2005; his coding journey started around 1989 for fun. He has a bachelor's degree in computer science. He has acquired a solid background in software architecture and expertise in ASP.NET Core through creating a wide range of web and cloud applications, from custom e-commerce websites to enterprise applications. He served many customers as an independent consultant, taught programming, and is now a Principal Architect at Export Development Canada. Passionate about C#, ASP.NET Core, AI, automation, and cloud computing, he fosters collaboration and the open-source ethos, sharing his expertise with the tech community.

I want to thank everyone who has supported me throughout my career, from my mom, who bought my first computers when I was a kid, to my other half and partner in life, Cathie, who is always there no matter the idea I pursue.

About the reviewer

Davide Bellone is a backend developer with over 10 years of professional experience. Based in Italy, he's worked with Microsoft platforms and tools since 2014. He has worked with .NET Core, SQL, Azure, and more. He loves learning new things and thinks the best way to learn is to share; that's why he started his journey as a content creator and conference speaker. He's the author of Code4IT.dev, a blog for C# and Azure developers. He's honoured to be a Microsoft MVP in Developer Technologies.

About the beta reader

Kevin Viera is a software engineer passionate about software architecture and emerging technologies. He has a diverse background covering various aspects of web development and computer science. Kevin's trajectory led him through a spectrum of languages and technologies such as C++, C#, JavaScript, and Python, before he began specializing in the .NET environment.

Throughout his career, Kevin has shown a strong interest in delving into the complexities of the .NET ecosystem. He began with the Windows-only .NET Framework, progressed to the cross-platform .NET Core, and finally focused on the current .NET environment as his main career path.

Learn more on Discord

To join the Discord community for this book – where you can share feedback, ask questions to the author, and learn about new releases – follow the QR code below:

`https://packt.link/ArchitectingASPNETCoreApps3e`

Table of Contents

Chapter 2: Automated Testing 19

Chapter 4: REST APIs 109

Section 2: Designing with ASP.NET Core 133

Chapter 5: Minimal APIs 135

Chapter 6: Model-View-Controller 185

Chapter 12: Behavioral Patterns 403

Section 4: Application Patterns 463

Chapter 14: Layering and Clean Architecture 467

Chapter 15: Object Mappers 503

Chapter 17: Getting Started with Vertical Slice Architecture 583

Chapter 18: Request-EndPoint-Response (REPR) 611

Chapter 19: Introduction to Microservices Architecture 647

Chapter 20: Modular Monolith 721

Preface

Design patterns are a set of solutions to many common problems in software development. They are essential for any experienced developer and professionals crafting software solutions.

We start by exploring automated testing, architectural principles like SOLID, and REST APIs. Then we learn about basic design patterns, dependency injection, and ASP.NET Core including minimal APIs, Model-View-Controller, and options. Next, we move on to learn how to design and manage applications using patterns and techniques. We finally explore higher-level patterns and how to structure the application as a whole.

The book covers many fundamental Gang of Four (GoF) patterns, such as Strategy, Singleton, Decorator, Façade, and Composite. The chapters are organized to build up your knowledge progressively, starting small with a strong base and building slowly on top of it, the same way you would build a program. Many use cases in the book combine more than one design pattern to display alternate usage. It also aims to show you that design patterns are tools to be used, not complex concepts to be feared.

This book is a journey to learn the reasoning behind the craft. By the end of the book, you will be able to mix and match design patterns and will have learned how to think about architecture. You will explore techniques to help you create the building blocks that you need to solve your unique day-to-day design problems.

Who this book is for

This book is for intermediate-level ASP.NET Core developers who want to improve their C# code structure. ASP.NET developers who want to modernize their knowledge and enhance their technical architecture skills will also like this book. It's also a good refresher for those in software design roles with more experience looking to update their expertise.

A good knowledge of C# programming and a basic understanding of web concepts is necessary to get the most out of this book, though some refreshers are included along the way.

What this book covers

Section 1: Principles and Methodologies

This section contains the book's foundations about automated testing, including xUnit, architectural principles like **SOLID**, and how to build REST APIs.

Chapter 1, Introduction, contains the prerequisites and an explanation of how the book works as well as a few important topics that will be useful to a software developer.

Chapter 2, Automated Testing, introduces you to the basics of unit testing and the xUnit testing framework as well as to some good practices and methodologies to help write tests.

Chapter 3, Architectural Principles, lays the architectural groundwork with crucial principles used throughout the book and extremely important to any engineer trying to write SOLID code.

Chapter 4, REST APIs, outlines HTTP basics, API versioning, the Data Transfer Object (DTO) pattern, and robust API contract design for RESTful services.

Section 2: Designing with ASP.NET Core

This section introduces ASP.NET Core-specific subjects, including Minimal API, Model-View-Controller (MVC), and other classic design patterns. We cover application configuration and logging patterns, two essential building blocks. We also deep dive into dependency injection and explore the evolved usage of certain patterns as pillars of modern software engineering.

Chapter 5, Minimal APIs, introduces the streamlined approach to building .NET applications. It emphasizes the advantages of minimal hosting and Minimal APIs offered in ASP.NET Core.

Chapter 6, Model-View-Controller, introduces you to the MVC pattern, focusing on web APIs. We also look at how to apply the DTO pattern with MVC.

Chapter 7, Strategy, Abstract Factory, and Singleton Design Patterns, introduces you to the traditional implementation of three GoF design patterns: Strategy, Abstract Factory, and Singleton, which influence algorithm encapsulation, object creation, and instance control.

Chapter 8, Dependency Injection, takes the ASP.NET Core dependency injection container for a ride, introducing you to one of the most important aspects of modern software development. This chapter connects ASP.NET Core and the SOLID principles. Once the basics of dependency injection are laid out, we review the previous three GoF design patterns and revisit them using dependency injection, opening up the way to build testable, flexible, and reliable software.

Chapter 9, Application Configuration and the Options Pattern, examines how to configure ASP.NET Core applications effectively using the Options pattern, which allows for loading configurations from multiple sources and using them seamlessly in our code.

Chapter 10, Logging Patterns, analyzes .NET's built-in logging framework, detailing essentials like log levels, providers, configuring logs, and the concept of structured logging.

Section 3: Component Patterns

This section focuses on component design, where we study how an individual piece of software can be crafted to achieve a particular goal. We explore a few more GoF patterns that should help you design SOLID data structures and components as well as simplifying the complexity of your code by encapsulating your logic in smaller units.

Chapter 11, Structural Patterns, introduces four new GoF structural design patterns demonstrating how to dynamically extend class behaviors and organize object hierarchies to boost flexibility and reusability.

Chapter 12, Behavioral Patterns, introduces the Template Method and Chain of Responsibility patterns, demonstrating how to streamline system behaviors and organize complex algorithmic structures for extensibility and maintainability. The chapter concludes by mixing them together as a final improvement on the code sample's design.

Chapter 13, Operation Result Pattern, explores the Operation Result pattern, detailing how to convey the success or failure of operations with messages and values, and how to implement this approach for robust error handling and status reporting in your applications.

Section 4: Application Patterns

This section takes a step toward application design and introduces layering, vertical slice architecture, Request-EndPoint-Response, microservices architecture, and Modular Monoliths. We overview each technique, making sure you know how to get started. We also cover different component-level patterns that help put those architectural styles together, like Object Mappers, Aggregate Services, Façade, Mediator, and CQRS patterns.

Chapter 14, Layering and Clean Architecture, introduces you to layering and Clean Architecture, covering the primary objectives behind the presentation, domain, data (persistence) layers, and their clean architecture counterparts, which is the apogee of layering. It also highlights the evolution of application design in the last few decades, helping you understand where it started (the beginning of the chapter) and where it is now (the end of the chapter).

Chapter 15, Object Mappers, covers object mapping techniques (copying an object into another) to simplify the transmission of model objects between layers using manual mapping and open source tools like AutoMapper and Mapperly. The chapter also introduces organization patterns like Aggregate Services and Façade.

Chapter 16, Mediator and CQS Patterns, introduces the Command Query Separation (CQS) and Mediator patterns. After covering those two patterns, we conclude with the practical application of MediatR—an open source library—to exemplify these concepts in real-world development.

Chapter 17, Getting Started with Vertical Slice Architecture, introduces Vertical Slice Architecture. It uses a number of the previous patterns and tools that we have explored to piece together a different way to see the design of an application. It also introduces FluentValidation, which gets added to MediatR and AutoMapper.

Chapter 18, Request-EndPoint-Response (REPR), introduces the REPR pattern, a method that refines application design with HTTP alignment, demonstrating its use with Minimal APIs and imparting strategies for building feature-centric software.

Chapter 19, Introduction to Microservices Architecture, outlines the core principles of microservices, what they are, what they are not, and discusses a few related patterns. It introduces many concepts, such as event-driven communication, Gateway, and Command Query Responsibility Segregation (CQRS) patterns, equipping you to design scalable systems.

Chapter 20, Modular Monolith, discusses the balance between traditional and microservices architecture with Modular Monoliths, offering a middle ground with segregated, well-defined modules for scalable, maintainable applications. This chapter also implements event-driven patterns using MassTransit—an open source library—to handle module communication.

Appendix

The *Appendix* explores numerous C# features spanning a wide range of versions, including .NET 8 and C# 12. If you don't understand a piece of code in the book, that feature is most likely covered in the *Appendix*. Even if you understood all the code, you may find some good tips there. You can consult the *Appendix* on GitHub (`https://adpg.link/net8-appendix`).

To get the most out of this book

You must know C# and how to program. Boolean logic, loops, and other basic programming constructs should be mastered, including object-oriented programming basics. Some knowledge of ASP.NET will be beneficial. Knowing how to read UML class and sequence diagrams is an asset, but not required.

The code samples and resources are available on GitHub (`https://adpg.link/net8`). The `README.md` file at the root of the repository is filled with information to help you find the code and resources you are looking for.

Most links are shortened in the form of `https://adpg.link/****` so readers of a physical copy of the book can easily type URLs quickly.

In the book, I use a mix of Visual Studio 2022 (which has a free version) and Visual Studio Code (free). I recommend that you use one or both of those. The IDE is unrelated to most of the content. You could use Notepad if you are impetuous enough (I don't recommend that). Unless you install Visual Studio, which comes with the .NET SDK, you may need to install the .NET 8 SDK. The SDK comes with the dotnet CLI as well as the building tools for running and testing your programs. I develop on Windows, but you should be able to use another OS. OS-related topics are very limited, even inexistent. The code compiles on both Windows and Linux.

Download the example code files

The code for the book is hosted on GitHub at `https://github.com/PacktPublishing/Architecting-ASP.NET-Core-Applications-3E`. We also have other code bundles from our rich catalog of books and videos available at `https://github.com/PacktPublishing/`. Check them out!

Download the color images

We also provide a PDF file that has color images of the screenshots/diagrams used in this book. You can download it here: `https://packt.link/gbp/9781805123385`.

Conventions used

There are a number of text conventions used throughout this book.

`CodeInText`: Indicates code words in text, database table names, folder names, filenames, file extensions, pathnames, dummy URLs, user input, and Twitter handles. For example: "Mount the downloaded `WebStorm-10*.dmg` disk image file as another disk in your system."

A block of code is set as follows:

```
public class FactTest
{
    [Fact]
    public void Should_be_equal()
    {
        var expectedValue = 2;
        var actualValue = 2;
        Assert.Equal(expectedValue, actualValue);
    }
}
```

When we wish to draw your attention to a particular part of a code block, the relevant lines or items are set in bold:

```
public class AsyncFactTest
{
    [Fact]
    public async Task Should_be_equal()
    {
        var expectedValue = 2;
        var actualValue = 2;
        await Task.Yield();
        Assert.Equal(expectedValue, actualValue);
    }
}
```

Any command-line input or output is written as follows:

```
Passed!  - Failed:     0, Passed:    23, Skipped:     0, Total:    23,
Duration: 22 ms - MyApp.Tests.dll (net6.0)
```

Bold: Indicates a new term, an important word, or words that you see on the screen, for example, in menus or dialog boxes, also appear in the text like this. For example: "Select **System info** from the **Administration** panel."

Warnings or important notes appear like this.

Tips and tricks appear like this.

Get in touch

Feedback from our readers is always welcome.

General feedback: Email feedback@packtpub.com and mention the book's title in the subject of your message. If you have questions about any aspect of this book, please email us at questions@packtpub.com.

Errata: Although we have taken every care to ensure the accuracy of our content, mistakes do happen. If you have found a mistake in this book, we would be grateful if you reported this to us. Please visit http://www.packtpub.com/submit-errata, click **Submit Errata**, and fill in the form.

Piracy: If you come across any illegal copies of our works in any form on the internet, we would be grateful if you would provide us with the location address or website name. Please contact us at copyright@packtpub.com with a link to the material.

If you are interested in becoming an author: If there is a topic that you have expertise in and you are interested in either writing or contributing to a book, please visit http://authors.packtpub.com.

Share your thoughts

Once you've read *Architecting ASP.NET Core Applications, Third Edition*, we'd love to hear your thoughts! Scan the QR code below to go straight to the Amazon review page for this book and share your feedback.

https://packt.link/r/1805123386

Your review is important to us and the tech community and will help us make sure we're delivering excellent quality content.

Download a free PDF copy of this book

Thanks for purchasing this book!

Do you like to read on the go but are unable to carry your print books everywhere?

Is your eBook purchase not compatible with the device of your choice?

Don't worry, now with every Packt book you get a DRM-free PDF version of that book at no cost.

Read anywhere, any place, on any device. Search, copy, and paste code from your favorite technical books directly into your application.

The perks don't stop there, you can get exclusive access to discounts, newsletters, and great free content in your inbox daily

Follow these simple steps to get the benefits:

1. Scan the QR code or visit the link below

`https://packt.link/free-ebook/9781805123385`

2. Submit your proof of purchase
3. That's it! We'll send your free PDF and other benefits to your email directly

Section 1

Principles and Methodologies

This section delves into the core architectural principles and testing methodologies that form the backbone of modern software engineering practices, setting a solid foundation for the book. By exploring these essential concepts, you gain the insights needed to navigate the complexities of software architecture and ASP.NET Core development.

We begin with an introduction to the book's structure and the essential knowledge required to make the most out of it, including a brief overview of design patterns, their significance, and the role of experience in shaping architectural decisions. We emphasize understanding rather than memorizing patterns, encouraging you to experiment and learn through hands-on experimentation.

The journey continues with a look at automated testing, a critical component of software quality assurance. *Chapter 2, Automated Testing,* introduces the fundamentals of testing, including unit tests, integration tests, and the principles of **test-driven development** (TDD). With a focus on the xUnit framework, you will learn how to apply various testing strategies to improve code reliability and maintainability. This chapter introduces integrating testing into the development process, emphasizing its role in modern workflows.

We explore architectural principles in *Chapter 3, Architectural Principles,* where we dissect the building blocks of software architecture, including discussions on responsibility segregation, the significance of design patterns, and strategies for creating robust and scalable systems. The chapter aims to equip you with the knowledge to make informed architectural decisions, emphasizing the rationale behind common design choices.

Chapter 4, REST APIs, covers REST APIs, an essential aspect of modern web development. This chapter provides a practical guide to designing and implementing RESTful APIs, including best practices and considerations for security, performance, and scalability. Through this exploration, you will understand how REST APIs fit into the architectural landscape.

By the end of these chapters, you will understand crucial concepts and have a strong foundation in testing methodologies, architectural principles, and REST APIs. Tying these concepts together lays the groundwork for a successful journey into software architecture, development, and the rest of the book.

This section comprises the following chapters:

- *Chapter 1, Introduction*
- *Chapter 2, Automated Testing*
- *Chapter 3, Architectural Principles*
- *Chapter 4, REST APIs*

1

Introduction

This book organizes chapters according to scale and topic, which allows you to start with a solid foundation and gradually build upon it, much like constructing a program. We aim to delve into the thought processes behind the systems we design from a software engineer's perspective.

While many resources focus on presenting just a handful of ways to apply design patterns, this book diverges from that path. We emphasize understanding the underlying principles and the rationale behind architectural choices hands-on.

This is not a magic recipe book. From experience, there is no magical recipe when designing software, only your logic, knowledge, experience, and analytical skills. Let's define "experience" as *your past successes and failures*. And don't worry, you will fail during your career, but don't get discouraged by it. The faster you fail, the faster you can recover and learn, leading to successful products. Many techniques covered in this book should help you achieve success. Everyone has failed and made mistakes; you aren't the first and certainly won't be the last. To paraphrase a well-known saying by Roosevelt: *The people who never fail are the ones who never do anything.*

At a high level, this book introduces you sequentially to topics including:

- **Principles and methodologies:** Automated testing, architectural principles, the fundamentals of REST APIs, and so on
- **Designing with ASP.NET Core:** ASP.NET Core mechanisms, such as minimal APIs, MVC, and dependency injection
- **Component patterns:** Create small chunks of software by leveraging Gang of Four structural and behavioral patterns
- **Application patterns:** Explore ways to structure an application, from layering to microservices architecture

Some subjects covered throughout the book could have a book of their own, so after this book, you should have plenty of ideas about where to continue your journey into software architecture.

Here are a few pointers about this book that are worth mentioning:

- The chapters are organized to start with small-scale patterns and then progress to higher-level ones, making the learning curve easier.
- Instead of giving you a recipe, the book focuses on the thinking behind the task at hand and shows the evolution of some techniques to help you understand why the shift happened.
- Many use cases combine more than one design pattern to illustrate alternate usage so you can understand and use the patterns efficiently. This also shows that design patterns are not beasts to tame but tools to use, manipulate, and bend to your will.
- As in real life, no textbook solution can solve all our problems; real problems are always more complicated than what's explained in textbooks. In this book, I will show you how to mix and match patterns to think "architecture" instead of giving you step-by-step instructions to reproduce.

The rest of this chapter introduces the concepts we explore throughout the book. We cover refreshers on a few notions—for intermediate and seasoned developers—to ensure everyone is on the same page. We also touch on .NET, its tooling, and some technical requirements.

In this chapter, we will cover the following topics:

- What is a design pattern?
- Anti-patterns and code smell
- Understanding the web: request/response
- Getting started with .NET

What is a design pattern?

Since you just purchased a book about design patterns, I guess you have some idea of what design patterns are, but let's make sure that we are on the same page.

> *"A design pattern is a proven technique that we can use to solve a specific problem."*

In this book, we apply different patterns to solve various problems and leverage some open-source tools to go further, faster! Abstract definitions make people sound smart, but understanding concepts requires more practice, and there is no better way to learn than by experimenting with something. Design patterns are no different.

If that definition does not make sense to you yet, don't worry. You should have enough information by the end of the book to correlate the multiple practical examples and explanations with that definition, making it crystal clear.

I like to compare programming to playing with LEGO® because what you must do is very similar: put small pieces together to create something bigger. With a lack of guidance and experience, your construction might not be as sturdy as it could be. With that analogy in mind, a design pattern is a plan to assemble a solution that fits one or more scenarios. For example, when building a castle, we could design a single tower (a plan) and produce it multiple times by following the same steps (instances of the plan). Design patterns act as that tower plan and give you the tools to assemble reliable pieces to improve your masterpiece (program).

However, instead of snapping LEGO® blocks together, you nest code blocks and interweave objects in a virtual environment.

Applying design patterns effectively will improve your designs, whether designing a small component or a whole system. However, be careful; throwing patterns into the mix just to use them can lead to the opposite result: over-engineering. Instead, **aim to write the least amount of readable code that solves your issue or automates your process.**

As we have briefly mentioned, design patterns apply to different software engineering levels, and in this book, we start small and grow to a cloud scale. We follow a smooth learning curve, starting with simpler patterns and code samples that bend good practices to focus on the patterns—and finally ending with more advanced topics and good practices.

Of course, some subjects are overviews more than deep dives, like automated testing, because no one can fit it all in a single book. Nonetheless, I have made sure to give you as much information about architecture-related subjects as possible to ensure the proper foundations are in place for you to get as much as possible out of the more advanced topics, and I sincerely hope you'll find this book a helpful and enjoyable read.

Let's start with the opposite of design patterns because it is essential to identify wrong ways of doing things to avoid making those mistakes or to correct them when you see them. Of course, knowing the right way to overcome specific problems using design patterns is also crucial.

Anti-patterns and code smells

Anti-patterns are proven bad architectural practices, while code smells are tips about possible flawed design. Learning about bad practices is as important as learning about the best ones. The book highlights multiple anti-patterns and code smells to help you get started. Here, we briefly explore a few of them.

Anti-patterns

An **anti-pattern** is the opposite of a design pattern: it is a proven flawed technique that will most likely cause you trouble and cost you time and money (and probably give you headaches).

An anti-pattern is a pattern that seems a good idea and seems to be the solution you were looking for, but it causes more harm than good. Some anti-patterns started as legitimate design patterns and were labeled anti-patterns later. Sometimes, it is a matter of opinion, and sometimes the classification can be influenced by the programming language or technologies.

Let's begin with an example. We will explore some other anti-patterns throughout the book.

Anti-pattern: God class

A **God class** is a class that handles too many things. Typically, this class serves as a central entity that many other classes inherit or use within the application. It is the class that knows and manages everything in the system; it is *the* class. On the other hand, it is also the class that nobody wants to update, which breaks the application every time somebody touches it: it is an evil class.

The best way to fix this is to segregate responsibilities and allocate them to multiple classes rather than concentrating them in a single class. We look at how to split responsibilities throughout the book, which helps create more robust software.

If you have a personal project with a *God class* at its core, start by reading the book and then try to apply the principles and patterns you learn to divide that class into multiple smaller classes that interact together. Try to organize those new classes into cohesive units, modules, or assemblies.

To help fix God classes, we dive into architectural principles in *Chapter 3, Architectural Principles*, opening the way to concepts such as responsibility segregation.

Code smells

A **code smell** is an indicator of a possible problem. It points to areas of your design that could benefit from a redesign. By "code smell," we mean "code that stinks" or "code that does not smell right."

It is important to note that a code smell only indicates the possibility of a problem; it does not mean a problem exists. Code smells are usually good indicators, so it is worth analyzing your software's "smelly" parts.

An excellent example is when a method requires many comments to explain its logic. That often means that the code could be split into smaller methods with proper names, leading to more readable code and allowing you to get rid of those pesky comments.

Another note about comments is that they don't evolve, so what often happens is that the code described by a comment changes but the comment remains the same. That leaves a false or obsolete description of a block of code that can lead a developer astray.

The same is also true with method names. Sometimes, the method's name and body tell a different story, leading to the same issues. Nevertheless, this happens less often than orphan or obsolete comments since programmers tend to read and write code better than spoken language comments. Nonetheless, keep that in mind when reading, writing, or reviewing code.

Code smell: Control Freak

An excellent example of a code smell is using the `new` keyword. This indicates a hardcoded dependency where the creator controls the new object and its lifetime. This is also known as the **Control Freak anti-pattern**, but I prefer to box it as a code smell instead of an anti-pattern since the `new` keyword is not intrinsically wrong.

At this point, you may be wondering how it is possible not to use the `new` keyword in object-oriented programming, but rest assured, we will cover that and expand on the Control Freak code smell in *Chapter 7, Strategy, Abstract Factory, and Singleton Design Patterns.*

Code smell: long methods

The **long methods** code smell is when a method extends to more than a certain number of lines of code. For most teams, 10 to 15 lines is enough to fall into this specific case. That is a good indicator that you should think about that method differently. Having comments that separate multiple code blocks is a good indicator of a method that may be too long.

Here are a few examples of what the case might be:

- The method contains complex logic intertwined in multiple conditional statements.
- The method contains a big `switch` block.
- The method does too many things.
- The method contains duplications of code.

To fix this, you could do the following:

- Extract one or more private methods.
- Extract some code to new classes.
- Reuse the code from external classes.
- If you have a lot of conditional statements or a huge `switch` block, you could leverage a design pattern such as the Chain of Responsibility, or CQS, which you will learn about in *Chapter 12, Behavioral Patterns*, and *Chapter 16, Mediator and CQS Patterns*.

Usually, each problem has one or more solutions; you need to spot the problem and then find, choose, and implement one of the solutions. Let's be clear: a method containing 16 lines does not necessarily need refactoring; it could be OK. Remember that a code smell indicates that there *might* be a problem, not that there necessarily *is* one—apply common sense.

Understanding the web: request/response

Before going any further, as an ASP.NET Core developer, it is imperative to understand the basic concept of the web. The idea behind HTTP 1.X is that a client sends an HTTP request to a server, and then the server responds to that client. That can sound trivial if you have web development experience. However, it is one of the most important web programming concepts, irrespective of whether you are building web APIs, websites, or complex cloud applications.

Let's reduce an HTTP request lifetime to the following:

1. The communication starts.
2. The client sends a request to the server.
3. The server receives the request.
4. The server does something with the request, like executing code/logic.
5. The server responds to the client.
6. The communication ends.

After that cycle, the server is no longer aware of the client. Moreover, if the client sends another request, the server is unaware that it responded to a request earlier for that same client because **HTTP is stateless.**

There are mechanisms for creating a sense of persistence between requests for the server to be "aware" of its clients. The most well-known of these is cookies.

If we dig deeper, an HTTP request comprises a header and an optional body. Then, requests are sent using a specific method. The most common HTTP methods are `GET` and `POST`. On top of those, extensively used by web APIs, we can add `PUT`, `DELETE`, and `PATCH` to that list.

Here is a quick reference table; we will explore the concept of idempotence afterward:

Method	Request has body	Response has body	Idempotent
`GET`	No*	Yes	Yes
`POST`	Yes	Yes	No
`PUT`	Yes	No	Yes
`PATCH`	Yes	Yes	No
`DELETE`	May	May	Yes

Table 1.1: Structure of common HTTP methods

* Sending a body with a `GET` request is not forbidden by the HTTP specifications, but the semantics of such a request are not defined either. It is best to avoid sending `GET` requests with a body.

An **idempotent** request is a request that always yields the same result, whether it is sent once or multiple times. For example, sending the same `DELETE` request multiple times should delete a single entity (idempotent), while sending the same `POST` request multiple times should create multiple similar entities (not idempotent). The status code of an idempotent request may vary, but the server state should remain the same. We explore those concepts in more depth in *Chapter 4, REST APIs.*

Now that we have explored HTTP methods, let's have a look at an example of a `GET` request to become more familiar with HTTP:

```
GET http: //www.forevolve.com/ HTTP/1.1
Host: www.forevolve.com
Connection: keep-alive
Upgrade-Insecure-Requests: 1
User-Agent: Mozilla/5.0 (Windows NT 10.0; Win64; x64)
AppleWebKit/537.36 (KHTML, like Gecko) Chrome/70.0.3538.110 Safari/537.36
Accept: text/html,application/xhtml+xml,application/xml;q=0.9,image/webp,image/
apng,*/*;q=0.8
Accept-Encoding: gzip, deflate
```

```
Accept-Language: en-US,en;q=0.9,fr-CA;q=0.8,fr;q=0.7
Cookie: ...
```

The HTTP header comprises a list of key/value pairs representing metadata that a client wants to send to the server. In this case, I queried my blog using the `GET` method, and Google Chrome attached some additional information to the request. I replaced the `Cookie` header's value with `...` because it can be pretty large and that information is irrelevant to this sample. Nonetheless, cookies are passed back and forth like any other HTTP header.

Important note about cookies and request size

The client sends cookies, and the server returns them for every request-response cycle. This could kill your bandwidth or slow down your application if you pass too much information back and forth (cookies or otherwise). An example would be a serialized identity cookie that is very large.

Another example, unrelated to cookies but that created such a back-and-forth, was the good old Web Forms `ViewState`. This was a hidden field sent with every request. That field could become very large when left unchecked.

Nowadays, with high-speed internet, it is easy to forget about those issues, but they can significantly impact the user experience of someone on a slow network.

When the server decides to respond to the request, it returns a header and an optional body, following the same principles as the request. The first line indicates the request's status: whether it was successful. In our case, the status code was `200`, which indicates success. Each server can add more or less information to its response. You can also customize the response with code.

Here is the response to the previous request, which mainly contains the response header as I removed most of the body for brevity reasons:

```
HTTP/1.1 200 OK
Server: GitHub.com
Content-Type: text/html; charset=utf-8
Last-Modified: Wed, 03 Oct 2018 21:35:40 GMT
ETag: W/"5bb5362c-f677"
Access-Control-Allow-Origin: *
Expires: Fri, 07 Dec 2018 02:11:07 GMT
Cache-Control: max-age=600
Content-Encoding: gzip
X-GitHub-Request-Id: 32CE:1953:F1022C:1350142:5C09D460
Content-Length: 10055
Accept-Ranges: bytes
Date: Fri, 07 Dec 2018 02:42:05 GMT
Via: 1.1 varnish
```

```
Age: 35
Connection: keep-alive
X-Served-By: cache-ord1737-ORD
X-Cache: HIT
X-Cache-Hits: 2
X-Timer: S1544150525.288285,VS0,VE0
Vary: Accept-Encoding
X-Fastly-Request-ID: 98a36fb1b5642c8041b88ceace73f25caaf07746

<!DOCTYPE html>
<html lang="en">
Response body truncated for brevity
</html>
```

Now that the browser has received the server's response, it renders the HTML web page. Then, for each resource, it sends another HTTP call to its URI and loads it. A resource is an external asset, such as an image, a JavaScript file, a CSS file, or a font.

After the response, the server is no longer aware of the client; the communication has ended. It is essential to understand that to create a pseudo-state between each request, we need to use an external mechanism. That mechanism could be ASP.NET Core *session state* (leveraging cookies under the hood), manually using cookies, or we could create a stateless application. I recommend going stateless whenever possible. We will write primarily stateless applications in the book.

If you want to learn more about session and state management, I left a link in the *Further reading* section at the end of the chapter.

As you can imagine, the backbone of the internet is its networking stack, built upon the **Open Systems Interconnection model** (**OSI model**), which defines seven layers. The **Hypertext Transfer Protocol** (**HTTP**) is the highest layer of that stack (layer 7). HTTP is an application layer built on the **Transmission Control Protocol** (**TCP**). TCP (layer 4) is the transport layer, which defines how data is moved over the network (for instance, the transmission of data, the amount of transmitted data, and error checking). TCP uses the **Internet Protocol** (**IP**) layer to reach the computer it tries to talk to. IP (layer 3) represents the network layer, which handles packet IP addressing. Understanding the book's content does not require OSI proficiency, but you cannot have too much foundational knowledge. See the *Further reading* section for more on this subject.

A packet is a chunk of data that is transmitted over the wire. We could send a large payload directly from a source to a destination machine, but that is not practical, so the network layer breaks down the payload into smaller packets. The network layer uses the **maximum transmission unit** (**MTU**) to know whether it needs to break down payloads.

For example, Machine A (source) sends a file to Machine B (destination), and the router (network layer) breaks the payload (file) into multiple packets, sends them to Machine B, and then Machine B reassembles the packets back into the file sent by Machine A. This process allows numerous senders to use the same wire instead of waiting for the first transmission to be done. If a packet gets lost in transit, the source machine can also send only that packet back to the target machine.

Rest assured, you don't need to understand every detail behind networking to program web applications, but it is always good to know that HTTP uses TCP/IP and chunks big payloads into smaller packets. Moreover, HTTP/1 limits the number of parallel requests a browser can open simultaneously. This knowledge can help you optimize your apps. For example, a high number of assets to load, their size, and the order in which they are sent to the browser can increase the page load time, the perceived page load time, or the paint time.

To conclude this subject and not dig too deep into networking, HTTP/1 is older but foundational. HTTP/2 is more efficient and supports streaming multiple assets using the same TCP connection. It also allows the server to send assets to the client before it requests the resources, called a server push.

If you find HTTP interesting, HTTP/2 is an excellent place to start digging deeper, as well as the HTTP/3 proposed standard that uses the QUIC transport protocol instead of HTTP (RFC 9114). ASP.NET Core 7.0+ supports HTTP/3, which is enabled by default in ASP.NET Core 8.0.

Next, let's quickly explore .NET.

Getting started with .NET

Let's start with a bit of history. .NET Framework 1.0 was first released in 2002. .NET is a managed framework that compiles your code into an **Intermediate Language** (**IL**) named **Microsoft Intermediate Language** (**MSIL**). That IL code is then compiled into native code and executed by the **Common Language Runtime** (**CLR**). The CLR is now known simply as the **.NET runtime**. After releasing several versions of .NET Framework, Microsoft never delivered on the promise of an interoperable stack. Moreover, many flaws were built into the core of .NET Framework, tying it to Windows.

Mono, an open-source project, was developed by the community to enable .NET code to run on non-Windows OSs. Mono was used and supported by Xamarin, acquired by Microsoft in 2016. Mono enabled .NET code to run on other OSes like Android and iOS. Later, Microsoft started to develop an official cross-platform .NET Software Development Kit (SDK) and runtime that they named .NET Core.

The .NET team did a magnificent job building ASP.NET Core from the ground up, cutting out compatibility with the older .NET Framework versions. That brought its share of problems at first, but .NET Standard alleviated the interoperability issues between the old .NET and the new .NET.

After years of improvements and two major versions in parallel (Core and Framework), Microsoft reunified most .NET technologies into .NET 5+ and the promise of a shared **Base Class Library** (**BCL**). With .NET 5, .NET Core simply became .NET while ASP.NET Core remained ASP.NET Core. There is no .NET "Core" 4, to avoid any potential confusion with .NET Framework 4.X.

New major versions of .NET are released every year now. Even-numbered are **Long-Term Support (LTS)** releases with free support for three years, and odd-numbered releases (Current) have free support for only 18 months.

The good thing behind this book is that the architectural principles and design patterns covered should remain relevant in the future and are not tightly coupled with the versions of .NET you are using. Minor changes to the code samples should be enough to migrate your knowledge and code to new versions.

Next, let's cover some key information about the .NET ecosystem.

.NET SDK versus runtime

You can install different binaries grouped under SDKs and runtimes. The SDK allows you to build and run .NET programs, while the runtime only allows you to run .NET programs.

As a developer, you want to install the SDK on your deployment environment. On the server, you want to install the runtime. The runtime is lighter, while the SDK contains more tools, including the runtime.

.NET 5+ versus .NET Standard

When building .NET projects, there are multiple types of projects, but basically, we can separate them into two categories:

- Applications
- Libraries

Applications target a version of .NET, such as `net5.0` and `net6.0`. Examples of that would be an ASP.NET Core application or a console application.

Libraries are bundles of code compiled together, often distributed as a NuGet package. .NET Standard class library projects allow sharing code between .NET 5+, and .NET Framework projects. .NET Standard came into play to bridge the compatibility gap between .NET Core and .NET Framework, which eased the transition. Things were not easy when .NET Core 1.0 first came out.

With .NET 5 unifying all the platforms and becoming the future of the unified .NET ecosystem, .NET Standard is no longer needed. Moreover, app and library authors should target the base **Target Framework Moniker (TFM)**, for example, `net8.0`. A TFM is a way to identify and target a certain version of .NET (`net8.0` targets .NET 8 while `net8.0-ios` targets .NET 8 for IOS devices). You can also target `netstandard2.0` or `netstandard2.1` when needed, for example, to share code with .NET Framework. Microsoft also introduced OS-specific TFMs with .NET 5+, allowing code to use OS-specific APIs like `net8.0-android` and `net8.0-tvos`, which give access to OS-specific APIs. You can also target multiple TFMs when needed.

I'm sure we will see .NET Standard libraries stick around for a while. All projects will not just migrate from .NET Framework to .NET 5+ magically, and people will want to continue sharing code between the two.

The next versions of .NET are built over .NET 5+, while .NET Framework 4.X will stay where it is today, receiving only security patches and minor updates. For example, .NET 8 is built over .NET 7, iterating over .NET 6 and 5.

Next, let's look at some tools and code editors.

The command-line interface versus Visual Studio Code versus Visual Studio

How can one of these projects be created? .NET Core comes with the `dotnet` **command-line interface (CLI)**, which exposes multiple commands, including `new`. Running the `dotnet new` command in a terminal generates a new project.

To create an empty class library, we can run the following commands:

```
md MyProject
cd MyProject
dotnet new classlib
```

That would generate an empty class library in the newly created `MyProject` directory.

The `-h` option helps discover available commands and their options. For example, you can use `dotnet -h` to find the available SDK commands or `dotnet new -h` to find out about options and available templates.

It is fantastic that .NET now has the `dotnet` CLI. The CLI enables us to automate our workflows in **continuous integration** (CI) pipelines while developing locally or through any other process.

The CLI also makes it easier to write documentation that anyone can follow; writing a few commands in a terminal is much easier and faster than installing programs like Visual Studio.

Visual Studio Code is my favorite text editor. I don't use it much for .NET coding, but I still do to reorganize projects, when it's CLI time, or for any other task that is easier to complete using a text editor, such as writing documentation using Markdown, writing JavaScript or TypeScript, or managing JSON, YAML, or XML files. To create a C# project, a Visual Studio solution, or to add a NuGet package using Visual Studio Code, open a terminal and use the CLI.

As for **Visual Studio**, my favorite C# IDE, it uses the same templating engine as the CLI under the hood to create the same projects, making it consistent between tools and just adding a user interface on top of it.

You can create and install additional `dotnet new` project templates in the CLI or even create global tools. You can also use another code editor or IDE if you prefer. Those topics are beyond the scope of this book.

An overview of project templates

Here is a subset of the templates that are installed by default (`dotnet new list`):

```
Template Name                                    Short Name
-----------------------------------------------  ------------
```

```
ASP.NET Core Empty                                  web
ASP.NET Core Web API                                webapi
ASP.NET Core Web App                                webapp,razor
ASP.NET Core Web App (Model-View-Controller)        mvc
Blazor WebAssembly App                              blazorwasm
Class Library                                       classlib
Console App                                         console
```

A study of all the templates is beyond the scope of this book, but I'd like to list the ones we use:

- `dotnet new console` creates a console application
- `dotnet new classlib` creates a class library
- `dotnet new xunit` creates an xUnit test project
- `dotnet new web` creates an empty web project
- `dotnet new mvc` scaffolds an MVC application
- `dotnet new webapi` scaffolds a web API application based on the MVC framework

Running and building your program

If you are using Visual Studio, you can always hit the *Play* button, or *F5*, and run your app. If you are using the CLI, you can use one of the following commands (and more). Each of them also offers different options to control their behavior. Add the `-h` flag with any command to get help on that command, such as `dotnet build -h`:

Command	Description
`dotnet restore`	Restore the dependencies (a.k.a. NuGet packages) based on the `.csproj` or `.sln` file present in the current directory.
`dotnet build`	Build the application based on the `.csproj` or `.sln` file present in the current directory. It implicitly runs the `restore` command first.
`dotnet run`	Run the current application based on the `.csproj` file present in the current directory. It implicitly runs the `build` and `restore` commands first.
`dotnet watch run`	Watch for file changes. When a file has changed, the CLI updates the code from that file using the hot-reload feature. When that is impossible, it rebuilds the application and then reruns it (equivalent to executing the `run` command again). If it is a web application, the page should refresh automatically.
`dotnet test`	Run the tests based on the `.csproj` or `.sln` file present in the current directory. It implicitly runs the `build` and `restore` commands first. We cover testing in the next chapter.
`dotnet watch test`	Watch for file changes. When a file has changed, the CLI reruns the tests (equivalent to executing the `test` command again).

`dotnet publish`	Publish the current application, based on the `.csproj` or `.sln` file present in the current directory, to a directory or remote location, such as a hosting provider. It implicitly runs the `build` and `restore` commands first.
`dotnet pack`	Create a NuGet package based on the `.csproj` or `.sln` file present in the current directory. It implicitly runs the `build` and `restore` commands first. You don't need a `.nuspec` file.
`dotnet clean`	Clean the build(s) output of a project or solution based on the `.csproj` or `.sln` file present in the current directory.

Table 1.2: Common CLI commands

Technical requirements

Throughout the book, we will explore and write code. I recommend installing Visual Studio, Visual Studio Code, or both to help with that. I use Visual Studio and Visual Studio Code. Other alternatives are Visual Studio for Mac, Riders, or any other text editor you choose.

You need to install the .NET SDK unless you install Visual Studio, which comes with it. The SDK comes with the CLI we explored earlier and the build tools for running and testing your programs. Look at the `README.md` file in the GitHub repository for more information and links to those resources.

The source code of all chapters is available for download on GitHub at the following address: `https://adpg.link/net8`.

Summary

This chapter introduced **design patterns**. Understanding design patterns provides us with blueprints to address common problems in software design. Like assembling LEGO®, design patterns are plans that guide us in piecing together solutions to fit various scenarios.

However, recognizing **anti-patterns** or approaches that can lead to inefficient, problematic designs is just as crucial. One such anti-pattern is the *God class*, which concentrates too many responsibilities within a single class. Proper application of design principles helps us avoid such pitfalls.

Furthermore, we delved into **code smells**, which might indicate areas of code needing revision. For example, a method extending beyond a certain length could signal that it's trying to handle too many responsibilities.

We also explained that, to build web applications, understanding **foundational web concepts** is critical. At its core, the web operates on a request/response mechanism, with the client making a request and the server responding. We overviewed HTTP, emphasizing its stateless nature. Knowing how the internet operates, including the OSI model, can prove valuable in the long term.

We continued by exploring **.NET essentials**, such as the SDK versus runtime and app targets versus .NET Standard. We then dug a little deeper into the .NET CLI, where I laid down a list of essential commands, including `dotnet build` and `dotnet watch run`. We also covered how to create new projects. This has set us up to explore the different possibilities we have when building our .NET applications.

In the next two chapters, we will explore automated testing and architectural principles. These are foundational chapters for building robust, flexible, and maintainable applications.

Questions

Let's take a look at a few practice questions:

1. Can we add a body to a `GET` request?
2. Why are long methods a code smell?
3. Is it true that .NET Standard should be your default target when creating libraries?
4. What is a code smell?

Further reading

Here are some links to consolidate what has been learned in the chapter:

- Overview of how .NET is versioned: `https://adpg.link/n52L`
- .NET CLI overview: `https://adpg.link/Lzx3`
- Custom templates for `dotnet new`: `https://adpg.link/74i2`
- Session and state management in ASP.NET Core: `https://adpg.link/Xzgf`
- OSI Model (Wikipedia): `https://adpg.link/LVc9`

Answers

Here are the answers to the earlier questions:

1. Yes, but don't. Sending a body with a `GET` request is not forbidden by the HTTP specifications, but such a request semantic is not defined either. It is preferable to avoid sending `GET` requests with a body.
2. Long methods are indicators that a method handles too many responsibilities and should be split into multiple methods or have some of the responsibilities extracted to other classes.
3. No. Target .NET Standard 2.0 when you want to support most runtime versions, like .NET Framework and .NET 6+. Targeting .NET Standard 2.1 is rarely needed, yet it adds around 4,000 APIs. In most cases, target .NET directly, like .NET 8.
4. A code smell represents a potential design flaw that could benefit from being rewritten. It helps identify potential problems.

Learn more on Discord

To join the Discord community for this book – where you can share feedback, ask questions to the author, and learn about new releases – follow the QR code below:

`https://packt.link/ArchitectingASPNETCoreApps3e`

2

Automated Testing

This chapter focuses on automated testing and how helpful it can be for crafting better software. It also covers a few different types of tests and the foundation of **test-driven development** (**TDD**). We also outline how testable ASP.NET Core is and how much easier it is to test ASP.NET Core applications than old ASP.NET MVC applications. This chapter overviews automated testing, its principles, the xUnit unit testing library, ways to sample test values, and more. While other books cover this topic in more depth, this chapter covers the foundational aspects of automated testing. We will use parts of this throughout the book, and this chapter ensures you have a strong enough base to understand the samples.

In this chapter, we cover the following topics:

- An overview of automated testing
- Testing approaches
- Testing techniques
- Test case creation
- Introducing the xUnit framework
- Arrange, Act, Assert
- Organizing your tests
- Writing ASP.NET Core integration tests
- Important testing principles

An overview of automated testing

Testing is an integral part of the development process, and automated testing becomes crucial in the long run. You can always run your ASP.NET Core website, open a browser, and click everywhere to test your features. That's a legitimate approach, but it is harder to test individual rules or more complex algorithms that way. Another downside is the lack of automation; when you first start with a small app containing a few pages, endpoints, or features, it may be fast to perform those tests manually. However, as your app grows, it becomes more tedious, takes longer, and increases the likelihood of making a mistake.

Of course, you will always need real users to test your applications, but you want those tests to focus on the UX, the content, some experimental features you are building, or what you can't automate. You do not want to waste time triaging bug reports filed by your users that automated tests could have caught early on.

There are multiple types of tests and techniques in the testing space. Here is a list of three broad categories that represent how we can divide automated testing from a code correctness standpoint:

- Unit tests
- Integration tests
- End-to-end (E2E) tests

Usually, you want a mix of those tests, so you have fast unit tests testing your algorithms, slower integration tests that ensure the integrations between components are correct, and even slower E2E tests that ensure the correctness of the system as a whole.

The test pyramid and testing diamond are good ways of explaining a few concepts around automated testing. You want different granularity of tests and a different number of tests depending on their complexity and speed of execution. The following test pyramid shows the three types of tests stated above. Moreover, that's just an abstract guideline to give you an idea. The most important aspect is the **return on investment** (**ROI**) and execution speed. If you can write one integration test that covers a large surface and is fast enough, this might be worth doing instead of multiple unit tests (see *Figure 2.2*, the testing diamond).

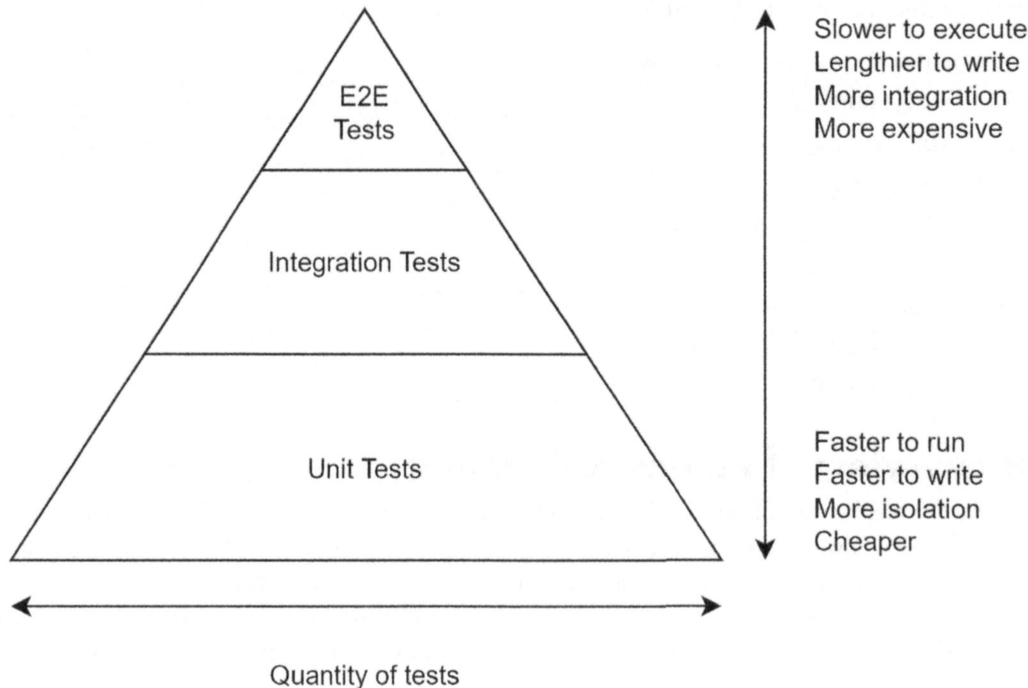

Figure 2.1: The test pyramid

I cannot stress this enough: the execution speed of your tests is essential to receive fast feedback and know immediately that you have broken something with your code changes. Layering different types of tests allows you to execute only the fastest subset often, the not-so-fast occasionally, and the very slow tests infrequently. If your test suite is fast enough, you don't even have to worry about it.

However, if you have a lot of manual or E2E UI tests that take hours to run, it slows development by delaying the feedback loop, which leads to delayed updates. As a result, we lose time and money, draining company resources and developers' morale, making maintaining a steady development pace challenging.

The testing diamond redistributes the test ratio to focus more on integration. It is a great strategy for integration-heavy systems, like REST APIs and microservices. In a nutshell, the testing diamond model prescribes writing mostly integration tests that cover a large part of your system and as many unit tests as needed to cover the complex algorithms of the system, and as the test pyramid, writing as few E2E tests as possible. The testing diamond is the strategy we employ the most in the book, especially in *Section 4, Application Patterns*.

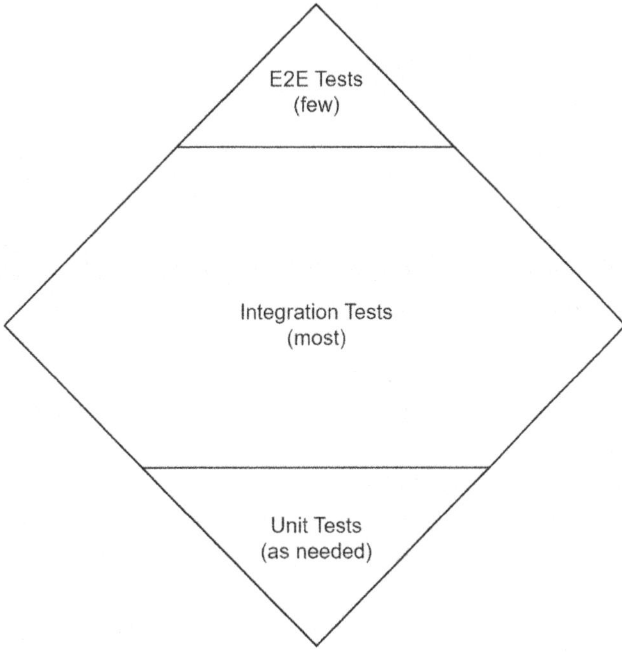

Figure 2.2: The testing diamond

Finally, on top of running your tests using a test runner, like in Visual Studio, VS Code, or the CLI, a great way to ensure code quality and leverage your automated tests is to run them in a **continuous integration** (CI) pipeline, validating code changes to detect issues.

CI/CD pipelines are automated processes in software development where the CI pipeline automatically tests code changes. Then, the **continuous deployment** (**CD**) pipeline deploys the application to a production environment. This process comes from the DevOps culture and allows us to frequently update our application with new features or fixes, ensuring a smoother and faster development cycle by leveraging automation. Automation reduces the risk of human error.

Tech-wise, back when .NET Core was in pre-release, I discovered that the .NET team was using xUnit to test their code and that it was the only testing framework available. xUnit has become my favorite testing framework since, and we use it throughout the book. Moreover, the ASP.NET Core team made our lives easier by designing ASP.NET Core for testability; testing is easier than before.

Why are we talking about tests in an architectural book? Because testability is a sign of a good design. It also allows us to use tests instead of words to prove some concepts. In many code samples, the test cases are the consumers, making the program lighter without building an entire UI and focusing on the patterns we are exploring instead of getting our focus scattered over some complex or lengthy UI code.

To ensure we do not deviate from the matter at hand, we use automated testing moderately in the book, but I strongly recommend that you continue to study it, as it will help improve your code and design.

Now that we have covered all that, let's explore those three types of tests, starting with unit testing.

Unit testing

Unit tests focus on individual units, like testing the outcome of a method. Unit tests should be fast and not rely on any infrastructure, such as a database. Those are the kinds of tests you want the most because they run fast, and each one tests a precise code path. They should also help you design your application better because you use your code in the tests, so you become its first consumer, leading to you finding some design flaws and making your code better. If you don't like using your code in your tests, that is a good indicator that nobody else will. Unit tests should focus on testing algorithms (what output is expected from certain inputs) and domain logic, not the code itself; how you wrote the code should have no impact on the intent of the test. For example, when testing a `Purchase` method, we must validate that it correctly handles buying items and not its implementation details.

Don't be discouraged if you find it challenging; writing a good test suite is not as easy as it sounds.

Integration testing

Integration tests focus on the interaction between components, such as what happens when a component queries the database or what happens when two components interact with each other.

Integration tests often require some infrastructure to interact with, which makes them slower to run. By following the classic testing model, you want integration tests, but you want fewer of them than unit tests. An integration test can be very close to an E2E test but without using a production-like environment.

In the book, we break the test pyramid rule and leverage the testing diamond instead, so always be critical of rules and principles; sometimes, breaking or bending them can be better. For example, having one good integration test can be better than *N* unit tests. See also the *Gray-box testing* section.

End-to-end testing

End-to-end tests focus on application-wide behaviors, such as what happens when a user clicks on a specific button, navigates to a particular page, posts a form, or sends a `PUT` request to some web API endpoint. E2E tests usually run on infrastructure to test your application and deployment.

Other types of tests

There are other types of automated tests. For example, we could do load testing, performance testing, regression testing, contract testing, penetration testing, functional testing, smoke testing, and more. You can automate tests for anything you want to validate, but some tests are more challenging to automate or more fragile than others, such as UI tests.

If you can automate a test in a reasonable timeframe, do it! Think about the ROI the test will provide. In the long run, this strategy will pay off.

One more thing; don't blindly rely on metrics such as code coverage. Those metrics make for cute badges in your GitHub project's `readme.md` file but can lead you off track, resulting in you writing useless tests. Don't get me wrong, code coverage is a great metric when used correctly, but remember that one good test can be better than a lousy test suite covering 100% of your code base. If you are using code coverage, ensure you and your team are not gaming the system.

Writing good tests is not easy and comes with practice.

One piece of advice: keep your test suite healthy by adding missing test cases and removing obsolete or useless tests. Think about use case coverage, not how many lines of code are covered by your tests.

Before moving forward to testing styles, let's inspect a hypothetical system and explore an efficient way to test it.

Finding the right balance

The next figure shows a dependency map of a hypothetical system. We use that diagram to pick the most meaningful type of test possible for each piece of the program. In real life, that diagram will most likely be in your head, but I drew it out in this case. Let's inspect that diagram before I explain its content:

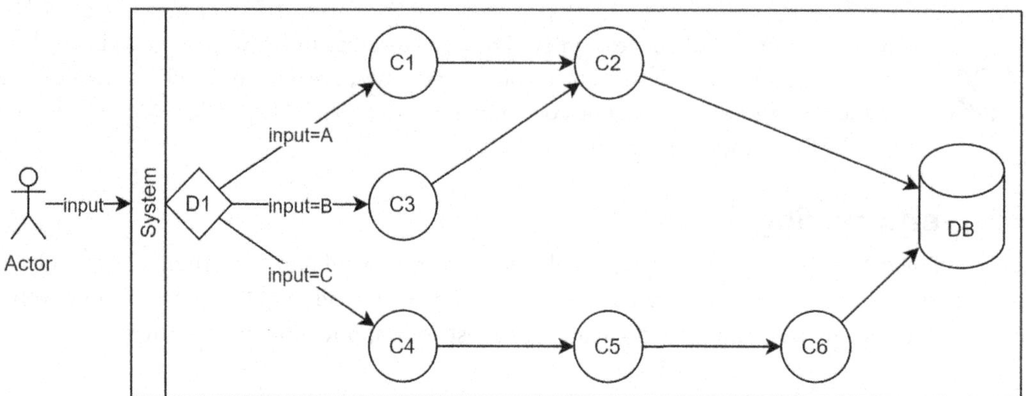

Figure 2.3: Dependency map of a hypothetical system

In the diagram, the **Actor** can be anything from a user to another system. The **System** is what the **Actor** interacts with. It forwards the **input** to **D1**, a component that has to decide what to do next based on the **input**. **C1** to **C6** are components of the system (could be classes or methods, for example). **DB** is a database.

D1 must choose between the flows **C1**, **C3**, or **C4**, based on the **Actor's input**. This type of logic is usually a good subject for unit tests, ensuring the algorithm yields the correct result based on the **input** parameter. Why pick a unit test? We can quickly test multiple scenarios, edge cases, out-of-bounds data cases, and more. We usually mock the dependencies away in this type of test and assert that the subject under test made the expected call to the desired component. The solid elements of the following diagram depicts this test (the dashed elements are not tested):

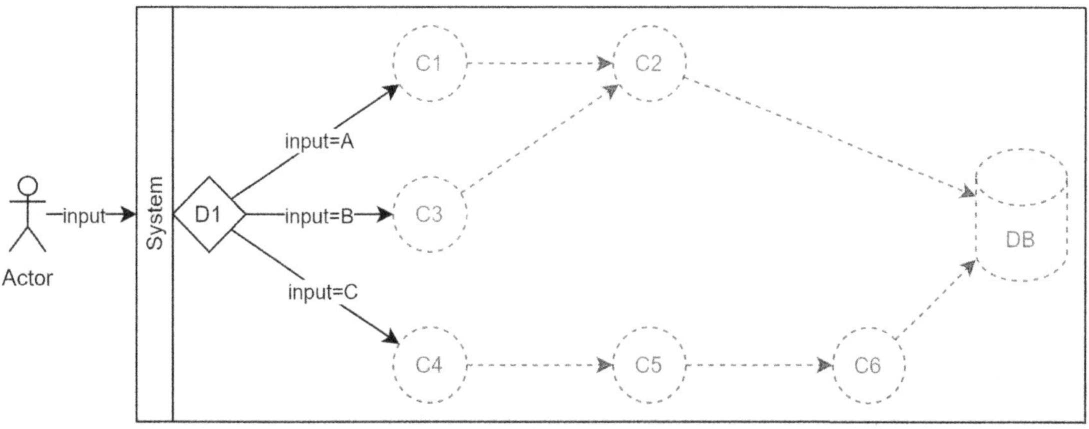

Figure 2.4: Unit testing D1

Then, if we look at the other flows, **C1** and **C3** are both using **C2**. Depending on the code (that does not exist here), we could write an integration test for **C1** and another one for **C3**, testing the integration with **C2** and the **DB** in the process. Here's a diagram that depicts the coverage of the **C1** and **C3** integration tests:

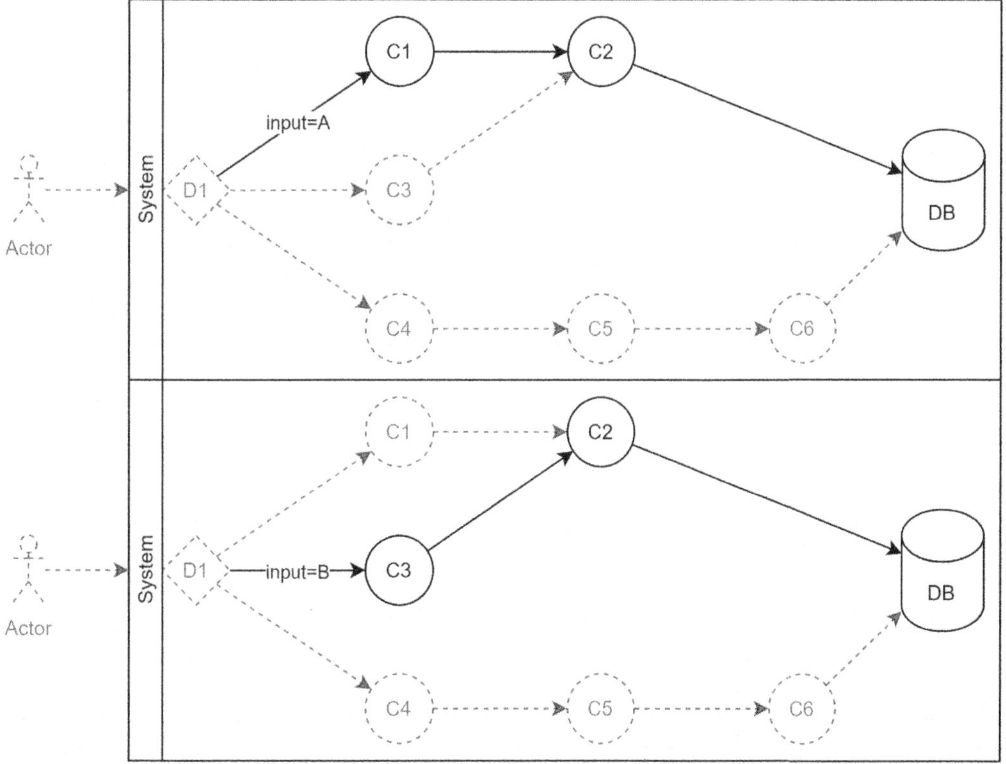

Figure 2.5: C1 (top) and C3 (bottom) integration test

Another way would be to unit test **C1** and **C3**, and then write integration tests between **C2** and the **DB**. Here's a diagram representing these three tests:

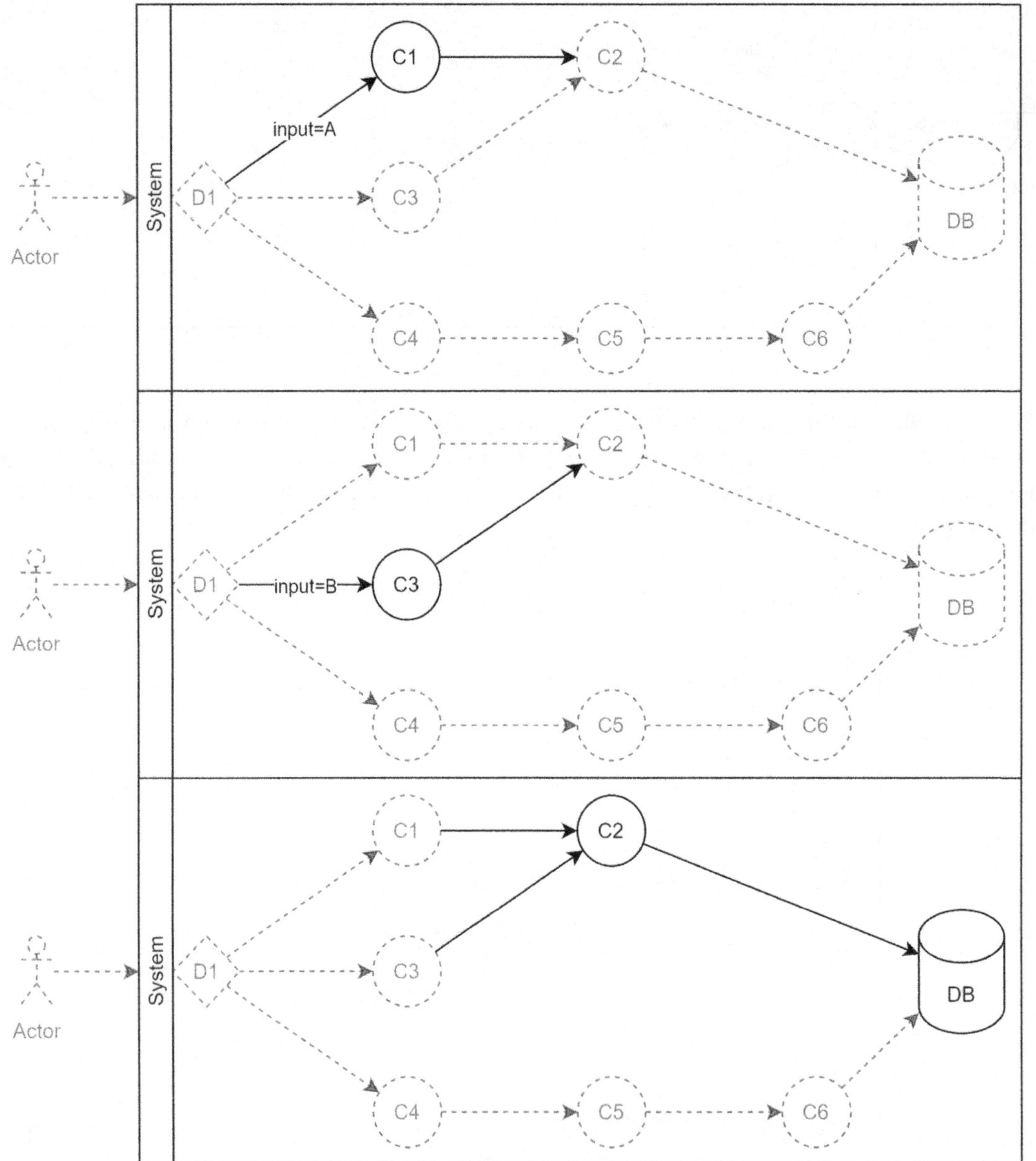

Figure 2.6: C1 (top) and C3 (middle) unit tests, and C2 (bottom) integration test

If **C2** has no logic, the latter could be the best and the fastest (two unit tests and one integration test). In comparison, the former will most likely yield results that give you more confidence in your test suite (two integration tests) because each one tests almost the end-to-end flow when **input** equals **A** or **B**, and the correct information reaches the **DB**.

Even if both techniques effectively tested the correctness of the system, the key is to ensure the minimal amount of effort needed to write and maintain the test suite while keeping a high degree of confidence.

For the last flow, we could write a single integration test for component **C4**, testing the whole chain in one go (**C4**, **C5**, and **C6**) instead of writing multiple mock-heavy unit tests for each component. If there is any logic that we need to test in components **C4**, **C5**, or **C6**, we can always add a few unit tests; that's what they are for. The following diagram depicts this test:

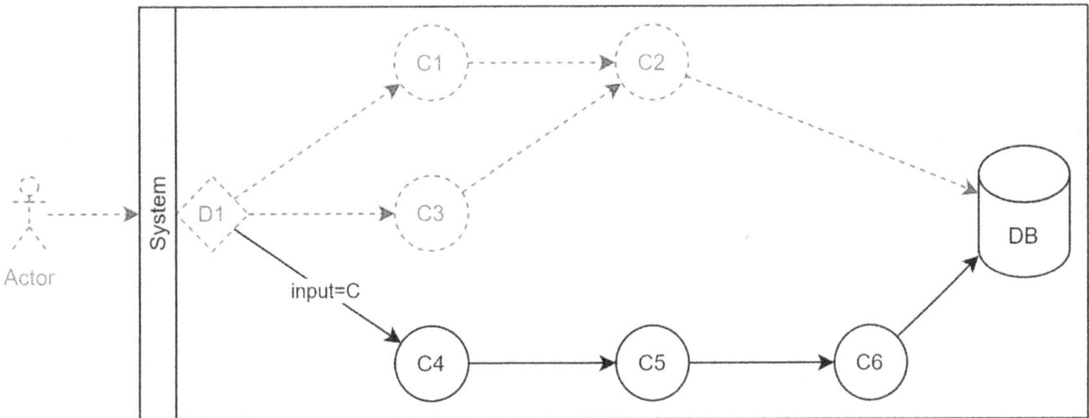

Figure 2.7: Integration testing C4

When it is an option, I recommend evaluating the possibility of writing fewer meaningful integration tests that assert the correctness of a use case over a suite of mock-heavy unit tests. Remember to always keep the execution speed in mind.

That may seem to go "against" the test pyramid but is aligned with the testing diamond model. If you spend less time (thus lower costs) testing more use cases (adding more value), that sounds like a win to me. Moreover, we must remember that mocking dependencies tends to make you waste time by fighting the framework or other libraries instead of testing something meaningful.

Let's explore how testing can help us enhance code quality.

Enhancing code quality

Testing is pivotal in application development, offering many benefits in supporting the product team. For the developers, these benefits include support with refactoring and managing technical debt, which is crucial for upholding and enhancing code quality, irrespective of the chosen testing approach or methodology. Let's delve into these benefits to understand their importance.

Improving quality with refactoring

Refactoring means changing the code to improve its structure and readability without altering its functionality. Think of it like tidying up a room: everything still works the same, but it's neater and easier to navigate.

Your automated test suite checks your code to ensure you haven't unintentionally changed how something works while refactoring. Whether or not you use TDD, it's a good idea to refactor regularly. This practice not only keeps your code clean but also reduces technical debt.

Of course, you must balance the time you spend refactoring with the gains it brings to the product or the team. Improving the readability of our code directly after writing it is cheap, while someone else trying to understand cryptic code or improve it two years later will cost way more.

Okay, but what is **technical debt**?

Managing technical debt

Technical debt refers to the cost of additional rework, the byproduct of cutting corners while developing a feature or a system. That happens no matter how hard you try because life is life, and there are delays, deadlines, budgets, and people—including developers (yes, that's us)—generating technical debt.

The most crucial point is understanding that you cannot avoid technical debt altogether, so it's better to embrace that fact and learn to live with it instead of fighting it. From that point forward, you can only try to limit the amount of technical debt you (or someone else) generate and ensure to always refactor some of it over time each sprint (or the unit of time that fits your projects/team/process).

One way to limit the piling up of technical debt is to refactor the code often. So, factor the refactoring time into your time estimates. Another way is to improve collaboration between all the parties involved. Everyone must work toward the same goal if you want your projects to succeed.

You will sometimes cut the usage of best practices short due to external forces like people or time constraints. The key is coming back at it as soon as possible to repay that technical debt, and automated tests are there to help you refactor that code and eliminate that debt elegantly. Depending on the size of your workplace, there will be more or fewer people between you and the decision of what to refactor and when.

Some of these things might be out of your control, so you may have to live with more technical debt than you would like. However, even when things are out of your control, nothing stops you from becoming a pioneer and working toward improving the enterprise's culture. Don't be afraid to become an agent of change and lead the charge.

Nevertheless, don't let the technical debt pile up too high, or you may not be able to pay it back and, at some point, the project may begin to break and fail. Don't be mistaken: a project in production can be a technical failure. Delivering a product does not guarantee its technical success; it can be broken, unmaintainable, and provide a bad user experience. I'm talking about the quality of the code and the application here, not the amount of generated revenue (I'll leave that to other people to evaluate).

Now that we have explored the fundamentals of automated testing, it is time to explore testing approaches, which are ways to apply those testing concepts.

Testing approaches

There are various approaches to testing, such as **test-driven development** (TDD), **acceptance test-driven development** (ATDD), and **behavior-driven development** (BDD).

The DevOps culture brings a mindset that embraces automated testing in line with its **CI** and **CD** ideals. We can enable CD with a robust and healthy suite of tests that gives a high degree of confidence in our code, high enough to deploy the program when all tests pass without fear of introducing a bug.

TDD

TDD is a software development method that states that you should write one or more tests before writing the actual code. In a nutshell, you invert your development flow by following the **Red-Green-Refactor** technique, which goes like this:

1. You write a failing test (red).
2. You write just enough code to make your test pass (green).
3. You refactor that code to improve the design by ensuring all the tests pass.

ATDD

ATDD takes a similar approach to TDD but at a broader level. In ATDD, we start by writing acceptance tests based on what the software should achieve from the user's perspective and define the expected behavior of a feature before developing it.

It's a collaborative approach, as customers (or product owners), developers, and testers come together to discuss and understand requirements, ensuring everyone is on the same page from the start. This collaboration of customers, developers, and testers is often called the "Three Amigos" as each of these roles brings a unique perspective to the table:

- **Customers** bring the user perspective, which can be substituted by product owners or product managers representing the business or the customers. Their main concern is the value a feature brings. They help define what the software should do, describe the desired functionality, and set the acceptance criteria. Their insights ensure that the product aligns with business goals and user needs.
- **Developers** provide the technical perspective. Developers are concerned with how the team will implement the feature, ensuring it's feasible and aligned with the system's architecture. They discuss potential challenges and help refine requirements into actionable tasks.
- **Testers** bring the quality and validation perspective. They think about edge cases, potential pitfalls, and overall system behavior. Their insights ensure that the feature is robust and reliable and that tests validate the desired behavior effectively.

This way, when developing the software using ATDD, we aim to meet the user's needs and expectations based on that collaborative consensus.

BDD

BDD is another complementary technique originating from TDD and ATDD. BDD is a form of ATDD that focuses on formulating test cases around application behaviors using spoken language and involves multiple parties like customers, developers, and testers. As we saw with ATDD, the voice of the customers is often provided by a product owner or a manager.

Practitioners of BDD often leverage the *User Story Template* and the *given-when-then* grammar to formalize their test cases, making them readable by non-developers. BDD test output must also be readable by non-developers to allow stakeholders to consult and understand the artifacts.

The **User Story Template**—*As a... I want to... So That...*—is a framework used in Agile development for articulating user stories, focusing on user requirements and their value. Its components are:

- **As a [type of user]**: This identifies the user or the role that will benefit from the feature. It sets the context by focusing on the specific user group.
- **I want to [an action or feature]**: This part specifies what the user needs or wants to do, essentially stating the requirement or the feature.
- **So that [benefit or reason]**: Here, we explain the feature's goal or value, showing why this feature is important for the user. This helps in understanding the purpose behind the requirement.

For example, in a project aimed at enhancing an e-commerce website, a user story could be:

```
As a frequent online shopper
I want to easily filter products by price range
So that I can quickly find items that fit my budget.
```

The *given-when-then* template defines the way to describe the behavior of a user story or acceptance test, like this:

- *Given* [one or more preconditions (context)]: This sets the stage, detailing the initial conditions or the state before the action takes place.
- *When* [something happens (behavior)]: This part describes the specific action or event that triggers the behavior.
- *Then* [one or more observable changes are expected (measurable side effects)]: This defines the expected outcome or changes resulting from the action.

Building upon our previous example of the online shopper, here's an example of given-when-then usage:

```
Given the following products:
| Product              | Price  |
| -------------------- | ------ |
| Wireless Mouse       | $20.99 |
| Bluetooth Headphones | $59.99 |
| Portable Charger     | $35.50 |
When I select the price range "Less than 50$" in the filter options
```

```
Then the list of products should include Wireless Mouse
And the list of products should include Portable Charger
```

ATDD and BDD are great areas to dig deeper into and can help design better apps; defining precise user-centric specifications can help build only what is needed, prioritize better, and improve communication between parties. Once the specifications (behaviors) are well defined, the team can continue leveraging unit tests, integration tests, and other tests during the development.

For the sake of simplicity, we stick to unit testing, integration testing, and a bit of TDD in the book.

Next, we look at different ways to write tests, requiring more or less knowledge of the inner workings of the code.

Testing techniques

Here we look at different ways to approach our tests. Should we know the code? Should we test user inputs and compare them against the system results? How do we identify a proper value sample?

Let's start with white-box testing.

White-box testing

White-box testing is a software testing technique that uses knowledge of the internal structure of the software to design tests. We can use white-box testing to find defects in the software's logic, data structures, and algorithms.

This type of testing is also known as clear-box testing, open-box testing, transparent-box testing, glass-box testing, and code-based testing.

Another benefit of white-box testing is that it can help optimize the code. By reviewing the code to write tests, developers can identify and improve inefficient code structures, improving overall software performance. The developer can also improve the application design by finding architectural issues while testing the code.

White-box testing encompasses most unit and integration tests.

Next, we look at black-box testing, the opposite of white-box testing.

Black-box testing

Black-box testing is a software testing method where a tester examines an application's functionality without knowing the internal structure or implementation details.

This form of testing focuses solely on the inputs and outputs of the system under test, treating the software as a "black box" that we can't see into.

The main goal of black-box testing is to evaluate the system's behavior against expected results based on requirements or user stories. Developers writing the tests do not need to know the codebase or the technology stack used to build the software.

We can use black-box testing to assess the correctness of several types of requirements, like:

- **Functional testing:** This type of testing is related to the software's functional requirements, emphasizing what the system does, a.k.a. behavior verification.
- **Non-functional testing:** This type of testing is related to non-functional requirements such as performance, usability, reliability, and security.
- **Regression testing:** This type of testing ensures the new code does not break existing functionalities and allows assessing the impact of new changes.

Next, let's explore a hybrid between white-box and black-box testing.

Gray-box testing

Gray-box testing is a blend of white-box and black-box testing. Testers need only partial knowledge of the application's internal workings and use a combination of the software's internal structure and external behavior to craft their tests.

Now, let's compare the three techniques.

White-box vs. black-box vs. gray-box testing

To start with a concise comparison, here's a table that compares the three broad techniques:

Feature	White-Box Testing	Black-Box Testing	Gray-Box Testing
Definition	Testing based on the internal design of the software	Testing focused on the behaviors and functionalities	Testing that leverages the internal design and focuses on the behaviors and functionalities
Knowledge of code required	Yes	No	Partially
Types of defects found	Logic, data structure, architecture, and performance issues	Functionality, usability, performance, and security issues	Most types of issues
Coverage per test	Small; targeted on a unit	Large; targeted on a use case	Up to large; can vary in scope

Testers	Usually performed by developers	Testers can write the tests without specific technical knowledge of the application's internal structure	Developers can write the tests, while testers also can with some knowledge of the code
When to use each style?	Write unit tests to validate complex algorithms or code that yields multiple results based on many inputs. These tests are usually high-speed so you can have many of them.	Write if you have specific scenarios you want to test, like UI tests, or if testers and developers are two distinct roles in your organization. These usually run the slowest and require you to deploy the application to test it. You want as few as possible to improve the feedback time.	Write to avoid writing black-box or white-box tests. Layer the tests to cover as much as possible with as few tests as possible. Depending on the application's architecture, this type of test can yield optimal results for many scenarios.

Table 2.1: Comparing the three broad techniques

Let's conclude next and explore a few advantages and disadvantages of each technique.

Conclusion

White-box testing includes unit and integration tests. Those tests run fast, and developers use them to improve the code and test complex algorithms. However, writing a large quantity of those tests takes time. Writing brittle tests that are tightly coupled with the code itself is easier due to the proximity to the code, increasing the maintenance cost of such test suites. It also makes it prone to overengineering your application in the name of testability.

Black-box testing encompasses different types of tests that tend toward E2E testing. Since the tests target the external surface of the system, they are less likely to break when the system changes. Moreover, they are excellent at testing behaviors, and since each test tests an E2E use case, we need fewer of them, leading to a decrease in writing time and maintenance costs. Testing the whole system has drawbacks, including the slowness of executing each test, so combining black-box testing with other types of tests is very important to find the right balance between the number of tests, test case coverage, and speed of execution of the tests.

Gray-box testing is a fantastic mix between the two others; you can treat any part of the software as a black box, leverage your inner workings knowledge to mock or stub parts of the test case (such as to assert whether the system persisted a record in the database), and test E2E scenarios more efficiently. It brings the best of both worlds, significantly reducing the number of tests while increasing the test surface considerably for each test case. However, doing gray-box testing on smaller units or heavily mocking the system may yield the same drawbacks as white-box testing.

Integration tests or almost-E2E tests are good candidates for gray-box testing. We implement gray-box testing use cases in *Chapter 18, Request-Endpoint-Response (REPR)*.

Meanwhile, let's explore a few techniques to help optimize our test case creation by applying different techniques.

Test case creation

Multiple ways exist to break down and create test cases to help find software defects with a minimal test count. Here are some techniques to help minimize the number of tests while maximizing the test coverage:

- Equivalence partitioning
- Boundary value analysis
- Decision table testing
- State transition testing
- Use case testing

I present the techniques theoretically. They apply to all sorts of tests and should help you write better test suites. Let's have a quick look at each.

Equivalence partitioning

This technique divides the input data of the software into different equivalence data classes and then tests these classes rather than individual inputs. An equivalence data class means that all values in that partition set should lead to the same outcome or yield the same result. Doing this allows for limiting the number of tests considerably.

For example, consider an application that accepts an integer value between 1 and 100 (inclusive). Using equivalence partitioning, we can divide the input data into two equivalence classes:

- Valid
- Invalid

To be more precise, we could further divide it into three equivalence classes:

- **Class 1:** Less than 1 (invalid)
- **Class 2:** Between 1 and 100 (valid)
- **Class 3:** Greater than 100 (invalid)

Then we can write three tests, picking one representative from each class (e.g., 0, 50, and 101) to create our test cases. Doing so ensures a broad coverage with minimal test cases, making our testing process more efficient.

Boundary value analysis

This technique focuses on the values at the boundary of the input domain rather than the center. This technique is based on the principle that errors are most likely to occur at the boundaries of the input domain.

The **input domain** represents the set of all possible inputs for a system. The **boundaries** are the edges of the input domain, representing minimum and maximum values.

For example, if we expect a function to accept an integer between 1 and 100 (inclusive), the boundary values would be 1 and 100. With boundary value analysis, we would create test cases for these values, values just outside the boundaries (like 0 and 101), and values just inside the boundaries (like 2 and 99).

Boundary value analysis is a very efficient testing technique that provides good coverage with a relatively small number of test cases. However, it's unsuitable for finding errors within the boundaries or for complex logic errors. Boundary value analysis should be used on top of other testing methods, such as equivalence partitioning and decision table testing, to ensure the software is as defect-free as possible.

Decision table testing

This technique uses a decision table to design test cases. A decision table is a table that shows all possible combinations of input values and their corresponding outputs.

It's handy for complex business rules that can be expressed in a table format, enabling testers to identify missing and extraneous test cases.

For example, our system only allows access to a user with a valid username and password. Moreover, the system denies access to users when it is under maintenance. The decision table would have three conditions (username, password, and maintenance) and one action (allow access). The table would list all possible combinations of these conditions and the expected action for each combination. Here is an example:

Valid Username	**Valid Password**	**System Under Maintenance**	**Allow Access**
True	True	False	Yes
True	True	True	No
True	False	False	No
True	False	True	No
False	True	False	No
False	True	True	No
False	False	False	No
False	False	True	No

Table 2.2: Sample of a decision table

The main advantage of decision table testing is that it ensures we test all possible input combinations. However, it can become complex and challenging to manage when systems have many input conditions, as the number of rules (and therefore, test cases) increases exponentially with the number of conditions.

State transition testing

We usually use **state transition testing** to test software with a state machine since it tests the different system states and their transitions. It's handy for systems where the system behavior can change based on its current state - for example, a program with states like "logged in" or "logged out."

To perform state transition testing, we need to identify the states of the system and then the possible transitions between the states. For each transition, we need to create a test case. The test case should test the software with the specified input values and verify that the software transitions to the correct state. For example, a user with the state "logged in" must transition to the state "logged out" after signing out.

The main advantage of state transition testing is that it tests sequences of events, not just individual events, which could reveal defects not found by testing each event in isolation. However, state transition testing can become complex and time-consuming for systems with many states and transitions.

Use case testing

This technique validates that the system behaves as expected when used in a particular way by a user. Use cases could have formal descriptions, be user stories, or take any other form that fits your needs.

A use case involves one or more actors executing steps or taking actions that should yield a particular result. A use case can include inputs and expected outputs. For example, when a user (actor) who is "signed in" (precondition) clicks the "sign out" button (action) and then navigates to the Profile page (action), the system denies access to the page and redirects the users to the Sign in page, displaying an error message (expected behaviors).

Use case testing is a systematic and structured approach to testing that helps identify defects in the software's functionality. It is very user-centric, ensuring the software meets the users' needs. However, creating test cases for complex use cases can be difficult. In the case of a user interface, the time to execute E2E tests of use cases can take a long time, especially as the number of tests grows.

Focus on testing behaviors and always center your test cases on functionality.

Now that we have explored these techniques, I'll introduce you to the xUnit framework and how to write tests, ensuring you're prepared for the examples in the book.

Introducing the xUnit framework

xUnit is a popular testing framework for writing and running unit tests. It provides tools and conventions to make testing more streamlined and effective. Whether you're a beginner or an experienced developer, xUnit helps ensure the code you write works as intended. We use xUnit throughout the book to write our unit and integration tests.

A crucial component of a testing framework is the **test runner**, which finds our tests, runs them, and then reports the results back to us. Think of it as an orchestra conductor, ensuring each test (or musician) performs its part. With xUnit, we benefit from seamless integration with various test runners, whether it's within our development environment or part of a CI process.

Visual Studio comes with the **Test Explorer** window and all the tools that you need to test your application. If unfamiliar, you can learn more about **Test Explorer** on Microsoft Learn: `https://adpg.link/Hg5r`.

Visual Studio Code also has built-in support for testing but requires us to install an extension by Microsoft. If unfamiliar, you can learn more about it on their website: `https://adpg.link/Mvr6`.

This section covers a lot of information, so feel free to use it as a reference. This medley of xUnit features aims to cover as much as possible to get you started with xUnit and ensure you understand the framework's possibilities and can follow along with the examples in the other chapters. It's important to note that this is not a step-by-step guide but a resource for future reference, as we use xUnit throughout the book. You can still follow along by recreating the examples if you want.

Let's dive in, starting with creating a test project.

How to create an xUnit test project

To create a new xUnit test project, you can run the `dotnet new xunit` command, and the CLI does the job for you by creating a project containing a `UnitTest1` class. That command does the same as creating a new xUnit project from Visual Studio.

For unit testing projects, name the project the same as the project you want to test and append `.Tests` to it. For example, `MyProject` would have a `MyProject.Tests` project associated with it. We explore more details in the *Organizing your tests* section below.

The template already defines all the required NuGet packages, so you can start testing immediately after adding a reference to your project under test.

You can also add project references using the CLI with the `dotnet add reference` command. Assuming we are in the `./test/MyProject.Tests` directory and the project file we want to reference is in the `./src/MyProject` directory, we can execute the following command to add a reference:

```
dotnet add reference ../../src/MyProject.csproj.
```

Next, we explore some xUnit features that will allow us to write test cases.

Key xUnit features

In xUnit, the `[Fact]` attribute is the way to create unique test cases, while the `[Theory]` attribute is the way to make data-driven test cases. Let's start with the `[Fact]` attribute, the simplest way to write a test case.

FactAttribute

In a test project, any method with no parameter can become a test method by decorating it with a `[Fact]` attribute, like this:

```
public class FactTest
{
    [Fact]
    public void Should_be_equal()
    {
        var expectedValue = 2;
        var actualValue = 2;
        Assert.Equal(expectedValue, actualValue);
    }
}
```

You can also decorate asynchronous methods with the `Fact` attribute when the code under test needs it:

```
public class AsyncFactTest
{
    [Fact]
    public async Task Should_be_equal()
    {
        var expectedValue = 2;
        var actualValue = 2;
        await Task.Yield();
        Assert.Equal(expectedValue, actualValue);
    }
}
```

In the preceding code, the highlighted line conceptually represents an asynchronous operation and does nothing more than allow the use of the `async`/`await` keywords. Nonetheless, having the ability to test async/await code, is mandatory nowadays, and xUnit supports it.

In our case, we created those two preceding classes as nested classes under the `xUnitFeaturesTest` class. Here's the complete code containing the preceding tests:

```
using Xunit;

namespace MyApp;
public class xUnitFeaturesTest
{
    public class FactTest
    {
        [Fact]
        public void Should_be_equal()
        {
            var expectedValue = 2;
            var actualValue = 2;
            Assert.Equal(expectedValue, actualValue);
        }
    }

    public class AsyncFactTest
    {
        [Fact]
        public async Task Should_be_equal()
        {
            var expectedValue = 2;
            var actualValue = 2;
            await Task.Yield(); // Async operation
            Assert.Equal(expectedValue, actualValue);
        }
    }
}
```

You can create test classes like any other classes in a test project. For example, we could write the preceding code in the `xUnitFeaturesTest.cs` file. To execute the tests, we can run the `dotnet test` CLI command in any terminal. When using Visual Studio Code, we can use the *C# Dev Kit* extension (see the information box at the beginning of this section). Let's start by running the tests from Visual Studio's **Test Explorer** (**View** | **Test Explorer**).

The test run result looks like this:

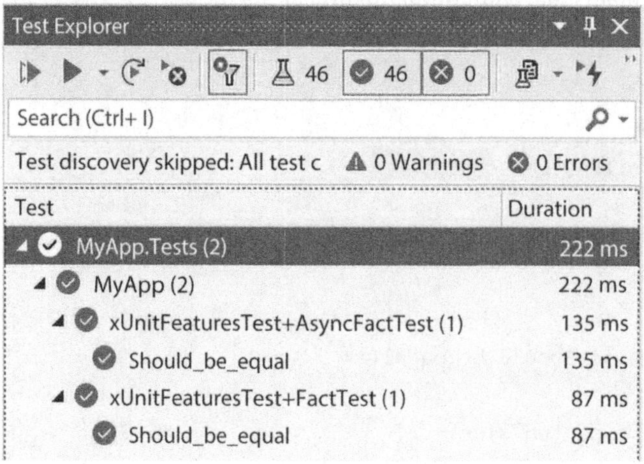

Figure 2.8: Test results in Visual Studio

You may have noticed from the screenshot that the **Test Explorer** window organizes our tests hierarchically:

- The project name: `MyApp.Tests`
- The namespace: `MyApp`
- The class name followed by a + sign and the nested class name: `xUnitFeaturesTest+FactTest` and `xUnitFeaturesTest+AsyncFactTest`
- The test method: `Should_be_equal`

If you are not using Visual Studio, running the `dotnet test` CLI command should yield a result similar to the following:

```
Starting test execution, please wait...
A total of 1 test files matched the specified pattern.

Passed!  - Failed:     0, Passed:     2, Skipped:     0, Total:     2,
Duration: 2 ms - MyApp.Tests.dll (net8.0)
```

As we can read from the preceding output, all tests have passed, none have failed, and none were skipped. It is as simple as that to create and run test cases using xUnit.

Learning the CLI commands can be very helpful in creating and debugging CI/CD pipelines, and you can use them, like the `dotnet test` command, in any script (like Bash and PowerShell).

Have you noticed the `Assert` keyword in the test code? If you are not familiar with it, we will explore assertions next.

Assertions

An assertion is a statement that checks whether a particular condition is `true` or `false`. If the condition is `true`, the test passes. If the condition is `false`, the test fails, indicating a problem with the subject under test.

Let's visit a few ways to assert correctness. We use barebone xUnit functionality in this section, but you can bring in the assertion library of your choice if you have one.

In xUnit, the assertion throws an exception when it fails, but you may never even realize that. You do not have to handle those; that's the mechanism to propagate the failure result to the test runner.

We won't explore all possibilities, but let's start with the following pieces of code. We cover the assertions one or two at a time instead of all at once. The following code should always be there, and the assertions replace the `Insert assertions here` comment:

```
public class AssertionTest
{
    [Fact]
    public void Exploring_xUnit_assertions()
    {
        object obj1 = new MyClass { Name = "Object 1" };
        object obj2 = new MyClass { Name = "Object 1" };
        object obj3 = obj1;
        object? obj4 = default(MyClass);
        //
        // Insert assertions here
        // The code we are covering next should be inserted here.
        //
        static void OperationThatThrows(string name)
        {
            throw new SomeCustomException { Name = name };
        }
    }
    private record class MyClass
    {
        public string? Name { get; set; }
    }
```

```
    private class SomeCustomException : Exception
    {
        public string? Name { get; set; }
    }
}
```

The two preceding classes, the `OperationThatThrows` method, and the variables are utilities used in the test to help us play with xUnit assertions. The variables are of the type `object` for exploration purposes, but you can use any type in your test cases. I omitted the assertion code that we are about to see to keep the code leaner.

If you have never seen the `record` keyword or other newer language features, you can consult the *Appendix* on GitHub (`https://adpg.link/net8-appendix`), where I packed lots of information about C# and .NET features.

The following two assertions are very explicit:

```
Assert.Equal(expected: 2, actual: 2);
Assert.NotEqual(expected: 2, actual: 1);
```

The first compares whether the actual value equals the expected value, while the second compares whether the two values are different. `Assert.Equal` is probably the most commonly used assertion method.

As a rule of thumb, it is better to assert equality (`Equal`) than assert that the values are different (`NotEqual`). Except in a few rare cases, asserting equality will yield more consistent results and close the door to missing defects.

The next two assertions are very similar to the equality ones but assert that the objects are the same instance or not (the same instance means the same reference):

```
Assert.Same(obj1, obj3);
Assert.NotSame(obj2, obj3);
```

The next one validates that the two objects are equal. Since we are using record classes, it makes it super easy for us; `obj1` and `obj2` are not the same (two instances) but are equal:

```
Assert.Equal(obj1, obj2);
```

Of course, we can assess the equality of any type, including primitives like number:

```
Assert.Equal(1, 2); // The test will fail because 1 does not equal 2
```

The next two are very similar and assert that the value is `null` or not:

```
Assert.Null(obj4);
Assert.NotNull(obj3);
```

The next line asserts that `obj1` is of the `MyClass` type and then returns the argument (`obj1`) converted to the asserted type (`MyClass`). If the type is incorrect, the `IsType` method will throw an exception:

```
var instanceOfMyClass = Assert.IsType<MyClass>(obj1);
```

Then we reuse the `Assert.Equal` method to validate that the value of the `Name` property is what we expect:

```
Assert.Equal(expected: "Object 1", actual: instanceOfMyClass.Name);
```

The following code block asserts that the `testCode` argument throws an exception of the `SomeCustomException` type:

```
var exception = Assert.Throws<SomeCustomException>(
    testCode: () => OperationThatThrows("Toto")
);
```

The `testCode` argument executes the `OperationThatThrows` inline function we saw initially. The `Throws` method allows us to test some exception properties by returning the exception in the specified type. The same behavior as the `IsType` method happens here; if the exception is of the wrong type or no exception is thrown, the `Throws` method will fail the test.

It is a good idea to ensure not only that the proper exception type is thrown, but the exception carries the correct values as well.

The following line asserts that the value of the `Name` property is what we expect it to be, ensuring our program would propagate the proper exception:

```
Assert.Equal(expected: "Toto", actual: exception.Name);
```

We covered a few assertion methods, but many others are part of xUnit, like the `Collection`, `Contains`, `False`, and `True` methods. We use many assertions throughout the book, so if these are still unclear, you will learn more about them.

Next, let's look at data-driven test cases using theories.

TheoryAttribute

For more complex test cases, we can use theories. A theory contains two parts:

- A `[Theory]` attribute that marks the method as a theory

- At least one data attribute that allows passing data to the test method: `[InlineData]`, `[MemberData]`, or `[ClassData]`

When writing a theory, your primary constraint is ensuring that the number of values matches the parameters defined in the test method. For example, a theory with one parameter must be fed one value. We look at some examples next.

You are not limited to only one type of data attribute; you can use as many as you need to suit your needs and feed a theory with the appropriate data.

InlineDataAttribute

The `[InlineData]` attribute is the most suitable for constant values or smaller sets of values. Inline data is the most straightforward way of the three because of the proximity of the test values and the test method.

Here is an example of a theory using inline data (`xUnitFeaturesTest.InlineDataTest.cs`):

```
public class InlineDataTest
{
    [Theory]
    [InlineData(1, 1)]
    [InlineData(2, 2)]
    [InlineData(5, 5)]
    public void Should_be_equal(int value1, int value2)
    {
        Assert.Equal(value1, value2);
    }
}
```

That test method yields three test cases in the Test Explorer, where each can pass or fail individually. Of course, since 1 equals 1, 2 equals 2, and 5 equals 5, all three test cases are passing, as shown here:

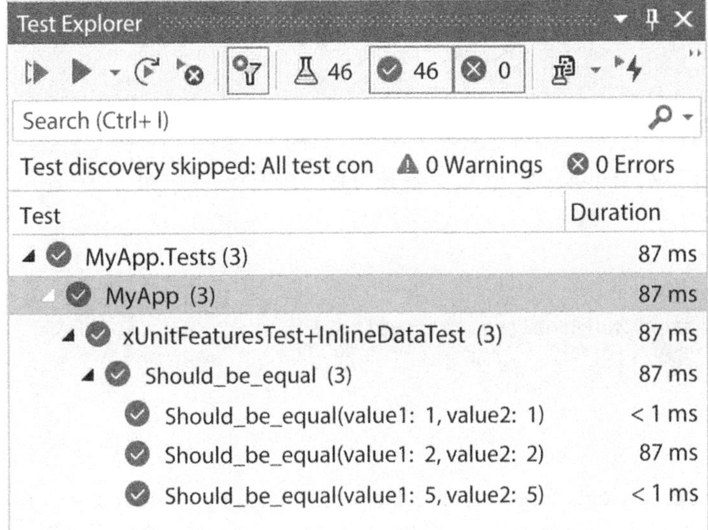

Figure 2.9: Inline data theory test results

MemberDataAttribute

We can also use the [MemberData] and [ClassData] attributes to simplify the test method's declaration when we have a large set of data to test. We can also do that when it is impossible to instantiate the data in the attribute, to reuse the data in multiple test methods, or to encapsulate the data away from the test class.

There are multiple ways to leverage the [MemberData] attribute. Here's the first we explore (xUnitFeaturesTest.MemberDataTestEnumerable.cs):

```
public class MemberDataTestEnumerable
{
    public static IEnumerable<object[]> Data => new[]
    {
        new object[] { 1, 2, false },
        new object[] { 2, 2, true },
        new object[] { 3, 3, true },
    };
```

```
    [Theory]
    [MemberData(nameof(Data))]
    public void Should_be_equal(int value1, int value2, bool shouldBeEqual)
    {
        if (shouldBeEqual)
        {
            Assert.Equal(value1, value2);
        }
        else
        {
            Assert.NotEqual(value1, value2);
        }
    }
}
```

The preceding test case yields three results. The code starts by loading a set of data from the `Data` property by decorating the test method with the `[MemberData(nameof(Data))]` attribute. This is how to load data from a member of the class in which the test method is declared. The member must be `static`. The test runner then executes the test case once per object array: three times in this case. Each value of the object array is then passed to the test method as an argument in the order they are declared.

Now, we explore another way of achieving the same result, which is very similar to the `Data` property but replaces `IEnumerable<object[]>` with a `TheoryData<…>` class, making it more readable and type-safe (`xUnitFeaturesTest.MemberDataTestTheoryData.cs`):

```
public class MemberDataTestTheoryData
{
    public static TheoryData<int, int, bool> TypedData => new()
    {
        { 3, 2, false },
        { 2, 3, false },
        { 5, 5, true },
    };

    [Theory]
    [MemberData(nameof(TypedData))]
    public void Should_be_equal(int value1, int value2, bool shouldBeEqual)
    {
        if (shouldBeEqual)
        {
            Assert.Equal(value1, value2);
        }
```

```
        else
        {
            Assert.NotEqual(value1, value2);
        }
    }
}
```

The preceding test case yields three results. It feeds a set of data to the test method by decorating it with the `[MemberData(nameof(TypedData))]` attribute. The member must be `static`. The big difference here is that the `TypedData` member is strongly typed using the `TheoryData` generic type, which is less prone to human error.

We can also leverage the `MemberData` attribute to load data that is not part of the class itself but part of another class. In that other class, we can leverage `TheoryData` or `IEnumerable<object[]>`. Here's an example (`xUnitFeaturesTest.MemberDataTestExternalProperty.cs`):

```
public class MemberDataTestExternalProperty
{
    [Theory]
    [MemberData(
        nameof(ExternalData.TypedData),
        MemberType = typeof(ExternalData))]
    public void Should_be_equal(int value1, int value2, bool shouldBeEqual)
    {
        if (shouldBeEqual)
        {
            Assert.Equal(value1, value2);
        }
        else
        {
            Assert.NotEqual(value1, value2);
        }
    }

    public class ExternalData
    {
        public static TheoryData<int, int, bool> TypedData => new()
        {
            { 20, 30, false },
            { 40, 50, false },
            { 50, 50, true },
        };
    }
}
```

The preceding test case yields three results, but its data originates from the `TypedData` property of the `ExternalData` class. To tell the `[MemberData(...)]` attribute about the external type, we leveraged the `MemberType` property of the attribute, which indicates to xUnit where to look for the specified member.

The `[MemberData]` attributes can also call methods. This is especially useful to parametrize the dataset and pass different arguments from one test case to the next. The next example divides the test case and the test data into two different classes. The test method uses the `ExternalData` class to get its data from. In this case, the `ExternalData` class is nested inside the same class as the `Should_be_equal` test method, but that is not a requirement. Here's the code (`xUnitFeaturesTest.MemberDataTestExternalMethod.cs`):

```
public class MemberDataTestExternalMethod
{
    [Theory]
    [MemberData(
        nameof(ExternalData.GetData),
        10,
        MemberType = typeof(ExternalData))]
    public void Should_be_equal(int value1, int value2, bool shouldBeEqual)
    {
        if (shouldBeEqual)
        {
            Assert.Equal(value1, value2);
        }
        else
        {
            Assert.NotEqual(value1, value2);
        }
    }

    public class ExternalData
    {
        public static TheoryData<int, int, bool> GetData(int start) => new()
        {
            { start, start, true },
            { start, start + 1, false },
            { start + 1, start + 1, true },
        };
    }
}
```

The preceding test case also yields three results, but in this case, we are sending `10` as an argument of the `GetData` method during the execution (the `start` parameter of the method). To do that, we specify the `MemberType` instance where the method is located so xUnit knows where to look. We pass the argument `10` as the second parameter of the `MemberData` constructor. We can pass as many arguments as we need, including none. The `GetData` method leverages the `start` parameter to generate its dataset.

We can also decorate the method with multiple `[MemberData]` attributes. Here's an example that combines what we have covered so far in this section (`xUnitFeaturesTest.MemberDataTest.cs`):

```
public class MemberDataTest
{
    public static IEnumerable<object[]> Data => new[]
    {
            new object[] { 1, 2, false },
            new object[] { 2, 2, true },
            new object[] { 3, 3, true },
        };

    public static TheoryData<int, int, bool> TypedData => new()
        {
            { 3, 2, false },
            { 2, 3, false },
            { 5, 5, true },
        };

    [Theory]
    [MemberData(nameof(Data))]
    [MemberData(nameof(TypedData))]
    [MemberData(
        nameof(ExternalData.GetData),
        10,
        MemberType = typeof(ExternalData))]
    [MemberData(
        nameof(ExternalData.TypedData),
        MemberType = typeof(ExternalData))]
    public void Should_be_equal(int value1, int value2, bool shouldBeEqual)
    {
        if (shouldBeEqual)
        {
            Assert.Equal(value1, value2);
        }
```

```
        else
        {
            Assert.NotEqual(value1, value2);
        }
    }

    public class ExternalData
    {
        public static IEnumerable<object[]> GetData(int start) => new[]
        {
                new object[] { start, start, true },
                new object[] { start, start + 1, false },
                new object[] { start + 1, start + 1, true },
            };

        public static TheoryData<int, int, bool> TypedData => new()
            {
                { 20, 30, false },
                { 40, 50, false },
                { 50, 50, true },
            };
    }
}
```

When running the tests, the data provided by the four `[MemberData]` attributes are combined and yield the following result when run from **Test Explorer** (12 results):

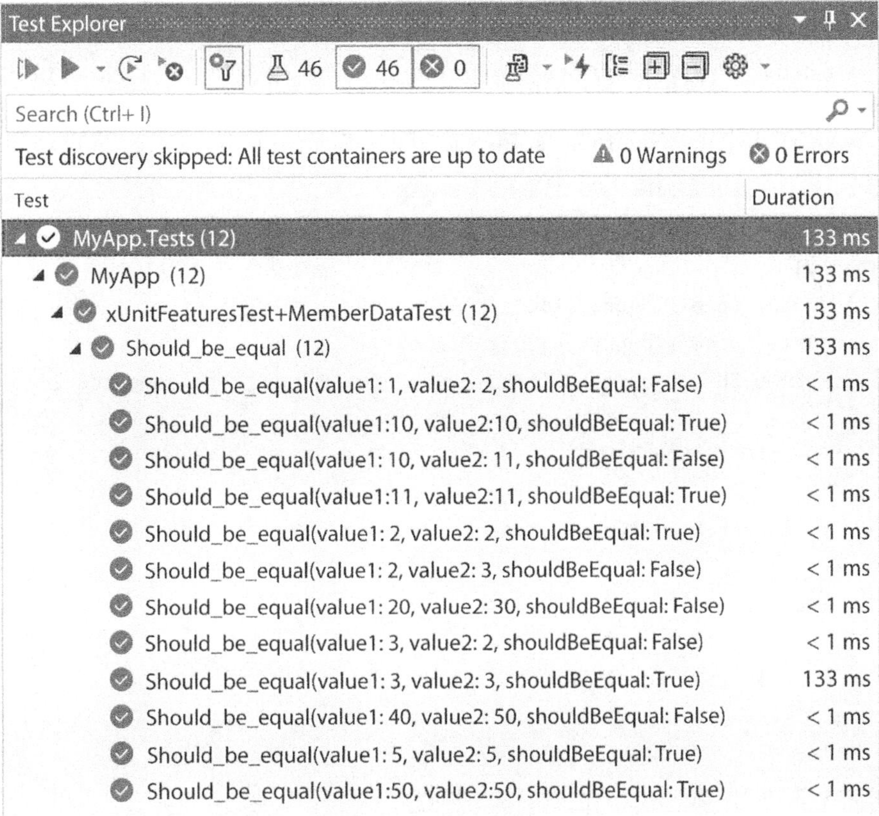

Figure 2.10: Member data theory test results

These are only a few examples of what we can do with the `[MemberData]` attribute. As you build more projects and tests, you'll find numerous ways to harness its data-driven testing capabilities, enhancing test flexibility and making it faster to test complex algorithms.

ClassDataAttribute

Last but not least, the `[ClassData]` attribute gets its data from a class implementing `IEnumerable<object[]>` or inheriting from `TheoryData<…>`. The concept is the same as the `[MemberData]` and `[InlineData]` attributes, but for class instead of members or inline. Here is an example:

```
public class ClassDataTest
{
    [Theory]
    [ClassData(typeof(TheoryDataClass))]
    [ClassData(typeof(TheoryTypedDataClass))]
    public void Should_be_equal(int value1, int value2, bool shouldBeEqual)
    {
        if (shouldBeEqual)
        {
            Assert.Equal(value1, value2);
        }
        else
        {
            Assert.NotEqual(value1, value2);
        }
    }
    public class TheoryDataClass : IEnumerable<object[]>
    {
        public IEnumerator<object[]> GetEnumerator()
        {
            yield return new object[] { 1, 2, false };
            yield return new object[] { 2, 2, true };
            yield return new object[] { 3, 3, true };
        }
        IEnumerator IEnumerable.GetEnumerator() => GetEnumerator();
    }

    public class TheoryTypedDataClass : TheoryData<int, int, bool>
    {
        public TheoryTypedDataClass()
        {
            Add(102, 104, false);
        }
    }
}
```

The preceding test case yields four results. The usage is very similar to `[MemberData]`, but we point xUnit to a type instead of a member.

In the `TheoryDataClass` class, implementing the `IEnumerable<object[]>` interface makes it easy to `yield return` the results. On the other hand, in the `TheoryTypedDataClass` class, by inheriting `TheoryData`, we can leverage a list-like `Add` method. Once again, I find inheriting from `TheoryData` more explicit, but either way works with xUnit. You have many options, so choose the best one for your use case.

Here is the result in **Test Explorer**, which is very similar to the other attributes:

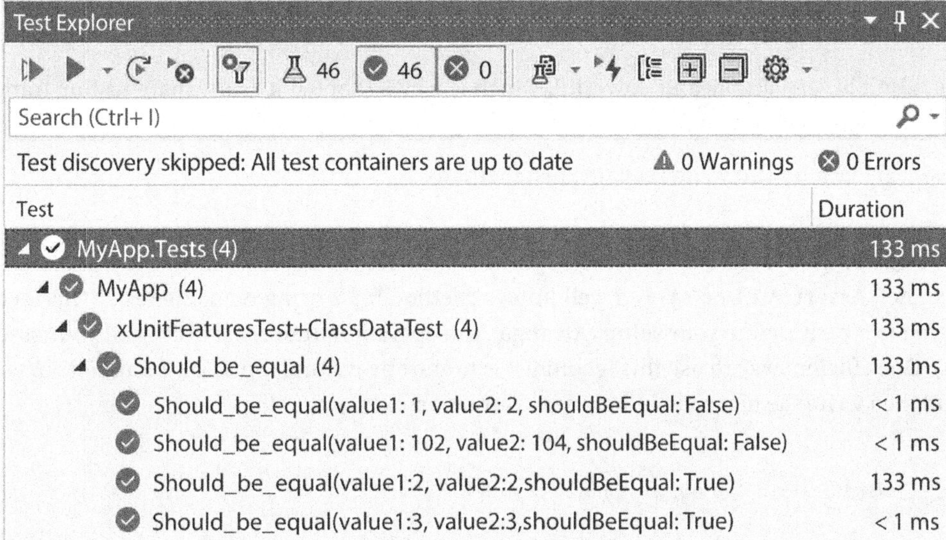

Figure 2.11: Test Explorer

That's it for the `TheoryAttribute`—next, a few words before organizing our tests.

Fixture

On top of the `FactAttribute`, `TheoryAttribute`, and assertions, xUnit offers other mechanisms that allow developers to inject dependencies into their test classes and share state between test cases. These are named fixtures. Fixtures allow dependencies to be reused by all test methods of a test class by implementing the `IClassFixture<T>` interface. Fixtures are very helpful for costly dependencies, like creating an in-memory database. With fixtures, you can create the dependency once and use it multiple times. The `HelloWorldControllerTest` class in the `MyApp.IntegrationTests` project shows that in action (see GitHub: `https://adpg.link/smFS`).

It is important to note that xUnit creates an instance of the test class for every test run, so your dependencies are recreated for every test unless you use fixtures.

You can also share the dependency provided by the fixture between multiple test classes by using `ICollectionFixture<T>`, `[Collection]`, and `[CollectionDefinition]` instead. We won't get into the details here, but at least you know it's possible and know what types to look for when you need something similar.

Finally, if you have worked with other testing frameworks, you might have encountered **setup** and **teardown** methods. In xUnit, there are no particular attributes or mechanisms for handling setup and teardown code. Instead, xUnit uses existing OOP concepts:

- To set up your tests, use the class constructor.
- To tear down (clean up) your tests, implement `IDisposable` or `IAsyncDisposable` and dispose of your resources there.

That's it; xUnit is very simple and powerful, which is why I adopted it as my main testing framework several years ago and chose it for this book.

Next, we will learn how to write readable test methods.

Arrange, Act, Assert

Arrange, Act, Assert (**AAA or 3A**) is a well-known method for writing readable tests. This technique allows you to clearly define your setup (Arrange), the operation under test (Act), and your assertions (Assert). One efficient way to use this technique is to start by writing the 3A as comments in your test case and then write the test code in between. Here is an example:

```
[Fact]
public void Should_be_equals()
{
    // Arrange
    var a = 1;
    var b = 2;
    var expectedResult = 3;

    // Act
    var result = a + b;

    // Assert
    Assert.Equal(expectedResult, result);
}
```

Of course, the preceding test case cannot fail, but the three blocks are easily identifiable with the 3A comments.

In general, *you want the Act block of your unit tests to be a single line*, making the test focus clear. If you need more than one line, the chances are that something is wrong in the test or the design.

When the tests are very small (only a few lines), removing the comments might help readability. Furthermore, when you have nothing to set up in your test case, delete the Arrange comment to improve its readability further.

Next, we learn how to organize tests into projects, directories, and files.

Organizing your tests

In a solution, we can organize our test projects in numerous ways. I typically set up a unit test project for each project within the solution, along with one or more dedicated integration test projects.

A unit test is directly related to a single unit of code, whether it's a method or a class. It is straightforward to associate a unit test project with its respective code project (assembly), leading to a one-to-one relationship. One unit test project per assembly makes them portable and easier to navigate, and even more so when the solution grows.

If you have a preferred way to organize yours that differs from what we are doing in the book, by all means, use that approach instead.

Integration tests, on the other hand, can span multiple projects, so having a single rule that fits all scenarios is challenging. One integration test project per solution is often enough. Sometimes, we can need more than one, depending on the context.

I recommend starting with one integration test project and adding more as needed during development instead of overthinking it before getting started. Trust your judgment; you can always change the structure as your project evolves.

Folder-wise, at the solution level, creating the application and its related libraries in an `src` directory helps isolate the actual solution code from the test projects created under a `test` directory, like this:

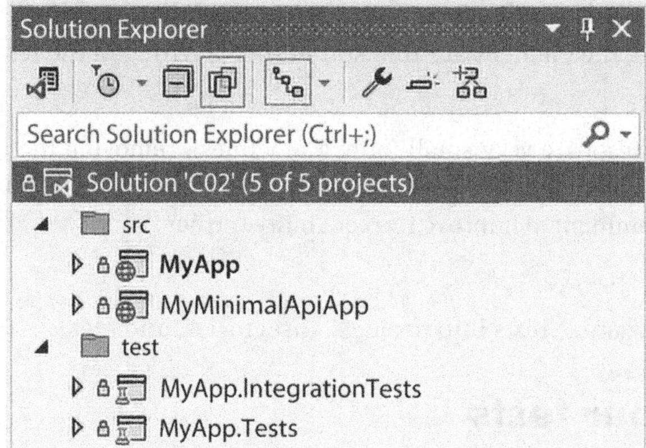

Figure 2.12: The Automated Testing Solution Explorer, displaying how the projects are organized

That's a well-known and effective way of organizing a solution in the .NET world.

Sometimes, it is not possible or it is unwanted to do that. One such use case would be multiple microservices written under a single solution. In that case, you might want the tests to live closer to your microservices and not split them between `src` and `test` folders. So you could organize your solution by microservice instead, like one directory per microservice that contains all the projects, including tests. This also applies to repositories that contain multiple applications, even if they are not microservices.

Let's now dig deeper into organizing unit tests.

Unit tests

How you organize your test projects may make a big difference between searching for your tests and making it easy to find them. Let's look at the different aspects, from the namespace to the test code itself.

Namespaces

I find it convenient to create unit tests in the same namespace as the subject under test when creating unit tests. That helps get tests and code aligned without adding any additional using statements.

To make it easier when creating files, you can change the default namespace used by Visual Studio when creating a new class in your test project by adding `<RootNamespace>[Project under test namespace]</RootNamespace>` to a `PropertyGroup` of the test project file (`*.csproj`), like this:

```
<PropertyGroup>
  ...
  <RootNamespace>MyApp</RootNamespace>
</PropertyGroup>
```

Here is an example in Visual Studio:

```
<Project Sdk="Microsoft.NET.Sdk">

  <PropertyGroup>
    <TargetFramework>net8.0</TargetFramework>
    <IsPackable>false</IsPackable>
    <RootNamespace>MyApp</RootNamespace>
    <Nullable>enable</Nullable>
  </PropertyGroup>

  <ItemGroup>...</ItemGroup>

  <ItemGroup>...</ItemGroup>

</Project>
```

Figure 2.13: A screenshot of the MyApp.Tests project file, showcasing the RootNamespace configuration

Test class names

By convention, I name test classes `[class under test]Test.cs` and create them in the same directory as in the original project. Finding tests is easy when following that simple rule since the test code is in the same location of the file tree as the code under test but in two distinct projects.

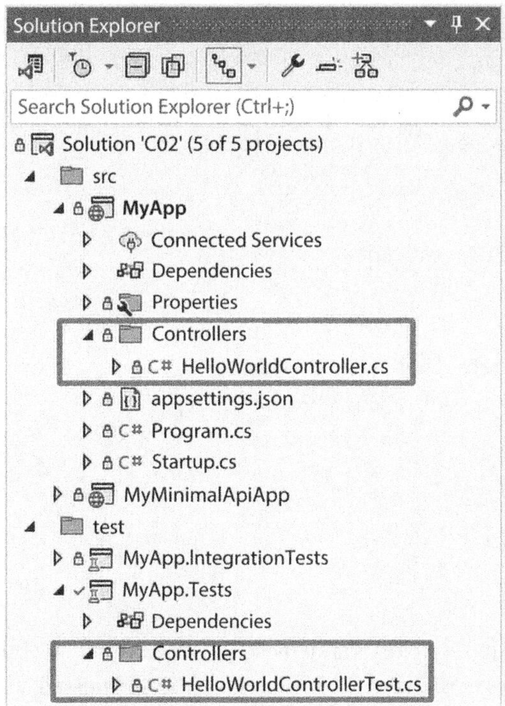

Figure 2.14: The Automated Testing Solution Explorer, displaying how tests are organized

Test code inside the test class

For the test code itself, I follow a multi-level structure similar to the following:

- One test class named the same as the class under test
- One nested test class per method to test from the class under test
- One test method per test case of the method under test

This technique helps organize tests by test case while keeping a clear hierarchy, leading to the following hierarchy:

- Class under test
- Method under test
- Test case using that method

In code, that translates to the following:

```
namespace MyApp.IntegrationTests.Controllers;
public class ValuesControllerTest
{
    public class Get : ValuesControllerTest
    {
        [Fact]
        public void Should_return_the_expected_strings()
        {
            // Arrange
            var sut = new ValuesController();

            // Act
            var result = sut.Get();

            // Assert
            Assert.Collection(result.Value,
                x => Assert.Equal("value1", x),
                x => Assert.Equal("value2", x)
            );
        }
    }
}
```

This convention allows you to set up tests step by step. For example, by inheriting the outer class (the `ValuesControllerTest` class here) from the inner class (the `Get` nested class), you can create top-level private mocks or classes shared by all nested classes and test methods. Then, for each method to test, you can modify the setup or create other private test elements in the nested classes.

Finally, you can do more configuration per test case inside the test method (the `Should_return_the_expected_strings` method here).

Don't go too hard on reusability inside your test classes, as it can make tests harder to read from an external eye, such as a reviewer or another developer who needs to play there. Unit tests should remain focused, small, and easy to read: a unit of code testing another unit of code. Too much reusability may lead to a brittle test suite.

Now that we have explored organizing unit tests, let's look at integration tests.

Integration tests

Integration tests are harder to organize because they depend on multiple units, can cross project boundaries, and interact with various dependencies.

We can create one integration test project for most simple solutions or many for more complex scenarios.

When creating one, you can name the project `IntegrationTests` or start with the entry point of your tests, like a REST API project, and name the project `[Name of the API project].IntegrationTests`. At this point, how to name the integration test project depends on your solution's structure and scope.

When you need multiple integration projects, you can follow a convention similar to unit tests and associate your integration projects one-to-one: `[Project under test].IntegrationTests`.

Inside those projects, it depends on how you want to approach the problem and the structure of the solution itself. Start by identifying the features under test. Name the test classes in a way that mimics your requirements, organize those into sub-folders (maybe a category or group of requirements), and code test cases as methods. You can also leverage nested classes, as we did with unit tests.

We will write tests throughout the book, so you will have plenty of examples to make sense of all this if it's not clear now.

Next, we implement an integration test by leveraging ASP.NET Core features.

Writing ASP.NET Core integration tests

When Microsoft developed ASP.NET Core from scratch, they addressed and enhanced numerous aspects, too many to list here, including testability.

Nowadays, there are two ways to structure a .NET program:

- The classic ASP.NET Core `Program` and the `Startup` classes. This model might be found in existing projects (created before .NET 6).

- The minimal hosting model introduced in .NET 6. This may look familiar to you if you know Node.js, as this model encourages you to write the startup code in the `Program.cs` file by leveraging top-level statements. You will most likely find this model in new projects (created after the release of .NET 6).

No matter how you write your program, that's the place to define the application's composition and how it boots.

In the case of a web application, the scope of our integration tests is often to call the endpoint of a controller over HTTP and assert the response. Luckily, in .NET Core 2.1, the .NET team added the `WebApplicationFactory<TEntry>` class to make the integration testing of web applications easier. With that class, we can boot up an ASP.NET Core application in memory and query it using the supplied `HttpClient` in a few lines of code. The test classes also provide extension points to configure the server, such as replacing implementations with mocks, stubs, or other test-specific elements.

To get started, we must create a test project. We can use the `dotnet new xunit` CLI command to achieve this. Then, we must reference the project under test from the test project. Whether using the classic or minimal hosting model, we can use the `dotnet add reference path_to_project_file.csproj` CLI command to do this. In the test project, we must install the `Microsoft.AspNetCore.Mvc.Testing` NuGet package to leverage the `WebApplicationFactory<TEntry>` class. You can use the `dotnet add package Microsoft.AspNetCore.Mvc.Testing` CLI command to achieve this.

The code in this section is available on GitHub:

- Classic web application: `https://adpg.link/QVgK`
- Classic web integration tests: `https://adpg.link/ZD1y`
- Minimal hosting application: `https://adpg.link/eWZT`
- Minimal hosting integration tests: `https://adpg.link/orFG`

With this in place, we are ready to start by booting up a classic web application test.

Classic web application

In a classic ASP.NET Core application, the `TEntry` generic parameter of the `WebApplicationFactory<TEntry>` class is usually the `Startup` or `Program` class of your project under test.

The test cases are in the `Automated Testing` solution under the `MyApp.IntegrationTests` project.

In this section, we test the following controller (we talk more about controllers and MVC in *Chapter 6, Model-View-Controller*):

```
using Microsoft.AspNetCore.Mvc;

namespace MyApp.Controllers;
```

```
[Route("")]
[ApiController]
public class HelloWorldController : ControllerBase
{
    [HttpGet]
    public string Hello()
    {
        return "Hello World!";
    }
}
```

Now, let's look at the test code:

```
using Microsoft.AspNetCore.Mvc.Testing;
using System.Net;
using Xunit;

namespace MyApp.IntegrationTests.Controllers;

public class HelloWorldControllerTest :
IClassFixture<WebApplicationFactory<Startup>>
{
    private readonly HttpClient _httpClient;
    public HelloWorldControllerTest(WebApplicationFactory<Startup>
webApplicationFactory)
    {
        _httpClient = webApplicationFactory.CreateClient();
    }
    public class Hello : HelloWorldControllerTest
    {
        public Hello(WebApplicationFactory<Startup> webApplicationFactory)
            : base(webApplicationFactory) { }

        [Fact]
        public async Task Should_respond_a_status_200_OK()
        {
            // Act
            var result = await _httpClient.GetAsync("/");

            // Assert
            Assert.Equal(HttpStatusCode.OK, result.StatusCode);
```

```
        }

        [Fact]
        public async Task Should_respond_hello_world()
        {
            // Act
            var result = await _httpClient.GetAsync("/");

            // Assert
            var contentText = await result.Content.ReadAsStringAsync();
            Assert.Equal("Hello World!", contentText);
        }
    }
}
```

The first piece of the preceding code that is relevant to us is how we get an instance of the `WebApplicationFactory<Startup>` class. We inject a `WebApplicationFactory<Startup>` object into the constructor by implementing the `IClassFixture<T>` interface.

Then, we have the nested `Hello` class that inherits the `HelloWorldControllerTest` class. The `Get` class contains the test cases. By inheriting the `HelloWorldControllerTest` class, we can leverage the `_httpClient` field from the test methods. This technique is especially useful for reusing the same test server from multiple test methods and speeding up the test execution at the cost of less test independence.

In the first test case, we use `HttpClient` to query the `http://localhost/` URI, accessible through the in-memory server. Then, we assert that the status code of the HTTP response was a success (`200 OK`):

```
[Fact]
public async Task Should_respond_a_status_200_OK()
{
    // Act
    var result = await _httpClient
        .GetAsync("/");

    // Assert
    Assert.Equal(HttpStatusCode.OK, result.StatusCode);
}
```

The second test case also sends an HTTP request to the in-memory server but reads the body and ensures its value is the same as expected:

```
[Fact]
public async Task Should_respond_hello_world()
```

```
{
    // Act
    var result = await _httpClient.GetAsync("/");

    // Assert
    var contentText = await result.Content.ReadAsStringAsync();
    Assert.Equal("Hello World!", contentText);
}
```

`WebApplicationFactory` preconfigured the `BaseAddress` property of the `HttpClient` class for us, so we don't need to prefix our requests with `http://localhost`.

When running those tests, an in-memory web server starts. Then, HTTP requests are sent to that server, testing the complete application. The tests are simple in this case, but you can create more complex test cases in more complex programs.

Next, we explore how to do the same for minimal APIs.

Minimal hosting

Now that we've delved into an MVC project, let's transition to minimal hosting. However, we'll need a workaround to ensure the `Program` class is discoverable.

Workaround

The workaround is to add a line at the bottom of the `Program.cs` file to change the autogenerated `Program` class visibility from `internal` to `public`. You can add that partial class anywhere, but keeping it in the `Program.cs` file makes it easier to find.

Here is the complete `Program.cs` file with that added line (highlighted):

```
var builder = WebApplication.CreateBuilder(args);
var app = builder.Build();
app.MapGet("/", () => "Hello World!");
app.Run();
public partial class Program { }
```

Then, we can write the same test cases as the ones we wrote for the classic web application explored previously. The only difference is that the value of the `TEntryPoint` generic argument is `Program` instead of `Startup`. Here's the full test class:

```
using Microsoft.AspNetCore.Mvc.Testing;
using System.Net;
using Xunit;
```

```
namespace MyMinimalApiApp;

public class ProgramTest : IClassFixture<WebApplicationFactory<Program>>
{
    private readonly HttpClient _httpClient;
    public ProgramTest(WebApplicationFactory<Program> webApplicationFactory)
    {
        _httpClient = webApplicationFactory.CreateClient();
    }

    public class Get : ProgramTest
    {
        public Get(WebApplicationFactory<Program> webApplicationFactory) :
base(webApplicationFactory) { }

        [Fact]
        public async Task Should_respond_a_status_200_OK()
        {
            // Act
            var result = await _httpClient.GetAsync("/");

            // Assert
            Assert.Equal(HttpStatusCode.OK, result.StatusCode);
        }

        [Fact]
        public async Task Should_respond_hello_world()
        {
            // Act
            var result = await _httpClient.GetAsync("/");

            // Assert
            var contentText = await result.Content.ReadAsStringAsync();
            Assert.Equal("Hello World!", contentText);
        }
    }
}
```

Like the tests of the classic web application, the preceding test methods expect that the endpoint returns a `200 OK` status code and the `text/plain` string `Hello World!` in the body.

Alternative to using fixtures

We can also instantiate `WebApplicationFactory` manually instead of leveraging a fixture. We must also use the preceding workaround to change the visibility of the `Program` class to `public` by adding the following line to the `Program.cs` file:

```
public partial class Program { }
```

However, instead of injecting the instance using the `IClassFixture` interface, we instantiate the factory manually. To ensure we dispose of the `WebApplicationFactory` instance, we can also implement the `IAsyncDisposable` interface.

Here's the complete example, which is very similar to the previous workaround:

```
namespace MyMinimalApiApp;
public class ProgramTestWithoutFixture : IAsyncDisposable
{
    private readonly WebApplicationFactory<Program> _webApplicationFactory;
    private readonly HttpClient _httpClient;

    public ProgramTestWithoutFixture()
    {
        _webApplicationFactory = new WebApplicationFactory<Program>();
        _httpClient = _webApplicationFactory.CreateClient();
    }

    public ValueTask DisposeAsync()
    {
        return ((IAsyncDisposable)_webApplicationFactory)
            .DisposeAsync();
    }
    // Omitted nested Get class
}
```

I omitted the test cases in the preceding code block because they are the same as the previous workarounds. The full source code is available on GitHub: `https://adpg.link/c5Na`.

Using class fixtures is more performant since the factory and the server get created only once per test run instead of recreated for every test method. However, you have better test isolation by creating one server per test.

Creating a reusable test application

Finally, we can encapsulate the creation of the `WebApplicationFactory` class in its own class. This leverages the `partial Program` class from the workaround we just explored but makes the test cases more readable. By encapsulating the setup of the test application in a class, you will improve the reusability and maintenance cost in most cases.

First, we need to change the `Program` class visibility by adding the following line to the `Project.cs` file:

```
public partial class Program { }
```

Now that we can access the `Program` class without the need to allow internal visibility to our test project, we can create our test application like this:

```
namespace MyMinimalApiApp;
public class MyTestApplication : WebApplicationFactory<Program> {}
```

Finally, we can reuse the same code to test our program but instantiate `MyTestApplication` instead of `WebApplicationFactory<Program>`, highlighted in the following code:

```
namespace MyMinimalApiApp;
public class MyTestApplicationTest
{
    public class Get : ProgramTestWithoutFixture
    {
        [Fact]
        public async Task Should_respond_a_status_200_OK()
        {
            // Arrange
            await using var app = new MyTestApplication();
            var httpClient = app.CreateClient();

            // Act
            var result = await httpClient.GetAsync("/");

            // Assert
            Assert.Equal(HttpStatusCode.OK, result.StatusCode);
        }
    }
}
```

You can also leverage fixtures, but for the sake of simplicity, I decided to show you how to instantiate our new test application manually.

This technique is wonderful for centralizing the custom initialization code of your test application. You can override certain bindings or services for all tests by configuring the test application (the `MyTestApplication` class in this case). We are leveraging this extensibility in some of the last chapters, for example, to configure in-memory databases.

And that's it. We have covered multiple ways to work around integration testing minimal APIs simplistically and elegantly. Next, we will explore a few testing principles before moving to architectural principles in the next chapter.

Important testing principles

One essential thing to remember when writing tests is to test use cases, not the code itself; we are testing features' correctness, not code correctness. Of course, if the expected outcome of a feature is correct, that also means the codebase is correct. However, it is not always true the other way around; correct code may yield an incorrect outcome. Also, remember that code costs money to write, while features deliver value.

To help with that, test requirements should revolve around **inputs and outputs**. When specific values go into your subject under test, you expect particular values to come out. Whether you are testing a simple `Add` method (where the inputs are two or more numbers and the output is the sum of those numbers) or a more complex feature (where the inputs come from a form and the output is the record getting persisted in a database), most of the time, we are testing that the inputs produced an output or an outcome.

Another concept is to divide those units as a query or a command. No matter how you organize your code, from a simple single-file application to a microservices-architecture-based Netflix clone, all simple or compounded operations are queries or commands. Thinking about a system this way should help you test the inputs and outputs. We discuss queries and commands in several chapters, so keep reading to learn more.

Now that we have laid this out, what if a unit must perform multiple operations, such as reading from a database, and then send multiple commands? You can create and test multiple smaller units (individual operations) and another unit that orchestrates those building blocks, allowing you to test each piece in isolation. We explore how to achieve this throughout the book.

In a nutshell, when writing automated tests:

- In the case of a query, we assert the output of the unit undergoing testing based on its input parameters.
- In the case of a command, we assert the outcome of the unit undergoing testing based on its input parameters.

We explore numerous techniques throughout the book to help you achieve that level of separation, starting with architectural principles in the next chapter.

Summary

This chapter covered automated testing, such as unit and integration tests. We also briefly covered end-to-end tests, but covering those in only a few pages is impossible. Still, we can apply the techniques for writing integration tests to end-to-end testing, particularly within the realm of REST APIs.

We explored different testing approaches from a bird's eye view, tackled technical debt, and explored multiple testing techniques like black-box, white-box, and gray-box testing. We also peeked at a few formal ways to choose the values to test, like equivalence partitioning and boundary value analysis.

We then looked at xUnit, the testing framework used throughout the book, and a way of organizing tests. We explored ways to pick the correct type of test and some guidelines about choosing the right quantity for each kind of test. Then we saw how easy it is to test our ASP.NET Core web applications by running the application under test in memory. Finally, we explored high-level concepts that should guide you in writing testable, flexible, and reliable programs.

Now that we have talked about testing, we are ready to explore a few architectural principles to help us increase programs' testability. Those are a crucial part of modern software engineering and go hand in hand with automated testing.

Questions

Let's take a look at a few practice questions:

1. Is it true that in TDD, you write tests before the code to be tested?
2. What is the role of unit tests?
3. How big can a unit test be?
4. What type of test is usually used when the subject under test has to access a database?
5. Is doing TDD required?
6. Do you need to know the inner workings of the application to do black-box testing?

Further reading

Here are some links to build upon what we have learned in the chapter:

- xUnit: `https://xunit.net/`.
- Run unit tests with Test Explorer: `https://adpg.link/Hg5r`.
- Testing with C# Dev Kit (VS Code): `https://adpg.link/Mvr6`.
- If you use Visual Studio, I have a few handy snippets to help improve productivity. They are available on GitHub: `https://adpg.link/5TbY`.
- Article: Testing Pyramid vs Testing Diamond (and how they affect Code Coverage): `https://adpg.link/12D1`.

Answers

Here are the answers to the earlier questions:

1. Yes, it is true.
2. To test a unit of code, such as the logical code path of a method.
3. As small as possible. A unit test aims to test the smallest possible unit of functionality in isolation.
4. Integration tests are usually used for that kind of task (integration between the system and the database).
5. No, there are multiple ways of writing code, with TDD being only one of them.
6. No, black-box testing does not require knowledge of the application; however, gray- and white-box testing do.

Learn more on Discord

To join the Discord community for this book – where you can share feedback, ask questions to the author, and learn about new releases – follow the QR code below:

`https://packt.link/ArchitectingASPNETCoreApps3e`

3

Architectural Principles

This chapter delves into fundamental architectural principles: pillars of contemporary software development practices. These principles help us create flexible, resilient, testable, and maintainable code.

We can use these principles to stimulate critical thinking, fostering our ability to evaluate trade-offs, anticipate potential issues, and create solutions that stand the test of time by influencing our decision-making process and helping our design choices.

As we embark on this journey, we constantly refer to those principles throughout the book, particularly the SOLID principles, which improve our ability to build flexible and robust software systems.

In this chapter, we cover the following topics:

- The **separation of concerns** (SoC) principle
- The **DRY** principle
- The **KISS** principle
- The **YAGNI** principle
- The **SOLID** principles

We also revise the following notions:

- Covariance
- Contravariance
- Interfaces

Separation of concerns (SoC)

As its name implies, the idea is to separate our software into logical blocks, each representing a concern. A "concern" refers to a specific aspect of a program. It's a particular interest or focus within a system that serves a distinct purpose. Concerns could be as broad as data management, as specific as user authentication, or even more specific, like copying an object into another. The SoC principle suggests that each concern should be isolated and managed separately to improve the system's maintainability, modularity, and understandability.

The SoC principle applies to all programming paradigms and all levels of architecture, like modules, subsystems, and microservices, as well as classes and methods. In a nutshell, this principle means factoring a program into the proper pieces, meaning they are fit to interact with each other yet are as independent as possible: separated by concern.

By correctly separating concerns, we can prevent changes in one area from affecting others, allow more efficient code reuse, and make it easier to understand and manage different parts of a system independently.

Here are a few examples:

- Security and logging are cross-cutting concerns.
- Rendering a user interface is a concern.
- Handling an HTTP request is a concern.
- Copying an object into another is a concern.
- Orchestrating a distributed workflow is a concern.

Before moving to the DRY principle, it is imperative to consider concerns when dividing software into pieces to create cohesive units. A good separation of concerns helps create modular designs and face design dilemmas more effectively, leading to a maintainable application.

Don't repeat yourself (DRY)

The DRY principle advocates the separation of concerns principle and aims to eliminate redundancy. It promotes the idea that each piece of knowledge or logic should have a single, unambiguous representation within a system.

So, when you have duplicated logic in your system, encapsulate it and reuse that new encapsulation in multiple places instead. If you find yourself writing the same or similar code in multiple places, refactor that code into a reusable component instead. Leverage functions, classes, modules, or other abstractions to refactor the code.

Adhering to the DRY principle makes your code more maintainable, less error-prone, and easier to modify because a change in logic or bug fix needs to be made in only one place, reducing the likelihood of introducing errors or inconsistencies.

However, it is imperative to regroup duplicated logic by concern, not only by the similarities of the code. Let's look at two classes that come from a hypothetical bookstore application:

```
public class AdminApp
{
    public async Task DisplayListAsync(
        IBookService bookService,
        IBookPresenter presenter)
    {
        var books = await bookService.FindAllAsync();
```

```
        foreach (var book in books)
        {
            await presenter.DisplayAsync(book);
        }
    }
}
public class PublicApp
{
    public async Task DisplayListAsync(
        IBookService bookService,
        IBookPresenter presenter)
    {
        var books = await bookService.FindAllAsync();
        foreach (var book in books)
        {
            await presenter.DisplayAsync(book);
        }
    }
}
```

The code of the two classes is very similar but encapsulating that code in a single class could very well be a mistake. Why? Keeping two separate classes is more logical because the admin program most likely has different reasons to change compared to the public program. Let's take an e-commerce website, for example. The customer application (`PublicApp`) will display different filters than the back office (`AdminApp`). There are very few reasons for an admin to sort the list by price, but a "search by SKU" field would probably need to be at the forefront. On the other hand, the `PublicApp` will address customer needs, like ordering items by price, to ensure the tools to help sell products are in place.

A **Stock Keeping Unit** (**SKU**) is a product's unique identifier used for inventory purposes.

So, encapsulating the list logic into the `IBookPresenter` interface could make sense and allow the program to pass a different implementation to `AdminApp` and `PublicApp`, leading to two different outcomes. For example, it would allow the program to react differently to both types of users as needed, like enabling filtering by SKU in the back office and sorting by price in the customer application. One way to implement this is by replacing the `foreach` loop with a `presenter.DisplayListAsync(books)` call, like the following highlighted code:

```
public class AdminApp
{
    public async Task DisplayListAsync(
        IBookService bookService,
```

```
        IBookPresenter presenter)
    {
        var books = await bookService.FindAllAsync();
        // We could filter the list here
        await presenter.DisplayListAsync(books);
    }
}
public class PublicApp
{
    public async Task DisplayListAsync(
        IBookService bookService,
        IBookPresenter presenter)
    {
        var books = await bookService.FindAllAsync();
        await presenter.DisplayListAsync(books);
    }
}
```

There is more to discuss here, like how to support multiple implementations of the interfaces, and we explore numerous options later in the book, so keep reading.

For now, remember that keeping our code DRY while following the SoC principles is imperative. Otherwise, what may seem like good code could become a maintenance nightmare.

Keep it simple, stupid (KISS)

This is another straightforward principle, yet one of the most important. Like in the physical world, the more moving pieces there are, the more chances that something breaks. This principle is a design philosophy that advocates for simplicity in design. It emphasizes the idea that systems work best when they are kept simple rather than made complex.

Striving for simplicity might involve writing shorter methods or functions, minimizing the number of parameters, avoiding over-architecting, and choosing the simplest solution to solve a problem.

Adding interfaces, abstraction layers, and complex object hierarchy adds complexity, but are the added benefits greater than the underlying complexity? If so, they are worth it; otherwise, they are not.

As a guiding principle, when you can write the same program with less complexity, do it. Predicting future requirements also often proves detrimental, as it may inadvertently inject unnecessary complexity into your codebase for features that might never materialize.

We study design patterns in the book, design systems using them, and learn how to apply a high degree of engineering to our code. However, mindlessly applying too many engineering techniques can lead to over-engineering. For example, a prototype does not require the same level of engineering as multi-million-dollar software. Toward the end of the book, we circle back on the KISS principle when exploring the vertical slice architecture and **request-endpoint-response** (**REPR**) patterns.

Next, let's continue keeping our application simple by exploring the YAGNI principle.

You Aren't Gonna Need It (YAGNI)

The "**You Aren't Gonna Need It**" (YAGNI) principle is a pragmatic approach to software development that advises against adding functionality until it's necessary to do so. It cautions us to resist the temptation to implement features or design elements that are not currently required, based on the speculation that they might be needed in the future.

By following YAGNI, we aim to avoid time wasted on unused code, reduce complexity, and increase productivity by focusing only on the immediate requirements of the software project at hand.

This principle supports agile methodologies, reinforcing the idea of delivering incremental value and maintaining the flexibility to adapt and evolve as actual needs emerge.

Next, we delve into the SOLID principles, which are the key to flexible software design.

The SOLID principles

SOLID is an acronym representing five principles that extend the basic OOP concepts of **Abstraction**, **Encapsulation**, **Inheritance**, and **Polymorphism**. They add more details about what to do and how to do it, guiding developers toward more robust and flexible designs.

It is crucial to remember that these are just guiding principles, not rules that you must follow no matter what. Think about what makes sense for your specific project. If you're building a small tool, it might be acceptable not to follow these principles as strictly as you would for a critical business application. In the case of business-critical applications, it might be a good idea to stick to them more closely. Still, it's usually a smart move to follow them, no matter the size of your app. That's why we discuss them before diving into design patterns and leverage them throughout the book.

The SOLID acronym represents the following:

- Single responsibility principle
- Open/closed principle
- Liskov substitution principle
- Interface segregation principle
- Dependency inversion principle

By following these principles, your systems should become easier to test and maintain.

Single responsibility principle (SRP)

Essentially, the SRP means that a single class should hold one, and only one, responsibility, leading to the following quote:

> *"There should never be more than one reason for a class to change."*
>
> *— Robert C. Martin, originator of the SRP*

OK, but why? Before answering, take a moment to remember a project you've worked on where someone changed one or more requirements along the way. I recall several projects that would have benefited from this principle. Now, imagine how much simpler it would have been if each part of your system had just one job, thereby leading to having only one reason to change.

Nothing is purely black or white—most things are a shade of gray. The same applies to software design: always do your best, learn from your mistakes, and stay humble (a.k.a. continuous improvement). You will not succeed at everything, and it's OK. Remember that behind each failure is an opportunity to learn.

The SRP helps make our classes more readable and reusable. It helps create flexible and maintainable systems, which helps when the system has to change. We must understand that applications and specifications vary constantly, and we can do nothing about it. However, the SRP can help mitigate the negative impact that changes may have on our system.

Moreover, when a class does only one thing, it's easier to see how changes will affect the system, which is more challenging with complex classes since one change might break other parts. Furthermore, fewer responsibilities mean less code. Less code is easier to understand, helping you grasp that part of the software more quickly.

Let's try this out in action.

Project – Single Responsibility

First, we look at the `Product` class used in the code sample. That class represents a simple fictional product:

```
public record class Product(int Id, string Name);
```

The code sample has no implementation because it is irrelevant to understanding the SRP. We focus on the class's API instead. Please assume we implemented the data-access logic using your favorite database.

The following class breaks the SRP:

```
namespace BeforeSRP;
public class ProductRepository
{
    public ValueTask<Product> GetOnePublicProductAsync(int productId)
        => throw new NotImplementedException();
    public ValueTask<Product> GetOnePrivateProductAsync(int productId)
        => throw new NotImplementedException();
    public ValueTask<IEnumerable<Product>> GetAllPublicProductsAsync()
        => throw new NotImplementedException();
    public ValueTask<IEnumerable<Product>> GetAllPrivateProductsAsync()
```

```
        => throw new NotImplementedException();
    public ValueTask CreateAsync(Product product)
        => throw new NotImplementedException();
    public ValueTask UpdateAsync(Product product)
        => throw new NotImplementedException();
    public ValueTask DeleteAsync(Product product)
        => throw new NotImplementedException();
}
```

What does not conform to the SRP in the preceding class? By reading the names of the methods, we can extract two responsibilities:

- Handling public products (highlighted code)
- Handling private products

The `ProductRepository` class mixes public and private product logic. From that API alone, there are many possibilities where an error could lead to leaking restricted data to public users. That is also true because the class exposes the private logic to the public-facing consumers.

We are ready to rethink the class now that we identified the responsibilities. We know it has two responsibilities, so breaking the class into two sounds like an excellent first step. Let's start with extracting a public API:

```
namespace AfterSRP;
public class PublicProductReader
{
    public ValueTask<IEnumerable<Product>> GetAllAsync()
        => throw new NotImplementedException();
    public ValueTask<Product> GetOneAsync(int productId)
        => throw new NotImplementedException();
}
```

The `PublicProductReader` class now contains only two methods: `GetAllAsync` and `GetOneAsync`. When reading the name of the class and its methods, it is clear that the class handles only public product data. By lowering the complexity of the class, we made it easier to understand.

Next, let's do the same for the private products:

```
namespace AfterSRP;
public class PrivateProductRepository
{
    public ValueTask<IEnumerable<Product>> GetAllAsync()
        => throw new NotImplementedException();
    public ValueTask<Product> GetOneAsync(int productId)
        => throw new NotImplementedException();
    public ValueTask CreateAsync(Product product)
```

```
        => throw new NotImplementedException();
    public ValueTask DeleteAsync(Product product)
        => throw new NotImplementedException();
    public ValueTask UpdateAsync(Product product)
        => throw new NotImplementedException();
}
```

The `PrivateProductRepository` class follows the same pattern. It includes the read methods, named the same as the `PublicProductReader` class, and the mutation methods only users with private access can use.

With these changes, we improved our code's readability, flexibility, and security by splitting the initial class into two. However, one thing to be careful about with the SRP is not to over-separate classes. The more classes there are in a system, the more complex assembling the system can become, and the harder it can be to debug and follow the execution paths. On the other hand, many well-separated responsibilities should lead to a better, more testable system.

It is tough to define one hard rule that defines "one reason" or "a single responsibility." However, as a rule of thumb, aim at packing a cohesive set of functionalities in a single class that revolves around its responsibility. You should strip out any excess logic and add missing pieces.

When you don't know how to name a class or a method, you may have identified a problem with your separation of concerns or responsibility segregation. This is a good indicator that you should go back to the drawing board. Nevertheless, naming is hard, so sometimes, that's just it, you can't find a good name.

Using precise names for variables, methods, classes, and other elements is very important and should not be overlooked.

Another good indicator is when a method becomes too big, maybe containing many `if` statements or loops. In that case, you can split that method into multiple smaller methods, classes, or any other construct that suits your requirements. That should make the code easier to read and make the initial method's body cleaner. It often also helps you get rid of the comments describing that bloated logic and improves testability.

Next, we explore how to change behaviors without modifying code.

Open/closed principle (OCP)

Let's start this section with a quote from Bertrand Meyer, the person who first wrote the term open/closed principle in 1988:

> *"Software entities (classes, modules, functions, and so on) should be open for extension but closed for modification."*

OK, but what does that mean? It means you should be able to change the class behaviors from the outside without altering the code.

As a bit of history, the first appearance of the OCP in 1988 referred to inheritance, and OOP has evolved a lot since then. Inheritance is still useful, but you should be careful as it is easily misused. Inheritance creates direct coupling between classes. You should, most of the time, opt for composition over inheritance.

"Composition over inheritance" is a principle that suggests it's better to build objects by combining simple, flexible parts (composition) rather than by inheriting properties from a larger, more complex object (inheritance).

Think of it like building with LEGO® blocks. It's easier to build and adjust your creation if you put together small blocks (composition) rather than trying to alter a big, single block that already has a fixed shape (inheritance).

In this section, we improve a business process multiple times to illustrate the OCP.

Project – Open Close

First, we look at the `Entity` and `EntityRepository` classes used in the code samples:

```
public record class Entity();
public class EntityRepository
{
    public virtual Task CreateAsync(Entity entity)
        => throw new NotImplementedException();
}
```

The `Entity` class represents a simple fictive entity with no properties; consider it anything you'd like. The `EntityRepository` class has a single `CreateAsync` method that inserts an instance of an `Entity` in a database (if it was implemented).

The code sample has few implementation details because it is irrelevant to understanding the OCP. Please assume we implemented the `CreateAsync` logic using your favorite database.

For the rest of the sample, we refactor the `EntityService` class, beginning with a version that inherits the `EntityRepository` class, breaking the OCP:

```
namespace OCP.NoComposability;
public class EntityService : EntityRepository
{
    public async Task ComplexBusinessProcessAsync(Entity entity)
    {
        // Do some complex things here
        await CreateAsync(entity);
        // Do more complex things here
    }
}
```

As the namespace implies, the preceding `EntityService` class offers no composability. Moreover, we tightly coupled it with the `EntityRepository` class. Since we just covered the *composition over inheritance* principle, we can quickly isolate the problem: **inheritance**.

As the next step to fix this mess, let's extract a private `_repository` field to hold an `EntityRepository` instance instead:

```
namespace OCP.Composability;
public class EntityService
{
    private readonly EntityRepository _repository
        = new EntityRepository();
    public async Task ComplexBusinessProcessAsync(Entity entity)
    {
        // Do some complex things here
        await _repository.CreateAsync(entity);
        // Do more complex things here
    }
}
```

Now the `EntityService` is composed of an `EntityRepository` instance, and there is no more inheritance. However, we still tightly coupled both classes, and it is impossible to change the behavior of the `EntityService` this way without changing its code.

To fix our last issues, we can inject an `EntityRepository` instance into the class constructor where we set our private field like this:

```
namespace OCP.DependencyInjection;
public class EntityService
{
    private readonly EntityRepository _repository;
    public EntityService(EntityRepository repository)
```

```
        {
            _repository = repository;
        }
        public async Task ComplexBusinessProcessAsync(Entity entity)
        {
            // Do some complex things here
            await _repository.CreateAsync(entity);
            // Do more complex things here
        }
    }
```

With the preceding change, we broke the tight coupling between the `EntityService` and the `EntityRepository` classes. We can also control the behavior of the `EntityService` class from the outside by deciding what instance of the `EntityRepository` class we inject into the `EntityService` constructor.

As we just explored, the OCP is a super powerful, yet simple, principle that allows controlling an object from the outside. For example, we could create two instances of the `EntityService` class with different `EntityRepository` instances that connect to different databases. Here's a rough example:

```
using OCP;
using OCP.DependencyInjection;

// Create the entity in database 1
var repository1 = new EntityRepository(/* connection string 1 */);
var service1 = new EntityService(repository1);

// Create the entity in database 2
var repository2 = new EntityRepository(/* connection string 2 */);
var service2 = new EntityService(repository2);

// Save an entity in two different databases
var entity = new Entity();
await service1.ComplexBusinessProcessAsync(entity);
await service2.ComplexBusinessProcessAsync(entity);
```

In the preceding code, assuming we implemented the `EntityRepository` class and configured `repository1` and `repository2` differently, the result of executing the `ComplexBusinessProcessAsync` method on `service1` and `service2` would create the entity in different databases. The behavior change between the two instances happened without changing the code of the `EntityService` class; composition wins over inheritance in this round.

The best way of implementing the OCP is the **Strategy pattern**, which we explore in *Chapter 7, Strategy, Abstract Factory, and Singleton Design Patterns,* and *Chapter 8, Dependency Injection*.

Next, we explore the principle that is the most complex yet the least applied.

Liskov substitution principle (LSP)

The LSP states that in a program, if we replace an instance of a superclass (supertype) with an instance of a subclass (subtype), the program should not break or behave unexpectedly.

Imagine we have a base class called `Bird` with a function called `Fly`, and we add the `Eagle` and `Penguin` subclasses. Since a penguin can't fly, replacing an instance of the `Bird` class with an instance of the `Penguin` subclass might cause problems because the program expects all birds to be able to fly.

So, according to the LSP, our subclasses should behave so the program can still work correctly, even if it doesn't know which subclass it's using, preserving system stability.

Next, we explore the formal definition of the LSP, which refers to covariance and contravariance. We explore covariance and contravariance afterward.

The LSP explained

The LSP came from Barbara Liskov at the end of the '80s and was revisited during the '90s by both Liskov and Jeannette Wing to create the principle that we know and use today. It is also similar to *Design by Contract*, by Bertrand Meyer.

Now, let's look at the formal subtype requirement definition:

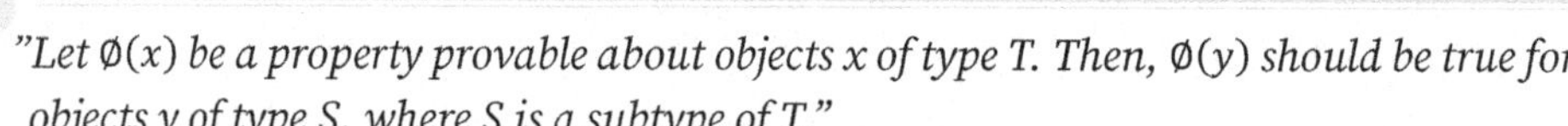

> *"Let Ø(x) be a property provable about objects x of type T. Then, Ø(y) should be true for objects y of type S, where S is a subtype of T."*

In simpler words, if `S` is a subtype of `T`, we can replace objects of type `T` with objects of type `S` without changing any of the expected behaviors of the program (correctness).

The LSP adds the following signature requirements:

- The parameters of methods in subtypes must be contravariant.
- The return type of methods in subtypes must be covariant.
- You can't throw a new type of exception in subtypes.

In C#, breaking the first two rules is challenging unless you intentionally try to.

Throwing a new type of exception in subtypes is also considered changing behaviors. You can, however, throw subtyped exceptions in subtypes because the existing consumers can handle them.

The LSP also adds the following behavioral conditions:

Conditions	Examples
Any precondition implemented in a supertype should yield the same outcome in its subtypes, but subtypes can be less strict about it, never more.	If a supertype validates that an argument cannot be `null`, the subtype could remove that validation but not add stricter validation rules.
Any postcondition implemented in a supertype should yield the same outcome in its subtypes, but subtypes can be more strict about it, never less.	If the supertype never returns `null`, the subtype should not return `null` either or risk breaking the consumers of the object that are not testing for `null`. If the supertype does not guarantee the returned value cannot be `null`, then a subtype could decide never to return `null`, making the instances interchangeable.
Subtypes must preserve the invariance of the supertype.	A subtype must pass all the tests written for the supertype, so there is no variance between them (they don't vary/they react the same).
The history constraint dictates that what happens in the supertype must still occur in the subtype, and you can't change this.	A subtype can add new properties (state) and methods (behaviors). A subtype must not modify the supertype state in any new way.

Table 3.1: LSP behavioral conditions

OK, at this point, you would be right to feel that this is rather complex. Yet, rest assured that this is the less important of the SOLID principles because we are moving as far as we can from inheritance, so the LSP should not apply often.

We can summarize the LSP as:

In your subtypes, add new behaviors and states; don't change existing ones.

In a nutshell, applying the LSP allows us to swap an instance of a class for one of its subclasses without breaking anything.

To make a LEGO® analogy: LSP is like swapping a 4x2 block with a 4x2 block with a sticker on it: neither the structure's structural integrity nor the block's role changed; the new block only has a new sticker state.

An excellent way of enforcing those behavioral constraints is automated testing. You can write a test suite and run it against all subclasses of a specific supertype to enforce the preservation of behaviors

Let's explore covariance and contravariance to ensure a full understanding of the LSP.

Covariance and contravariance

We won't go too deep into this, so we don't move too far away from the LSP, but since the formal definition mentions the terms, we must understand these at least a minimum.

Covariance and contravariance represent specific polymorphic scenarios. They allow reference types to be converted into other types implicitly. They apply to generic type arguments, delegates, and array types. Chances are, you will never need to remember this, as most of it is implicit, yet, here's an overview:

- **Covariance** (`out`) enables us to use a more derived type (a subtype) instead of the supertype. Covariance is usually applicable to method return types. For instance, if a base class method returns an instance of a class, the equivalent method of a derived class can return an instance of a subclass.
- **Contravariance** (`in`) is the reverse situation. It allows a less derived type (a supertype) to be used instead of the subtype. Contravariance is usually applicable to method argument types. If a method of a base class accepts a parameter of a particular class, the equivalent method of a derived class can accept a parameter of a superclass.

Let's use some code to understand this more, starting with the model:

```
public record class Weapon { }
public record class Sword : Weapon { }
public record class TwoHandedSword : Sword { }
```

Simple class hierarchy: we have a `TwoHandedSword` class that inherits from the `Sword` class and the `Sword` class that inherits from the `Weapon` class.

Covariance

To demo covariance, we leverage the following generic interface:

```
public interface ICovariant<out T>
{
    T Get();
}
```

In C#, the `out` modifier, the highlighted code, explicitly specifies that the generic parameter `T` is covariant. Covariance applies to return types, hence the `Get` method that returns the generic type `T`.

Before testing this out, we need an implementation. Here's a bare-bones one:

```
public class SwordGetter : ICovariant<Sword>
{
    private static readonly Sword _instance = new();
    public Sword Get() => _instance;
}
```

The highlighted code, which represents the `T` parameter, is of type `Sword`, a subclass of `Weapon`. Since covariance means you can **return (output) the instance of a subtype as its supertype**, using the `Sword` subtype allows exploring this with the `Weapon` supertype.

Here's the xUnit fact that demonstrates covariance:

```
[Fact]
public void Generic_Covariance_tests()
{
    ICovariant<Sword> swordGetter = new SwordGetter();
    ICovariant<Weapon> weaponGetter = swordGetter;
    Assert.Same(swordGetter, weaponGetter);

    Sword sword = swordGetter.Get();
    Weapon weapon = weaponGetter.Get();

    var isSwordASword = Assert.IsType<Sword>(sword);
    var isWeaponASword = Assert.IsType<Sword>(weapon);

    Assert.NotNull(isSwordASword);
    Assert.NotNull(isWeaponASword);
}
```

The highlighted line represents covariance, showing that we can implicitly convert the `ICovariant<Sword>` subtype to the `ICovariant<Weapon>` supertype.

The code after that showcases what happens with that polymorphic change. For example, the `Get` method of the `weaponGetter` object returns a `Weapon` type, not a `Sword`, even if the underlying instance is a `SwordGetter` object. However, that `Weapon` is, in fact, a `Sword`, as the assertions demonstrate.

Next, let's explore contravariance.

Contravariance

To demonstrate contravariance, we leverage the following generic interface:

```
public interface IContravariant<in T>
{
    void Set(T value);
}
```

In C#, the `in` modifier, the highlighted code, explicitly specifies that the generic parameter `T` is contravariant. Contravariance applies to input types, hence the `Set` method that takes the generic type `T` as a parameter.

Before testing this out, we need an implementation. Here's one:

```
public class WeaponSetter : IContravariant<Weapon>
{
    private Weapon? _weapon;
    public void Set(Weapon value)
        => _weapon = value;
}
```

The highlighted code, which represents the `T` parameter, is of type `Weapon`, the topmost class in our class hierarchy; other classes derive from it. Since contravariance means you can **input the instance of a subtype as its supertype**, using the `Weapon` supertype allows exploring this with the `Sword` and `TwoHandedSword` subtypes.

Here's the xUnit fact that demonstrates contravariance:

```
[Fact]
public void Generic_Contravariance_tests()
{
    IContravariant<Weapon> weaponSetter = new WeaponSetter();
    IContravariant<Sword> swordSetter = weaponSetter;
    Assert.Same(swordSetter, weaponSetter);

    // Contravariance: Weapon > Sword > TwoHandedSword
    weaponSetter.Set(new Weapon());
    weaponSetter.Set(new Sword());
    weaponSetter.Set(new TwoHandedSword());

    // Contravariance: Sword > TwoHandedSword
    swordSetter.Set(new Sword());
    swordSetter.Set(new TwoHandedSword());
}
```

The highlighted line represents contravariance. We can implicitly convert the `IContravariant<Weapon>` supertype to the `IContravariant<Sword>` subtype.

The code after that showcases what happens with that polymorphic change. For example, the `Set` method of the `weaponSetter` object can take a `Weapon`, a **`Sword`**, or a `TwoHandedSword` instance because they are all subtypes of the `Weapon` type (or the `Weapon` type itself).

The same happens with the `swordSetter` instance, but it only takes a `Sword` or a `TwoHandedSword` instance, starting at the `Sword` type in the inheritance hierarchy because the compiler considers the `swordSetter` instance to be an `IContravariant<Sword>`, even if the underlying implementation is of the `WeaponSetter` type.

Writing the following yields a compiler error:

```
swordSetter.Set(new Weapon());
```

The error is:

```
Cannot convert from Variance.Weapon to Variance.Sword.
```

That means that, for the compiler, `swordSetter` is of type `IContravariant<Sword>`, not `IContravariant<Weapon>`.

I left a link in the *Further reading* section that explains covariance and contravariance if you want to know more since we just covered the basics here.

Now that we have discussed covariance and contravariance, let's jump into some code to visualize the LSP in practice.

Project – Liskov Substitution

To demonstrate the LSP, we will explore some scenarios. Each scenario is a test class that follows the same structure:

```
namespace LiskovSubstitution;
public class TestClassName
{
    public static TheoryData<SuperClass> InstancesThatThrowsSuperExceptions =
new TheoryData<SuperClass>()
    {
        new SuperClass(),
        new SubClassOk(),
        new SubClassBreak(),
    };
    [Theory]
    [MemberData(nameof(InstancesThatThrowsSuperExceptions))]
    public void Test_method_name(SuperClass sut)
    {
        // Scenario
    }
    // Other classes, like SuperClass, SubClassOk,
    // and SubClassBreak
}
```

In the preceding code structure, the highlighted code changes for every test. The setup is simple; I use the test method to simulate code that a program could execute, and just by running the same code three times on different classes, each theory fails once:

- The initial test passes.
- The test of a subtype respecting the LSP passes.
- The test of a subtype violating the LSP fails.

The parameter `sut` is the subject under test, a well-known acronym.

Of course, we can't explore all scenarios, so I picked three; let's check the first one.

Scenario 1: ExceptionTest

This scenario explores what can happen when a subtype throws a new exception type.

The following code is the consumer of the subject under test:

```
try
{
    sut.Do();
}
catch (SuperException ex)
{
    // Some code
}
```

The preceding code is very standard. We wrapped the execution of some code (the `Do` method) in a try-catch block to handle a specific exception.

The initial subject under test (`SuperClass`) simulates that at some point during the execution of the `Do` method, it throws an exception of type `SuperException`. When we execute the code, the `try-catch` block catches the `SuperException`, and everything goes as planned. Here's the code:

```
public class SuperClass
{
    public virtual void Do()
        => throw new SuperException();
}
public class SuperException : Exception { }
```

Next, the `SubClassOk` class simulates that the execution changed, and it throws a `SubException` that inherits the `SuperException` class. When we execute the code, the `try-catch` block catches the `SubException`, because it's a subtype of `SuperException`, and everything goes as planned. Here's the code:

```
public class SubClassOk : SuperClass
{
    public override void Do()
        => throw new SubException();
}
public class SubException : SuperException { }
```

Finally, the `SubClassBreak` class simulates that it is throwing `AnotherException`, a new type of exception. When we execute the code, the program stops unexpectedly because we did not design the `try-catch` block for that. Here's the code:

```
public class SubClassBreak : SuperClass
{
    public override void Do()
        => throw new AnotherException();
}
public class AnotherException : Exception { }
```

So as trivial as it may sound, throwing that exception breaks the program and goes against the LSP.

Scenario 2: PreconditionTest

This scenario explores that any precondition implemented in a supertype should yield the same outcome in its subtypes, but subtypes can be less strict about it, never more.

The following code is the consumer of the subject under test (`sut`):

```
var value = 5;
var result = sut.IsValid(value);
Console.WriteLine($"Do something with {result}");
```

The preceding code is very standard. We have the `value` variable that could come from anywhere. Then we pass it to the `IsValid` method. Finally, we do something with the `result`; in this case, we write a line to the console. The same code is executed for each class we are about to see.

The initial subject under test (`SuperClass`) simulates that a precondition exists that enforces that the value must be positive. Here's the code:

```
public class SuperClass
{
    public virtual bool IsValid(int value)
    {
        if (value < 0)
        {
            throw new ArgumentException(
                "Value must be positive.",
                nameof(value)
```

```
            );
        }
        return true;
    }
}
```

Next, the `SubClassOk` class simulates that the execution changed and tolerates negative values up to -10. Everything is fine when executing the code because the precondition is less strict. Here's the code:

```
public class SubClassOk : SuperClass
{
    public override bool IsValid(int value)
    {
        if (value < -10)
        {
            throw new ArgumentException(
                "Value must be greater or equal to -10.",
                nameof(value)
            );
        }
        return true;
    }
}
```

Finally, the `SubClassBreak` class simulates that the execution changed and restricts using values under 10. When executing the code (remember that the test value is 5), the test breaks because it is not expecting that error. The precondition of the `SubClassBreak` class is stricter than the one in the `SuperClass` class. Here's the code:

```
public class SubClassBreak : SuperClass
{
    public override bool IsValid(int value)
    {
        if (value < 10) // Break LSP
        {
            throw new ArgumentException(
                "Value must be greater than 10.",
                nameof(value)
            );
        }
        return true;
    }
}
```

This is yet another example of how a simple change can break its consumers and the LSP. Of course, this is an overly simplified example focusing only on the precondition, but the same applies to more complex scenarios. Coding is like playing with blocks.

Scenario 3: PostconditionTest

This scenario explores that postconditions implemented in a supertype should yield the same outcome in its subtypes, but subtypes can be more strict about it, never less.

The following code is the consumer of the subject under test:

```
var value = 5;
var result = sut.Do(value);
Console.WriteLine($"Do something with {result.Value}");
```

The preceding code is very standard and very similar to the second scenario. We have the `value` variable that could come from anywhere. Then we pass it to the `Do` method. Finally, we do something with the `result`; in this case, we write a line to the console. The `Do` method returns an instance of a `Model` class, which has only a `Value` property. Here's the code:

```
public record class Model(int Value);
```

The initial subject under test (`SuperClass`) simulates that at some point during the execution, it returns a `Model` instance and sets the value of the `Value` property to the value of the `value` parameter. Here's the code:

```
public class SuperClass
{
    public virtual Model Do(int value)
    {
        return new(value);
    }
}
```

Next, the `SubClassOk` class simulates that the execution changed and returns a `SubModel` instance instead. The `SubModel` class inherits the `Model` class and adds a `DoCount` property. When executing the code, everything is fine because the output is invariant (a `SubModel` is a `Model` and behaves the same). Here's the code:

```
public class SubClassOk : SuperClass
{
    private int _doCount = 0;
    public override Model Do(int value)
    {
        var baseModel = base.Do(value);
        return new SubModel(baseModel.Value, ++_doCount);
    }
}
public record class SubModel(int Value, int DoCount) : Model(Value);
```

Finally, the `SubClassBreak` class simulates that the execution changed and returns `null` when the value of the `value` parameter is `5`. When executing the code, it breaks at runtime with a `NullReferenceException` when accessing the `Value` property during the interpolation that happens in the `Console.WriteLine` call. Here's the code:

```
public class SubClassBreak : SuperClass
{
    public override Model Do(int value)
    {
        if (value == 5)
        {
            return null;
        }
        return base.Do(value);
    }
}
```

This last scenario shows once again how a simple change can break our program. Of course, this is also an overly simplified example focusing only on the postcondition and history constraint, but the same applies to more complex scenarios.

What about the history constraint? We added a new state element to the `SubClassOk` class by creating the `_doCount` field. Moreover, by adding the `SubModel` class, we added the `DoCount` property to the return type. That field and property were nonexistent in the supertype, and they did not alter its behaviors: LSP followed!

Conclusion

The key idea of the LSP is that the consumer of a supertype should remain unaware of whether it's interacting with an instance of a supertype or an instance of a subtype.

We could also name this principle the backward-compatibility principle because everything that worked in a way before must still work at least the same after the substitution, which is why this principle is essential.

Once again, this is only a principle, not a law. You can also see a violation of the LSP as a *code smell*. From there, analyze whether you have a design problem and its impact. Use your analytical skills on a case-by-case basis and conclude whether or not it would be acceptable to break the LSP in that specific case. Sometimes you want to change the program's behavior and break the LSP, but beware that you might break certain execution paths you did not account for and introduce defects.

The more we are progressing in the book and with our engineering skills, the more we are moving away from inheritance, and the less we need to worry about this principle. However, if you use inheritance and want to ensure your subtypes don't break the program, apply the LSP, and you will be rewarded by improving your chances of producing defect-free, backward-compatible changes.

Let's look at the ISP next.

Interface segregation principle (ISP)

Let's start with another famous quote by Robert C. Martin:

> *"Many client-specific interfaces are better than one general-purpose interface."*

What does that mean? It means the following:

- You should create interfaces.
- You should value small interfaces more.
- You should not create multipurpose interfaces.

You can see a multipurpose interface as "an interface to rule them all" or a God class, introduced in *Chapter 1, Introduction.*

An interface could refer to a class interface (the public members of a class) or a C# interface. We focus on C# interfaces in the book, as we use them extensively. Moreover, C# interfaces are very powerful.

Speaking of interfaces, let's quickly look at them before digging into some code.

What is an interface?

Interfaces are among the most valuable tools in the C# toolbox for creating flexible and maintainable software. It can be tough to understand and grasp the power of interfaces at first, especially from an explanation, so don't worry if you don't; you will see plenty in action throughout the book.

You can see an interface as allowing a class to impersonate different things (APIs), bringing polymorphism to the next level.

Next are some more details that overview interfaces:

- The role of an interface is to define a cohesive contract (public methods, properties, and events). In its theoretical form, an interface contains no code; it is only a contract. In practice, since C# 8, we can create default implementation in interfaces, which could be helpful to limit breaking changes in a library (such as adding a method to an interface without breaking any class implementing that interface).
- An interface following the ISP should be small. Its members should commit to the SRP and strive toward a common goal (cohesion).
- In C#, a class can implement multiple interfaces, exposing multiples of those public contracts or, more accurately, be any and all of them. By leveraging polymorphism, we can consume a class as if it were any of the interfaces it implements or its supertype if it inherits another class.

A class does not inherit from an interface; it implements an interface. However, an interface can inherit from another interface.

Let's explore the ISP example now that we refreshed our memory.

Project – Interface Segregation

In this project, we start with the same class as the SRP example but extract an interface from the `ProductRepository` class.

Let's start by looking at the `Product` class, which represents a simple fictitious product:

```
public record class Product(int Id, string Name);
```

The code sample has no implementation because it is irrelevant to understanding the ISP. We focus on the interfaces instead. Please assume we implemented the data-access logic using your favorite database.

Now, let's look at the interface extracted from the `ProductRepository` class:

```
namespace InterfaceSegregation.Before;
public interface IProductRepository
{
    public ValueTask<IEnumerable<Product>> GetAllPublicProductAsync();
    public ValueTask<IEnumerable<Product>> GetAllPrivateProductAsync();
    public ValueTask<Product> GetOnePublicProductAsync(int productId);
    public ValueTask<Product> GetOnePrivateProductAsync(int productId);
    public ValueTask CreateAsync(Product product);
    public ValueTask UpdateAsync(Product product);
    public ValueTask DeleteAsync(Product product);
}
```

At this point, the `IProductRepository` interface breaks the SRP and the ISP the same way the `ProductRepository` class did before. We already identified the SRP issues earlier but did not reach the point of extracting interfaces.

The `ProductRepository` class implements the `IProductRepository` interface and is the same as the SRP example (all methods `throw new NotImplementedException()`).

In the SRP example, we identified the following responsibilities:

- Handling public products
- Handling private products

Based on our previous analysis, we have two functional requirements (public and private access). By digging deeper, we can also identify five different database operations. Here's the result in a grid:

	Public	Private
Read one product	Yes	Yes
Read all products	Yes	Yes
Create a product	No	Yes
Update a product	No	Yes
Delete a product	No	Yes

Table 3.2: A grid that shows what the software needs to do (functional requirements) and what needs to happen in the database (database operation requirements)

We can extract the following families of database operations from *Table 3.2*:

- Read products (read one, read all).
- Write or alter products (create, update, delete).

Based on that thorough analysis, we can extract the `IProductReader` and `IProductWriter` interfaces representing the database operation. Then we can create the `PublicProductReader` and `PrivateProductRepository` classes to implement our functional requirements.

Let's start with the `IProductReader` interface:

```
namespace InterfaceSegregation.After;
public interface IProductReader
{
    public ValueTask<IEnumerable<Product>> GetAllAsync();
    public ValueTask<Product> GetOneAsync(int productId);
}
```

With this interface, we cover the *read one product* and *read all products* use cases. Next, the `IProductWriter` interface covers the other three database operations:

```
namespace InterfaceSegregation.After;
public interface IProductWriter
{
    public ValueTask CreateAsync(Product product);
    public ValueTask UpdateAsync(Product product);
    public ValueTask DeleteAsync(Product product);
}
```

We can cover all the database use cases with the preceding interfaces. Next, let's create the `PublicProductReader` class:

```
namespace InterfaceSegregation.After;
public class PublicProductReader : IProductReader
{
    public ValueTask<IEnumerable<Product>> GetAllAsync()
        => throw new NotImplementedException();
    public ValueTask<Product> GetOneAsync(int productId)
        => throw new NotImplementedException();
}
```

In the preceding code, the `PublicProductReader` only implements the `IProductReader` interface, covering the identified scenarios.

We do the `PrivateProductRepository` class next before exploring the advantages of the ISP:

```
namespace InterfaceSegregation.After;
public class PrivateProductRepository : IProductReader, IProductWriter
{
    public ValueTask<IEnumerable<Product>> GetAllAsync()
        => throw new NotImplementedException();
    public ValueTask<Product> GetOneAsync(int productId)
        => throw new NotImplementedException();
    public ValueTask CreateAsync(Product product)
        => throw new NotImplementedException();
    public ValueTask DeleteAsync(Product product)
        => throw new NotImplementedException();
    public ValueTask UpdateAsync(Product product)
        => throw new NotImplementedException();
}
```

In the preceding code, the `PrivateProductRepository` class implements the `IProductReader` and `IProductWriter` interfaces, covering all the database needs.

Now that we have covered the building blocks, let's explore what this can do. Here's the `Program.cs` file:

```
using InterfaceSegregation.After;

var publicProductReader = new PublicProductReader();
var privateProductRepository = new PrivateProductRepository();

ReadProducts(publicProductReader);
ReadProducts(privateProductRepository);
```

```
// Error: Cannot convert from PublicProductReader to IProductWriter
// ModifyProducts(publicProductReader); // Invalid
WriteProducts(privateProductRepository);

ReadAndWriteProducts(privateProductRepository, privateProductRepository);
ReadAndWriteProducts(publicProductReader, privateProductRepository);

void ReadProducts(IProductReader productReader)
{
    Console.WriteLine(
        "Reading from {0}.",
        productReader.GetType().Name
    );
}
void WriteProducts(IProductWriter productWriter)
{
    Console.WriteLine(
        "Writing to {0}.",
        productWriter.GetType().Name
    );
}
void ReadAndWriteProducts(IProductReader productReader, IProductWriter
productWriter)
{
    Console.WriteLine(
        "Reading from {0} and writing to {1}.",
        productReader.GetType().Name,
        productWriter.GetType().Name
    );
}
```

From the preceding code, the `ReadProducts`, `ModifyProducts`, and `ReadAndUpdateProducts` methods write messages in the console to demonstrate the advantages of applying the ISP.

The `publicProductReader` (instance of `PublicProductReader`) and `privateProductRepository` (instance of `PrivateProductRepository`) variables are passed to the methods to show what we can and cannot do with the current design.

Before getting into the weeds, when we execute the program, we obtain the following output:

```
Reading from PublicProductReader.
Reading from PrivateProductRepository.
Writing to PrivateProductRepository.
Reading from PrivateProductRepository and writing to PrivateProductRepository.
Reading from PublicProductReader and writing to PrivateProductRepository.
```

First operation: Read products

The following code represents the first operation:

```
ReadProducts(publicProductReader);
ReadProducts(privateProductRepository);
```

Since the `PublicProductReader` and `PrivateProductRepository` classes implement the `IProductReader` interface, the `ReadProducts` method accepts them, leading to the following output:

```
Reading from PublicProductReader.
Reading from PrivateProductRepository.
```

That means we can centralize some code that reads from both implementations.

Second operation: Write products

The following code represents the second operation:

```
WriteProducts(privateProductRepository);
```

Since only the `PrivateProductRepository` class implements the `IProductWriter` interface, the `WriteProducts` method accepts only the `privateProductRepository` variable and outputs the following:

```
Writing to PrivateProductRepository.
```

This is one advantage of well-segregated interfaces and responsibilities; if we try to execute the following line, the compiler yields the error saying that we `cannot convert from PublicProductReader to IProductWriter`:

```
ModifyProducts(publicProductReader);
```

That error makes sense because `PublicProductReader` does not implement the `IProductWriter` interface.

Third operation: Read and write products

The following code represents the third operation:

```
ReadAndWriteProducts(
    privateProductRepository,
    privateProductRepository
);
ReadAndWriteProducts(
    publicProductReader,
    privateProductRepository
);
```

Let's analyze the two calls to the `ReadAndWriteProducts` method individually, but before that, let's look at the console output:

```
Reading from PrivateProductRepository and writing to PrivateProductRepository.
Reading from PublicProductReader and writing to PrivateProductRepository.
```

The first execution reads and writes to the `PrivateProductRepository` instance, which is possible because it implements both the `IProductReader` and `IProductWriter` interfaces.

The second call, however, reads from the public reader but writes using the private writer.

The last example shows the power of the ISP, especially when mixed with the SRP, and how easy it is to swap one piece for another when segregating our interfaces correctly and designing our code for the program's use cases.

You should not divide all your repositories into readers and writers; this sample only demonstrates some possibilities. Always design your programs for the specifications that you have.

Conclusion

To summarize the idea behind the ISP, if you have multiple smaller interfaces, it is easier to reuse them and expose only the features you need instead of exposing APIs that part of your program doesn't need. Furthermore, it is easier to compose bigger pieces using multiple specialized interfaces by implementing them as needed than remove methods from a big interface if we don't need them in one of its implementations.

The main takeaway is to **only depend on the interfaces that you consume.**

If you don't see all of the benefits yet, don't worry. All the pieces should come together as we move on to the last SOLID principle, dependency injection, and as you practice applying the SOLID principles throughout the book and beyond.

Like the SRP, be careful not to overuse the ISP mindlessly. Think about cohesion and what you are trying to achieve, not how granular an interface can become. The finer-grained your interfaces, the more flexible your system will be but remember that flexibility has a cost, which can become very high very quickly. For example, your highly flexible system may be very hard to navigate and understand, increasing the cognitive load required to work on the project.

Next, we explore the last of the SOLID principles.

Dependency inversion principle (DIP)

The DIP provides flexibility, testability, and modularity by reducing tight coupling between classes or modules.

Let's continue with another quote from Robert C. Martin:

> *"depend upon abstractions, not concretions."*

In the previous section, we explored interfaces (abstractions), one of the pivotal elements of our SOLID arsenal, and using interfaces is the best way to approach the DIP.

> Are you wondering why not use abstract classes? While helpful at providing default behaviors over inheritance, they're not fully abstract. If one is, it's better to use an interface instead.
>
> Interfaces are more flexible and powerful, acting as contracts between parts of a system. They also allow a class to implement multiple interfaces, boosting flexibility. However, don't discard abstract classes mindlessly. Actually, don't discard anything mindlessly.

Exposing interfaces can save countless hours of struggling to find complex workarounds when writing unit tests. That is even more true when building a framework or library that others use. In that case, please pay even more attention to providing your consumers with interfaces to mock if necessary.

All that talk about interfaces again is great, but how can we invert the flow of dependencies? Spoiler alert: interfaces!

Let's compare a direct dependency and an inverted dependency first.

Direct dependency

A direct dependency occurs when a particular piece of code (like a class or a module) relies directly on another. For example, if Class A uses a method from Class B, then Class A directly depends on Class B, which is a typical scenario in traditional programming.

Say we have a `SomeService` class that uses the `SqlDataPersistence` class for production but the `LocalDataPersistence` class during development and testing. Without inverting the dependency flow, we end up with the following **Unified Modeling Language** (**UML**) dependency graph:

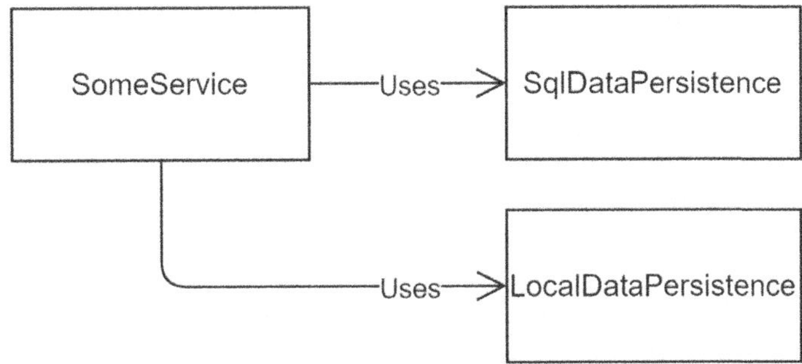

Figure 3.1: Direct dependency graph schema

With the preceding system, we could not change the `SqlDataPersistence` or `LocalDataPersistence` classes by the `CosmosDbDataPersistence` class (not in the diagram) without impacting the `SomeService` class.

We call direct dependencies like these **tight coupling.**

Inverted dependency

An inverted dependency occurs when high-level modules (which provide complex logic) are independent of low-level modules (which provide basic, foundational operations).

We can achieve this by introducing an abstraction (like an interface) between the modules. This means that instead of Class A depending directly on Class B, Class A would rely on an abstraction that Class B implements.

Here is the updated schema that improves the direct dependency example:

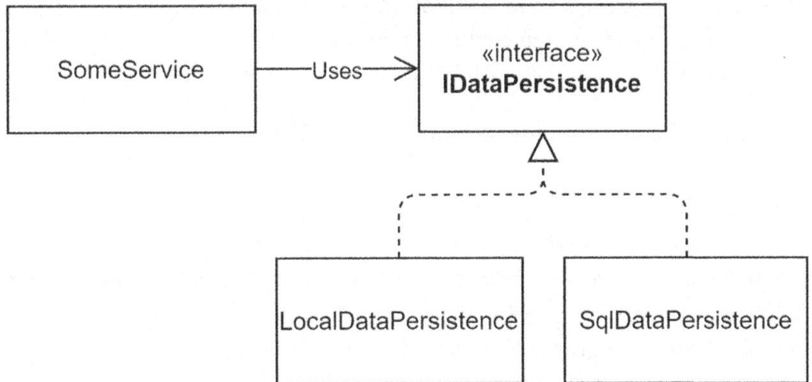

Figure 3.2: Indirect dependency graph schema

In the preceding diagram, we successfully inverted the dependency flow by ensuring the `SomeService` class depends only on an `IDataPersistance` interface (abstraction) that the `SqlDataPersistence` and `LocalDataPersistence` classes implement. We could then use the `CosmosDbDataPersistence` class (not in the diagram) without impacting the `SomeService` class.

We call inverted dependencies like these **loose coupling.**

Now that we have covered how to invert the dependency flow of classes, we will look at inverting subsystems.

Direct subsystems dependency

The preceding direct dependency example divided into packages, which have the same issue, would look like the following:

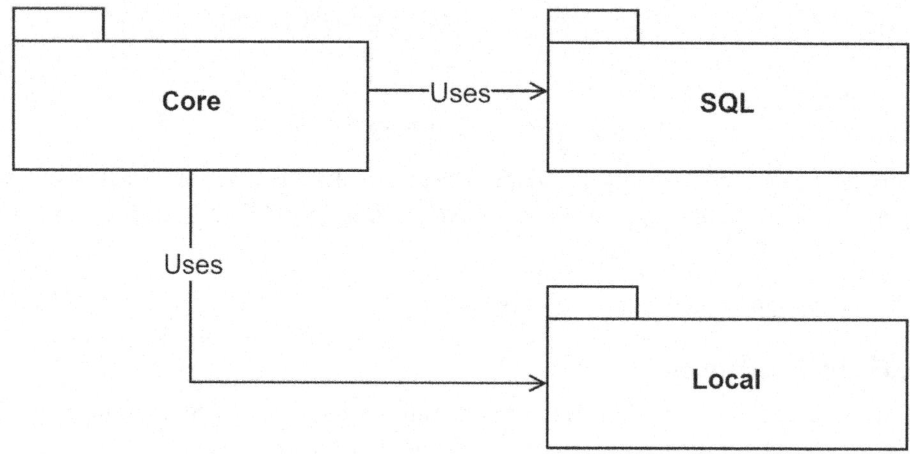

Figure 3.3: Direct dependency graph divided into packages

The `Core` package depends on the `SQL` and `Local` packages leading to tight coupling.

Packages usually represent assemblies or namespaces. However, dividing responsibilities around assemblies allows loading only the implementations that the program needs. For example, one program could load the `Local` assembly, another could load the SQL assembly, and a third could load both.

Enough said; let's invert the dependency flow of those subsystems.

Inverted subsystems dependency

This section explores inverting the dependency flow of subsystems to reduce the tight coupling between them and make the system more maintainable. A subsystem can be a module, a package, or an assembly. We'll talk mostly about assemblies since code compiles to assemblies in .NET. This approach helps us create more flexible programs by arranging our code in separate loosely coupled assemblies, improving our applications' modularity.

To continue the inverted dependency example, we can do the following:

1. Create an abstraction assembly containing only interfaces.
2. Create other assemblies that contain the implementation of the contracts from that first assembly.
3. Create assemblies that consume the code through the abstraction assembly.

There are multiple examples of this in .NET, such as the `Microsoft.Extensions.DependencyInjection.Abstractions` and `Microsoft.Extensions.DependencyInjection` assemblies. We explore this concept further in *Chapter 14, Layering and Clean Architecture*.

Then, if we divide the inverted dependency examples into multiple packages, it would look like the following:

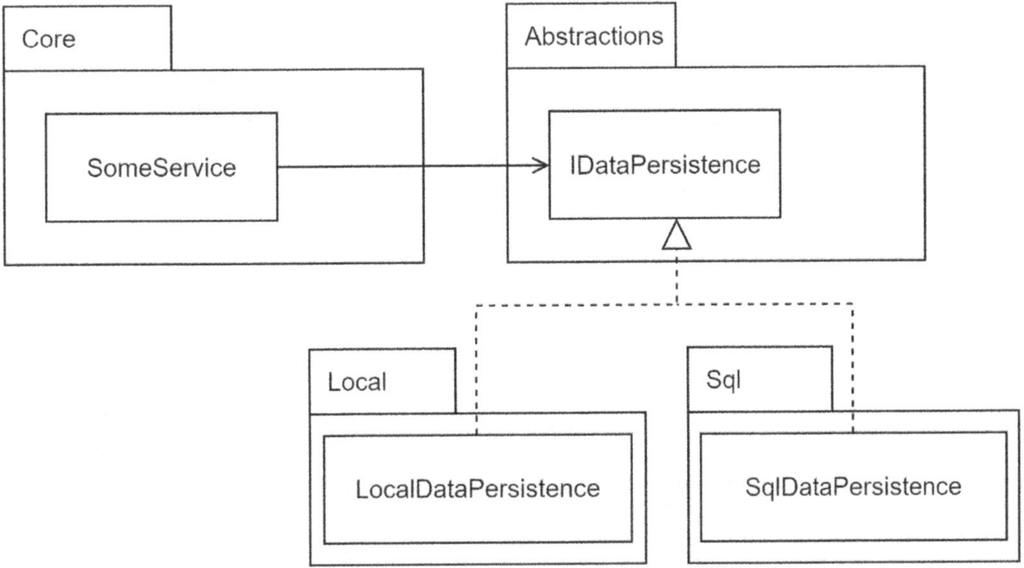

Figure 3.4: Inverted dependency examples divided into multiple packages

In the diagram, the `Core` package directly depends on the `Abstractions` package, while two implementations are available: `Local` and `Sql`. Since we only rely on abstractions, we can swap one implementation for the other without impacting `Core`, and the program will run just fine unless something is wrong with the implementation itself (but that has nothing to do with the DIP).

We could also create a new `CosmosDb` package and a `CosmosDbDataPersistence` class that implements the `IDataPersistence` interface, and then use it in the `Core` without breaking anything. Why? Because we are only directly depending on abstractions, leading to a loosely coupled system.

Next, we dig into some code.

Project – Dependency inversion

In this section, we translate the preceding iteration of the inverted dependency example in code. We create the following assemblies to align with the preceding diagram:

- `App` is a console application that references all projects to showcase different use cases.
- `Core` is a class library that depends on the `Abstractions` package.
- `Abstractions` is a class library that contains the `IDataPersistence` interface.

- `Sql` and `Local` are class libraries that reference the `Abstractions` project and implement the `IDataPersistence` interface.

The code sample has few implementation details because it is irrelevant to understanding the DIP. Please assume we implemented the `Persist` methods logic using your favorite in-memory and SQL databases.

Visually, the relationships between the packages look like the following:

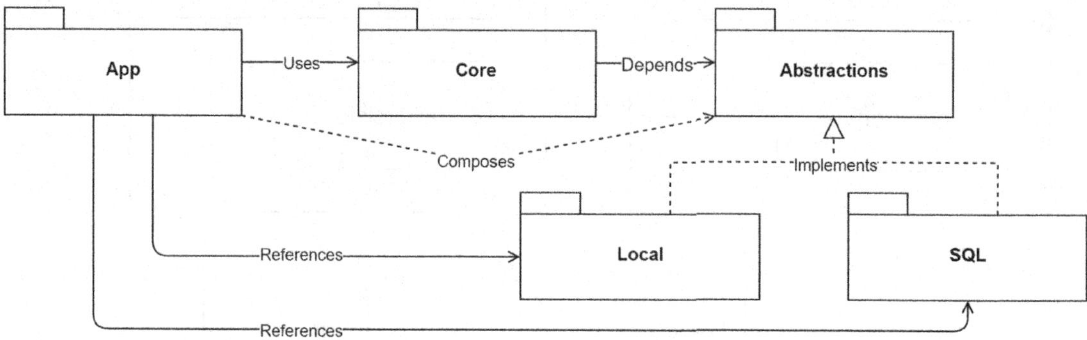

Figure 3.5: The visual representation of the packages and their relationships

Code-wise, our abstraction contains a `Persist` method that we use to showcase the DIP:

```
namespace Abstractions;
public interface IDataPersistence
{
    void Persist();
}
```

Next, the `LocalDataPersistence` class depends on the `Abstractions` package and outputs a line to the console, allowing us to trace what happens in the system:

```
using Abstractions;
namespace Local;
public class LocalDataPersistence : IDataPersistence
{
    public void Persist()
    {
        Console.WriteLine("Data persisted by LocalDataPersistence.");
    }
}
```

Next, the SqlDataPersistence class is very similar to the LocalDataPersistence class; it depends on the Abstractions package and outputs a line in the console, allowing us to trace what happens in the system:

```
using Abstractions;
namespace Sql;
public class SqlDataPersistence : IDataPersistence
{
    public void Persist()
    {
        Console.WriteLine("Data persisted by SqlDataPersistence.");
    }
}
```

Before we get to the program flow, we still have the SomeService class to look at, which depends on the Abstractions package:

```
using Abstractions;
namespace App;
public class SomeService
{
    public void Operation(IDataPersistence someDataPersistence)
    {
        Console.WriteLine("Beginning SomeService.Operation.");
        someDataPersistence.Persist();
        Console.WriteLine("SomeService.Operation has ended.");
    }
}
```

The highlighted code shows that the SomeService class calls the Persist method of the provided IDataPersistence interface implementation. The SomeService class is not aware of where the data goes. In the case of full implementation, the someDataPersistence instance is responsible for where the data would be persisted. Other than that, the Operation method writes lines to the console so we can trace what happens.

Now, from the App package, the Program.cs file contains the following code:

```
using Core;
using Local;
using Sql;

var sqlDataPersistence = new SqlDataPersistence();
var localDataPersistence = new LocalDataPersistence();

var service = new SomeService();
```

```
service.Operation(localDataPersistence);
service.Operation(sqlDataPersistence);
```

In the preceding code, we create a `SqlDataPersistence` and a `LocalDataPersistence` instance. Doing that forced us to depend on both packages, but we could have chosen otherwise.

Then we create an instance of the `SomeService` class. We then pass both `IDataPersistence` implementations to the `Operation` method one after the other.

When we execute the program we get the following output:

```
Beginning SomeService.Operation.
Data persisted by LocalDataPersistence.
SomeService.Operation has ended.
Beginning SomeService.Operation.
Data persisted by SqlDataPersistence.
SomeService.Operation has ended.
```

The first half of the preceding terminal output represents the first call to the `Operation` method, where we passed the `LocalDataPersistence` instance. The second half represents the second call, where we passed the `SqlDataPersistence` instance.

The highlighted lines show that depending on an interface allowed us to change this behavior (OCP). Moreover, we could create a `CosmosDb` package, reference it from the `App` package, then pass an instance of a `CosmosDbDataPersistence` class to the `Operation` method, and the `Core` package would not know about it. Why? Because we inverted the dependency flow, creating a loosely coupled system. We even did some *dependency injection*.

Dependency injection, or **Inversion of Control** (**IoC**), is a design principle that is a first-class citizen of ASP.NET Core. It allows us to map abstractions to implementations, and when we need a new type, the whole object tree gets created automatically based on our configuration. We start that journey in *Chapter 8*, *Dependency Injection*.

Conclusion

The core idea is to depend on abstractions. Interfaces are pure contracts, which makes them more flexible than abstract classes. Abstract classes are still helpful, and we explore ways to leverage them in the book.

Depending on implementations (classes) creates tight coupling between classes, which leads to a system that can be harder to maintain. The cohesion between your dependencies is essential in whether the coupling will help or hurt you in the long run.

Summary

In this chapter, we covered many architectural principles. We began by exploring DRY, KISS, and SoC principles before learning about the SOLID principles and their importance in modern software engineering. By following those principles, you should be able to build better, more maintainable software.

As we also covered, principles are only principles, not laws. You must always be careful not to abuse them so they remain helpful instead of harmful. The context is always essential; internal tools and critical business applications require different levels of tinkering.

The key takeaways from this chapter are:

- Don't over-engineer your solutions (KISS).
- Encapsulate and reuse business logic (DRY).
- Organize elements around concerns and responsibilities (SoC/SRP).
- Aim at composability (OCP).
- Support backward compatibility (LSP).
- Write granular interfaces/contracts (ISP).
- Depend on abstractions and invert the dependency flow (DIP).

With all those principles in our toolbox, we are ready to jump into design patterns and get our design level one step further, with the next chapter covering REST APIs.

Questions

Let's take a look at a few practice questions:

1. How many principles are represented by the SOLID acronym?
2. Is it true that when following the SOLID principles, the idea is to create big components that can each manage more elements of a program by creating God classes?
3. By following the DRY principle, you want to remove all code duplication from everywhere, irrespective of the source, and encapsulate that code into a reusable component. Is this affirmation correct?
4. Is it true that the ISP tells us that creating multiple small interfaces is better than creating one large one?
5. What principle tells us that creating multiple small classes that handle a single responsibility is better than one class handling multiple responsibilities?

Further reading

Here is a link to build upon what we learned in the chapter:

- Covariance and contravariance (C#): `https://adpg.link/BxBG`

Answers

1. Five: S.O.L.I.D. (SRP, OCP, LSP, ISP, and DIP).
2. No, the idea is the opposite: create small components that interact with each other in a loosely coupled manner.
3. No, you want to encapsulate similar logic, not similar-looking blocks of code.
4. Yes, it is easier to reuse small pieces than adapt enormous ones.
5. It is the SRP. The SoC principle also advocates that idea but applies at all design levels.

Learn more on Discord

To join the Discord community for this book – where you can share feedback, ask questions to the author, and learn about new releases – follow the QR code below:

`https://packt.link/ArchitectingASPNETCoreApps3e`

4

REST APIs

This chapter delves into the heart of web application communication — REST APIs. In today's connected digital world, effective communication between different applications is paramount, and RESTful APIs play a pivotal role in facilitating this interaction.

We start by exploring the basic fabric of the web: HTTP. We touch on the core HTTP methods, such as GET, POST, PUT, and DELETE, to see how they carry out **Create, Read, Update, and Delete** (**CRUD**) operations in a RESTful context. We then turn our attention to HTTP status codes — the system's way of informing clients about the status of their requests — and HTTP headers.

Since APIs evolve and managing these changes without disrupting existing clients is a significant challenge, we'll look at different strategies for API versioning and the trade-offs involved with each.

Then, we learn about the **Data Transfer Object** (**DTO**) pattern. Packaging data into DTOs can provide many benefits, from reducing the number of calls to better encapsulation and improved performance when sending data over the network.

Finally, we explore the importance of defining clear and robust API contracts, which ensures API stability. We discuss techniques for designing and documenting these contracts, ensuring they serve as practical guides for API consumers.

By the end of this chapter, you'll know how REST APIs work and will be ready to start building some using ASP.NET Core as we move further through our architectural journey in the next few chapters.

In this chapter, we cover the following topics:

- REST and HTTP
- The Data Transfer Object (DTO) pattern
- API contracts

Let's begin with REST.

REST and HTTP

REST, or **REpresentational State Transfer**, is a way to create internet-based services, like web services, web APIs, REST APIs, or RESTful APIs. Those services commonly use HTTP as their transport protocol. REST reuses well-known HTTP specifications instead of recreating new ways of exchanging data. For example, returning an HTTP status code `200 OK` indicates success, while `400 Bad Request` indicates failure.

Here are some defining characteristics:

- **Statelessness:** In a RESTful system, every client-to-server request should contain all the details necessary for the server to comprehend and execute it. The server retains no information about the client's most recent HTTP request. This enhances both reliability and scalability.
- **Caching capabilities:** Clients should be able to cache responses to enhance performance.
- **Simplicity and loose coupling:** REST uses HTTP to ensure a simplified, decoupled architecture. This makes the development, maintenance, and scaling of REST APIs easier and facilitates their usage.
- **Resource identifiability:** Each REST API endpoint is a distinct resource, enabling us to secure each piece of the system separately.
- **Interface as a contract:** The REST API layer serves as an exchange contract or an abstraction. It effectively conceals the backend system's underlying implementation, fostering streamlined interactions.

While we could delve much deeper into the intricacies of REST APIs, the preceding characteristics serve as foundational knowledge, providing good enough knowledge to get started with RESTful services. Having navigated through these essentials, let's shift our focus toward understanding how REST APIs harness the power of HTTP.

HTTP methods

HTTP methods, also known as verbs, define the type of action a client can perform on a resource in a RESTful API. Each method represents a specific operation that defines the endpoint's intent on a resource.

Here is a list of the most frequently used methods, what they are for, and their expected success status code:

Method	Typical role	Success status code
`GET`	Retrieve a resource (read data).	200 OK
`POST`	Create a new resource.	201 CREATED
`PUT`	Replace a resource.	200 OK or 204 No Content
`DELETE`	Delete a resource.	200 OK or 204 No Content
`PATCH`	Partially update a resource.	200 OK

Table 4.1: Most common HTTP methods and their expected status code

We use those methods to build CRUD and more complex APIs alike. CRUD stands for Create, Read, Update, and Delete, representing the four basic operations that a client can perform on data. These actions are fundamental in managing data, whether it's adding new records (Create: `POST`), viewing existing data (Read: `GET`), modifying existing records (Update: `PUT` or `PATCH`), or removing them (Delete: `DELETE`).

Next, we explore the commonly used status codes.

HTTP status codes

HTTP status codes are part of the HTTP response and provide the client with information about the success or failure of their request, that is, the status of the request.

Status codes touching similar subjects are grouped under the same broad "hundredth" categories:

- `1XX` (informational) codes indicate that the request was received and the process is continuing, such as **100 Continue** and **101 Switching Protocols**.
- `2XX` (successful) codes indicate that the request was received successfully.
- `3XX` (redirection) codes indicate that the client must take further action to complete the redirection request.
- `4XX` (client error) codes indicate an error on the client's part, such as validation errors. The client sent an empty required field, for example.
- `5XX` (server error) codes indicate that the server failed to fulfill an apparently valid request and that the client cannot do anything about it (retrying the request is not an option).

The following table explains some of the most common ones:

Status code	**Role**
200 OK	Indicates the request has succeeded. It usually includes data related to the resource in the response body.
201 CREATED	Indicates the request has succeeded and the system created a resource. It should also include a `Location` HTTP header pointing to the newly created resource and can include the new entity in the response body.
202 ACCEPTED	Indicates the request has been accepted for processing but has not been processed yet. We use this code for asynchronous operations. In an event-driven system (see *Chapter 17, Getting Started with Vertical Slice Architecture*), this could mean that an event has been published, the current resource has completed its job (published the event), but to know more, the client needs to contact another resource, wait for a notification, just wait, or can't know.
204 NO CONTENT	Indicates the request has succeeded with no content in the response body.
302 FOUND	Indicates that the requested resource resides temporarily under a different URL specified in the `Location` header. We commonly use this status code for redirection.

400 BAD REQUEST	Indicates that the server could not understand or process the request. This usually relates to a validation error like a bad input or a missing field.
401 UNAUTHORIZED	Indicates that the request requires user authentication to access the resource.
403 FORBIDDEN	Indicates that the server understood the request but refused to authorize it. This usually means the client lacks access rights for the resource (authorization).
404 NOT FOUND	Indicates the resource does not exist or was not found. REST APIs often return this from valid endpoints.
409 CONFLICT	Indicates that the server cannot complete the request due to a conflict with the current state of the resource. A typical scenario would be that the entity has changed between its read operation (`GET`) and the current update (`PUT`) operation.
500 INTERNAL SERVER ERROR	Indicates that an unhandled error occurred on the server side and prevented it from fulfilling the request.

Table 4.2: Most common HTTP status codes and their meaning

Now that we have covered the HTTP methods and status codes, we look at how to pass more metadata between the client and the server.

HTTP headers

REST APIs leverage HTTP headers to transmit clients' information and describe their options and capabilities. Headers are part of both the request and the response.

Header	Description
`Location`	We can use the `Location` header for different purposes, usually to tell the client where to go next. It takes the form of a URL. For example: • After creating an entity (`201 Created`), the `Location` header should point to the `GET` endpoint where the client can access that new entity. • After starting an asynchronous operation (`202 Accepted`), the `Location` header could point to the status endpoint where you can poll for the state of the operation (has it completed or failed, or is it still ongoing?). • When a server wants to instruct a client to load another page (a redirection), the `Location` header contains the destination URL. The following status codes are the most common for redirections: `301 Moved Permanently`, `302 Found`, `303 See Other`, `307 Temporary Redirect`, and `308 Permanent Redirect`.

`Retry-After`	The `Retry-After` header informs the client when to try the request again, usually used after maintenance or when a server is busy. For example: • After a `202 Accepted`, the `Retry-After` header indicates the time to wait before querying the `Location` header to get the result of the asynchronous call. • After a `301 Moved Permanently`, the `Retry-After` header indicates the time to wait before redirecting the user and following the URL in the `Location` header. • After a `429 Too Many Requests`, the `Retry-After` header indicates the wait time before sending a new request to the server. This is issued when rate limits are in place on an API. • After a 503 Service Unavailable, the Retry-After header indicates the service's expected downtime and the time the client should wait before resending the request.
`ETag`	`ETag`, or entity tag, is a unique identifier for a specific version of a resource, helpful for managing conflicts and caching. For example: • The `ETag` header (sent by the server) used in conjunction with the `If-Match` header (sent back by the client) helps avoid *mid-air collisions*, meaning the server will reject an update if the entity changed between the time the client requested the entity (`ETag`) and when it sent the update request to the server (`If-Match`). In this context, the `ETag` and `If-Match` headers form a sort of *optimistic concurrency* mechanism. • The `ETag` header (sent by the server) used in conjunction with the `If-None-Match` header (sent back by the client) allows a server to return a `304 Not Modified` status code when the client requests a resource that has not changed.
`Allow`	The `Allow` header should list the HTTP methods (like GET or POST) supported by the requested resource when the server responds with a `405 Method Not Allowed` status code. This header should guide the client in interacting with the resource.
`Authorization`	The `Authorization` header is key for security, as it carries credentials proving the authenticity of a user making a request.
`Cache-Control`	The `Cache-Control` header directs how resources are stored in the cache, influencing the freshness and reusability of the content. Requests (clients) and responses (servers) use this header to control the caching. The `Cache-Control` header contains directives instructing the other party on how to treat the cache. For example, a client can use `Cache-Control: no-cache` and `Cache-Control: max-age=0` to force the reload of a resource.

Table 4.3: Most used HTTP headers and their description

This information should be enough theory to get you started with HTTP and REST. If you want to know more, I've left links to the MDN web docs about HTTP in the *Further reading* section at the end of the chapter.

Next, we look at versioning because nothing stays the same forever; business needs change, and APIs must evolve with them.

Versioning

Versioning is a crucial aspect of a REST API. Whether the version of the API is long-lived or transitory (during the decommissioning cycle of an old endpoint, for example), both ends of the pipe must know what to expect and what API contract to respect. Unless you are your only consumer, you'll need a way for the API clients to query specific API versions when the contract changes.

This section explores a few ways to think about our versioning strategy.

Default versioning strategy

The default strategy is the first thing to consider when versioning an API. What happens when no version is specified? Will the endpoint return an error, or the first or the latest version?

If the API returns an error, you should implement the default versioning strategy from day one so clients know a version is required. In this case, there is no real drawback. On the other hand, putting this strategy in place after the fact will break all clients that do not specify a version number, which might not be the best way to keep your consumers happy.

The second way is always to return the first version. This method is an excellent way to preserve backward compatibility. You can add more endpoint versions without breaking your consumers.

The opposite way is always to return the latest version. For consumers, this means specifying a version to consume or be up to date or break, and this might not be the best user experience to provide to your consumers. Nonetheless, many have opted for this default strategy.

Another way to go is to pick any version as the default baseline for the API (like version 3.2, for example) or even choose a different version per endpoint. Say you default to 3.2, then deploy 4.0. Since the clients must opt in to access the new API, they won't break automatically and will have the time to update from 3.2 to 4.0 following their own roadmap. This is a good strategy to default to a well-known and stable API version before moving forward with breaking changes.

No matter what you choose, always think it through by weighing the pros and cons.

Next, we explore ways to define those versions.

Versioning strategy

Of course, there are multiple ways to think this through. You can leverage URL patterns to define and include the API version, like `https://localhost/v2/some-entities`. This strategy is easier to query from a browser, making it simple to know the version at a glance, but the endpoint is not pointing to a unique resource anymore (a key principle of REST), as each resource has one endpoint for each version. Nonetheless, this way of versioning an API is used extensively and is one of the most popular ways, if not *the* most popular way, of doing REST versioning, even if it violates one of its core principles (debatably).

The other way is to use HTTP headers. You can use a custom header like `api-version` or `Accept-version`, for example, or the standard `Accept` header. This way allows resources to have unique endpoints (URIs) while enabling multiple versions of each entity (multiple versions of each API contract describing the same entity).

For example, a client could specify an HTTP header while calling the endpoint like this (custom header):

```
GET https://localhost/some-entities
Accept-version: v2
```

Or like the following, by leveraging the `Accept` header for *content negotiation*:

```
GET https://localhost/some-entities
Accept: application/vnd.api.v2+json
```

Different people use different values for the `Accept` headers, for example:

- `application/vnd.myapplication.v2+json`
- `application/vnd.myapplication.entity.v2+json`
- `application/vnd.myapplication.api+json; version=2`
- `application/json; version=2`

Whicher way you use, you'll most likely need to version your APIs at some point. Some people are strong advocates of one way or the other, but ultimately, you should decide on a case-by-case basis what best covers your needs and capacities: simplicity, formality, or a mix of both.

Wrapping up

With a method (verb), the client (and the endpoint) can express the intent to create, update, read, or delete an entity. With a status code, the endpoint can tell the client the state of the operation. Adding HTTP headers, clients, and servers can add more metadata to the request or response. Finally, by adding versioning, the REST API can evolve without breaking existing clients while giving them options to consume specific versions.

With what we just covered, you should have more than enough information to follow along with the examples in this book and build a few REST APIs along the way. Next, we explore data transfer objects and then piece all this together when learning about API contracts.

The Data Transfer Object (DTO) pattern

The **Data Transfer Object (DTO)** design pattern is a robust approach to managing and transferring data in a service-oriented architecture like REST APIs. The DTO pattern is about organizing the data to deliver it to API clients optimally. DTOs are an integral part of the API contract, which we explore next.

Goal

A DTO's objective is to *control an endpoint's inputs and outputs* by loosely coupling the exposed API surface from the application's inner workings. DTOs empower us to craft our web services the way we want the consumers to interact with them. So, no matter the underlying system, we can use DTOs to design endpoints that are easier to consume, maintain, and evolve.

Design

Each DTO represents an entity with all the necessary properties. That entity is either an input or an output and allows crafting the interaction between the clients and the API.

DTOs serve to loosely couple our domain from the data exposed over the API by adding a level of abstraction. This allows us to change the underlying domain model without affecting the data exposed to the API consumers and vice versa.

Another way to use a DTO is by packaging related pieces of information together, allowing a client to make a single call to fetch all necessary data, thereby eliminating the need for multiple requests.

Based on REST and HTTP, the flow of a request goes like the following: an HTTP request comes in, some code is executed (domain logic), and an HTTP response goes back to the client. The following diagram represents this flow:

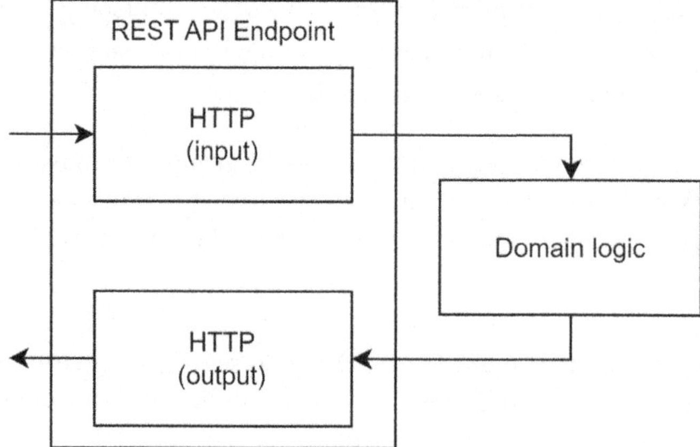

Figure 4.1: An HTTP request getting in and out of a REST API endpoint

Now, if we take that flow and change HTTP to DTO, we can see that a DTO can be part of the data contract as an input or an output:

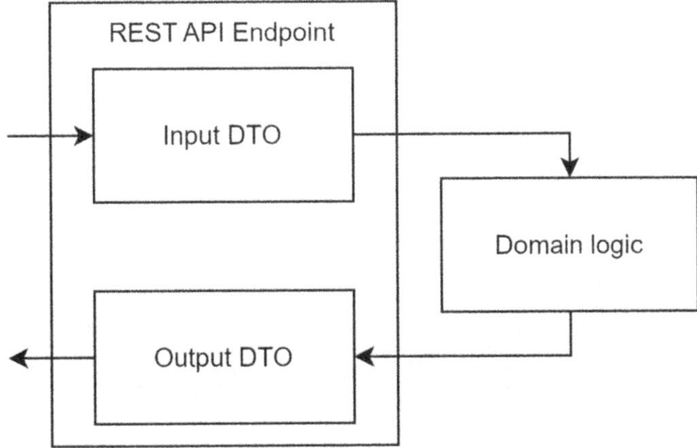

Figure 4.2: An input DTO hitting some domain logic, then the endpoint returning an output DTO

How can the HTTP request become an object? Most of the time:

- We use deserialization or data binding for inputs.
- We use serialization for outputs.

Let's look at a few examples.

Conceptual examples

Conceptually, say that we are building a web application allowing people to register for events. We explore two use cases next.

Registering for an activity

The first scenario we are exploring is a user registering for an activity. An activity is a sort of event in the system. We use an external payment gateway, so our application never handles financial data. Nevertheless, we must send transaction data to our backend to associate and complete the payment. The following diagram depicts the workflow:

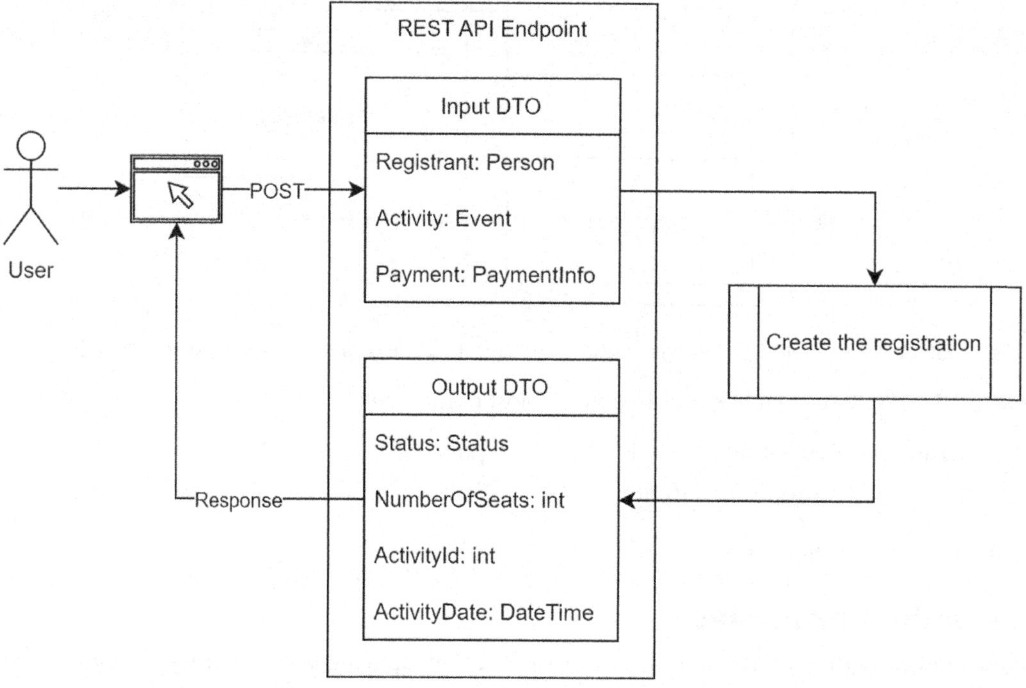

Figure 4.3: The DTOs implicated in an activity registration flow

The body of the request could look like the following JSON snippet:

```
{
    "registrant": {
        "firstname": "John",
        "lastname": "Doe"
    },
    "activity": {
        "id": 123,
        "seats": 2
    },
    "payment": {
        "nonce": "abc123"
    }
}
```

Next, the following JSON snippet could represent the body of the response:

```
{
    "status": "Success",
    "numberOfSeats": 2,
    "activityId": 123,
    "activityDate": "2023-06-03T20:00:00"
}
```

Of course, this is a very lightweight version of a registration system. The objective is to show that:

1. Three entities came in as an HTTP POST request (a registrant, an activity, and payment information).
2. The system executed some business logic to register the person to the activity and to complete the financial transaction.
3. The API returned mixed information to the client.

This pattern is handy to input and output only what you need. If you are designing the user interface that consumes the API, outputting a well-thought DTO can ensure that the UI renders the next screen just by reading the response from the server, saving your UI from having to fetch more data, speeding up the process, and improving the user experience.

We explore fetching information about an activity registration next.

Fetching activity registration details

In the same system, the user wants to review the details of an activity they registered using the preceding process.

In this case, the flow goes like this:

1. The client sends the registration identifier over a `GET` request.
2. The system fetches the registrant information, the activity information, and the number of seats the user reserved for that activity.
3. The server returns the data to the client.

The following diagram visually represents the use case:

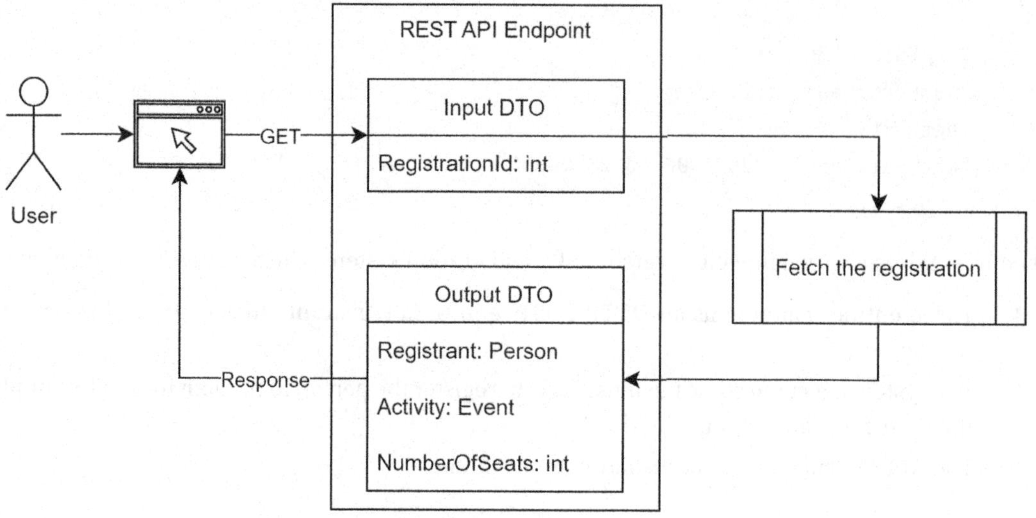

Figure 4.4: The DTOs implicated in fetching the info related to a registered activity

In this case, the input would be part of the URL, like `/registrations/123`. The output would be part of the response body, and could look like the following:

```
{
    "registrant": {
        "firstname": "John",
        "lastname": "Doe"
    },
    "activity": {
        "id": 123,
        "name": "Super Cool Show",
        "date": "2023-06-03T20:00:00"
    },
    "numberOfSeats": 2
}
```

By creating that endpoint using a well-crafted output DTO, we condensed three HTTP requests into one: the registrant, the activity, and the registration (number of seats). This powerful technique applies to any technology, not just ASP.NET Core, and allows us to design APIs without connecting clients directly to our data (loose coupling).

Conclusion

A DTO allows us to design an API endpoint with specialized input and output instead of exposing the domain or data model. Those DTOs shield our internal business logic, which improves our ability to design our APIs and also helps us make them more secure.

By defining DTOs, we can avoid a malicious actor trying to bind data that they should not have access to. For example, when using an input "Login DTO" that only contains the `username` and `password` properties, a malicious user could be prevented from binding the `IsAdmin` field available in our domain and database. There are other ways to mitigate this, but they are out of the scope of this chapter; yet, a DTO is a great candidate to mitigate this attack vector.

This separation between the presentation and domain is a crucial element that leads to having multiple independent components instead of a bigger, more fragile one or leaking the internal data structure to the clients consuming the API.

We explore building APIs in the next few chapters and explore some topics in more depth in *Section 4, Application Patterns.*

Using the DTO pattern helps us follow the SOLID principles in the following ways:

- S: A DTO adds clear boundaries between the domain logic or the data and the API contract, dividing one model into several distinct responsibilities to help keep things isolated.
- O: N/A.
- L: N/A.
- I: A DTO is a smaller, specifically crafted model that serves a clear purpose. With a DTO, we now have two models (domain and API contract) and several classes (input DTO, output DTO, and domain or data entities) instead of a generic one (only the domain or data entity).
- D: N/A.

Next, we look at how we can glue the pieces that we have explored so far into API contracts.

API contracts

API contracts serve as an essential blueprint, outlining the rules of engagement between your API and its consumers. This includes available endpoints, the HTTP methods they support, the expected request formats, and potential response structures, including HTTP status codes.

These contracts provide clarity, robustness, consistency, and interoperability, facilitating seamless system interactions, no matter the language they are built with. Moreover, well-documented API contracts are a reliable reference guide, helping developers understand and utilize your API effectively. Thus, designing comprehensive and clear API contracts is critical in building high-quality, maintainable, and user-friendly APIs.

An API contract describes a REST API, so a consumer should know how to call an endpoint and what to expect from it in return. What an endpoint does or the capability it provides should be clear just by reading its contract.

Each endpoint in a REST API should provide at least the following signature:

- A **Uniform Resource Identifier** (**URI**) that indicates where to access it.

- An HTTP method that describes the type of operation it does.
- An input that defines what is needed for the operation to happen. For example, the input can be the HTTP body, URL parameters, query parameters, HTTP headers, or even a combination.
- One or more outputs defining what the client should expect. Successful requests typically return data in the body and a status code, while failures might only provide a status code or include error details in the body.

The input and output of an endpoint are often DTOs, making DTOs even more important.

There are multiple ways to define API contracts. For example, to define an API contract, we could do the following:

- Open any text editor, such as MS Word or Notepad, and start writing a document describing the web APIs; this is probably the most tedious and least flexible way. I do not recommend this for many reasons.
- Write specifications in Markdown files and save those files within your project Git repository for easy discoverability. This is very similar to MS Word, but more accessible for all team members to consume. This approach is better than Word, yet not optimal since you need to manually update those files when the API changes.
- Use an existing standard, such as the OpenAPI Specification (formerly Swagger). This technique implies a learning curve, but the result is easier to consume. Moreover, many tools allow us to create automation using the OpenAPI specs. This approach is starting to remove the need for manual intervention.
- Use a code-first approach and ASP.NET Core tooling to extract the OpenAPI specs from your code.
- Use any other tools that fit your requirements.

Postman is a fantastic tool for building web API documentation and test suites and experimenting with your APIs. It supports OpenAPI specifications, allows you to create mock servers, supports environments, and more.

No matter the tools, there are two major trends in how to design the API contract of a REST API:

- Design the contract first, then build the API (contract-first).
- Build the API, then extract the contract for the code (code-first).

To design the contract first, one must adopt a tool to write the specifications, then code the API according to the specs.

I left a link in the *Further reading* section about OpenAPI.

On the other hand, to use a code-first approach and automatically extract the OpenAPI specifications from the API, we must ensure our endpoints are discoverable by the .NET `ApiExplorer`.

No matter how you do it, in ASP.NET Core, we use classes and structs to represent the data contract of our REST APIs; whether it happens before or after you write the API contract does not matter. Next, we explore how to leverage Swagger to generate an API contract in a code-first manner. We could also write OpenAPI specs by hand using YAML or JSON, but I prefer imperative languages like C# to declarative programming.

Imperative programming languages focus on the "how" by defining explicit steps to achieve a result, while declarative languages focus on the "what" by specifying the desired outcome without detailing the process to get there.

People often prefer imperative programming languages because they offer explicit control over program flow and step-by-step instructions, which can feel more intuitive.

In our case, the tooling support for C# is just plain better, making it easier to write and refactor the specs. On top of this, the specs come from our endpoints (living documentation), so that's one less static artifact to maintain (YAML or JSON file).

Code-first API contract

In this example, we start with an empty project (`dotnet new web`) and create a tiny API that exposes the following endpoints:

- Read the specified entity.
- Create a new entity.

The code doesn't do much and returns fake data, but it is enough to explore its data contract.

Remember that coding is like playing with LEGO® blocks, but we connect many tiny patterns to create our software and create value. Understanding and learning that skill will lead you beyond just being able to use some canned magic recipe, which would limit you to using just what people share with you.

In this example, we use the OpenAPI Specification to describe our API. To save ourselves from writing JSON and go code-first instead, we leverage the SwaggerGen package.

To use SwaggerGen, we must install the `Swashbuckle.AspNetCore.SwaggerGen` NuGet package.

Here's the `Program.cs` file, without the endpoints, showing how to leverage SwaggerGen:

```
var builder = WebApplication.CreateBuilder(args);
builder.Services.AddEndpointsApiExplorer();
builder.Services.AddSwaggerGen();

var app = builder.Build();
app.UseSwagger();
// Omitted endpoints
app.Run();
```

The highlighted lines are the only things we must add to use SwaggerGen in a project, which generates the API contract in the **OpenAPI Specification** (**OAS**) format for us. That auto-generated OAS file is very long (113 lines), so I only pasted some snippets in the book for clarity. However, you can run the project and navigate to the `/swagger/v1/swagger.json` URL in a browser to access the complete OAS.

I created the `swagger.json` file in the project for convenience so you can consult the file without running the program. The tool does not generate a physical file.

Let's have a look at those endpoints.

The first endpoint

The code of the first endpoint that allows a client to read an entity looks like this:

```
app.MapGet(
    "/{id:int}",
    (int id) => new ReadOneDto(
        id,
        "John Doe"
    )
);
public record class ReadOneDto(int Id, string Name);
```

Here's the API contract we can extract from the preceding code:

Contract segment	Value
HTTP method	`GET`
URI	`/{id}` (for example, `/123`)
Input	The `id` parameter
Output	An instance of the `ReadOneDto` class

If you open the `ReadOneEntity.http` file from Visual Studio or VS Code and send the `GET` request in that file to the running application, the server will respond with a similar HTTP response to the one that follows.

The HTTP request is:

```
GET https://localhost:7000/123
```

The trimmed-down response is:

```
HTTP/1.1 200 OK
Content-Type: application/json; charset=utf-8
Server: Kestrel

{
  "id": 123,
  "name": "John Doe"
}
```

The `.http` files are new to VS 2022 (version 17.6 or higher) and allow us to write and execute HTTP requests from VS itself. In a nutshell, you should see a **Send request** link above the request. When you click on it, VS sends the HTTP request to the server and displays the response. The program must be running for the request to hit the server. Achieving the same result is possible using a VS Code extension.

I left links in the *Further reading* section if you want to know more or need the VS Code extension.

As we can see, when we query the API for the entity `id=123`, the endpoint returns that entity with a `200 OK` status code, and the response body is a serialized instance of the `ReadOneDto` class.

SwaggerGen generated the following OpenAPI specs for the first endpoint:

```
"/{id}": {
  "get": {
    "parameters": [
      {
```

```
                "name": "id",
                "in": "path",
                "required": true,
                "schema": {
                  "type": "integer",
                  "format": "int32"
                }
              }
            ],
            "responses": {
              "200": {
                "description": "Success",
                "content": {
                  "application/json": {
                    "schema": {
                      "$ref": "#/components/schemas/ReadOneDto"
                    }
                  }
                }
              }
            }
          }
        },
```

That snippet describes the endpoint and references our output model (highlighted line). The schemas are at the bottom of the JSON file. Here's the schema that represents the `ReadOneDto`:

```
"ReadOneDto": {
  "type": "object",
  "properties": {
    "id": {
      "type": "integer",
      "format": "int32"
    },
    "name": {
      "type": "string",
      "nullable": true
    }
  },
  "additionalProperties": false
}
```

As we can see from the highlighted lines, that schema has a property name of type string and a property id of type integer, the same as our ReadOneDto class.

Fortunately, we don't need to write that JSON since the tool generates it based on our code. Next, we look at the second endpoint.

The second endpoint

The code of the second endpoint that allows a client to create an entity looks like this:

```
app.MapPost(
    "/",
    (CreateDto input) => new CreatedDto(
        Random.Shared.Next(int.MaxValue),
        input.Name
    )
);
public record class CreateDto(string Name);
public record class CreatedDto(int Id, string Name);
```

Here's the API contract we can extract from the preceding code:

Contract segment	Value
HTTP method	POST
URI	/
Input	An instance of the CreateDto class
Output	An instance of the CreatedDto class

Sending the following HTTP request (you can use the CreateEntity.http file) results in the output that follows:

```
POST / HTTP/1.1
Content-Type: application/json
Host: localhost:7000
Accept: application/json
Connection: keep-alive
Content-Length: 28

{
    "name": "Jane Doe"
}
```

The trimmed-down response is:

```
HTTP/1.1 200 OK
Content-Type: application/json; charset=utf-8
Date: Sat, 03 Jun 2023 17:59:25 GMT
Server: Kestrel
Alt-Svc: h3=":7000"; ma=86400
Transfer-Encoding: chunked

{"id":1624444431,"name":"Jane Doe"}
```

As we can see from the preceding request, the client sent a serialized instance of the `CreateDto` class, set the name to Jane Doe, and received that same entity back but with a numeric `id` property (an instance of the `CreatedDto` class).

The OpenAPI specs of our endpoint look like the following:

```
"/": {
  "post": {
    "requestBody": {
      "content": {
        "application/json": {
          "schema": {
            "$ref": "#/components/schemas/CreateDto"
          }
        }
      },
      "required": true
    },
    "responses": {
      "200": {
        "description": "Success",
        "content": {
          "application/json": {
            "schema": {
              "$ref": "#/components/schemas/CreatedDto"
            }
          }
        }
      }
    }
  }
}
```

The input and output schemas are:

```
"CreateDto": {
  "type": "object",
  "properties": {
    "name": {
      "type": "string",
      "nullable": true
    }
  },
  "additionalProperties": false
},
"CreatedDto": {
  "type": "object",
  "properties": {
    "id": {
      "type": "integer",
      "format": "int32"
    },
    "name": {
      "type": "string",
      "nullable": true
    }
  },
  "additionalProperties": false
},
```

Similar to the first endpoint, SwaggerGen translates our C# classes into OpenAPI specs. Let's wrap this up.

Wrapping up

Some ASP.NET Core templates come with SwaggerGen preconfigured. They also come with the Swagger UI, which lets you visually explore the API contract from your application and even query it. `NSwag` is another tool that offers similar features. Plenty of online documentation shows how to take advantage of those tools.

Besides exploring tooling, we defined that an API contract is fundamental and promotes robustness and reliability. Each endpoint has the following pieces as part of the overall API contract:

- The URI it is accessible from
- The HTTP method that best defines the operation
- An input
- One or more outputs

A single URI can lead to multiple endpoints by combining different HTTP methods and inputs. For example, `GET /api/entities` may return a list of entities, while `POST /api/entities` may create a new entity.

Using the entity's name in its plural form is a convention many use because it intuitively signifies that the endpoint deals with collections of resources rather than a single instance. For example, an endpoint like `/users` suggests that it gives access to a list of all user entities, and you can perform operations such as retrieval, creation, and deletion on the collection. In contrast, when interacting with an individual record within that collection, the convention is to specify an identifier, such as `/users/123`, with `123` being the user's ID. This naming convention differentiates between actions on the entire set and actions on a specific element of the set, making the API's structure more understandable and its usage more predictable.

Summary

REST APIs facilitate communication between applications in today's interconnected digital world. We explored HTTP, HTTP methods, HTTP status codes, and HTTP headers. We then explored API versioning, DTOs, and the importance of API contracts.

Here are a few key takeaways:

- **REST and HTTP**: REST APIs are integral to web application communication. They use HTTP as their transport protocol, leveraging its methods, status codes, and headers to facilitate interaction between different applications.
- **HTTP methods**: HTTP methods or verbs (GET, POST, PUT, DELETE, and PATCH) define the type of action a client can perform on a resource in a RESTful API. Understanding these methods is crucial for carrying out CRUD operations.
- **HTTP status codes and headers**: HTTP status codes inform clients about the success or failure of their requests. HTTP headers transmit additional information and describe clients' options and capabilities. Both are essential components of HTTP communication.
- **Versioning**: Managing changes in APIs without disrupting existing clients is a significant challenge. Different strategies for API versioning can help address this issue, but each comes with its own trade-offs.
- **Data Transfer Object (DTO)**: DTOs package data into a format that can provide many benefits, including reducing the number of HTTP calls, improving encapsulation, and enhancing performance when sending data over the network.
- **API contracts**: Clear and robust API contracts ensure API stability. They serve as a blueprint for interaction between an API and its consumers, outlining available endpoints, supported HTTP methods, expected request formats, and potential response structures.
- **Practical application**: Understanding these concepts is not only theoretically important but also practically helpful in building and working with REST APIs using ASP.NET Core or any other similar technology.

By now, you should have a solid understanding of REST APIs and be ready to explore how to implement one using ASP.NET Core. ASP.NET Core makes writing REST APIs using MVC or minimal APIs a breeze. MVC is a well-used pattern that is almost impossible to avoid. However, the new minimal API model makes the process leaner. Moreover, with application patterns like **Request-EndPoint-Response (REPR)** or Vertical Slice Architecture, we can organize our API per feature instead of by layer, leading to an improved organization. We cover those topics in *Section 4, Application Patterns*.

Next, we explore designing with ASP.NET Core, starting with Minimal APIs.

Questions

Let's look at a few practice questions:

1. What is the most common status code sent in a REST API after creating an entity?
2. If you introduce a default strategy that returns the lowest possible version when no version is specified, would it break existing clients?
3. If you want to read data from the server, what HTTP method would you use?
4. Can DTOs add flexibility and robustness to a system?
5. Are DTOs part of an API contract?

Further reading

Here are some links to build on what we have learned in the chapter:

- HTTP request methods (MDN): `https://adpg.link/MFWb`
- HTTP response status codes (MDN): `https://adpg.link/34Jq`
- HTTP headers (MDN): `https://adpg.link/Hx55`
- Use `.http` files in Visual Studio 2022: `https://adpg.link/cbhv`
- REST Client, a VS Code extension to use `.http` files: `https://adpg.link/UCGv`
- OpenAPI Specification: `https://adpg.link/M4Uz`

Answers

1. An API usually returns the status code `201 Created` after creating a new entity.
2. No, it will not break clients because they will either be using the lowest API version or have already specified a specific version.
3. We typically use the HTTP GET method to read data from a REST API.
4. Yes, DTOs add flexibility and robustness to a system. They allow you to control exactly what data you expose to the client and can reduce the amount of unnecessary data that needs to be sent over the network.
5. Yes, DTOs are part of an API contract. They define the data format exchanged between the client and server, ensuring both sides understand the data being sent and received.

Learn more on Discord

To join the Discord community for this book – where you can share feedback, ask questions to the author, and learn about new releases – follow the QR code below:

`https://packt.link/ArchitectingASPNETCoreApps3e`

Section 2

Designing with ASP.NET Core

This section begins with an introduction to building ASP.NET Core web applications, focusing on the simplified approach to using the Minimal API model. It then discusses the **Model View Controller** (**MVC**) pattern, emphasizing its importance in developing structured web APIs. The section also delves into REST APIs, highlighting the role of **Data Transfer Objects** (**DTOs**) and API contracts in facilitating data exchange.

We then focus on understanding and applying classic Gang of Four design patterns like Strategy, Abstract Factory, and Singleton, setting the stage for more advanced concepts like **dependency injection** (**DI**). We thoroughly explore DI—**a crucial element of modern ASP.NET Core development**—emphasizing its significance in enhancing application maintainability and scalability.

Furthermore, the section examines ASP.NET Core-specific patterns, including the Options pattern and logging abstractions, providing a comprehensive guide to effectively leveraging these features in application development.

With those chapters on Minimal APIs, MVC, design patterns, dependency injection, configuration, and logging, this section offers a holistic view of designing applications with ASP.NET Core, equipping developers with the knowledge to build robust, efficient, and maintainable web applications. The section progresses from basic to advanced concepts, preparing developers with practical knowledge and skills for complex designs that real life confronts us with, and ensures a deep, practical understanding of ASP.NET Core's capabilities and design patterns, paving the way for the rest of the book.

This section comprises the following chapters:

- *Chapter 5, Minimal APIs*
- *Chapter 6, Model-View-Controller*
- *Chapter 7, Strategy, Abstract Factory, and Singleton Design Patterns*

- *Chapter 8, Dependency Injection*
- *Chapter 9, Application Configuration and the Options Pattern*
- *Chapter 10, Logging Patterns*

5

Minimal APIs

This chapter covers Minimal APIs, a simplified way of setting up and running .NET applications. We explore what makes minimal hosting and Minimal APIs a pivotal update in ASP.NET Core as we unravel the simplicity of creating APIs with less ceremony. We cover many possibilities that ASP.NET Core Minimal APIs bring, like how to configure, customize, and organize those endpoints.

We also explore using Minimal APIs with **Data Transfer Objects** (**DTOs**), combining simplicity with effective data transfer management to structure API contracts effectively.

Inspired by technologies like Express and Node.js, Minimal APIs bring a fresh perspective to the .NET world, allowing us to build lean and performant APIs without compromising resiliency.

In this chapter, we cover the following topics:

- Top-level statements
- Minimal hosting
- Minimal APIs
- Using Minimal APIs with Data Transfer Objects

Let's begin with top-level statements.

Top-level statements

The .NET team introduced top-level statements to the language in .NET 5 and C# 9. From that point, writing statements before declaring namespaces and other members became possible. Under the hood, the compiler emits those statements in a `Program.Main` method.

With top-level statements, a minimal .NET "Hello World" console program looked like this (`Program.cs`):

```
using System;
Console.WriteLine("Hello world!");
```

Unfortunately, we still need a project to run it, so we have to create a `.csproj` file with the following content (for example, `MyProject.csproj`):

```
<Project Sdk="Microsoft.NET.Sdk">
    <PropertyGroup>
        <TargetFramework>net8.0</TargetFramework>
        <OutputType>Exe</OutputType>
    </PropertyGroup>
</Project>
```

From there, we can use the .NET CLI to `dotnet run` the application, and it will output the following in the console before the program terminates:

```
Hello world!
```

On top of such statements, we can also declare other members, like classes, and use them in our application. However, we must declare classes at the end of the top-level code.

Be aware that the top-level statement code is not part of any namespace, and creating classes in a namespace is recommended, so you should limit the number of declarations done in the `Program.cs` file to what is internal to its inner workings, if anything.

Top-level statements are great for getting started with C#, writing code samples, and cutting out boilerplate code.

The highlighted line of the preceding C# code (`using System;`) is unnecessary when the *implicit usings* feature is enabled, which is the default in .NET 6+ projects. The templates add the following line to the `.csproj` file:

```
<ImplicitUsings>enable</ImplicitUsings>
```

Next, we explore the minimal hosting model built using top-level statements.

Minimal hosting

.NET 6 introduced the minimal hosting model. It combines the `Startup` and `Program` classes into a single `Program.cs` file. It leverages top-level statements to minimize the boilerplate code necessary to bootstrap the application. It also uses *global using directives* and the *implicit usings* feature to reduce the amount of boilerplate code further. This model only requires one file with the following three lines of code to create a web application (remember you can use `dotnet new web` to create an empty web application project):

```
WebApplicationBuilder builder = WebApplication.CreateBuilder(args);
```

```
WebApplication app = builder.Build();
app.Run();
```

The preceding code is way leaner than before. Of course, it starts an app that does nothing, but doing the same before would have required tens of lines of code.

The minimal hosting code is divided into two pieces:

- The *web application builder* we use to configure the application, register services, settings, environment, logging, and more (the highlighted code)
- The *web application* we use to configure the HTTP pipeline and routes (the non-highlighted lines)

That simplified model led to Minimal APIs that we explore next.

Minimal APIs

ASP.NET Core's Minimal APIs are built on the minimal hosting model and bring a streamlined approach to constructing web applications. Highly inspired by Node.js, they facilitate the development of APIs by reducing the boilerplate code.

By emphasizing simplicity and performance, they enhance readability and maintainability. They are an excellent fit for microservices architecture and applications that aim to remain efficient.

You can also build large applications using Minimal APIs; the word minimal refers to their lean approach, not the type of application you can make with them.

This minimalist approach does compromise a little on functionalities but improves flexibility and speed. Here's a comparative table:

Feature	ASP.NET Core Minimal API	ASP.NET Core MVC
Purpose	Designed for building APIs with minimal dependencies and minimal boilerplate code	Designed for building web applications and APIs following the Model-View-Controller pattern
Functionality	Includes essential features like model binding, dependency injection, filters, and a route-to-delegate model	Offers additional advanced features, like Razor views, Razor Pages, model validation, and MVC filters
Pros	• Closer to HTTP • The URL space is at the forefront • Easier to get started • Ideal for microservices • Lower resource consumption • Performance boost	• Full-featured framework, suitable for UI and APIs • Mature and well-known framework with a rich ecosystem and tooling support

Cons	• Compromises on some functionalities • Harder to organize a large number of endpoints in bigger projects [1]	• More boilerplate code for simple APIs • Can be overkill for small, simple services • Heavy usage of attributes • Requires more knowledge to get started

Table 5.1: Comparison of ASP.NET Core Minimal API and ASP.NET Core MVC

[1] We explore ways to organize Minimal API endpoints in *Chapter 18, Request-EndPoint-Response (REPR)*, and *Chapter 20, Modular Monolith.*

The Minimal API model has enough features for most applications, but ASP.NET Core MVC remains a robust choice, especially if you can't use external libraries or if you don't want to implement missing features yourself. Remember, choosing between Minimal APIs and MVC doesn't have to be binary; depending on your project's needs, you can use both in tandem and leverage the strengths of each.

We explore the Model-View-Controller (MVC) pattern in *Chapter 6, Model-View-Controller.*

Now that we have explored how to create a minimal API project, let's look at mapping HTTP requests to code next.

Mapping a route to a delegate

Minimal APIs bring multiple extension methods to configure the HTTP pipeline and configure endpoints. We can use those methods to map a route (a URL pattern) to a `RequestDelegate` delegate. Here's an example—the delegate (lambda expression) is highlighted:

```
app.MapGet("some/url/pattern", (HttpContext context) => {
    // Do something
});
```

That preceding endpoint allows us to control the HTTP request directly from the `HttpContext` object. We can also register many different delegates to handle the requests. Here's the most basic endpoint one can register, which returns a `200 OK` status code and no body—the endpoint does nothing since the lambda expression has an empty body; the delegate (lambda expression) is highlighted:

```
app.MapGet("most/basic/delegate", () => { });
```

To better control our endpoints, we can use the following methods to map different HTTP methods:

Method	Description
`MapGet`	Maps a `GET` request to a `RequestDelegate`
`MapPost`	Maps a `POST` request to a `RequestDelegate`
`MapPut`	Maps a `PUT` request to a `RequestDelegate`
`MapDelete`	Maps a `DELETE` request to a `RequestDelegate`
`MapMethods`	Maps a route pattern and multiple HTTP methods to a `RequestDelegate`
`Map`	Maps a route pattern to a `RequestDelegate`
`MapFallback`	Maps a fallback `RequestDelegate`, which runs when no other routes match
`MapGroup`	Allows configuring a route pattern and properties that apply to all endpoints defined under that group

Table 5.2: Map route-to-delegate extension methods

Here's a minimal GET example:

```
app.MapGet("minimal-endpoint-inline", () => "GET!");
```

When executing the program, navigating to the `/minimal-endpoint-inline` URI routes the request to the registered `RequestDelegate` (highlighted code), which outputs the following string:

```
GET!
```

As simple as that, we can route requests to delegates and create endpoints.

On top of registering endpoints, we can also register middleware like any other ASP.NET Core application. Moreover, the built-in middleware, like authentication and CORS, works the same with Minimal APIs.

Next, we explore ways to configure endpoints so we can create better APIs than an endpoint returning a literal string.

Configuring endpoints

Now that we know that, with Minimal APIs, we map routes to delegates, and we have learned of a few methods to do that, let's explore how to register the delegates:

- Inline, as with the preceding examples
- Using a method

To declare the delegate inline, we can do the following:

```
app.MapGet("minimal-endpoint-inline", () => "GET!");
```

To use a method, we can do the following:

```
app.MapGet("minimal-endpoint-method", MyMethod);
void MyMethod() { }
```

When enabled, ASP.NET Core registers the class name that contains the method with the `ApiExplorer` as a tag. We dig deeper into metadata further in the chapter.

All the concepts we explore in this chapter apply to both ways of registering delegates. Let's start by studying how to input data in our endpoints.

Inputs

An endpoint rarely has no parameter (no input value). Minimal APIs, like MVC, support a wide variety of binding sources. A binding source represents the conversion from the HTTP request into a strongly typed C# object, input as a parameter.

Most of the parameter binding happens implicitly, but in case you need to bind a parameter explicitly, here are the supported binding sources:

Source	Attribute	Description
`Route`	`[FromRoute]`	Binds the route value that matches the name of the parameter.
`Query`	`[FromQuery]`	Binds the query string value that matches the name of the parameter.
`Header`	`[FromHeader]`	Binds the HTTP header value that matches the name of the parameter.
`Body`	`[FromBody]`	Binds the JSON body of the request to the parameter's type.
`Form`	`[FromForm]`	Binds the form value that matches the name of the parameter.
`Services`	`[FromServices]`	Injects the service from the ASP.NET Core IoC container.
`Custom`	`[AsParameters]`	Binds the form values to a type. The matches happen between the form keys and the properties' names. It also allows binding multiple sources to a type.

Table 5.3: Supported binding sources

Next is a demo where we implicitly bind the `id` parameter from the route (highlighted code) to a parameter in the delegate. It is important to note that the parameter type is used to validate the input value, so both must be the same type. Here's that simple binding:

```
app.MapGet(
    "minimal-endpoint-input-route-implicit/{id}",
    (int id) => $"The id was {id}."
);
```

In most cases, the bindings work implicitly. However, you can explicitly bind the delegate's parameters like this:

```
using Microsoft.AspNetCore.Mvc;
// ...
app.MapGet(
    "minimal-endpoint-input-route-explicit/{id}",
    ([FromRoute] int id) => $"The id was {id}."
);
```

We can also implicitly inject dependencies into our delegates and even mix that with a route parameter like this (complete `Program.cs` file):

```
var builder = WebApplication.CreateBuilder(args);
builder.Services.AddSingleton<SomeInternalService>();
var app = builder.Build();
app.MapGet(
    "minimal-endpoint-input-service/{value}",
    (string value, SomeInternalService service)
        => service.Respond(value)
);
app.Run();
public class SomeInternalService {
    public string Respond(string value)
        => $"The value was {value}";
}
```

Following this pattern opens endless possibilities to input data into our endpoints.

If you are unfamiliar with **Dependency Injection** (**DI**), we explore DI in more depth in *Chapter 8*, *Dependency Injection*. Meanwhile, remember that we can bind objects to parameters, whether they are a DTO or a service.

On top of that, ASP.NET Core provides us with a few special types, which we explore next.

Special types

We can inject the following objects into our delegates as parameters, and ASP.NET Core manages them for us:

Class	Description
`HttpContext`	The `HttpContext` encompasses all the current HTTP request and response details. The `HttpContext` exposes all the other special types we are exploring here, so if you need more than one, you can inject the `HttpContext` directly to reduce the number of parameters.
`HttpRequest`	We can use the `HttpRequest` to do basic HTTP operations on the current request, like to query the parameters manually and bypass the ASP.NET Core data-binding mechanism. This is the same as the `HttpContext.Request` property.
`HttpResponse`	Like the `HttpRequest`, we can leverage the `HttpResponse` object to execute manual operations on the HTTP response, like writing directly to the response stream, managing HTTP headers manually, etc. This is the same as the `HttpContext.Response` property.
`CancellationToken`	Passing a cancellation token to an asynchronous operation is a recommended practice. It lets you stop the operation and its related tasks so they don't complete and use up resources unnecessarily. In this case, it allows canceling the related tasks when the client cancels the request. This is the same as the `HttpContext.RequestAborted` property.
`ClaimsPrincipal`	To access the current user, we can inject a `ClaimsPrincipal` instance. This is the same as the `HttpContext.User` property.

Table 5.4: Special HTTP types

Here's an example where two endpoints write to the response stream, one using the `HttpContext` and the other the `HttpResponse` object:

```
app.MapGet(
    "minimal-endpoint-input-HttpContext/",
    (HttpContext context)
        => context.Response.WriteAsync("HttpContext!")
);
app.MapGet(
    "minimal-endpoint-input-HttpResponse/",
    (HttpResponse response)
```

```
        => response.WriteAsync("HttpResponse!")
);
```

We can treat those special types like any other bindings and seamlessly integrate them with other types, such as route values and services.

We cover one last piece of data binding next.

Custom binding

We can manually bind data from the request to an instance of a custom class. We can achieve this in the following ways:

- Create a static `TryParse` method that parses a string from a route, query, or header value
- Create a static `BindAsync` method that directly controls the binding process using the `HttpContext`

We must write those static methods in the class we intend to create using the HTTP request's data. We explore those two scenarios next.

Manual parsing

The `TryParse` method takes a string and an `out` parameter of the type itself. The framework uses that method to parse a value into the desired type.

The parsing API supports the implementation of one of the following methods:

```
public static bool TryParse(string value, TSelf out result);
public static bool TryParse(string value, IFormatProvider provider, TSelf out
result);
```

Implementing the `IParsable<TSelf>` interface provides the appropriate `TryParse` method.

Here is an example that parses latitude and longitude coordinates:

```
using System.Diagnostics.CodeAnalysis;
// ...
app.MapGet(
    "minimal-endpoint-input-Coordinate/",
    (Coordinate coordinate) => coordinate
);
// ...
public class Coordinate : IParsable<Coordinate>
{
    public double Latitude { get; set; }
```

```
    public double Longitude { get; set; }

    public static Coordinate Parse(
        string value,
        IFormatProvider? provider)
    {
        if (TryParse(value, provider, out var result))
        {
            return result;
        }
        throw new ArgumentException(
            "Cannot parse the value into a Coordinate.",
            nameof(value)
        );
    }

    public static bool TryParse(
        [NotNullWhen(true)] string? s,
        IFormatProvider? provider,
        [MaybeNullWhen(false)] out Coordinate result)
    {
        var segments = s?.Split(
            ',',
            StringSplitOptions.TrimEntries |
            StringSplitOptions.RemoveEmptyEntries
        );
        if (segments?.Length == 2)
        {
            var latitudeIsValid = double.TryParse(
                segments[0],
                out var latitude
            );
            var longitudeIsValid = double.TryParse(
                segments[1],
                out var longitude
            );
            if (latitudeIsValid && longitudeIsValid)
            {
                result = new() {
                    Latitude = latitude,
                    Longitude = longitude
```

```
                };
                return true;
            }
        }
        result = null;
        return false;
    }
}
```

In the preceding code, the endpoint returns a JSON representation of the `Coordinate` class, while the `TryParse` method parses the input string into a `Coordinate` object.

The `Parse` method of the `Coordinate` class comes from the `IParsable<TSelf>` interface and is not needed for model binding.

For example, if we request the following URI:

```
/minimal-endpoint-input-Coordinate?coordinate=45.501690%2C%20-73.567253
```

The endpoint returns:

```
{
  "latitude": 45.50169,
  "longitude": -73.567253
}
```

Parsing a string into an object is a viable choice for simple scenarios. However, more complex scenarios require another technique that we explore next.

Manual binding

The `BindAsync` method takes an `HttpContext` and a `ParameterInfo` parameter and returns a `ValueTask<TSelf>` where `TSelf` is the type we are writing data binding for. The `HttpContext` represents the source of the data (the HTTP request), and the `ParameterInfo` represents the delegate's parameter from which we could want to know something, like its name.

The data-binding API supports the implementation of one of the following methods:

```
public static ValueTask<TSelf?> BindAsync(HttpContext context, ParameterInfo
parameter);
public static ValueTask<TSelf?> BindAsync(HttpContext context);
```

Implementing the `IBindableFromHttpContext<TSelf>` interface provides the appropriate `BindAsync` method.

Here is an example that binds a `Person` from the HTTP request's query parameters:

```
using System.Reflection;
// ...
app.MapGet(
    "minimal-endpoint-input-Person/",
    (Person person) => person
);
// ...
public class Person : IBindableFromHttpContext<Person>
{
    public required string Name { get; set; }
    public required DateOnly Birthday { get; set; }

    public static ValueTask<Person?> BindAsync(
        HttpContext context,
        ParameterInfo parameter)
    {
        var name = context.Request.Query["name"].Single();
        var birthdayIsValid = DateOnly.TryParse(
            context.Request.Query["birthday"],
            out var birthday
        );
        if (name is not null && birthdayIsValid) {
            var person = new Person() {
                Name = name,
                Birthday = birthday
            };
            return ValueTask.FromResult(person)!;
        }
        return ValueTask.FromResult(default(Person));
    }
}
```

The preceding code returns a JSON representation of the person. For example, if we request the following URI:

```
/minimal-endpoint-input-Person?name=John%20Doe&birthday=2023-06-14
```

The endpoint returns:

```
{
  "name": "John Doe",
```

```
    "birthday": "2023-06-14"
}
```

As we can see, the `BindAsync` method is way more powerful than the `TryParse` method because we can access a broader range of options using the `HttpContext`, allowing us to cover complex use cases.

However, in this case, we could have leveraged the `[AsParameters]` attribute to achieve the same result and get the data from the query without needing to write the data-binding code manually. What a great opportunity to explore this attribute; here's the updated version of the same code:

```
app.MapGet(
    "minimal-endpoint-input-Person2/",
    ([AsParameters] Person2 person) => person
);
public class Person2
{
    public required string Name { get; set; }
    public required DateOnly Birthday { get; set; }
}
```

That's it; the `AsParameters` attribute did the work for us!

Now that we have covered reading the input values from different places in the HTTP request, it is time to explore how to output results.

Outputs

There are several ways to output data from our delegates:

- Return a serializable object.
- Return an `IResult` implementation.
- Return a `Results<TResult1, TResult2, …, TResultN>` where the `TResult` generic parameters represent the different `IResult` implementations the endpoint can return.

We explore those possibilities next.

Serializable object

The first is to return a serializable object, as we did in the previous section about inputs. ASP.NET Core serializes the object into a JSON string and sets the `Content-Type` header to `application/json`. This is the easiest way to do it but also the least flexible.

For example, the following code:

```
app.MapGet(
    "minimal-endpoint-output-coordinate/",
    () => new Coordinate {
        Latitude = 43.653225,
```

```
        Longitude = -79.383186
    }
);
```

outputs the following JSON string:

```
{
  "latitude": 43.653225,
  "longitude": -79.383186
}
```

The problem with this approach is that we don't control the status code, nor can we return multiple different results from the endpoint—for example, if the endpoint returns `200 OK` in one case and `404 Not Found` in another. To help us with this, we explore the `IResult` abstraction next.

IResult

The next option is to return the `IResult` interface. We can leverage the `Results` or `TypedResults` classes from the `Microsoft.AspNetCore.Http` namespace to do that.

I recommend defaulting to using `TypedResults`, which .NET 7 introduced.

The main difference between the two is that the methods in the `Results` class return `IResult`, while those in `TypedResults` return a typed implementation of the `IResult` interface. This difference may sound insignificant, but it changes everything regarding discoverability by the API Explorer. The API Explorer can't automatically discover the API contract of the former, while it can for the latter. This is possible because the compiler can infer the return type, but it creates challenges when returning more than one result type.

This choice impacts the amount of work you'll have to put into getting well-crafted OpenAPI specifications automatically (or not so automatically).

The following two endpoints explicitly state the result is `200 OK`, one with each class:

```
app.MapGet(
    "minimal-endpoint-output-coordinate-ok1/",
    () => Results.Ok(new Coordinate {
        Latitude = 43.653225,
        Longitude = -79.383186
    })
);
```

```
app.MapGet(
    "minimal-endpoint-output-coordinate-ok2/",
    () => TypedResults.Ok(new Coordinate {
        Latitude = 43.653225,
        Longitude = -79.383186
    })
);
```

When looking at the generated OpenAPI specifications, the first endpoint has no return value, while the other has a `Coordinate` definition mimicking our C# class.

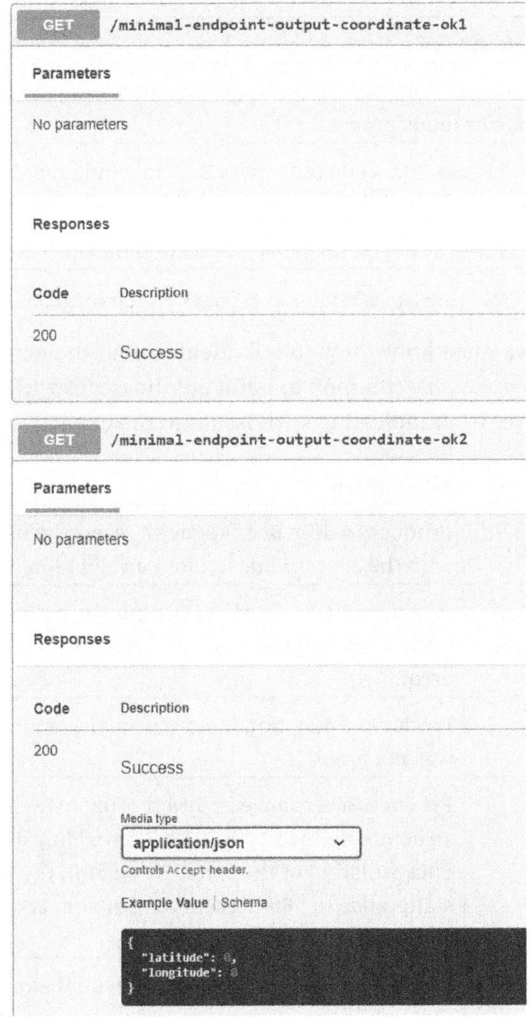

Figure 5.1: A screenshot of the generated OpenAPI specifications, one endpoint with more details than the other

Next, we dig deeper into the `TypedResults` class.

TypedResults

We can use the methods of the `TypedResults` class to generate strongly-typed outputs. They allow us to control the output while informing ASP.NET Core of the specifics, like the status code and return type.

Please note that for the sake of simplicity, I've omitted variants and overloads, focusing solely on the fundamentals of each method in the tables.

Let's start with the successful status code, where the `200 OK` status code is most likely the most common:

Method	Description
`Accepted`	Produces a `202 Accepted` response, indicating the beginning of an asynchronous process.
`Created`	Produces a `201 Created` response, indicating the system created the entity, the location of the entity, and the entity itself.
`Ok`	Produces a `200 OK` response, indicating the operation was successful.

Table 5.5: TypedResults successful status code methods

On top of the successes, we must know how to tell clients about the errors. For example, `400 Bad Request` and `404 Not Found` are very common to point out the issues with the request. The following table contains methods to assist in indicating such issues to the clients:

Method	Description
`BadRequest`	Produces a `400 Bad Request` response, indicating an issue with the client request, often a validation error.
`Conflict`	Produces a `409 Conflict` response, indicating a conflict occurred when processing the request, often a concurrency error.
`NotFound`	Produces a `404 Not Found` response, indicating the resource was not found.
`Problem`	Produces a response body adhering to the *Problem Details* structure defined by **RFC7807**, providing a standardized encapsulation of the error. By default, the method sets the status code to `500 Internal Server Error`, but we can customize that.
`UnprocessableEntity`	Produces a `422 Unprocessable Content` response, indicating that, while the server comprehends the request's content type and the syntax is correct, it cannot process the instructions or the entity.

`ValidationProblem`	Produces a `400 Bad Request` status code response with a body adhering to the *Problem Details* structure defined by **RFC7807**. We use this method to communicate input validation errors to clients in a standard format compared to the `BadRequest` method, which allows us to respond with any type. This method ensures consistency.

Table 5.6: TypedResults problematic status code

Leveraging the *Problem Details* structure improves the interoperability of our API by choosing a standard instead of crafting a custom way of returning our API errors.

It is rarer in APIs than with conventional web applications to send redirections to clients, yet, we can redirect the clients to another URL with one of the following methods when needed:

Method	Description
`LocalRedirect`	Produces a `301 Moved Permanently`, `302 Found`, `307 Temporary Redirect`, or `308 Permanent Redirect` response based on the specified arguments. This method throws an exception at runtime if the URL is not local, which is an excellent option to ensure dynamically generated URLs are not sending users away. For example, when the URL is composed using user inputs.
`Redirect`	Produces a `301 Moved Permanently`, `302 Found`, `307 Temporary Redirect`, or `308 Permanent Redirect` response based on the specified arguments.

Table 5.7: TypedResults redirection status code

Sending files to the client is another helpful feature; for example, the API could protect the files using authorization. The following table showcases a few helper methods to send files to the client:

Method	Description
`File`	Writes the file content to the response stream. The `File` methods are aliases for the `Bytes` and `Stream` methods. We look at those soon.
`PhysicalFile`	Writes the content of a physical file to the response using an absolute or relative path. Caution: do not expose this method to raw user inputs because it can read files outside the web content root. So a malicious actor could craft a request to access restricted files.

`VirtualFile`	Writes the content of a physical file to the response using an absolute or relative path. This method limits the file's location to the web content root and is safer when dealing with user inputs.

Table 5.8: TypedResults methods for downloading files

On top of the methods we have explored so far, the following table lists ways to handle the content directly in its raw format. These content-handling methods can become handy when you need more control over what is happening:

Method	**Description**
`Bytes`	Writes the byte array or `ReadOnlyMemory<byte>` content directly to the response. It defaults to sending an `application/octet-stream` MIME type to the client. This default behavior can be customized as needed.
`Content`	Writes the specified content `string` to the response stream. It defaults to sending a `text/plain` MIME type to the client. This default behavior can be customized as needed.
`Json`	Serializes the specified object to JSON. It defaults to sending an `application/json` MIME type to the client with a `200 OK` status code. These default behaviors can be customized as needed. Compared to the other methods, like the `Ok` method, the primary advantage is that it allows us to use a non-default instance of the `JsonSerializerOptions` class to configure the serialization of the response.
`NoContent`	Produces an empty `204 No Content` response.
`StatusCode`	Produces an empty response with the specified status code.
`Stream`	Allows writing directly to the response stream from another `Stream`. It defaults to sending an `application/octet-stream` MIME type to the client. This default behavior can be customized as needed. This method is highly customizable, returns a `200 OK` status code by default, and supports range requests that produce the status code `206 Partial Content` or `416 Range Not Satisfiable`.
`Text`	Writes the content string to the HTTP response. It defaults to sending a `text/plain` MIME type to the client. This default behavior can be customized as needed, as well as the text encoding.

Table 5.9: TypedResults raw content handling methods

The `application/octet-stream` MIME type suggests that the response body is a file without specifying its type, which typically prompts the browser to download the file.

Finally, we can leverage the following methods of the `TypedResults` class to create security flows. Most of these methods rely on the current implementation of the `IAuthenticationService` interface, which dictates their behavior:

Method	Description
`Challenge`	Initiates a challenge for authentication when an unauthenticated user requests an endpoint that necessitates authentication.
`Forbid`	Invokes when an authenticated user tries to access a resource for which they do not have the necessary permissions. By default, it produces a `403 Forbidden` response, although the behavior may vary depending on the specific authentication scheme.
`SignIn`	Commences the sign-in process for a user, based on the specified authentication scheme.
`SignOut`	Initiates the sign-out process for the given authentication scheme.
`Unauthorized`	Produces a `401 Unauthorized` response which specifies that the user is not authenticated

Table 5.10: TypedResults security-related methods

Now that we have covered the `TypedResults` possibilities, we explore how to return those typed results next.

Returning multiple typed results

While returning a single typed result is helpful, the capability to produce multiple results is better aligned with real-life scenarios. As we previously examined, it's possible to return multiple `IResult` objects, but we're restricted to a single typed result. This limitation arises from the compiler's inability to identify a shared interface and deduce an `IResult` return type from the typed results. Even if the compiler could, that wouldn't enhance discoverability.

To overcome this limitation, .NET 7 introduced the `Results<T1, TN>` types, allowing us to return up to six different typed results.

Here's an example that returns `200 OK` when the random number is even and `209 Conflict` when it is odd:

```
app.MapGet(
    "multiple-TypedResults/",
    Results<Ok, Conflict> ()
        => Random.Shared.Next(0, 100) % 2 == 0
            ? TypedResults.Ok()
            : TypedResults.Conflict()
);
```

This also works with methods like this:

```
app.MapGet(
    "multiple-TypedResults-delegate/",
    MultipleResultsDelegate
);
Results<Ok, Conflict> MultipleResultsDelegate()
{
    return Random.Shared.Next(0, 100) % 2 == 0
        ? TypedResults.Ok()
        : TypedResults.Conflict();
}
```

Adopting this approach enhances the API Explorer's comprehension of the API, thereby allowing tools like Swagger to automatically generate more accurate and detailed API documentation.

Next, we explore adding more metadata to endpoints.

Metadata

Sometimes, relying solely on automatic metadata is not enough. That's why ASP.NET Core offers different helper methods to fine-tune the metadata of our endpoints.

We can use most helper methods with groups and routes. In the case of a group, the metadata cascades to its children, whether it is another group or a route. However, a child can override the inherited values by changing the metadata.

Here's a partial list of helpers and their usage:

Method	Description
`Accepts`	Specifies the supported request content types. *Only applicable to routes.*
`AllowAnonymous`	Specifies that anonymous users can access the endpoint(s).
`CacheOutput`	Adds an output caching policy to the endpoint(s).
`DisableRateLimiting`	Turns off the rate-limiting feature on the endpoint(s).
`ExcludeFromDescription`	Excludes the item from the API Explorer data.

`Produces`
`ProducesProblem`
`ProducesValidationProblem`
	Describes a response, including its type, content type, and status code.
	Only applicable to routes.

`RequireAuthorization`	Specifies that only authorized users can access the endpoint(s). We can be more granular by using one of the overloads. For example, we can specify a policy name or an `AuthorizationPolicy` instance. *You must configure authorization for this to work.*
`RequireCors`	Specifies that the endpoint(s) must follow a CORS policy. *You must configure CORS for this to work.*
`RequireRateLimiting`	Adds a rate-limiting policy to the endpoint(s). *You must configure rate-limiting for this to work.*
`WithDescription`	Describes the route. When used on a group, the description cascades to all routes within that group.
`WithName`	Attributes a name to the route. We can use this name to identify the route, which must be unique. For example, we can use the route name with the `LinkGenerator` class to generate the URL of that endpoint.
`WithOpenApi`	Ensures the builder adds the compatible metadata about the endpoint so tools like Swagger can generate the OpenAPI specifications. The `Microsoft.AspNetCore.OpenApi` NuGet package provides this method. **You must add this package to your project** before being able to use the `WithOpenApi` method. We can also use this method to configure the operation and parameters instead of the other extension methods. *Other methods, like* `WithDescription` *and* `WithSummary`*, depend on the* `WithOpenApi` *method, which must also be called on the endpoint or group.*
`WithSummary`	Adds a summary to the route. When used on a group, the summary cascades to all routes within that group.
`WithTags`	Adds tags to the route. When used on a group, the tags cascade to all routes within that group.

Table 5.11: Metadata helper methods

Next, we are leveraging SwaggerGen to create Open API specifications (OAS). Everything is set up for us when creating a project using the `webapi` template (`dotnet new webapi`). Otherwise, we must install the following packages:

- `Microsoft.AspNetCore.OpenApi` provides the `WithOpenApi` method.
- `Swashbuckle.AspNetCore` is a tool that generates OAS and a UI on top of the specs.

At this point, the `csproj` file should look like this (versions may differ):

```
<Project Sdk="Microsoft.NET.Sdk.Web">
  <PropertyGroup>
    <TargetFramework>net8.0</TargetFramework>
    <Nullable>enable</Nullable>
    <ImplicitUsings>enable</ImplicitUsings>
    <InvariantGlobalization>true</InvariantGlobalization>
  </PropertyGroup>
  <ItemGroup>
    <PackageReference Include="Microsoft.AspNetCore.OpenApi" Version="8.0.0" />
    <PackageReference Include="Swashbuckle.AspNetCore" Version="6.4.0" />
  </ItemGroup>
</Project>
```

Then, in the `Program.cs` file, we must register the following dependencies:

```
builder.Services.AddEndpointsApiExplorer();
builder.Services.AddSwaggerGen();
```

Finally, we must configure the following middleware:

```
app.UseSwagger();
app.UseSwaggerUI();
```

In the source code, `Program.cs` calls the `app.UseDarkSwaggerUI()` method instead of `app.UseSwaggerUI()`. The `UseDarkSwaggerUI` method wraps `UseSwaggerUI` and registers a CSS file that converts the UI to dark mode. The code is available on GitHub.

With that setup in place, let's look at an example that creates a group, tags it, and then ensures that all routes under that group have their metadata harvestable by SwaggerGen (the API Explorer):

```
var metadataGroup = app
    .MapGroup("minimal-endpoint-metadata")
    .WithTags("Metadata Endpoints")
    .WithOpenApi()
;
```

We can now define endpoints on that group using the `metadataGroup` as if it were the app variable.

Next, we create an endpoint that we name `"Named Endpoint"` and describe it using the `WithOpenApi` method, including deprecating it:

```
const string NamedEndpointName = "Named Endpoint";
metadataGroup
    .MapGet(
        "with-name",
        () => $"Endpoint with name '{NamedEndpointName}'."
    )
    .WithName(NamedEndpointName)
    .WithOpenApi(operation => {
        operation.Description = "An endpoint that returns its name.";
        operation.Summary = $"Endpoint named '{NamedEndpointName}'.";
        operation.Deprecated = true;
        return operation;
    })
;
```

Next, we generate a URL based on the preceding named endpoint; we describe the endpoint using the `WithDescription` method and add metadata to the `endpointName` parameter, including an example. Once again, we leverage the `WithOpenApi` method:

```
metadataGroup
    .MapGet(
        "url-of-named-endpoint/{endpointName?}",
        (string? endpointName, LinkGenerator linker) => {
            var name = endpointName ?? NamedEndpointName;
            return new {
                name,
                uri = linker.GetPathByName(name)
            };
        }
    )
    .WithDescription("Return the URL of the specified named endpoint.")
    .WithOpenApi(operation => {
        var endpointName = operation.Parameters[0];
        endpointName.Description = "The name of the endpoint to get the URL
for.";
        endpointName.AllowEmptyValue = true;
        endpointName.Example = new OpenApiString(NamedEndpointName);
        return operation;
```

```
    })
;
```

When requesting the preceding endpoint, we get the URL of the specified route. By default, we get the URL of the `"Named Endpoint"` route—our only named route—in the following JSON format:

```
{
  "name": "Named Endpoint",
  "uri": "/minimal-endpoint-metadata/with-name"
}
```

As a last example, we can exclude a route from the metadata with the `ExcludeFromDescription` method:

```
metadataGroup
    .MapGet("excluded-from-open-api", () => { })
    .ExcludeFromDescription()
;
```

When looking at the Swagger UI, we can see the following section representing the group we just defined:

Metadata Endpoints

GET ~~/minimal-endpoint-metadata/with-name~~ Endpoint named 'Named Endpoint'

GET /minimal-endpoint-metadata/url-of-named-endpoint/{endpointName}

Figure 5.2: A screenshot of the Swagger UI "Metadata Endpoints" route group

We can see two endpoints in the preceding screenshot and, as expected, the third endpoint was excluded.

The first route is marked as deprecated and shows a summary. When we open it, we see a warning, a description, no parameters, and one `200 OK` response with a MIME type `text/plain`.

I omitted adding a screenshot of Swagger UI for the first endpoint since it does not add much and would be hard to read. To explore the Swagger UI by yourself, you can run the `Minimal.API` program and navigate to the `/swagger/index.html` URL.

The second route does not have a summary but, when we open it, we have a description. The metadata we added for the `endpointName` parameter is there, and most interestingly, the example became the default value:

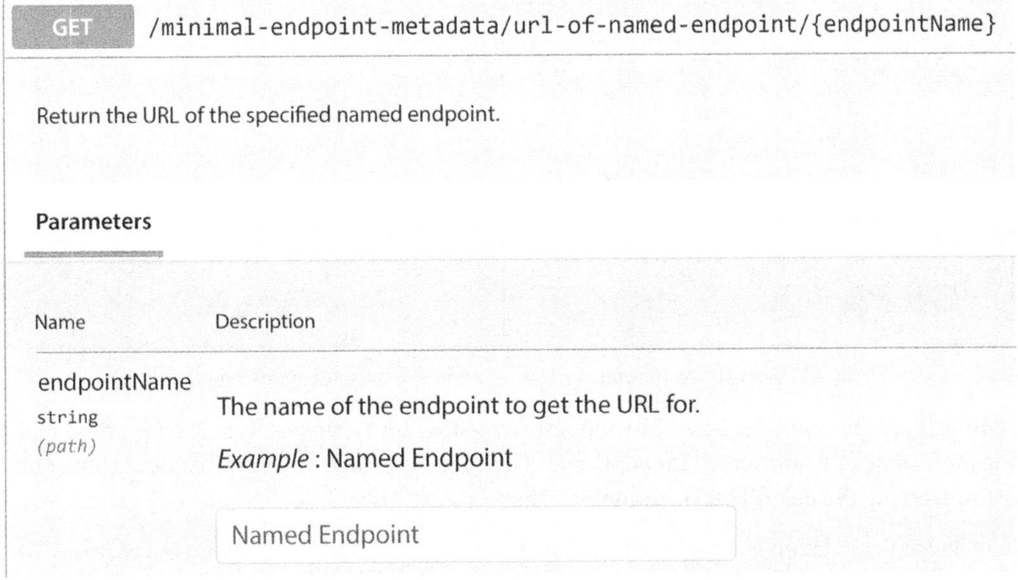

Figure 5.3: A screenshot of Swagger UI showcasing the metadata of the endpointName parameter

Swagger UI can become very handy for manually calling our API during development or leveraging other OpenAPI compatible tools. For example, we could generate code based on the OpenAPI specs, like a TypeScript client.

Next, we explore how to configure the Minimal API JSON serializer.

Configuring JSON serialization

In ASP.NET Core, we can customize the JSON serializer globally or create a new one for a specific scenario.

To change the default serializer behaviors, we can invoke the `ConfigureHttpJsonOptions` method, which configures the `JsonOptions` object. From there, we can change the options like this:

```
builder.Services.ConfigureHttpJsonOptions(options => {
    options.SerializerOptions.PropertyNamingPolicy = JsonNamingPolicy.
KebabCaseLower;
});
```

With the preceding code in the `Program.cs` file, we tell the serializer to serialize the property name following a `lower-case-kebab` naming convention. Here is an example:

Endpoint	Response

<pre>jsonGroup.MapGet(
    "kebab-person/",
    () => new {
        FirstName = "John",
        LastName = "Doe"
    }
);</pre>
	<pre>{
	  "first-name": "John",
	  "last-name": "Doe"
	}</pre>

Table 5.12: Showcasing the output of the JsonNamingPolicy.KebabCaseLower policy

We can achieve the same for specific endpoints by using the `TypedResults.Json` method and specifying an instance of `JsonSerializerOptions`. The following code accomplishes the same outcome while preserving the default serialization options:

```
var kebabSerializer = new JsonSerializerOptions(JsonSerializerDefaults.Web)
{
    PropertyNamingPolicy = JsonNamingPolicy.KebabCaseLower
};
jsonGroup.MapGet(
    "kebab-person/",
    () => TypedResults.Json(new {
        FirstName = "John",
        LastName = "Doe"
    }, kebabSerializer)
);
```

I highlighted the changes between this code and the previous example. First, we create an instance of the `JsonSerializerOptions` class. To simplify the configuration, we start with the default web serialization values by passing the `JsonSerializerDefaults.Web` argument to the constructor. Then, in the object initializer, we set the value of the `PropertyNamingPolicy` property to `JsonNamingPolicy.KebabCaseLower`, which ends up with the same result as before. Finally, to use our options, we pass the `kebabSerializer` variable as the second argument of the `TypedResults.Json` method.

Serializing enums as strings

I often find myself changing a configuration to output the string representation of an `enum` value. To do so, we must register an instance of the `JsonStringEnumConverter` class. We can find this class in the `System.Text.Json.Serialization` namespace. Afterward, enums will be serialized as strings. Here is an example:

```
using System.Text.Json.Serialization;
// ...
var enumSerializer = new JsonSerializerOptions(JsonSerializerDefaults.Web);
enumSerializer.Converters.Add(new JsonStringEnumConverter());
jsonGroup.MapGet(
    "enum-as-string/",
    () => TypedResults.Json(new {
        FirstName = "John",
        LastName = "Doe",
        Rating = Rating.Good,
    }, enumSerializer)
);
// ...
public enum Rating
{
    Bad = 0,
    Ok,
    Good,
    Amazing
}
```

When executing the preceding code, we obtain the following result:

```
{
  "firstName": "John",
  "lastName": "Doe",
  "rating": "Good"
}
```

Using the default options yields the following instead:

```
{
  "firstName": "John",
  "lastName": "Doe",
  "rating": 2
}
```

I usually change this option globally since having a human-readable value instead of a number is more explicit, easier to understand for a human, and easier to leverage for a client (machine).

Many other options exist to tweak the serializer, but we can't explore them all here. Next, we look at endpoint filters.

Leveraging endpoint filters

ASP.NET Core 7.0 added the possibility to register endpoint filters. This way, we can encapsulate and reuse cross-cutting concerns and logic across endpoints.

An example of reusability is that I prefer FluentValidation to .NET attributes, so I created an open-source project implementing a filter that ties Minimal APIs with FluentValidation. I can then reuse that filter across projects by referencing a NuGet package. We explore FluentValidation in *Section 4: Application Patterns*, and I left a link to that project in the *Further reading* section.

How does it work?

- We can register endpoint filters inline or by creating a class
- We can add filters to an endpoint or a group using the `AddEndpointFilter` method
- When adding a filter to a group, it applies to all its children
- We can add multiple filters per endpoint or group
- ASP.NET Core executes the filters in the order they are registered

Let's look at a simple inline filter:

```
inlineGroup
    .MapGet("basic", () => { })
    .AddEndpointFilter((context, next) =>
    {
        return next(context);
    });
```

The highlighted code represents the filter in the form of a delegate. The filter does nothing but execute the next delegate in the chain—in this case, the endpoint delegate itself.

In the following example, we use the `Rating` enum and only accept positive ratings in the endpoint. To achieve this, we add a filter that validates the input value before reaching the endpoint:

```
public enum Rating
{
    Bad = 0,
    Ok,
    Good,
    Amazing
}
// ...
inlineGroup
```

```
    .MapGet("good-rating/{rating}", (Rating rating)
        => TypedResults.Ok(new { Rating = rating }))
    .AddEndpointFilter(async (context, next) =>
    {
        var rating = context.GetArgument<Rating>(0);
        if (rating == Rating.Bad)
        {
            return TypedResults.Problem(
                detail: "This endpoint is biased and only accepts positive
ratings.",
                statusCode: StatusCodes.Status400BadRequest
            );
        }
        return await next(context);
    });
```

From the filter, we leveraged the `EndpointFilterFactoryContext` to access the rating argument. The code then validates that the rating is not `Bad`. If the rating is `Bad`, the filter immediately returns a *problem details* object and a `400 Bad Request` status code before reaching the endpoint delegate. Otherwise, the endpoint code is executed.

You probably wonder how useful writing code like this can be; well, this case is purely educational and not that useful in a real-world scenario. We could have validated the parameter in the endpoint delegate directly and saved ourselves the trouble of accessing it through its index. Nonetheless, it shows how filters work so that you can build helpful real-life filters with this knowledge; remember that coding is like playing with LEGO® blocks.

To improve on this foundation and make the previous example reusable, we can extract the filter logic into a class and apply it to multiple endpoints. We could also move the inline implementation to a group so it affects all its children. Let's have a look at making our inline filter a class.

A filter class must implement the `IEndpointFilter` interface. Here's the reimplementation of the previous logic in the `GoodRatingFilter` class:

```
public class GoodRatingFilter : IEndpointFilter
{
    public async ValueTask<object?> InvokeAsync(
        EndpointFilterInvocationContext context,
        EndpointFilterDelegate next)
    {
        var rating = context.GetArgument<Rating>(0);
        if (rating == Rating.Bad)
        {
            return TypedResults.Problem(
```

```
                detail: "This endpoint is biased and only accepts positive
ratings.",
                statusCode: StatusCodes.Status400BadRequest
            );
        }
        return await next(context);
    }
}
```

The GoodRatingFilter class InvokeAsync method code is the same as the inline version.

We can configure the filter on the group or individual endpoints to recreate the same behavior. Here's an example of a group:

```
var groupWithAnEndpointFilter = app.MapGroup("leveraging-endpoint-filters")
    .WithTags("Leveraging Endpoint Filters")
    .AddEndpointFilter<GoodRatingFilter>()
;
```

When doing this, all endpoints registered on that group inherit the filter. For example, the following two endpoints inherit the filter:

```
groupWithAnEndpointFilter
    .MapGet("good-rating/{rating}", (Rating rating)
        => TypedResults.Ok(new { Rating = rating }))
;
groupWithAnEndpointFilter
    .MapGet("good-rating/{rating}-{review}", (Rating rating, string review)
        => TypedResults.Ok(new { Rating = rating, Review = review }))
;
```

On top of this, one of the most interesting benefits of a filter is the ability to reuse it on different endpoints—also applicable to groups—like this:

```
var appOrGroupA = app.MapGroup("appOrGroupA");
appOrGroupA
    .MapGet("good-rating/{rating}", (Rating rating)
        => TypedResults.Ok(new { Rating = rating }))
    .AddEndpointFilter<GoodRatingFilter>();
;
```

The preceding endpoint—part of the appOrGroupA group—uses the filter (highlighted line). Next is another endpoint that leverages the same filter—part of the appOrGroupB group:

```
var appOrGroupB = app.MapGroup("appOrGroupB");
appOrGroupB
```

```
    .MapPut("good-rating/{rating}", (Rating rating)
        => TypedResults.Ok(new { Rating = rating }))
    .AddEndpointFilter<GoodRatingFilter>();
;
```

Using filters this way allows us to keep our code DRY. Encapsulating pieces of logic in filters is very beneficial to avoid repetitive code that makes our codebase harder to maintain, whether it is input validation, logging, exception handling, or another scenario.

And this is not all; there is one more thing about filters we must explore.

Leveraging the endpoint filter factory

We can use an endpoint filter factory to run code when ASP.NET Core builds the endpoint (makes the `RequestDelegate`) before declaring the filter. Then, from the factory, we control the creation of the filter itself.

We explore the factory pattern in *Chapter 7, Strategy, Abstract Factory, and Singleton Design Patterns.*

The following code registers an endpoint filter factory:

```
inlineGroup
    .MapGet("endpoint-filter-factory", () => "RAW")
    .AddEndpointFilterFactory((filterFactoryContext, next) =>
    {
        // Building RequestDelegate code here.
        var logger = filterFactoryContext.ApplicationServices
            .GetRequiredService<ILoggerFactory>()
            .CreateLogger("endpoint-filter-factory");
        logger.LogInformation("Code that runs when ASP.NET Core builds the
RequestDelegate");

        // Returns the EndpointFilterDelegate ASP.NET Core executes as part of
the pipeline.
        return async invocationContext =>
        {
            logger.LogInformation("Code that ASP.NET Core executes as part of
the pipeline");
            // Filter code here
            return await next(invocationContext);
        };
    });
```

The preceding code adds an endpoint filter factory that logs some information to the console, which allows us to track what is happening. The highlighted code represents the filter itself. For example, we could write the same code as the `GoodRatingFilter` class there.

Next, let's look at what happens when we execute the program and load the endpoint five times:

```
[11:22:56.673] info: Microsoft.Hosting.Lifetime[14]
      Now listening on: https://localhost:7298
[11:22:56.698] info: Microsoft.Hosting.Lifetime[14]
      Now listening on: http://localhost:5085
[11:22:56.702] info: Microsoft.Hosting.Lifetime[0]
      Application started. Press Ctrl+C to shut down.
[11:22:56.705] info: Microsoft.Hosting.Lifetime[0]
      Hosting environment: Development
[11:22:56.708] info: Microsoft.Hosting.Lifetime[0]
      Content root path: .../C05/Minimal.API
[11:23:28.349] info: endpoint-filter-factory[0]
      Code that runs when ASP.NET Core builds the RequestDelegate
[11:23:45.181] info: endpoint-filter-factory[0]
      Code that runs when ASP.NET Core builds the RequestDelegate
[11:24:56.043] info: endpoint-filter-factory[0]
      Code that ASP.NET Core executes as part of the pipeline
[11:24:57.439] info: endpoint-filter-factory[0]
      Code that ASP.NET Core executes as part of the pipeline
[11:24:58.443] info: endpoint-filter-factory[0]
      Code that ASP.NET Core executes as part of the pipeline
[11:24:59.262] info: endpoint-filter-factory[0]
      Code that ASP.NET Core executes as part of the pipeline
[11:25:00.154] info: endpoint-filter-factory[0]
      Code that ASP.NET Core executes as part of the pipeline
```

Here's what happened from the preceding output:

1. The API starts (the first 10 lines).
2. ASP.NET Core executes the factory code when building the `RequestDelegate` from the `EndpointRoutingMiddleware` (the next two lines).
3. `SwaggerGen`, using the `ApiExplorer`, also does the same from the `SwaggerMiddleware`, hence the second factory call (the next two lines).
4. Afterward, ASP.NET Core only executes the filters during requests—in this case, five times (the last 10 lines).

Now that we've seen how it runs, it is time to learn how it works.

Don't worry if you don't understand how the `GetRequiredService` method or the `ILoggerFactory` interface works; we explore those topics in *Chapter 8, Dependency Injection*, and *Chapter 10, Logging Patterns*.

We start by registering the endpoint filter factory using the `AddEndpointFilterFactory` method, which applies to groups and individual routes (we dig deeper into groups next). The factory delegate is of the type `Func<EndpointFilterFactoryContext, EndpointFilterDelegate, EndpointFilterDelegate>`.

Inside the delegate, using the `EndpointFilterFactoryContext` parameter named `filterFactoryContext`, we have access to the following objects:

- The `ApplicationServices` property provides access to an `IServiceProvider` interface, allowing us to extract services from the container, as demonstrated with the `ILoggerFactory` interface.
- The `MethodInfo` property offers a `MethodInfo` object granting access to the caller to which we add the endpoint filter factory. This object encapsulates the reflection data, including types, generic parameters, attributes, and more.

Finally, the factory delegate returns the filter that ASP.NET Core executes when a request hits the endpoint(s). In this case, the filter is the following:

```
async invocationContext =>
{
    logger.LogInformation("Code that ASP.NET Core executes as part of the 
pipeline");
    return await next(invocationContext);
};
```

The `next` parameter (highlighted code) represents the next filter in line or the endpoint itself—it works the same here as with any endpoint filter. Not calling the `next` parameter means ASP.NET Core will never execute the endpoint code, which is a way to control the flow of the application.

To make an endpoint filter factory more reusable, we could create a class, an extension method, or return an existing filter class. We can also combine those ways to craft a more testable and DRY implementation of an endpoint filter factory. While we won't delve into these specific approaches in this context, by the end of the book, you should have acquired enough knowledge to achieve these tasks by yourself.

Next, we look at organizing our endpoints.

Organizing endpoints

Grouping endpoints using the `MapGroup` method is an effective organizational strategy. However, defining all routes directly within the `Program.cs` file can result in a long and challenging-to-navigate file.

To mitigate this, we can arrange these groups of endpoints in separate classes and create an extension method to add these endpoints to the `IEndpointRouteBuilder`. We can also encapsulate the groups, or even multiple groups, within another assembly, which we can load from the API.

We explore ways to design applications in *Section 4: Application Patterns*, including in *Chapter 18, Request-EndPoint-Response (REPR)*, and *Chapter 20, Modular Monolith*.

Let's start with simple groups.

MapGroup

Creating groups is the first tool to organize the routes of our APIs. It comes with the following advantages:

- We can create a shared URL prefix for the group's children
- We can add metadata that applies to the group's children
- We can add endpoint filters that apply to the group's children

Here is an example of a group that configures those three items:

```
// Create a reusable logger
var loggerFactory = app.ServiceProvider
    .GetRequiredService<ILoggerFactory>();
var groupLogger = loggerFactory
    .CreateLogger("organizing-endpoints");

// Create the group
var group = app
    .MapGroup("organizing-endpoints")
    .WithTags("Organizing Endpoints")
    .AddEndpointFilter(async (context, next) => {
        groupLogger.LogTrace("Entering organizing-endpoints");
        // Omitted argument logging
        var result = await next(context);
        groupLogger.LogTrace("Exiting organizing-endpoints");
        return result;
    })
;
// Map endpoints in the group
group.MapGet("demo/", ()
    => "GET endpoint from the organizing-endpoints group.");
group.MapGet("demo/{id}", (int id)
```

```
    => $"GET {id} endpoint from the organizing-endpoints group.");
```

The highlighted code does the following:

- Configures the `organizing-endpoints` URL prefix
- Adds the `Organizing Endpoints` tag (metadata)
- Adds an inline filter that logs information about the requests

We can reach the endpoints at the following URLs:

- `/organizing-endpoints/demo`
- `/organizing-endpoints/demo/123`

As the following Swagger UI screenshot shows, the two endpoints are tagged correctly:

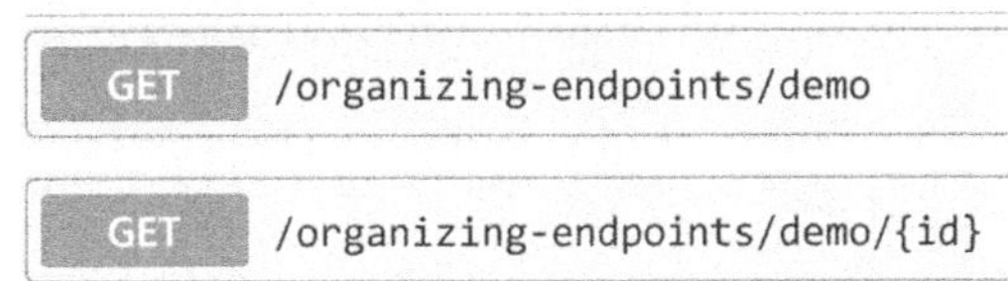

Figure 5.4: The two endpoints under the Organizing Endpoints tag

Then, after requesting the two endpoints, we end up with the following log excerpt:

```
[23:55:01.516] trce: organizing-endpoints[0]
      Entering organizing-endpoints
[23:55:01.516] trce: organizing-endpoints[0]
      Exiting organizing-endpoints
[23:55:06.028] trce: organizing-endpoints[0]
      Entering organizing-endpoints
[23:55:06.028] dbug: organizing-endpoints[0]
      Argument 1: Int32 = 123
[23:55:06.028] trce: organizing-endpoints[0]
      Exiting organizing-endpoints
```

As demonstrated, leveraging groups for shared configuration streamlines the process of setting up aspects like authorization rules, caching, and more. By adopting this approach, we uphold the DRY (Don't Repeat Yourself) principle, improving the maintainability of our code.

Next, we encapsulate mapping endpoints into classes.

Creating a custom Map extension method

Now that we have explored how to create groups, it is time to move the endpoints out of the `Program.cs` file. One way is to create an extension method that registers the route. To achieve this, we must extend the `IEndpointRouteBuilder` interface as follows:

```
namespace Minimal.API;
```

```
public static class OrganizingEndpoints
{
    public static void MapOrganizingEndpoints(
        this IEndpointRouteBuilder app)
    {
        // Map endpoints and groups here
    }
}
```

Then, we must call our extension method in the `Program.cs` file, as follows:

```
var builder = WebApplication.CreateBuilder(args);
var app = builder.Build();
app.MapOrganizingEndpoints();
app.Run();
```

And with that, we've seen how a simple technique allows us to group our routes together, offering an organized way to structure our APIs.

We can improve on this technique by returning the `IEndpointRouteBuilder` instead of `void` in our extension method, which makes our extension "fluent," as demonstrated below:

```
namespace Minimal.API;
public static class OrganizingEndpoints
{
    public static IEndpointRouteBuilder MapOrganizingEndpointsFluently(
        this IEndpointRouteBuilder app)
    {
        var group = app
            .MapGroup("organizing-endpoints-fluently")
            .WithTags("Organizing Fluent Endpoints")
        ;
        // Map endpoints and groups here
        return app;
    }
}
```

Then, from the `Program.cs` file, we can call multiple maps in a "single line of code" like the following:

```
app
    .MapOrganizingEndpointsFluently()
    .MapOrganizingEndpoints()
;
```

Creating fluent APIs is very convenient, especially in such cases. Fluent APIs are highly readable and intuitive, emphasizing a flow resembling natural language or a chain of actions. In this case, it improves readability, ease of use, and discoverability, keeping the startup configuration tidy and easy to follow.

This technique allows you to create fluent APIs for anything, not just registering routes.

Another variation of this pattern exists that's worth noting. Rather than returning the `IEndpointRouteBuilder`, the extension method can return the `RouteGroupBuilder` instead, granting the caller access to the group itself. Here is an example:

```
namespace Minimal.API;
public static class OrganizingEndpoints
{
    public static RouteGroupBuilder MapOrganizingEndpointsComposable(
        this IEndpointRouteBuilder app)
    {
        var group = app
            .MapGroup("organizing-endpoints-composable")
            .WithTags("Organizing Composable Endpoints")
        ;
        // Map endpoints and groups here
        return group;
    }
}
```

We can use such methods to create a complex hierarchy of routes and groups by splitting the registration into multiple files.

The fluent version is the most common way. It does not expose the group to the outside (encapsulation) and allows fluent chaining of other method calls.

And voilà! We now know how basic extension methods can help us organize our endpoints. Next, we explore how to move those extension methods into class libraries.

Class libraries

This last technique allows us to create and register routes from class libraries using the previously explored techniques.

First, we must create a class library project, which we can do using the `dotnet new classlib` CLI command.

Unfortunately, a class library project cannot access everything we need, like the `IEndpointRouteBuilder` interface. The good news is that it is trivial to change this fact. All we have to do is add a `FrameworkReference` element in an `ItemGroup` element in the `csproj` file, as follows:

```
<Project Sdk="Microsoft.NET.Sdk">
    <PropertyGroup>
        <TargetFramework>net8.0</TargetFramework>
        <ImplicitUsings>enable</ImplicitUsings>
        <Nullable>enable</Nullable>
    </PropertyGroup>
    <ItemGroup>
        <FrameworkReference Include="Microsoft.AspNetCore.App" />
    </ItemGroup>
</Project>
```

That minor addition equips us with everything necessary to create an ASP.NET Core-enabled library, including mapping endpoints! Transferring the preceding C# code into this class library project yields the same functional results as in a web application.

To use the class library from an ASP.NET Core project, you must reference the project using the CLI, Visual Studio, or by adding a `ProjectReference` tag in the `csproj` file, like any other project reference. For example, the following references a `Shared.csproj` file that is in a `Shared` directory:

```
<ItemGroup>
  <ProjectReference Include="..\Shared\Shared.csproj" />
</ItemGroup>
```

Then, you can register the dependencies, endpoints, and middleware with the ASP.NET Core project using the technique we explored previously.

I used this technique in the `Shared` project of the solution we explore in this chapter and the next. If you are curious, the complete source code is available on GitHub (`https://adpg.link/SPm5`).

Next, we mix Minimal APIs and DTOs.

Using Minimal APIs with Data Transfer Objects

This section explores leveraging the **Data Transfer Object** (**DTO**) pattern with Minimal APIs.

This section is the same as we explore in *Chapter 6, Model-View-Controller*, but in the context of Minimal APIs. Moreover, the two code projects are part of the same Visual Studio solution for convenience, allowing you to compare the two implementations.

Goal

As a reminder, DTOs aim to *control the inputs and outputs of an endpoint* by decoupling the API contract from the application's inner workings. DTOs empower us to define our APIs without thinking about the underlying data structures, leaving us to craft our REST APIs how we want.

We discuss REST APIs and DTOs in more depth in *Chapter 4, REST APIs*.

Other possible objectives are to save bandwidth by limiting the amount of information the API transmits, flattening the data structure, or adding API features that cross multiple entities.

Design

Let's start by analyzing a diagram that shows how Minimal APIs work with DTOs:

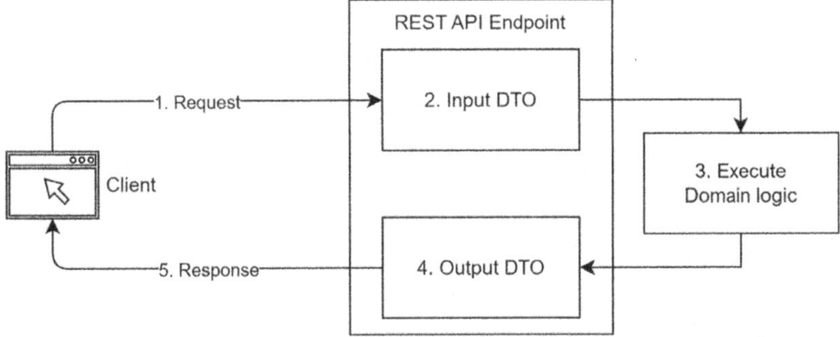

Figure 5.5: An input DTO hitting some domain logic, then the endpoint returning an output DTO

DTOs allow the decoupling of the domain (3) from the request (1) and the response (5). This model empowers us to manage the inputs and outputs of our REST APIs independently from the domain logic. Here's the flow:

1. The client sends a request to the server.
2. ASP.NET Core leverages its data binding and parsing mechanism to convert the information of the HTTP request to C# (input DTO).
3. The endpoint does what it is supposed to do.
4. ASP.NET Core serializes the output DTO to the HTTP response.
5. The client receives and handles the response.

Let's explore some code to understand the concept better.

Project – Minimal API

This code sample is similar to the next chapter but uses Minimal APIs instead of the MVC framework. Both versions are part of the same solution to make it easy to compare them—for example, `DTOEndpoints.GetCustomersSummaryAsync` is almost the same implementation as `CustomersController.GetAllAsync`, but one uses the Minimal API model while the other uses the MVC model.

Context: We must build an application to manage customers and contracts. We must track the state of each contract and have a primary contact in case the business needs to contact the customer. Finally, we must display the number of contracts and the number of opened contracts for each customer on a dashboard.

The model is the following:

```
namespace Shared.Models;
public record class Customer(
    int Id,
    string Name,
    List<Contract> Contracts
);
public record class Contract(
    int Id,
    string Name,
    string Description,
    WorkStatus Status,
    ContactInformation PrimaryContact
);
public record class WorkStatus(int TotalWork, int WorkDone)
{
    public WorkState State =>
        WorkDone == 0 ? WorkState.New :

        WorkDone == TotalWork ? WorkState.Completed :
        WorkState.InProgress;
}
public record class ContactInformation(
    string FirstName,
    string LastName,
    string Email
);
public enum WorkState
```

```
{
    New,
    InProgress,
    Completed
}
```

The preceding code is straightforward. The only piece of logic is the `WorkStatus.State` property, which returns `WorkState.New` when the work has not yet started on that contract, `WorkState.Completed` when all the work is completed, or `WorkState.InProgress` otherwise.

The endpoints (`CustomersEndpoints.cs`) leverage the `ICustomerRepository` interface to simulate database operations. The implementation uses `List<Customer>` as the database, but the interface and the implementation details are unimportant.

When starting the application, the following line of code seeds the database, adding test data to it for us to get started quickly:

```
app.InitializeSharedDataStore();
```

Now that we know the underlying foundation, let's explore CRUD endpoints that do not leverage DTOs.

Raw CRUD endpoints

Many issues can arise if we create CRUD endpoints to manage the customers directly (see `CustomersEndpoints.cs`). First, a little mistake from the client could erase several data points. For example, if the client forgets to send the contracts during a `PUT` operation, that would delete all the contracts associated with that customer. Here's the endpoint code:

```
// PUT raw/customers/1
group.MapPut("/{customerId}", async (int customerId, Customer input,
ICustomerRepository customerRepository, CancellationToken cancellationToken) =>
{
    var updatedCustomer = await customerRepository.UpdateAsync(
        input,
        cancellationToken
    );
    if (updatedCustomer == null)
    {
        return Results.NotFound();
    }
    return Results.Ok(updatedCustomer);
});
```

The highlighted code represents the customer update. So, to mistakenly remove all contracts, a client could send the following HTTP request (from the `Minimal.API.http` file):

```
PUT {{Minimal.API.BaseAddress}}/customers/1
```

```
Content-Type: application/json

{
  "id": 1,
  "name": "Some new name",
  "contracts": []
}
```

That request would result in the following response entity:

```
{
  "id": 1,
  "name": "Some new name",
  "contracts": []
}
```

Previously, however, that customer had contracts (seeded when we started the application). By exposing our entities directly, we are giving a lot of power to the consumers of our API.

Another issue with this design is if we want to aggregate and calculate statistics, like when creating a dashboard. In that case, the UI would have to calculate the statistics about the contracts. Moreover, if we implement a paging mechanism over the contract list, the UI could become increasingly complex and even over-query the database, hindering our performance.

I implemented the entire API, which is available on GitHub but without the UI.

Next, we explore how we can fix those two use cases using DTOs.

DTO-enabled endpoints

To solve our problems, we reimplement the endpoints using DTOs. These endpoints use methods instead of inline delegates and return `Results<T1, T2, …>` instead of `IResult`. We explore the `UpdateCustomerAsync` and `GetCustomersSummaryAsync` methods afterward. The complete code is available on GitHub.

Let's start by declaring a group and the endpoints:

```
var group = app
    .MapGroup("/dto/customers")
    .WithTags("Customer DTO")
    .WithOpenApi()
;
group.MapGet("/", GetCustomersSummaryAsync);
```

```
group.MapPut("/{customerId}", UpdateCustomerAsync);
```

Next, to make it easier to follow along, here are the DTOs the two methods are using:

```
namespace Shared.DTO;
public record class ContractDetails(
    int Id,
    string Name,
    string Description,
    int StatusTotalWork,
    int StatusWorkDone,
    string StatusWorkState,
    string PrimaryContactFirstName,
    string PrimaryContactLastName,
    string PrimaryContactEmail
);
public record class CustomerDetails(
    int Id,
    string Name,
    IEnumerable<ContractDetails> Contracts
);
public record class CustomerSummary(
    int Id,
    string Name,
    int TotalNumberOfContracts,
    int NumberOfOpenContracts
);
public record class UpdateCustomer(string Name);
```

First, let's fix our update problem, starting with the reimplementation of the update endpoint leveraging DTOs (see the `DTOEndpoints.cs` file):

```
// PUT dto/customers/1
private static async Task<Results<
    Ok<CustomerDetails>,
    NotFound,
    Conflict
>> UpdateCustomerAsync(
        int customerId,
        UpdateCustomer input,
        ICustomerRepository customerRepository,
        CancellationToken cancellationToken)
```

```
{
    // Get the customer
    var customer = await customerRepository.FindAsync(
        customerId,
        cancellationToken
    );
    if (customer == null)
    {
        return TypedResults.NotFound();
    }

    // Update the customer's name using the UpdateCustomer DTO
    var updatedCustomer = await customerRepository.UpdateAsync(
        customer with { Name = input.Name },
        cancellationToken
    );
    if (updatedCustomer == null)
    {
        return TypedResults.Conflict();
    }

    // Map the updated customer to a CustomerDetails DTO
    var dto = MapCustomerToCustomerDetails(updatedCustomer);

    // Return the DTO
    return TypedResults.Ok(dto);
}
```

In the preceding code, the main differences are (highlighted):

- The request body is now bound to the `UpdateCustomer` class instead of the `Customer` itself
- The action method returns an instance of the `CustomerDetails` class instead of the `Customer` itself when the operation succeeds

However, we can see more code in our endpoint than before. That's because it now handles the changes instead of the clients. The action now does the following:

1. Loads the data from the database
2. Ensures the entity exists
3. Uses the input DTO to update the data, limiting the clients to a subset of properties
4. Proceeds with the update
5. Ensures the entity still exists (handles conflicts)

6. Copies the `Customer` into the output DTO and returns it

By doing this, we now control what the clients can do when they send a `PUT` request through the input DTO (`UpdateCustomer`). Moreover, we encapsulated the logic to calculate the statistics on the server. We hid the computation behind the output DTO (`CustomerDetails`), which lowers the complexity of our UI and allows us to improve the performance without impacting any of our clients (loose coupling).

Furthermore, we now use the `customerId` parameter.

If we send the same HTTP request as before, which sends more data than we accept, only the customer's name will change. On top of that, we get all the data we need to display the customer's statistics. Here's a response example:


```
{
  "id": 1,
  "name": "Some new name",
  "contracts": [
    {
      "id": 1,
      "name": "First contract",
      "description": "This is the first contract.",
      "statusTotalWork": 100,
      "statusWorkDone": 100,
      "statusWorkState": "Completed",
      "primaryContactFirstName": "John",
      "primaryContactLastName": "Doe",
      "primaryContactEmail": "john.doe@jonnyboy.com"
    },
    {
      "id": 2,
      "name": "Some other contract",
      "description": "This is another contract.",
      "statusTotalWork": 100,
      "statusWorkDone": 25,
      "statusWorkState": "InProgress",
      "primaryContactFirstName": "Jane",
      "primaryContactLastName": "Doe",
      "primaryContactEmail": "jane.doe@jonnyboy.com"
    }
  ]
}
```


As we can see from the preceding response, only the customer's name changed, but we now received the `statusWorkDone` and `statusTotalWork` fields. Lastly, we flattened the data structure.

DTOs are a great resource to flatten data structures. Keep in mind that you must always design your systems, including DTOs and data contracts, for specific use cases.

As for the dashboard, the "get all customers" endpoint achieves this by doing something similar. It outputs a collection of `CustomerSummary` objects instead of the customers themselves. In this case, the endpoint executes the calculations and copies the entity's relevant properties to the DTO. Here's the code:

```
// GET: dto/customers
private static async Task<Ok<IEnumerable<CustomerSummary>>>
GetCustomersSummaryAsync(
    ICustomerRepository customerRepository,
    CancellationToken cancellationToken)
{
    // Get all customers
    var customers = await customerRepository
        .AllAsync(cancellationToken);

    // Map customers to CustomerSummary DTOs
    var customersSummary = customers.Select(customer => new CustomerSummary(
        Id: customer.Id,
        Name: customer.Name,
        TotalNumberOfContracts: customer.Contracts.Count,
        NumberOfOpenContracts: customer.Contracts
            .Count(x => x.Status.State != WorkState.Completed)
    ));

    // Return the DTOs
    return TypedResults.Ok(customersSummary);
}
```

In the preceding code, the method does the following:

1. Reads the entities.
2. Creates the DTOs and calculates the number of open contracts.
3. Returns the DTOs.

As simple as that, we have now encapsulated the computation on the server.

You should optimize such code based on your real-life data source. In this case, `static List<T>` is low latency. However, querying the whole database to get a count can become a bottleneck.

Calling the endpoint results in the following:

```
[
  {
    "id": 1,
    "name": "Some new name",
    "totalNumberOfContracts": 2,
    "numberOfOpenContracts": 1
  },
  {
    "id": 2,
    "name": "Some mega-corporation",
    "totalNumberOfContracts": 1,
    "numberOfOpenContracts": 1
  }
]
```

It is now super easy to build our dashboard. We can query that endpoint once and display the data in the UI. The UI offloaded the calculation to the backend.

User interfaces tend to be more complex than APIs because they are stateful. As such, offloading as much complexity as you can to the backend helps. You can use a **backend-for-frontend** (**BFF**) to help with this task. We explore ways to layer APIs, including the BFF pattern in *Chapter 19, Introduction to Microservices Architecture*.

Lastly, you can play with the API using the HTTP requests in the `MVC.API.DTO.http` file. I implemented all the endpoints using a similar technique.

If your endpoints become too complex, it is good practice to encapsulate them into other classes. We explore many techniques to organize application code in *Section 4: Application Patterns*.

Conclusion

A data transfer object allows us to design an API endpoint with a specific data contract (input and output) instead of exposing the domain or data model. This separation between the presentation and the domain is a crucial element that leads to having multiple independent components instead of a bigger, more fragile one.

We use DTOs to control the endpoints' inputs and outputs, giving us more control over what the clients can do or receive.

Using the data transfer object pattern helps us follow the SOLID principles in the following ways:

- S: A DTO adds clear boundaries between the domain or data model and the API contract. Moreover, having an input and an output DTO helps further separate the responsibilities.
- O: N/A.
- L: N/A.
- I: A DTO is a small, specifically crafted data contract (abstraction) with a clear purpose in the API contract.
- D: Due to those smaller interfaces (ISPs), DTOs allow changing the implementation details of the endpoint without affecting the clients because they depend only on the API contract (the abstraction).

You should now understand the added value of DTOs and what part they play in an API contract. Finally, you should have a strong base of Minimal API possibilities.

Summary

Throughout the chapter, we explored ASP.NET Core Minimal APIs and their integration with the DTO pattern. Minimal APIs simplify web application development by reducing boilerplate code. The DTO pattern helps us decouple the API contract from the application's inner workings, allowing flexibility in crafting REST APIs. DTOs can also save bandwidth and flatten or change data structures. Endpoints exposing their domain or data entities directly can lead to issues, while DTO-enabled endpoints offer better control over data exchanges.

We also discussed numerous Minimal API aspects, including input binding, outputting data, metadata, JSON serialization, endpoint filters, and endpoint organization. With this foundational knowledge, we can begin to design ASP.NET Core Minimal APIs.

For more information about Minimal APIs and what they have to offer, you can visit the *Minimal APIs quick reference* page of the official documentation: `https://adpg.link/S47i`.

In the next chapter, we revisit the same notions in an ASP.NET Core MVC context.

Questions

Let's look at a few practice questions:

1. How can we map different HTTP requests to delegates with Minimal APIs?
2. Can we use middleware with Minimal APIs?
3. Can you name at least two binding sources that Minimal APIs support?
4. What is the difference between using the `Results` and `TypedResults` classes?
5. What is the purpose of endpoint filters?

Further reading

Here are some links to build on what we have learned in the chapter:

- Minimal APIs quick reference: `https://adpg.link/S47i`
- Problem Details for HTTP APIs (RFC7807): `https://adpg.link/1hpM`
- `FluentValidation.AspNetCore.Http`: `https://adpg.link/sRtU`

Answers

1. Minimal APIs provide extension methods such as `MapGet`, `MapPost`, `MapPut`, and `MapDelete` to configure the HTTP pipeline and map specific HTTP requests to delegates.
2. Yes, we can use middleware with Minimal APIs, just like any other ASP.NET Core application.
3. Minimal APIs support various binding sources, including `Route`, `Query`, `Header`, `Body`, `Form`, and `Services`.
4. The methods in the `Results` class return `IResult`, while those in `TypedResults` return a typed implementation of the `IResult` interface. This difference is significant because the API Explorer can automatically discover the API contract from the typed results (`TypedResults` methods) but not from the generic `IResult` interface (`Results` methods).
5. Endpoint filters allow encapsulation and reuse of cross-cutting logic across endpoints. For example, they're helpful for input validation, logging, exception handling, and promoting code reusability.

Learn more on Discord

To join the Discord community for this book – where you can share feedback, ask questions to the author, and learn about new releases – follow the QR code below:

`https://packt.link/ArchitectingASPNETCoreApps3e`

6

Model-View-Controller

This chapter delves into the **Model-View-Controller** (**MVC**) design pattern, a cornerstone of modern software architecture that intuitively structures your code around entities. MVC is perfect for CRUD operations or to tap into the advanced features unavailable in minimal APIs.

The MVC pattern partitions your application into three interrelated parts:

- **Models** represent our data and business logic.
- **Views** are the user-facing components.
- **Controllers** act as intermediaries, mediating the interaction between models and views.

With its emphasis on the separation of concerns, the MVC pattern is a proven pattern for creating scalable and robust web applications. In the context of ASP.NET Core, MVC has provided a practical approach to building applications efficiently for years.

While we discussed REST APIs in *Chapter 4*, this chapter provides insight into how to use MVC to create REST APIs. We also address using **Data Transfer Objects** (**DTOs**) within this framework.

In this chapter, we cover the following topics:

- The MVC design pattern
- Using MVC with DTOs

Our ultimate goal is clean, maintainable, and scalable code; the ASP.NET Core MVC framework is a favored tool to achieve this. Let's dive in!

The MVC design pattern

Now that we have explored the basics of REST and minimal APIs, it is time to explore the MVC pattern to build ASP.NET Core REST APIs.

MVC is a design pattern commonly used in web development. It has a long history of being used to build REST APIs in ASP.NET and is widely used and praised by many.

As previously established, this pattern divides an application into three interconnected components: the model, the view, and the controller. A view in MVC formerly represented a user interface. However, in our case, the view is a data contract that reflects the REST API's data-oriented nature.

Dividing responsibilities this way aligns with the **Single Responsibility Principle** (**SRP**) explored in *Chapter 3, Architectural Principles*. However, this is not the only way to build REST APIs with ASP.NET Core, as we saw in *Chapter 5, Minimal APIs*.

The new minimal API model mixed with the **Request-EndPoint-Response** (**REPR**) pattern can make building REST APIs leaner. We cover that pattern in *Chapter 18, Request-EndPoint-Response (REPR)*. We can see REPR as what ASP.NET Core Razor Pages are to page-oriented web applications, but for REST APIs instead.

We often design MVC applications around entities, and each one has a controller that orchestrates its endpoints. We call those CRUD controllers. However, you can design your controller to fit your needs. In the past few decades, the number of REST APIs has just exploded to a gazillion; everybody builds APIs nowadays – not because people follow the trend but for good reasons.

REST APIs have fundamentally transformed how systems communicate, offering various benefits that make them indispensable in modern software architecture. Here are a few key factors that contribute to their widespread appeal:

- **Data efficiency**: REST APIs promote efficient data sharing across different systems, fostering seamless interoperability.
- **Universal communication**: REST APIs leverage universally recognized data formats like JSON or XML, ensuring broad compatibility and interoperability.
- **Backend centralization**: REST APIs enable the backend to serve as a centralized hub, supporting multiple frontend platforms, including mobile, desktop, and web applications.
- **Layered backends**: REST APIs facilitate the stratification of backends, allowing for the creation of foundational, low-level APIs that provide basic functionalities. These, in turn, can be consumed by higher-level, product-centric APIs that offer specialized capabilities, thus promoting a flexible and modular backend architecture.
- **Security measures**: REST APIs can function as gateways, providing security measures to protect downstream systems and ensuring data access is appropriately regulated—a good example of layering APIs.
- **Encapsulation**: REST APIs allow for the encapsulation of specific units of logic into reusable, independent modules, often leading to cleaner, more maintainable code.
- **Scalability**: Due to their stateless nature, REST APIs are easier to scale up to accommodate increasing loads.

These advantages greatly facilitate the reuse of backend systems across various user interfaces or even other backend services. Consider, for instance, a typical mobile application that needs to support iOS, Android, and web platforms. By utilizing a shared backend through REST APIs, development teams can streamline their efforts, saving significant time and cost. This shared backend approach ensures consistency across platforms while reducing the complexity of maintaining multiple code bases.

We explore different patterns in *Chapter 19, Introduction to Microservices Architecture*.

Goal

In the context of REST APIs, the MVC pattern aims to streamline the process of managing an entity by breaking it down into three separate, interacting components. Rather than struggling with large, bloated blocks of code that are hard to test, developers work with smaller units that enhance maintainability and promote efficient testing. This compartmentalization results in small, manageable pieces of functionality that are simpler to maintain and test.

Design

MVC divides an application into three distinct parts, with each having a single responsibility:

- **Model:** The model represents the data and business logic we are modeling.
- **View:** The view represents what the user sees. In the context of REST APIs, that usually is a serialized data structure.
- **Controller:** The controller represents a key component of MVC. It orchestrates the flow between the client request and the server response. The primary role of the controller is to act as an HTTP bridge. Essentially, the controller facilitates the communication in and out of the system.

The code of a controller should remain minimalistic and not contain complex logic, serving as a thin layer between the clients and the domain.

We explore alternative points of view in *Chapter 14, Layering and Clean Architecture*.

Here is a diagram that represents the MVC flow of a REST API:

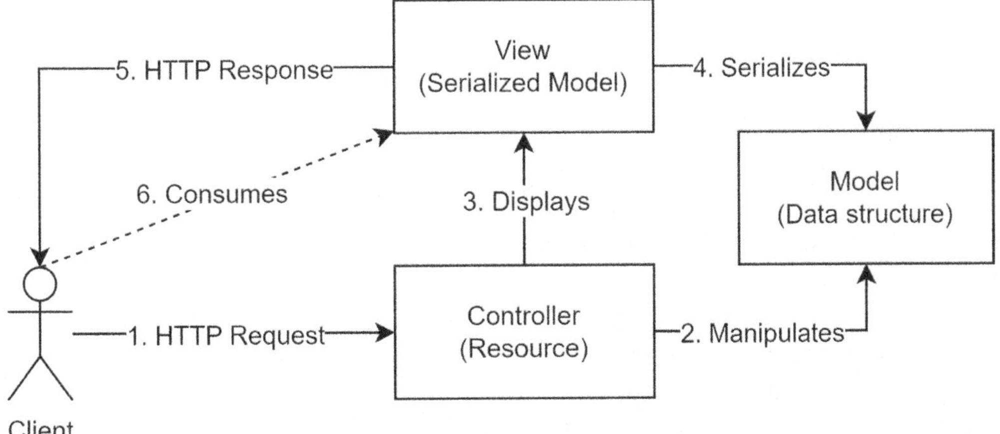

Figure 6.1: Workflow of a REST API using MVC

In the preceding diagram, the controller sends the serialized model to the client. In most scenarios, this is not ideal. We generally prefer sending only the necessary data portion, formatted according to our requirements. We can design robust API contracts by leveraging the DTO pattern to achieve that. However, before we delve into that, let's first explore the basics of ASP.NET Core MVC.

Anatomy of ASP.NET Core web APIs

There are many ways to create a REST API project in .NET, including the `dotnet new` CLI command and Visual Studio. In this case, we bootstrap the project manually so that you can create an empty web project, using the `dotnet new web` command.

Using the .NET 8 CLI, you can scaffold a web API project using controllers by executing the following command:

```
dotnet new webapi --use-controllers
```

Next, we explore a few pieces of the MVC framework, starting with the entry point.

The entry point

The first piece of the MVC framework is the entry point: the `Program.cs` file. Since .NET 6, there is no more `Startup` class by default, and the compiler autogenerates the `Program` class. As explored in the previous chapter, using the minimal hosting model leads to a simplified `Program.cs` file with less boilerplate code.

Here is an example:

```
using Shared;
using System.Text.Json.Serialization;

var builder = WebApplication.CreateBuilder(args);
builder.Services.AddCustomerRepository();

builder.Services
    .AddControllers()
    .AddJsonOptions(options => options
        .JsonSerializerOptions
        .Converters
        .Add(new JsonStringEnumConverter())
    )
;
builder.Services.AddEndpointsApiExplorer();
builder.Services.AddSwaggerGen();

var app = builder.Build();
```

```
if (app.Environment.IsDevelopment())
{
    app.UseSwagger();
    app.UseDarkSwaggerUI();
}
app.MapControllers();
app.InitializeSharedDataStore();
app.Run();
```

In the preceding `Program.cs` file, the highlighted lines identify the minimum code required to enable ASP.NET Core MVC. The rest is very similar to the minimal API code.

Directory structure

The default directory structure contains a `Controllers` folder to host the controllers.

On top of that, we can create a `Models` folder to store our model classes or use any other structure.

While controllers are typically housed in the `Controllers` directory for organizational purposes, this convention is more for the benefit of developers than a strict requirement. ASP.NET Core is indifferent to the file's location, offering us the flexibility to structure our project as we see fit.

Section 4, Application Patterns, explores many ways of designing applications.

Next, we look at the central part of this pattern—the controllers.

Controller

The easiest way to create a controller is to create a class inheriting from `ControllerBase`. However, while `ControllerBase` adds many utility methods, the only requirement is to decorate the controller class with the `[ApiController]` attribute.

By convention, we write the controller's name in its plural form and suffix it with `Controller`. For example, if the controller relates to the `Employee` entity, we'd name it `EmployeesController`, which, by default, leads to an excellent URL pattern that is easy to understand:

- Get all employees: `/employees`
- Get a specific employee: `/employees/{id}`, and so on

Once we have a controller class, we must add actions. Actions are public methods that represent the operations that a client can perform. Each action represents an HTTP endpoint.

More precisely, the following defines a controller:

- A controller exposes one or more actions.
- An action can take zero or more input parameters.
- An action can return zero or one output value.
- The action is what handles the HTTP request.

We should group cohesive actions under the same controller, thus contributing to a more organized, maintainable, and efficient codebase.

For example, the following represents the `SomeController` class containing a single `Get` action:

```
[Route("api/[controller]")]
[ApiController]
public class SomeController : ControllerBase
{
    [HttpGet]
    public IActionResult Get() => Ok();
}
```

The preceding `Get` method (action) returns an empty `200 OK` response to the client. We can reach the endpoint at the `/api/some` URI. From there, we can add more actions.

The `ControllerBase` class gives us access to most of the same utility methods that we had with the minimal APIs' `TypedResults` class.

Next, we look at returning values.

Returning values

The aim of building a REST API is to return data to clients and execute remote operations. Most of the plumbing is done for us by the ASP.NET Core code, including serialization.

Most of the ASP.NET Core pipeline is customizable, which is out of the scope of this chapter.

Before returning values, let's look at a few valuable helper methods provided by the `ControllerBase` class:

Method	Description
`StatusCode`	Produces an empty response with the specified status code. We can optionally include an argument to serialize in the response body.
`Ok`	Produces a `200 OK` response, indicating that the operation was successful. We can optionally include an argument to serialize in the response body.
`Created`	Produces a `201 Created` response, indicating that the system created the entity. We can optionally specify the location where to read the entity and the entity itself as arguments. The `CreatedAtAction` and `CreatedAtRoute` methods give us options to compose the location value.
`NoContent`	Produces an empty `204 No Content` response.
`NotFound`	Produces a `404 Not Found` response, indicating that the resource was not found.
`BadRequest`	Produces a `400 Bad Request` response, indicating an issue with the client request, often a validation error.
`Redirect`	Produces a `302 Found` response, accepting the `Location` URL as an argument. Different `Redirect*` methods produce `301 Moved Permanently`, `307 Temporary Redirect`, and `308 Permanent Redirect` responses instead.
`Accepted`	Produces a `202 Accepted` response, indicating the beginning of an asynchronous process. We can optionally specify the location the client can query to learn about the status of the asynchronous operation. We can also optionally specify an object to serialize in the response body. The `AcceptedAtAction` and `AcceptedAtRoute` methods give us options to compose the location value.
`Conflict`	Produces a `409 Conflict` response, indicating that a conflict occurred when processing the request, often a concurrency error.

Table 6.1: A subset of the `ControllerBase` *methods producing an* `IActionResult`

Other methods in the `ControllerBase` class are self-discoverable using IntelliSense (code completion) or in the official documentation. Most, if not all, of what we covered in *Chapter 5, Minimal APIs*, is also available to controllers.

The advantage of using a helper method is leveraging the ASP.NET Core MVC mechanism, making our lives easier. However, you could manually manage the HTTP response, using lower-level APIs like `HttpContext`, or create custom classes that implement the `IActionResult` interface to hook your custom response classes into the MVC pipeline.

Now, let's look at the multiple ways we can use to return data to the client:

Return type	Description
`void`	We can return `void` and manually manage the HTTP response using the `HttpContext` class. This is the most low-level and complex way.
`TModel`	We can directly return the model, which ASP.NET Core will serialize. The problem with this approach is that we don't control the status code, and neither can we return multiple different results from the action.
`ActionResult` `IActionResult`	We can return one of those two abstractions. The concrete result can take many forms, depending on the implementation that the action method returns. However, doing this makes our API less auto-discoverable by tools like SwaggerGen.
`ActionResult<TModel>`	We can return the `TModel` directly and other results, like a `NotFoundResult` or a `BadRequestResult`. This is the most flexible way to make the API the most discoverable by the `ApiExplorer`.

Table 6.2: Multiple ways to return data

Let's start with an example, where the actions return an instance of the `Model` class by leveraging the `Ok` method (highlighted code):

```
using Microsoft.AspNetCore.Mvc;
namespace MVC.API.Controllers;
[Route("api/[controller]")]
[ApiController]
public class ValuesController : ControllerBase
{
    [HttpGet("IActionResult")]
    public IActionResult InterfaceAction()
        => Ok(new Model(nameof(InterfaceAction)));

    [HttpGet("ActionResult")]
    public ActionResult ClassAction()
        => Ok(new Model(nameof(ClassAction)));
```

```
    // ...

    // The custom Model class we are using in the controller
    public record class Model(string Name);
}
```

The problem with the preceding code is API discoverability. The `ApiExplorer` can't know what the endpoints return. The `ApiExplorer` describes the actions as returning `200 OK` but doesn't know about the `Model` class.

To overcome this limitation, we can decorate our actions with the `ProducesResponseType` attribute, effectively circumventing the limitation, as shown below:

```
[ProducesResponseType(typeof(Model), StatusCodes.Status200OK)]
public IActionResult InterfaceAction() { ... }
```

In the preceding code, we specify the return type as the first argument and the status code as the second. Using the constants of the `StatusCodes` class is a convenient way to reference standard status codes.

We can decorate each action with multiple `ProducesResponseType` attributes to define alternate states, such as `404` and `400`.

With ASP.NET Core MVC, we can also define conventions that apply broad rules to our controllers, allowing us to define those conventions once and reuse them throughout our application. I left a link in the *Further reading* section.

Next, we explore how we can return a `Model` instance directly. The `ApiExplorer` can discover the return value of the method this way, so we do not need to use the `ProducesResponseType` attribute:

```
[HttpGet("DirectModel")]
public Model DirectModel()
    => new Model(nameof(DirectModel));
```

Next, thanks to **class conversion operators** (see *Appendix* on GitHub [`https://adpg.link/net8-appendix`] for more info), we can do the same with `ActionResult<T>`, like this:

```
[HttpGet("ActionResultT")]
public ActionResult<Model> ActionResultT()
    => new Model(nameof(ActionResultT));
```

The main benefit of using `ActionResult<T>` is to return other types of results. Here is an example showing this, where the method returns either `Ok` or `NotFound`:

```
[HttpGet("MultipleResults")]
public ActionResult<Model> MultipleResults()
{
```

```
    var condition = Random.Shared
        .GetItems(new[] { true, false }, 1)
        .First();
    return condition
        ? Ok(new Model(nameof(MultipleResults)))
        : NotFound();
}
```

However, the `ApiExplorer` does not know about the `404 Not Found`, so we must document it using the `ProducesResponseType` attribute.

We can return a `Task<T>` or a `ValueTask<T>` from the action method when the method body is asynchronous. Doing so lets you write the async/await code from the controller.

I highly recommend returning a `Task<T>` or a `ValueTask<T>` whenever possible because it allows your REST API to handle more requests using the same resources without effort. Nowadays, non-Task-based methods in libraries are infrequent, so you will most likely have little choice.

We learned multiple ways to return values from an action. The `ActionResult<T>` class is the most flexible regarding feature support. On the other hand, `IActionResult` is the most abstract one.

Next, we look at routing requests to those action methods.

Attribute routing

Attribute routing maps an HTTP request to a controller action. Those attributes decorate the controllers and the actions to create the complete routes. We have already used some of those attributes. Nonetheless, let's visit them:

```
namespace MVC.API.Controllers.Empty;
[Route("empty/[controller]")]
[ApiController]
public class CustomersController : ControllerBase
{
    [HttpGet]
    public Task<IEnumerable<Customer>> GetAllAsync(
        ICustomerRepository customerRepository)
        => throw new NotImplementedException();
    [HttpGet("{id}")]
    public Task<ActionResult<Customer>> GetOneAsync(
        int id, ICustomerRepository customerRepository)
        => throw new NotImplementedException();
    [HttpPost]
```

```
    public Task<ActionResult> PostAsync(
        [FromBody] Customer value, ICustomerRepository customerRepository)
        => throw new NotImplementedException();
    [HttpPut("{id}")]
    public Task<ActionResult<Customer>> PutAsync(
        int id, [FromBody] Customer value,
        ICustomerRepository customerRepository)
        => throw new NotImplementedException();
    [HttpDelete("{id}")]
    public Task<ActionResult<Customer>> DeleteAsync(
        int id, ICustomerRepository customerRepository)
        => throw new NotImplementedException();
}
```

The `Route` attributes and `Http[Method]` attributes define what a user should query to reach a specific resource. The `Route` attribute allows us to define a routing pattern that applies to all HTTP methods under the decorated controller. The `Http[Method]` attributes determine the HTTP method used to reach that action method. They also offer the possibility to set an optional and additive route pattern to handle more complex routes, including specifying route parameters. Those attributes are beneficial in crafting concise and clear URLs while keeping the routing system close to the controller.

All routes must be unique.

Based on the code, `[Route("empty/[controller]")]` means that the actions of this controller are reachable through `empty/customers` (MVC ignores the `Controller` suffix).

Then, the other attributes tell ASP.NET to map specific requests to specific methods:

Routing attribute	HTTP method	URL
`HttpGet`	`GET`	`empty/customers`
`HttpGet("{id}")`	`GET`	`empty/customers/{id}`
`HttpPost`	`POST`	`empty/customers`
`HttpPut("{id}")`	`PUT`	`empty/customers/{id}`
`HttpDelete("{id}")`	`DELETE`	`empty/customers/{id}`

Table 6.3: routing attributes of the example controller and their final URL

As we can see from the preceding table, we can even use the same attribute for multiple actions as long as the URL is unique. In this case, the `id` parameter is the `GET` discriminator.

Next, we can use the `FromBody` attribute to tell the model binder to use the HTTP request body to get the value of that parameter. There are many such attributes; here's a list:

Attribute	Description
`FromBody`	Binds the JSON body of the request to the parameter's type.
`FromForm`	Binds the form value that matches the name of the parameter.
`FromHeader`	Binds the HTTP header value that matches the name of the parameter.
`FromQuery`	Binds the query string value that matches the name of the parameter.
`FromRoute`	Binds the route value that matches the name of the parameter.
`FromServices`	Inject the service from the ASP.NET Core dependency container.

Table 6.4: MVC binding sources

ASP.NET Core MVC does a lot of implicit binding, so you don't always need to decorate all parameters with an attribute. For example, .NET injects the services we needed in the code samples, and we never used the `FromServices` attribute. It's the same with the `FromRoute` attribute.

Now, if we look back at `CustomersController`, the route map looks like the following (I excluded non-route-related code to improve readability):

URL	Action/method
`GET empty/customers`	`GetAllAsync()`
`GET empty/customers/{id}`	`GetOneAsync(int id)`
`POST empty/customers`	`PostAsync([FromBody] Customer value)`
`PUT empty/customers/{id}`	`PutAsync(int id, [FromBody] Customer value)`
`DELETE empty/customers/{id}`	`DeleteAsync(int id)`

Table 6.5: The map between the URLs and their respective action methods

ASP.NET Core MVC maps a *route parameter* to the *method parameter*, and both names must be identical. For example, as the preceding table illustrates, the route parameter `id` matches the method parameter `id`.

When designing a REST API, the URL leading to our endpoints should be clear and concise, making it easy for consumers to discover and learn. Hierarchically grouping our resources by responsibility (concern) and creating a cohesive URL space help achieve that goal. Consumers (a.k.a. other developers) should understand the logic behind the endpoints easily. Think about your endpoints as if you were the consumer of the REST API. I would even extend that suggestion to any API; always consider the consumers of your code to create the best possible APIs.

Conclusion

This section explored the MVC pattern, how to create controllers and action methods, and how to route requests to those actions.

We could talk about MVC for the remainder of the book, but we would be missing the point. The subset of features we covered here should be enough theory to fill any knowledge gaps you might have had, allowing you to understand the code samples that leverage ASP.NET Core MVC.

Using the MVC pattern helps us follow the SOLID principles in the following ways:

- **S**: The MVC pattern divides the rendering of a data structure into three different roles. The framework handles most of the serialization portion (the view), leaving us only two pieces to manage: the model and the controller.
- **O**: N/A
- **L**: N/A
- **I**: Each controller handles a subset of features and represents a smaller interface in the system. MVC makes the system easier to manage than having a single entry point for all routes, like a single controller.
- **D**: N/A

Next, we explore the **Data Transfer Object** pattern to isolate the API's model from the domain.

Using MVC with DTOs

This section explores leveraging the **DTO** pattern with the MVC framework.

This section is the same as we explored in *Chapter 5, Minimal APIs*, but in the context of MVC. Moreover, the two code projects are part of the same Visual Studio solution for convenience, allowing you to compare the two implementations.

Goal

As a reminder, DTOs aim to *control the inputs and outputs of an endpoint* by decoupling the API contract from the application's inner workings. DTOs empower us to define our APIs without thinking about the underlying data structures, leaving us to craft our REST APIs how we want.

We discuss REST APIs and DTOs in more depth in *Chapter 4, REST APIs*.

Other possible objectives are to save bandwidth by limiting the amount of information the API transmits, flattening the data structure, or adding API features that cross multiple entities.

Design

Let's start by analyzing a diagram that expands MVC to work with DTOs:

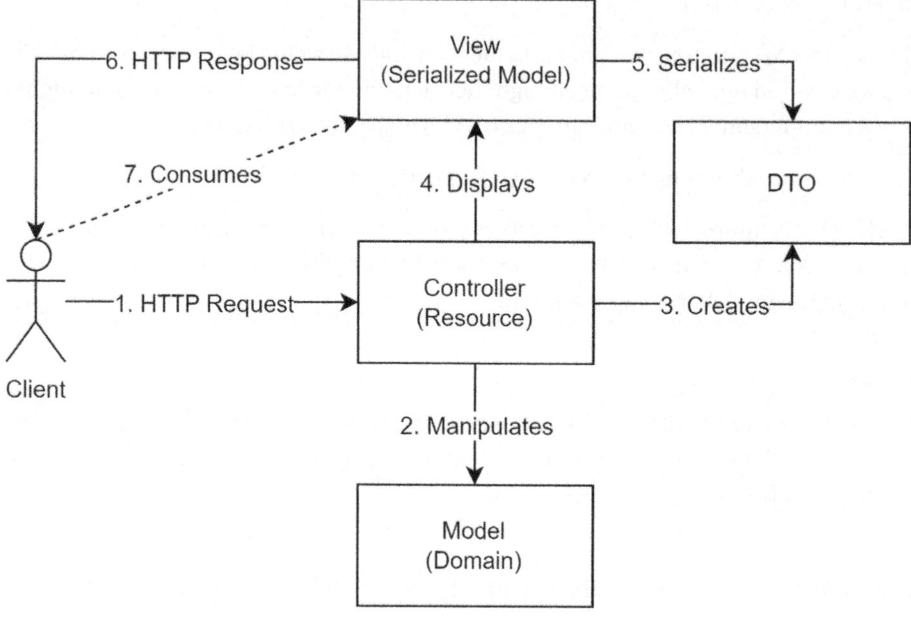

Figure 6.2: MVC workflow with a DTO

DTOs allow the decoupling of the domain from the view (data) and empower us to manage the inputs and outputs of our REST APIs independently from the domain. The controller still manipulates the domain model but returns a serialized DTO instead.

Project – MVC API

This code sample is similar to the previous chapter but uses the MVC framework instead of minimal APIs. Both versions are part of the same solution to make it easy to compare them—for example, `DTOEndpoints.GetCustomersSummaryAsync` is almost the same implementation as `CustomersController.GetAllAsync`, but one uses the minimal API model while the other uses the MVC model.

Therefore, I kept most of the code out of the book so that it does not feel redundant. You can refer to the previous chapter or GitHub if you are uncertain of some shared code.

Context (reminder): We must build an application to manage customers and contracts. We must track the state of each contract and have a primary contact in case a business needs to contact a customer. Finally, we must display the number of contracts and the number of opened contracts for each customer on a dashboard.

Let's first explore a CRUD controller that does not leverage DTOs.

Raw CRUD controller

The same issues that we explored in the previous chapter can arise if we create a CRUD controller to manage the customers directly.

The controller code of this section is in the `RawCustomersController.cs` file. The minimal API model's equivalent is in the `CustomersEndpoints.cs` file. The rest of the code is mostly the same.

For example, the controller action that returns all customers looks like this:

```
using Microsoft.AspNetCore.Mvc;
using Shared.Data;
using Shared.Models;

namespace MVC.API.Controllers.Raw;

[Route("raw/[controller]")]
[ApiController]
[Tags("Customers Raw")]
public class CustomersController : ControllerBase
{
    // GET: raw/customers
    [HttpGet]
    public async Task<IEnumerable<Customer>> GetAllAsync(
        ICustomerRepository customerRepository)
    {
        return await customerRepository
            .AllAsync(HttpContext.RequestAborted);
    }

    // Other actions are omitted
}
```

Here's the minimal API version:

```
var group = routes
    .MapGroup("/raw/customers")
    .WithTags("Customers Raw")
;
group.MapGet("/", async (ICustomerRepository customerRepository,
CancellationToken cancellationToken) =>
{
    return await customerRepository
        .AllAsync(cancellationToken);
});
```

As we can see from the preceding two code blocks, both models use a different semantic to declare the endpoint and configure the routing, but the logic is the same (the highlighted code). The controller uses the routing attributes, while the minimal API endpoint uses extension methods like `WithTags` and `MapGet`.

Next, we explore a controller when using DTOs.

DTO controller

We can use DTOs with controllers to solve our problems, as we did with minimal APIs. For example, the controller action that returns the customer summaries looks like this:

```
using Microsoft.AspNetCore.Mvc;
using Shared.Data;
using Shared.DTO;
using Shared.Models;

namespace MVC.API.Controllers.DTO;

[Route("dto/[controller]")]
[ApiController]
[Tags("Customers DTO")]
public class CustomersController : ControllerBase
{
    [HttpGet]
    public async Task<IEnumerable<CustomerSummary>>
GetAllAsync(ICustomerRepository customerRepository)
    {
        // Get all customers
        var customers = await customerRepository.AllAsync(
            HttpContext.RequestAborted
        );

        // Map customers to CustomerSummary DTOs
        var customersSummary = customers
            .Select(customer => new CustomerSummary(
                Id: customer.Id,
                Name: customer.Name,
                TotalNumberOfContracts: customer.Contracts.Count,
                NumberOfOpenContracts: customer.Contracts.Count(x => x.Status.
State != WorkState.Completed)
```

```
            ))
        ;

        // Return the DTOs
        return customersSummary;
    }

    // Other actions are omitted
}
```

Its minimal API counterpart, pointing to the `GetCustomersSummaryAsync` method, looks like this:

```
var group = routes
    .MapGroup("/dto/customers")
    .WithTags("Customers DTO")
;
group.MapGet("/", GetCustomersSummaryAsync);

static async Task<Ok<IEnumerable<CustomerSummary>>> GetCustomersSummaryAsync(
    ICustomerRepository customerRepository,
    CancellationToken cancellationToken)
{
    // Get all customers
    var customers = await customerRepository.AllAsync(cancellationToken);

    // Map customers to CustomerSummary DTOs
    var customersSummary = customers.Select(customer => new CustomerSummary(
        Id: customer.Id,
        Name: customer.Name,
        TotalNumberOfContracts: customer.Contracts.Count,
        NumberOfOpenContracts: customer.Contracts
            .Count(x => x.Status.State != WorkState.Completed)
    ));

    // Return the DTOs
    return TypedResults.Ok(customersSummary);
}
```

The highlighted code of the two preceding code blocks shows the difference between the two routing models, while the body of the `GetAllAsync` and `GetCustomersSummaryAsync` methods are very similar.

The entire API is available on GitHub to compare other methods and explore the codebase more. Moreover, you can play with the API using the HTTP requests in the `MVC.API.DTO.http` file.

If your controller logic becomes too complex, it is good practice to encapsulate it in other classes. We explore many techniques to organize application code in *Section 4, Application Patterns*.

Conclusion

In this section, we revisited the added value of DTOs using the MVC framework. As explored in *Chapter 5, Minimal APIs*, a DTO used in conjunction with MVC allows us to design an API endpoint with a specific data contract (input and output), instead of exposing the domain or data model. This separation between the presentation and the domain is a crucial element that results in having multiple independent components, instead of a bigger, more fragile one. Using DTOs to control the inputs and outputs gives us more control over what clients can do or receive.

Summary

This chapter explored the MVC design pattern, a well-established framework in the ASP.NET ecosystem that offers more advanced features than its newer minimal APIs counterpart. Minimal APIs don't compete against MVC; we can use them together.

The MVC pattern emphasizes the separation of concerns, making it a proven pattern for creating maintainable, scalable, and robust web applications. We broke down the MVC pattern into its three core components: models, views, and controllers. Models represent data and business logic, views are user-facing components (serialized data structures), and controllers act as intermediaries, mediating the interaction between models and views.

We also discussed using DTOs to package data in the format we need, providing many benefits, including flexibility, efficiency, encapsulation, and improved performance. DTOs are a crucial part of the API contract.

Now that we have explored principles and methodologies, the following two chapters explore our first **Gang of Four** (**GoF**) design patterns and deep dive into ASP.NET Core Dependency Injection. All of this will help us continue on the path we started: learning to design better software.

Questions

Let's look at a few practice questions:

1. What are the three components of the MVC design pattern?
2. What is the role of a controller in the MVC pattern?
3. What are DTOs, and why are they important?
4. How does the MVC pattern contribute to the maintainability of an application?
5. How does attribute routing work in MVC?

Further reading

Here are some links to build on what we have learned in the chapter:

- Using web API conventions: `https://adpg.link/ioKV`
- Getting started with Swashbuckle and ASP.NET Core: `https://adpg.link/ETja`

Answers

1. The three components of the MVC design pattern are models, views, and controllers.
2. In the MVC pattern, a controller acts as an intermediary, mediating the interaction between models and views.
3. We use DTOs to package data into a format that provides many benefits, including efficient data sharing, encapsulation, and improved maintainability.
4. The MVC pattern contributes to the maintainability of an application by separating concerns. Each component (model, view, controller) has a specific role and responsibility, making the code easier to manage, test, and extend.
5. Attribute routing in MVC maps an HTTP request to a controller action. These attributes decorate the controllers and the actions to create the complete routes.

Learn more on Discord

To join the Discord community for this book – where you can share feedback, ask questions to the author, and learn about new releases – follow the QR code below:

`https://packt.link/ArchitectingASPNETCoreApps3e`

7

Strategy, Abstract Factory, and Singleton Design Patterns

This chapter explores object creation using a few classic, simple, and yet powerful design patterns from the **Gang of Four** (**GoF**). These patterns allow developers to encapsulate and reuse behaviors, centralize object creation, add flexibility to our designs, or control object lifetime. Moreover, you will most likely use some of them directly or indirectly in all the software you build.

The GoF is the name given to Erich Gamma, Richard Helm, Ralph Johnson, and John Vlissides, authors of *Design Patterns: Elements of Reusable Object-Oriented Software* (1994). In that book, they introduced 23 design patterns, some of which we revisit in this book.

Why are they that important? Because they are the building blocks of robust object composition and help create flexibility and reliability. I grouped these patterns in this chapter because they are the building blocks of *Chapter 8, Dependency Injection*, where we will reuse them, make them even more potent, and learn about the foundational knowledge that makes a difference between programming and designing programs. Learning to walk before running is crucial, so visiting the base implementation of those patterns here is only the first step.

In this chapter, we cover the following topics:

- The Strategy design pattern
- The Abstract Factory design pattern
- The Singleton design pattern

The Strategy design pattern

The Strategy pattern is a behavioral design pattern that allows us to change object behaviors at runtime.

We can also use this pattern to compose complex object trees and rely on it to follow the **Open/Closed Principle** (**OCP**) without much effort. Moreover, it plays a significant role in the *composition over inheritance* way of thinking and is the backbone of dependency injection.

In this chapter, we focus on the behavioral part of the Strategy pattern. The next chapter covers how to use this pattern to compose systems dynamically.

Goal

The Strategy pattern aims to extract an algorithm (a strategy) from the host class that needs it (the context or consumer). That allows the consumer to decide on the strategy (algorithm) to use at runtime.

Design

Before any further explanation, let's take a look at the following class diagram:

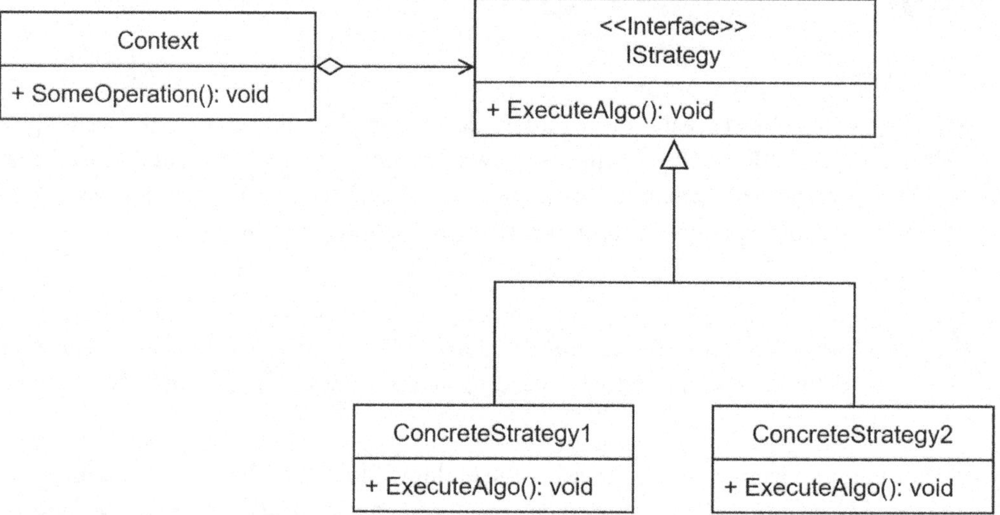

Figure 7.1: Strategy pattern class diagram

Based on the preceding diagram, the building blocks of the Strategy pattern are the following:

- `Context` is a class that depends on the `IStrategy` interface and leverages an implementation of the `IStrategy` interface to execute the `ExecuteAlgo` method.
- `IStrategy` is an interface defining the strategy API.
- `ConcreteStrategy1` and `ConcreteStrategy2` represent different concrete implementations of the `IStrategy` interface.

In the following diagram, we explore what happens at runtime. The actor represents any code consuming the `Context` object.

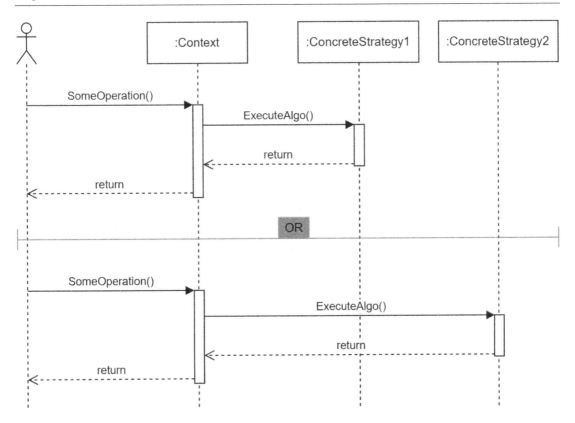

Figure 7.2: Strategy pattern sequence diagram

When the consumer calls the `Context.SomeOperation()` method, it does not know which implementation is executed, which is an essential part of this pattern. The `Context` class should not be aware of the strategy it uses either. It should run the strategy through the interface, unaware of the implementation.

That is the strength of the Strategy pattern: it abstracts the implementation away from both the `Context` class and its consumers. Because of that, we can change the strategy during either the object creation or at runtime without the object knowing, changing its behavior on the fly.

We could even generalize that last sentence and extend it to any interface. Depending on an interface breaks the ties between the consumer and the implementation by relying on that abstraction instead.

Project – Strategy

Context: We want to sort a collection differently, eventually even using different sort algorithms (out of the scope of the example but possible). Initially, we want to support sorting the elements of any collection in ascending or descending order.

To achieve this, we need to implement the following building blocks:

- The `Context` is the `SortableCollection` class.
- The `IStrategy` is the `ISortStrategy` interface.
- The concrete strategies are:
  - `SortAscendingStrategy`
  - `SortDescendingStrategy`

The consumer is a small REST API that allows the user to change the strategy, sort the collection, and display the items. Let's start with the `ISortStrategy` interface:

```
public interface ISortStrategy
{
    IOrderedEnumerable<string> Sort(IEnumerable<string> input);
}
```

That interface contains only one method that expects a string collection as input and returns an ordered string collection. Now, let's inspect the two implementations:

```
public class SortAscendingStrategy : ISortStrategy
{
    public IOrderedEnumerable<string> Sort(IEnumerable<string> input)
        => input.OrderBy(x => x);
}
public class SortDescendingStrategy : ISortStrategy
{
    public IOrderedEnumerable<string> Sort(IEnumerable<string> input)
        => input.OrderByDescending(x => x);
}
```

Both implementations are super simple, using **Language Integrated Query** (**LINQ**) to sort the input and return the result directly.

When using expression-bodied methods, please ensure you do not make the method harder to read for your colleagues (or future you) by creating very complex one-liners. Writing multiple lines often makes code easier to read.

The next building block to inspect is the `SortableCollection` class. It is composed of multiple string items (the `Items` property), and you can sort them using an `ISortStrategy`. Here's the class:

```
using System.Collections.Immutable;
namespace MySortingMachine;
public sealed class SortableCollection
```

```
{
    private ISortStrategy _sortStrategy;
    private ImmutableArray<string> _items;
    public IEnumerable<string> Items => _items;
    public SortableCollection(IEnumerable<string> items)
    {
        _items = items.ToImmutableArray();
        _sortStrategy = new SortAscendingStrategy();
    }

    public void SetSortStrategy(ISortStrategy strategy)
        => _sortStrategy = strategy;

    public void Sort()
    {
        _items = _sortStrategy
            .Sort(Items)
            .ToImmutableArray()
        ;
    }
}
```

The SortableCollection class is the most complex one so far, so let's take a more in-depth look:

- The _sortStrategy field references the algorithm: an ISortStrategy implementation.
- The _items field references the strings themselves.
- The Items property exposes the strings to the consumers of the class.
- The constructor initializes the Items property using the items parameter and sets the default sorting strategy.
- The SetSortStrategy method allows consumers to change the strategy at runtime.
- The Sort method uses the _sortStrategy field to sort the items.

With that code, we can see the Strategy pattern in action. The _sortStrategy field represents the current algorithm, respecting an ISortStrategy contract, which is updatable at runtime using the SetSortStrategy method. The Sort method delegates the work to the ISortStrategy implementation (the concrete strategy).

Therefore, changing the value of the _sortStrategy field leads to a change of behavior of the Sort method, making this pattern very powerful yet simple. The highlighted code represents this pattern.

The _items field is an ImmutableArray<string>, which makes changing the list impossible from the outside. For example, a consumer cannot pass a List<string> to the constructor and then change it later. Immutability has many advantages.

Let's experiment with this by looking at the `Consumer.API` project, a REST API application that uses the previous code. The following is a breakdown of the `Program.cs` file:

```
using MySortingMachine;
SortableCollection data = new(new[] {
    "Lorem", "ipsum", "dolor", "sit", "amet." });
```

The `data` member is the context, our sortable collection of items. Next, we look at some boilerplate code to create the application and serialize `enum` values as strings:

```
var builder = WebApplication.CreateBuilder(args);
builder.Services.ConfigureHttpJsonOptions(options => {
    options.SerializerOptions.Converters
        .Add(new JsonStringEnumConverter());
});
var app = builder.Build();
```

Finally, the last part represents the consumer of the context:

```
app.MapGet("/", () => data);
app.MapPut("/", (ReplaceSortStrategy sortStrategy) =>
{
    ISortStrategy strategy = sortStrategy.SortOrder == SortOrder.Ascending
        ? new SortAscendingStrategy()
        : new SortDescendingStrategy();
    data.SetSortStrategy(strategy);
    data.Sort();
    return data;
});
app.Run();

public enum SortOrder
{
    Ascending,
    Descending
}
public record class ReplaceSortStrategy(SortOrder SortOrder);
```

In the preceding code, we declared the following endpoints:

- The first endpoint returns the `data` object when a client sends a `GET` request.
- The second endpoint allows you to change the sort strategy based on the `SortOrder` enum when a client sends a `PUT` request. Once the strategy is modified, it sorts the collection and returns the sorted data.

The highlighted code represents the consumption of this implementation of the strategy pattern.

The `ReplaceSortStrategy` class is an input DTO. Combined with the `SortOrder` enum, they represent the API contract of the second endpoint.

When we run the API and request the first endpoint, it responds with the following JSON body:

```
[
  "Lorem",
  "ipsum",
  "dolor",
  "sit",
  "amet."
]
```

As we can see, the items are in the order we set them because the code never called the `Sort` method.

Next, let's send the following HTTP request to the API to change the sort strategy to `"Descending"`:

```
PUT https://localhost:7280/
Content-Type: application/json

{
    "sortOrder": "Descending"
}
```

After the execution, the endpoint responds with the following JSON data:

```
[
  "sit",
  "Lorem",
  "ipsum",
  "dolor",
  "amet."
]
```

As we can see from the content, the sorting algorithm worked. Afterward, the list will remain in the same order if we query the GET endpoint.

Next, let's look at this use case using a sequence diagram:

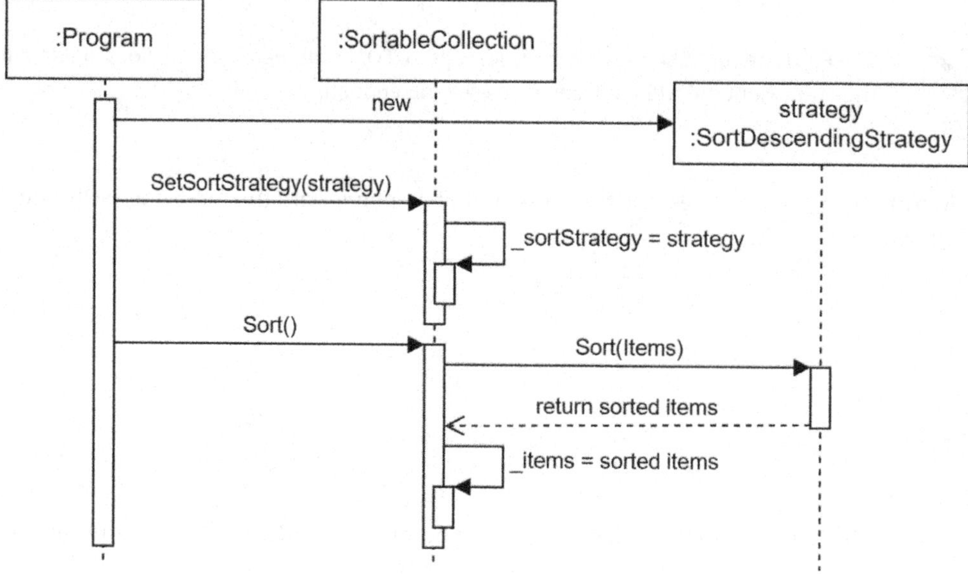

Figure 7.3: Sequence diagram sorting the items using the sort descending strategy

The preceding diagram shows the `Program` creating a strategy and assigning it to `SortableCollection`, using its `SetSortStrategy` method. Then, when the `Program` calls the `Sort()` method, the `SortableCollection` instance delegates the sorting computation to the underlying implementation of the `ISortStrategy` interface. That implementation is the `SortDescendingStrategy` class (the **strategy**) that was set by the `Program` at the beginning.

Sending another `PUT` request but specifying the `Ascending` sort order ends up with a similar result, but the items would be sorted alphabetically.

The HTTP requests are available in the `Consumer.API.http` file.

From a strategy pattern perspective, the `SortableCollection` class (the **context**) is responsible for referencing and using the current strategy.

Conclusion

The Strategy design pattern is very effective at delegating responsibilities to other objects, allowing you to hand over the responsibility of an algorithm to other objects while keeping its usage trivial. It also allows you to have a rich interface (context) with behaviors that can change at runtime.

As we can see, the Strategy pattern is excellent at helping us follow the **SOLID** principles:

- **S**: It helps extract responsibilities to external classes and use them interchangeably.
- **O**: It allows you to extend classes without updating the code by changing the current strategy at runtime, which is pretty much the literal definition of the OCP.

- **L:** It does not rely on inheritance. Moreover, it plays a large role in the *composition over inheritance principle*, helping us avoid inheritance altogether and, in turn, the **Liskov Substitution Principle** (**LSP**).
- **I:** By creating smaller strategies based on lean and focused interfaces, the Strategy pattern is an excellent enabler of the ISP.
- **D:** The creation of dependencies is moved from the class using the strategy (the context) to the class's consumer. That makes the context depend on abstraction instead of implementation, inverting the flow of control.

If you notice C# features you are less familiar with, the *Appendix* on GitHub (`https://adpg.link/net8-appendix`) explains many of them briefly.

Next, we explore the Abstract Factory pattern.

The Abstract Factory design pattern

The Abstract Factory design pattern is a creational design pattern from the GoF. We use creational patterns to create other objects, and factories are a very popular way of doing that.

We use factories to create complex objects that can't be assembled automatically by a dependency injection library. There'll be more on that in the next chapter.

Goal

The Abstract Factory pattern is used to abstract the creation of a family of objects. It usually implies the creation of multiple object types within that family. A family is a group of related or dependent objects (classes).

Let's think about creating automotive vehicles. There are multiple vehicle types, and there are multiple models and makes for each type. We can use the Abstract Factory pattern to model this sort of scenario.

The *Factory Method* pattern also focuses on creating a single type of object instead of a family. We only cover Abstract Factory here, but we use other types of factories later in the book.

Design

With Abstract Factory, the consumer asks for an abstract object and gets one. The factory is an abstraction, and the resulting objects are also abstractions, decoupling the creation of an object from its consumers.

That allows you to add or remove families of objects produced together without impacting the consumers (all actors communicate through abstractions).

In our case, the family (the set of objects the factory can produce) is composed of a car and a bike, and each factory (family) must produce both objects.

If we think about vehicles, we could have the ability to create low- and high-end models of each vehicle type. Here is a diagram representing how to achieve that using the Abstract Factory pattern:

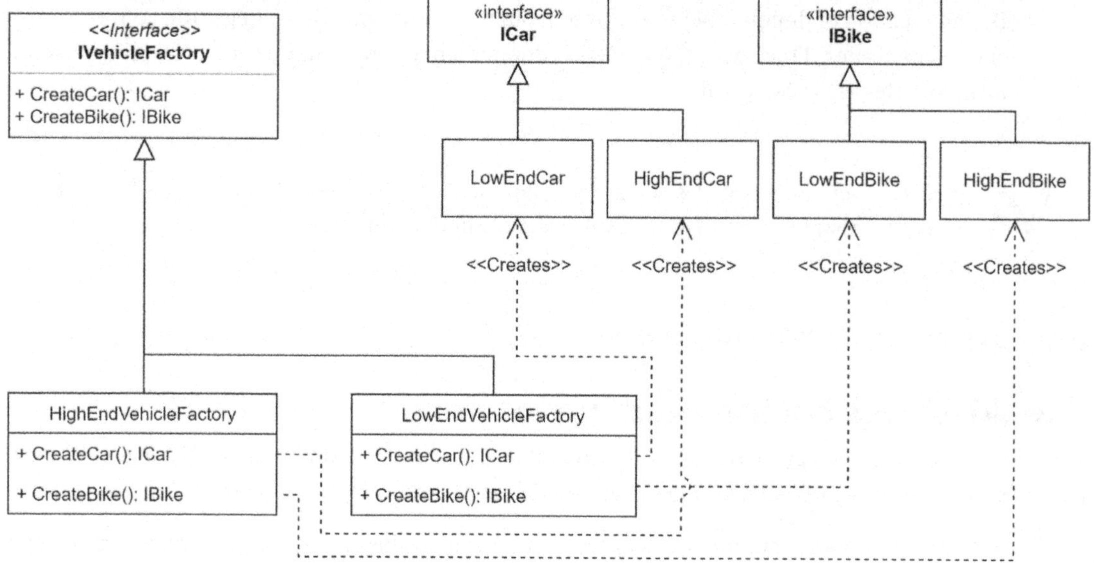

Figure 7.4: Abstract Factory class diagram

In the diagram, we have the following elements:

- The `IVehicleFactory` interface represents the Abstract Factory. It defines two methods: one that creates cars of type `ICar` and another that creates bikes of type `IBike`.
- The `HighEndVehicleFactory` class is a concrete factory implementing the `IVehicleFactory` interface. It handles high-end vehicle model creation, and its methods return `HighEndCar` or `HighEndBike` instances.
- The `LowEndVehicleFactory` is a second concrete factory implementing the `IVehicleFactory` interface. It handles low-end vehicle model creation, and its methods return `LowEndCar` or `LowEndBike` instances.
- `LowEndCar` and `HighEndCar` are two implementations of `ICar`.
- `LowEndBike` and `HighEndBike` are two implementations of `IBike`.

Based on that diagram, consumers use the concrete factories through the `IVehicleFactory` interface and should not be aware of the implementation used underneath. Applying this pattern abstracts away the vehicle creation process.

Project – Abstract Factory

Context: We need to support the creation of multiple models of vehicles. We also need to be able to add new models as they become available without impacting the system. To begin with, we only support high-end and low-end models (cars and bikes), but we know this will change sooner rather than later.

For the sake of our demo, the vehicles are just empty classes and interfaces because learning how to model vehicles is not necessary to understand the pattern; that would be noise. The following code represents those entities:

```
public interface ICar { }
public interface IBike { }
public class LowEndCar : ICar { }
public class LowEndBike : IBike { }
public class HighEndCar : ICar { }
public class HighEndBike : IBike { }
```

Next, we look at the part that we want to study—the factories:

```
public interface IVehicleFactory
{
    ICar CreateCar();
    IBike CreateBike();
}
public class LowEndVehicleFactory : IVehicleFactory
{
    public IBike CreateBike() => new LowEndBike();
    public ICar CreateCar() => new LowEndCar();
}
public class HighEndVehicleFactory : IVehicleFactory
{
    public IBike CreateBike() => new HighEndBike();
    public ICar CreateCar() => new HighEndCar();
}
```

The factories are simple implementations that describe the pattern well:

- `LowEndVehicleFactory` creates low-end models.
- `HighEndVehicleFactory` creates high-end models.

The consumer of this code is an xUnit test project. Unit tests are often your first consumers, especially if you are doing **test-driven development (TDD)**.

I created the following base test class to reuse the same test methods for each factory and abstract its implementation (the test cases are not aware of the factory's type, only its interface):

```
using Xunit;
namespace Vehicles;
public abstract class BaseAbstractFactoryTest<TConcreteFactory, TExpectedCar, TExpectedBike>
    where TConcreteFactory : IVehicleFactory, new()
{
    // Test methods here
}
```

The key to that class is the following generic parameters:

- The `TConcreteFactory` parameter represents the type of concrete factory we want to test. Its generic constraint specifies that it must implement the `IVehicleFactory` interface and have a parameterless constructor.
- The `TExpectedCar` parameter represents the type of `ICar` we expect from the `CreateCar` method.
- The `TExpectedBike` parameter represents the type of `IBike` we expect from the `CreateBike` method.

The first test method contained by that class is the following:

```
[Fact]
public void Should_create_a_ICar_of_type_TExpectedCar()
{
    // Arrange
    IVehicleFactory vehicleFactory = new TConcreteFactory();
    var expectedCarType = typeof(TExpectedCar);

    // Act
    ICar result = vehicleFactory.CreateCar();

    // Assert
    Assert.IsType(expectedCarType, result);
}
```

The preceding test method creates a vehicle factory using the `TConcreteFactory` generic parameter, and then creates a car using that factory. Finally, it asserts that the `ICar` instance is of the expected type.

The second test method contained by that class is the following:

```
[Fact]
public void Should_create_a_IBike_of_type_TExpectedBike()
```

```
{
    // Arrange
    IVehicleFactory vehicleFactory = new TConcreteFactory();
    var expectedBikeType = typeof(TExpectedBike);

    // Act
    IBike result = vehicleFactory.CreateBike();

    // Assert
    Assert.IsType(expectedBikeType, result);
}
```

The preceding test method is very similar and creates a vehicle factory using the `TConcreteFactory` generic parameter, but then it creates a bike instead of a car using that factory. Finally, it asserts that the `IBike` instance is of the expected type.

I used the `ICar` and `IBike` interfaces to type the variables instead of `var`, to clarify the `result` variable type. The same applies to the `IVehicleFactory` interface.

Now, to test the low-end factory, we declare the following test class:

```
namespace Vehicles.LowEnd;
public class LowEndVehicleFactoryTest :
BaseAbstractFactoryTest<LowEndVehicleFactory, LowEndCar, LowEndBike>
{
}
```

That class solely depends on the `BaseAbstractFactoryTest` class and specifies the types to test for (which are highlighted).

Next, to test the high-end factory, we declare the following test class:

```
namespace Vehicles.HighEnd;
public class HighEndVehicleFactoryTest :
BaseAbstractFactoryTest<HighEndVehicleFactory, HighEndCar, HighEndBike>
{
}
```

Like the low-end factory, that class depends on the `BaseAbstractFactoryTest` class and specifies the types to test for (which are highlighted).

In a more complex scenario where we can't use the `new()` generic constraint, we can leverage an IoC container to create the instance of `TConcreteFactory` and optionally mock its dependencies.

We could also create concrete test classes instead of relying on such a base class, which showcases the abstraction that the pattern brings to the table.

With that test code, we created the following two sets of two tests:

- A `LowEndVehicleFactory` class that should create a `LowEndCar` instance.
- A `LowEndVehicleFactory` class that should create a `LowEndBike` instance.
- A `HighEndVehicleFactory` class that should create a `HighEndCar` instance.
- A `HighEndVehicleFactory` class that should create a `HighEndBike` instance.

We now have four tests: two for bikes and two for cars.

If we review the tests' execution, both test methods are unaware of types. They use Abstract Factory (`IVehicleFactory`) and test the `result` against the expected type, without knowing what they are testing except for the abstraction. That shows how loosely coupled the consumers (tests) and the factories are.

We would use the `ICar` or the `IBike` instances in a real-world program to do something relevant based on the specifications. That could be a racing game or a rich person's garage management system—who knows?

The important part of this project is **the abstraction of the object creation process**. The test code (consumer) is not aware of the implementations.

Next, we extend our implementation.

Project – the mid-range vehicle factory

To prove the flexibility of our design based on the Abstract Factory pattern, let's add a new concrete factory named `MidRangeVehicleFactory`. That factory should return a `MidRangeCar` or `MidRangeBike` instance.

Once again, the car and bike are just empty classes (of course, in your programs, they will do something):

```
public class MiddleGradeCar : ICar { }
public class MiddleGradeBike : IBike { }
```

The new `MidRangeVehicleFactory` looks pretty much the same as the other two:

```
public class MidRangeVehicleFactory : IVehicleFactory
{
    public IBike CreateBike() => new MiddleGradeBike();
```

```
    public ICar CreateCar() => new MiddleGradeCar();
}
```

Now, to test the mid-range factory, we declare the following test class:

```
namespace Vehicles.MidRange;
public class MidRangeVehicleFactoryTest :
BaseAbstractFactoryTest<MidRangeVehicleFactory, MidRangeCar, MidRangeBike>
{
}
```

Like the low-end and high-end factories, the mid-range test class depends on the `BaseAbstractFactoryTest` class and specifies the types to test for (which are highlighted).

If we run the tests, we now have the following six passing tests:

Test	Duration
Vehicles.Tests (6)	255 ms
Vehicles.HighEnd (2)	85 ms
HighEndVehicleFactoryTest (2)	85 ms
Should_create_a_IBike_of_type_TExpectedBike	85 ms
Should_create_a_ICar_of_type_TExpectedCar	< 1 ms
Vehicles.LowEnd (2)	85 ms
LowEndVehicleFactoryTest (2)	85 ms
Should_create_a_IBike_of_type_TExpectedBike	< 1 ms
Should_create_a_ICar_of_type_TExpectedCar	85 ms
Vehicles.MidRange (2)	85 ms
MidRangeVehicleFactoryTest (2)	85 ms
Should_create_a_IBike_of_type_TExpectedBike	< 1 ms
Should_create_a_ICar_of_type_TExpectedCar	85 ms

Figure 7.5: Visual Studio Test Explorer showcasing the six passing tests

So, without updating the consumer (the `AbstractFactoryTest` class), we added a new family of vehicles, the mid-range cars and bikes; kudos to the Abstract Factory pattern for that wonderfulness!

Impacts of the Abstract Factory

Before concluding, what would happen if we packed everything in a large interface instead of using an Abstract Factory (breaking the ISP along the way)? We could have created something like the following interface:

```
public interface ILargeVehicleFactory
{
```

```
    HighEndBike CreateHighEndBike();
    HighEndCar CreateHighEndCar();
    LowEndBike CreateLowEndBike();
    LowEndCar CreateLowEndCar();
}
```

As we can see, the preceding interface contains four specific methods and seems docile.

However, the consumers of that code would be tightly coupled with those specific methods. For example, to change a consumer's behavior, we'd need to update its code, like changing the call from `CreateHighEndBike` to `CreateLowEndBike`, which breaks the OCP. On the other hand, with the factory method, we can set a different factory for the consumers to spit out different results, which moves the flexibility out of the object itself and becomes a matter of composing the object graph instead (there'll be more on that in the next chapter).

Moreover, when we want to add mid-range vehicles, we must update the `ILargeVehicleFactory` interface, which becomes a breaking change—the implementation(s) of the `ILargeVehicleFactory` must be updated. Here's an example of the two new methods:

```
public interface ILargeVehicleFactory
{
    HighEndBike CreateHighEndBike();
    HighEndCar CreateHighEndCar();
    LowEndBike CreateLowEndBike();
    LowEndCar CreateLowEndCar();
    MidRangeBike CreateMidRangeBike();
    MidRangeCar CreateMidRangeCar();
}
```

From there, once the implementation(s) are updated, if we want to consume the new mid-range vehicles, we need to open each consumer class and apply the changes there, which once again breaks the OCP.

The most crucial part is understanding and seeing the coupling and its impacts.

Now, let's conclude before exploring the last design pattern of the chapter.

Conclusion

The Abstract Factory pattern is excellent for abstracting away the creation of object families, isolating each family and its concrete implementation, and leaving the consumers unaware of the family created at runtime by the factory.

We talk more about factories in the next chapter; meanwhile, let's see how the Abstract Factory pattern can help us follow the **SOLID** principles:

- S: Each concrete factory is solely responsible for creating a family of objects. You could combine Abstract Factory with other creational patterns, such as the **Prototype** and **Builder** patterns, for more complex creational needs.
- O: We can create and use new families of objects, like the mid-range vehicles, without breaking existing client code.
- L: We aim at composition, so there's no need for any inheritance, implicitly discarding the need for the LSP. If you use abstract classes in your design, you must ensure you don't break the LSP when creating new abstract factories.
- I: Extracting a small abstraction with many implementations, where each concrete factory focuses on one family, makes that interface very focused on one task, instead of having a large interface that exposes all types of products (like the `ILargeVehicleFactory` interface).
- D: By depending only on interfaces, the consumer is unaware of the concrete types it uses.

Next, we explore the last design pattern of the chapter.

The Singleton design pattern

The Singleton design pattern allows you to create and reuse a single instance of a class. We could use a static class to achieve almost the same goal, but not everything is doable using static classes. For example, a static class can't implement an interface. We can't pass an instance of a static class as an argument because there is no instance. We can only use static classes directly, which leads to tight coupling every time.

The Singleton pattern in C# is an anti-pattern. As a rule of thumb, we should never use it and use dependency injection instead. .NET and C# offer the tools to implement similar functionalities without the drawbacks, hence the recommendation to not use this pattern. One such drawback is poor testability. That said, it is a classic design pattern worth learning to at least avoid implementing it. We explore a better alternative in the next chapter.

Here are a few reasons why we are covering this pattern:

- It translates into a singleton scope in the next chapter.
- Without knowing about it, you cannot locate it, try to remove it, or avoid its usage.
- It is a simple pattern to explore.
- It leads to other patterns, such as the **Ambient Context** pattern.

Goal

The Singleton pattern limits the number of instances of a class to one. Then, the idea is to reuse the same instance subsequently. A singleton encapsulates both the object logic itself and its creational logic. For example, the Singleton pattern could lower the cost of instantiating an object with a large memory footprint, since the program instantiates it only once.

Can you think of a SOLID principle that gets broken right there?

The Singleton pattern asserts that one object must have two responsibilities, breaking the **Single Responsibility Principle** (**SRP**). A singleton is the object itself and its own factory.

Design

This design pattern is straightforward and is limited to a single class. Let's start with a class diagram:

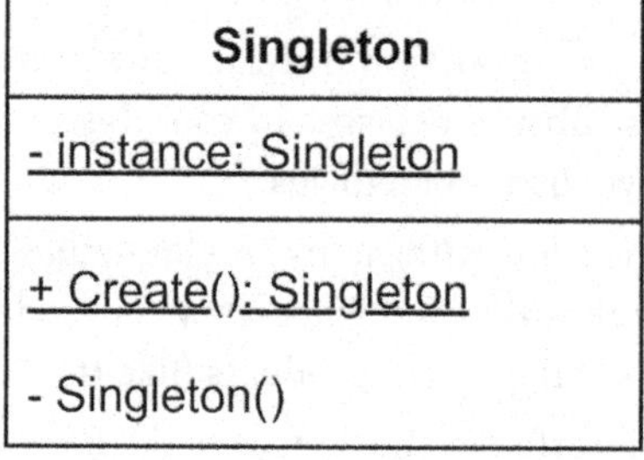

Figure 7.6: Singleton pattern class diagram

The `Singleton` class is composed of the following:

- A private static field that holds its unique instance.
- A public static `Create` method that creates or returns the unique instance.
- A private constructor, so external code cannot instantiate it without passing by the `Create` method.

You can name the `Create()` method anything or even get rid of it, as we see in the next example. We could name it `GetInstance()`, or it could be a static property named `Instance` or bear any other relevant name.

We can translate the preceding diagram to the following code:

```
public class MySingleton
{
    private static MySingleton? _instance;
    private MySingleton() { }
    public static MySingleton Create()
    {
        _instance ??= new MySingleton();
        return _instance;
    }
}
```

The null-coalescing assignment operator `??=` only assigns the new instance of `MySingleton` if the `_instance` member is `null`. That line is equivalent to writing the following `if` statement:

```
if (_instance == null)
{
    _instance = new MySingleton();
}
```

Before discussing the code further, let's explore our new class's behavior. We can see in the following unit test that `MySingleton.Create()` always returns the same instance as expected:

```
public class MySingletonTest
{
    [Fact]
    public void Create_should_always_return_the_same_instance()
    {
        var first = MySingleton.Create();
        var second = MySingleton.Create();
        Assert.Same(first, second);
    }
}
```

And voilà! We have a working Singleton pattern, which is extremely simple—probably the most simple design pattern that I can think of.

Here is what happens under the hood:

1. The first time that a consumer calls `MySingleton.Create()`, it creates the first instance of `MySingleton`. Since the constructor is `private`, it can only be created from the inside.
2. The `Create` method then persists that first instance to the `_instance` field for future use.
3. When a consumer calls `MySingleton.Create()` a second time, it returns the `_instance` field, reusing the class's previous (and only) instance.

Now that we understand the logic, there is a potential issue with that design: it is not thread-safe.

Thread safety ensures that a piece of code can safely be used by multiple threads at the same time, without leading to data corruption or conflicting outcomes. It commonly involves using synchronization mechanisms to manage concurrent access to shared resources.

If we want our singleton to be thread-safe, we can lock the instance creation like this:

```
public class MySingletonWithLock
{
    private static readonly object _myLock = new();
    private static MySingletonWithLock? _instance;
    private MySingletonWithLock() { }
    public static MySingletonWithLock Create()
    {
        lock (_myLock)
        {
            _instance ??= new MySingletonWithLock();
        }
        return _instance;
    }
}
```

In the preceding code, we ensure two threads do not attempt to access the Create method simultaneously, in turn ensuring that they do not get different instances. Next, we improve our thread-safe example by making it shorter.

An alternative (better) way

Previously, we used the "long way" of implementing the Singleton pattern and had to implement a thread-safe mechanism. Now, that classic method is behind us. We can shorten that code and even get rid of the Create() method, like this, which gives us thread safety out of the box:

```
public class MySimpleSingleton
{
    public static MySimpleSingleton Instance { get; } = new();
    private MySimpleSingleton() { }
}
```

The preceding code relies on the static initializer to ensure that only one instance of the MySimpleSingleton class is created and assigned to the Instance property.

This simple technique should do the trick unless the singleton's constructor executes some heavy processing.

With the property instead of a method, we can use the singleton class like this:

```
MySimpleSingleton.Instance.SomeOperation();
```

We can prove the correctness of that claim by executing the following test method:

```
[Fact]
public void Create_should_always_return_the_same_instance()
{
    var first = MySimpleSingleton.Instance;
    var second = MySimpleSingleton.Instance;
    Assert.Same(first, second);
}
```

It is usually best to delegate responsibilities to the language or the framework whenever possible, as we did here with the property initializer. Using a static constructor would also be a valid, thread-safe alternative, once again delegating the job to language features.

Beware of the arrow operator

It may be tempting to use the arrow operator `=>` to initialize the `Instance` property, like this: `public static MySimpleSingleton Instance => new MySimpleSingleton();`. However, doing so would return a new instance every time. This would defeat the purpose of what we want to achieve. On the other hand, the property initializer runs only once.

The arrow operator makes the `Instance` property an expression-bodied member, equivalent to creating the following getter: `get { return new MySimpleSingleton(); }`. You can consult the *Appendix* on GitHub (`https://adpg.link/net8-appendix`), for more information about expression-bodied statements.

Before we conclude the chapter, we should discuss how the Singleton (anti-)pattern also leads to a code smell.

Code smell – Ambient Context

That last implementation of the **Singleton** pattern led us to the **Ambient Context** pattern. **An ambient context is a global state**, which we could even call an anti-pattern, but let's just say that it is a consequential code smell.

I do not recommend using ambient contexts for multiple reasons. First, I do my best to avoid anything global. Globals, like static members in C#, can look very convenient because they are easy to access and use. They are always there and accessible whenever needed – easy. However, they have many drawbacks in terms of flexibility and testability.

When using an ambient context, the following occurs:

- **Tight coupling:** Global states lead to less flexible systems; consumers are tightly coupled with the ambient context.
- **Testing difficulty:** Global objects are harder to replace, and we cannot easily swap them for other objects, like a mock.

- **Unforeseen impacts:** If some part of your system messes up your global state, that may have unexpected consequences on other parts of your system, and you may have difficulty finding out the root cause of those errors.
- **Potential misuse:** Developers could be tempted to add non-global concerns to the ambient context, leading to a bloated component.

Fun fact

Many years ago, before the JavaScript frameworks era, I fixed a bug in a system where some function was overriding the value of `undefined`, due to a subtle error. This is an excellent example of how global variables could significantly impact your whole system and make it more brittle. The same applies to the Ambient Context and Singleton patterns in C#; globals can be dangerous and annoying.

Rest assured that, nowadays, browsers won't let developers update the value of `undefined`, but it was possible back then.

Keeping in mind our earlier discussion on global objects, an ambient context is a global instance usually available through a static property, just like a singleton. That global instance usually provides some shared state across an application. The Ambient Context pattern can bring good things, but it is a code smell that smells bad.

There are a few examples in .NET Framework, such as `System.Threading.Thread.CurrentPrincipal` and `System.Threading.Thread.CurrentThread`, that are scoped to a thread instead of being purely global, like most static members. Ambient contexts do not have to be singletons, but that is what they are most of the time. Creating a non-global (scoped) ambient context is harder and requires more work.

Is the Ambient Context pattern good or bad? I'd go with both! It is useful primarily because of its convenience and ease of use. Most of the time, it could and should be designed differently to reduce its drawbacks. As a rule of thumb, do not implement the Ambient Context pattern unless you have no other choice.

There are many ways of implementing an ambient context, but to keep it brief and straightforward, we focus only on the singleton version of the ambient context. The following code is a good example:

```
public class MyAmbientContext
{
    public static MyAmbientContext Current { get; } = new MyAmbientContext();
    private MyAmbientContext() { }
    public void WriteSomething(string something)
    {
        Console.WriteLine($"This is your something: {something}");
    }
}
```

That code is an exact copy of the MySimpleSingleton class, with a few subtle changes:

- Instance is named Current.
- The WriteSomething method is new but has nothing to do with the Ambient Context pattern itself; it is just to make the class do something.

If we take a look at the test method that follows, we can see that we use the ambient context by calling MyAmbientContext.Current, just like we did with the last singleton implementation:

```
[Fact]
public void Should_echo_the_inputted_text_to_the_console()
{
    // Arrange (make the console write to a StringBuilder
    // instead of the actual console)
    var expectedText = "This is your something: Hello World!" + Environment.
NewLine;
    var sb = new StringBuilder();
    using (var writer = new StringWriter(sb))
    {
        Console.SetOut(writer);
        // Act
        MyAmbientContext.Current.WriteSomething("Hello World!");
    }
    // Assert
    var actualText = sb.ToString();
    Assert.Equal(expectedText, actualText);
}
```

The property could include a public setter or support more complex logic. Building the right classes and exposing the right behaviors is up to you and your specifications.

To conclude this interlude, avoid ambient contexts and use instantiable classes instead. We will see how to replace a singleton with a single instance of a class using dependency injection in the next chapter. That gives us a more flexible alternative to the Singleton pattern. We can also create a single instance per HTTP request, which saves us the trouble of coding it while eliminating the disadvantages.

Conclusion

The Singleton pattern allows you to create a single instance of a class for the whole lifetime of a program. It leverages a private static field and a private constructor to achieve its goal, exposing the instantiation through a public static method or property. We can use a field initializer, the Create method itself, a static constructor, or any other valid C# options to encapsulate the initialization logic.

Now, let's see how the Singleton pattern can help us follow (or not) the SOLID principles:

- **S**: The singleton violates this principle because it has two clear responsibilities:
  - It has the responsibility for which it has been created (not illustrated here), like any other class.
  - It has the responsibility of creating and managing itself (lifetime management).
- **O**: The Singleton pattern also violates this principle. It enforces a single static instance, locked in place by itself, which limits extensibility. It is impossible to extend the class without changing its code.
- **L**: There is no inheritance directly involved, which is the only good point.
- **I**: Building a small targeted singleton class with a streamlined API (class interface) would satisfy this principle.
- **D**: The singleton class has a rock-solid hold on itself. It also suggests using its static property (or method) directly without using an abstraction, breaking the **dependency inversion principle (DIP)** with a sledgehammer.

As you can see, the Singleton pattern violates almost all the SOLID principles and, thus, should be used cautiously. Having only a single instance of a class and always using that same instance is a common concept. However, we explore more appropriate ways to do this in the next chapter, leading me to the following advice: do not use the Singleton pattern, and if you see it used somewhere, try refactoring it out.

I suggest avoiding static members that create global states as a general good practice. They can make your system less flexible and more brittle. There are occasions where static members are worth using, but try keeping their number as low as possible. Ask yourself if you can replace that static member or class with something else before coding one.

Some may argue that the Singleton design pattern is a legitimate way of doing things. However, in ASP.NET Core, I am afraid I have to disagree: we have a powerful mechanism to do it differently, called dependency injection. When using other technologies, maybe, but not with modern .NET.

Summary

In this chapter, we explored our first GoF design patterns. These patterns expose some of the essential basics of software engineering—not necessarily the patterns themselves but the concepts behind them:

- The Strategy pattern is a behavioral pattern that we use to compose most of our future classes. It allows you to swap behavior at runtime by composing an object with small pieces and coding against interfaces, following the SOLID principles.
- The Abstract Factory pattern introduces the idea of abstracting away object creation, leading to a better separation of concerns. More specifically, it aims to abstract the creation of object families and follow the SOLID principles.

- Even if we defined it as an anti-pattern, the Singleton pattern brings application-level objects to the table. It allows you to create a single instance of an object that lives for the whole lifetime of a program. The pattern violates most SOLID principles.

We also peeked at the Ambient Context code smell, which is used to create an omnipresent entity accessible from everywhere. It is often implemented as a singleton and introduces a global state object to a program.

The next chapter explores how dependency injection helps us compose complex yet maintainable systems. We also revisit the Strategy, Factory, and Singleton patterns to see how to use them in a dependency injection-oriented context and how powerful they really are.

Questions

Let's take a look at a few practice questions:

1. Why is the Strategy pattern a behavioral pattern?
2. What is the goal of creational patterns?
3. If I write the code `public MyType MyProp => new MyType();` and I call the property twice (`var v1 = MyProp; var v2 = MyProp;`), are `v1` and `v2` the same instance or two different instances?
4. Is it true that the Abstract Factory pattern allows us to add new families of elements without modifying the existing consuming code?
5. Why is the Singleton pattern an anti-pattern?

Answers

1. It helps manage behaviors at runtime, such as changing an algorithm in the middle of a running program.
2. Creational patterns are responsible for creating objects.
3. `v1` and `v2` are two different instances. The code on the right-hand side of the arrow operator is executed every time you call the property's getter.
4. Yes, it is true. That's the primary goal of the pattern, as we demonstrated in the `MidRangeVehicleFactory` code sample.
5. The Singleton pattern violates the SOLID principles and encourages the use of global (static) state objects. We can avoid this pattern most of the time.

Learn more on Discord

To join the Discord community for this book – where you can share feedback, ask questions to the author, and learn about new releases – follow the QR code below:

https://packt.link/ArchitectingASPNETCoreApps3e

8

Dependency Injection

This chapter explores the ASP.NET Core **dependency injection** (**DI**) system, how to leverage it efficiently, and its limits and capabilities.

We learn to compose objects using DI and delve into the **inversion of control** (**IoC**) principle. As we traverse the landscape of the built-in DI container, we explore its features and potential uses.

Beyond practical examples, we lay down the conceptual foundation of DI to understand its purpose, its benefits, and the problems it solves and to lay down the ground for the rest of the book as we rely heavily on DI.

We then return to the first three **Gang of Four** (**GoF**) design patterns we encountered, but this time, through the lens of DI. By refactoring these patterns using DI, we gain a more holistic understanding of how this powerful design tool influences the structure and flexibility of our software.

DI is a cornerstone for mastering modern application design and plays a transformative role in developing efficient, adaptable, testable, and maintainable software.

In this chapter, we cover the following topics:

- What is DI?
- Revisiting the Strategy pattern
- Revisiting the Singleton pattern
- Understanding guard clauses
- Understanding the Service Locator pattern
- Revisiting the Factory pattern

What is dependency injection?

DI is a way to apply the **IoC** principle. IoC is a broader version of the dependency inversion principle (the *D* in SOLID). In essence, while IoC is about shifting the control of the program's flow to a separate component or framework to increase modularity, the DIP focuses on how modules or classes are interconnected.

The idea behind DI is to move the creation of dependencies from the objects themselves to the **composition root**. That way, we can delegate the management of dependencies to an **IoC container**, which does the heavy lifting.

An IoC container and a **DI container** are the same thing—they're just different words people use. I use both interchangeably in real life, but I stick to the IoC container in the book because it seems more accurate than a DI container.

IoC is the concept (the principle), while DI is a way of inverting the flow of control (applying IoC). For example, you apply the IoC principle (inverting the flow) by injecting dependencies at runtime (doing DI) using a container.

Here, we explore an example programmed using traditional code that directly couples two classes. We then create the same class hierarchy using manual DI.

Let's look at a diagram that represents a `Client` class tightly coupled with a `Service` class:

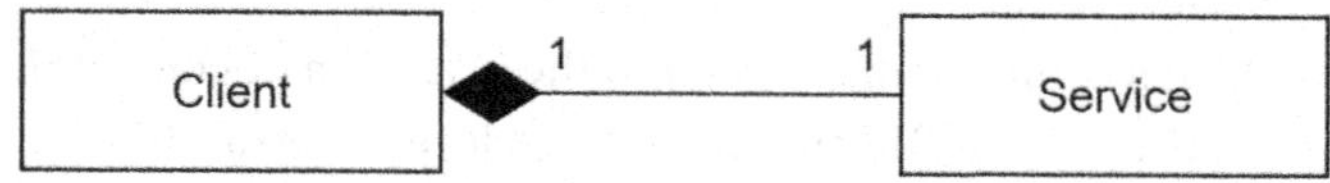

Figure 8.1: Tight coupling relationship between two classes

The preceding diagram shows that an instance of the `Client` class is composed of an instance of the `Service` class. On top of that, the `Client` class controls the lifetime of the `Service` class.

We do not cover UML in this book, but in the GitHub README file, you will find links to UML resources online to help you understand UML diagrams.

Next is a code example that depicts the `Client` class creating an instance of the `Service` class in its `Operation` method (highlighted lines):

```
namespace CoreConcepts.Raw;
public class Client
{
    public void Operation()
    {
        // Direct control over dependency
        var service = new Service(); // Dependency
        service.ExecuteSomeTask();
    }
}
public class Service
```

```
{
    public void ExecuteSomeTask()
        => throw new NotImplementedException();
}
```

Now, based on that code, let's explore what happens when a `Consumer` object calls the `Operation` method of a `Client` object using a sequence diagram:

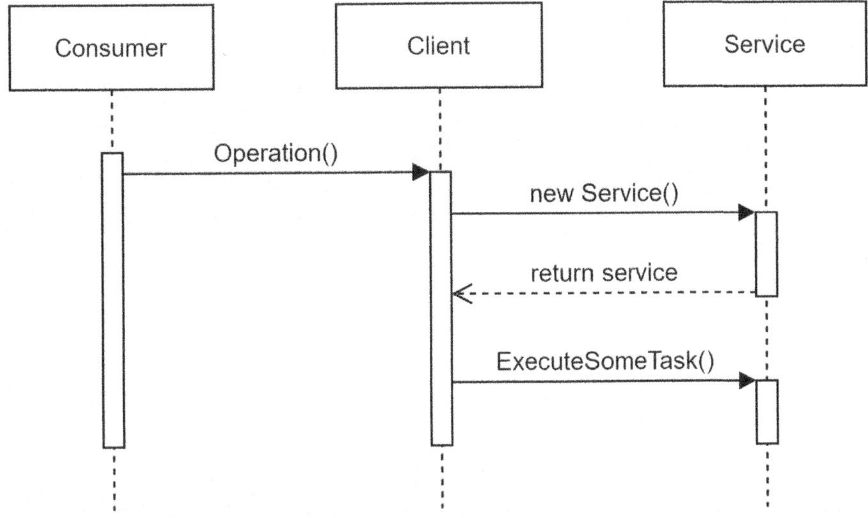

Figure 8.2: Sequence diagram showcasing the direct dependency between the Client and Service classes

The diagram clearly shows that the `Client` class creates an instance of the `Service` class before calling its `ExecuteSomeTask` method. On top of being tightly coupled, the `Client` class directly controls when the `Service` instance is created and destroyed, leading to a direct dependency.

Now, to remove the dependency creation from the `Client` class and invert the dependency flow, let's create a manual and very barebone `Container` class to simulate the use of an IoC container. Let's start with a diagram that shows the relationship between that container, a client (consumer of a service), and a service:

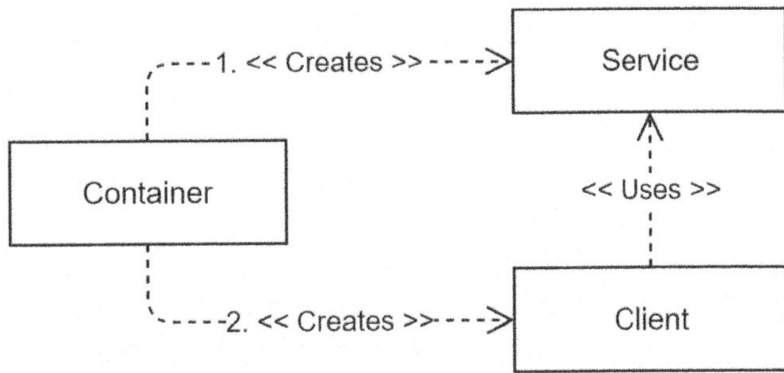

Figure 8.3: Relationships between the different actors involved in DI

The preceding diagram showcases that the `Container` class manages the creation of objects and does so in the following order:

1. The `Container` creates a `Service` object.
2. The `Container` creates a `Client` object that depends on and uses the `Service` object.

Now, to make this clearer, let's investigate that diagram as a sequence of events where we add a `Consumer` class that uses the `Container` to obtain an instance of the `Client` class and call its `Operation` method:

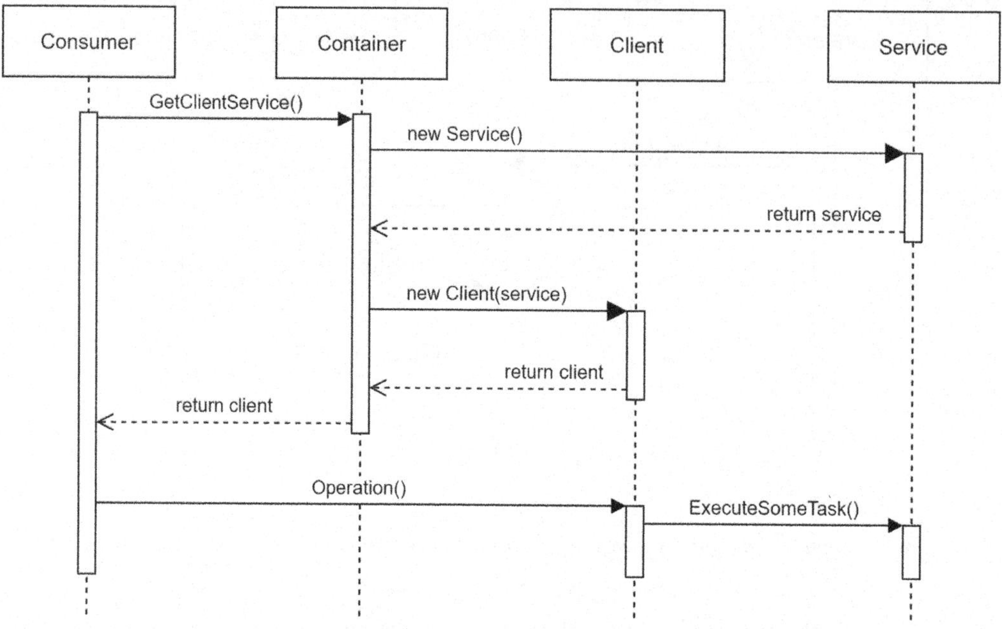

Figure 8.4: The sequence in which the Container inverts the dependency flow

The preceding sequence diagram illustrates the IoC container's role in orchestrating the creation and management of objects and their dependencies. On top of that, the `Client` class no longer controls the creation process or the lifetime of the `Service` class, which **inverts the dependency flow**. As we are about to see, the `Container` class injects the `Service` instance in the `Client` class. The following code depicts this new reality:

```
namespace CoreConcepts;
public class Container
{
    public Client GetClientService()
    {
        // Inversion of Control
        var service = new Service(); // Dependency
        var client = new Client(service); // Dependency injection
        return client;
    }
```

```
}
public class Client(Service service) // Dependency
{
    private readonly Service _service = service;
    public void Operation()
    {
        // Using but not controlling the dependency
        _service.ExecuteSomeTask();
    }
}
public class Service
{
    public void ExecuteSomeTask()
        => throw new NotImplementedException();
}
```

The highlighted lines show the IoC principle in action where the `Client` class is no longer responsible for creating the `Service` class, but the `Container` class is. That small change inverted the dependency flow. We build upon this concept during this chapter and the rest of the book.

The IoC principle is crucial in building flexible, testable, and reliable systems.

Next, we define the composition root.

The composition root

A critical concept behind DI is the composition root. The composition root is where we tell the container about our dependencies and their expected lifetime: where we compose our dependency trees.

The composition root should be as close to the program's starting point as possible, so from ASP.NET Core 8 onward, the composition root is in the `Program.cs` file. In previous versions prior to ASP.NET Core 6, it was in the `Program` or `Startup` classes.

Next, we explore how to leverage DI to create highly adaptable systems.

Striving for adaptability

To achieve a high degree of flexibility with DI, we can apply the following formula, driven by the SOLID principles.

Object `A` should not know that it is using object `B`. Instead, `A` should use an interface, `I`, implemented by `B`, and `B` should be resolved and injected at runtime.

Let's decompose this:

- Object `A` should depend on interface `I` instead of concrete type `B`
- Instance `B`, injected into `A`, should be resolved by the IoC container at runtime

- `A` should not be aware of the existence of `B`
- `A` should not control the lifetime of `B`

We can also inject objects directly without passing by an interface. It all depends on what we inject, in what context, and our requirements. We tackle many use cases throughout the book to help you understand DI.

Next, we translate this equation into an analogy that helps explain the reasons to use a container.

Understanding the use of the IoC container

To better understand the use of the IoC container and to create an image around the previous adaptability concept, let's start with a LEGO® analogy where IoC is the equivalent of drawing a plan to build a LEGO® castle:

1. We draw the plan.
2. We gather the blocks.
3. We press the start button on a hypothetical robot builder.
4. The robot assembles the blocks by following our plan.
5. The castle is complete.

By following this logic, we can create a new 4x4 block with a unicorn painted on its side (concrete type), update the plan (composition root), and then press the restart button to rebuild the castle with that new block inserted into it, replacing the old one without affecting the structural integrity of the castle (program). As long as we respect the 4x4 block contract (interface), everything is updatable without impacting the rest of the castle, leading to great flexibility.

Following that idea, if we need to manage every single LEGO® block one by one, it would quickly become incredibly complex! Therefore, managing all dependencies by hand in a project would be super tedious and error prone, even in the smallest program. This situation is where an IoC container (the hypothetical robot builder) comes into play.

The role of an IoC container

An IoC container manages objects for us. We configure it, and then, when we ask for a service, the container resolves and injects it.

On top of that, the container manages the lifetime of dependencies, leaving our classes to do only one thing: the job we designed them to do. No more need to think about their dependencies!

The bottom line is that an IoC container is a DI framework that does the auto-wiring for us. We can conceptualize DI as follows:

1. The *consumer* of a dependency states its needs about one or more dependencies (contracts).
2. The IoC container injects that dependency (implementation) upon creating the *consumer*, fulfilling its needs at runtime.

Next, we explore a code smell that applying DI helps us avoid.

Code smell – Control Freak

Control Freak is a code smell and even an anti-pattern that forbids us from using the new keyword. Yes, using the new keyword is the code smell! Using the new keyword to create a dependency within the class consuming that dependency violates the IoC principle, hence why we call that concept the Control Freak code smell.

The following code is wrong, violates the IoC principle, and blocks us from leveraging DI, which reduces the flexibility and testability of the code:

```
namespace CompositionRoot.ControlFreak;
public class Consumer
{
    public void Do()
    {
        var dependency = new Dependency();
        dependency.Operation();
    }
}
public class Dependency
{
    public void Operation()
        => throw new NotImplementedException();
}
```

The highlighted line shows the anti-pattern in action. To enable the Consumer class to use DI, we could update it to the following:

```
public class Consumer
{
    private readonly Dependency _dependency;
    public DIEnabledConsumer(Dependency dependency)
    {
        _dependency = dependency;
    }
    public void Do()
    {
        _dependency.Operation();
    }
}
```

The preceding code removes the new keyword and is now open for modification. The highlighted lines represent the constructor injection pattern we explore subsequently in this chapter.

Nevertheless, do not ban the `new` keyword just yet. Instead, every time you use it, ask yourself whether the object you instantiated using the `new` keyword is a dependency that could be managed by the container and injected instead.

To help with that, I borrowed two terms from Mark Seemann's book *Dependency Injection in .NET*; the name *Control Freak* also comes from that book. He describes the following two categories of dependencies:

- Stable dependencies
- Volatile dependencies

Next is my take on defining them.

Stable dependencies

Stable dependencies should not break our application when a new version is released. They should use deterministic algorithms (input `X` should always produce output `Y`), and you should not expect to change them with something else in the future.

Most data structures devoid of behaviors, like **Data Transfer Objects** (**DTOs**), fall into this category. You can also consider the .NET BCL as stable dependencies.

We can still instantiate objects using the `new` keyword when they fall into this category because the dependencies are stable and unlikely to break anything if they change.

Next, we look at their counterpart.

Volatile dependencies

Volatile dependencies can change at runtime, like extendable elements with contextual behaviors. They may also be likely to change for various reasons like new features development.

Most classes we create, such as data access and business logic code, are volatile dependencies.

The primary way to break the tight coupling between classes is to rely on interfaces and DI and no longer instantiate those volatile dependencies using the `new` keyword.

Volatile dependencies are why DI is key to building flexible, testable, and maintainable software.

Conclusion

To conclude this interlude: don't be a control freak anymore; those days are behind you!

When in doubt, inject the dependency instead of using the `new` keyword.

Next, we explore the available lifetimes we can attribute to our volatile dependencies.

Object lifetime

Now that we understand we should no longer use the `new` keyword with volatile dependencies and limit its use as much as possible with stable dependencies, we need a way to create those classes. From now on, the IoC container will play that role and manage object instantiation and their lifetime for us.

What's an object's lifetime?

When we create an instance manually, using the `new` keyword, we create a hold on that object; we know when we create it and when its life ends. That's the lifetime of the object.

Of course, using the `new` keyword leaves no chance to control these objects from the outside, enhance them, intercept them, or swap them for another implementation—as covered in the preceding *Code smell – Control Freak* section.

.NET object lifetime

With DI, we need to forget about controlling objects and start to think about using dependencies, or more explicitly, depending on their interfaces.

In ASP.NET Core, there are three possible lifetimes to choose from:

Lifetime	Description
Transient	The container creates a new instance every time the dependency is requested.
Scoped	The container creates an instance per HTTP request and reuses it. In some rare cases, we can also create custom scopes.
Singleton	The container creates a single instance of that dependency and reuses that object for the whole lifespan of the application.

Table 8.1: ASP.NET Core objects lifetime description

We can now manage our volatile dependencies using one of those three scopes. Here are some questions to help you choose:

- Do I need a single instance of my dependency? Yes? Use the **singleton** lifetime.
- Do I need a single instance of my dependency shared over an HTTP request? Yes? Use the **scoped** lifetime.
- Do I need a new instance of my dependency every time? Yes? Use the **transient** lifetime.

A general approach to object lifetime is to design the components to be *singletons*. When impossible, we go for *scoped*. When *scoped* is also impossible, go for *transient*. This way, we maximize instance reuse, lower the overhead of creating objects, lower the memory cost of keeping those objects in memory, and lower the amount of garbage collection needed to remove unused instances.

For example, we can pick *singleton* mindlessly for stateless objects, which are the easiest to maintain and less likely to break.

For stateful objects, where multiple consumers use the same instance, we must ensure the object is thread-safe if the lifetime is *singleton* or *scoped* because multiple consumers could try to access it simultaneously.

One essential aspect to consider when choosing a lifetime is the consumers of stateful objects. For example, if we load data related to the current user, we must ensure that data does not leak to other users. To do so, we can define the lifetime of that object to *scoped*, which is limited to a single HTTP request. If we don't want to reuse that state between multiple consumers, we can choose a *transient* lifetime to ensure every consumer gets their own instance.

How does that translate into code? .NET offers multiple extension methods to help us configure the lifetimes of our objects, like `AddTransient`, `AddScoped`, and `AddSingleton`, which explicitly state their lifetimes.

We explore the registration process next, but meanwhile, let's look at how the lifetime behaves using code, starting with the `ObjectLifetime` class that exposes an `Id` property. That property is set to a random `Guid` when the class is initialized. The class implements three interfaces that each expose the `Id` property. We use those interfaces to inject dependencies into the `ServiceConsumer` class and register each of them with a different lifetime. Here's that code:

```
namespace CoreConcepts;
public class ObjectLifetime : ITransient, IScoped, ISingleton
{
    public Guid Id { get; } = Guid.NewGuid();
}
public interface ISingleton
{
    Guid Id { get; }
}
public interface IScoped
{
    Guid Id { get; }
}
public interface ITransient
```

```
{
    Guid Id { get; }
}
```

Next, let's have a look at the ServiceConsumer class that depends on the three interfaces:

```
public class ServiceConsumer(ISingleton singleton, IScoped scoped, ITransient
transient)
{
    private readonly ISingleton _singleton = singleton;
    private readonly IScoped _scoped = scoped;
    private readonly ITransient _transient = transient;

    public Guid SingletonId => _singleton.Id;
    public Guid ScopedId => _scoped.Id;
    public Guid TransientId => _transient.Id;
}
```

The preceding class expects three objects to be injected in its constructor and expose three properties that each return the ID of one dependency. This class is about to allow us to test those lifetimes. Before executing the program, let's add the following code to the Program.cs file:

```
using CoreConcepts;

var builder = WebApplication.CreateBuilder(args);
builder.Services.AddSingleton<ISingleton, ObjectLifetime>();
builder.Services.AddScoped<IScoped, ObjectLifetime>();
builder.Services.AddTransient<ITransient, ObjectLifetime>();
builder.Services.AddTransient<ServiceConsumer>();

var app = builder.Build();
app.MapGet("/", (ServiceConsumer serviceConsumer1, ServiceConsumer
serviceConsumer2) =>
{
    return TypedResults.Ok(new[] {
        serviceConsumer1,
        serviceConsumer2
    });
});
app.Run();
```

The preceding code registers the dependencies with their expected lifetime and exposes an endpoint that takes ServiceConsumer instances and returns them. This highlighted code is what interests us here.

Each `ServiceConsumer` instance has three dependencies, one singleton, one scoped, and one transient. Having two instances allows us to test the scoped lifetime. Here's what happens when we execute the program:

```
[
  {
    "singletonId": "23f9a45e-c667-436f-8704-688220e99696",
    "scopedId": "30ddcc63-9874-4002-8376-56e25f907803",
    "transientId": "4428e377-8778-4590-b433-ab5539d52d15"
  },
  {
    "singletonId": "23f9a45e-c667-436f-8704-688220e99696",
    "scopedId": "30ddcc63-9874-4002-8376-56e25f907803",
    "transientId": "b650bb84-f295-4ae5-ad46-89be3e9bab53"
  }
]
```

As we can see, the two `singletonId` instances are the same and the two `scopedId` instances are the same, but the two `transientId` instances are different. Now, if we call the endpoint a second time, here's the result:

```
[
  {
    "singletonId": "23f9a45e-c667-436f-8704-688220e99696",
    "scopedId": "2e81f97e-92b1-4c1a-b794-a27bd3d8b70d",
    "transientId": "7a88b245-197c-4ead-9f60-b7f73d464d78"
  },
  {
    "singletonId": "23f9a45e-c667-436f-8704-688220e99696",
    "scopedId": "2e81f97e-92b1-4c1a-b794-a27bd3d8b70d",
    "transientId": "e100ec02-eb0b-455b-b3db-94ec7e63c499"
  }
]
```

Now, the two `singletonId` instances are the same and are the same as the previous request, because the container injects the same object in all instances of the `ServiceConsumer` class, across HTTP requests. The two `scopedId` instances are the same, but different than the previous request because the container injects the same object only for the lifetime of its scope (the HTTP request by default). Once again, the `transientId` instances are different because the container injects a new instance every time.

We use the built-in container throughout the book with many of its registration methods, so you should grow familiar with it very quickly. It has good discoverability, so you can explore the built-in IoC container possibilities using IntelliSense while writing code or reading the documentation.

Next, let's explore those Add methods and explore how to register dependencies with the container in more detail.

Registering our dependencies

In ASP.NET Core, we register our dependencies in the Program.cs file, which represents the composition root. The minimal hosting model, the WebApplicationBuilder, exposes the Services property we use to add our dependencies to the container. Afterward, .NET creates the container when it builds the WebApplication instance.

Next is a minimal Program.cs file depicting this concept:

```
var builder = WebApplication.CreateBuilder(args);
// Register dependencies
var app = builder.Build();
// The IoC container is now available
app.Run();
```

We use the builder.Services property to register our dependencies in that IServiceCollection implementation. Here's an example of registering some dependencies:

```
builder.Services.AddSingleton<Dependency1>();
builder.Services.AddScoped<Dependency2>();
builder.Services.AddTransient<Dependency3>();
```

The preceding code registers the dependencies using the three lifetimes we studied, ensuring we receive the same instance of Dependency1 for every request, the same instance of Dependency2 for the duration of an HTTP request (but distinct instances across different HTTP requests), and a unique instance of Dependency3 for each request.

Remember to compose the program in the composition root. That removes the need for those pesky new keywords spread around your codebase and all the tight coupling that comes with them. Moreover, it centralizes the application's composition into that location, creating the plan to assemble the LEGO® blocks.

As you may be thinking right now, that can lead to a lot of registration statements in a single location, and you are correct; maintaining such a composition root would be a challenge in almost any application. To address this concern, we introduce an elegant way to encapsulate the registration code next, ensuring it remains manageable.

Registering your features elegantly

As we've just discovered, while we should register dependencies in the composition root, we can also arrange our registration code in a structured manner. For example, we can break down our application's composition into several methods or classes and invoke them from our composition root. Another strategy could be to use an auto-discovery system to automate the registration of certain services.

The critical part is to centralize the program composition in one place.

A common pattern in ASP.NET Core is having special methods like `Add[Feature name]`. These methods register their dependencies, letting us add a group of dependencies with just one method call. This pattern is convenient for breaking down program composition into smaller, easier-to-handle parts, like individual features. This also makes the composition root more readable.

A feature is the correct size as long as it stays cohesive. If your feature becomes too big, does too many things, or starts to share dependencies with other features, it may be time for a redesign before losing control over it. That's usually a good indicator of undesired coupling.

To implement this pattern, we use extension methods, making it trivial. Here's a guide:

1. Create a static class named `[subject]Extensions` in the `Microsoft.Extensions.DependencyInjection` namespace.
2. Create an extension method that returns the `IServiceCollection` interface, which allows method calls to be chained.

According to Microsoft's recommendation, we should create the class in the same namespace as the element we extend. In our case, the `IServiceCollection` interface lives in the `Microsoft.Extensions.DependencyInjection` namespace.

Of course, this is not mandatory, and we can adapt this process to our needs. For example, we can define the class in another namespace if we want consumers to add a `using` statement explicitly. We can also return another type, then the registration process can continue beyond that first method, like a builder interface.

Builder interfaces are used to configure more complex features, like ASP.NET Core MVC. For example, the `AddControllers` extension method returns an `IMvcBuilder` interface that contains a `PartManager` property. Moreover, some extension methods target the `IMvcBuilder` interface, allowing further configuration of the feature by requiring its registration first; that is, you can't configure `IMvcBuilder` before calling `AddControllers`. You can also design your features to leverage that pattern when needed.

Let's explore a demo.

Project – Registering the demo feature

Let's explore registering the dependencies of the demo feature. That feature contains the following code:

```
namespace CompositionRoot.DemoFeature;
public class MyFeature
{
    private readonly IMyFeatureDependency _myFeatureDependency;
    public MyFeature(IMyFeatureDependency myFeatureDependency)
    {
        _myFeatureDependency = myFeatureDependency;
    }

    public void Operation()
    {
        // use _myFeatureDependency
    }
}

public interface IMyFeatureDependency { }
public class MyFeatureDependency : IMyFeatureDependency { }
```

As we can see, there is nothing complex but two empty classes and an interface. Remember that we are exploring the registration of dependencies, not what to do with them or what they can do—yet.

Now, we want the container to serve an instance of the `MyFeatureDependency` class when a dependency requests the `IMyFeatureDependency` interface as the `MyFeature` class does. We want a singleton lifetime.

To achieve this, in the `Program.cs` file, we can write the following code:

```
builder.Services.AddSingleton<MyFeature>();
builder.Services.AddSingleton<IMyFeatureDependency, MyFeatureDependency>();
```

We can also chain the two method calls instead:

```
builder.Services
    .AddSingleton<MyFeature>()
    .AddSingleton<IMyFeatureDependency, MyFeatureDependency>()
;
```

However, this is not yet elegant. What we want to achieve is this:

```
builder.Services.AddDemoFeature();
```

To build that registration method, we can write the following extension method:

```
using CompositionRoot.DemoFeature;
namespace Microsoft.Extensions.DependencyInjection;
public static class DemoFeatureExtensions
{
    public static IServiceCollection AddDemoFeature(this IServiceCollection
services)
    {
        return services
            .AddSingleton<MyFeature>()
            .AddSingleton<IMyFeatureDependency, MyFeatureDependency>()
        ;
    }
}
```

As highlighted, the registration is the same but uses the `services` parameter, which is the extended type, instead of the `builder.Services` (`builder` does not exist in that class, yet the `services` parameter is the same object as the `builder.Services` property).

If you are unfamiliar with extension methods, they come in handy for extending existing classes, like we just did. Besides having a static method inside a static class, the `this` keyword next to the first parameter determines whether it is an extension method.

For example, we can build sophisticated libraries that are easy to use with a set of extension methods. Think `System.Linq` for such a system.

Now that we have learned the basics of DI, there is one last thing to cover before revisiting the Strategy design pattern.

Using external IoC containers

ASP.NET Core provides an extensible built-in IoC container out of the box. It is not the most powerful IoC container because it lacks some advanced features, but it does the job for most applications.

Rest assured; we can change it to another one if need be. You might also want to do that if you are used to another IoC container and want to stick to it.

Here's the strategy I recommend:

1. Use the built-in container, as per Microsoft's recommendation.
2. When you can't achieve something with it, look at your design and see if you can redesign your feature to work with the built-in container and simplify your design.
3. If it is impossible to achieve your goal, see if extending the default container using an existing library or coding the feature yourself is possible.
4. If it is still impossible, explore swapping it for another IoC container.

Assuming the container supports ASP.NET Core, it is super simple to swap. Yet, using a third-party library might be regulated in your workplace or you may want to keep the number of third-party libraries low in your project to reduce the maintenance and risks of such dependencies. On top of that, the default container is the standard in official documentation, which makes it easier to understand and adapt the example you will find online.

To register a third-party container, it must implement the `IServiceProviderFactory<TContainerBuilder>` interface. Then, in the `Program.cs` file, we must register that factory using the `UseServiceProviderFactory<TContainerBuilder>` method like this:

```
var builder = WebApplication.CreateBuilder(args);
builder.Host.UseServiceProviderFactory<ContainerBuilder>(new
ContainerBuilderFactory());
```

In this case, the `ContainerBuilder` and `ContainerBuilderFactory` classes are just wrappers around ASP.NET Core (see GitHub for the implementation), but your third-party container of choice should provide you with those types. I suggest you visit their documentation to know more.

Once that factory is registered, we can configure the container using the `ConfigureContainer<TContainerBuilder>` method and register our dependencies as usual, like this:

```
builder.Host.ConfigureContainer<ContainerBuilder>((context, builder) =>
{
    builder.Services.AddSingleton<Dependency1>();
    builder.Services.AddSingleton<Dependency2>();
    builder.Services.AddSingleton<Dependency3>();
});
```

That's the only difference; the rest of the `Program.cs` file remains the same.

As I sense you don't feel like implementing your own IoC container, multiple third-party integrations already exist. Here is a non-exhaustive list taken from the official documentation:

- Autofac
- DryIoc
- Grace
- LightInject
- Lamar
- Stashbox
- Simple Injector

On top of replacing the container entirely, some libraries extend the default container and add functionalities to it. We explore this option in *Chapter 11, Structural Patterns*.

Now that we have covered most of the theory, we revisit the Strategy pattern as the primary tool to compose our applications and add flexibility to our systems.

Revisiting the Strategy pattern

In this section, we leverage the Strategy pattern to compose complex object trees and use DI to dynamically create those instances without using the `new` keyword, moving away from being control freaks and toward writing DI-ready code.

The Strategy pattern is a behavioral design pattern we can use to compose object trees at runtime, allowing extra flexibility and control over objects' behavior. Composing our objects using the Strategy pattern makes our classes smaller, easier to test and maintain, and puts us on the SOLID path.

From now on, we want to compose objects and lower the amount of inheritance to a minimum. We call that principle **composition over inheritance**. The goal is to inject dependencies (composition) into the current class instead of depending on base class features (inheritance).

Additionally, this approach enables us to pull out behaviors and place them in separate classes, adhering to the **Single Responsibility Principle** (**SRP**) and **Interface Segregation Principle** (**ISP**). We can reuse these behaviors in one or more different classes through their interface, embodying the **Dependency Inversion Principle** (**DIP**). This strategy promotes code reuse and composition.

The following list covers the ways of injecting dependencies into objects, allowing us to control their behaviors from the outside by composing our objects:

- Constructor injection
- Property injection
- Method injection

We can also get dependencies directly from the container. This is known as the Service Locator (anti-)pattern. We explore the Service Locator pattern later in this chapter.

Let's look at some theory and then jump into the code to see DI in action.

Constructor injection

Constructor injection consists of injecting dependencies into the constructor as parameters. This is the most popular and preferred technique by far. Constructor injection is useful for injecting required dependencies; you can add null checks to ensure that, also known as the guard clause (see the *Understanding guard clauses* section).

Property injection

Property injection is about injecting **optional dependencies** into properties. However, the built-in IoC container does not support **property injection** out of the box.

Most of the time, you want to avoid doing this because property injection results in optional dependencies, meaning the properties are nullable, requiring null checks in the code that uses those properties, which introduces avoidable code complexity. So, when we think about it, it is good that ASP.NET Core left this one out of the built-in container.

You can usually remove the property injection requirements by reworking your design, leading to a better design. If you cannot avoid using property injection, use a third-party container or find a way to build the dependency tree yourself (maybe leveraging one of the Factory patterns).

Nevertheless, from a high-level view, the container would do something like this:

1. Create a new instance of the class and inject all required dependencies into the constructor.
2. Find extension points by scanning properties (this could be attributes, contextual bindings, or something else).
3. For each extension point, inject (set) a dependency, leaving unconfigured properties untouched, hence its definition of an optional dependency.

There are a couple of exceptions to the previous statement regarding the lack of support by ASP.NET Core:

- Razor components (powering Blazor for example) support property injection using the `[Inject]` attribute
- Razor contains the `@inject` directive, which generates a property to hold a dependency (ASP.NET Core manages to inject it)

We can't call that property injection per se because they are not optional but required, and the `@inject` directive is more about generating code than doing DI. They are more about an internal workaround than "real" property injection. That is as close as .NET gets from property injection.

I recommend aiming for constructor injection instead. Not having property injection should not cause you any problems. Often, our need for property injection stems from less-than-optimal design choices, whether from our design strategies or a framework we're utilizing.

Next, we look at method injection.

Method injection

Method injection is used to inject **optional dependencies** into classes through method parameters. We can also validate those at runtime using null checks or any other required logic.

ASP.NET Core supports method injection only at a few locations, such as in a controller's actions (methods), the `Startup` class (if you are using the pre-.NET 6 hosting model), and the middleware's `Invoke` or `InvokeAsync` methods. We cannot liberally use method injection in our classes without some work on our part.

I recommend aiming for constructor injection whenever you can. We should only resort to method injection when it's our sole option or when it brings added value to our design.

For example, in a controller, injecting a transient service in the only action that needs it instead of using constructor injection could save a lot of useless object instantiation and, by doing so, increase performance (less instantiation and less garbage collection). This can also lower the number of class-level dependencies a single class has.

Manually injecting a dependency in a method as an argument is valid. Here's an example, starting with the classes:

```
namespace CompositionRoot.ManualMethodInjection;
public class Subject
{
    public int Operation(Context context)
    {
        // ...
        return context.Number;
    }
}
public class Context
{
    public required int Number { get; init; }
}
```

The preceding code represents the `Subject` class that consumes an instance of the `Context` class from its `Operation` method. It then returns the value of its `Number` property.

This example follows a similar pattern to injecting an `HttpContext` into an endpoint delegate. In that case, the `HttpContext` represents the current HTTP request. In our case, the `Context` contains only an arbitrary number we use in the consuming code.

To test that our code does as it should, we can write the following test:

```
[Fact]
public void Should_return_the_value_of_the_Context_Number_property()
{
    // Arrange
    var subject = new Subject();
    var context = new Context { Number = 44 };

    // Act
```

```
        var result = subject.Operation(context);

        // Assert
        Assert.Equal(44, result);
    }
```

When we run the test, it works. We manually injected the `context` into the `subject` (highlighted code).

Now, to simulate a more complex system, let's have a look at a theory that injects the `subject` and the `context` in the test method (method injection) so we can manually inject the `context` into the `subject` without instantiating them inside the test method:

```
    public static IEnumerable<object[]> GetData() {
        // Return a set of test data; omitted for brevity.
    }
    [Theory]
    [MemberData(nameof(GetData))]
    public void Showcase_manual_method_injection(
        Subject subject, Context context, int expectedNumber)
    {
        // Manually injecting the context into the
        // Operation method of the subject.
        var number = subject.Operation(context);

        // Validate that we got the specified context.
        Assert.Equal(expectedNumber, number);
    }
```

The preceding code showcases the same concept, but xUnit injects the dependencies into the method, which is closer to what would happen in a real program. Remember, we want to remove the `new` keywords from our lives!

In a controller or a minimal API endpoint, we can use the `[FromServices]` attribute to inject a dependency as a method parameter, like the following highlighted code:

```
    using Microsoft.AspNetCore.Mvc;
    // ...
    public IActionResult GetUsingMethodInjection([FromServices] IMyService
    myService)
    {
        // ...
    }
```

Having explored how to inject dependencies, we are ready to roll up our sleeves and dive into hands-on coding.

Project – Strategy

In the Strategy project, we delve into various methods of injecting dependencies, transitioning from the Control Freak approach to a SOLID one. Through this exploration, we evaluate the advantages and drawbacks of each technique.

The project takes the form of a travel agency's location API returning a list of cities. Initially, the API returns only hardcoded cities. We've implemented the same endpoint five times across different controllers to facilitate comparison and trace the progression. Each controller comes in a pair except for one. The pairs comprise a base controller that uses an in-memory service (dev) and an updated controller that simulates a SQL database (production). Here's the breakdown of each controller:

- The `ControlFreakLocationsController` instantiates the `InMemoryLocationService` class using the `new` keyword
- The `ControlFreakUpdatedLocationsController` instantiates the `SqlLocationService` class and its dependency using the `new` keyword
- The `InjectImplementationLocationsController` leverages constructor injection to get an instance of the `InMemoryLocationService` class from the container
- The `InjectImplementationUpdatedLocationsController` leverages constructor injection to get an instance of the `SqlLocationService` class from the container
- The `InjectAbstractionLocationsController` leverages DI and interfaces to let its consumers change its behavior at runtime

The controllers share the same building blocks; let's start there.

Shared building blocks

The `Location` data structure is the following:

```
namespace Strategy.Models;
public record class Location(int Id, string Name, string CountryCode);
```

The `LocationSummary` DTO returned by the controller is the following:

```
namespace Strategy.Controllers;
public record class LocationSummary(int Id, string Name);
```

The service interface is the following and has only one method that returns one or more `Location` objects:

```
using Strategy.Models;
namespace Strategy.Services;
public interface ILocationService
{
    Task<IEnumerable<Location>> FetchAllAsync(CancellationToken
cancellationToken);
}
```

The two implementations of this interface are an in-memory version to use when developing and an SQL version to use when deploying (let's call this production to keep it simple).

The in-memory service returns a predefined list of cities:

```
using Strategy.Models;
namespace Strategy.Services;
public class InMemoryLocationService : ILocationService
{
    public async Task<IEnumerable<Location>> FetchAllAsync(CancellationToken
cancellationToken)
    {
        return new Location[] {
            new Location(1, "Paris", "FR"),
            // ...
            new Location(10, "Toronto", "CA"),
        };
    }
}
```

The SQL implementation uses an `IDatabase` interface to access the data:

```
using Strategy.Data;
using Strategy.Models;
namespace Strategy.Services;
public class SqlLocationService : ILocationService
{
    private readonly IDatabase _database;
    public SqlLocationService(IDatabase database) {
        _database = database;
    }

    public Task<IEnumerable<Location>> FetchAllAsync(CancellationToken
cancellationToken) {
        return _database.ReadManyAsync<Location>(
            "SELECT * FROM Location",
            cancellationToken
        );
    }
}
```

That database access interface is simply the following:

```
namespace Strategy.Data;
```

```
public interface IDatabase
{
    Task<IEnumerable<T>> ReadManyAsync<T>(string sql, CancellationToken
cancellationToken);
}
```

In the project itself, the `IDatabase` interface has only the `NotImplementedDatabase` implementation, which throws a `NotImplementedException` when its `ReadManyAsync` method is called:

```
namespace Strategy.Data;
public class NotImplementedDatabase : IDatabase
{
    public Task<IEnumerable<T>> ReadManyAsync<T>(string sql, CancellationToken
cancellationToken)
        => throw new NotImplementedException();
}
```

Since the goal is not to learn about database access, I mocked that part in a test case in an xUnit test using the controller and the `SqlLocationService` class.

With those shared pieces, we can start with the first two controllers.

Control Freak controllers

This first version of the code showcases the lack of flexibility that creating dependencies using the `new` keyword brings when the time to update the application arises. Here's the initial controller that leverages an in-memory collection:

```
using Microsoft.AspNetCore.Mvc;
using Strategy.Services;
namespace Strategy.Controllers;
[Route("travel/[controller]")]
[ApiController]
public class ControlFreakLocationsController : ControllerBase
{
    [HttpGet]
    public async Task<IEnumerable<LocationSummary>> GetAsync(CancellationToken
cancellationToken)
    {
        var locationService = new InMemoryLocationService();
        var locations = await locationService
            .FetchAllAsync(cancellationToken);
```

```
        return locations
            .Select(l => new LocationSummary(l.Id, l.Name));
    }
}
```

Executing this code works and returns the `LocationSummary` equivalent of the `Location` objects returned by the `FetchAllAsync` method of the `InMemoryLocationService` class. However, changing the `InMemoryLocationService` to a `SqlLocationService` is impossible without changing the code like this:

```
public class ControlFreakUpdatedLocationsController : ControllerBase
{
    [HttpGet]
    public async Task<IEnumerable<LocationSummary>> GetAsync(CancellationToken
cancellationToken)
    {
        var database = new NotImplementedDatabase();
        var locationService = new SqlLocationService(database);
        var locations = await locationService.FetchAllAsync(cancellationToken);
        return locations.Select(l => new LocationSummary(l.Id, l.Name));
    }
}
```

The changes are highlighted in the two code blocks. We could also create an if statement to load one or the other conditionally, but exporting this to a whole system makes a lot of duplication.

Advantages:

- It is easy to understand the code and what objects the controller uses

Disadvantages:

- The controller is tightly coupled with its dependencies, leading to a lack of flexibility
- Going from `InMemoryLocationService` to `SqlLocationService` requires updating the code

Let's improve on that design next with the next controller pair.

Injecting an implementation in the controllers

This second version of the code base improves flexibility by leveraging DI. In the following controller, we inject the `InMemoryLocationService` class in its constructor:

```
using Microsoft.AspNetCore.Mvc;
using Strategy.Services;
namespace Strategy.Controllers;
[Route("travel/[controller]")]
[ApiController]
public class InjectImplementationLocationsController : ControllerBase
```

```
{
    private readonly InMemoryLocationService _locationService;
    public InjectImplementationLocationsController(
        InMemoryLocationService locationService)
    {
        _locationService = locationService;
    }

    [HttpGet]
    public async Task<IEnumerable<LocationSummary>> GetAsync(CancellationToken
cancellationToken)
    {
        var locations = await _locationService.
FetchAllAsync(cancellationToken);
        return locations.Select(l => new LocationSummary(l.Id, l.Name));
    }
}
```

Assuming the `InMemoryLocationService` class is registered with the container, running this code would yield the same result as the Control Freak version and return the in-memory cities.

To register a class with the container, we can do the following:

```
builder.Services.AddSingleton<InMemoryLocationService>();
```

Unfortunately, to change that service for the `SqlLocationService`, we need to change the code again. This time, however, we must only change the constructor injection code like this:

```
public class InjectImplementationUpdatedLocationsController : ControllerBase
{
    private readonly SqlLocationService _locationService;
    public InjectImplementationUpdatedLocationsController(SqlLocationService
locationService)
    {
        _locationService = locationService;
    }
    // ...
}
```

This is yet another not ideal outcome, as the controller is tightly coupled with the `SqlLocationService` class.

Advantages:

- It is easy to understand the code and what objects the controller uses
- Using constructor injection allows changing the dependency in one place, and all the methods get it (assuming we have more than one method)
- We can inject subclasses without changing the code

Disadvantages:

- The controller is tightly coupled with its dependencies, leading to a lack of flexibility
- Going from `InMemoryLocationService` to `SqlLocationService` requires updating the code

We are getting there but still have a last step to make the controller flexible.

Injecting an abstraction in the controller

In this last controller, we leverage the SOLID principles, constructor injection, and, inherently, the Strategy pattern to build a controller that we can change from the outside.

All we have to do to make the code flexible is inject the interface instead of its implementation, like this:

```
using Microsoft.AspNetCore.Mvc;
using Strategy.Services;
namespace Strategy.Controllers;
[Route("travel/[controller]")]
[ApiController]
public class InjectAbstractionLocationsController : ControllerBase
{
    private readonly ILocationService _locationService;
    public InjectAbstractionLocationsController(ILocationService
locationService)
    {
        _locationService = locationService;
    }

    [HttpGet]
    public async Task<IEnumerable<LocationSummary>> GetAsync(CancellationToken
cancellationToken)
    {
        var locations = await _locationService.
FetchAllAsync(cancellationToken);
        return locations.Select(l => new LocationSummary(l.Id, l.Name));
    }
}
```

The highlighted lines showcase the changes. Injecting the `ILocationService` interface lets us control whether we inject an instance of the `InMemoryLocationService` class, the `SqlLocationService` class, or any other implementation we'd like.

This is the most flexible possibility we can get.

Advantages:

- Using constructor injection allows changing the dependency in one place, and all the methods get it (assuming we have more than one method).
- Injecting the `ILocationService` interface allows us to inject any of its implementations without changing the code.
- Because of the `ILocationService` interface, the controller is loosely coupled with its dependencies.

Disadvantages:

- Understanding what objects the controller uses is harder since the dependencies are resolved at runtime. However, this forces us to program against an interface instead (a good thing).

Let's have a look at this flexibility in action.

Constructing the InjectAbstractionLocationsController

I created a few xUnit tests to explore the possibilities.

I used Moq to **mock** implementations. A mock mimics the behavior of an object in a simulated way and is used primarily in unit testing to isolate and test how a piece of software interacts with an external dependency.

If you are unfamiliar with Moq and want to learn more, I left a link in the *Further reading* section.

Two of the tests refer to the following member, a static `Location` object:

```
public static Location ExpectedLocation { get; }
    = new Location(11, "Montréal", "CA");
```

The test cases are not to assess the correctness of our code but to explore how easy it is to compose the controller differently. Let's explore the first test case.

Use the InMemoryLocationService

The first test method uses the in-memory location service to compose the controller like this:

```
var inMemoryLocationService = new InMemoryLocationService();
var devController = new InjectAbstractionLocationsController(
    inMemoryLocationService);
```

As we can see from the preceding code, we inject a different service into the controller, changing its behavior. This time, after calling the `GetAsync` method, the controller returns the `Location` object from the `InMemoryLocationService`.

The visual representation of our object tree is as follows:

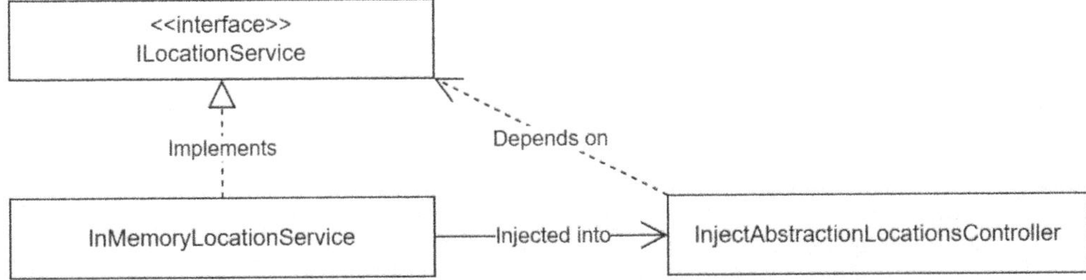

Figure 8.5: Composition of the controller in a test that injects an InMemoryLocationService instance

It is harder to write assertions for the preceding test because we inject an instance of the `InMemoryLocationService` class, which ties the result to its implementation. For this reason, we won't look at that code here.

Nonetheless, we succeeded at composing the controller differently. Let's have a look at the next test case.

Mock the ILocationService

This unit test mocks the `ILocationService` directly. The mock service returns a collection of one item. That item is the `Location` instance referenced by the `ExpectedLocation` property. Here's that code:

```
var locationServiceMock = new Mock<ILocationService>();
locationServiceMock.Setup(x => x.FetchAllAsync(It.IsAny<CancellationToken>())).
ReturnsAsync(() => new Location[] { ExpectedLocation });

var testController = new InjectAbstractionLocationsController(
    locationServiceMock.Object);
```

When executing the `GetAsync` method, we get the same result as in the first test case: a collection of a single test `Location` object.

We can assert the correctness of the method by comparing values like this:

```
Assert.Collection(result,
    location =>
    {
        Assert.Equal(ExpectedLocation.Id, location.Id);
        Assert.Equal(ExpectedLocation.Name, location.Name);
    }
);
```

We can also leverage Moq to verify that the controller called the `FetchAllAsync` method using the following code:

```
locationServiceMock.Verify(x => x
    .FetchAllAsync(It.IsAny<CancellationToken>()),
    Times.Once()
);
```

The object tree is very similar to the previous diagram, but we mocked the service implementation, focusing the test on a single unit:

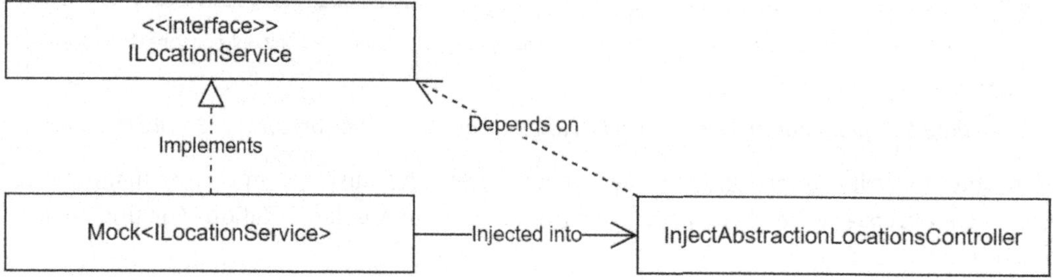

Figure 8.6: Composition of the controller in a test that mocks the ILocationService interface

As we explored in this project, with the right design and DI, we can easily compose different object trees using the same building blocks. However, with a bad design, it is hard or even impossible to do so without altering the code.

As you may have noticed, we used the `new` keyword in the controller to instantiate the DTO. DTOs are stable dependencies. We also explore object mappers in *Chapter 15, Object Mappers,* which is a way to encapsulate the logic of copying an object into another.

Let's have a look at the last test case.

Mock the IDatabase

The last test case is an integration test that injects an instance of the `SqlLocationService` class into the controller and mocks the database. The fake database returns a collection of one item. That item is the `Location` instance referenced by the `ExpectedLocation` property. Here's that code:

```
var databaseMock = new Mock<IDatabase>();
databaseMock.Setup(x => x.ReadManyAsync<Location>(It.IsAny<string>(),
It.IsAny<CancellationToken>()))
    .ReturnsAsync(() => new Location[] { ExpectedLocation })
;
```

```
var sqlLocationService = new SqlLocationService(
    databaseMock.Object);
var sqlController = new InjectAbstractionLocationsController(
    sqlLocationService);
```

The preceding code shows how we can control the dependency we inject into the classes because of how the `InjectAbstractionLocationsController` was designed. We can't say the same about the four other controller versions.

Next, we call the `GetAsync` method to verify that everything works as expected:

```
var result = await sqlController.GetAsync(CancellationToken.None);
```

Finally, let's verify we received that collection of one object:

```
Assert.Collection(result,
    location =>
    {
        Assert.Equal(ExpectedLocation.Id, location.Id);
        Assert.Equal(ExpectedLocation.Name, location.Name);
    }
);
```

Optionally, or instead, we could validate the service called the database mock, like this:

```
databaseMock.Verify(x => x
    .ReadManyAsync<Location>(
        It.IsAny<string>(),
        It.IsAny<CancellationToken>()
    ),
    Times.Once()
);
```

There are a lot of useful features in the Moq library.

Validating that the code is correct is not important for this example. The key is to understand the composition of the controller, which the following diagram represents:

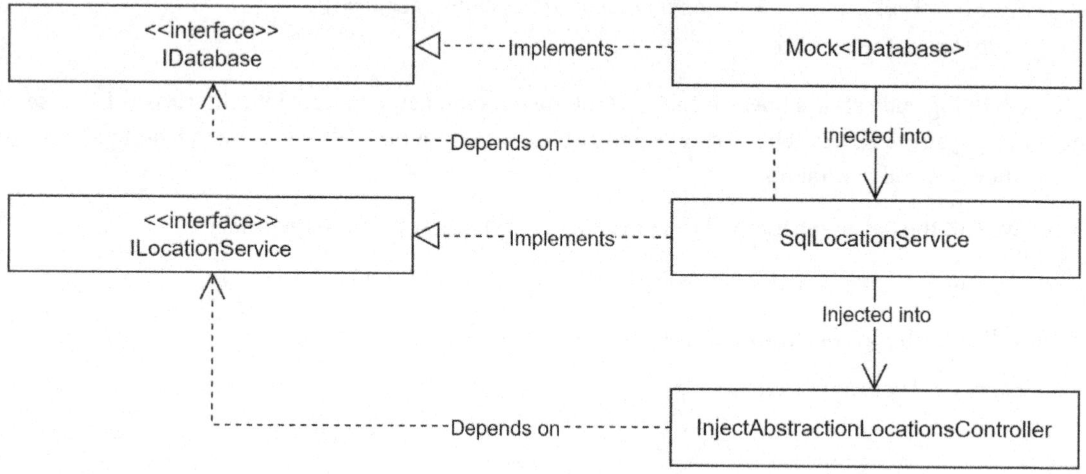

Figure 8.7: Composition of the controller in a test that mocks the IDatabase interface

As we can see from the diagram, the classes depend on interfaces, and we inject implementations when building them.

Let's conclude before our next subject.

Conclusion

In this section, we saw that the strategy pattern went from a simple behavioral GoF pattern to the cornerstone of DI. We explored different ways of injecting dependencies with a strong focus on constructor injection.

Constructor injection is the most commonly used approach as it injects required dependencies, which we want the most. Method injection allows injecting algorithms, shared states, or contexts in a method that could not otherwise access that information. We can use property injection to inject optional dependencies, which should rarely happen and be avoided if possible.

You can see optional dependencies as code smells because if the class has an optional role to play, it also has a primary role resulting in dual responsibilities. Moreover, if a role is optional, it could be better to move it to another class or rethink the system's design in that specific area.

To practice what you just learned, you could connect the code sample to a real database, an Azure Table, Redis, a JSON file, or any other data source. As a starting point, you can create a class that implements the `ILocationService` interface for each data source you want to connect to.

As we covered, we can inject classes into other classes directly. There is nothing wrong with that. However, I suggest injecting interfaces as your initial approach until you are confident that you have mastered the different architectural principles and patterns covered in this book.

Next, we revisit an (anti-)pattern while exploring the singleton lifetime replacing it.

Revisiting the Singleton pattern

The Singleton pattern is obsolete, goes against the SOLID principles, and we replace it with a lifetime, as we've already seen. This section explores that lifetime and recreates the good old application state, which is nothing more than a singleton-scoped dictionary.

We explore two examples: one about the application state, in case you were wondering where that feature disappeared to. Then, the Wishlist project also uses the singleton lifetime to provide an application-level feature. There are also a few unit tests to play with testability and to allow safe refactoring.

Project – Application state

You might remember the application state if you programmed ASP.NET using .NET Framework or the "good" old classic ASP with VBScript. If you don't, the application state was a key/value dictionary that allowed you to store data globally in your application, shared between all sessions and requests. That is one of the things that ASP always had and other languages, such as PHP, did not (or do not easily allow).

For example, I remember designing a generic reusable typed shopping cart system with classic ASP/VBScript. VBScript was not a strongly typed language and had limited object-oriented capabilities. The shopping cart fields and types were defined at the application level (once per application), and then each user had their own "instance" containing the products in their "private shopping cart" (created once per session).

In ASP.NET Core, there is no more `Application` dictionary. To achieve the same goal, you could use a static class or static members, which is not the best approach; remember that global objects (`static`) make your application harder to test and less flexible. We could also use the Singleton pattern or create an ambient context, allowing us to create an application-level instance of an object. We could even mix that with a factory to create end user shopping carts, but we won't; these are not the best solution either.

For most cases requiring an application state-like feature, the best approach would be to create a standard class and an interface and then register the binding with a singleton lifetime in the container. Finally, you inject it into the component that needs it, using constructor injection. Doing so allows the mocking of dependencies and changing the implementations without touching the code but the composition root.

Sometimes, the best solution is not the technically complex ones or design pattern-oriented; the best solution is often the simplest. Less code means less maintenance and fewer tests, resulting in a simpler application.

Let's implement a small program that simulates the application state. The API is a single interface with two implementations. The program also exposes part of the API over HTTP, allowing users to get or set a value associated with the specified key. We use the singleton lifetime to ensure the data is shared between all requests.

The interface looks like the following:

```
public interface IApplicationState
{
    TItem? Get<TItem>(string key);
    bool Has<TItem>(string key);
    void Set<TItem>(string key, TItem value) where TItem : notnull;
}
```

We can get the value associated with a key, associate a value with a key (set), and validate whether a key exists.

The `Program.cs` file contains the code responsible for handling HTTP requests. We can swap the implementations by commenting or uncommenting the first line of the `Program.cs` file, which is `#define USE_MEMORY_CACHE`. That changes the dependency registration, as highlighted in the following code:

```
var builder = WebApplication.CreateBuilder(args);
#if USE_MEMORY_CACHE
        builder.Services.AddMemoryCache();
        builder.Services.AddSingleton<IApplicationState,
ApplicationMemoryCache>();
#else
        builder.Services.AddSingleton<IApplicationState,
ApplicationDictionary>();
#endif
var app = builder.Build();
app.MapGet("/", (IApplicationState myAppState, string key) =>
{
    var value = myAppState.Get<string>(key);
    return $"{key} = {value ?? "null"}";
});
app.MapPost("/", (IApplicationState myAppState, SetAppState dto) =>
{
    myAppState.Set(dto.Key, dto.Value);
    return $"{dto.Key} = {dto.Value}";
});
app.Run();
public record class SetAppState(string Key, string Value);
```

Let's now explore the first implementation.

First implementation

The first implementation uses the memory cache system, and I thought it would be educational to show that to you. Caching data in memory is something you might need to do sooner rather than later. However, we are hiding the cache system behind our implementation, which is also educational.

You must register the memory cache by adding the following line to your `Program.cs` file:

```
builder.Services.AddMemoryCache();
```

Here is the `ApplicationMemoryCache` class:

```
public class ApplicationMemoryCache : IApplicationState
{
    private readonly IMemoryCache _memoryCache;
    public ApplicationMemoryCache(IMemoryCache memoryCache)
    {
        _memoryCache = memoryCache ?? throw new
ArgumentNullException(nameof(memoryCache));
    }
    public TItem Get<TItem>(string key)
    {
        return _memoryCache.Get<TItem>(key);
    }
    public bool Has<TItem>(string key)
    {
        return _memoryCache.TryGetValue<TItem>(key, out _);
    }
    public void Set<TItem>(string key, TItem value)
    {
        _memoryCache.Set(key, value);
    }
}
```

The `ApplicationMemoryCache` class is a thin wrapper over `IMemoryCache`, hiding the implementation details. Such a wrapper is similar to the Façade and Adapter patterns we explore in *Chapter 11, Structural Patterns*.

This simple class and two lines in our composition root make it an application-wide key-value store; done already! Let's now explore the second implementation.

Second implementation

The second implementation uses `ConcurrentDictionary<string, object>` to store the application state data and ensure thread safety, as multiple users could use the application state simultaneously. The `ApplicationDictionary` class is almost as simple as `ApplicationMemoryCache`:

```
using System.Collections.Concurrent;
namespace ApplicationState;
public class ApplicationDictionary : IApplicationState
{
    private readonly ConcurrentDictionary<string, object> _cache = new();

    public TItem? Get<TItem>(string key)
    {
        return _cache.TryGetValue(key, out var item)
            ? (TItem)item
            : default;
    }

    public bool Has<TItem>(string key)
    {
        return _cache.TryGetValue(key, out var item) && item is TItem;
    }

    public void Set<TItem>(string key, TItem value)
        where TItem : notnull
    {
        _cache.AddOrUpdate(key, value, (k, v) => value);
    }
}
```

The preceding code leverages the `TryGetValue` and `AddOrUpdate` methods to ensure thread safety while keeping the logic to a minimum and ensuring we avoid coding mistakes.

Can you spot the flaw that might cause some problems in this design? See the solution at the end of the project section.

Let's explore how to use the implementations.

Using the implementations

We can now use any of the two implementations without impacting the rest of the program. That demonstrates the strength of DI when it comes to dependency management. Moreover, we control the lifetime of the dependencies from the composition root.

If we were to use the `IApplicationState` interface in another class, say `SomeConsumer`, its usage could look similar to the following:

```
namespace ApplicationState;
public class SomeConsumer
{
    private readonly IApplicationState _myApplicationWideService;
    public SomeConsumer(IApplicationState myApplicationWideService)
    {
        _myApplicationWideService = myApplicationWideService ?? throw new
ArgumentNullException(nameof(myApplicationWideService));
    }
    public void Execute()
    {
        if (_myApplicationWideService.Has<string>("some-key"))
        {
            var someValue = _myApplicationWideService.Get<string>("some-key");
            // Do something with someValue
        }
        // Do something else like:
        _myApplicationWideService.Set("some-key", "some-value");
        // More logic here
    }
}
```

In that code, `SomeConsumer` depends only on the `IApplicationState` interface, not `ApplicationDictionary` or `ApplicationMemoryCache`, and even less on `IMemoryCache` or `ConcurrentDictionary<string, object>`. Using DI allows us to hide the implementation by inverting the flow of dependencies. It also breaks direct coupling between concrete implementations. This approach also promotes programming against interfaces, as recommended by the DIP, and facilitates the creation of open-closed classes, in accordance with the **Open/Closed Principle** (OCP).

Here is a diagram illustrating our application state system, making it visually easier to notice how it breaks coupling:

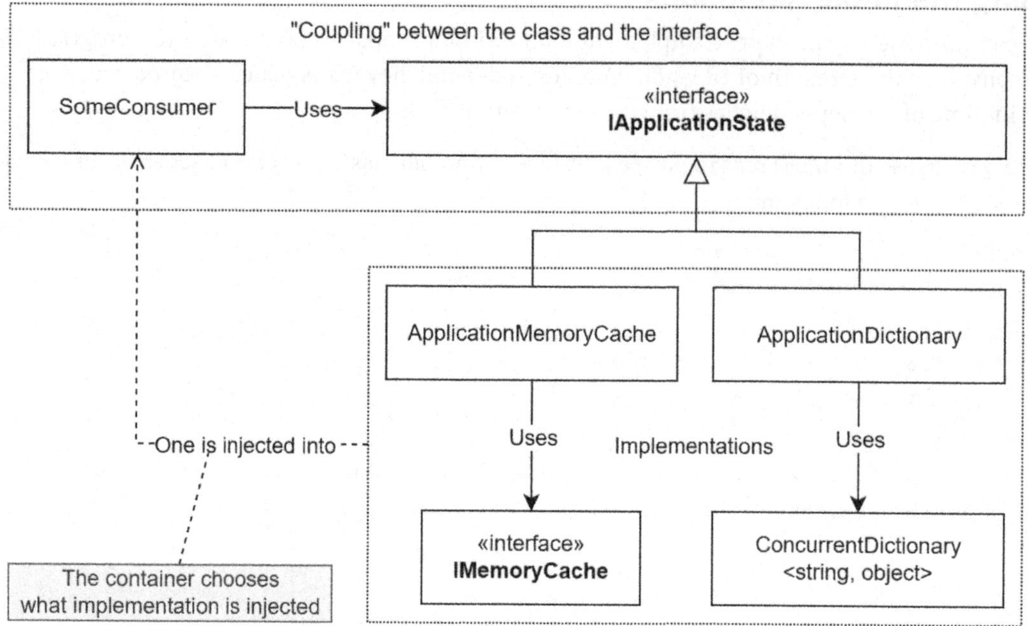

Figure 8.8: DI-oriented diagram representing the application state system

From this sample, let's remember that the singleton lifetime allows us to reuse objects between requests and share them application-wide. Moreover, hiding implementation details behind interfaces can improve the flexibility of our design.

It is important to note that the singleton scope is only valid in a single process, so you can't rely purely on in-memory mechanisms for larger applications that span multiple servers. We could use the `IDistributedCache` interface to circumvent this limitation and persist our application state system to a persistent caching tool, like Redis.

The flaw: If we look closely at the `Has<TItem>` method, it returns true only when an entry is present for the specified key AND has the right type. So, we could override an entry of a different type without knowing it exists.

For example, `ConsumerA` sets an item of type `A` for the key `K`. Elsewhere in the code, `ConsumerB` looks to see if an item of type `B` exists for the key `K`. The method returns `false` because it's a different type. `ConsumerB` overrides the value of the `K` with an object of type `B`. Here's the code representing this:

```
// Arrange
var sp = new ServiceCollection()
    .AddSingleton<IApplicationState, ApplicationDictionary>()
    .BuildServiceProvider()
;

// Step 1: Consumer A sets a string
var consumerA = sp.GetRequiredService<IApplicationState>();
consumerA.Set("K", "A");
Assert.True(consumerA.Has<string>("K")); // true

// Step 2: Consumer B overrides the value with an int
var consumerB = sp.GetRequiredService<IApplicationState>();
if (!consumerB.Has<int>("K")) // Oops, key K exists but it's of
type string, not int
{
    consumerB.Set("K", 123);
}
Assert.True(consumerB.Has<int>("K")); // true

// Consumer A is broken!
Assert.False(consumerA.Has<string>("K")); // false
```

Improving the design to support such a scenario could be a good practice exercise. You could, for example, remove the `TItem` type from the `Has` method or, even better, allow storing multiple items under the same key, as long as their types are different.

Let's now explore the next project.

Project – Wishlist

Let's get into another sample to illustrate using the singleton lifetime and DI. Seeing DI in action should help understand it and then leverage it to create SOLID software.

Context: The application is a site-wide wishlist where users can add items. Items expire every 30 seconds. When a user adds an existing item, the system must increment the count and reset the item's expiration time. That way, popular items stay on the list longer, making it to the top. When displayed, the system must sort the items by count (highest count first).

An expiration time of 30 seconds is very fast, but I'm sure you don't want to wait days before an item expires when running the app. It is a test config.

The program is a tiny web API that exposes two endpoints:

- Add an item to the wishlist (`POST`)
- Read the wishlist (`GET`)

The wishlist interface looks like this:

```
public interface IWishList
{
    Task<WishListItem> AddOrRefreshAsync(string itemName);
    Task<IEnumerable<WishListItem>> AllAsync();
}
public record class WishListItem(string Name, int Count, DateTimeOffset
Expiration);
```

The two operations are there, and by making them async (returning a `Task<T>`), we could implement another version that relies on a remote system, such as a database, instead of an in-memory store. Then, the `WishListItem` record class is part of the `IWishList` contract. To keep it simple, the wishlist only stores the names of items.

Trying to foresee the future is not usually a good idea, but designing APIs to be awaitable is generally a safe bet. Other than this, I'd recommend you stick to the simplest code that satisfies the program's needs (KISS). When you try to solve problems that do not exist yet, you usually end up coding a lot of useless stuff, leading to additional unnecessary maintenance and testing time.

In the composition root, we must serve the `IWishList` implementation instance in a singleton scope (highlighted) so all requests share the same instance. Let's start with the first half of the `Program.cs` file:

```
var builder = WebApplication.CreateBuilder(args);
builder.Services
    .AddSingleton<InMemoryWishListOptions>()
    .AddSingleton<IWishList, InMemoryWishList>()
;
```

Let's now look at the second half of the `Program.cs` file that contains the minimal API code to handle the HTTP requests:

```
var app = builder.Build();
app.MapGet("/", async (IWishList wishList) =>
    await wishList.AllAsync());
app.MapPost("/", async (IWishList wishList, CreateItem? newItem) =>
{
    if (newItem?.Name == null)
    {
        return Results.BadRequest();
    }
    var item = await wishList.AddOrRefreshAsync(newItem.Name);
    return Results.Created("/", item);
});
app.Run();
public record class CreateItem(string? Name);
```

The `GET` endpoint delegates the logic to the injected `IWishList` implementation and returns the result, while the `POST` endpoint validates the `CreateItem` DTO before delegating the logic to the wishlist.

To help us implement the `InMemoryWishList` class, we started by writing some tests to back our specifications up. Since static members are hard to configure in tests (remember globals?), I borrowed a concept from the ASP.NET Core memory cache and created an `ISystemClock` interface that abstracts away the static call to `DateTimeOffset.UtcNow` or `DateTime.UtcNow`. This way, we can program the value of `UtcNow` in our tests to create expired items. Here's the clock interface and implementation:

```
namespace Wishlist.Internal;
public interface ISystemClock
{
    DateTimeOffset UtcNow { get; }
}
public class SystemClock : ISystemClock
{
    public DateTimeOffset UtcNow => DateTimeOffset.UtcNow;
}
```

.NET 8 adds a new `TimeProvider` class to the `System` namespace, which does not help us much here. However, if we want to leverage that API, we could update the `SystemClock` class to the following:

```
public class CustomClock : ISystemClock
{
    private readonly TimeProvider _timeProvider;
    public CustomClock(TimeProvider timeProvider)
    {
        _timeProvider = timeProvider ?? throw new
ArgumentNullException(nameof(timeProvider));
    }
    public DateTimeOffset UtcNow => _timeProvider.GetUtcNow();
}
```

The preceding code leverages the new API by injecting a `TimeProvider` object into the constructor. That change would only complicate the code, so we'll stick to our simple implementation instead.

Let's look at the outline of the unit tests next because the whole code would take pages and be of low value:

```
namespace Wishlist;
public class InMemoryWishListTest
{
    // Constructor and private fields omitted
    public class AddOrRefreshAsync : InMemoryWishListTest
    {
        [Fact]
        public async Task Should_create_new_item();
        [Fact]
        public async Task Should_increment_Count_of_an_existing_item();
        [Fact]
        public async Task Should_set_the_new_Expiration_date_of_an_existing_
item();
        [Fact]
        public async Task Should_set_the_Count_of_expired_items_to_1();
        [Fact]
        public async Task Should_remove_expired_items();
    }
    public class AllAsync : InMemoryWishListTest
    {
```

```
        [Fact]
        public async Task Should_return_items_ordered_by_Count_Descending();
        [Fact]
        public async Task Should_not_return_expired_items();
    }
    // Private helper methods omitted
}
```

The full source code is on GitHub: `https://adpg.link/d4HR`. In the test class, we can mock the `ISystemClock` interface and program it to obtain the desired results based on each test case. We can also program some helper methods to make it easier to read the tests. Those helpers use tuples to return multiple values (see the *Appendix* on GitHub—`https://adpg.link/net8-appendix`—for more information on language features).

Here's the mock field:

```
private readonly Mock<ISystemClock> _systemClockMock = new();
```

Here's an example of such a helper method setting the clock to the present time and the `ExpectedExpiryTime` to a later time (`UtcNow + ExpirationInSeconds` later):

```
private (DateTimeOffset UtcNow, DateTimeOffset ExpectedExpiryTime) SetUtcNow()
{
    var utcNow = DateTimeOffset.UtcNow;
    _systemClockMock.Setup(x => x.UtcNow).Returns(utcNow);
    var expectedExpiryTime = utcNow.AddSeconds(_options.ExpirationInSeconds);
    return (utcNow, expectedExpiryTime);
}
```

Here is an example of another helper method setting the clock and the `ExpectedExpiryTime` to the past (two-time `ExpirationInSeconds` for the clock and once `ExpirationInSeconds` for the `ExpectedExpiryTime`):

```
private (DateTimeOffset UtcNow, DateTimeOffset ExpectedExpiryTime)
SetUtcNowToExpired()
{
    var delay = -(_options.ExpirationInSeconds * 2);
    var utcNow = DateTimeOffset.UtcNow.AddSeconds(delay);
    _systemClockMock.Setup(x => x.UtcNow).Returns(utcNow);
    var expectedExpiryTime = utcNow.AddSeconds(_options.ExpirationInSeconds);
    return (utcNow, expectedExpiryTime);
}
```

We have five tests covering the `AddOrRefreshAsync` method and two covering the `AllAsync` method. Here is the implementation of the `InMemoryWishList` class:

```
namespace Wishlist;
public class InMemoryWishList : IWishList
{
    private readonly InMemoryWishListOptions _options;
    private readonly ConcurrentDictionary<string, InternalItem> _items = new();
    public InMemoryWishList(InMemoryWishListOptions options)
    {
        _options = options ?? throw new ArgumentNullException(nameof(options));
    }
    public Task<WishListItem> AddOrRefreshAsync(string itemName)
    {
        // Remove expired items
        var expirationTime = _options.SystemClock.UtcNow.AddSeconds(_options.
ExpirationInSeconds);
        _items
            .Where(x => x.Value.Expiration < _options.SystemClock.UtcNow)
            .Select(x => x.Key)
            .ToList()
            .ForEach(key => _items.Remove(key, out _))
        ;

        // Add the item or update the count
        var item = _items.AddOrUpdate(
            itemName,
            new InternalItem(Count: 1, Expiration: expirationTime),
            (string key, InternalItem item) => item with {
                Count = item.Count + 1,
                Expiration = expirationTime
            }
        );

        // Convert the InternalItem to a WishListItem
        var wishlistItem = new WishListItem(
            Name: itemName,
            Count: item.Count,
            Expiration: item.Expiration
        );
        return Task.FromResult(wishlistItem);
    }
```

```
    public Task<IEnumerable<WishListItem>> AllAsync()
    {
        var items = _items
            // Filter out the expired items
            .Where(x => x.Value.Expiration >= _options.SystemClock.UtcNow)
            // Project InternalItem to WishListItem
            .Select(x => new WishListItem(
                Name: x.Key,
                Count: x.Value.Count,
                Expiration: x.Value.Expiration
            ))
            .OrderByDescending(x => x.Count)
            .AsEnumerable()
        ;
        return Task.FromResult(items);
    }
    private record class InternalItem(int Count, DateTimeOffset Expiration);
}
```

The `InMemoryWishList` class uses `ConcurrentDictionary<string, InternalItem>` internally to store the items and make the wishlist thread-safe. It also uses a `with` expression to manipulate and copy the `InternalItem` record class.

The `AllAsync` method filters out expired items, while the `AddOrRefreshAsync` method removes expired items. This might not be the most advanced logic ever, but that does the trick.

You might have noticed that the code is not the most elegant of all, and I left it this way on purpose. While using the test suite, I invite you to refactor the methods of the `InMemoryWishList` class to be more readable.

I took a few minutes to refactor it myself and saved it as `InMemoryWishListRefactored`. You can also uncomment the first line of `InMemoryWishListTest.cs` to test that class instead of the main one. My refactoring is a way to make the code cleaner and to give you ideas. It is not the only way, nor the best way, to write that class (the "best way" being subjective).

Lastly, optimizing for readability and performance are often very different things.

Back to DI, the line that makes the wishlist shared between users is in the composition root we explored earlier. As a reference, here it is:

```
builder.Services.AddSingleton<IWishList, InMemoryWishList>();
```

Yes, only that line makes all the difference between creating multiple instances and a single shared instance. Setting the lifetime to Singleton allows you to open multiple browsers and share the wishlist.

To `POST` to the API, I recommend using the `Wishlist.http` file in the project. You can also use the Swagger UI that I added to the project.

That's it! All that code to demo what a single line of code in the composition root can do, and we have a working program, as tiny as it may be.

Conclusion

This section explored replacing the classic Singleton pattern with a standard instantiable class registered with a singleton lifetime. We looked at the old application state, learned that it was no more, and implemented two versions of it. We no longer need that, but it was a good way of learning about singletons.

We then implemented a wishlist system as a second example. We concluded that the whole thing was managed by and working due to a single line of the composition root: the call to the `AddSingleton` method. Changing that line could drastically change the system's behavior, making it unusable.

The Singleton pattern is an anti-pattern in .NET, and unless you find strong reasons to implement it, you should stick to normal classes and DI instead. Doing this moves the creation responsibility from the singleton class to the IoC container and the configuration to the composition root, leaving the class with only one responsibility.

Next, we explore guard clauses.

Understanding guard clauses

A guard clause represents a condition the code must meet before executing a method. Essentially, it's a type of code that "guards" against continuing the execution of the method if certain conditions aren't met.

In most cases, guard clauses are implemented at the beginning of a method to throw an exception early when the conditions necessary for the method's execution are not satisfied. Throwing an exception allows callers to catch the error without the need to implement a more complex communication mechanism.

We already stated that we use constructor injection to inject the required dependencies reliably. However, nothing fully guarantees us that the dependencies are not `null`. Ensuring a dependency is not `null` is one of the most common guard clauses, which is trivial to implement. For example, we could check for nulls in the controller by replacing the following:

```
_locationService = locationService;
```

With the following:

```
_locationService = locationService ?? throw new
ArgumentNullException(nameof(locationService));
```

The preceding code uses a `throw` expression from C# 7 (See the *Appendix on GitHub* for more information). The `ArgumentNullException` type makes it evident that the `locationService` parameter is `null`. So, if the `locationService` parameter is `null`, an `ArgumentNullException` is thrown; otherwise, the `locationService` parameter is assigned to the `_locationService` member.

Of course, with the introduction of the nullable reference types (see the *Appendix* on GitHub—`https://adpg.link/net8-appendix`), receiving a `null` argument is less likely yet still possible.

The built-in container will automatically throw an exception if it can't fulfill all dependencies during the instantiation of a class (such as a controller). That does not mean that all third-party containers act the same.

Moreover, that does not protect you from passing `null` to a class you manually instantiate, nor that a method will not receive a `null` value. I recommend adding guards even though they are less mandatory now. The tooling can handle most of the work for us, leading to only a minor time overhead.

Furthermore, suppose you are writing code consumed by other projects, like a library. In that case, adding guards is more important since nothing guarantees that the consumers of that code have nullable reference type checks enabled.

When we need to validate a parameter and don't need an assignment, like with most parameters of a constructor, we can use the following helper, and the BCL handles the check for us:

```
ArgumentNullException.ThrowIfNull(locationService);
```

When we need to validate a string and want to ensure it is not empty, we can use the following instead:

```
ArgumentException.ThrowIfNullOrEmpty(name);
```

Of course, we can always revert to `if` statements to validate parameters. When doing so, we must ensure we throw relevant exceptions. If no pertinent exceptions exist, we can create one. Creating custom exceptions is a great way to write manageable applications.

Next, we explore the Service Locator anti-pattern/code smell.

Understanding the Service Locator pattern

Service Locator is an anti-pattern that reverts the IoC principle to its Control Freak roots. The only difference is that you use the IoC container to build the dependency tree instead of the `new` keyword.

There is some use of this pattern in ASP.NET, and we may argue that there are some reasons for using the Service Locator pattern, but it should happen rarely or never in most applications. For that reason, let's call the Service Locator pattern a **code smell** instead of an **anti-pattern**.

My strong recommendation is *don't use the Service Locator pattern* unless you know you are not creating hidden coupling or have no other option.

As a rule of thumb, you want to avoid injecting an `IServiceProvider` in your application's code base. Doing so reverts to the classic flow of control and defeats the purpose of DI.

A good use of Service Locator could be to migrate a legacy system that is too big to rewrite. So, you could build the new code using DI and update the legacy code using the Service Locator pattern, allowing both systems to live together or migrate one into the other, depending on your goal.

Fetching dependencies dynamically is another potential use of the Service Locator pattern; we explore this in *Chapter 15, Object Mappers*.

Without further ado, let's jump into some more code.

Project – ServiceLocator

The best way to avoid something is to know about it, so let's see how to implement the Service Locator pattern using `IServiceProvider` to find a dependency.

The service we want to use is an implementation of `IMyService`. Let's start with the interface:

```
namespace ServiceLocator;
public interface IMyService : IDisposable
{
    void Execute();
}
```

The interface inherits from the `IDisposable` interface and contains a single `Execute` method. Here is the implementation, which does nothing more than throw an exception if the instance has been disposed of (we leverage this later):

```
namespace ServiceLocator;
public class MyServiceImplementation : IMyService
{
    private bool _isDisposed = false;
    public void Dispose() => _isDisposed = true;
    public void Execute()
    {
        if (_isDisposed)
        {
            throw new NullReferenceException("Some dependencies have been
disposed.");
        }
    }
}
```

Then, let's add a controller that implements the Service Locator pattern:

```
namespace ServiceLocator;
public class MyController : ControllerBase
{
    private readonly IServiceProvider _serviceProvider;
    public MyController(IServiceProvider serviceProvider)
    {
        _serviceProvider = serviceProvider ?? throw new
ArgumentNullException(nameof(serviceProvider));
    }
    [Route("/service-locator")]
    public IActionResult Get()
    {
        using var myService = _serviceProvider
            .GetRequiredService<IMyService>();
        myService.Execute();
        return Ok("Success!");
    }
}
```

In the preceding code, instead of injecting `IMyService` into the constructor, we are injecting `IServiceProvider`. Then, we use it (highlighted line) to locate the `IMyService` instance. Doing so shifts the responsibility for creating the object from the container to the consumer (`MyController`, in this case). `MyController` should not be aware of `IServiceProvider` and should let the container do its job without interference.

To run the application, we must register our dependencies in the `Program.cs` file, as follows:

```
var builder = WebApplication.CreateBuilder(args);
builder.Services
    .AddSingleton<IMyService, MyServiceImplementation>()
    .AddControllers()
;
var app = builder.Build();
app.MapControllers();
app.Run();
```

The preceding code enables controller support and registers our service.

What could go wrong when running the program? If we run the application and navigate to `/service-locator`, everything works as expected. However, if we reload the page, we get an error thrown by the `Execute` method because the `using` declaration implicitly called the `Dispose()` method. `MyController` should not control the lifetime of its dependencies, but it is, because of the Service Locator pattern, which is the point that I am trying to emphasize: leave the container to control the lifetime of dependencies rather than trying to be a control freak. Using the Service Locator pattern opens pathways toward those wrong behaviors, which will likely cause more harm than good in the long run.

Moreover, even though the ASP.NET Core container does not natively support this, we lose the ability to inject dependencies contextually when using the Service Locator pattern because the consumer controls its dependencies. What do I mean by contextually? Let's assume we have two classes, `A` and `B`, implementing interface `I`. We could inject an instance of `A` into `Consumer1` but an instance of `B` into `Consumer2`.

To fix the controller, we must either remove the using statement or even better: move away from the Service Locator pattern and inject our dependencies instead. Of course, you are reading a DI chapter, so I picked moving away from the Service Locator pattern. Here's what we are about to tackle:

- Method injection
- Constructor injection
- Minimal API

Let's start with method injection.

Implementing method injection

The following controller uses *method injection* instead of the Service Locator pattern. Here's the code that demonstrates this:

```
public class MethodInjectionController : ControllerBase
{
    [Route("/method-injection")]
    public IActionResult GetUsingMethodInjection([FromServices] IMyService
myService)
    {
        ArgumentNullException.ThrowIfNull(myService, nameof(myService));
        myService.Execute();
        return Ok("Success!");
    }
}
```

Let's analyze the code:

- The `[FromServices]` attribute tells the model binder about method injection
- We added a guard clause to protect us from `null`
- Finally, we kept the original code except for the `using` statement

Method injection like this is convenient when a controller has multiple actions but only one uses the service.

Let's reexplore constructor injection.

Implementing constructor injection

At this point, you should be familiar with constructor injection. Nonetheless, next is the controller's code after migrating the Service Locator pattern to constructor injection:

```
namespace ServiceLocator;
public class ConstructorInjectionController : ControllerBase
{
    private readonly IMyService _myService;
    public ConstructorInjectionController(IMyService myService)
    {
        _myService = myService ?? throw new
ArgumentNullException(nameof(myService));
    }
    [Route("/constructor-injection")]
    public IActionResult GetUsingConstructorInjection()
    {
        _myService.Execute();
        return Ok("Success!");
    }
}
```

When using constructor injection, we ensure that `IMyService` is not `null` upon class instantiation. Since it is a class member, it is even less tempting to call its `Dispose()` method in an action method, leaving that responsibility to the container (as it should be).

Let's analyze the code before moving to the next possibility:

- We implemented the strategy pattern with constructor injection
- We added a guard clause to ensure no `null` value could get in at runtime
- We simplified the action to the bare minimum

Both techniques are an acceptable replacement for the Service Locator pattern.

Implementing a minimal API

Of course, we can do the same with a minimal API. Here is the code of that endpoint:

```
app.MapGet("/minimal-api", (IMyService myService) =>
```

```
{
    myService.Execute();
    return "Success!";
});
```

That code does the same as the method injection sample without the guard clause that I omitted because no external consumer will likely inject nulls into it: the endpoint is a delegate passed directly to the `MapGet` method.

Refactoring out the Service Locator pattern is often as trivial as this.

Conclusion

Most of the time, by following the Service Locator anti-pattern, we only hide that we are taking control of objects instead of decoupling our components. The code sample demonstrated a problem when disposing of an object, which could also happen using constructor injection. However, when thinking about it, it is more tempting to dispose of an object that we create than one we inject.

Moreover, the service locator takes control away from the container and moves it into the consumer, against the OCP. You should be able to update the consumer by updating the composition root's bindings.

In the case of the sample code, we could change the binding, and it would work. In a more advanced case, binding two implementations to the same interface and injecting them contextually depending on the class it is injected in can be quite tough with the built-in container.

The IoC container is responsible for weaving the program's thread, connecting its pieces together where each independent piece should be as clueless as possible about the others.

On top of that, the Service Locator pattern complicates testing. When unit testing your class, you must mock a container that returns a mocked service instead of mocking only the service.

One place where I can see its usage justified is in the composition root, where bindings are defined, and sometimes, especially when using the built-in container, we can't avoid it to compensate for the lack of advanced features. Another good place would be a library that adds functionalities to the container. Other than that, try to stay away!

Beware

Moving the service locator elsewhere does not make it disappear; it only moves it around, like any dependency. However, moving it to the composition root can improve the maintainability of that code and remove the tight coupling.

Next, we revisit our third and final pattern of this chapter.

Revisiting the Factory pattern

A factory creates other objects; it is like a literal real-world factory. We explored in the previous chapter how to leverage the Abstract Factory pattern to create families of objects. A factory can be as simple as an interface with one or more `Create[Object]` methods or, even more, a simple delegate. We explore a DI-oriented simple factory in this section. We are building on top of the Strategy pattern example.

In that example, we coded two classes implementing the `ILocationService` interface. The composition root used the `#define` preprocessor directive to tell the compiler what bindings to compile. In this version, we want to choose the implementation at runtime.

Not compiling the code we don't need is good for many reasons, including security (lowering the attack surface). In this case, we are simply using an alternative strategy useful for many scenarios.

To achieve our new goal, we can extract the construction logic of the `ILocationService` interface into a factory.

Project – Factory

In the project, a copy from the Strategy project, we start by renaming the `InjectAbstractionLocationsController` class to `LocationsController`. We can then delete the other controllers.

Now, we want to change the `ILocationService` bindings to reflect the following logic:

- When developing the application, we use the `InMemoryLocationService` class
- When deploying to any environment, we must use the `SqlLocationService` class

To achieve this, we use the `Environment` property of the `WebApplicationBuilder` object. That property of type `IWebHostEnvironment` contains some useful properties like the `EnvironmentName`, and .NET adds extension methods, like the `IsDevelopment` method that returns true when the `EnvironmentName` equals `Development`. Here's the `Program.cs` file code:

```
using Factory.Data;
using Factory.Services;
var builder = WebApplication.CreateBuilder(args);
builder.Services.AddControllers();

builder.Services.AddSingleton<ILocationService>(sp =>
{
    if (builder.Environment.IsDevelopment())
    {
        return new InMemoryLocationService();
    }
    return new SqlLocationService(new NotImplementedDatabase());
```

```
});

var app = builder.Build();
app.MapControllers();
app.Run();
```

The preceding code is fairly straightforward; it registers a delegate to act as a factory, which builds the appropriate service based on the ASP.NET Core **Environment**.

We are using the `new` keyword here, but is this wrong? The composition root is where we should create or configure elements, so instantiating objects there is correct, as it is to use the Service Locator pattern. It is best to avoid the `new` keyword and the Service Locator pattern whenever possible, but using the default container makes it harder than with a full-featured third-party one. Nevertheless, we can avoid doing that in many cases, and even if we must use the `new` keyword and the Service Locator pattern, we often don't need a third-party container.

When we run the program, the right instance is injected into the controller based on the logic we added to the factory. The flow is similar to the following:

1. The application starts.
2. A client sends an HTTP request to the controller (`GET /travel/locations`).
3. ASP.NET Core creates the controller and leverages the IoC container to inject the `ILocationService` dependency.
4. Our factory creates the correct instance based on the current environment.
5. The action method runs, and the client receives the response.

We could also create a factory class and an interface, as explored in the previous chapter. However, in this case, it would likely just create noise.

An essential thing to remember is that *moving code around your codebase does not make that code, logic, dependencies, or coupling disappear*. Coding a factory doesn't make all your design issues disappear. Moreover, adding more complexity adds a cost to your project, so factory or not, each time you try to break tight coupling or remove a dependency, ensure that you are not just moving the responsibility elsewhere or overengineering your solution.

Of course, to keep our composition root clean, we could create an extension method that does the registration, like an `AddLocationService` method. I'll leave you to try this one out, find other ways to improve the project, or even improve one of your own projects.

The possibilities are almost endless when you think about the Factory patterns. Now that you've seen a few in action, you may find other uses for a factory when injecting some classes with complex instantiation logic into other objects.

Summary

This chapter delved into DI, understanding its crucial role in crafting adaptable systems. We learned how DI applies the IoC principle, shifting dependency creation from the objects to the composition root. We explored the IoC container's role in object management, service resolution and injection, and dependency lifetime management. We tackled the Control Freak anti-pattern, advocating for DI over using the `new` keyword.

We revisited the Strategy pattern and explored how to use it with DI to compose complex object trees. We learned about the principle of composition over inheritance, which encourages us to inject dependencies into the classes instead of relying on base class features and inheritance. We explored different ways of injecting dependencies into objects, including constructor injection, property injection, and method injection.

We learned that a guard clause is a condition that must be met before a method is executed, often used to prevent null dependencies. We explored how to implement guard clauses. We also discussed the importance of adding guard clauses, as nullable reference type checks offer no guarantee at runtime.

We revisited the Singleton pattern and how to replace it with a lifetime. We explored two examples utilizing the singleton lifetime to provide application-level features.

We delved into the Service Locator pattern, often considered an anti-pattern, as it can create hidden coupling and revert the IoC principle. We learned that avoiding using the Service Locator pattern is generally best. We explored how to implement the Service Locator pattern and discussed the potential issues that could arise.

We revisited the Factory pattern and learned how to build a simple, DI-oriented factory that replaces the object creation logic of the IoC container.

Here are the key takeaways from this substantial chapter:

- DI is a technique applying the IoC principle for effective dependency management and lifetime control.
- An IoC container resolves and manages dependencies, offering varying control over object behavior.
- We can categorize dependencies into stable and volatile, the latter justifying DI.
- The lifetime of a service is Transient, Scoped, or Singleton.
- DI allows us to avoid the Control Freak anti-pattern and stop creating objects with the `new` keyword, improving flexibility and testability.
- The Service Locator pattern often creates hidden coupling and should be avoided but in the composition root.
- The composition root is where we register our service bindings with the IoC container; in the `Program.cs` file.
- Composing objects using the Strategy pattern alongside constructor injection facilitates handling complex object trees, emphasizing the principle of composition over inheritance.

- On top of constructor injection, there's also method injection and property injection, which are less supported. It is best to prioritize constructor injection over the others.
- Guard clauses safeguard method execution from unmet conditions.
- It is better to avoid the Singleton pattern in favor of binding a class and an interface with a singleton lifetime in the container.
- The Factory pattern is ideal for creating objects with complex instantiation logic.
- Moving code around doesn't eliminate dependencies or coupling; it's important not to overengineer solutions.

In subsequent sections, we explore tools that add functionalities to the default built-in container. Meanwhile, we explore options, settings, and configurations in the next chapter. These ASP.NET Core patterns aim to make our lives easier when managing such common problems.

Questions

Let's take a look at a few practice questions:

1. What are the three DI lifetimes that we can assign to objects in ASP.NET Core?
2. What is the composition root for?
3. Is it true that we should avoid the `new` keyword when instantiating volatile dependencies?
4. What is the pattern that we revisited in this chapter that helps compose objects to eliminate inheritance?
5. Is the Service Locator pattern a design pattern, a code smell, or an anti-pattern?
6. What is the principle of composition over inheritance?

Further reading

Here are some links to build upon what we have learned in the chapter:

- Moq: `https://adpg.link/XZv8`
- If you need more options, such as contextual injections, you can check out an open-source library I built. It adds support for new scenarios: `https://adpg.link/S3aT`
- Official documentation, Default service container replacement: `https://adpg.link/5ZoG`

Answers

1. Transient, Scoped, Singleton.
2. The composition root holds the code that describes how to compose the program's object graph—the types bindings.
3. Yes, it is true. Volatile dependencies should be injected instead of instantiated.
4. The Strategy pattern.

5. The Service Locator pattern is all three. It is a design pattern used by DI libraries internally but becomes a code smell in application code. If misused, it is an anti-pattern with the same drawbacks as using the `new` keyword directly.
6. The principle of composition over inheritance encourages us to inject dependencies into classes and use them instead of relying on base class features and inheritance. This approach promotes flexibility and code reuse. It also negates the need for the LSP.

Learn more on Discord

To join the Discord community for this book – where you can share feedback, ask questions to the author, and learn about new releases – follow the QR code below:

`https://packt.link/ArchitectingASPNETCoreApps3e`

Learn more on Discord

Application Configuration and the Options Pattern

This chapter delves into the **Options** pattern and the configuration of applications, using features provided by ASP.NET Core to simplify the management and implementation of configuration. We explore a range of tools and methodologies that allow us to divide our configuration into multiple smaller objects (Separation of Concerns), configure them during different stages of the startup flow, and validate them. Additionally, we cover a broad spectrum of scenarios, including watching for runtime changes with minimal effort and managing, injecting, and loading configurations into our ASP.NET Core applications.

The new options system repurposed the `ConfigurationManager` class as an internal piece. We can no longer use it as the old .NET Framework-era static methods are gone. The new patterns and mechanisms help avoid useless coupling, add flexibility to our designs, and are DI-native. The system is also simpler to extend.

The Options pattern's goal is to use settings at runtime, allowing changes to the application to happen without changing the code. The settings could be as simple as a `string`, a `bool`, a database connection string, or a complex object that holds an entire subsystem's configuration.

By the end of the chapter, you will know how to leverage the .NET options and settings infrastructure.

In this chapter, we cover the following topics:

- Loading the configuration
- Learning the options interfaces
- Exploring common usage scenarios
- Learning options configuration
- Validating our options objects
- Validating options using FluentValidation

- Injecting options objects directly
- Centralizing the configuration for easier management
- Using the configuration-binding source generator
- Using the options validation source generator
- Using the `ValidateOptionsResultBuilder` class

Let's get started!

Loading the configuration

ASP.NET Core allows us to load settings from multiple sources seamlessly by using configuration providers. We can customize these sources from the `WebApplicationBuilder`, or use the defaults set by the `WebApplication.CreateBuilder(args)` method.

The default sources, in order, are as follows:

1. `appsettings.json`
2. `appsettings.{Environment}.json`
3. User secrets; these are only loaded when the environment is `Development`
4. Environment variables
5. Command-line arguments

The order is essential, as the last to be loaded overrides previous values. For example, you can set a value in `appsettings.json` and override it in `appsettings.Staging.json` by redefining the value in that file, user secrets, or an environment variable or by passing it as a command-line argument when you run your application.

You can name your environments as you want, but by default, ASP.NET Core has built-in helper methods for Development, Staging, and Production.

On top of the default providers, we can register other configuration sources out of the box, like `AddIniFile`, `AddInMemoryCollection`, and `AddXmlFile`, for example.

We can also load NuGet packages to install custom providers, like Azure KeyVault and Azure App Configuration, to centralize secrets and configuration management into the Azure cloud. The most interesting part of those configuration providers is that no matter the sources, it does not affect the consumption of the settings, only the composition root. This means we can start loading settings one way, then change our mind later or have different strategies for dev and prod, and none of that affects the codebase but the composition root.

We'll explore a few building blocks next.

Learning the options interfaces

There are four main interfaces to use settings:

- `IOptionsMonitor<TOptions>`
- `IOptionsFactory<TOptions>`
- `IOptionsSnapshot<TOptions>`
- `IOptions<TOptions>`

We must inject one of those interfaces into a class to use the available settings. `TOptions` is the type that represents the settings that we want to access.

The framework returns an empty instance of your options class if you don't configure it. We learn how to configure options properly in the next subsection; meanwhile, remember that using property initializers inside your options class can also be a great way to ensure certain defaults are used. You can also use constants to centralize those defaults somewhere in your codebase (making them easier to maintain). Proper configuration and validation are always preferred, but both combined can add a safety net.

Don't use initializers or constants for default values that change based on the environment (dev, staging, or production) or for secrets such as connection strings and passwords. It will be easier to avoid configuration issues by validating that the properties are set. For example, if an initializer exists, it will be hard to know if the property was overridden by an environment-specific value, making it hard to catch misconfiguration during startup. Without an initializer, all we have to do is ensure the property has a value. Of course, the validation logic can be more complex based on your scenario. We explore validation later in the chapter.

You should always keep secrets out of your Git history because once they're committed and pushed, they become accessible to anyone who can view the repository's history. This advice is valid for C# code and setting files (any files). Why? Malicious actors could use the value from Git history to gain unauthorized access or compromise your systems.

To remove secrets from Git history, you must rewrite the history and exclude the commits that contain sensitive data. Removing secrets from Git history after the fact is challenging, can cause all sorts of issues, and doesn't guarantee that others haven't accessed the secrets already. If that ever happens, ensure you change the secrets to ensure no one can access the vulnerable resource using the potentially leaked credentials.

A simple tip is always to assume that a secret pushed to Git is leaked and treat that value as public. We can extend this to treating private Git repositories as open source (public); you don't want your credentials publicly available, do you? Then don't commit them to Git.

To circumvent adding secrets to Git, use ASP.NET Core secrets locally and a secret store like Azure Key Vault for remote environments like Staging and Production. When using a secret store, follow the vendor's best practices, like using one Key Vault per application per environment to reduce the number of secrets an attacker can compromise in one go.

If we create the following class, since the default value of an `int` is `0`, the default number of items to display per page would be 0, leading to an empty list:

```
public class MyListOption
{
    public int ItemsPerPage { get; set; }
}
```

However, we can configure this using a property initializer, as follows:

```
public class MyListOption
{
    public int ItemsPerPage { get; set; } = 20;
}
```

The default number of items to display per page is now 20.

In the source code for this chapter, I've included a few tests in the `CommonScenarios.Tests` project that assert the lifetime of the different options interfaces. I haven't included this code here for brevity, but it describes the behavior of the different options via unit tests. See `https://adpg.link/AXa5` for more information.

The options served by each interface have different DI lifetimes and other features. The following table exposes some of those features:

Interface	Lifetime	Support named options	Support change notification
`IOptionsMonitor<TOptions>`	Singleton	Yes	Yes
`IOptionsFactory<TOptions>`	Transient	Yes	No
`IOptionsSnapshot<TOptions>`	Scoped	Yes	No
`IOptions<TOptions>`	Singleton	No	No

Table 9.1: The different options interfaces, their DI lifetime, and support for other features.

Next, we explore those interfaces in more depth.

IOptionsMonitor<TOptions>

This interface is the most versatile of them all:

- It supports receiving notifications about reloading the configuration (like when the settings file changed).
- It supports caching.
- It supports named configuration (identifying multiple different `TOptions` with a name).

- The injected `IOptionsMonitor<TOptions>` instance is always the same (**singleton lifetime**).
- It supports unnamed default settings through its `Value` property.

If we only configure named options or no instance at all, the consumer will receive an empty `TOptions` instance (`new TOptions()`).

IOptionsFactory<TOptions>

This interface is a factory, as we saw in *Chapter 7, Strategy, Abstract Factory, and Singleton Design Patterns*, and in *Chapter 8, Dependency Injection*, we use factories to create instances; this interface is no different.

How a factory works is simple: the container creates a new factory every time you ask for one (transient lifetime), and the factory creates a new options instance every time you call its `Create(name)` method (**transient lifetime**).

To get the default instance (non-named options), you can use the `Options.DefaultName` field or pass an empty string; this is usually handled for you by the framework.

If we only configure named options or no instance at all, the consumer will receive an empty `TOptions` instance (`new TOptions()`) after calling `factory.Create(Options.DefaultName)`.

The `IOptionsFactory<TOptions>` interface is closer to an internal building block you want to consume directly from your classes to avoid moving the object creation and lifetime management to those. However, the factory can be useful to create a highly dynamic or advanced configuration system. Meanwhile, do not use the `IOptionsFactory<TOptions>` interface in your classes unless you are building such a system. Using the factory in the composition root is an option, yet you should need this only on rare occasions.

IOptionsSnapshot<TOptions>

This interface is useful when you need a snapshot of the settings for the duration of an HTTP request. How this works is as follows:

- The container creates only one instance per request (**scoped lifetime**).
- It supports named configuration.
- It supports unnamed default settings through its `CurrentValue` property.

If we only configure named options or no instance at all, the consumer will receive an empty `TOptions` instance (`new TOptions()`).

IOptions<TOptions>

This interface is the first that was added to ASP.NET Core. How this works is as follows:

- It does not support advanced scenarios such as what snapshots and monitors do.
- Whenever you request an `IOptions<TOptions>` instance, you get the same instance (**singleton lifetime**), so after changing a configuration, you must restart the application for the changes to take effect.

`IOptions<TOptions>` does not support named options, so you can only access the default instance.

Now that we've looked at the building blocks, let's dig into some code to explore leveraging these interfaces.

Exploring common usage scenarios

This first example covers multiple basic use cases, such as injecting options, using named options, and storing options values in settings.

The name of the project in the source code is `CommonScenarios`.

Let's start by manually changing the configuration values.

Manual configuration

In the composition root, we can manually configure options, which is very useful for configuring ASP.NET Core MVC, the JSON serializer, other pieces of the framework, or our own handcrafted options.

Here's the first options class we use in the code, which contains only a `Name` property:

```
namespace CommonScenarios;
public class MyOptions
{
    public string? Name { get; set; }
}
```

In the composition root, we can use the `Configure` extension method, which extends the `IServiceCollection` interface to configure our object. Here's how we can set the default options of the `MyOptions` class:

```
builder.Services.Configure<MyOptions>(myOptions =>
```

```
{
    myOptions.Name = "Default Option";
});
```

With that code, if we inject that options instance into a class, the value of the `Name` property will be the string `Default Option`.

We explore loading settings from a non-hardcoded configuration source next.

Using the settings file

Loading configurations from a file is often more convenient than hard coding the values in C#. Moreover, the mechanism allows overriding the configurations using different sources, bringing even more advantages.

To load `MyOptions` from the `appsettings.json` file, we must first reference the configuration section, then configure the options, like the following:

```
var defaultOptionsSection = builder.Configuration
    .GetSection("defaultOptions");
builder.Services
    .Configure<MyOptions>(defaultOptionsSection);
```

The preceding code loads the following data from the `appsettings.json` file:

```
{
  "defaultOptions": {
    "name": "Default Options"
  }
}
```

The `defaultOptions` section maps to objects with the same key in the JSON file (see the highlighted code). The `name` property of the `defaultOptions` section translates to the `Name` property of the `MyOptions` class.

That code does the same as the preceding hardcoded version. However, manually loading the section in this way allows us to load a different section for different named options.

This is just another way we can leverage the ASP.NET Core Options pattern and configuration system. Now that we know how to configure the options, it is time to use them.

Injecting options

Let's start by learning how to leverage the `IOptions<TOptions>` interface, the first and simplest interface that came out of .NET Core.

To try this out, let's create an endpoint and inject the `IOptions<MyOptions>` interface as a parameter:

```
app.MapGet(
    "/my-options/",
```

```
    (IOptions<MyOptions> options) => options.Value
);
```

In the preceding code, the `Value` property returns the configured value, which is the following, serialized as JSON:

```
{
  "name": "Default Options"
}
```

And voilà! We can also use constructor injection or any other method we know to use the value of our options object.

Next, we explore configuring multiple instances of the same options class.

Named options

Now, let's explore named options by configuring two more instances of the `MyOptions` class. The concept is to associate a configuration of the options with a name. Once that is done, we can request the configuration we need.

Unfortunately, the ways we explore named options and most online examples break the Inversion of Control principle.

Why? By injecting an interface that is directly tied to a lifetime, the consuming class controls that part of the dependency.

Rest assured, we revisit this at the end of the chapter.

First, in the `appsettings.json` file, let's add the highlighted sections:

```
{
  "defaultOptions": {
    "name": "Default Options"
  },
  "options1": {
    "name": "Options 1"
  },
  "options2": {
    "name": "Options 2"
  }
}
```

Now that we have those configs, let's configure them in the `Program.cs` file by adding the following lines:

```
builder.Services.Configure<MyOptions>(
    "Options1",
```

```
    builder.Configuration.GetSection("options1")
);
builder.Services.Configure<MyOptions>(
    "Options2",
    builder.Configuration.GetSection("options2")
);
```

In the preceding code, the highlighted strings represent the names of the options we are configuring. We associate each configuration section with a named instance.

It is important to note that when we only configure named instances, there are no default options, so we must consume named instances. Otherwise, as we covered previously, injecting a default—unnamed—instance will result in injecting empty objects.

Now to consume those named options, we have multiple choices. We can inject an `IOptionsFactory<MyOptions>`, `IOptionsMonitor<MyOptions>`, or `IOptionsSnapshot<MyOptions>` interface. The final choice depends on the lifetime the consumer of the options needs. However, in our case, we use all of them to ensure we explore them all.

IOptionsFactory<MyOptions>

Let's start with creating an endpoint where we inject a factory:

```
app.MapGet(
    "/factory/{name}",
    (string name, IOptionsFactory<MyOptions> factory)
        => factory.Create(name)
);
```

The factory interface forces us to pass in a name—which is convenient for us. When we execute the program, the endpoint serves us the options based on the specified name. For example, when we send the following request:

```
GET https://localhost:8001/factory/Options1
```

The endpoint returns the following JSON:

```
{
  "name": "Options 1"
}
```

If we pass `Options2` instead, we get the following JSON:

```
{
  "name": "Options 2"
}
```

As simple as that, we can now choose between three different options, the default (unnamed) and the two named options. Of course, once again, we can leverage any other technique we know, like constructor injection.

Let's explore the next interface.

IOptionsMonitor<MyOptions>

We use the `IOptionsMonitor` interface similarly to the `IOptionsFactory` interface when we need named options. So, let's start by creating a similar endpoint:

```
app.MapGet(
    "/monitor/{name}",
    (string name, IOptionsMonitor<MyOptions> monitor)
        => monitor.Get(name)
);
```

The preceding code is almost the same as the factory one, but the `IOptionsMonitor` interface exposes a `Get` method instead of a `Create` method. This semantically expresses that the code is getting an options instance (singleton) instead of creating a new one (transient).

Again, similarly, if we send the following request:

```
GET https://localhost:8001/monitor/Options2
```

The server returns the following JSON:

```
{
  "name": "Options 2"
}
```

One difference is that we can access the default options as well; here's how:

```
app.MapGet(
    "/monitor",
    (IOptionsMonitor<MyOptions> monitor)
        => monitor.CurrentValue
);
```

In the preceding code, the `CurrentValue` property returns the default options. So, when calling this endpoint, we should receive the following JSON:

```
{
  "name": "Default Options"
}
```

As simple as that, we can either access the default value or a named value. We explore one other scenario that the `IOptionsMonitor` interface supports after we cover the `IOptionsSnapshot` interface next.

IOptionsSnapshot<MyOptions>

The `IOptionsSnapshot` interface inherits the `IOptions` interface, contributing its `Value` property, and also offers a `Get` method (scoped lifetime) that works like the `IOptionsMonitor` interface.

Let's start with the first endpoint:

```
app.MapGet(
    "/snapshot",
    (IOptionsSnapshot<MyOptions> snapshot)
        => snapshot.Value
);
```

It should be no surprise that the preceding endpoint returns the following:

```
{
  "name": "Default Options"
}
```

Then the following parametrized endpoint returns the specified named options:

```
app.MapGet(
    "/snapshot/{name}",
    (string name, IOptionsSnapshot<MyOptions> snapshot)
        => snapshot.Get(name)
);
```

Say we are passing the name `Options1`; then the endpoint will return the following option:

```
{
  "name": "Options 1"
}
```

And we are done. It is quite simple to use options as .NET does most of the work for us. The same goes for configuring options classes.

Bind options to an existing object

Alternatively, we can also "bind" a configuration section to an existing object using the `Bind` method like this:

```
var options = new MyOptions();
builder.Configuration.GetSection("options1").Bind(options);
```

That code loads the settings and assigns them to the object's properties, matching the settings key to the property's name. However, **this does not add the object to the IoC container.**

To overcome this, if we do not want to register the dependency manually and don't need the object, we can use the `Bind` or `BindConfiguration` method from `OptionsBuilder<TOptions>`. We create that object with the `AddOptions` method, like for `Bind`:

```
builder.Services.AddOptions<MyOptions>("Options3")
    .Bind(builder.Configuration.GetSection("options3"));
```

The preceding code loads the `options3` configuration section using the `GetSection` method (highlighted), then `OptionsBuilder<TOptions>` binds that value to the name `Options3` through the `Bind` method. This registers a named instance of `MyOptions` with the container. We dig into named options later.

Then, again, we can skip the use of the `GetSection` method by using the `BindConfiguration` method instead, like this:

```
builder.Services.AddOptions<MyOptions>("Options4")
    .BindConfiguration("options4");
```

The preceding code loads the settings from the `options4` section, then registers that new setting with the IoC container.

But wait, our exploration isn't over yet! Up next, we delve into the process of reloading options at runtime.

Reloading options at runtime

A fascinating aspect of the ASP.NET Core options is that the system reloads the value of the options when someone updates a configuration file like `appsettings.json`. To try it out, you can:

1. Run the program.
2. Query an endpoint using the request available in the `CommonScenarios.http` file.
3. Change the value of that option in the `appsettings.json` file and save the file.
4. Query the same endpoint again, and you should see the updated value.

This is an out-of-the-box feature. However, the system rebuilds the options instance, which does not update the references on the previous instance. The good news is that we can hook into the system and react to the changes.

For most scenarios, we don't need to manually check for change since the value of the `CurrentValue` property gets updated. However, if you directly reference that value, this mechanism can be useful.

In this scenario, we have a notification service that sends emails. The SMTP client's configurations are settings. In this case, we only have the `SenderEmailAddress` since sending actual emails is unnecessary. We are logging the notification in the console instead, allowing us to see the configuration changes appear live.

Let's start with the `EmailOptions` class:

```
namespace CommonScenarios.Reload;
public class EmailOptions
```

```
{
    public string? SenderEmailAddress { get; set; }
}
```

Next, we have the `NotificationService` class itself. Let's start with its first iteration:

```
namespace CommonScenarios.Reload;
public class NotificationService
{
    private EmailOptions _emailOptions;
    private readonly ILogger _logger;

    public NotificationService(IOptionsMonitor<EmailOptions>
emailOptionsMonitor, ILogger<NotificationService> logger)
    {
        _logger = logger ?? throw new ArgumentNullException(nameof(logger));
        ArgumentNullException.ThrowIfNull(emailOptionsMonitor);
        _emailOptions = emailOptionsMonitor.CurrentValue;
    }

    public Task NotifyAsync(string to)
    {
        _logger.LogInformation(
            "Notification sent by '{SenderEmailAddress}' to '{to}'.",
            _emailOptions.SenderEmailAddress,
            to
        );
        return Task.CompletedTask;
    }
}
```

In the preceding code, the class holds a reference on the `EmailOptions` class upon creation (highlighted lines). The `NotifyAsync` method writes an information message in the console and then returns.

We explore logging in the next chapter.

Because the `NotificationService` class has a singleton lifetime and references the options class itself, if we change the configuration, the value will not update since the system recreates a new instance with the updated configuration. Here's the service registration method:

```
public static WebApplicationBuilder AddNotificationService(
```

```
        this WebApplicationBuilder builder)
    {
        builder.Services.Configure<EmailOptions>(builder.Configuration
            .GetSection(nameof(EmailOptions)));
        builder.Services.AddSingleton<NotificationService>();
        return builder;
    }
```

How do we fix this? In this case, we could fix the issue by referencing the `IOptionsMonitor` interface instead of its `CurrentValue` property. However, if you face a scenario where it's impossible—because of object lifetimes or how a class references the configuration value, for example—you can tap into the `OnChange` method of the `IOptionsMonitor` interface. In the constructor, you could add the following code:

```
emailOptionsMonitor.OnChange((options) =>_emailOptions = options);
```

With that code, when the `appsettings.json` file changes, the code updates the `_emailOptions` field. As easy as this, we reactivated the reloading feature.

One more thing: the `OnChange` method returns an `IDisposable` we can dispose of to stop listening for changes. I implemented two additional methods in the source code: `StartListeningForChanges` and `StopListeningForChanges`, and three endpoints: one to send notifications, one to stop listening for changes, and one to start listening for changes again.

Now that we know how to use options, let's explore additional ways to configure them.

Learning options configuration

Now that we have covered basic usage scenarios, let's attack some more advanced possibilities, such as creating types to configure, initialize, and validate our options.

The name of the project in the source code is `OptionsConfiguration`.

We start by configuring options, which happens in two phases:

1. The configuration phase.
2. The post-configuration phase

In a nutshell, the post-configuration phase happens later in the process. This is a good place to enforce that some values are configured a certain way or to override configuration, for example, in integration tests.

To configure an options class, we have many options, starting with the following interfaces:

Interface	Description
`IConfigureOptions<TOptions>`	Configure the default `TOptions` type.
`IConfigureNamedOptions<TOptions>`	Configure the default and named `TOptions` type.
`IPostConfigureOptions<TOptions>`	Configure the default and named `TOptions` type during the post-configuration phase.

Table 9.2: Interfaces to configure options classes

If a configuration class implements both `IConfigureOptions` and `IConfigureNamedOptions` interfaces, the `IConfigureNamedOptions` interface will take precedence, and the `Configure` method of the `IConfigureOptions` interface will not be executed.

You can configure the default instance using the `Configure` method of the `IConfigureNamedOptions` interface; the name of the options will be empty (equal to the member `Options.DefaultName`).

We can also leverage the following methods that extend the `IServiceCollection` interface:

Method	Description
`Configure<TOptions>`	Configure the default and named `TOptions` type inline or from a configuration section.
`ConfigureAll<TOptions>`	Configure all options of type `TOptions` inline.
`PostConfigure<TOptions>`	Configure the default and named `TOptions` type inline during the post-configuration phase.
`PostConfigureAll<TOptions>`	Configure all options of type `TOptions` inline during the post-configuration phase.

Table 9.3: Configuration methods

As we are about to see, the registration order is very important. The configurators are executed in order of registration within a phase. Each phase is independent of the other; thus, the sequence in which we declare the configuration and post-configuration phases doesn't have an effect, the configuration always gets executed before the post-configuration.

First, we must lay out the groundwork for our little program.

Creating the program

After creating an empty web application, the first building block is to create the options class that we want to configure:

```
namespace OptionsConfiguration;
public class ConfigureMeOptions
```

```
{
    public string? Title { get; set; }
    public IEnumerable<string> Lines { get; set; } = Enumerable.
Empty<string>();
}
```

We use the `Lines` property as a trace bucket. We add lines to it to visually confirm the order that the configurators are executed.

Next, we define application settings in the `appsettings.json` file:

```
{
  "configureMe": {
    "title": "Configure Me!",
    "lines": [
      "appsettings.json"
    ]
  }
}
```

We use the configuration as a starting point. It defines the value of the `Title` property and adds a first line to the `Lines` property, allowing us to trace the order it is executed.

Next, we need an endpoint to access the settings, serialize the result to a JSON string, and then write it to the response stream:

```
app.MapGet(
    "/configure-me",
    (IOptionsMonitor<ConfigureMeOptions> options) => new {
        DefaultInstance = options.CurrentValue,
        NamedInstance = options.Get(NamedInstance)
    }
);
```

By calling this endpoint, we can consult the values of the default and named instances we are about to create. We define the `NamedInstance` constant next.

ASP.NET Core configures the options when they are requested for the first time. In this case, both instances of the `ConfigureMeOptions` class are configured when calling the `/configure-me` endpoint for the first time.

If we run the program now, we'll end up with two empty instances, so before doing that, we need to tell ASP.NET about the `configureMe` configuration section we added to the `appsettings.json` file.

Configuring the options

We want two different options to test out many possibilities:

- A default option (unnamed)
- A named instance

To achieve this, we must add the following lines in the `Program.cs` file:

```
const string NamedInstance = "MyNamedInstance";
builder.Services
    .Configure<ConfigureMeOptions>(builder.Configuration
        .GetSection("configureMe"))
    .Configure<ConfigureMeOptions>(NamedInstance, builder.Configuration
        .GetSection("configureMe"))
;
```

The preceding code registers a default instance (see the highlighted code) and a named instance. Both use the `configureMe` configuration section and so start with the same initial values, as we can see when running the project:

```
{
  "defaultInstance": {
    "title": "Configure Me!",
    "lines": [
      "appsettings.json"
    ]
  },
  "namedInstance": {
    "title": "Configure Me!",
    "lines": [
      "appsettings.json"
    ]
  }
}
```

The `defaultInstance` and `namedInstance` properties are self-explanatory and relate to their respective options instance.

Now that we've configured the options, we are ready to explore using the `IConfigureOptions<TOptions>` interface.

Implementing a configurator object

We can encapsulate the configuration logic into classes to apply the **single responsibility principle (SRP)**. To do so, we must implement an interface and create the binding with the IoC container.

First, we must create a class that we name `ConfigureAllConfigureMeOptions`, which configures all `ConfigureMeOptions` instances, default and named:

```
namespace OptionsConfiguration;
public class ConfigureAllConfigureMeOptions :
IConfigureNamedOptions<ConfigureMeOptions>
{
    public void Configure(string? name, ConfigureMeOptions options)
    {
        options.Lines = options.Lines.Append(
            $"ConfigureAll:Configure name: {name}");
        if (name != Options.DefaultName)
        {
            options.Lines = options.Lines.Append(
                $"ConfigureAll:Configure Not Default: {name}");
        }
    }

    public void Configure(ConfigureMeOptions options)
        => Configure(Options.DefaultName, options);
}
```

In the preceding code, we implement the interface (see the highlighted code), which contains two methods. The second `Configure` method is never called by the framework, but just in case, we can simply redirect the call to the other method if it happens. The body of the first `Configure` method (highlighted) adds a line to all options and a second line when the option is not the default one.

Instead of testing if the option is not the default one (`name != Options.DefaultName`), you can check for the option's name or use a `switch` to configure specific options by name.

We can tell the IoC container about this code, so ASP.NET Core executes it like this:

```
builder.Services.AddSingleton<IConfigureOptions<ConfigureMeOptions>,
ConfigureAllConfigureMeOptions>();
```

Now, with this binding in place, ASP.NET Core will run our configuration code the first time we request our endpoint. Here's the result:

```
{
  "defaultInstance": {
    "title": "Configure Me!",
    "lines": [
```

```
      "appsettings.json",
      "ConfigureAll:Configure name: "
    ]
  },
  "namedInstance": {
    "title": "Configure Me!",
    "lines": [
      "appsettings.json",
      "ConfigureAll:Configure name: MyNamedInstance",
      "ConfigureAll:Configure Not Default: MyNamedInstance"
    ]
  }
}
```

As we can see from that JSON output, the configurator ran and added the expected lines to each instance.

It is important to note that you must bind `IConfigureOptions<TOptions>` to your configuration class even if you implemented the `IConfigureNamedOptions<TOptions>` interface.

And voilà! We have a neat result that took almost no effort. This can lead to so many possibilities! Implementing `IConfigureOptions<TOptions>` is probably the best way to configure the default values of an options class.

Next, we add post-configuration to the mix!

Adding post-configuration

We must take a similar path to add post-configuration values but implement `IPostConfigureOptions<TOptions>` instead. To achieve this, we update the `ConfigureAllConfigureMeOptions` class to implement that interface:

```
namespace OptionsConfiguration;
public class ConfigureAllConfigureMeOptions :
    IPostConfigureOptions<ConfigureMeOptions>,
    IConfigureNamedOptions<ConfigureMeOptions>
{
    // Omitted previous code
    public void PostConfigure(string? name, ConfigureMeOptions options)
    {
        options.Lines = options.Lines.Append(
            $"ConfigureAll:PostConfigure name: {name}");
    }
}
```

In the preceding code, we implemented the interface (see the highlighted lines). The `PostConfigure` method simply adds a line to the `Lines` property.

To register it with the IoC container, we must add the following line:

```
builder.Services.AddSingleton<IPostConfigureOptions<ConfigureMeOptions>,
ConfigureAllConfigureMeOptions>();
```

The big difference is that this runs during the post-configuration phase, independent of the initial configuration phase. Executing the application now leads to the following result:

```
{
  "defaultInstance": {
    "title": "Configure Me!",
    "lines": [
      "appsettings.json",
      "ConfigureAll:Configure name: ",
      "ConfigureAll:PostConfigure name: "
    ]
  },
  "namedInstance": {
    "title": "Configure Me!",
    "lines": [
      "appsettings.json",
      "ConfigureAll:Configure name: MyNamedInstance",
      "ConfigureAll:Configure Not Default: MyNamedInstance",
      "ConfigureAll:PostConfigure name: MyNamedInstance"
    ]
  }
}
```

In the preceding JSON, the highlighted lines represent our post-configuration code that was added at the end. You might tell yourself, of course, it's the last line; it's the last code we registered, which is a legitimate assumption. However, here's the complete registration code, which clearly shows the `IPostConfigureOptions<TOptions>` interface was registered first (highlighted), proving the post-configuration code runs last:

```
builder.Services
    .AddSingleton<IPostConfigureOptions<ConfigureMeOptions>,
ConfigureAllConfigureMeOptions>()
    .Configure<ConfigureMeOptions>(builder.Configuration
        .GetSection("configureMe"))
    .Configure<ConfigureMeOptions>(NamedInstance, builder.Configuration
        .GetSection("configureMe"))
```

```
    .AddSingleton<IConfigureOptions<ConfigureMeOptions>,
ConfigureAllConfigureMeOptions>()
;
```

Next, we create a second configuration class.

Using multiple configurator objects

A very interesting concept with the ASP.NET Core options pattern is that we can register as many configuration classes as we want. This creates many possibilities, including code from one or more assemblies configuring the same options class.

Now that we know how this works, let's add the `ConfigureMoreConfigureMeOptions` class, which also adds a line to the `Lines` property:

```
namespace OptionsConfiguration;
public class ConfigureMoreConfigureMeOptions :
IConfigureOptions<ConfigureMeOptions>
{
    public void Configure(ConfigureMeOptions options)
    {
        options.Lines = options.Lines.Append("ConfigureMore:Configure");
    }
}
```

This time, we want that class only to augment the default instance, so it implements the **`IConfigureOptions<TOptions>`** interface (see the highlighted lines).

Next, we must register the binding:

```
builder.Services.AddSingleton<IConfigureOptions<ConfigureMeOptions>,
ConfigureMoreConfigureMeOptions>();
```

As we can see, it's the same binding but pointing to the `ConfigureMoreConfigureMeOptions` class instead of the `ConfigureAllConfigureMeOptions` class.

Executing the application and querying the endpoint outputs the following JSON:

```
{
  "defaultInstance": {
    "title": "Configure Me!",
    "lines": [
      "appsettings.json",
      "ConfigureAll:Configure name: ",
      "ConfigureMore:Configure",
      "ConfigureAll:PostConfigure name: "
    ]
```

```
  },
  "namedInstance": {
    "title": "Configure Me!",
    "lines": [
      "appsettings.json",
      "ConfigureAll:Configure name: MyNamedInstance",
      "ConfigureAll:Configure Not Default: MyNamedInstance",
      "ConfigureAll:PostConfigure name: MyNamedInstance"
    ]
  }
}
```

The preceding JSON shows the line our new class added to only the default instance (highlighted) before the post-configure option.

The possibilities are great, right? The code can configure objects in one of the two phases, which is very flexible.

Next, we explore a few more possibilities.

Exploring other configuration possibilities

We can mix those configuration classes with extension methods. For example:

- We can call the `Configure` and `PostConfigure` methods multiple times.
- We can call the `ConfigureAll` and `PostConfigureAll` methods to configure all the options of a given `TOptions`.

Here, we use the `PostConfigure` method to demonstrate that. Let's add the following lines of code (highlighted):

```
const string NamedInstance = "MyNamedInstance";
var builder = WebApplication.CreateBuilder(args);
builder.Services.PostConfigure<ConfigureMeOptions>(
    NamedInstance,
    x => x.Lines = x.Lines.Append("Inline PostConfigure Before")
);
builder.Services
    .AddSingleton<IPostConfigureOptions<ConfigureMeOptions>,
ConfigureAllConfigureMeOptions>()
    .Configure<ConfigureMeOptions>(builder.Configuration
        .GetSection("configureMe"))
    .Configure<ConfigureMeOptions>(NamedInstance, builder.Configuration
        .GetSection("configureMe"))
    .AddSingleton<IConfigureOptions<ConfigureMeOptions>,
ConfigureAllConfigureMeOptions>()
```

```
    //.AddSingleton<IConfigureNamedOptions<ConfigureMeOptions>,
ConfigureAllConfigureMeOptions>()
    .AddSingleton<IConfigureOptions<ConfigureMeOptions>,
ConfigureMoreConfigureMeOptions>()
;
builder.Services.PostConfigure<ConfigureMeOptions>(
    NamedInstance,
    x => x.Lines = x.Lines.Append("Inline PostConfigure After")
);
// ...
```

The preceding code registers two configuration delegates that target our named instance. They both run in the post-configuration phase. So running the app and accessing the endpoint shows the order in which all lines are added:

```
{
  "defaultInstance": {
    "title": "Configure Me!",
    "lines": [
      "appsettings.json",
      "ConfigureAll:Configure name: ",
      "ConfigureMore:Configure",
      "ConfigureAll:PostConfigure name: "
    ]
  },
  "namedInstance": {
    "title": "Configure Me!",
    "lines": [
      "appsettings.json",
      "ConfigureAll:Configure name: MyNamedInstance",
      "ConfigureAll:Configure Not Default: MyNamedInstance",
      "Inline PostConfigure Before",
      "ConfigureAll:PostConfigure name: MyNamedInstance",
      "Inline PostConfigure After"
    ]
  }
}
```

In the preceding JSON, we can see that the two highlighted lines are the ones we just added, loaded in order, and not applied to the default options.

There is one more configuration possibility, which comes from the validation API. This is most likely an unintended side effect, but it works nonetheless.

The following code adds the "Inline Validate" line after the post-configuration phase:

```
builder.Services.AddOptions<ConfigureMeOptions>().
Validate(options =>
{
    // Validate was not intended for this, but it works
nonetheless...
    options.Lines = options.Lines.Append("Inline Validate");
    return true;
});
```

In terms of separation of concerns, we should stay away from this. However, knowing this may help you work around a post-configuration order issue one day.

Now that we know the options interface types, their lifetimes, and many ways to configure their values, it is time to validate them and enforce a certain level of integrity in our programs.

Validating our options objects

Another feature that comes out of the box is options validation, which allows us to run validation code when a `TOptions` object is created. The validation code is guaranteed to run the first time an option is created and does not account for subsequent option modifications. Depending on the lifetime of your options object, the validation may or may not run. For example:

Interface	Lifetime	Validation
`IOptionsMonitor<TOptions>`	Singleton	Validate the options once.
`IOptionsFactory<TOptions>`	Transient	Validate the options every time the code calls the `Create` method.
`IOptionsSnapshot<TOptions>`	Scoped	Validate the options once per HTTP request (per scope).
`IOptions<TOptions>`	Singleton	Validate the options once.

Table 9.4: The effect of validation on options lifetime

I wrote three test cases in the `ValidateLifetime.cs` file if you are interested in seeing this in action.

We can create validation types to validate options classes. They must implement the `IValidateOptions<TOptions>` interface or use data annotations such as `[Required]`. Implementing the interface works very similarly to the options configuration.

The name of the project in the source code is `OptionsValidation`.

First, let's see how to force the validation when the program starts.

Eager validation

Eager validation has been added to .NET 6 and allows catching incorrectly configured options at startup time in a fail-fast mindset. The `Microsoft.Extensions.Hosting` assembly adds the `ValidateOnStart` extension method to the `OptionsBuilder<TOptions>` type. There are different ways of using this, including the following, which binds a configuration section to an options class:

```
services.AddOptions<Options>()
    .Configure(o => /* Omitted configuration code */)
    .ValidateOnStart()
;
```

The highlighted line is all we need to apply our validation rules during startup. I recommend using this as your new default so you know that options are misconfigured at startup time instead of later at runtime, limiting unexpected issues.

Now that we know that, let's look at how to configure options validation.

Data annotations

Let's start by using `System.ComponentModel.DataAnnotations` types to decorate our options with validation attributes. We activate this feature with the `ValidateDataAnnotations` extension method. This also works with eager validation by chaining both methods.

If you are unfamiliar with `DataAnnotations`, they are attributes used to validate EF Core and MVC model classes. Don't worry, they are very explicit, so you should understand the code.

To demonstrate this, let's look at the skeleton of two small tests:

```
using Microsoft.Extensions.DependencyInjection;
```

```
using Microsoft.Extensions.Options;
using System.ComponentModel.DataAnnotations;
using Xunit;

namespace OptionsValidation;
public class ValidateOptionsWithDataAnnotations
{
    [Fact]
    public void Should_pass_validation() { /*omitted*/ }
    [Fact]
    public void Should_fail_validation() { /*omitted*/ }

    private class Options
    {
        [Required]
        public string? MyImportantProperty { get; set; }
    }
}
```

The preceding code shows that the `MyImportantProperty` property of the `Options` class is required and cannot be `null` (see the highlighted line).

There are many data annotation attributes that we can use to validate settings. `Required`, `MinLength`, `MaxLength`, `StringLength`, `Range`, `EmailAddress`, `Phone`, `Url`, and `RegularExpression` are a few examples. We can also create our own.

Next, we'll look at the test cases.

The first test is expecting the validation to pass:

```
[Fact]
public void Should_pass_validation()
{
    // Arrange
    var services = new ServiceCollection();
    services.AddOptions<Options>()
        .Configure(o => o.MyImportantProperty = "A value")
        .ValidateDataAnnotations()
        .ValidateOnStart() // eager validation
    ;
    var serviceProvider = services.BuildServiceProvider();
    var options = serviceProvider
```

```
            .GetRequiredService<IOptionsMonitor<Options>>();

        // Act & Assert
        Assert.Equal(
            "A value",
            options.CurrentValue.MyImportantProperty
        );
    }
```

The test simulates the execution of a program where the IoC container creates the options class, and its consumer (the test) leverages it. The highlighted line sets the property to `"A value"`, making the validation pass. The code also enables eager validation (`ValidateOnStart`) on top of the validation of data annotations (`ValidateDataAnnotations`).

The second test is expecting the validation to fail:

```
    [Fact]
    public void Should_fail_validation()
    {
        // Arrange
        var services = new ServiceCollection();
        services.AddOptions<Options>()
            .ValidateDataAnnotations()
            .ValidateOnStart() // eager validation
        ;
        var serviceProvider = services.BuildServiceProvider();

            // Act & Assert
            var error = Assert.Throws<OptionsValidationException>(
                () => options.CurrentValue);
            Assert.Collection(error.Failures,
                f => Assert.Equal("DataAnnotation validation failed for 'Options'
    members: 'MyImportantProperty' with the error: 'The MyImportantProperty field
    is required.'.", f)
            );
        );
    }
```

In the preceding code, the `MyImportantProperty` is never set (see the highlighted code), leading to the validation failing and throwing an `OptionsValidationException`. The test simulates catching that exception.

The eager validation does not work in the tests because it is not an ASP.NET Core program but xUnit test cases.

That's it—.NET does the job for us and validates our instance of the `Options` class using the data annotation like you can do when using EF Core or MVC model.

Next, we explore how to create validation classes to validate our options objects manually.

Validation types

To implement options validation types—options validators—we can create a class that implements one or more `IValidateOptions<TOptions>` interfaces. One type can validate multiple options, and multiple types can validate the same options, so the possible combinations can cover all use cases.

Using a custom class is no harder than using data annotations. However, it allows us to remove the validation concerns from the options class and code more complex validation logic. You should pick the way that makes the most sense for your project.

On top of personal preferences, say you use a third-party library with options. You load that library into your application and expect the configuration to be a certain way. You could create a class to validate that the options class provided by the library is configured appropriately for your application and even validate this at startup time.

You can't use data annotations for that because you don't control the code. Moreover, it is not a general validation that should apply to all consumers but a specific validation for that one app.

Let's start with the skeleton of the test class:

```
using Microsoft.Extensions.DependencyInjection;
using Microsoft.Extensions.Options;
using Xunit;

namespace OptionsValidation;
public class ValidateOptionsWithTypes
{
    [Fact]
    public void Should_pass_validation() {}
    [Fact]
    public void Should_fail_validation() {}

    private class Options
```

```
    {
        public string? MyImportantProperty { get; set; }
    }

    private class OptionsValidator : IValidateOptions<Options>
    {
        public ValidateOptionsResult Validate(
            string name, Options options)
        {
            if (string.IsNullOrEmpty(options.MyImportantProperty))
            {
                return ValidateOptionsResult.Fail(
                    "'MyImportantProperty' is required.");
            }
            return ValidateOptionsResult.Success;
        }
    }
}
```

In the preceding code, we have the `Options` class, which is similar to the previous example but without the data annotation. The difference is that instead of using the `[Required]` attribute, we created the `OptionsValidator` class (highlighted) containing the validation logic.

`OptionsValidator` implements `IValidateOptions<Options>`, which only contains a `Validate` method. This method allows named and default options to be validated. The `name` argument represents the options' names. In our case, we implemented the required logic for all options.

To return the state of the validation process, the `ValidateOptionsResult` class exposes a few members to help us, such as the `Success` and `Skip` fields, and two `Fail()` methods. `ValidateOptionsResult.Success` indicates success. `ValidateOptionsResult.Skip` indicates that the validator did not validate the options, most likely because it only validates certain named options but not the given one. The `ValidateOptionsResult.Fail(message)` and `ValidateOptionsResult.Fail(messages)` methods indicate a failure and take a single message or a collection of messages as an argument.

To make this work, we must make the validator available to the IoC container, as we did with the options configuration. We explore the two test cases next, which are very similar to the data annotation example.

Here's the first test case that passes the validation:

```
[Fact]
public void Should_pass_validation()
{
    // Arrange
    var services = new ServiceCollection();
    services.AddSingleton<IValidateOptions<Options>, OptionsValidator>();
    services.AddOptions<Options>()
```

```
        .Configure(o => o.MyImportantProperty = "A value")
        .ValidateOnStart()
    ;
    var serviceProvider = services.BuildServiceProvider();

    // Act & Assert
    var options = serviceProvider
        .GetRequiredService<IOptionsMonitor<Options>>();
    Assert.Equal(
        "A value",
        options.CurrentValue.MyImportantProperty
    );
}
```

The test case simulates an application that configures `MyImportantProperty` correctly, which passes validation. The highlighted line shows how to register the validator class. The rest is done by the framework when using the options class.

Next, we explore a test that fails the validation:

```
[Fact]
public void Should_fail_validation()
{
    // Arrange
    var services = new ServiceCollection();
    services.AddSingleton<IValidateOptions<Options>, OptionsValidator>();
    services.AddOptions<Options>().ValidateOnStart();
    var serviceProvider = services.BuildServiceProvider();

    // Act & Assert
    var options = serviceProvider
        .GetRequiredService<IOptionsMonitor<Options>>();
    var error = Assert.Throws<OptionsValidationException>(
        () => options.CurrentValue);
    Assert.Collection(error.Failures,
        f => Assert.Equal("'MyImportantProperty' is required.", f)
    );
}
```

The test simulates a program where the `Options` class is not configured appropriately. When accessing the `options` object, the framework builds the class and validates it, throwing an `OptionsValidationException` because of the validation rules (see the highlighted lines).

Using types to validate options is handy when you don't want to use data annotations, can't use data annotations, or need to implement certain logic that is easier within a method than with attributes.

Next, we glance at how to leverage options with FluentValidation.

Validating options using FluentValidation

In this project, we validate options classes using FluentValidation. FluentValidation is a popular open-source library that provides a validation framework different from data annotations. One of the primary advantages of FluentValidation is that it allows encapsulating validation rules in another class than the one being validated. That makes the validation logic easier to test and more explicit than depending on metadata added by attributes. We explore FluentValidation more in *Chapter 17, Getting Started with Vertical Slice Architecture*, but that should not hinder you from following this example.

The name of the project in the source code is `OptionsValidationFluentValidation`.

Here, I want to show you how to leverage a few patterns we've learned so far to implement this ourselves with only a few lines of code. In this micro-project, we leverage:

- Dependency injection
- The Strategy design pattern
- The Options pattern
- Options validation: Validation types
- Options validation: Eager validation

Let's start with the options class itself:

```
public class MyOptions
{
    public string? Name { get; set; }
}
```

The options class is very thin, containing only a nullable `Name` property. Next, let's look at the FluentValidation validator, which validates that the `Name` property is not empty:

```
public class MyOptionsValidator : AbstractValidator<MyOptions>
{
    public MyOptionsValidator()
    {
        RuleFor(x => x.Name).NotEmpty();
    }
}
```

If you have never used FluentValidation before, the `AbstractValidator<T>` class implements the `IValidator<T>` interface and adds utility methods like `RuleFor`. The `MyOptionsValidator` class contains the validation rules.

To make ASP.NET Core validate `MyOptions` instances using FluentValidation, we must implement an `IValidateOptions<TOptions>` interface as we did in the previous example, inject our validator in it, and then leverage it to ensure the validity of `MyOptions` objects. This implementation of the `IValidateOptions` interface creates a bridge between the FluentValidation features and the ASP.NET Core options validation.

Here is a generic implementation of such a class that could be reused for any type of options:

```
public class FluentValidateOptions<TOptions> : IValidateOptions<TOptions>
    where TOptions : class
{
    private readonly IValidator<TOptions> _validator;
    public FluentValidateOptions(IValidator<TOptions> validator)
    {
        _validator = validator;
    }
    public ValidateOptionsResult Validate(string name, TOptions options)
    {
        var validationResult = _validator.Validate(options);
        if (validationResult.IsValid)
        {
            return ValidateOptionsResult.Success;
        }
        var errorMessages = validationResult.Errors.Select(x =>
x.ErrorMessage);
        return ValidateOptionsResult.Fail(errorMessages);
    }
}
```

In the preceding code, the `FluentValidateOptions<TOptions>` class adapts the `IValidateOptions<TOptions>` interface to the `IValidator<TOptions>` interface by leveraging FluentValidation in the `Validate` method. In a nutshell, we use the output of one system and make it the input of another system.

This type of adaptation is known as the Adapter design pattern. We explore the Adapter pattern in the next chapter.

Now that we have all the building blocks, let's have a look at the composition root:

```
using FluentValidation;
using Microsoft.Extensions.Options;
var builder = WebApplication.CreateBuilder(args);
builder.Services
    .AddSingleton<IValidator<MyOptions>, MyOptionsValidator>()
    .AddSingleton<IValidateOptions<MyOptions>,
FluentValidateOptions<MyOptions>>()
;
builder.Services
    .AddOptions<MyOptions>()
    .ValidateOnStart()
;
var app = builder.Build();
app.MapGet("/", () => "Hello World!");
app.Run();
```

The highlighted code is the key to this system:

- It registers the FluentValidation `MyOptionsValidator` that contains the validation rules.
- It registers the generic `FluentValidateOptions` instance, so .NET uses it to validate the `MyOptions` class.
- Under the hood, the `FluentValidateOptions` class uses the `MyOptionsValidator` to validate the options internally.

When running the program, the console yields the following error, as expected:

```
Hosting failed to start
Unhandled exception. Microsoft.Extensions.Options.OptionsValidationException:
'Name' must not be empty.
[...]
```

This may look like a lot of trouble for a simple required field; however, `FluentValidateOptions<TOptions>` is reusable. We could also scan one or more assemblies to register all the validators with the IoC container automatically.

Now that we've explored many ways to configure and validate options objects, it is time to look at a way to inject options classes directly, either by choice or to work around a library capability issue.

Injecting options objects directly

The only negative point about the .NET Options pattern is that we must tie our code to the framework's interfaces. We must inject an interface like `IOptionsMonitor<MyOptions>` instead of the `MyOptions` class itself. By letting the consumers choose the interface, we let them control the lifetime of the options, which breaks the inversion of control, dependency inversion, and open/closed principles.

We should move that responsibility out of the consumer up to the composition root.

As we explored at the beginning of this chapter, the `IOptions`, `IOptionsFactory`, `IOptionsMonitor`, and `IOptionsSnapshot` interfaces define the options object's lifetime.

In most cases, I prefer to inject `MyOptions` directly, controlling its lifetime from the composition root, instead of letting the class itself control its dependencies. I'm a little *anti-control-freak*, I know. Moreover, writing tests using the `MyOptions` class directly over mocking an interface like `IOptionsSnapshot` is easier.

The source code of this section is part of the `OptionsValidation` project.

It just so happens that we can circumvent this easily with the following two-part trick:

1. Set up the options class normally, as explored in this chapter.
2. Create a dependency binding that instructs the container to inject the options class directly using the Options pattern.

The xUnit test of the `ByPassingInterfaces` class from the `OptionsValidation` project demonstrates this. Here's the skeleton of that test class:

```
using Microsoft.Extensions.DependencyInjection;
using Microsoft.Extensions.Options;
using Xunit;

namespace OptionsValidation;
public class ByPassingInterfaces
{
    [Fact]
    public void Should_support_any_scope() { /*...*/ }

    private class MyOptions
    {
        public string? Name { get; set; }
    }
}
```

The preceding `MyOptions` class has only a `Name` property. We use it next to explore the workaround in the test case:

```
[Fact]
public void Should_support_any_scope()
{
    // Arrange
    var services = new ServiceCollection();
    services.AddOptions<MyOptions>()
        .Configure(o => o.Name = "John Doe");
    services.AddScoped(serviceProvider => {
        var snapshot = serviceProvider
            .GetRequiredService<IOptionsSnapshot<MyOptions>>();
        return snapshot.Value;
    });
    var serviceProvider = services.BuildServiceProvider();

    // Act & Assert
    using var scope1 = serviceProvider.CreateScope();
    var options1 = scope1.ServiceProvider.GetService<MyOptions>();
    var options2 = scope1.ServiceProvider.GetService<MyOptions>();
    Assert.Same(options1, options2);

    using var scope2 = serviceProvider.CreateScope();
    var options3 = scope2.ServiceProvider.GetService<MyOptions>();
    Assert.NotSame(options2, options3);
}
```

In the preceding code block, we registered the `MyOptions` class using a factory method. That way, we can inject the `MyOptions` class directly (with a scoped lifetime). Moreover, the implementation factory now controls the `MyOptions` class's creation and lifetime (see the highlighted code).

And voilà! This workaround allows us to inject `MyOptions` directly into our system without tying our classes with any .NET-specific options interface.

As a reminder, consuming options through the `IOptionsSnapshot<TOptions>` interface results in a *scoped* lifetime.

The *Act & Assert* section of the test validates the correctness of the setup by creating two scopes and ensuring that each scope returns a different instance while returning the same instance within the scope. For example, both `options1` and `options2` come from `scope1`, so they should be the same. On the other hand, `options3` comes from `scope2`, so it should be different than `options1` and `options2`.

This workaround also applies to existing systems that could benefit from the Options pattern without updating its code—assuming the system is dependency injection-ready. We can also use this trick to compile an assembly that does not depend on `Microsoft.Extensions.Options`.

By using this trick, we can set the lifetime of the options from the composition root, which is a more classic dependency injection-enabled flow. To change the lifetime, use a different interface, like `IOptionsMonitor` or `IOptionsFactory`.

Next, we explore a way to organize all this code.

Centralizing the configuration for easier management

Creating tons of classes is very object-oriented and follows the single responsibility principle, among others. However, dividing responsibilities into programming concerns does not always lead to the easiest code to understand because it creates a lot of classes and files, often spread across multiple layers.

An alternative is to regroup the initialization and validation with the options class itself, shifting the multiple responsibilities to a single one: an end-to-end options class management.

The name of the project in the source code is `CentralizingConfiguration`.

In this example, we explore the `ProxyOptions` class, which carries the name of the service and the time the proxy service should cache items in seconds. We want to set a default value for the `CacheTimeInSeconds` property and validate that the `Name` property is not empty.

On the other hand, we don't want the consumer of that class to have access to any other methods, like `Configure` or `Validate`.

To achieve this, we can implement the interfaces explicitly, hiding them from the `ProxyOptions` but showing them to the consumers of the interfaces. For example, binding the `ProxyOptions` class to the `IValidateOptions<ProxyOptions>` interface gives the consumer access to the `Validate` method through the `IValidateOptions<ProxyOptions>` interface. Explaining this should be simpler in code; here's the class:

```
using Microsoft.Extensions.Options;

namespace CentralizingConfiguration;
public class ProxyOptions : IConfigureOptions<ProxyOptions>,
IValidateOptions<ProxyOptions>
```

```
{
    public static readonly int DefaultCacheTimeInSeconds = 60;

    public string? Name { get; set; }
    public int CacheTimeInSeconds { get; set; }

    void IConfigureOptions<ProxyOptions>.Configure(
        ProxyOptions options)
    {
        options.CacheTimeInSeconds = DefaultCacheTimeInSeconds;
    }

    ValidateOptionsResult IValidateOptions<ProxyOptions>.Validate(
        string? name, ProxyOptions options)
    {
        if (string.IsNullOrWhiteSpace(options.Name))
        {
            return ValidateOptionsResult.Fail(
                "The 'Name' property is required.");
        }
        return ValidateOptionsResult.Success;
    }
}
```

The preceding code implements both the `IConfigureOptions<ProxyOptions>` and `IValidateOptions<ProxyOptions>` interfaces explicitly (highlighted) by omitting the visibility modifier and prefixing the name of the method with the name of the interface, like the following:

```
ValidateOptionsResult IValidateOptions<ProxyOptions>.Validate(...)
```

Now, to leverage it, we must register it with the IoC container like this:

```
builder.Services
    .AddSingleton<IConfigureOptions<ProxyOptions>, ProxyOptions>()
    .AddSingleton<IValidateOptions<ProxyOptions>, ProxyOptions>()
    .AddSingleton(sp => sp
        .GetRequiredService<IOptions<ProxyOptions>>()
        .Value
    )
    .Configure<ProxyOptions>(options
        => options.Name = "High-speed proxy")
    .AddOptions<ProxyOptions>()
    .ValidateOnStart()
;
```

In the preceding code, we combined many notions we explored, like:

- Registering the options class
- Using the workaround to inject the `ProxyOptions` class directly
- Configuring the options inline and through a configurator class
- Leveraging a validation class
- Enforcing the validation by eager loading our options during the startup

If you comment out the highlighted line, the application will throw an exception on startup.

The only endpoint defined in the application is the following:

```
app.MapGet("/", (ProxyOptions options) => options);
```

When we run the application, we get the following output:

```
{
  "name": "High-speed proxy",
  "cacheTimeInSeconds": 60
}
```

As expected, the value of the `cacheTimeInSeconds` property equals the value of the `DefaultCacheTimeInSeconds` field, and the value of the `name` property is what we configured in the `Program.cs` file.

When using the IntelliSense feature inside your favorite IDE (I'm using Visual Studio 2022 here), you can see only the properties—because we implicitly implemented the interfaces—and don't see the methods:

```
(ProxyOptions options) => options.|);
```

Figure 9.1: VS IntelliSense not showing explicitly implemented interface members

That's it; we are done with this organizational technique.

To keep the composition cleaner, we could encapsulate the bindings in an extension method, and, even better, make that extension method register the whole proxy feature, for example, `services.AddProxyService()`.

I'll let you practice this one on your own as we already explored this.

Next, we explore code generators!

Using the configuration-binding source generator

.NET 8 introduces a **configuration-binding source generator** that provides an alternative to the default reflection-based implementation. In simple terms, the name of the options class properties and the settings keys are now hard-coded, accelerating the configuration retrieval.

Beware: the settings keys are case-sensitive and map one-on-one with the C# class property name, unlike the non-generated code.

Web applications using native AOT deployment (ahead-of-time compilation to native code) or trimming self-contained deployments to ship only the bits in use now leverage this option by default.

The native AOT deployment model compiles the code to a single runtime environment like Windows x64. It does not need the **just-in-time (JIT)** compiler since the code is already compiled to the native version of the targeted environment. AOT deployments are self-contained and do not need the .NET runtime to work.

You can use the `EnableConfigurationBindingGenerator` property in your `csproj` file to manually activate or deactivate the generator:

```
<PropertyGroup>
  <EnableConfigurationBindingGenerator>true</
EnableConfigurationBindingGenerator>
</PropertyGroup>
```

Now that the generator is enabled, let's see how this works.

The generator looks for a few options, including the `Configure` and `Bind` methods. It then generates the binding code.

The name of the project in the source code is `ConfigurationGenerators`.

In this first part of the project, we create an options class and register it with the IoC container to consume it through an API endpoint.

We use the following options class:

```
namespace ConfigurationGenerators;
public class MyOptions
{
    public string? Name { get; set; }
}
```

In the `Program.cs` file, we can use the source generator like this:

```
builder.Services
    .AddOptions<MyOptions>()
    .BindConfiguration("MyOptions")
;
```

As you may have noticed, the preceding code is the same as we used before and does what you expect it to do, but the new source generator generates the code under the hood—no functional or usage changes. The generated source code is too long to include here and is not very interesting.

Let's explore another source generator next.

Using the options validation source generator

.NET 8 introduces the **options validation source generator**, which generates the validation code based on data annotations. The idea is similar to the configuration-binding source generator but for the validation code.

To leverage the validation generator, we must add a reference on the `Microsoft.Extensions.Options.DataAnnotations` package.

Afterward, we must:

1. Create an empty validator class.
2. Ensure the class is `partial`.
3. Implement the `IValidateOptions<TOptions>` interface (but not the methods).
4. Decorate the validator class with the `[OptionsValidator]` attribute.
5. Register the validator class with the container.

This procedure sounds complicated but is way simpler in code; let's look at that now.

The name of the project in the source code is `ConfigurationGenerators`.

In this second part of the project, we continue to build on the previous pieces and add validation to our MyOptions class. Of course, we also want to test the new source generator.

Here's the updated MyOptions class:

```
using System.ComponentModel.DataAnnotations;
namespace ConfigurationGenerators;
public class MyOptions
{
    [Required]
    public string? Name { get; set; }
}
```

The highlighted line represents the changes. We want to ensure the Name property is not empty.

Now that we've updated our options class, let's create the following validator class:

```
using Microsoft.Extensions.Options;
namespace ConfigurationGenerators;
[OptionsValidator]
public partial class MyOptionsValidator : IValidateOptions<MyOptions>
{
}
```

The preceding code is an empty shell that prepares the class for the code generator. The [OptionsValidator] attribute represents the generator hook (that is, the flag the generator is looking for). And with this code, we are done with steps 1 to 4; simpler than English, right?

Now, for the last step, we register our validator like normal:

```
builder.Services.AddSingleton<IValidateOptions<MyOptions>,
MyOptionsValidator>();
```

To test this out, let's add a valid named options instance bound to the following configuration section in the appsettings.json file:

```
{
  "MyOptions": {
    "Name": "Options name"
  }
}
```

Here's how we bind it in the Program.cs file:

```
builder.Services
    .AddOptions<MyOptions>("valid")
    .BindConfiguration("MyOptions")
    .ValidateOnStart()
;
```

The preceding code registers the `valid` named option, binds it to the configuration section `MyOptions`, and validates the values when the application starts.

Other ways to register the named options also work. I used this one for convenience purposes only.

If we were to inspect the content of the options at runtime, it would be what we expect; nothing is different from what we explored throughout the chapter:

```
{
  "name": "Options name"
}
```

At this point, the program should start.

Next, to test this out, let's add another named options class, but an invalid one this time. We won't change anything in the `appsettings.json` file, and add the following registration code:

```
builder.Services
    .AddOptions<MyOptions>("invalid")
    .BindConfiguration("MissingSection")
    .ValidateOnStart()
;
```

The preceding code binds a missing section to the `invalid` named options, making the `Name` property equal to `null`. That object will not pass our validation because the `Name` property is required.

If we run the application now, we get the following message:

```
Hosting failed to start
Microsoft.Extensions.Options.OptionsValidationException: Name: The invalid.Name
field is required.
```

From that error, we know the validation works as expected. It is not every day that we are happy when our application doesn't start but this is one of those times.

That's it for the code generation; it behaves the same, but the code under the hood is different, enabling technologies like AOT and trimming that do not support reflection-based mechanisms well. Moreover, code generation should speed up the program execution because the behaviors are hard-coded instead of relying on a dynamic reflection-based approach.

Next, let's dig into another class introduced in .NET 8.

Using the ValidateOptionsResultBuilder class

`ValidateOptionsResultBuilder` is a new type in .NET 8. It allows us to dynamically accumulate validation errors and create a `ValidateOptionsResult` object representing its current state.

The name of the project in the source code is `ValidateOptionsResultBuilder`.

Its basic usage is straightforward, as we are about to see.

In this project, we are validating the `MyOptions` object. The type has multiple validation rules, and we want to ensure we are not stopping after the first rule fails validation so a consumer would know all the errors in one go. To achieve this, we decided to use the `ValidateOptionsResultBuilder` class.

Let's start with the options class:

```
namespace ValidateOptionsResultBuilder;
public class MyOptions
{
    public string? Prop1 { get; set; }
    public string? Prop2 { get; set; }
}
```

Next, let's implement a validator class that enforces that both properties can't be empty:

```
using Microsoft.Extensions.Options;
namespace ValidateOptionsResultBuilder;
public class SimpleMyOptionsValidator : IValidateOptions<MyOptions>
{
    public ValidateOptionsResult Validate(string? name, MyOptions options)
    {
        var builder = new Microsoft.Extensions.Options.
ValidateOptionsResultBuilder();
        if (string.IsNullOrEmpty(options.Prop1))
        {
            builder.AddError(
                "The value cannot be empty.",
                nameof(options.Prop1)
            );
        }
        if (string.IsNullOrEmpty(options.Prop2))
```

```
        {
            builder.AddError(
                "The value cannot be empty.",
                nameof(options.Prop2)
            );
        }
        return builder.Build();
    }
}
```

In the preceding code, we created a `ValidateOptionsResultBuilder` object, added errors to it, and then returned an instance of the `ValidateOptionsResult` class by leveraging its `Build` method. The usage of the `ValidateOptionsResultBuilder` class is highlighted.

Next, to test this out, we must register the options. Let's also create an endpoint. Here's the `Program.cs` file:

```
using ValidateOptionsResultBuilder;
using Microsoft.Extensions.Options;

var builder = WebApplication.CreateBuilder(args);
builder.Services
    .AddSingleton<IValidateOptions<MyOptions>, SimpleMyOptionsValidator>()
    .AddOptions<MyOptions>("simple")
    .BindConfiguration("SimpleMyOptions")
    .ValidateOnStart()
;

var app = builder.Build();
app.MapGet("/", (IOptionsFactory<MyOptions> factory) => new
{
    simple = factory.Create("simple")
});
app.Run();
```

The preceding code is as familiar as it can get after a whole chapter on the Options pattern. We register our options class and the validator and create an endpoint.

When we call the endpoint, we get the following result:

```
Hosting failed to start
Microsoft.Extensions.Options.OptionsValidationException: Property Prop1: The value cannot be empty.; Property Prop2: The value cannot be empty.
```

As expected, the application failed to start because the validation of the `MyOptions` class failed. One difference is that we have two combined error messages instead of one.

As a reference, a validator doing the same without using the `ValidateOptionsResultBuilder` type would look like this:

```
using Microsoft.Extensions.Options;
namespace ValidateOptionsResultBuilder;
public class ClassicMyOptionsValidator : IValidateOptions<MyOptions>
{
    public ValidateOptionsResult Validate(string? name, MyOptions options)
    {
        if (string.IsNullOrEmpty(options.Prop1))
        {
            return ValidateOptionsResult.Fail(
                $"Property {nameof(options.Prop1)}: The value cannot be empty."
            );
        }
        if (string.IsNullOrEmpty(options.Prop2))
        {
            return ValidateOptionsResult.Fail(
                $"Property {nameof(options.Prop2)}: The value cannot be empty."
            );
        }
        return ValidateOptionsResult.Success;
    }
}
```

The highlighted code represents the standard process that gets replaced by the use of the `ValidateOptionsResultBuilder` type in the `SimpleMyOptionsValidator` class.

This concludes our project. It was nothing very complex, yet it is a nice addition to help accumulate multiple error messages. On top of that, the `ValidateOptionsResultBuilder` type can also accumulate `ValidationResult` and `ValidateOptionsResult` objects, which can lead to more complex systems like collecting results from multiple validators. I'll let you play around with implementing this one.

Let's briefly wrap up the chapter next.

Wrapping up

In this chapter, we learned how the Options pattern helps enhance application flexibility and reliability when we need configurations. We explored multiple elements of the framework to use configuration, load configurations, and validate configurations. We learned about tools that can help us validate our objects, how to inject our settings directly into their consumers, and more.

Now, on top of that, let's explore how the Options pattern helps us adhere to the SOLID principles:

- S: The Options pattern divides managing settings into multiple pieces where each has a single responsibility. Loading unmanaged settings into strongly typed classes is one responsibility, validating options using classes is another, and configuring options from multiple independent sources is one more.
- O: The different `IOptions*<TOptions>` interfaces break this principle by forcing the consumer to decide what lifetime and capabilities the options should have. To change the lifetime of a dependency, we must update the consuming class when using those interfaces. On the other hand, we explored an easy and flexible workaround that allows us to bypass this issue for many scenarios and inject the options directly, inverting the dependency flow again, leading to open/closed consumers.
- L: N/A.
- I: The `IValidateOptions<TOptions>` and `IConfigureOptions<TOptions>` interfaces are two good examples of segregating a system into smaller interfaces where each has a single purpose.
- D: The options framework is built around interfaces, allowing us to depend on abstractions.

Again, the `IOptions*<TOptions>` interfaces are the exceptions to this. Even if they are interfaces, they tie us to implementation details like the options lifetime. In this case, I think it is more beneficial to inject the options object directly (a data contract) instead of those interfaces.

Let's recap this chapter before jumping into ASP.NET Core logging.

Summary

This chapter explored the Options pattern, a powerful tool allowing us to configure our ASP.NET Core applications. It enables us to change the application without altering the code. The capability even allows the application to reload the options at runtime when a configuration file is updated without downtime.

We learned how to load settings from multiple sources, with the last loaded source overriding previous values. We discovered the following interfaces to access settings and learned that the choice of interface influences the lifetime of the options object:

- `IOptionsMonitor<TOptions>`
- `IOptionsFactory<TOptions>`
- `IOptionsSnapshot<TOptions>`
- `IOptions<TOptions>`

We delved into manually configuring options in the composition root and loading them from a settings file. We also learned how to inject options into a class and configure multiple instances of the same options type using named options. We explored encapsulating the configuration logic into classes to apply the **single responsibility principle** (**SRP**). We achieved this by implementing the following interfaces:

- `IConfigureOptions<TOptions>`
- `IConfigureNamedOptions<TOptions>`
- `IPostConfigureOptions<TOptions>`

We also learned that we could mix configuration classes with inline configurations using the `Configure` and `PostConfigure` methods and that the registration order of configurators is crucial as they are executed in order of registration.

We also delved into options validation. We learned that the frequency at which options objects are validated depends on the lifetime of the options interface used. We also discovered the concept of eager validation, which allows us to catch incorrectly configured options classes at startup time. We learned how to use data annotations to decorate our options with validation attributes such as `[Required]`. We can create validation classes to validate our options objects for more complex scenarios. Those validation classes must implement the `IValidateOptions<TOptions>` interface. We also learned how to bridge other validation frameworks like FluentValidation to complement the out-of-the-box functionalities or accommodate your taste for a different validation framework.

We explored a workaround allowing us to inject options classes directly into their consumers. Doing this allows us to control their lifetime from the composition root instead of letting the types consuming them control their lifetime. This approach aligns better with the dependency injection and Inversion of Control principles. That also makes testing the classes easier.

Finally, we looked at the .NET 8 code generators that change how the options are handled but do not impact how we use the Options pattern. We also explored the `ValidateOptionsResultBuilder` type, also introduced in .NET 8.

Next, we explore .NET logging, which is another very important aspect of building applications; good traceability can make all the difference when observing or debugging applications.

Questions

Let's take a look at a few practice questions:

1. Name one interface we can use to inject a settings class.
2. Name the two phases ASP.NET Core uses when configuring options.
3. How significant is the order in which we register configuration objects and inline delegates?
4. Can we register multiple configuration classes?
5. What is eager validation, and why should you use it?
6. What interface must we implement to create a validator class?

Further reading

Here are some links to build upon what we learned in the chapter:

- Options pattern in ASP.NET Core (official docs): `https://adpg.link/RTGc`

- Quickstart: Create an ASP.NET Core app with Azure App Configuration: https://adpg.link/qhLV
- Secret storage in the Production environment with Azure Key Vault: https://adpg.link/Y5D7

Answers

1. We can use one of the following interfaces: IOptionsMonitor<TOptions>, IOptionsFactory<TOptions>, IOptionsSnapshot<TOptions>, or IOptions<TOptions>.
2. The configuration and the post-configuration phases.
3. Configurators are executed in the order of their registration, so their order is crucial.
4. Yes, we can register as many configuration classes as we want.
5. Eager validation allows catching incorrectly configured options at startup time, which can prevent runtime issues.
6. We must implement the IValidateOptions<TOptions> interface.

Learn more on Discord

To join the Discord community for this book – where you can share feedback, ask questions to the author, and learn about new releases – follow the QR code below:

https://packt.link/ArchitectingASPNETCoreApps3e

10

Logging Patterns

This chapter delves into logging, an integral feature of .NET, and concludes the *Designing for ASP.NET Core* section. Logging is a fundamental building block for applications, allowing us to capture valuable information during runtime, and ASP.NET Core conveniently provides built-in support for it. In this chapter, we will explore the logging framework provided by ASP.NET Core and learn how to implement it effectively in our applications.

Logging is essential and adds visibility to production systems. Without logs, you don't know what is happening in your system unless you are the only one using it, which is very unlikely. ASP.NET Core offers a logging system with clean interfaces, eliminating the need for third-party libraries and presenting a flexible and robust approach to integrating logging into our applications. Like many other systems, the logging system is provider-based, allowing us to add and configure the logging providers that suit our needs.

At the end of this chapter, you will have a firm grasp of what logging is and how to integrate it into your applications.

In this chapter, we cover the following topics:

- What is logging?
- Writing logs
- Log levels
- Logging providers
- Configuring logging
- Structured logging

Let's start by exploring what logging is.

What is logging?

Logging is the practice of writing messages into a log and cataloging information for later use. Logging is a cross-cutting concern, meaning it applies to every piece of your application. We talk about layers in *Chapter 14, Layering and Clean Architecture*, but until then, let's just say that a cross-cutting concern affects all layers and cannot be centralized in just one; it affects a bit of everything.

Logging is essential for several reasons, including:

- **Error diagnosis:** Logging helps capture runtime errors and stack traces, which are invaluable for diagnosing issues after they occur, especially once an application is in production
- **Debugging support:** Detailed logs can provide context when debugging, helping developers understand the application's state at the time of an error or exception
- **Performance monitoring:** By logging performance metrics, you can identify bottlenecks and optimize the efficiency of your application
- **Security auditing:** Tracking security events can aid security auditing and response to threats more quickly
- **Compliance:** Many industries require logs for regulatory compliance, ensuring that the application meets legal data handling and privacy standards
- **Behavioral analytics:** Logging user actions and system events can provide insights into user behavior and help drive product improvements

A log is made up of log entries. We can view each log entry as an event that happened during the program's execution. Those events are then written to the log. This log can be a file, a remote system, `stdout`, or a combination of multiple destinations. Next is an example of an ASP.NET Core console log. The first four info messages are about ASP.NET Core booting up the server, while the last four are information about a GET request:

```
info: Microsoft.Hosting.Lifetime[14]
      Now listening on: http://localhost:5094
info: Microsoft.Hosting.Lifetime[0]
      Application started. Press Ctrl+C to shut down.
info: Microsoft.Hosting.Lifetime[0]
      Hosting environment: Development
info: Microsoft.Hosting.Lifetime[0]
      Content root path: {omitted}
info: Microsoft.AspNetCore.Hosting.Diagnostics[1]
      Request starting HTTP/1.1 GET http://localhost:5094/ - - -
info: Microsoft.AspNetCore.Routing.EndpointMiddleware[0]
      Executing endpoint 'HTTP: GET /'
info: Microsoft.AspNetCore.Routing.EndpointMiddleware[1]
      Executed endpoint 'HTTP: GET /'
info: Microsoft.AspNetCore.Hosting.Diagnostics[2]
```

```
        Request finished HTTP/1.1 GET http://localhost:5094/ - 200 - text/
plain;+charset=utf-8 2.6690ms
```

When creating a log entry, we must also think about the severity of that log entry. The severity level represents the type of message or the level of importance of the message we are logging. We can also use it to filter those logs. `Trace`, `Error`, and `Debug` are examples of log entry levels. The log levels can vary depending on the technology but are usually somewhat similar to the one ASP.NET Core exposes. Those levels are defined in the `Microsoft.Extensions.Logging.LogLevel` enum.

Another important aspect of a log entry is how it is structured. You can log a single string. Everyone on your team could log single strings in their own way. But what happens when someone searches for information? Chaos ensues! Unstructured logs can lead to frustration while searching for specific information because they lack a uniform format, making it difficult to query and filter the data effectively. As a result, searching through these logs can be time-consuming and error-prone and can significantly hinder an individual's ability to identify the information they need quickly. One way to fix this is by using structured logging.

Structured logging is simple yet complex; you must create a structure the program follows for all log entries. That structure does not have to be overly complex to begin with; your structure can also use well-known formats like JSON. The important part is that the log entries are structured. We introduce this subject in the *Structured logging* section. For now, let's just say that if you must decide on a logging strategy, I recommend digging into structured logging first. If you are part of a team, then chances are someone else already did. If that's not the case, you can always bring it up. Continuous improvement is a key aspect of life.

We could write a whole book on logging, best logging practices, and structured logging, but this chapter aims to teach you how to use .NET logging abstractions.

Writing logs

Now that we understand what logs are, it is time to translate that knowledge into C#. Most of what we need is part of the `Microsoft.Extensions.Logging.Abstractions` assembly, which is included by default in ASP.NET Core projects, so we don't need to do anything to tap into the logging system. The `Microsoft.Extensions.Logging` namespace contains most of the logging building blocks.

The logging system is provider-based, meaning we must register one or more `ILoggerProvider` instances if we want our log entries to be recorded somewhere, like in stdout or a file. By default, when calling `WebApplication.CreateBuilder(args)`, it registers the Console, Debug, EventSource, and EventLog (Windows only) providers, but we can modify this list. We can add and remove providers if you need to. The required dependencies for using the logging system are also registered as part of this process.

Before we look at the code, let's learn how to create log entries, which is the objective behind logging. To create an entry, we can use one of the following interfaces: `ILogger`, `ILogger<T>`, or `ILoggerFactory`.

Let's take a look at them in more detail:

Interface	Description
ILogger	Base type that allows us to perform logging operations.
ILogger<T>	Base type that allows us to perform logging operations. Inherits from the ILogger interface. The system uses the generic parameter T as the log entry's category.
ILoggerFactory	A factory interface that allows creating ILogger objects and specifying the category name manually as a string.

Table 10.1: The logging interfaces

The following code represents the most commonly used pattern, which consists of injecting an `ILogger<T>` interface and storing it in an `ILogger` field before using it, like this:

```
namespace LoggingConsole;

public class ServiceUsingILogger(ILogger<ServiceUsingILogger> logger)
{
    private readonly ILogger _logger = logger ?? throw new
ArgumentNullException(nameof(logger));

    public string Generate()
    {
        _logger.LogInformation("ServiceUsingILogger generating a GUID...");
        var guid = Guid.NewGuid();
        _logger.LogDebug("ServiceUsingILogger generated the GUID {guid}.",
guid);
        return guid.ToString();
    }
}
```

The preceding `ServiceUsingILogger` class has a private `_logger` field. The primary constructor takes an `ILogger<Service>` logger as a parameter and stores it in that field. The `Generate` method uses the `_logger` field to write information-level and debug-level messages to the log.

If you find the declaration of the `ServiceUsingILogger` class strange, that's because I used a **primary constructor**, which is new in C# 12. Have a look at the *Appendix* on GitHub (`https://adpg.link/net8-appendix`) for more information about primary constructors.

We can write the following content in the `Program.cs` file to try the logger:

```
using LoggingConsole;

var builder = WebApplication.CreateBuilder(args);
builder.Services.AddSingleton<ServiceUsingILogger>();

var app = builder.Build();
app.MapGet("/", (ServiceUsingILogger service) => service.Generate());
app.Run();
```

In the preceding code, the first highlighted line registers `ServiceUsingILogger` with the IoC container, which allows injecting an instance in the endpoint (the second highlighted line). From there, the endpoint calls the `Generate` method and returns its value.

If we execute the program at this point, the console output will resemble the following:

```
info: Microsoft.Hosting.Lifetime[14]
      Now listening on: https://localhost:7170
info: Microsoft.Hosting.Lifetime[14]
      Now listening on: http://localhost:5020
info: Microsoft.Hosting.Lifetime[0]
      Application started. Press Ctrl+C to shut down.
info: Microsoft.Hosting.Lifetime[0]
      Hosting environment: Development
info: Microsoft.Hosting.Lifetime[0]
      Content root path: ...\C10\LoggingConsole
info: LoggingConsole.ServiceUsingILogger[0]
      ServiceUsingILogger generating a GUID...
```

As we can see in the preceding listing, only the information-level entry was logged to the console. That's because the default minimum log level is `Information`.

In an ASP.NET Core application, all that logging goes to the console by default. Logging is a great way to know what is happening in the background when running the application.

The `ServiceUsingILogger` class is a simple consumer of an `ILogger<T>` interface (`ILogger<ServiceUsingILogger>`). You can use the same pattern for any class you want to add logging support to. Change the generic value (`ServiceUsingILogger`, in this case) by the class you are injecting the `ILogger<T>` interface into. That generic argument becomes the logger's category name when writing log entries (`LoggingConsole.ServiceUsingILogger` in the preceding console output).

To wrap this up, this simple example allowed us to implement the most commonly used logging pattern in ASP.NET Core. You can also log what is happening in your application and infrastructure and run real-time security analysis on those log streams to quickly identify security breaches, intrusion attempts, or system failures. These subjects are out of the scope of this book, but having strong logging capabilities at the application level can only help your overall observability and debugging strategy.

Before moving on to the next subject, let's explore an example that leverages the `ILoggerFactory` interface. The code sets a custom category name and uses the created `ILogger` instance to log a message. This is very similar to the previous example. Here's the consumer's code:

```
namespace LoggingConsole;

public class ServiceUsingLoggerFactory
{
    public const string CategoryName = "My Service";
    private readonly ILogger _logger;
    public ServiceUsingLoggerFactory(ILoggerFactory loggerFactory)
    {
        ArgumentNullException.ThrowIfNull(loggerFactory,
nameof(loggerFactory));
        _logger = loggerFactory.CreateLogger(CategoryName);
    }

    public string Generate()
    {
        _logger.LogInformation("ServiceUsingLoggerFactory generating a
GUID...");
        var guid = Guid.NewGuid();
        _logger.LogDebug("ServiceUsingLoggerFactory generated the GUID
{guid}.", guid);
        return guid.ToString();
    }
}
```

The preceding code should look very familiar. Let's focus on the highlighted lines, which relate to the current pattern:

1. We inject the `ILoggerFactory` interface into the class constructor (instead of an `ILogger<Service>`).
2. We create an `ILogger` instance with the `"My Service"` category name.

3. We assign the logger to the `_logger` field.
4. We then use that `ILogger` from the `Generate` method.

Now, let's modify the `Program.cs` file to execute this new code and add the following lines:

```
builder.Services.AddSingleton<ServiceUsingLoggerFactory>();
// ...
app.MapGet("/factory", (ServiceUsingLoggerFactory service) => service.
Generate());
```

The preceding code is similar to how we registered the `ServiceUsingILogger` class. So now, if we run the program and call the `/factory` endpoint, we should get an output similar to the following:

```
info: Microsoft.Hosting.Lifetime[14]
      Now listening on: https://localhost:7170
info: Microsoft.Hosting.Lifetime[14]
      Now listening on: http://localhost:5020
info: Microsoft.Hosting.Lifetime[0]
      Application started. Press Ctrl+C to shut down.
info: Microsoft.Hosting.Lifetime[0]
      Hosting environment: Development
info: Microsoft.Hosting.Lifetime[0]
      Content root path: ...\C10\LoggingConsole
info: My Service[0]
      ServiceUsingLoggerFactory generating a GUID...
```

The preceding console output is also very similar to the previous one, but the category name is `My Service`, as defined when creating the `ILogger` using the `ILoggerFactory`.

As a rule of thumb, I recommend using the `ILogger<T>` interface by default because it is the simplest way; it removes the need to manage the category name manually, and it lowers the chances of making a mistake while naming the category. If it's impossible because you need to specify a different category than the class name, for example, or if you need a more dynamic way of setting the category name for your log entries, leverage the `ILoggerFactory` instead. By default, when using `ILogger<T>`, the category name is the type name of the `T` parameter, which should be the name of the class creating log entries. The `ILoggerFactory` interface is more of an internal piece than something made for us to consume; nonetheless, it exists and can satisfy some use cases.

Now that we have covered how to write log entries, it's time to learn how to manage their severity.

Log levels

In the previous examples, we used the `LogInformation` method to log information messages, but there are other levels as well, shown in the following table:

Level	Method	Description	Production
Trace	`LogTrace`	This is used to capture detailed information about the program, instrument execution speed, and debugging. You can also log sensitive information when using traces.	Disabled.
Debug	`LogDebug`	This is used to log debugging and development information.	Disabled unless troubleshooting.
Information	`LogInformation`	This is used to track the flow of the application. Normal events that occur in the system are often information-level events, such as for when the system started, the system stopped, and a user has signed in.	Enabled for your application. Depending on the amount of information-level logs your application generates, you may want to adjust this. You should disable ASP.NET Core information-level logs and may want to tweak your third-party dependencies.
Warning	`LogWarning`	This is used to log abnormal behavior in the application flow that does not cause the program to stop, but that may need to be investigated; for example, handled exceptions, failed network calls, and accessing resources that do not exist.	Enabled.

Error	`LogError`	This is used to log errors in the application flow that do not cause the application to stop. Errors must usually be investigated. Examples include the failure of the current operation and an exception that cannot be handled.	Enabled.
Critical	`LogCritical`	This is used to log errors that require immediate attention and represent a catastrophic state. The program is most likely about to stop, and the integrity of the application might be compromised; for example, a hard drive is full, the server is out of memory, or the database is in a deadlocked state.	Enabled with some alerts that could be configured to trigger automatically.

Table 10.2: Log severity levels

As described in the preceding table, each log level serves one or more purposes. Those log levels tell the logger what severity a log entry is. Then, we can configure the system to log only entries of at least a certain level so we don't fill out production logs with traces and debug entries, for example.

In a project I led, we benchmarked multiple ways to log simple and complex messages using ASP.NET Core to build clear and optimized guidelines around that. We could not reach a fair conclusion when the messages were logged due to a large time variance between benchmark runs. However, we observed a trend when messages were skipped—not logged—like a *trace* log with the minimum logging level configured to *debug*, for example.

Based on our findings, I recommend using **log message templates** for `Trace`, `Debug`, and `Information` messages. This approach is preferred over string interpolation (e.g., `_logger.LogTrace($"Some: {variable}")`) and other methods like `string.Format`. While it may seem unusual to focus on optimizing logging for messages often not logged due to being below the configured minimum logging level, this method proves beneficial, especially in production. Here are examples of log message templates, which are the fastest way to handle log entries that might be skipped:

```
_logger.LogTrace("Some: {variable}", variable);
// Or
_logger.LogTrace("Some: {0}", variable);
```

As shown in the preceding code, log message templates allow the logging framework to delay the processing of the message template and arguments until it's sure it must log the message. If the logging level for these messages is disabled, the application incurs only a minimal overhead, without unnecessary string processing. This optimization can save valuable computing time.

When the log level for these messages is disabled, such as in production environments, you benefit from the efficiency of not processing the message, thus reducing overhead. This contrasts with string interpolation, where the string and variables are processed regardless of whether the log message is ultimately written. Here's an example of string interpolation (a.k.a. what not to do):

```
_logger.LogTrace($"Some: {variable}");
```

For warning and higher levels, where messages are likely to be logged regardless of the environment, using either log message templates or interpolation is generally acceptable. However, adopting the log message template approach for all levels ensures consistency and optimizes performance across your application.

One last note. I suggest you don't try to over-optimize your code before there is a need for that. The action of investing a lot of effort in optimizing something that does not need optimizing is known as **premature optimization.** The idea is to optimize just enough upfront and fix the performance when you find real issues.

Now that we know the log levels that .NET offers us, let's look at the logging providers.

Logging providers

To give you an idea of the possible built-in logging providers, here is a list from the official documentation (see the *Further reading* section at the end of this chapter):

- **Console:** The `Console` provider sends log messages, typically seen in the terminal, to the standard output stream (stdout).
- **Debug:** The `Debug` provider writes log messages to a debugger monitor, such as the Visual Studio Output window, using the `System.Diagnostics.Debug` class.
- **EventSource:** The `EventSource` provider is a fast, structured logging solution built into the .NET Runtime. The logs (or traces) can be consumed by advanced monitoring tools and used for performance analysis. It leverages the `System.Diagnostics.Tracing.EventSource` class under the hood.
- **EventLog:** the `EventLog` provider writes logs to the Windows event log.
- **ApplicationInsights:** This provider integrates with Azure Application Insights.

The following is a list of third-party logging providers, also from the official documentation:

- elmah.io
- Gelf
- JSNLog

- KissLog.net
- Log4Net
- NLog
- PLogger
- Sentry
- Serilog
- Stackdriver

Now, if you need any of those or your favorite logging library is part of the preceding list, you know you can use it. If it is not, maybe it supports ASP.NET Core but was not part of the documentation when I consulted it.

Next, let's learn how to configure the logging system.

Configuring logging

As with most features of ASP.NET Core, we can configure logging. The default `WebApplicationBuilder` does a lot of that for us, but if we want to tweak the defaults, we can. On top of that, the system loads the `Logging` section of the configuration. That section is present, by default, in the `appsettings.json` file. Like all configurations, it is cumulative, so we can redefine part of it in another file or configuration provider.

We won't dig too deep into customization, but it is good to know that we can customize the minimum level of what we are logging. We can also use transformation files (such as `appsettings.Development.json`) to customize those levels per environment.

For example, we can define our defaults in `appsettings.json`, then update a few for development purposes in `appsettings.Development.json`, change the production settings in `appsettings.Production.json`, then change the staging settings in `appsettings.Staging.json`, and add some testing settings in `appsettings.Testing.json`.

First, let's take a peek at the default settings:

```
{
  "Logging": {
    "LogLevel": {
      "Default": "Information",
      "Microsoft": "Warning"
    }
  }
}
```

We can define default levels (using `Logging:LogLevel:Default`) and a custom level for each category (such as `Logging:LogLevel:Microsoft`) representing base namespaces. For example, from that configuration file, the minimum level is `Information`, while every item part of the `Microsoft` or `Microsoft.*` namespaces have a minimum level of `Warning`.

That allows for removing noise when running the application. We can also leverage these configurations to debug certain parts of the application by lowering the log level to `Debug` or `Trace` for only a subset of items (items from one or more namespaces, for example).

We can also filter what we want to log on a provider basis, using configuration or code. In the configuration file, we can change the default level of the console provider to `Trace`, like this:

```
{
  "Logging": {
    "LogLevel": {
      "Default": "Information",
      "Microsoft": "Warning"
    },
    "Console": {
      "LogLevel": {
        "Default": "Trace"
      }
    }
  }
}
```

We kept the same default values but added the `Logging:Console` section (see the highlighted code) with a default `LogLevel` set to `Trace`. We can define as many settings as we need.

Instead of configurations, we can use the `AddFilter` extension methods, as shown in the following code, or in conjunction with configurations.

To log Debug-level messages, we can add the following to the `Program.cs` file:

```
using Microsoft.Extensions.Logging.Console;
// ...
builder.Logging.AddFilter<ConsoleLoggerProvider>(
    level => level >= LogLevel.Debug
);
```

The preceding code tells the `ConsoleLoggerProvider` to log Debug-level messages and above. The `ConsoleLoggerProvider` is the provider of `ConsoleLogger` instances and allows us to configure how the console logging behaves.

However, when we run the program, we now get a lot of noise in our console because we told ASP.NET Core to log Debug information for everything, not just our code. To overcome this, we can make our filter more precise and target only a specific category. If we replace the preceding line with the following in the `Program.cs` file, only the entries that are in the `My Service` category will be logged:

```
builder.Logging.AddFilter<ConsoleLoggerProvider>(
    ServiceUsingLoggerFactory.CategoryName,
```

```
    level => level >= LogLevel.Debug
);
```

The preceding code uses another overload of the `AddFilter` method to filter using the `CategoryName` constant of the `ServiceUsingLoggerFactory` class. Now if we run the application and navigate to the `/factory` endpoint, we should get an output like the following:

```
info: Microsoft.Hosting.Lifetime[14]
      Now listening on: https://localhost:7170
info: Microsoft.Hosting.Lifetime[14]
      Now listening on: http://localhost:5020
info: Microsoft.Hosting.Lifetime[0]
      Application started. Press Ctrl+C to shut down.
info: Microsoft.Hosting.Lifetime[0]
      Hosting environment: Development
info: Microsoft.Hosting.Lifetime[0]
      Content root path: ...\C10\LoggingConsole
info: LoggingConsole.ServiceUsingILogger[0]
      ServiceUsingILogger generating a GUID...
info: My Service[0]
      ServiceUsingLoggerFactory generating a GUID...
dbug: My Service[0]
      ServiceUsingLoggerFactory generated the GUID 8bcc3fa4-0fb5-42fe-b16e-
55433c5ba5d1.
```

As the preceding terminal output shows, only the `My Service` category was allowed to log Debug-level entries.

We now know of two ways to set the minimum logging levels:

- Code
- Configuration

We can tweak the way we configure our logging policies as needed. Code can be more testable, while configurations can be updated at runtime without redeploying. Moreover, with the cascading model, which allows us to override configuration, we can cover most use cases using configurations.

The biggest downside of configuration is that writing strings in a JSON file is more error-prone than writing code (assuming you are not reverting to using strings there either but using constants as we did in the code sample). However, I usually stick with configurations to set those values, as they do not change often. If you prefer code, the drawback is that you need to recompile or redeploy your application to update your logging configuration, which can be a bad strategy.

Next, let's look at a brief example of structured logging.

Structured logging

As stated at the beginning, structured logging can be a game changer that opens opportunities. Querying a data structure is always more versatile than querying a single line of text. That is even more true if there is no clear guideline around logging, whether a line of text or a JSON-formatted data structure.

To keep it simple, we leverage a built-in formatter (highlighted line below) that serializes our log entries into JSON. Here is the `Program.cs` file:

```
var builder = WebApplication.CreateBuilder(args);
builder.Logging.AddJsonConsole();
var app = builder.Build();
app.MapGet("/", (ILoggerFactory loggerFactory) =>
{
    const string category = "root";
    var logger = loggerFactory.CreateLogger(category);
    logger.LogInformation("You hit the {category} URL!", category);
    return "Hello World!";
});
app.Run();
```

The preceding code transforms the console to logging JSON. For example, every time we hit the / endpoint, the console displays the following JSON:

```
{
  "EventId": 0,
  "LogLevel": "Information",
  "Category": "root",
  "Message": "You hit the root URL!",
  "State": {
    "Message": "You hit the root URL!",
    "category": "root",
    "{OriginalFormat}": "You hit the {category} URL!"
  }
}
```

Without that formatter, the usual output would have been:

```
info: root[0]
      You hit the root URL!
```

Based on that comparison, it is more versatile to query the JSON logs programmatically than the `stdout` line.

The biggest benefit of structured logging is improved searchability. You can run more precise queries at scale with a predefined data structure.

Of course, if you are setting up a production system, you would probably want more information attached to such log items like the correlation ID of the request, optionally some information about the current user, the server's name on which the code is running, and possibly more details depending on the application.

You may need more than the out-of-the-box features to utilize structured logging fully. Some third-party libraries like Serilog offer those additional capabilities. However, defining the way to send plain text to the logger could be a start.

Each project should dictate the needs and depth of each feature, including logging. Moreover, structured logging is a broader subject that merits studying independently. Nonetheless, I wanted to touch on this subject a bit, and hopefully, you learned enough about logging to get started.

Summary

In this chapter, we delved into the concept of logging. We learned that logging is the practice of recording messages into a log for later use, such as debugging errors, tracing operations, and analyzing usage.

Logging is essential, and ASP.NET Core offers us various ways to log information independently of third-party libraries while allowing us to use our favorite logging framework. We can customize the way the logs are written and categorized. We can use zero or more logging providers. We can also create custom logging providers like `AssertableLoggerProvider` and `XunitTestOutputLoggerProvider`, which we used to experiment with the ASP.NET Core logging system (not depicted in the chapter, but available on GitHub). Finally, we can use configurations or code to filter logs and much more.

Here is the default logging pattern to remember:

1. Inject an `ILogger<T>`, where `T` is the type of the class into which the logger is injected. `T` becomes the category.
2. Save a reference of that logger into a `private readonly ILogger` field.
3. Use that logger in your methods to log messages using the appropriate log level.

The logging system is a great addition to .NET Core compared to .NET Framework. It allows us to standardize the logging mechanism, making our systems easier to maintain in the long run. For example, suppose you want to use a new third-party library or even a custom-made one. In that case, you can load the provider into your `Program`, and the entire system will adapt and start using it without any further changes as long as you depend only on the logging abstractions. This is a good example of what well-designed abstractions can bring to a system.

This chapter closes the second section of this book with ASP.NET Core at its center. We explore design patterns to create flexible and robust components in the next few chapters.

Questions

Let's take a look at a few practice questions:

1. Can we write log entries to the console and a file at the same time?
2. Is it true that we should log the Trace- and Debug-level log entries in a production environment?
3. What is the purpose of structured logging?
4. How can we create a log entry in .NET?

Further reading

Here is a link to build upon what we learned in the chapter:

- [Official docs] Logging in .NET Core and ASP.NET Core: `https://adpg.link/MUVG`

Answers

1. Yes, you can configure as many providers as you want. One could be for the console, and another could append entries to a file.
2. No, you should not log Trace-level entries in production. You should only log Debug-level entries when debugging an issue.
3. Structured logging maintains a consistent structure across all log entries, making searching and analyzing logs easier.
4. We can create a log entry using interfaces like `ILogger`, `ILogger<T>`, and `ILoggerFactory`.

Learn more on Discord

To join the Discord community for this book – where you can share feedback, ask questions to the author, and learn about new releases – follow the QR code below:

`https://packt.link/ArchitectingASPNETCoreApps3e`

Section 3

Component Patterns

This section takes you on a journey through component design, focusing on creating and enhancing software components to fulfill specific goals. It navigates the architectural landscapes of software design, employing renowned Gang of Four design patterns to craft robust, maintainable, and flexible components.

Chapter 11, Structural Patterns, introduces structural patterns, showcasing the Decorator, Composite, Adapter, and Façade patterns. These patterns empower developers to extend classes dynamically (open-closed principle), manage complex object structures, bridge incompatible interfaces without changing existing code, and provide simpler interfaces to complex systems, which can significantly ease the integration and maintenance effort of subsystems.

Chapter 12, Behavioral Patterns, focuses on the Template Method and Chain of Responsibility patterns—two behavioral patterns crucial for managing shared logic and simplifying complex operations. The Template Method pattern simplifies the reuse of a shared algorithm and allows algorithm customization without altering its structure, while the Chain of Responsibility pattern facilitates dynamic or complex request handling through a chain of handlers.

Chapter 13, Operation Result Pattern, discusses the Operation Result pattern and its role in defining a method's capability to return a complex result. This result indicates the operation's success or failure and conveys additional details such as the operation's outcome, reasons for failure, and other pertinent information. This pattern can be valuable in structuring and enhancing communication between components when you want to avoid throwing exceptions.

Throughout the section, we learn to design and refine software components by applying structural and behavioral patterns and the Operation Result pattern. At the end of the section, developers will be equipped to tackle the complexities of software design, ensuring the system's components are functional, adaptable, and easy to maintain.

This section comprises the following chapters:

- *Chapter 11, Structural Patterns*
- *Chapter 12, Behavioral Patterns*
- *Chapter 13, Operation Result Pattern*

11

Structural Patterns

This chapter explores four structural design patterns from the well-known **Gang of Four** (**GoF**).

We use structural patterns to build and organize complex object hierarchies in a maintainable fashion. They allow us to dynamically add behaviors to existing classes, whether we designed the initial system this way or as an afterthought that emerges out of necessity later in the program's lifecycle. Structural patterns promote reusability and enhance the overall flexibility of the system.

In this chapter, we cover the following topics:

- The Decorator design pattern
- The Composite design pattern
- The Adapter design pattern
- The Façade design pattern

The first two patterns help us extend a class dynamically and efficiently manage a complex object structure. The Adapter pattern helps us connect an existing interface to another incompatible interface, enabling communication between two different systems. The Façade pattern provides a simpler interface to a complex system, shielding it or making it easier for consumers to interact with.

Let's unlock the power and simplicity of structural patterns.

The Decorator design pattern

The Decorator pattern allows us to dynamically add new functionality to an object by wrapping it with one or more decorator objects. This pattern allows us to add additional behaviors to objects at runtime without modifying the existing code, which helps us follow the Open-Closed principle. This pattern enables us to separate responsibilities into multiple smaller pieces. It is a simple but powerful pattern.

In this section, we explore how to implement this pattern in the traditional way and how to leverage an open-source library named **Scrutor** to help us create powerful dependency injection-ready decorators.

Goal

The Decorator pattern aims to extend an existing object at runtime without changing its code. Moreover, the decorated object should remain unaware of the decoration process, making this approach an excellent fit for complex or long-lasting systems that necessitate evolution.

The Decorator pattern makes it easier to encapsulate responsibilities into multiple classes, instead of packing multiple responsibilities inside a single class. Having multiple classes with a single responsibility makes the system easier to manage.

I often use this pattern to add flexibility and create adaptability in a program for next to no cost. In addition, small classes are easier to test, so the Decorator pattern adds ease of testability into the mix, making it worth mastering.

Design

A **decorator** class wraps and extends the functionality of the **decorated** class. For this to work, the decorator must both implement the same interface as the decorated class and hold a reference to an instance of it. Let's see this step by step, starting with a non-decorated class design:

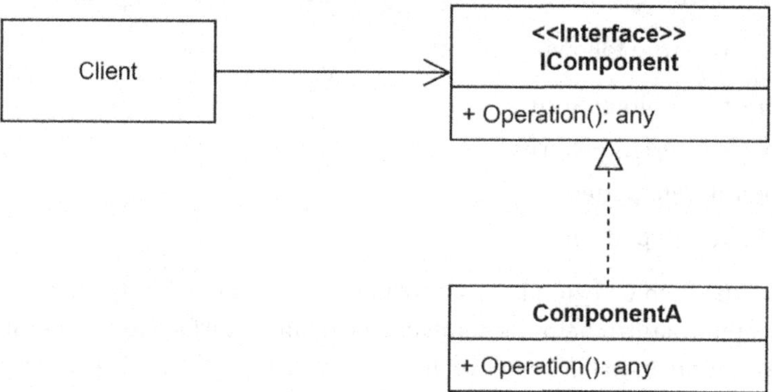

Figure 11.1: A class diagram representing the ComponentA class implementing the IComponent interface

In the preceding diagram, we have the following components:

- A client that calls the `Operation()` method of the `IComponent` interface.
- `ComponentA`, which implements the `IComponent` interface.

This translates into the following sequence diagram:

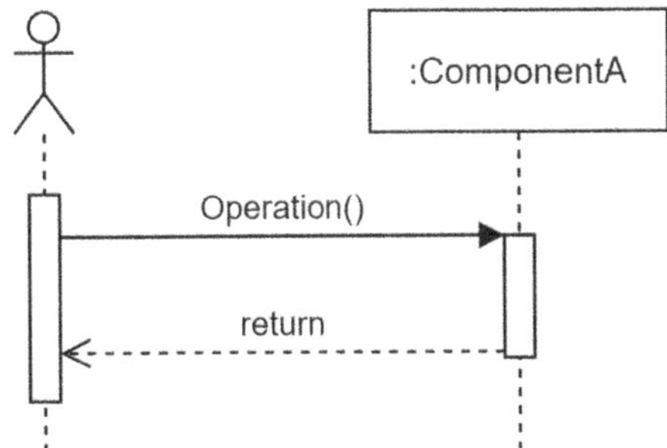

Figure 11.2: A sequence diagram showing a consumer calling the Operation method of the ComponentA class

Now, say that we want to add a behavior to `ComponentA`, but only in some cases. In other cases, we want to keep the initial behavior. To do so, we could choose the Decorator pattern and implement it as follows:

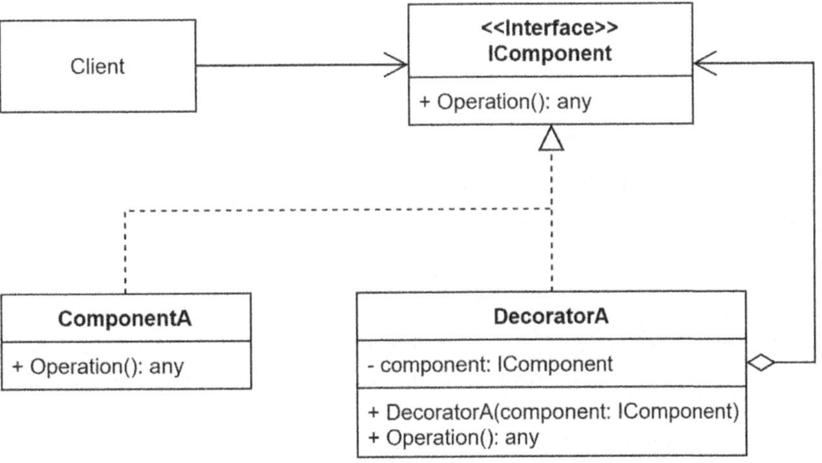

Figure 11.3: Decorator class diagram

Instead of modifying the `ComponentA` class, we created `DecoratorA`, which also implements the `IComponent` interface. This way, the `Client` object can use an instance of `DecoratorA` instead of `ComponentA` and leverage the new behavior without impacting the other consumers of `ComponentA`. Then, to avoid rewriting the whole component, an implementation of the `IComponent` interface (say an instance of `ComponentA`) is injected when creating a new `DecoratorA` instance (constructor injection). This new instance is stored in the `component` field and used by the `Operation()` method (implicitly using the **Strategy** pattern).

We can translate the updated sequence like so:

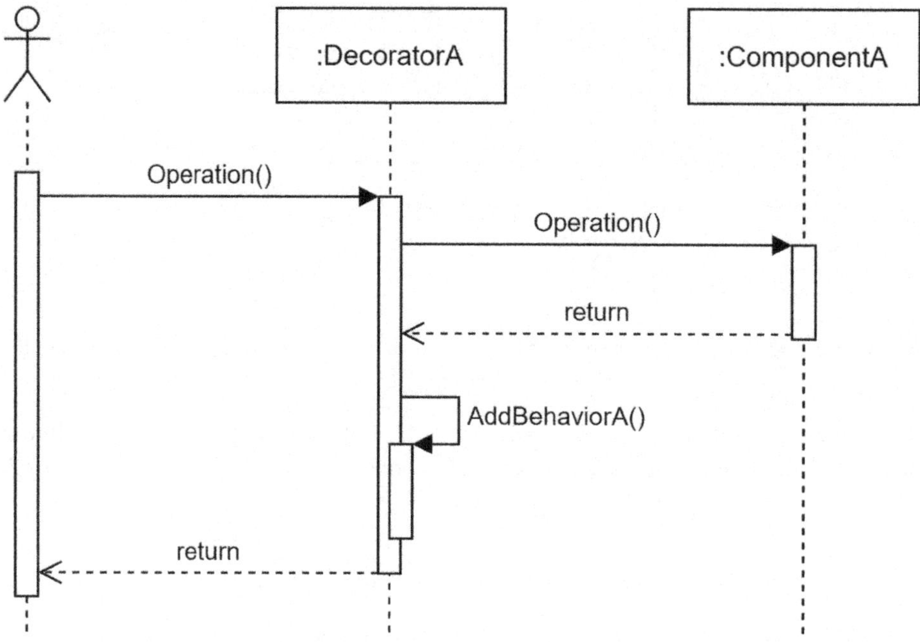

Figure 11.4: Decorator sequence diagram

In the preceding diagram, instead of calling `ComponentA` directly, `Client` calls `DecoratorA`, which in turn calls `ComponentA`. Finally, `DecoratorA` does some postprocessing by calling its private method, `AddBehaviorA()`.

Nothing from the Decorator pattern limits us from doing preprocessing, postprocessing, wrapping the decorated class's call (the `Operation` method in this example) with some logic (like an `if` statement or a `try-catch`), or all of that combined. The use of adding a postprocessing behavior is only an example.

To show you how powerful the Decorator pattern is before we jump into the code, know this: we can chain decorators! Since our decorator depends on the interface (not the implementation), we could inject another decorator, let's call it `DecoratorB`, inside `DecoratorA` (or vice versa). We could then create a long chain of rules that decorate one another, leading to a very powerful yet simple design.

Let's take a look at the following class diagram, which represents our chaining example:

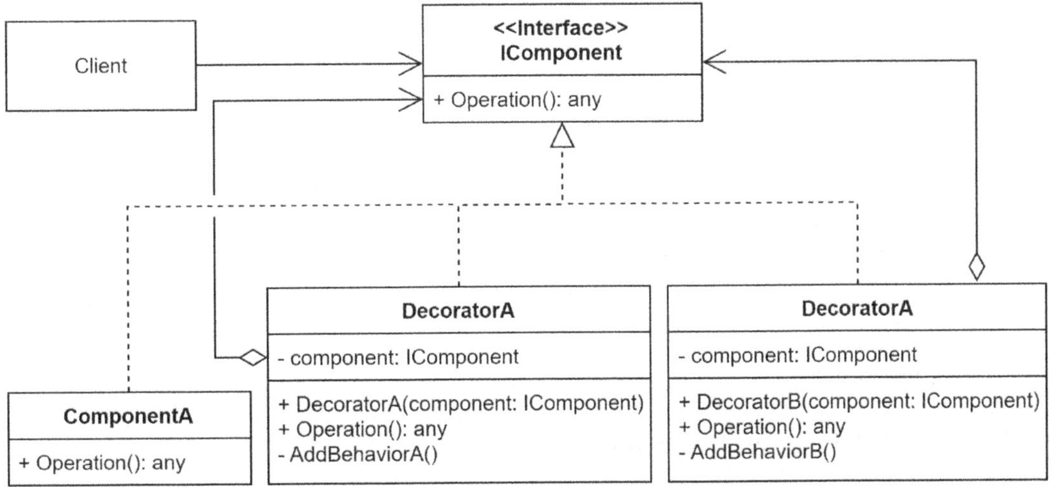

Figure 11.5: Decorator class diagram, including two decorators

Here, we created the `DecoratorB` class, which looks very similar to `DecoratorA` but has a private `AddBehaviorB()` method instead of `AddBehaviorA()`.

How we implement the decorator logic is irrelevant to the pattern, so I excluded the `AddBehaviorA()` method from *Figure 11.3* to show you only the pattern. However, I added it to *Figure 11.5* to clarify the idea behind having a second decorator.

Let's take a look at the sequence diagram for this:

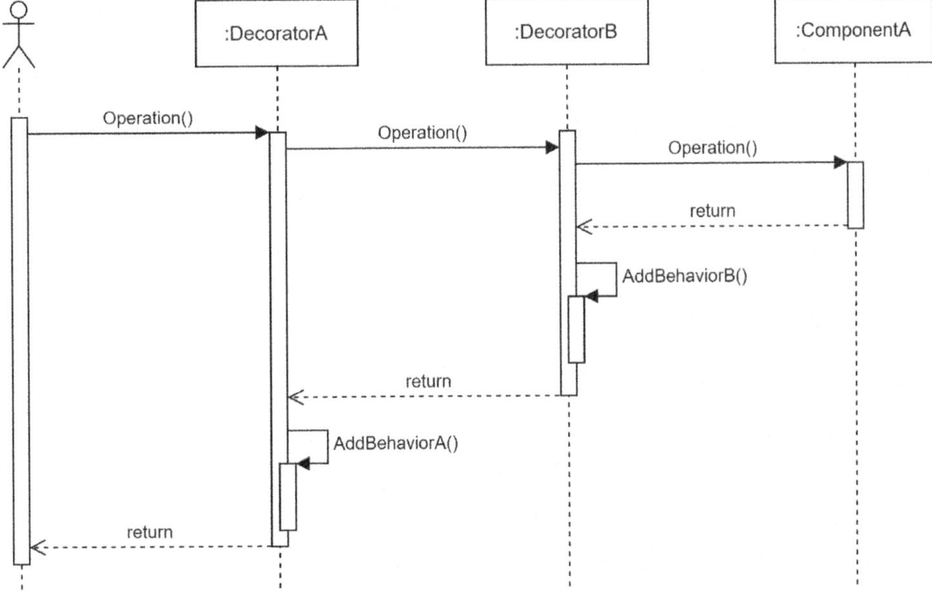

Figure 11.6: Sequence diagram of two nested decorators

With this, we are beginning to see the power of decorators. In the preceding diagram, we can assess that the behaviors of `ComponentA` have been changed twice without `Client` knowing about it. All those classes are unaware of the next `IComponent` in the chain. They don't even know that they are being decorated. They only play their role in the plan—that's all.

It is also important to note that the decorator's power resides in its dependency on the interface, not on an implementation, making it reusable. Based on that fact, we could swap `DecoratorA` and `DecoratorB` to invert the order the new behaviors are applied without touching the code itself. We could also apply the same decorator (say `DecoratorC`) to multiple `IComponent` implementations, like decorating both `DecoratorA` and `DecoratorB`. A decorator could even decorate itself.

Let's now dig into some code.

Project – Adding behaviors

Let's implement the previous example to help visualize the Decorator pattern. In the code we are about to implement, the `Operation` method of the component class returns a literal string. The `Operation` method of the decorator classes returns a modified version of the string provided by the class they are decorating. The program writes the string received from an `Operation` method to the response stream. It is not fancy but visually shows how the pattern works and allows us to build on top of our initial scenario, showcasing the flexibility the Decorator pattern brings.

First, let's look at the `IComponent` interface:

```
public interface IComponent
{
    string Operation();
}
```

The `IComponent` interface only states that an implementation should have an `Operation()` method that returns a `string`.

Next, let's look at the `ComponentA` class:

```
public class ComponentA : IComponent
{
    public string Operation()
    {
        return "Hello from ComponentA";
    }
}
```

The `Operation()` method of the `ComponentA` class returns a literal string.

Now that we've described the first pieces, let's look at the consumer:

```
var builder = WebApplication.CreateBuilder(args);
```

```
builder.Services.AddSingleton<IComponent, ComponentA>();
var app = builder.Build();
app.MapGet("/", (IComponent component) => component.Operation());
app.Run();
```

In the preceding `Program.cs` file, we register `ComponentA` as the implementation of `IComponent`, with a singleton lifetime. We then inject an `IComponent` implementation when an HTTP request hits the / endpoint. The delegate then calls the `Operation()` method and outputs the result to the response.

At this point, running the application results in the following response:

```
Hello from ComponentA
```

So far, it's pretty simple; the client calls the endpoint, the container injects an instance of the `ComponentA` class into the endpoint delegate, then the endpoint returns the results of `Operation` method to the client.

Next, we add the first decorator.

DecoratorA

Here, we want to modify the response without touching the code of the `ComponentA` class. To do so, we chose to create a decorator named `DecoratorA` that wraps the `Operation()` result into a `<DecoratorA>` tag:

```
public class DecoratorA : IComponent
{
    private readonly IComponent _component;
    public DecoratorA(IComponent component)
    {
        _component = component ?? throw new
ArgumentNullException(nameof(component));
    }
    public string Operation()
    {
        var result = _component.Operation();
        return $"<DecoratorA>{result}</DecoratorA>";
    }
}
```

`DecoratorA` implements and depends on the `IComponent` interface. It uses the injected `IComponent` implementation in its `Operation()` method and wraps its result in an HTML-like (XML) tag.

Now that we have a decorator, we need to tell the IoC container to send an instance of `DecoratorA` instead of `ComponentA` when injecting an `IComponent` interface.

`DecoratorA` should decorate `ComponentA`. More precisely, the container should inject an instance of the `ComponentA` class into the `DecoratorA` class.

To achieve this, we could register it as follows:

```
builder.Services.AddSingleton<IComponent>(serviceProvider => new DecoratorA(new
ComponentA()));
```

Here, we are telling ASP.NET Core to inject an instance of `DecoratorA` that decorates an instance of `ComponentA` when injecting an `IComponent` interface. When we run the application, we should see the following result in the browser:

```
<DecoratorA>Hello from ComponentA</DecoratorA>
```

You may have noticed a few `new` keywords there, but even though it is not very elegant, we can manually create new instances in the composition root without jeopardizing our application's health. We learn how to get rid of some of them later with the introduction of Scrutor.

Next, let's create the second decorator.

DecoratorB

Now that we have a decorator, it is time to create a second decorator to demonstrate the power of chaining decorators.

Context: We need another content wrapper but don't want to modify existing classes. To achieve this, we concluded that creating a second decorator would be perfect, so we created the following `DecoratorB` class:

```
public class DecoratorB : IComponent
{
    private readonly IComponent _component;
    public DecoratorB(IComponent component)
    {
        _component = component ?? throw new
ArgumentNullException(nameof(component));
    }
    public string Operation()
    {
        var result = _component.Operation();
        return $"<DecoratorB>{result}</DecoratorB>";
    }
}
```

The preceding code is similar to `DecoratorA`, but the XML tag is `DecoratorB` instead.

The important part is that the decorator depends on and implements the `IComponent` interface and doesn't depend on a concrete class. This is what gives us the flexibility of decorating any `IComponent`, and this is what enables us to chain decorators.

To complete this example, we need to update our composition root like this:

```
builder.Services.AddSingleton<IComponent>(serviceProvider => new DecoratorB(new
DecoratorA(new ComponentA())));
```

Now, `DecoratorB` decorates `DecoratorA`, which decorates `ComponentA`. When running the application, you see the following output:

```
<DecoratorB><DecoratorA>Hello from ComponentA</DecoratorA></DecoratorB>
```

And voilà! These decorators allowed us to modify the behavior of `ComponentA` without impacting the code. However, our composition root is beginning to get messy as we instantiate multiple dependencies inside each other, making our application harder to maintain. Moreover, the code is becoming harder to read. Furthermore, the code would be even harder to read if the decorators were also depending on other classes.

We can use decorators to change the behavior or state of an object. We can be very creative with decorators; for example, you could create a class that queries remote resources over HTTP and then decorate that class with a small component that manages a memory cache of the results, limiting the round trip to the remote server. You could create another decorator that monitors the time needed to query those resources and then log that to Application Insights—so many possibilities.

Next, we eliminate the `new` keywords and clean up our composition root.

Project – Decorator using Scrutor

This project aims to simplify the composition of the system we just created. To achieve this, we use **Scrutor**, an open-source library that allows us to do just that, among other things.

We first need to install the Scrutor NuGet package using Visual Studio or the CLI. When using the CLI, run the following command:

```
dotnet add package Scrutor
```

Once Scrutor is installed, we can use the `Decorate` extension method on the `IServiceCollection` to add decorators.

By using Scrutor, we can update the following messy code:

```
builder.Services.AddSingleton<IComponent>(serviceProvider => new DecoratorB(new
DecoratorA(new ComponentA())))
```

And convert it into this more elegant code:

```
builder.Services
    .AddSingleton<IComponent, ComponentA>()
    .Decorate<IComponent, DecoratorA>()
```

```
    .Decorate<IComponent, DecoratorB>()
;
```

In the preceding code, we register `ComponentA` as the implementation of `IComponent`, with a singleton lifetime, just like the first time.

Then, by using Scrutor, we told the IoC container to override that first binding and to decorate the already registered `IComponent` (`ComponentA`) with an instance of `DecoratorA` instead.

Then, we overrode the second binding by telling the IoC container to return an instance of `DecoratorB` that decorates the last known binding of `IComponent` instead (`DecoratorA`).

The result is the same as we did previously, but the code is now more elegant. On top of that improved readability, this lets the container create the instances instead of us using the `new` keyword, adding more flexibility and stability to our system.

As a reminder, the IoC container serves the equivalent of the following `instance` when an `IComponent` interface is requested:

```
var instance = new DecoratorB(new DecoratorA(new ComponentA()));
```

Why am I talking about elegance and flexibility? This code is a simple example, but if we add other dependencies to those classes, it could quickly become a complex code block that could become a maintenance nightmare, very hard to read, and have manually managed lifetimes. Of course, if the system is simple, you can always instantiate the decorators manually without loading an external library.

Whenever possible, keep your code simple. Using Scrutor is one way of achieving this. Code simplicity helps in the long run as it is easier to read and follow, even for someone else reading it. Consider that someone will most likely read your code one day.

Moreover, adding any external dependency to a project should be considered carefully. Remember that you must keep the dependency up to date, so having too many can take maintenance time. The library's author can also stop maintaining it, and the library will become outdated. The library may introduce breaking changes forcing you to update your code, and so on.

Furthermore, there is the security aspect to consider. Supply chain attacks are not uncommon. If you work in a regulated place, you may have to go through a cybersecurity vetting process, etc.

Besides those general tips, I've been using Scrutor for many years; I find it very stable and don't remember any breaking changes that caused me issues.

To ensure both programs behave the same, with or without Scrutor, let's explore the following integration test that runs for both projects, ensuring their correctness:

```
namespace Decorator.IntegrationTests;
//...
[Fact]
public async Task Should_return_a_double_decorated_string()
{
    // Arrange
    var client = _webApplicationFactory.CreateClient();

    // Act
    var response = await client.GetAsync("/");

    // Assert
    response.EnsureSuccessStatusCode();
    var body = await response.Content.ReadAsStringAsync();
    Assert.Equal(
        "Operation: <DecoratorB><DecoratorA>Hello from ComponentA</
DecoratorA></DecoratorB>",
        body
    );
}
```

The preceding test sends an HTTP request to one of the applications running in memory and compares the server response to the expected value. Since both projects should have the same output, we reuse this test in both the `DecoratorPlainStartupTest` and `DecoratorScrutorStartupTest` classes. They are empty and only route the test to the correct program. Here's an example of the Visual Studio Test Explorer:

Test	Duration
Decorator.IntegrationTests (2)	290 ms
Decorator.IntegrationTests (2)	290 ms
DecoratorPlainStartupTest (1)	145 ms
Should_return_a_double_decorated_string	145 ms
DecoratorScrutorStartupTest (1)	145 ms
Should_return_a_double_decorated_string	145 ms

Figure 11.7: A Visual Studio Test Explorer screenshot displaying the Decorator integration tests

You can also do assembly scanning using Scrutor (`https://adpg.link/xvfS`), which allows you to perform automatic dependency registration. This is outside the scope of this chapter, but it is worth looking into. Scrutor allows you to use the built-in IoC container for more complex scenarios, postponing the need to replace it with a third-party one.

Conclusion

The Decorator pattern is one of our toolbox's simplest yet most powerful design patterns. It augments existing classes without modifying them. A decorator is an independent block of logic that we can use to create complex and granular object trees that fit our needs.

We also explored the Scrutor open-source library to assist us in registering our decorator with the container.

The Decorator pattern helps us stay in line with the **SOLID** principles (and vice versa), as follows:

- **S**: The Decorator pattern suggests creating small classes to add behaviors to other classes, segregating responsibilities, and fostering reuse.
- **O**: Decorators add behaviors to other classes without modifying them, which is literally the definition of the OCP.
- **L**: N/A.
- **I**: By following the ISP, creating decorators for your specific needs should be easy. However, implementing the Decorator pattern may become difficult if your interfaces are too complex. Having a hard time creating a decorator is a good indicator that the interface may be too big—a code smell. A well-segregated interface should be easy to decorate.
- **D**: Depending on abstractions is the key to the Decorator's power.

Next, we explore the Composite pattern, which helps us manage complex objects' structures differently than the Decorator pattern does.

The Composite design pattern

The Composite design pattern is another structural GoF pattern that helps us manage complex object structures. This pattern is best suited for representing part-whole hierarchies and treating individual objects and compositions uniformly. In contrast, the Decorator pattern is ideal for adding responsibilities to objects dynamically without altering their structure. Choose the Composite pattern when you work with tree-like structures and the Decorator pattern when you need to extend an object's behavior without modifying its class.

Goal

The goal behind the Composite pattern is to create a hierarchical data structure where you don't need to differentiate groups from single components, making the traversal and manipulation of the hierarchy easy for its consumers.

You could think of the Composite pattern as a way of building a graph or a tree with self-managing nodes.

Design

The design of the Composite pattern is straightforward; we have *components* and *composites*. Both implement a common interface that defines the shared operations. The *components* are single nodes, while the *composites* are collections of *components*. Let's take a look at a diagram:

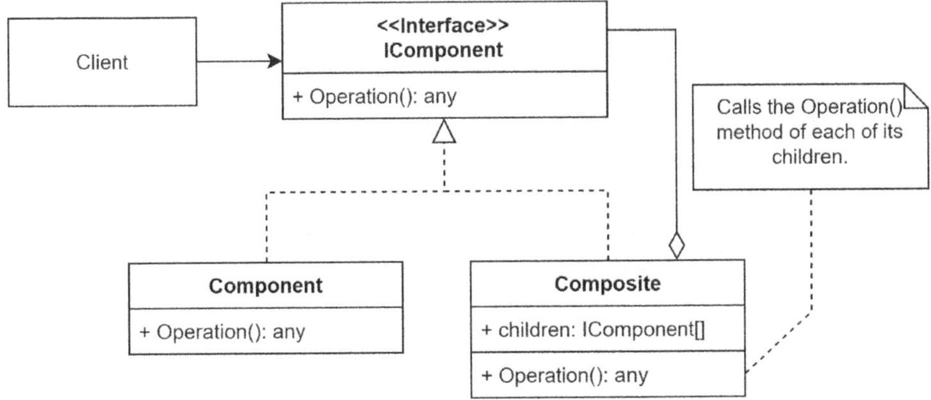

Figure 11.8: Composite class diagram

In the preceding diagram, `Client` depends on an `IComponent` interface and is unaware of the underlying implementation—it could be an instance of a `Component` or a `Composite`; it does not matter.

Then, we have two implementations:

- `Component` represents a single element; a leaf.
- `Composite` represents a collection of `IComponent`. The `Composite` object uses its children to manage the hierarchy's complexity by delegating part of the process to them.

Those three pieces, when put together, create the Composite design pattern. Considering that it is possible to add instances of the `Composite` and `Component` classes as children of other `Composite` objects, it is possible to create complex, non-linear, and self-managed data structures with next to no effort.

You are not limited to one type of component and one type of composite; you can create as many implementations of the `IComponent` interface as you need. Then, you can even mix and match them to create a non-linear tree.

Project – BookStore

Context: We built a program in the past to support a bookstore. However, the store is going so well that our little program is not enough anymore. Our fictional company now owns multiple stores. They want to divide those stores into sections and manage book sets and single books. After a few minutes of gathering information and asking them questions, we realize they can have sets of sets, subsections, and possibly sub-stores, so we need a flexible design.

We decide to use the Composite pattern to solve this problem. Here's our class hierarchy:

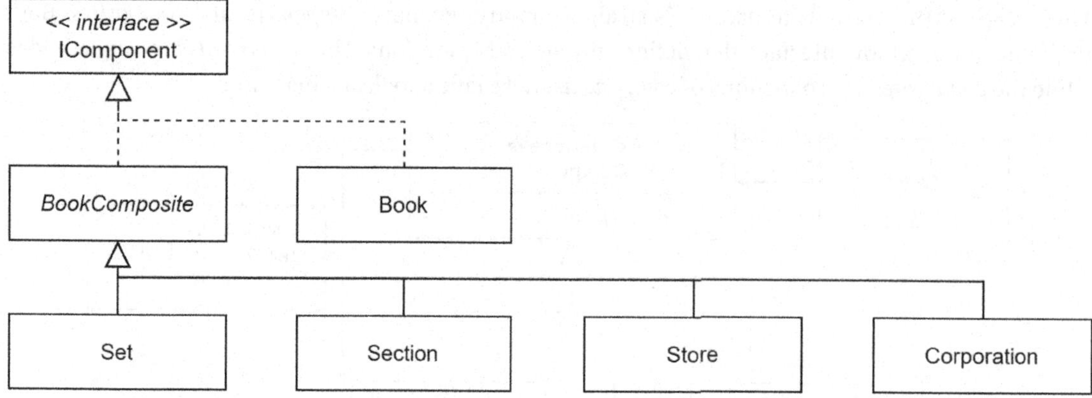

Figure 11.9: The BookStore project composite class hierarchy

Due to the complexity of our class hierarchy and the uncertainty of a project in an early stage, we decided that a factory would be adequate to create our class hierarchy, showcase our design, and validate it with the customer. Here's the high-level design:

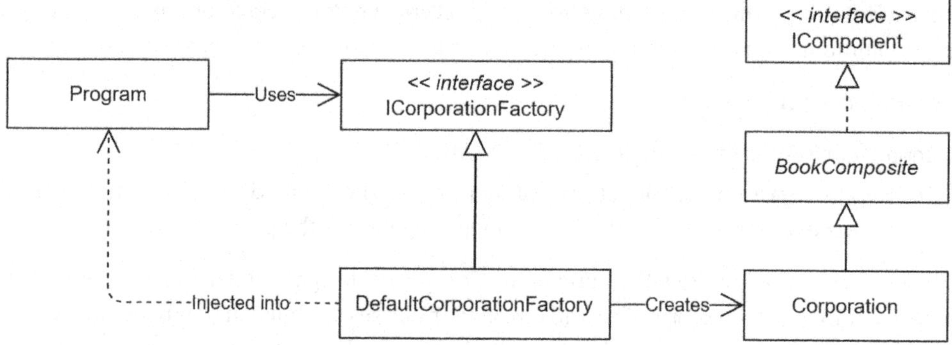

Figure 11.10: High-level design of the BookStore project

We decided to aim for the smallest possible interface to get the ball rolling. Since we want to know how many items are available in any part of the store and what type of component we are interacting with, we created the following interface:

```
namespace Composite.Models;
public interface IComponent
{
    int Count { get; }
    string Type { get; }
}
```

The Count property allows us to calculate how many items are available under the corporation, a store, a section, a set, or any other composite component we create in the future. The Type property forces each component to display its type linearly.

We can create such a minimal interface because we are not executing any operations on the data structure but rather counting the elements, then serializing it to JSON. The serializer will take care of navigating the class hierarchy for us. In another context, the minimal subset of properties might be more than this.

Next, let's create our composite structure, starting with the Book class (the *Component*):

```
namespace Composite.Models;
public class Book : IComponent
{
    public Book(string title)
    {
        Title = title ?? throw new ArgumentNullException(nameof(title));
    }

    public string Title { get; }
    public string Type => "Book";
    public int Count { get; } = 1;
}
```

The preceding Book class implements the interface by always returning a count of 1 because it is a single book, a leaf in the tree. The Type property is also hard-coded. As a book, the class requires a title upon construction that it stores in the Title property (not inherited and only available to Book instances).

In a real scenario, we'd have more properties, like the ISBN and author, but doing so here would just clutter the example. We are not designing a real bookstore but learning about the Composite pattern.

Next, let's create our composite component, the BookComposite class:

```
using System.Collections;
using System.Collections.ObjectModel;
namespace Composite.Models;
public abstract class BookComposite : IComponent
{
    protected readonly List<IComponent> children = new();
```

```
    public BookComposite(string name)
    {
        Name = name ?? throw new ArgumentNullException(nameof(name));
    }

    public string Name { get; }
    public virtual string Type => GetType().Name;
    public virtual int Count
        => children.Sum(child => child.Count);
    public virtual IEnumerable Children
        => new ReadOnlyCollection<IComponent>(children);

    public virtual void Add(IComponent bookComponent)
    {
        children.Add(bookComponent);
    }

    public virtual void Remove(IComponent bookComponent)
    {
        children.Remove(bookComponent);
    }
}
```

The `BookComposite` class implements the following shared features:

- Children management (highlighted in the code)
- Setting the `Name` property of the composite object and forcing the classes inheriting it to set a name upon construction
- Automatically finds and sets the `Type` name of its derived class
- Counting the number of children (and, implicitly, the children's children)
- Exposing the children through the `Children` property and ensuring consumers can't modify the collection from the outside by returning a `ReadOnlyCollection` object

Using the LINQ `Sum()` extension method in the `children.Sum(child => child.Count());` expression allowed us to replace a more complex `for` loop and an accumulator variable.

Adding the `virtual` modifier to the `Type` property allows sub-types to override the property in case their type's name does not reflect the type that should be displayed in the program.

Now, we can start implementing the other classes of our complex composite hierarchy and assign a responsibility to each class, showing how flexible the Composite pattern is.

The following classes inherit from the BookComposite class:

- The Corporation class represents the corporation that owns multiple stores. However, it is not limited to owning stores; a corporation could own other corporations, stores, or any other IComponent.
- The Store class represents a bookstore.
- The Section class represents a section of a bookstore, an aisle, or a category of books.
- The Set class represents a book set, such as a trilogy.

These can be composed of any IComponent, making this an ultra-flexible data structure.

Let's look at the code for these BookComposite sub-types, starting with the Corporation class:

```
namespace Composite.Models;
public class Corporation : BookComposite
{
    public Corporation(string name, string ceo)
        : base(name)
    {
        CEO = ceo;
    }

    public string CEO { get; }
}
```

The corporation contributes a CEO to the model because someone has to manage the place.

Next, we look at the Store class:

```
namespace Composite.Models;
public class Store : BookComposite
{
    public string Location { get; }
    public string Manager { get; }
    public Store(string name, string location, string manager)
        : base(name)
    {
        Location = location;
        Manager = manager;
    }
}
```

On top of the BookComposite members, a store has a manager and a location.

Now, the `Section` class does not add anything, but we can use it as a flexible organizer:

```
namespace Composite.Models;
public class Section : BookComposite
{
    public Section(string name) : base(name) { }
}
```

Finally, the `Set` class allows creating the book set upon construction through the books parameter:

```
namespace Composite.Models;
public class Set : BookComposite
{
    public Set(string name, params IComponent[] books)
        : base(name)
    {
        foreach (var book in books)
        {
            Add(book);
        }
    }
}
```

Composing a set of books upon creation of the instance will be convenient later when we assemble the tree.

Next, let's explore the last part of the program that helps encapsulate the data structure's creation: the factory.

The factory is not part of the Composite pattern, but now that we know what a factory is, we can use one to encapsulate the creation logic of our data structure and talk about it.

The factory interface looks like the following:

```
public interface ICorporationFactory
{
    Corporation Create();
}
```

The default concrete implementation of the `ICorporationFactory` interface is the `DefaultCorporationFactory` class. It creates a large non-linear data structure with sections, subsections, sets, and subsets.

This whole structure is defined using our composite model in the `DefaultCorporationFactory` class. Due to its large size, let's start with the class's skeleton and its `Create` method:

```
using Composite.Models;
namespace Composite.Services;
public class DefaultCorporationFactory : ICorporationFactory
{
    public Corporation Create()
    {
        var corporation = new Corporation(
            "Boundless Shelves Corporation",
            "Bosmang Kapawu"
        );
        corporation.Add(CreateTaleTowersStore());
        corporation.Add(CreateEpicNexusStore());
        return corporation;
    }
    // ...
}
```

In the preceding `Create` method, we create the corporation, add two stores, then return the result.

The `CreateTaleTowersStore` and `CreateEpicNexusStore` methods create a store, set their name, address, and manager, and create three sections each:

```
private IComponent CreateTaleTowersStore()
{
    var store = new Store(
        "Tale Towers",
        "125 Enchantment Street, Storyville, SV 72845",
        "Malcolm Reynolds"
    );
    store.Add(CreateFantasySection());
    store.Add(CreateAdventureSection());
    store.Add(CreateDramaSection());
    return store;
}
private IComponent CreateEpicNexusStore()
{
    var store = new Store(
        "Epic Nexus",
        "369 Parchment Plaza, Novelty, NV 68123",
```

```
        "Ellen Ripley"
    );
    store.Add(CreateFictionSection());
    store.Add(CreateFantasySection());
    store.Add(CreateAdventureSection());
    return store;
}
```

Both stores share two sections (have the same books; highlighted code), each with a unique section.

If we look at the `CreateFictionSection` method, it adds an imaginary book and a subsection:

```
private IComponent CreateFictionSection()
{
    var section = new Section("Fiction");
    section.Add(new Book("Some alien cowboy"));
    section.Add(CreateScienceFictionSection());
    return section;
}
```

The `CreateScienceFictionSection` method adds an invented book and the *Star Wars* book set composed of three trilogies (a set of sets):

```
private IComponent CreateScienceFictionSection()
{
    var section = new Section("Science Fiction");
    section.Add(new Book("Some weird adventure in space"));
    section.Add(new Set(
        "Star Wars",
        new Set(
            "Prequel trilogy",
            new Book("Episode I: The Phantom Menace"),
            new Book("Episode II: Attack of the Clones"),
            new Book("Episode III: Revenge of the Sith")
        ),
        new Set(
            "Original trilogy",
            new Book("Episode IV: A New Hope"),
            new Book("Episode V: The Empire Strikes Back"),
            new Book("Episode VI: Return of the Jedi")
        ),
        new Set(
            "Sequel trilogy",
```

```
                new Book("Episode VII: The Force Awakens"),
                new Book("Episode VIII: The Last Jedi"),
                new Book("Episode IX: The Rise of Skywalker")
            )
        ));
        return section;
    }
```

Now, if we look at this part of the data structure, we have the following:

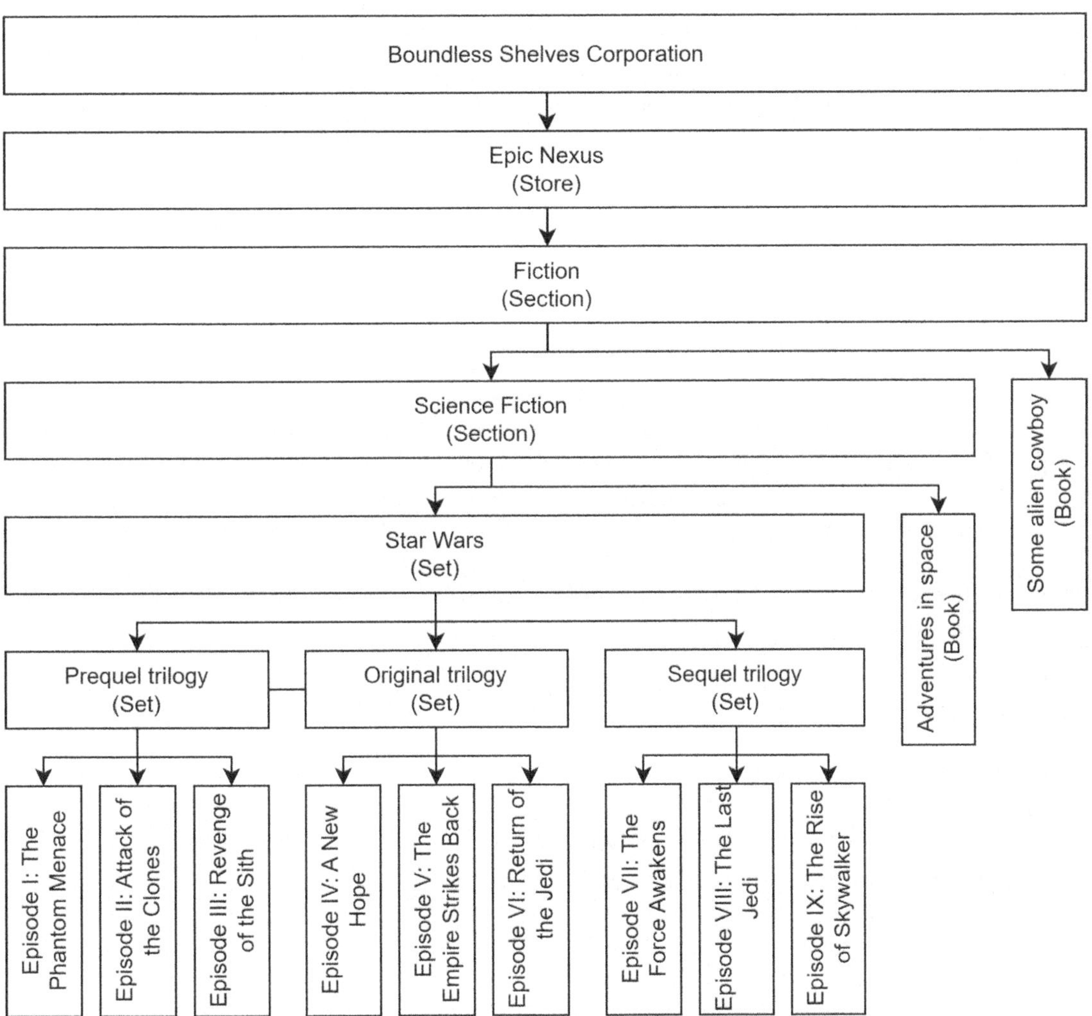

Figure 11.11: The Fiction section of the Epic Nexus store data

On a broader level, the whole organizational structure, down to the section level (without the books and sets), looks like this:

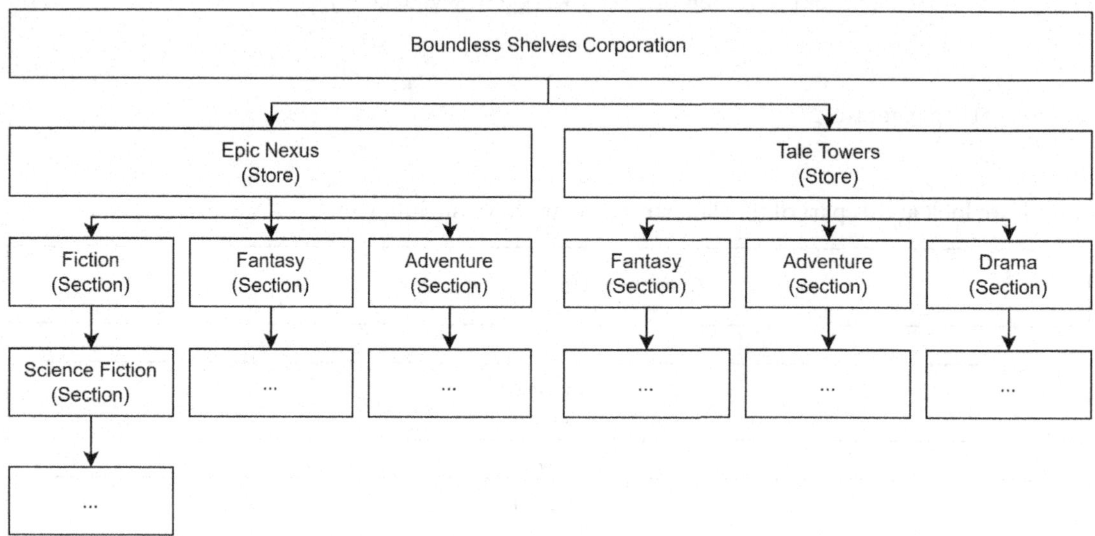

Figure 11.12: The composite hierarchy without the books and sets

I omitted publishing the whole data structure, including the books, as an image because it is too large and would be hard to read. Rest assured, the content itself is unimportant, and the section we are studying is enough to understand the flexibility the composite pattern brings to the design.

As we explore this, we can see how flexible the design is. We can create almost any organizational structure we want.

Now, let's look at the `Program.cs` file and register our dependencies and an endpoint to query the data structure:

```
using Composite.Services;

var builder = WebApplication.CreateBuilder(args);
builder.Services.AddSingleton<ICorporationFactory,
DefaultCorporationFactory>();

var app = builder.Build();

app.MapGet(
    "/",
    (ICorporationFactory corporationFactory)
        => corporationFactory.Create()
```

```
);
app.Run();
```

The preceding code registers the factory that creates the corporation data structure with the container and an endpoint to serve it.

When we execute the code, we get the full data structure of the corporation. For brevity reasons, the following JSON represents the fiction section, excluding the books:


```
{
  "ceo": "Bosmang Kapawu",
  "name": "Boundless Shelves Corporation",
  "type": "Corporation",
  "count": 43,
  "children": [
    {
      "location": "369 Parchment Plaza, Novelty, NV 68123",
      "manager": "Ellen Ripley",
      "name": "Epic Nexus",
      "type": "Store",
      "count": 25,
      "children": [
        {
          "name": "Fiction",
          "type": "Section",
          "count": 11,
          "children": [
            {
              "name": "Science Fiction",
              "type": "Section",
              "count": 10,
              "children": [
                {
                  "name": "Star Wars",
                  "type": "Set",
                  "count": 9,
                  "children": [
                    {
                      "name": "Prequel trilogy",
                      "type": "Set",
                      "count": 3,
```

```
                      "children": []
                    },
                    {
                      "name": "Original trilogy",
                      "type": "Set",
                      "count": 3,
                      "children": []
                    },
                    {
                      "name": "Sequel trilogy",
                      "type": "Set",
                      "count": 3,
                      "children": []
                    }
                  ]
                }
              ]
            }
          ]
        }
      ]
    }
  ]
}
```

The values of the `count` fields reflect the total count. If you run the program and play with the preprocessor symbols defined in the `DefaultCorporationFactory.cs` file (`ADD_BOOKS`, `ADD_SETS`, and `ONLY_FICTION`), you will end up with different numbers.

For example, if you use the following combination, the count will equal 0 because there is no book (component) in any collection (composite):

```
#undef ADD_BOOKS
#define ADD_SETS // OR #undef ADD_SETS
#define ONLY_FICTION
```

The Composite pattern allowed us to render a complex data structure in a small method call. Since each component autonomously handles itself, the Composite pattern removes the burden of managing this complexity from the consumer.

I encourage you to play around with the existing data structure so that you understand the pattern. You could also try adding a `Movie` class to manage movies; a bookstore must diversify its activities. You could also differentiate movies from books so that customers are not confused. The bookstores could have both physical and digital books as well.

If you are keen to try more, try building a new application from scratch and use the Composite pattern to create, manage, and display a multi-level menu structure or a file system API.

Conclusion

The Composite pattern effectively builds, manages, and maintains complex non-linear data structures. Its power is primarily in its self-management capabilities. Each node, component, or composite is responsible for its own logic, leaving little to no work for the composite's consumers. Of course, a more complex scenario would have led to a more complex interface.

Using the Composite pattern helps us follow the **SOLID** principles in the following ways:

- **S**: It helps divide multiple elements of a complex data structure into small classes to split responsibilities.
- **O**: By allowing us to "mix and match" different implementations of `IComponent` interface, the Composite pattern allows us to extend the data structure without impacting the other existing classes. For example, you could create a new class that implements `IComponent` and start using it immediately without modifying any other component classes.
- **L**: N/A.
- **I**: The Composite pattern may violate the ISP when single items implement operations that only impact the collections, like the `Add` and `Remove` methods, but we have not done this here.
- **D**: The Composite pattern actors depend solely on `IComponent`, which inverts the dependency flow.

Next, we move to a different type of structural pattern that adapts one interface to another.

The Adapter design pattern

The Adapter pattern is another structural design pattern that allows two incompatible interfaces to work together without modifying their existing code. This pattern introduces a wrapper class called the *Adapter*, which bridges the gap between the interfaces.

Goal

The Adapter design pattern is applicable when we want to use an existing class, but its interface is incompatible with what we want to use it for. Instead of refactoring the class, which could introduce bugs or errors in the existing codebase or even cascade changes to other parts of the system, we can use an *Adapter* class to make the class's interface compatible with the *Target* interface.

The Adapter pattern is handy when we cannot change the *Adaptee's* code or do not want to change it.

Design

You can think of the adapter as a power outlet's universal adapter; you can connect a North American device to a European outlet by connecting it to the adapter and then to the power outlet. The Adapter design pattern does precisely that but for APIs.

Let's start by looking at the following diagram:

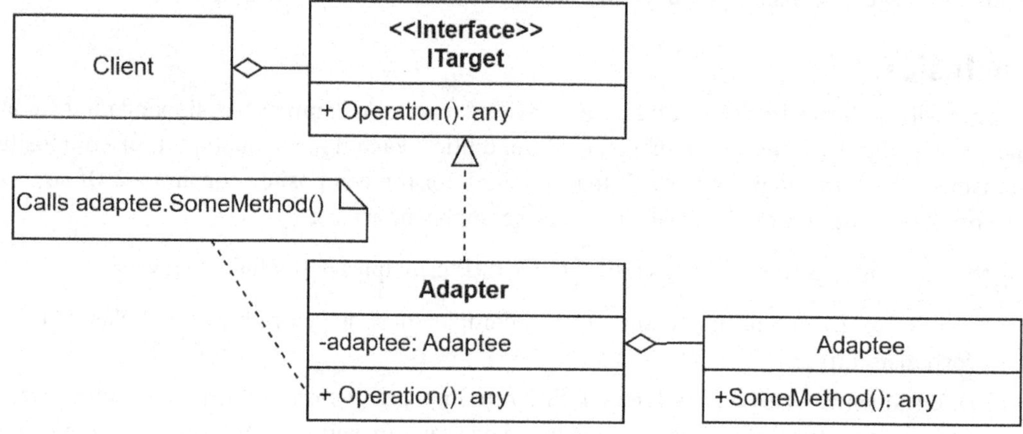

Figure 11.13: Adapter class diagram

In the preceding diagram, we have the following actors:

- The `ITarget` interface holds the contract we want (or have) to use.
- The `Adaptee` class represents the concrete component we want to use that does not conform to `ITarget`.
- The `Adapter` class adapts the `Adaptee` class to the `ITarget` interface.

There is a second way of implementing the Adapter pattern that implies inheritance. If you can go for composition, go for it, but if you need access to `protected` members of `Adaptee`, you can go for inheritance instead, like this:

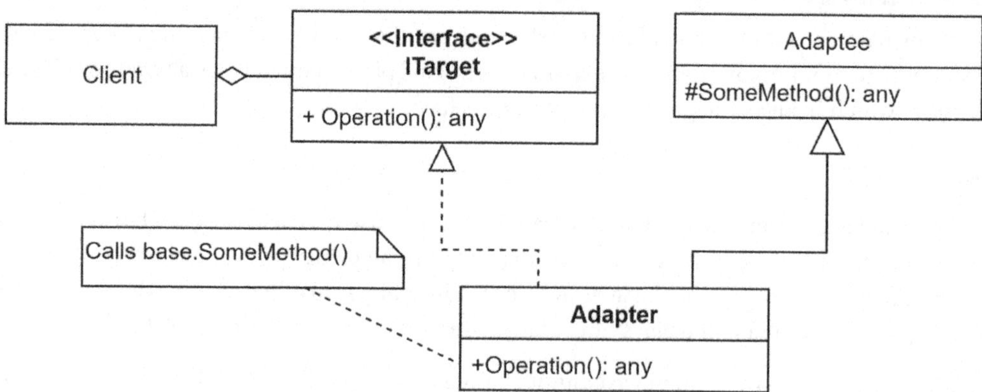

Figure 11.14: Adapter class diagram inheriting the Adaptee

The actors are the same, but instead of composing the `Adapter` class with the `Adaptee` class, the `Adapter` class inherits from the `Adaptee` class. This design makes the `Adapter` class become both an `Adaptee` and an `ITarget`.

Let's explore how to implement the Adapter pattern hands-on.

Project – Greeter

Context: We've programmed a highly sophisticated greeting system that we want to reuse in a new program. However, its interface does not match the new design, and we cannot modify it because other systems use that greeting system.

To fix this problem, we decided to apply the Adapter pattern.

Let's start with the external greeter (`ExternalGreeter`) class:

```
public class ExternalGreeter
{
    public string GreetByName(string name)
    {
        return $"Adaptee says: hi {name}!";
    }
}
```

Next, let's look at the new interface (`IGreeter`) used in our new system:

```
public interface IGreeter
{
    string Greeting();
}
```

The `ExternalGreeter` class does not implement the `IGreeter` interface, and we must not directly modify the `ExternalGreeter` class to prevent any breaking changes from occurring in other systems. To solve this problem, we decided to use the Adapter pattern, so now we must create an adapter. Here's how we can adapt the external greeter to meet the latest requirements:

```
public class ExternalGreeterAdapter : IGreeter
{
    private readonly ExternalGreeter _adaptee;
    public ExternalGreeterAdapter(ExternalGreeter adaptee)
    {
        _adaptee = adaptee ?? throw new ArgumentNullException(nameof(adaptee));
    }
    public string Greeting()
    {
        return _adaptee.GreetByName("ExternalGreeterAdapter");
    }
}
```

In the preceding code blocks, the actors are as follows:

- The `IGreeter` interface represents the *Target* and is the interface that we must use.

- The `ExternalGreeter` class represents the *Adaptee* and is the external component that already contains all the logic that someone programmed and tested. That code could be in an external assembly or installed from a NuGet package.
- The `ExternalGreeterAdapter` class represents the *Adapter* and is where the adapter does its job. In this case, the `Greeting` method calls the `GreetByName` method of the `ExternalGreeter` class, which implements the greeting logic.

Now, we can call the `Greeting` method and get the result of the `GreetByName` call. With this in place, we can reuse the existing logic through the `ExternalGreeterAdapter` class.

We can also test `IGreeter` consumers by mocking the `IGreeter` interface without dealing with the `ExternalGreeterAdapter` class.

In this case, the "complex logic" is pretty simple, but we are here for the Adapter pattern, not for imaginary business logic. Now, let's take a look at the consumer:

```
var builder = WebApplication.CreateBuilder(args);
builder.Services.AddSingleton<ExternalGreeter>();
builder.Services.AddSingleton<IGreeter, ExternalGreeterAdapter>();
var app = builder.Build();
app.MapGet("/", (IGreeter greeter) => greeter.Greeting());
app.Run();
```

In the preceding code, we composed our application by registering the `ExternalGreeterAdapter` class as a singleton bound to the `IGreeter` interface. We also informed the container to provide a single instance of the `ExternalGreeter` class whenever requested (in this case, we inject it into the `ExternalGreeterAdapter` class).

The consumer (*Client* in the class diagrams) is the highlighted endpoint where the `IGreeter` interface is injected as a parameter. Then, the delegate calls the `Greeting` method on that injected instance and outputs the greeting message to the response.

The following diagram represents what's happening in this system:

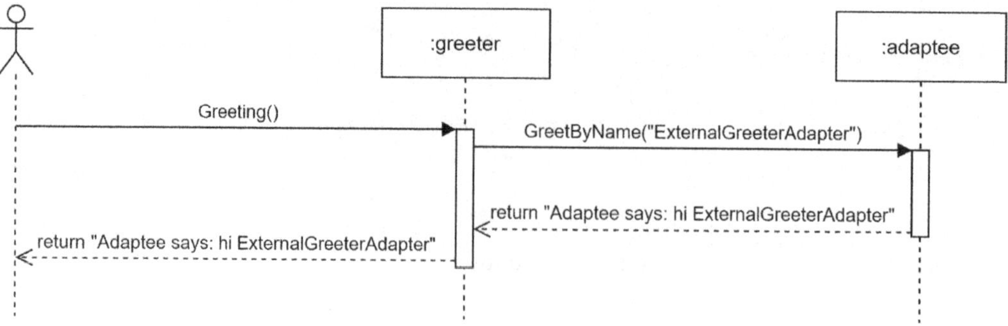

Figure 11.15: Greeter system sequence diagram

And voilà! We've adapted the `ExternalGreeterAdapter` class to the `IGreeter` interface with little effort.

Conclusion

The Adapter pattern is another simple pattern that offers flexibility. With it, we can use older or non-conforming components without rewriting them. Of course, depending on the *Target* and *Adaptee* interfaces, you may need to put more or less effort into writing the code of the *Adapter* class.

Now, let's learn how the Adapter pattern can help us follow the **SOLID** principles:

- **S**: The Adapter pattern has only one responsibility: make an interface work with another interface.
- **O**: The Adapter pattern allows us to modify the *Adaptee's* interface without the need to modify its code.
- **L**: Inheritance is not much of a concern regarding the Adapter pattern, so this principle does not apply once again. If *Adapter* inherits from *Adaptee*, the goal is to change its interface, not its behavior, which should conform to the LSP.
- **I**: We can view the *Adapter* class as a facilitator to the ISP, with the *Target* interface as the ultimate destination. The Adapter pattern relies on the design of the *Target* interface but doesn't directly influence it. Per this principle, our primary focus should be to design the *Target* interface in a manner that abides by the ISP.
- **D**: The Adapter pattern introduces only an implementation of the *Target* interface. Even if the *Adapter* depends on a concrete class, it breaks the direct dependency on that external component by adapting it to the *Target* interface.

Next, we explore the last structural pattern of the chapter that teaches foundational concepts.

The Façade design pattern

The Façade pattern is a structural pattern that simplifies the access to a complex system. It is very similar to the Adapter pattern, but it creates a wall (a façade) between one or more subsystems. The big difference between the adapter and the façade is that instead of adapting an interface to another, the façade simplifies the use of a subsystem, typically by using multiple classes of that subsystem.

We can apply the same idea to shielding one or more programs, but in this case, we call the façade a gateway—more on that in *Chapter 19, Introduction to Microservices Architecture*.

The Façade pattern is extremely useful and can be adapted to multiple situations.

Goal

The Façade pattern aims to simplify the use of one or more subsystems by providing an interface that is easier to use than the subsystems themselves, shielding the consumers from that complexity.

Design

Imagine a system with a multitude of complex classes. Direct interaction between the consuming code and these classes can become problematic due to coupling, complexity, and low code readability and maintainability. The Façade design pattern offers a solution by providing a unified interface to a set of APIs in a subsystem, making it easier to use.

The `Facade` class contains references to the objects of the complex subsystem and delegates client requests to the appropriate subsystem object. From a client's perspective, it only interacts with a single, simplified interface represented by the Façade. Behind the scenes, the Façade coordinates with the subsystem's components to fulfill the client's request.

We could create multiple diagrams representing a multitude of subsystems, but let's keep things simple. Remember that you can replace the single subsystem shown in the following diagram with as many subsystems as you need to adapt:

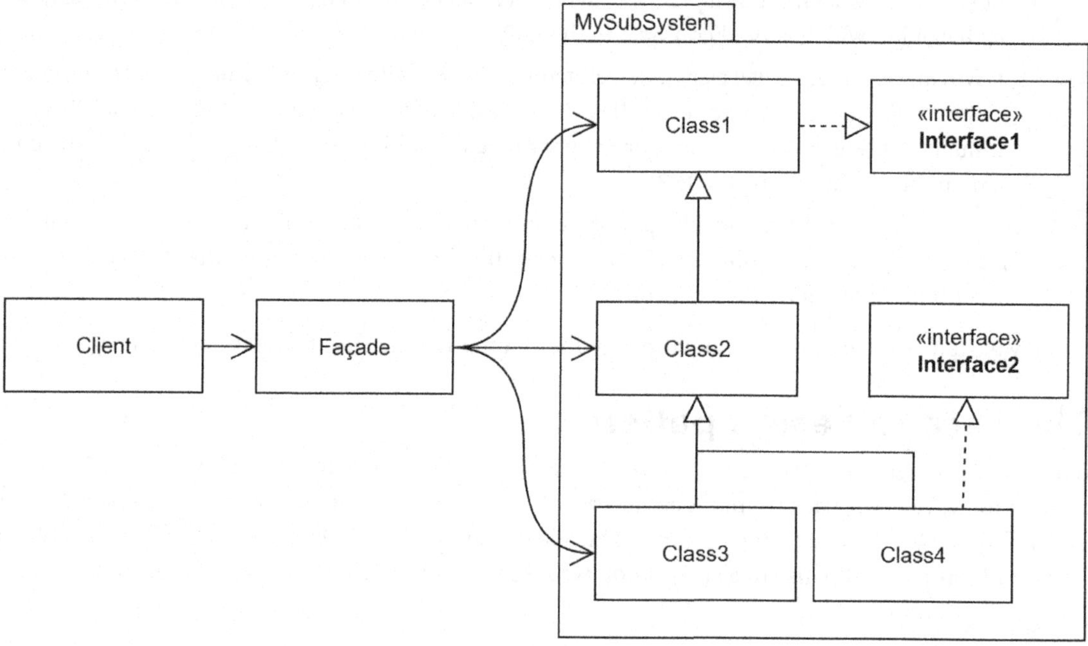

Figure 11.16: A class diagram representing a Façade object that hides a complex subsystem

The *Façade* plays the intermediary between the *Client* and the subsystem, simplifying its usage. Let's see this in action as a sequence diagram:

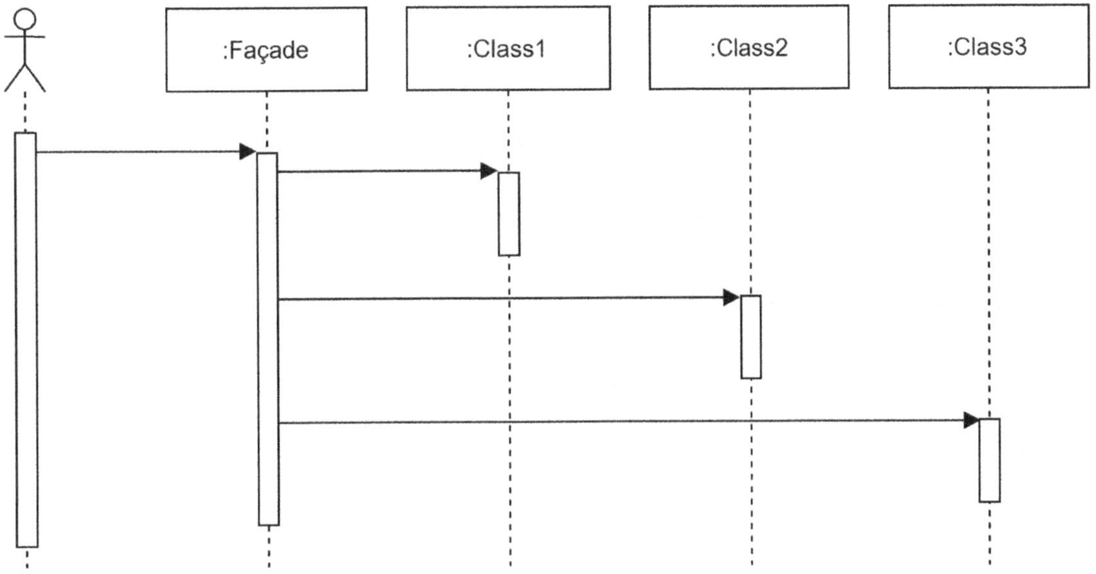

Figure 11.17: A sequence diagram representing a Façade object that interacts with a complex sub-system

In the preceding diagram, the *Client* calls the *Façade* once, while the *Façade* places multiple calls against different classes.

There are multiple ways of implementing a façade:

- **Opaque façades:** In this form, the `Façade` class is inside the subsystem. All other classes of the subsystem have an `internal` visibility modifier. This way, only the classes inside the subsystem can interact with the other internal classes, forcing the consumers to use the `Façade` class.
- **Transparent façades:** In this form, the classes can have a `public` modifier, allowing the consumers to use them directly or to use the `Façade` class. This way, we can create the `Façade` class inside or outside the subsystem.
- **Static façades:** In this form, the `Façade` class is `static`. We can implement a static façade as opaque or transparent.

I recommend using static façades as a last resort because `static` elements limit flexibility and testability.

We look at some code next.

Project – The façades

In this example, we play with the following C# projects:

- The `OpaqueFacadeSubSystem` class library showcases an **opaque façade**.
- The `TransparentFacadeSubSystem` class library showcases a **transparent façade**.
- The `Facade` project is a REST API that consumes the façades. It exposes two endpoints to access the `OpaqueFacadeSubSystem` project, and two others that target the `TransparentFacadeSubSystem` project.

Let's start with the class libraries.

To follow the SOLID principles, adding some interfaces representing the elements of the subsystem seemed appropriate. In subsequent chapters, we explore how to organize our abstractions to be more reusable, but for now, both abstractions and implementations live in the same assembly.

Opaque façade

In this assembly, only the façade is public; all the other classes are internal, which means they are hidden from the external world. In most cases, this is not ideal; hiding everything makes the subsystem less flexible and harder to extend. However, in some scenarios, you may want to control access to your internal APIs. This may be because they are not mature enough and you don't want any third party to depend on them, or for any other reasons you deem appropriate for your specific use case.

Let's start by taking a look at the following abstraction:

```
namespace OpaqueFacadeSubSystem.Abstractions;
public interface IECommerceOpaqueFacade
{
    string PlaceOrder(string productId, int quantity);
    string CheckOrderStatus(int orderId);
}
```

The preceding interface represents our e-commerce system façade. Next, let's look at the hidden (`internal` visibility) subsystems that the façade fronts, starting with the inventory subsystem:

```
namespace OpaqueFacadeSubSystem;
internal class InventoryService
{
    public bool CheckStock(string productId, int quantity)
    {
        // Check if the product is available in the desired quantity
        return true; // Simplified for example
```

```
    }
}
```

The `InventoryService` class has one `CheckStock` method that always returns true. This is to keep the code simple.

Next, let's look at the order processing subsystem:

```
namespace OpaqueFacadeSubSystem;
internal class OrderProcessingService
{
    public int CreateOrder(string productId, int quantity)
    {
        // Logic to create an order
        return 123; // Returns a mock order ID
    }

    public string GetOrderStatus(int orderId)
    {
        // Logic to get order status
        return "Order Shipped"; // Simplified for example
    }
}
```

The `OrderProcessingService` class exposes `CreateOrder`, which simulates creating an order by always returning `123`, and `GetOrderStatus`, which simulates finding the status of one's order by always returning `"Order Shipped"`.

Next, let's look at the shipping subsystem:

```
namespace OpaqueFacadeSubSystem;
// A hidden Shipping Subsystem
internal class ShippingService
{
    public void ScheduleShipping(int orderId)
    {
        // Logic to schedule shipping
    }
}
```

The `ShippingService` class exposes only the `ScheduleShipping` method, which simulates scheduling the shipping of an order.

Now, with those services, we can create our `IECommerceOpaqueFacade` implementation:

```
using OpaqueFacadeSubSystem.Abstractions;
```

```
namespace OpaqueFacadeSubSystem;
// The opaque façade implementation
public class ECommerceFacade : IECommerceOpaqueFacade
{
    private readonly InventoryService _inventoryService;
    private readonly OrderProcessingService _orderProcessingService;
    private readonly ShippingService _shippingService;

    internal ECommerceFacade(InventoryService inventoryService,
OrderProcessingService orderProcessingService, ShippingService shippingService)
    {
        _inventoryService = inventoryService ?? throw new
ArgumentNullException(nameof(inventoryService));
        _orderProcessingService = orderProcessingService ?? throw new
ArgumentNullException(nameof(orderProcessingService));
        _shippingService = shippingService ?? throw new
ArgumentNullException(nameof(shippingService));
    }

    public string PlaceOrder(string productId, int quantity)
    {
        if (_inventoryService.CheckStock(productId, quantity))
        {
            var orderId = _orderProcessingService.CreateOrder(productId,
quantity);
            _shippingService.ScheduleShipping(orderId);
            return $"Order {orderId} placed successfully.";
        }
        return "Order failed due to insufficient stock.";
    }

    public string CheckOrderStatus(int orderId)
    {
        return _orderProcessingService.GetOrderStatus(orderId);
    }
}
```

The `ECommerceFacade` class is coupled with `InventoryService`, `OrderProcessingService`, and `ShippingService` directly. There was no point in extracting any `internal` interfaces since the subsystem is not extensible anyway. We could have done this to offer some internal flexibility, but there was no advantage in this case.

Besides that tight coupling, the `ECommerceFacade` class implements the `PlaceOrder` method, which leverages the three services to simulate passing an order. The class also exposes `CheckOrderStatus`, which directly delegates requests to the order processing service. Those two methods hide the complexity of the subsystems behind an easy-to-use interface.

This is a classic use of a façade; the façade queries other objects that are more or less complex and then does something with the results, taking away the caller's burden of knowing the subsystem.

However, since the members use the `internal` visibility modifier, we can't directly register the dependencies with the IoC container from the program. To solve this problem, the `OpaqueFacadeSubSystem` project can register its dependencies by adding an extension method. The following extension method is accessible by the consuming application:

```
using OpaqueFacadeSubSystem;
using OpaqueFacadeSubSystem.Abstractions;

namespace Microsoft.Extensions.DependencyInjection;

public static class StartupExtensions
{
    public static IServiceCollection AddOpaqueFacadeSubSystem(this
IServiceCollection services)
    {
        services.AddSingleton<IECommerceOpaqueFacade>(serviceProvider
            => new ECommerceFacade(new InventoryService(), new
OrderProcessingService(), new ShippingService()));
        return services;
    }
}
```

The preceding code manually creates the dependencies and adds a binding to the `IECommerceOpaqueFacade` interface so the system can use it. This hides everything but the interface from the consumer.

Before exploring the consumer—the REST API—we look at the transparent façade implementation.

Transparent façade

The transparent façade is the most flexible type of façade and is very suitable for a system that leverages dependency injection. The implementation is similar to the opaque façade, but the `public` visibility modifier changes how consumers can access the class library elements. For this system, it was worth adding interfaces to allow the consumers of the subsystem to extend it when needed.

First, let's take a look at the new abstractions:

```
namespace TransparentFacadeSubSystem.Abstractions;

public interface IInventoryService
```

```
{
    bool CheckStock(string productId, int quantity);
}

public interface IOrderProcessingService
{
    int CreateOrder(string productId, int quantity);
    string GetOrderStatus(int orderId);
}

public interface IShippingService
{
    void ScheduleShipping(int orderId);
}
```

The API of this subsystem is the same as the opaque façade. The only difference is how we can use and extend the subsystem (from a consumer standpoint). The implementations are mostly the same as well, but the classes implement the preceding interfaces and are `public` instead of `internal`; the highlighted elements represent those changes:

```
using TransparentFacadeSubSystem.Abstractions;

namespace TransparentFacadeSubSystem;

// Subsystem: Inventory
public class InventoryService : IInventoryService
{
    public bool CheckStock(string productId, int quantity)
    {
        // Check if the product is available in the desired quantity
        return true; // Simplified for example
    }
}

// Subsystem: Order Processing
public class OrderProcessingService : IOrderProcessingService
{
    public int CreateOrder(string productId, int quantity)
    {
        // Logic to create an order
        return 123; // Returns a mock order ID
    }
```

```
    public string GetOrderStatus(int orderId)
    {
        // Logic to get order status
        return "Order Shipped"; // Simplified for example
    }
}

// Subsystem: Shipping
public class ShippingService : IShippingService
{
    public void ScheduleShipping(int orderId)
    {
        // Logic to schedule shipping
    }
}

// The transparent e-commerce façade
public class ECommerceFacade : IECommerceTransparentFacade
{
    private readonly IInventoryService _inventoryService;
    private readonly IOrderProcessingService _orderProcessingService;
    private readonly IShippingService _shippingService;

    public ECommerceFacade(IInventoryService inventoryService,
IOrderProcessingService orderProcessingService, IShippingService
shippingService)
    {
        _inventoryService = inventoryService ?? throw new
ArgumentNullException(nameof(inventoryService));
        _orderProcessingService = orderProcessingService ?? throw new
ArgumentNullException(nameof(orderProcessingService));
        _shippingService = shippingService ?? throw new
ArgumentNullException(nameof(shippingService));
    }

    public string PlaceOrder(string productId, int quantity)
    {
        if (_inventoryService.CheckStock(productId, quantity))
        {
            var orderId = _orderProcessingService.CreateOrder(productId,
quantity);
```

```
            _shippingService.ScheduleShipping(orderId);
            return $"Order {orderId} placed successfully.";
        }
        return "Order failed due to insufficient stock.";
    }

    public string CheckOrderStatus(int orderId)
    {
        return _orderProcessingService.GetOrderStatus(orderId);
    }
}
```

To simplify the use of the e-commerce subsystem, we will create the following extension method as a good practice that makes consuming the subsystem easier. Everything that we define in that method can be overridden from the composition root (which is not the case for the opaque façade):

```
using Microsoft.Extensions.DependencyInjection.Extensions;
using TransparentFacadeSubSystem;
using TransparentFacadeSubSystem.Abstractions;

namespace Microsoft.Extensions.DependencyInjection;

public static class StartupExtensions
{
    public static IServiceCollection AddTransparentFacadeSubSystem(this
IServiceCollection services)
    {
        services.TryAddSingleton<IInventoryService, InventoryService>();
        services.TryAddSingleton<IOrderProcessingService,
OrderProcessingService>();
        services.TryAddSingleton<IShippingService, ShippingService>();
        services.TryAddSingleton<IECommerceTransparentFacade,
ECommerceFacade>();
        return services;
    }
}
```

All the new elements of the opaque façade code are gone and have been replaced by simple dependency registration (singleton lifetimes, in this case). These little differences give us the tools to reimplement any part of the subsystem if we want to, as we will soon see.

We can register bindings in the transparent façade extension method because classes and interfaces are `public`. The container needs a public constructor to do its work.

In the opaque façade, we had to define the constructor of the `ECommerceFacade` class as `internal` because the type of its parameters (`InventoryService`, `OrderProcessingService`, and `ShippingService`) are `internal`, making it impossible to leverage the container. Changing the visibility modifier of the opaque façade constructor from `internal` to `public` would have yielded a *CS0051 Inconsistent accessibility* error.

Besides those differences, the transparent façade plays the same role as the opaque façade, outputting the same result.

We consume those two façades next.

The program

Now, let's analyze the consumer, an ASP.NET Core application that forwards HTTP requests to the façades and returns the result as their response.

The first step is to register the dependencies in `Program.cs` like this:

```
using OpaqueFacadeSubSystem.Abstractions;
using TransparentFacadeSubSystem.Abstractions;

var builder = WebApplication.CreateBuilder(args);
builder.Services
    .AddOpaqueFacadeSubSystem()
    .AddTransparentFacadeSubSystem()
;
```

With these extension methods, the application root is so clean that it is hard to know that we registered two subsystems against the IoC container. This is a good way of keeping your code organized and clean, especially when you're building class libraries or complex applications.

Now that everything has been registered, the second thing we need to do is route those HTTP requests to the façades. Let's take a look at the code first:

```
var app = builder.Build();
app.MapPost(
    "/opaque/PlaceOrder",
    (PlaceOrder order, IECommerceOpaqueFacade eCommerceOpaqueFacade)
        => eCommerceOpaqueFacade.PlaceOrder(order.ProductId, order.Quantity)
);
```

```
app.MapGet(
    "/opaque/CheckOrderStatus/{orderId}",
    (int orderId, IECommerceOpaqueFacade eCommerceOpaqueFacade)
        => eCommerceOpaqueFacade.CheckOrderStatus(orderId)
);
app.MapPost(
    "/transparent/PlaceOrder",
    (PlaceOrder order, IECommerceTransparentFacade eCommerceTransparentFacade)
        => eCommerceTransparentFacade.PlaceOrder(order.ProductId, order.
Quantity)
);
app.MapGet(
    "/transparent/CheckOrderStatus/{orderId}",
    (int orderId, IECommerceTransparentFacade eCommerceTransparentFacade)
        => eCommerceTransparentFacade.CheckOrderStatus(orderId)
);
app.Run();

public record class PlaceOrder(string ProductId, int Quantity);
```

In the preceding block, we define four routes. Each route dispatches the request to one of the façade's methods (highlighted code) using the façade that is injected in its delegate. The two `PlaceOrder` endpoints leverage the `PlaceOrder` record class (last line) as a DTO.

To test the program, I created a `Facade.http` file in the project that contains the following:

```
@Facade_HostAddress = https://localhost:9004

GET {{Facade_HostAddress}}/opaque/CheckOrderStatus/123
###

POST {{Facade_HostAddress}}/opaque/PlaceOrder
Content-Type: application/json

{
    "productId": "P12345",
    "quantity": 5
}

###

GET {{Facade_HostAddress}}/transparent/CheckOrderStatus/123
```

```
###

POST {{Facade_HostAddress}}/transparent/PlaceOrder
Content-Type: application/json

{
    "productId": "P12345",
    "quantity": 5
}
```

The first two requests hit the opaque façade while the last two hit the transparent façade. Now, if we run the program and execute the `CheckOrderStatus` method from the transparent or the opaque façade, the response should be the following:

```
Order Shipped
```

What happened is located inside the delegates. It uses the injected `IECommerceOpaqueFacade` or `IECommerceTransparentFacade` service, calls its `CheckOrderStatus` method, and outputs the result to the response stream.

A similar result happens if we send the `PlaceOrder` requests, but the result is the following instead:

```
Order 123 placed successfully.
```

Now, let's explore how the IoC container composes the service that gets injected as an `IECommerceTransparentFacade` interface when the program executes that operation. The `ECommerceFacade` class is bound to the interface and the `InventoryService`, `OrderProcessingService`, and `ShippingService` classes are injected in its constructor based on their respective interface (as we defined in the bindings).

Visually, the following flow happens:

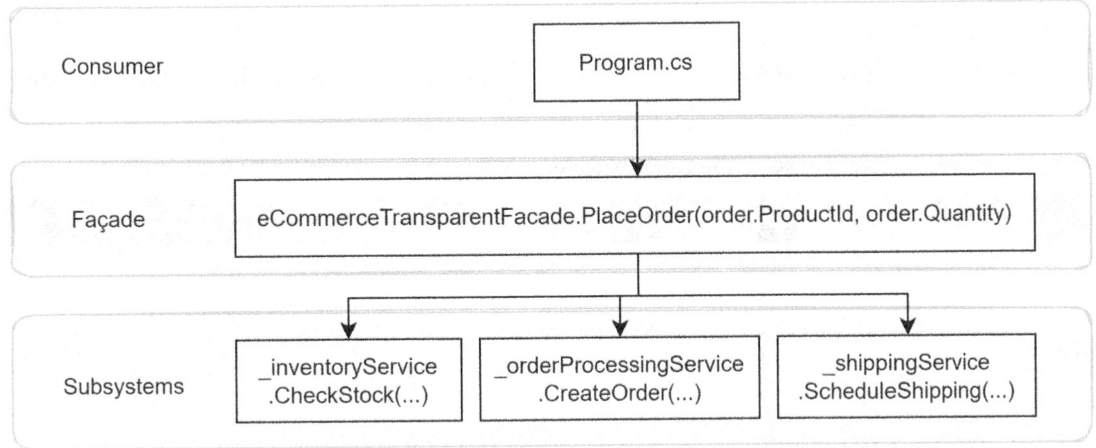

Figure 11.18: A representation of the call hierarchy that occurs when the consumer executes the PlaceOrder method on the transparent façade

In the preceding diagram, we can see the shielding that's done by the façade and how it has made the consumer's life easier: one call instead of three.

One of the hardest parts of using dependency injection is its abstractness. If you are not sure how all those parts are assembled, add a breakpoint into Visual Studio (on the `eCommerceTransparentFacade.PlaceOrder(...)` line, for example) and run the application in debug mode. You can right-click the `PlaceOrder` method, then select **Breakpoint** > **Insert Breakpoint** to insert a breakpoint to the right-hand side of a lambda expression. The result should look like the following:

```
app.MapPost(
    "/transparent/PlaceOrder",
    (PlaceOrder order, IECommerceTransparentFacade eCommerceTransparentFacade)
        => eCommerceTransparentFacade.PlaceOrder(order.ProductId, order.Quantity)
);
```

Figure 11.19: A breakpoint in debug mode

From there, once the breakpoint is hit, **Step Into** each method call. That should help you figure out what is happening. Using the debugger to find the concrete types and their states can help find details about a system or diagnose bugs.

To use **Step Into**, you can use the following button or hit *F11*:

Figure 11.20: The Visual Studio Step Into (F11) button

Next, let's update the result of the `PlaceOrder` endpoint (transparent façade) without changing the subsystem's code.

Flexibility in action

As discussed, the transparent façade adds more flexibility. Here, we explore this flexibility in action.

Context: We want to change the behavior of the `ECommerceFacade` class. At the moment, the result of the `/transparent/PlaceOrder` endpoint looks like this:

```
Order 123 placed successfully.
```

However, to demonstrate we can extend and change the subsystem without altering it, we implement a new version of the `IInventoryService` interface. Here's the code for that class:

```
using TransparentFacadeSubSystem.Abstractions;
namespace Facade;
public class UpdatedInventoryService : IInventoryService
{
    public bool CheckStock(string productId, int quantity)
    {
        return false; // Simplified for example
    }
}
```

The preceding code (highlighted line) makes the `CheckStock` method always return `false`, which changes the result of the endpoint. As a reminder, here's the content of the `PlaceOrder` method:

```
public string PlaceOrder(string productId, int quantity)
{
    if (_inventoryService.CheckStock(productId, quantity))
    {
        var orderId = _orderProcessingService.CreateOrder(productId, quantity);
        _shippingService.ScheduleShipping(orderId);
        return $"Order {orderId} placed successfully.";
    }
    return "Order failed due to insufficient stock.";
}
```

With the `CheckStock` method returning `false`, the result will be:

```
Order failed due to insufficient stock.
```

The only step that remains is to register our new binding with the IoC container, like this:

```
using Facade;
// ...
builder.Services
    .AddSingleton<IInventoryService, UpdatedInventoryService>()
    .AddOpaqueFacadeSubSystem()
    .AddTransparentFacadeSubSystem()
;
```

With this change, if we run the program, we should see the desired result!

Adding a dependency for a second time makes the container resolves that dependency, thus overriding the first one. However, both registrations remain in the services collection; for example, calling `GetServices<IInventoryService>()` on `IServiceProvider` would return two dependencies. Do not confuse the `GetServices()` and `GetService()` methods (plural versus singular); one returns a collection while the other returns a single instance. That single instance is always the last that has been registered.

In this case, since the extension methods are using the `TryAddSingleton` extension method instead, by registering our custom binding before the call to `AddTransparentFacadeSubSystem`, the IoC container will only contain one binding. The `TryAddSingleton` extension method only adds the binding if it does not exist, which is perfect for this type of scenario.

That's it! We updated the system without modifying it. This is what dependency injection can do for you when designing a program around it.

Alternative façade patterns

One alternative would be to create a *hybrid between a transparent façade and an opaque façade* by exposing the abstractions using the `public` visibility modifier (all of the interfaces) while keeping the implementations hidden under an `internal` visibility modifier. This hybrid design offers a balance between **control and flexibility**.

Another alternative would be to create *a façade outside of the subsystem*. In the previous examples, we created the façades inside the class libraries, but this is not mandatory; the façade is just a class that creates an accessible wall between your system and one or more subsystems. It should be located wherever you see fit. Creating external façades like this would be especially useful when you do not control the source code of the subsystem(s), such as if you only have access to the binaries. This could also be used to create project-specific façades over the same subsystem, giving you extra flexibility without cluttering your subsystems with multiple façades, shifting the maintenance cost from the subsystems to the client applications that use them.

You do not need to create an assembly per subsystem; you can create multiple subsystems in the same assembly. You can even create a single assembly that includes all your subsystems, façades, and the client code (all in a single project). We explore ways to organize applications in *Section 4: Application Patterns*.

That said, whether talking about subsystems or REST APIs, layering APIs (multiple assemblies) is an excellent way to create low-level functionalities that are atomic but harder to use (subsystem) while providing a higher-level API to access them through the façade (Gateway pattern for REST API), leading to a better consumer experience and the potential to tap into reusing the low-level building blocks (improved reusability/flexibility).

Conclusion

The Façade pattern is handy for simplifying consumers' lives, allowing us to hide subsystems' implementation details behind a wall. There are multiple flavors to it; the two most prominent ones are:

- The **opaque façade**, which controls access by hiding most of the subsystem(s)
- The **transparent façade**, which increases flexibility by exposing at least part of the subsystem(s)

Now, let's see how the **opaque façade** pattern can help us follow the **SOLID** principles:

- **S**: A well-designed **opaque façade** serves this exact purpose by providing a cohesive set of functionalities to its clients by hiding overly complex subsystems or internal implementation details.
- **O**: By hiding the subsystem, the **opaque façade** limits our ability to extend it. However, we could implement a **hybrid façade** to help with that.
- **L**: N/A.
- **I**: The **opaque façade** does not help nor diminish our ability to apply the ISP.
- **D**: The Façade pattern does not specify anything about interfaces, so it is up to you to enforce this principle by using other patterns, principles, and best practices.

Finally, let's see how the **transparent façade** pattern can help us follow the **SOLID** principles:

- **S**: A well-designed **transparent façade** serves this exact purpose by providing a cohesive set of functionalities to its consumers by hiding overly complex subsystems or internal implementation details.
- **O**: A well-designed **transparent façade** and its underlying subsystem's components can be extended without direct modification, as we saw in the *Flexibility in action* section.
- **L**: N/A.
- **I**: By exposing a façade that uses different smaller objects implementing small interfaces, we could say that the segregation is done at both the façade and the component levels.
- **D**: The Façade pattern does not specify anything about interfaces, so it is up to you to enforce this principle by using other patterns, principles, and best practices.

Summary

In this chapter, we covered multiple fundamental GoF structural design patterns. They help us extend our systems from the outside without modifying the actual classes, leading to a higher degree of cohesion by composing our object graph dynamically.

We started with the Decorator pattern, a powerful tool that allows us to dynamically add new functionality to an object without altering its original code. Decorators can also be chained, allowing even greater flexibility (decorating other decorators). We learned that this pattern adheres to the Open-Closed principle and promotes the separation of responsibilities into smaller, manageable pieces.

We also used an open-source tool named Scrutor that simplifies the decorator pattern usage by extending the built-in ASP.NET Core dependency injection system.

Then, we covered the Composite pattern, which allows us to create complex, non-linear, and self-managed data structures with minimal effort. That hierarchical data structure where groups and single components are indistinguishable makes the hierarchy's traversal and manipulation easier. We use this pattern to build graphs or trees with self-managing nodes.

After that, we covered the Adapter pattern, which allows two incompatible interfaces to work together without modifying their code. This pattern is very helpful when we need to adapt the components of external systems that we have no control over, do not want to change, or can't change.

Finally, we dug into different variations of the Façade pattern, which allows us to create a wall in front of one or more subsystems, simplifying its usage. It could also be used to hide the implementation details of a subsystem from its consumers.

The next chapter explores two GoF behavioral design patterns: the Template method and the Chain of Responsibility design pattern.

Questions

Here are a few revision questions:

1. What is the main advantage of the Decorator pattern?
2. Can we decorate a decorator with another decorator?
3. What is the primary goal of the Composite design pattern?
4. Can we use the Adapter pattern to migrate an old API to a new system in order to adapt its APIs before rewriting it?
5. What is the primary responsibility of the Adapter pattern?
6. What is the difference between the Adapter and the Façade patterns?
7. What is the main difference between an Opaque façade and a Transparent façade?

Further reading

- To learn more about Scrutor, please visit `https://adpg.link/xvfS`.

Answers

1. The Decorator pattern allows us to dynamically add new functionality to an object at runtime without modifying its original code, promoting flexibility, testability, and manageability.
2. Yes, we can decorate decorators by depending only on interfaces because they are just another implementation of the interface, nothing more.
3. The Composite design pattern aims to simplify handling complex structures by treating individual and group elements indistinguishably.
4. Yes, we could use an adapter for this.
5. The Adapter pattern's primary responsibility is to adapt one interface to work with another interface that is incompatible with direct use.

6. The Adapter and Façade design patterns are almost the same but are applied to different scenarios. The Adapter pattern adapts an API to another API, while the Façade pattern exposes a unified or simplified API, hiding one or more complex subsystems.
7. An Opaque façade hides most of the subsystem (`internal` visibility), controlling access to it, while a Transparent façade exposes at least part of the subsystem (`public` visibility), increasing flexibility.

Learn more on Discord

To join the Discord community for this book – where you can share feedback, ask questions to the author, and learn about new releases – follow the QR code below:

`https://packt.link/ArchitectingASPNETCoreApps3e`

12

Behavioral Patterns

This chapter explores two new design patterns from the well-known **Gang of Four** (GoF). They are behavioral patterns, meaning they help simplify system behavior management.

Often, we need to encapsulate some core algorithm while allowing other pieces of code to extend that implementation. That is where the **Template Method** pattern comes into play. Other times, we have a complex process with multiple algorithms that all apply to one or more situations, and we need to organize it in a testable and extensible fashion. This is where the **Chain of Responsibility** pattern can help.

In this chapter, we cover the following topics:

- The Template Method pattern
- The Chain of Responsibility pattern
- Mixing the Template Method and Chain of Responsibility patterns

The Template Method pattern

The **Template Method pattern** is a GoF behavioral pattern that uses inheritance to share code between the base class and its subclasses. It is another very powerful yet simple design pattern.

Goal

The goal of the Template Method pattern is to encapsulate the outline of an algorithm in a base class while leaving some parts of that algorithm open for modification by the subclasses, which adds flexibility at a low cost.

Design

First, we need to define a base class that contains the `TemplateMethod` method and then define one or more sub-operations that need to be implemented by its subclasses (`abstract`) or that can be overridden (`virtual`).

Using UML, it looks like this:

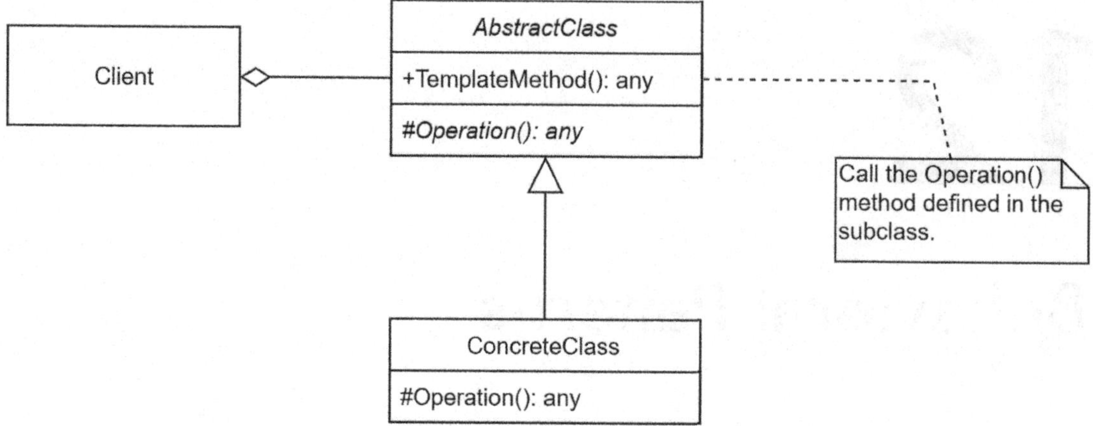

Figure 12.1: Class diagram representing the Template Method pattern

How does this work?

- `AbstractClass` implements the shared code: the algorithm in its `TemplateMethod` method
- `ConcreteClass` implements its specific part of the algorithm in its inherited `Operation` method
- `Client` calls `TemplateMethod`, which calls the subclass implementation of one or more specific algorithm elements (the `Operation` method in this case)

We could also extract an interface from `AbstractClass` to allow even more flexibility, but that's beyond the scope of the Template Method pattern.

Let's now get into some code to see the Template Method pattern in action.

Project – Building a search machine

Let's start with the simple example of building a search machine to demonstrate how the Template Method pattern works.

Context: We want to use a different search algorithm depending on the collection. We want to use a *binary search* for sorted collections, but we want to use a *linear search* for unsorted collections.

To achieve that, we decided to leverage the Template Method pattern so we can encapsulate the core logic into a base class, defer the sort algorithm part to a subclass, each responsible for one algorithm (**single responsibility principle** (**SRP**) and separation of concerns), and use the base class as an abstraction so consumers of the sort can use one or the other without the need to know (polymorphism).

Let's start to explore the supertype, the `SearchMachine` class:

```
namespace TemplateMethod;
```

```
public abstract class SearchMachine
{
    protected int[] Values { get; }
    protected SearchMachine(params int[] values)
    {
        Values = values ?? throw new ArgumentNullException(nameof(values));
    }
    public int? IndexOf(int value)
    {
        if (Values.Length == 0) { return null; }
        var result = Find(value);
        return result;
    }
    protected abstract int? Find(int value);
}
```

The `SearchMachine` class represents the *AbstractClass* in the design. It exposes the `IndexOf` template method, which uses the required hook represented by the `abstract Find` method (see highlighted code). The hook is required because each subclass must implement that method, thereby making that method a required extension point (or hook). The algorithm is simple here, as it only ensures that the `Find` method is not called if there are no values to search for (directly return `null` because it's impossible to find any number in an empty collection).

Now that we looked at this shared piece of the pattern, let's explore our first implementation of the *ConcreteClass* from the design, the `LinearSearchMachine` class:

```
namespace TemplateMethod;
public class LinearSearchMachine : SearchMachine
{
    public LinearSearchMachine(params int[] values)
        : base(values) { }

    protected override int? Find(int value)
    {
        for (var i = 0; i < Values.Length; i++)
        {
            if (Values[i] == value) { return i; }
        }
        return null;
    }
}
```

The `LinearSearchMachine` class is a *ConcreteClass* representing the linear search implementation used by `SearchMachine`. It contributes a part of the `IndexOf` algorithm through its `Find` method. To achieve that, the `LinearSearchMachine` class inherits from the `SearchMachine` class, which requires implementing the `Find` method.

Now, let's move to the second implementation of the *ConcreteClass* block from the design, the `BinarySearchMachine` class:

```
namespace TemplateMethod;
public class BinarySearchMachine : SearchMachine
{
    public BinarySearchMachine(params int[] values)
        : base(values.OrderBy(v => v).ToArray()) { }

    protected override int? Find(int value)
    {
        var index = Array.BinarySearch(Values, value);
        return index < 0 ? null : index;
    }
}
```

The `BinarySearchMachine` class is another *ConcreteClass*, but it represents the binary search implementation of `SearchMachine` instead of a linear search. As with the `LinearSearchMachine` class, the preceding class inherits from the `SearchMachine` class and implements the `Find` method. In this case, we skipped the implementation of the binary search algorithm by delegating it to the built-in `Array.BinarySearch` method. Thanks to the .NET team! On top of that, this class ensures the array is ordered during instantiation (highlighted code)—in the constructor.

The binary search algorithm requires an ordered collection to work; hence, the sorting is done in the constructor when passing the values to the base class (`OrderBy`). That may not be the most performant way of ensuring the array is sorted (precondition/guard), but it is a very fast and readable way to write it. Moreover, in our case, performance is not an issue.

If you must optimize such an algorithm to work with a large data set, you can leverage parallelism (multithreading) to help out. In any case, run a proper benchmark to ensure you optimize the right thing and assess your real gains. Look at BenchmarkDotNet (`https://adpg.link/C5E9`) if you are looking at benchmarking .NET code.

Now that we have the building blocks in place, it's time to explore the `Program.cs` file so we can start the server and test this out. Let's begin with the dependency registration:

```
using TemplateMethod;
var builder = WebApplication.CreateBuilder(args);
builder.Services
```

```
    .AddSingleton<SearchMachine>(x
        => new LinearSearchMachine(1, 10, 5, 2, 123, 333, 4))
    .AddSingleton<SearchMachine>(x
        => new BinarySearchMachine(1, 2, 3, 4, 5, 6, 7, 8, 9, 10))
;
```

As highlighted in the preceding code, we configure `LinearSearchMachine` and `BinarySearchMachine` as two `SearchMachine` implementations and initialize them using a different sequence of numbers.

Next, let's look at the REST endpoint that performs the search and returns the results:

```
var app = builder.Build();
app.MapGet("/search/{number}", SearchForIndex);
app.Run();

IEnumerable<SearchResult> SearchForIndex(
    int number, IEnumerable<SearchMachine> searchMachines)
{
    foreach (var searchMachine in searchMachines)
    {
        var name = searchMachine.GetType().Name;
        var index = searchMachine.IndexOf(number);
        var found = index.HasValue;
        yield return new SearchResult(number, name, found, index);
    }
}
public record class SearchResult(
    int SearchedNumber,
    string Name,
    bool Found,
    int? Index
);
```

In the preceding code, we define a search endpoint that delegates the requests to the `SearchForIndex` method. When called, ASP.NET Core injects all registered `SearchMachine` services into the endpoint, and the method calls the `IndexOf` method of each instance (highlighted in the code block). The `SearchForIndex` method then returns an instance of the `SearchResult` class (a DTO) that is created using the return value of the `IndexOf` method of each `SearchMachine` instance. The results then get serialized to JSON by the endpoint.

Here's an example of the JSON when searching for the number 123:

```
[
  {
    "searchedNumber": 123,
```

```
        "name": "LinearSearchMachine",
        "found": true,
        "index": 4
    },
    {
        "searchedNumber": 123,
        "name": "BinarySearchMachine",
        "found": false,
        "index": null
    }
]
```

To test the endpoint, you can use the predefined requests in the `TemplateMethod.http` file or any HTTP Client you choose, including a web browser. The preceding JSON comes from the following request:

```
GET https://localhost:10004/search/123
```

The preceding output shows the two algorithms at play. One of the two `SearchMachine` implementations contains the value `123` (index 4), but not the other. Here is a reminder of the values with the 123 value highlighted at index 4:

```
new LinearSearchMachine(1, 10, 5, 2, 123, 333, 4)
new BinarySearchMachine(1, 2, 3, 4, 5, 6, 7, 8, 9, 10)
```

As a reminder, the `Find` method returns `null` when it does not find a value, and, by extension, so does the `IndexOf` method, hence why the `index` property of the `BinarySearchMachine` result is `null`.

Here's what happened in more detail:

1. The client sends an HTTP request to the server.
2. The search endpoint handles it and delegates the request to the `SearchForIndex` method for convenience. We can't use `yield return` inside an anonymous method or lambda expression, so this keeps the code cleaner.
3. The `SearchForIndex` method iterates the collection of `SearchMachine` implementations injected by the IoC container.

4. For each of the `SearchMachine` implementations, the `SearchForIndex` method calls the `IndexOf` method. The base class implements the `IndexOf` method and delegates the search algorithm to the subclasses' `Find` method. The Template Method pattern is at play here; each `SearchMachine` subtype can execute the expected task by implementing only the `Find` piece of the overall algorithm.
5. Afterward, the results cascade back to the user and get serialized to JSON by ASP.NET Core.

Now, let's look at a sequence diagram that mimics this interaction. I removed the `foreach` loop to simplify the diagram and the `SearchForIndex` method of the `Program` class directly calls each instance instead:

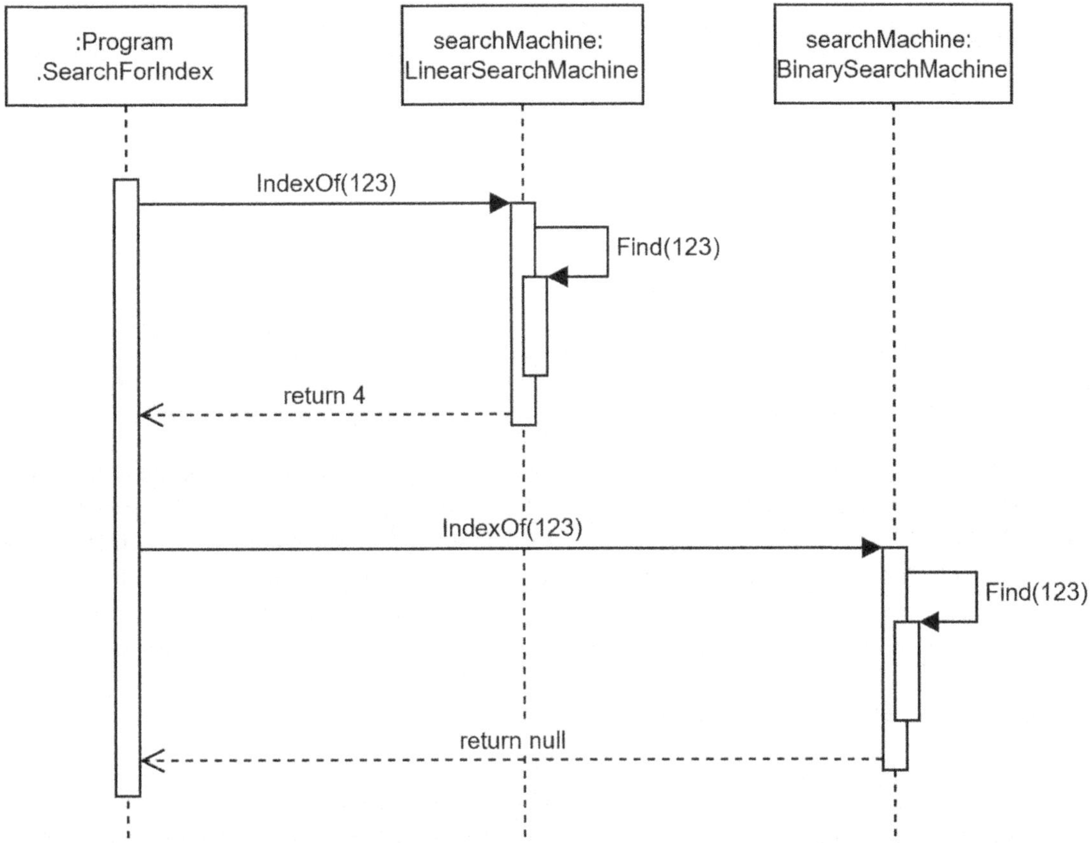

Figure 12.2: A sequence diagram representing the SearchForIndex method calling the IndexOf method of the two SearchMachine implementations

The diagram shows that the `IndexOf` method of each object calls its `Find` method. However, based on that sequence, the Template Method pattern is hard to see since the `IndexOf` method is part of the supertype, and only the `Find` method is part of the subtypes.

For that reason, I created a sequence-inspired diagram to showcase what is happening at the code level:

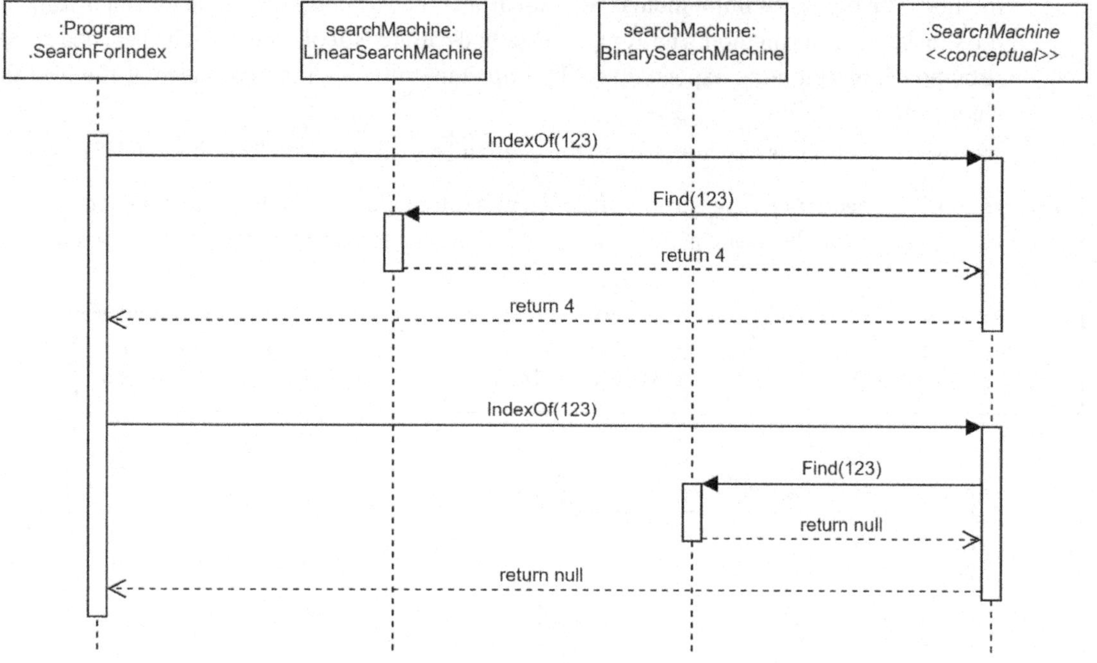

Figure 12.3: A sequence-inspired diagram that conceptually shows the sequence of events of the Template Method pattern, showcasing the parts played by the supertype and its subtypes

The preceding diagram shows that the `SearchMachine` class is responsible for the main algorithm code—the `IndexOf` method. At the same time, each subtype is responsible for implementing the `Find` method—their piece of the algorithm. The sequence diagram 12.2 shows that the `IndexOf` method call is sent to an instance of the `LinearSearchMachine` or `BinarySearchMachine` class, which is correct. However, as shown by diagram 12.3, the code itself is inherited and encapsulated in the `SearchMachine` class, hence the conceptual lifeline. So, here we can see that the inherited code—the `IndexOf` method—is in the `SearchMachine` class, but when executed, it calls the `Find` method of its current subtype—the `LinearSearchMachine` or `BinarySearchMachine` class.

The preceding diagram is not a UML sequence diagram, but creating a sequence-inspired diagram is the best way I found to visually explain the Template Method pattern concept and ensure we clearly see what class is responsible for what part of the algorithm.

Voilà! We have covered the Template Method pattern, as easy as that. Of course, our algorithm was trivial, but the concept remains.

We can add `virtual` methods in the base class to create optional hooks. Those methods become optional extension points that subclasses can implement. That allows a more complex and more versatile scenario to be supported. We will not cover this here because it is not part of the pattern itself, even if it is very similar and complementary.

There are many examples of optional extension points in the .NET **base class library** (**BCL**), like most methods of the `ComponentBase` class (in the `Microsoft.AspNetCore.Components` namespace). For example, when overriding the `OnInitialized` method in a Razor component, we leverage an optional extension hook. The base method does nothing and is for extensibility purposes, allowing us to run code as part of the component's life cycle. You can consult the `ComponentBase` class code in the official .NET repo on GitHub: `https://adpg.link/1WYq`.

Let's have a look at a few unit tests before moving on.

Unit tests

Now that we are done with the pattern itself, I also created some unit tests to ensure the correctness of the implementations. Testing your code is a good habit, and unit tests are perfect to ensure the correctness of "complex" algorithms.

Here's a test for the `LinearSearchMachine` class:

```
namespace TemplateMethod;
public class LinearSearchMachineTest
{
    public class IndexOf
    {
        [Theory]
        [InlineData(1, 0)]
        [InlineData(2, 4)]
        [InlineData(3, 2)]
        [InlineData(7, null)]
        public void Should_return_the_expected_result(
            int value, int? expectedIndex)
        {
            // Arrange
            var sorter = new LinearSearchMachine(1, 5, 3, 4, 2);

            // Act
            var index = sorter.IndexOf(value);

            // Assert
```

```
            Assert.Equal(expectedIndex, index);
        }
    }
}
```

The preceding test ensures that the correct values are found or not by the `IndexOf` method of the `LinearSearchMachine` class.

Next is a similar test for the `BinarySearchMachine` class:

```
namespace TemplateMethod;
public class BinarySearchMachineTest
{
    public class IndexOf
    {
        [Theory]
        [InlineData(1, 0)]
        [InlineData(8, 5)]
        [InlineData(3, 2)]
        [InlineData(7, null)]
        public void Should_return_the_expected_result(int value, int?
expectedIndex)
        {
            // Arrange
            var sorter = new BinarySearchMachine(1, 2, 3, 4, 5, 8);

            // Act
            var index = sorter.IndexOf(value);

            // Assert
            Assert.Equal(expectedIndex, index);
        }
    }
}
```

The preceding test does a similar job of ensuring that the correct values are found or not by the `IndexOf` method of the `BinarySearchMachine` class.

Finally, I've created two tests to cover the `SearchMachine` class and ensure it guards against `null` and returns `null` when the `Values` property is empty. Let's look at the building blocks first, and we'll come back to the tests after (highlighted code):

```
namespace TemplateMethod;
public class SearchMachineTest
```

```
{
    public class Ctor : SearchMachineTest { }
    public class IndexOf : SearchMachineTest { }

    private class FakeSearchMachine : SearchMachine
    {
        public FakeSearchMachine(params int[] values)
            : base(values) { }

        protected override int? Find(int value)
        {
            throw new NotImplementedException();
        }
    }
}
```

The `FakeSearchMachine` class allows us to instantiate a `SearchMachine` in a controlled environment, hence why it has a `private` visibility modifier, so only the tests can access it. The `Find` method should never be called, and for that reason, it throws an exception. It is important to note that an unhandled exception will make an xUnit test fail, which is what we want here.

Now, let's have a look at the guard test, which expects the constructor to throw an `ArgumentNullException` when the `values` argument is `null`:

```
public class Ctor : SearchMachineTest
{
    [Fact]
    public void Should_guard_against_null_values()
    {
        Assert.Throws<ArgumentNullException>(() => new
FakeSearchMachine(null!));
    }
}
```

The last test ensures that when the `Values` property is empty, the `IndexOf` method returns `null` before calling the `Find` method:

```
public class IndexOf : SearchMachineTest
{
    [Fact]
    public void Should_return_null_when_Values_is_empty()
    {
        // Arrange
        var searchMachine = new FakeSearchMachine();
```

```
        // Act
        var result = searchMachine.IndexOf(5);

        // Assert
        Assert.Null(result);
    }
}
```

These few tests yield 100% code coverage of the `TemplateMethod` namespace, which represents the implementation of the Template Method pattern. The global namespace has 0% coverage—the code in the `Program.cs` file—because it just shows how to use the pattern. Of course, you should also test your endpoints in an actual application, as we do for many code samples in the book. We cover more of that in *Section 4: Application Patterns.*

This concludes our study of another simple yet powerful design pattern.

Conclusion

The Template Method pattern is a powerful and easy-to-implement design pattern, allowing subclasses to reuse the algorithm's skeleton while implementing (abstract) or overriding (virtual) subparts. It allows implementation-specific classes to extend the core algorithm. It can reduce the duplication of logic and improve maintainability while not cutting out any flexibility in the process. There are many examples in the .NET BCL, and we leverage this pattern at the end of the chapter based on a real-world scenario.

Now, let's see how the Template Method pattern can help us follow the **SOLID** principles:

- **S**: The Template Method pattern pushes algorithm-specific portions of the code to subclasses while keeping the core algorithm in the base class. Doing that helps follow the SRP by distributing responsibilities.
- **O**: By opening extension hooks, it opens the template for extensions (allowing subclasses to extend it) and closes it from modifications (no need to modify the base class since the subclasses can extend it).
- **L**: As long as the subclasses are the implementations and do not alter the base class per se, following the **Liskov substitution principle** (**LSP**) should not be a problem. However, this principle is tricky, so it is possible to break it; by throwing a new type of exception or altering the state of a more complex base class in a way that changes its behavior, for example.
- **I**: As long as the base class implements the smallest cohesive surface possible, using the Template Method pattern should not negatively impact the program. On top of this, having a smaller interface surface in classes diminishes the chances of breaking the LSP.
- **D**: The Template Method pattern is based on an abstraction, so as long as consumers depend on that abstraction, it should help to get in line with the **dependency inversion principle** (**DIP**).

Next, we move to the Chain of Responsibility design pattern before mixing the Template Method and Chain of Responsibility patterns to improve our code.

The Chain of Responsibility pattern

The **Chain of Responsibility pattern** is a GoF behavioral pattern that chains classes to handle complex scenarios efficiently, with limited effort. Once again, the goal is to take a complex problem and break it into multiple smaller units.

Goal

The Chain of Responsibility pattern aims to chain multiple handlers that each solve a limited number of problems. A handler decides to process the request or pass it on to the next handler in the chain.

We often create a default handler that executes logic at the end of the chain as the terminal handler. Such a handler can throw an exception (for example, `OperationNotHandledException`) to cascade the issue up the call stack to a consumer who knows how to handle and react to it. Another strategy is creating a terminal handler that does the opposite and ensures nothing happens.

Design

The most basic Chain of Responsibility starts by defining an interface that handles a request (`IHandler`). Then, we add classes that deal with one or more scenarios (`Handler1` and `Handler2`). Conceptually, each handler references the *next handler*, allowing us to create a chain (a linked list of handlers).

Here's a conceptual diagram representing the pattern:

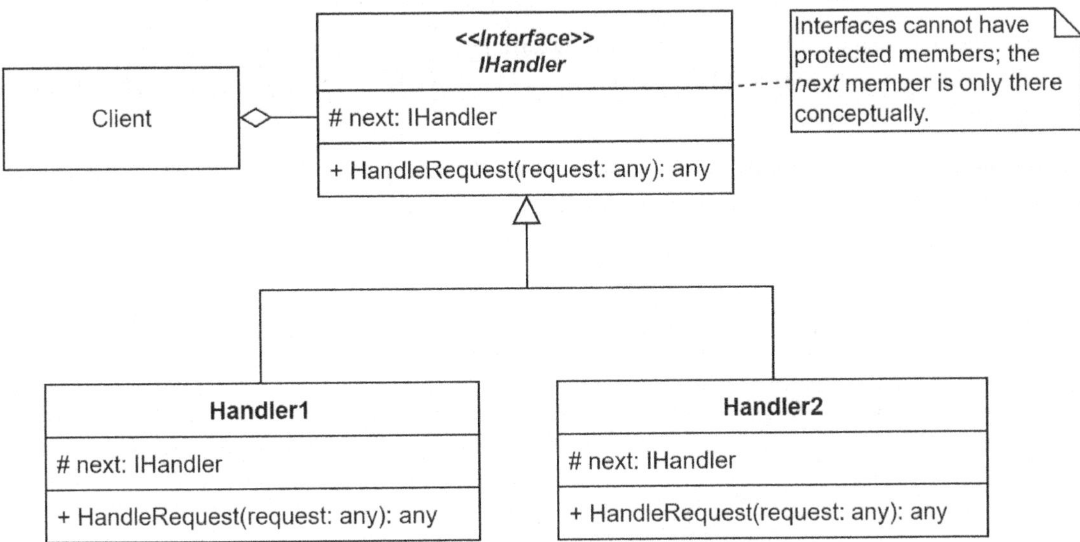

Figure 12.4: Class diagram conceptually representing the Chain of Responsibility pattern

Each handler in the chain can pass control to the next handler or not, potentially becoming a terminal handler by deciding to conclude the process. For this reason, the `IHandler` interface should not include the `next` member.

Moreover, we can't create `private` or `protected` members in an interface. We could add a `SetNextHandler` method, yet we should leverage constructor injection, which inverts the dependency flow and delegates the chain creation to the IoC container. Here's an updated diagram without the `protected` interface member that also adapts the visibility of the `next` field to `private`:

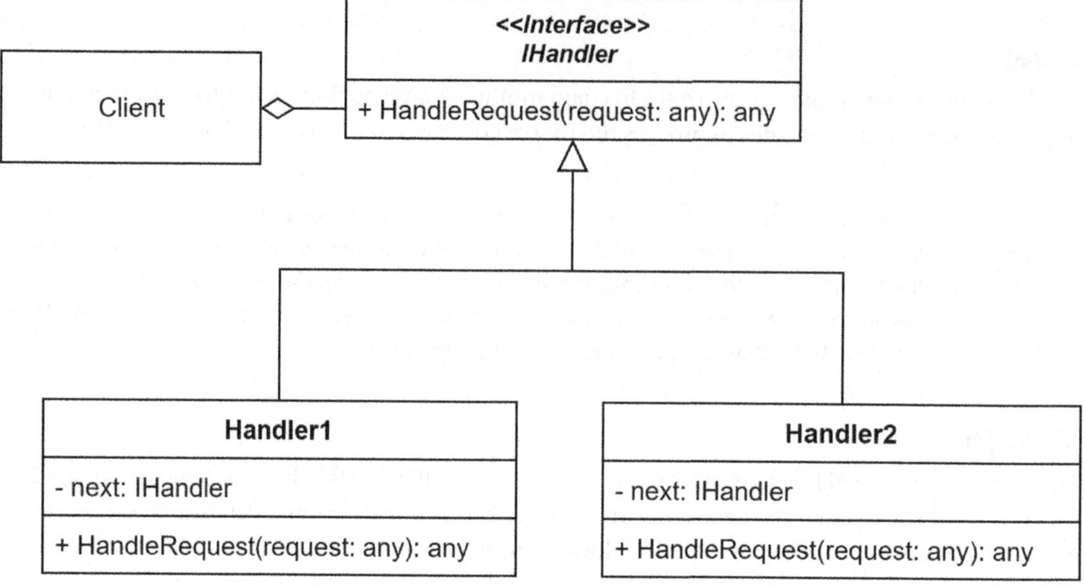

Figure 12.5: Class diagram representing the Chain of Responsibility pattern

A difference between the Chain of Responsibility pattern and many other patterns is that no central dispatcher knows the handlers; all handlers are independent. The consumer receives a handler and tells it to handle the request.

Each handler determines if it can process the request. If it can, it processes it. Otherwise, it decides if it should forward the request to the next handler in the chain.

This pattern allows us to divide complex logic into multiple pieces that handle a single responsibility, improving testability, reusability, and extensibility in the process. Since no orchestrator exists, each chain element is independent, leading to a cohesive and loosely coupled design.

When creating the chain of responsibility, you can order the handlers so that the most requested handlers are closer to the beginning of the chain and the least requested handlers are closer to the end. This helps limit the number of "chain links" that are visited for each request before reaching the right handler.

The Chain of Responsibility and Decorator patterns are very similar in their implementation. Nevertheless, the Decorator pattern attaches new responsibilities to objects, while the Chain of Responsibility pattern divides the processing capabilities into multiple objects.

For example, the Decorator pattern is like putting your smartphone in a protective case; the case makes the phone more secure or looks better, but underneath, it's still the same phone. On the other hand, the Chain of Responsibility pattern is like troubleshooting a phone issue, where you first try restarting it yourself, then search for solutions online, call customer support if needed, and finally take it to a service center, passing the problem along until it's solved.

We can construct a pipeline using the Chain of Responsibility pattern by lifting the limitation that restricts a single handler to either handle a request or pass it along. In the case of a pipeline, the handler can execute some logic or pass the request along in any order, as the Decorator pattern prescribes, yet it can also be terminal. The ASP.NET Core middleware pipeline is a good example, where each component can inspect and act on the request.

Enough theory; let's look at some code.

Project – Message interpreter

Context: We need to create the receiving end of a messaging application where each message is unique, making it impossible to create a single algorithm to handle them all.

After analyzing the problem, we decided to build a chain of responsibility where each handler can manage a single message. The pattern seems more than perfect!

This project is based on something that I built years ago. IoT devices were sending bytes (messages) due to limited bandwidth. Then, we had to associate those bytes with real values in a web application. Each message had a fixed header size but a variable body size. The headers were handled in a base handler (template method), and each handler in the chain managed a different message type. For the current example, we keep it simpler than parsing bytes, but the concept is the same.

For our demo application, the messages are as simple as this:

```
namespace ChainOfResponsibility;
public record class Message(string Name, string? Payload);
```

The `Name` property is used as a discriminator to differentiate messages, and each handler is responsible for doing something with the `Payload` property.

We won't do anything with the payload as it is irrelevant to the pattern, but conceptually, that is the logic that should happen.

The handlers are very simple; here's the interface:

```
namespace ChainOfResponsibility;
public interface IMessageHandler
```

```
{
    void Handle(Message message);
}
```

The only thing a handler can do is handle a message.

Our initial application can handle the following messages:

- The `AlarmTriggeredHandler` class handles `AlarmTriggered` messages
- The `AlarmPausedHandler` class handles `AlarmPaused` messages
- The `AlarmStoppedHandler` class handles `AlarmStopped` messages

The real-world logic is that a machine can send an alarm to a REST API indicating it has reached a certain threshold. Then, the REST API can push that information to a UI, send an email, a text message, or whatnot.

An alerted human can then pause the alarm while investigating the issue so other people know the alarm is being handled.

Finally, a human can go to the physical device and stop the alarm because the person has resolved the issue.

We could extrapolate on many more sub-scenarios, but this is the gist.

The three handlers are very similar and share quite a bit of logic, but we fix that later.

In the meantime, we have the following handlers:

```
namespace ChainOfResponsibility;
public class AlarmTriggeredHandler : IMessageHandler
{
    private readonly IMessageHandler? _next;
    public AlarmTriggeredHandler(IMessageHandler? next = null)
    {
        _next = next;
    }
    public void Handle(Message message)
    {
        if (message.Name == "AlarmTriggered")
        {
            // Do something clever with the Payload
        }
        else
        {
            _next?.Handle(message);
```

```
        }
    }
}
public class AlarmPausedHandler : IMessageHandler
{
    private readonly IMessageHandler? _next;
    public AlarmPausedHandler(IMessageHandler? next = null)
    {
        _next = next;
    }
    public void Handle(Message message)
    {
        if (message.Name == "AlarmPaused")
        {
            // Do something clever with the Payload
        }
        else
        {
            _next?.Handle(message);
        }
    }
}
public class AlarmStoppedHandler : IMessageHandler
{
    private readonly IMessageHandler? _next;
    public AlarmStoppedHandler(IMessageHandler? next = null)
    {
        _next = next;
    }
    public void Handle(Message message)
    {
        if (message.Name == "AlarmStopped")
        {
            // Do something clever with the Payload
        }
        else
        {
            _next?.Handle(message);
        }
    }
}
```

Each handler does two things:

- It receives an optional "next handler" from its constructor (highlighted in the code). This creates a chain similar to a singly linked list.
- It handles only the requests it knows about, delegating the others to the next handler in the chain.

Let's use `Program.cs` as the consumer of the Chain of Responsibility (the Client) and use POST requests to interface with our REST API and build the message.

Here is the first part of our REST API:

```
var builder = WebApplication.CreateBuilder(args);
builder.Services.AddSingleton<IMessageHandler>(
    new AlarmTriggeredHandler(
        new AlarmPausedHandler(
            new AlarmStoppedHandler())));
```

In the preceding code, we manually create the Chain of Responsibility and register it as a singleton bound to the `IMessageHandler` interface. In that registration code, each handler is manually injected in the previous constructor (created with the `new` keyword).

The next code represents the second half of the `Program.cs` file:

```
var app = builder.Build();
app.MapPost(
    "/handle",
    (Message message, IMessageHandler messageHandler) =>
    {
        messageHandler.Handle(message);
        return $"Message '{message.Name}' handled successfully.";
    });
app.Run();
```

The consuming endpoint is reachable through the `/handle` URL and expects a `Message` object in its body. It then uses the injected implementation of the `IMessageHandler` interface and passes the message to it.

If we run any of the HTTP requests in the `ChainOfResponsibility.http` file, we get a successful result similar to this:

```
Message 'AlarmTriggered' handled successfully.
```

The problem with the current implementation is that even if we send an invalid message, the consumer can't know because there is no feedback mechanism, so the endpoint always returns a valid response even when no handler picks up the message.

To handle this scenario, let's add a fourth handle—a terminal handler—that notifies the consumers of invalid requests:

```
public class DefaultHandler : IMessageHandler
{
    public void Handle(Message message)
    {
        throw new NotSupportedException(
            $"Messages named '{message.Name}' are not supported.");
    }
}
```

This new terminal handler throws an exception that notifies the consumers about the error.

We can create custom exceptions to simplify differentiating between system and application errors. In this case, throwing a system exception is good enough. In a real-world application, I recommend creating a custom exception that represents the end of the chain. Ensure it contains the relevant information for the consumers to react to it according to your use case.

Next, let's register our new terminal handler in the chain (highlighted):

```
builder.Services.AddSingleton<IMessageHandler>(
    new AlarmTriggeredHandler(
        new AlarmPausedHandler(
            new AlarmStoppedHandler(
                new DefaultHandler()
            ))));
```

Of course, manually registering the chain can become tedious and hard to read. To circumvent that, we can use Scrutor, which we used in *Chapter 11, Structural Patterns*. Here's an updated version of the previous code using Scrutor (don't forget to add the NuGet package to your project):

```
builder.Services
    .AddSingleton<IMessageHandler, DefaultHandler>()
    .Decorate<IMessageHandler, AlarmStoppedHandler>()
    .Decorate<IMessageHandler, AlarmPausedHandler>()
    .Decorate<IMessageHandler, AlarmTriggeredHandler>()
;
```

It is important to note that the preceding code does the same thing as manually instantiating the chain of responsibility. However, the registration order is reversed because we treat each handler as a decorator, so we start with the terminal handler of the chain, which is the `DefaultHandler` class in this case.

That code is available in the project named *FinalChainOfResponsibility*, which is the last code sample of the chapter. That said, the code works with all three versions as long as you install the Scrutor package.

Now, let's test the terminal handler by sending a POST request with the name `SomeUnhandledMessageName`. The endpoint yields the following exception:

```
System.NotSupportedException: Messages named 'SomeUnhandledMessageName' are not supported.
   at ChainOfResponsibility.DefaultHandler.Handle(Message message) in C12\src\ChainOfResponsibility\DefaultHandler.cs:line 7
   at ChainOfResponsibility.AlarmStoppedHandler.Handle(Message message) in C12\src\ChainOfResponsibility\AlarmStoppedHandler.cs:line 19
   at ChainOfResponsibility.AlarmPausedHandler.Handle(Message message) in C12\src\ChainOfResponsibility\AlarmPausedHandler.cs:line 19
   at ChainOfResponsibility.AlarmTriggeredHandler.Handle(Message message) in C12\src\ChainOfResponsibility\AlarmTriggeredHandler.cs:line 19
   at Program.<>c.<<Main>$>b__0_0(Message message, IMessageHandler messageHandler) in C12\src\ChainOfResponsibility\Program.cs:line 22
   at lambda_method1(Closure, Object, HttpContext, Object)
   at Microsoft.AspNetCore.Http.RequestDelegateFactory.<>c__DisplayClass100_2.<<HandleRequestBodyAndCompileRequestDelegateForJson>b__2>d.MoveNext()
--- End of stack trace from previous location ---
   at Microsoft.AspNetCore.Routing.EndpointMiddleware.<Invoke>g__AwaitRequestTask|6_0(Endpoint endpoint, Task requestTask, ILogger logger)
   at Microsoft.AspNetCore.Diagnostics.DeveloperExceptionPageMiddlewareImpl.Invoke(HttpContext context)

HEADERS
=======
Host: localhost:10001
Content-Type: application/json
traceparent: 00-5d737fdbb1018d5b7d060b74baf26111-2805f137fe1541af-00
Content-Length: 77
```

So far, so good, but the experience is not great, so let's add a `try...catch` block to handle this in the endpoint:

```
app.MapPost(
    "/handle",
    (Message message, IMessageHandler messageHandler) =>
    {
        try
        {
            messageHandler.Handle(message);
            return $"Message '{message.Name}' handled successfully.";
        }
```

```
            catch (NotSupportedException ex)
            {
                return ex.Message;
            }
    });
```

Now, when we send an invalid message, the API gently returns the following message to us:

```
Messages named 'SomeUnhandledMessageName' are not supported.
```

Voilà. We have built a simple Chain of Responsibility that handles many types of messages.

Conclusion

The Chain of Responsibility pattern is another great GoF pattern. It divides a large problem into smaller, cohesive units, each doing one job: handling its specific requests.

Now, let's see how the Chain of Responsibility pattern can help us follow the **SOLID** principles:

- S: The Chain of Responsibility pattern aims to achieve this exact principle: create a single unit of logic per class!
- O: The Chain of Responsibility pattern allows the addition, removal, and reordering of handlers without touching the code but by altering the chain's composition in the composition root.
- L: N/A.
- I: The Chain of Responsibility pattern helps with the ISP if we create a small interface. The handler interface is not limited to a single method; it can expose multiple.
- D: By using the handler interface, no element of the chain, nor the consumers, depends on a specific handler; they only depend on the interface that represents the chain (and the handlers), which helps invert the dependency flow.

Next, let's use the Template Method and Chain of Responsibility patterns to encapsulate our handlers' duplicated logic.

Mixing the Template Method and Chain of Responsibility patterns

This section explores a combination of two powerful design patterns: the Template Method and the Chain of Responsibility. As we are about to explore, those two patterns fit together well.

We use the Template Method pattern as the base structure, providing the handlers' blueprint. Meanwhile, the Chain of Responsibility pattern manages the handling sequence, ensuring each request is routed to the correct handler.

When these two patterns work in tandem, they form a robust framework that facilitates easy management, maintains order, and increases the adaptability of our system.

Project – Improved message interpreter

Now that we know both the **Chain of Responsibility** and **Template Method** patterns, it is time to *DRY* out our handlers by extracting the shared logic into an abstract base class using the Template Method pattern and providing extension points to the subclasses.

We covered the *DRY* principle—Don't Repeat Yourself—in *Chapter 3, Architectural Principles*.

OK, so what logic is duplicated?

- The `next` handler injection code is the same in all but the terminal handlers. Moreover, this is an important part of the pattern we should encapsulate in the base class.
- The logic testing whether the current handler can handle the message is also the same in all but the terminal handlers.

Let's create a new base class that implements the Template Method pattern and a large part of the logic of our chain of responsibility:

```
namespace ImprovedChainOfResponsibility;
public abstract class MessageHandlerBase : IMessageHandler
{
    private readonly IMessageHandler? _next;
    public MessageHandlerBase(IMessageHandler? next = null)
    {
        _next = next;
    }
    public void Handle(Message message)
    {
        if (CanHandle(message))
        {
            Process(message);
        }
        else if (HasNext())
        {
            _next.Handle(message);
        }
    }
    [MemberNotNullWhen(true, nameof(_next))]
    private bool HasNext()
    {
        return _next != null;
```

```
    }
    protected virtual bool CanHandle(Message message)
    {
        return message.Name == HandledMessageName;
    }
    protected abstract string HandledMessageName { get; }
    protected abstract void Process(Message message);
}
```

In the preceding code, the `MessageHandlerBase` class adds the `Handle` template method and exposes the following extension points:

- The `CanHandle` method tests whether `HandledMessageName` is equal to the value of the `message.Name` property. A subclass can override this method if it requires a different comparison logic. This method is an optional hook.
- All subclasses must implement the `HandledMessageName` property, which is the key driver of the `CanHandle` method. This property is a mandatory hook.
- All subclasses must implement the `Process` method, allowing them to run their logic against the message. This method is a mandatory hook.

In the preceding code, the `MemberNotNullWhen` attribute tells the compiler that the `_next` field is not `null` when `HasNext` returns `true`. Without that attribute, Visual Studio complains with a *CS8602 - Dereference of a possibly null reference.* warning message on the line `_next.Handle(message);`. You can use many similar attributes to tell the compiler about your code behaviors relating to null states. Here's the full code snippet as a reminder:

```
[MemberNotNullWhen(true, nameof(_next))]
private bool HasNext()
{
    return _next != null;
}
```

Now, to understand how these hooks play out, let's take a look at the three simplified alarm handlers:

```
public class AlarmTriggeredHandler : MessageHandlerBase
{
    protected override string HandledMessageName => "AlarmTriggered";
    public AlarmTriggeredHandler(IMessageHandler? next = null)
        : base(next) { }
    protected override void Process(Message message)
    {
        // Do something clever with the Payload
```

```
    }
}
public class AlarmPausedHandler : MessageHandlerBase
{
    protected override string HandledMessageName => "AlarmPaused";
    public AlarmPausedHandler(IMessageHandler? next = null)
        : base(next) { }
    protected override void Process(Message message)
    {
        // Do something clever with the Payload
    }
}
public class AlarmStoppedHandler : MessageHandlerBase
{
    protected override string HandledMessageName => "AlarmStopped";
    public AlarmStoppedHandler(IMessageHandler? next = null)
        : base(next) { }
    protected override void Process(Message message)
    {
        // Do something clever with the Payload
    }
}
```

As we can see from the updated alarm handlers, they are now limited to a single responsibility: processing the messages they can handle. In contrast, `MessageHandlerBase` now handles the chain of responsibility's plumbing.

We left the `DefaultHandler` class unchanged since it is the end of the chain and does not support having a next handler and does not process messages.

Mixing those two patterns creates a complex messaging system that divides responsibilities into handlers. There is one handler per message, and the chain logic is pushed into a base class.

The beauty of such a system is that we don't have to think about all the messages simultaneously; we can focus on just one message at a time, thereby reducing the cognitive load. When dealing with a new type of message, we can focus on that precise message, implement its handler, and forget about the other types of message. The consumers can also be super dumb, sending the request into the pipe without knowing about the Chain of Responsibility, and like magic, the right handler shall prevail!

Nonetheless, have you noticed an issue with this design? Let's have a look at it next.

Project – A final, finer-grained design

In the last example, we used `HandledMessageName` and `CanHandle` to decide whether a handler could handle a request.

There is one problem with that code: if a subclass decides to override `CanHandle`, and then decides that it no longer requires `HandledMessageName`, we would end up having a lingering, unused property in our system.

There are worse situations, but we are talking component design here, so why not push that system a little further toward a better design?

One way to fix this is to create a finer-grained class hierarchy, as follows:

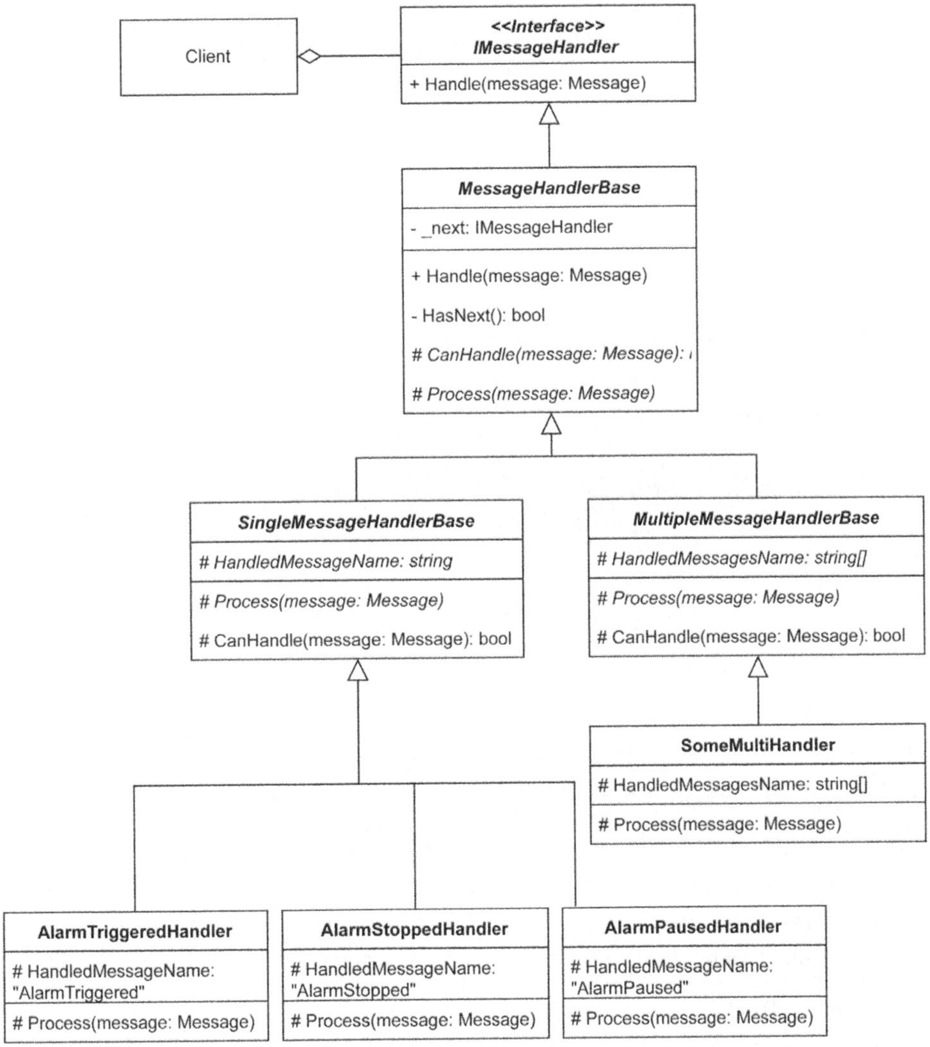

Figure 12.6: Class diagram representing the design of the finer-grained project that implements the Chain of Responsibility and Template Method patterns

The preceding diagram looks more complicated than it is. But let's look at our refactored code first, starting with the new `MessageHandlerBase` class:

```
namespace FinalChainOfResponsibility;
public interface IMessageHandler
{
    void Handle(Message message);
}
public abstract class MessageHandlerBase : IMessageHandler
{
    private readonly IMessageHandler? _next;
    public MessageHandlerBase(IMessageHandler? next = null)
    {
        _next = next;
    }
    public void Handle(Message message)
    {
        if (CanHandle(message))
        {
            Process(message);
        }
        else if (HasNext())
        {
            _next.Handle(message);
        }
    }
    [MemberNotNullWhen(true, nameof(_next))]
    private bool HasNext()
    {
        return _next != null;
    }
    protected abstract bool CanHandle(Message message);
    protected abstract void Process(Message message);
}
```

The `MessageHandlerBase` class manages the Chain of Responsibility by handling the next handler logic and by exposing two hooks (the Template Method pattern) for subclasses to extend:

- `bool CanHandle(Message message)`
- `void Process(Message message)`

This class is similar to the previous one, but the `CanHandle` method is now abstract, and we removed the `HandledMessageName` property, leading to better responsibility segregation and better hooks.

Next, let's look at the `SingleMessageHandlerBase` class, which replaces the logic we removed from the `MessageHandlerBase` class:

```
public abstract class SingleMessageHandlerBase : MessageHandlerBase
{
    public SingleMessageHandlerBase(IMessageHandler? next = null)
        : base(next) { }
    protected override bool CanHandle(Message message)
    {
        return message.Name == HandledMessageName;
    }
    protected abstract string HandledMessageName { get; }
}
```

The `SingleMessageHandlerBase` class inherits from the `MessageHandlerBase` class and overrides the `CanHandle` method. It implements the logic related to it and adds the `HandledMessageName` property that subclasses must define for the `CanHandle` method to work (a required extension point).

The `AlarmPausedHandler`, `AlarmStoppedHandler`, and `AlarmTriggeredHandler` classes now inherit from `SingleMessageHandlerBase` instead of `MessageHandlerBase`, but nothing else has changed. Here's the code as a reminder:

```
namespace FinalChainOfResponsibility;
public class AlarmPausedHandler : SingleMessageHandlerBase
{
    protected override string HandledMessageName => "AlarmPaused";
    public AlarmPausedHandler(IMessageHandler? next = null)
        : base(next) { }
    protected override void Process(Message message)
    {
        // Do something clever with the Payload
    }
}
public class AlarmStoppedHandler : SingleMessageHandlerBase
{
    protected override string HandledMessageName => "AlarmStopped";
    public AlarmStoppedHandler(IMessageHandler? next = null)
        : base(next) { }
    protected override void Process(Message message)
    {
        // Do something clever with the Payload
    }
}
```

```
public class AlarmTriggeredHandler : SingleMessageHandlerBase
{
    protected override string HandledMessageName => "AlarmTriggered";
    public AlarmTriggeredHandler(IMessageHandler? next = null)
        : base(next) { }
    protected override void Process(Message message)
    {
        // Do something clever with the Payload
    }
}
```

Those subclasses of `SingleMessageHandlerBase` implement the `HandledMessageName` property, which returns the message name they can handle, and they implement the handling logic by overriding the `Process` method as before.

Next, we look at the `MultipleMessageHandlerBase` class, which enables its sub-types to handle more than one message type:

```
public abstract class MultipleMessageHandlerBase : MessageHandlerBase
{
    public MultipleMessageHandlerBase(IMessageHandler? next = null)
        : base(next) { }
    protected override bool CanHandle(Message message)
    {
        return HandledMessagesName.Contains(message.Name);
    }
    protected abstract string[] HandledMessagesName { get; }
}
```

The `MultipleMessageHandlerBase` class does the same as `SingleMessageHandlerBase`, but it uses a string array instead of a single string, supporting multiple handler names.

The `DefaultHandler` class has not changed.

For demonstration purposes, let's add the `SomeMultiHandler` class that simulates a message handler that can handle `"Foo"`, `"Bar"`, and `"Baz"` messages:

```
namespace FinalChainOfResponsibility;
public class SomeMultiHandler : MultipleMessageHandlerBase
{
    public SomeMultiHandler(IMessageHandler? next = null)
        : base(next) { }

    protected override string[] HandledMessagesName
        => new[] { "Foo", "Bar", "Baz" };
```

```
        protected override void Process(Message message)
        {
            // Do something clever with the Payload
        }
    }
```

This class hierarchy may sound complicated, but what we did was to allow extensibility without the need to keep any unnecessary code in the process, leaving each class with a single responsibility:

- The `MessageHandlerBase` class handles `_next`
- The `SingleMessageHandlerBase` class handles the `CanHandle` method of handlers supporting a single message
- The `MultipleMessageHandlerBase` class handles the `CanHandle` method of handlers supporting multiple messages
- Other classes implement their version of the `Process` method to handle one or more messages

This is another example demonstrating the strength of the Template Method and Chain of Responsibility patterns working together. That last example also emphasizes the importance of the SRP by allowing greater flexibility while keeping the code reliable and maintainable.

Another strength of that design is the interface at the top. Anything that does not fit the class hierarchy can be implemented directly from the interface instead of trying to adapt logic from inappropriate structures. The `DefaultHandler` class is a good example of that.

Tricking code into doing your bidding instead of properly designing that part of the system leads to half-baked solutions that become hard to maintain.

Conclusion

Mixing the Template Method and Chain of Responsibility patterns led to smaller classes with a single responsibility each. We removed the lingering property while keeping that logic out of the handlers. We even extended the logic to more use cases.

Summary

In this chapter, we covered two GoF behavioral patterns. These patterns can help us create flexible yet easy-to-maintain systems. As the name suggests, behavioral patterns aim at encapsulating application behaviors into cohesive pieces.

First, we looked at the Template Method pattern, which allows us to encapsulate an algorithm's outline inside a base class, leaving some parts open for modification by subclasses. Tricking code into doing your bidding instead of properly designing that part of the system leads to half-baked solutions that become hard to maintain.

The subclasses then fill in the gaps and extend that algorithm to those predefined locations. These locations can be required (abstract) or optional (virtual).

Then, you learned about the Chain of Responsibility pattern, which opens the possibility of chaining multiple small handlers into a chain of processing, inputting the message to be processed at the beginning of the chain (the interface), and waiting for one or more handlers to execute the logic related to that message against it.

You don't have to stop the chain's execution at the first handler. The Chain of Responsibility can become a pipeline instead of associating one message to one handler, as we explored.

Lastly, leveraging the Template Method pattern to encapsulate the Chain of Responsibility's chaining logic led us to a simpler, robust, flexible, and testable implementation without any sacrifices. The two design patterns fit very well together.

In the next chapter, we dig into the Operation Result design pattern to discover efficient and flexible ways of managing return values.

Questions

Let's take a look at a few practice questions:

1. What is the main goal of the Template Method pattern?
2. What is the main goal of the Chain of Responsibility pattern?
3. Is it true that we can only add one `abstract` method when implementing the Template Method design pattern?
4. Can we use the Strategy pattern in conjunction with the Template Method pattern?
5. Is it true that there is a limit of 32 handlers in a Chain of Responsibility?
6. In a Chain of Responsibility, can multiple handlers process the same message?
7. In what way can the Template Method pattern help implement the Chain of Responsibility pattern?

Answers

1. The Template Method pattern encapsulates an algorithm's outline in a base class while leaving some parts of that algorithm open for modification by its subclasses.
2. The Chain of Responsibility pattern divides a larger problem into small pieces (handlers). Each piece is self-governed, while the chain's existence is abstracted from its consumers.
3. False; you can create as many `abstract` (required) or `virtual` (optional) extension points (hooks) as you need.

4. Yes, there is no reason not to.
5. No, there isn't a specific limit of 32 handlers in a Chain of Responsibility pattern. However, in practice, the number of handlers is limited by system resources and performance considerations, similar to other coding constructs.
6. In the stricter sense, a handler must either process the message or defer it to the next handler in the chain. However, allowing more than one handler to process a message creates a pipeline, which opens a lot of possibilities.
7. It helps divide responsibilities between classes by encapsulating the shared logic into one or more base classes.

Learn more on Discord

To join the Discord community for this book – where you can share feedback, ask questions to the author, and learn about new releases – follow the QR code below:

`https://packt.link/ArchitectingASPNETCoreApps3e`

13

Operation Result Pattern

This chapter explores the **Operation Result** pattern, starting simple and progressing to more complex cases. An operation result aims to communicate the success or failure of an operation to its caller. It also allows that operation to return both a value and one or more messages to the caller.

This pattern builds upon foundational object-oriented programming concepts. In this chapter, we iterate and design different forms of operation result objects incrementally. Of course, you should always base your final design on your needs, so learning multiple ways to implement this pattern will help you make the right choices.

The Operation Result pattern is also known as the **Result Object pattern.** I prefer Operation Result because the name specifies that it represents the result of an operation, while Result Object has a broader meaning. Nonetheless, both are basically the same.

In this chapter, we cover how to implement the Operation Result design pattern, which includes using the pattern to return a value, return error messages, return messages with severity levels, and use sub-classes and static factory methods for improved isolation of successes and failures. We also visit a lifelike example at the end to put all of the hands-on theory into a more real-life context.

The Operation Result pattern

The Operation Result design pattern can have a very simple or complex implementation, depending on how much information you want the operation to return to its caller. In this section, we explore multiple ways to use this pattern. We start with its simplest form and build on that until we can return messages and values and add severity levels as the result of an operation.

Imagine any system where you want to display user-friendly error messages, achieve some small speed gain by returning an object instead of throwing an exception, or even handle failure easily and explicitly. The **Operation Result** design pattern can help you achieve these goals.

One excellent use case is to handle the result of a remote operation, such as after querying a remote web service.

Goal

The role of the **Operation Result** pattern is to give an operation (a method) the possibility to return a complex result (an object) that describes whether the operation was successful and that can contain more information, like an actual result. Here is a short list of possibilities:

Description	Mandatory information
Access the success indicator of the operation—whether the operation succeeded or not.	Yes
Access the operation result, if there is one. In other circumstances, this would be the value the method (operation) would return.	No
Access the cause of the failure if the operation was unsuccessful—for example, one or more error messages.	No
Access other information that documents the operation's result. This additional information could be a list of messages or properties that describe the result of the operation.	No

Table 13.1: A list of information the result object can contain

The list can go even further, such as returning the severity of a failure or adding any other relevant information for the specific use case. The success indicator could be binary (`true` or `false`), or there could be more than two states, such as success, partial success, and failure. The operation result object can contain anything a regular class would.

Always focus on your needs first, then use your imagination and knowledge to find the best solution. Software engineering is not only about applying techniques that others tell you to. It's an art! The difference is that you are crafting software instead of painting or woodworking, and most people won't see any of that art (code) or get it even if they do.

Design

It is easy to rely on throwing exceptions when an operation fails. However, the Operation Result pattern is an alternative way of communicating success or failure between components when you don't want to use exceptions. This pattern is useful when the messages are not errors, such as warning messages, or when treating an erroneous result is part of the main flow rather than a side `catch` flow.

A method must return an object containing one or more elements presented in the *Goal* section to be used effectively. As a rule of thumb, a method returning an operation result should not throw exceptions. This way, consumers don't have to handle anything other than the operation result itself.

You can throw exceptions for special cases but, at this point, it is a judgment call based on clear specifications or facing a real problem. For example, a critical event that happens, like the disk being full, would be a valid use case for an exception because it has nothing to do with the main flow, and the code must alert the rest of the program about the system failure.

Let's start by taking a look at a diagram—which contains no implementation details—that describes the sequence of events of any implementation of this pattern:

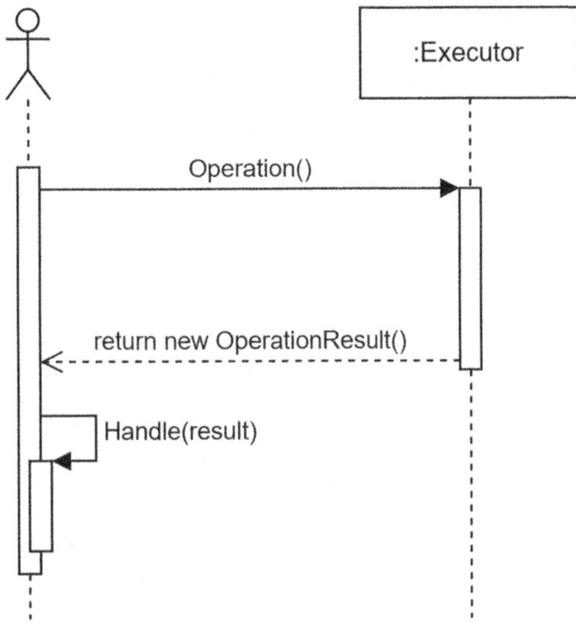

Figure 13.1: Sequence diagram of the Operation Result design pattern

The preceding diagram shows that:

1. The consumer calls the `Operation` method.
2. The executor runs its logic and then returns a result (an object).
3. The consumer handles the `OperationResult` instance returned by the `Operation` method.

Since the design of the `OperationResult` object is directly linked to the use case you are dealing with and the possibilities are endless, I can't show you a class diagram that represents all possibilities. So, instead, let's explore many examples that explain and showcase hands-on possibilities of what we can include in that result object. From there, you can leverage your object-oriented programming skills to design your own operation result implementation.

Project – Implementing different Operation Result patterns

In this project, a consumer (REST API) routes the HTTP requests to the correct handler. We are visiting each of those handlers one by one to create an incremental learning flow, from simple to more complex operation results. This project shows you many ways to implement the Operation Result pattern to help you understand it, make it your own, and implement it as required in your projects.

Let's start with the REST API.

The Program.cs file

For that to work, we must register the `Executor` classes that each example uses, like this (`Program.cs` file):

```
builder.Services
    .AddSingleton<OperationResult.SimplestForm.Executor>()
    .AddSingleton<OperationResult.SingleError.Executor>()
    .AddSingleton<OperationResult.SingleErrorWithValue.Executor>()
    .AddSingleton<OperationResult.MultipleErrorsWithValue.Executor>()
    .AddSingleton<OperationResult.WithSeverity.Executor>()
    .AddSingleton<OperationResult.StaticFactoryMethod.Executor>()
;
```

The preceding code registers all `Executor` classes of all the examples we are about to see. Each example has one `Executor` class. So, if you implement each example one by one, you don't need all that code, just one line.

Also, the consumers of all examples are HTTP GET endpoints defined in the `Program.cs` file. The following code (from `Program.cs`) routes the HTTP requests toward a handler (omitted here):

```
app.MapGet("/simplest-form", ...);
app.MapGet("/single-error", ...);
app.MapGet("/single-error-with-value", ...);
app.MapGet("/multiple-errors-with-value", ...);
app.MapGet("/multiple-errors-with-value-and-severity", ...);
app.MapGet("/static-factory-methods", ...);
```

Like the previous dependency registration, the preceding code covers all the examples we are about to see, so if you implement each example one by one, you can implement each endpoint individually; you don't need all of them.

Next, we dig into each case one by one.

The simplest form of the Operation Result pattern

The following diagram represents the simplest form of the Operation Result pattern:

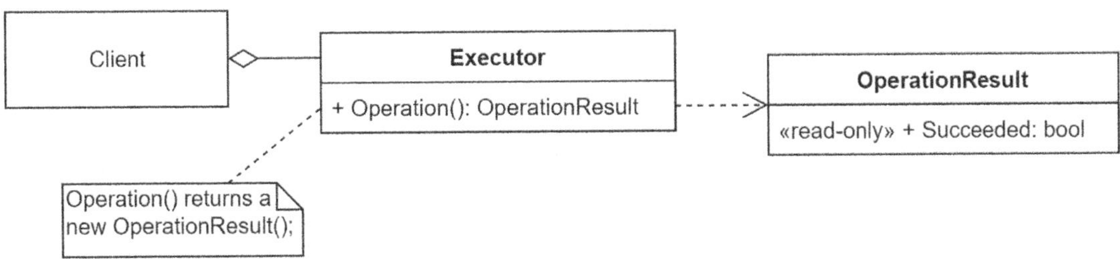

Figure 13.2: Class diagram of the Operation Result design pattern

In the diagram, we have all the actors from the sequence diagram we explored in the *Design* section, and we started to design the `OperationResult` class by adding a read-only `Succeeded` property.

We can translate that class diagram into the following blocks of code:

```
app.MapGet(
    "/simplest-form",
    (OperationResult.SimplestForm.Executor executor) =>
    {
        var result = executor.Operation();
        if (result.Succeeded)
        {
            // Handle the success
            return "Operation succeeded";
        }
        else
        {
            // Handle the failure
            return "Operation failed";
        }
    }
);
```

The preceding code handles the `/simplest-form` HTTP requests. The highlighted code consumes the following operation:

```
namespace OperationResult.SimplestForm;
public class Executor
{
    public OperationResult Operation()
    {
        // Randomize the success indicator
        // This should be real logic
        var randomNumber = Random.Shared.Next(100);
```

```
        var success = randomNumber % 2 == 0;
        // Return the operation result
        return new OperationResult(success);
    }
}
public record class OperationResult(bool Succeeded);
```

The Executor class contains the operation to execute represented by the Operation method. That method returns an instance of the OperationResult class. The implementation is based on a random number. Sometimes it succeeds, and sometimes it fails. You would usually code real application logic in that method instead. Moreover, in an actual application, the method should have a proper name representing the operation, like PayRegistrationFees or CreateConcert. We explore a real-world-like example at the end of the chapter.

The OperationResult record class represents the result of the operation. In this case, a simple read-only Boolean value is stored in the Succeeded property (highlighted).

I chose a record class because there is no reason for the result to change. To learn more about record classes, have a look at the *Appendix* for this book, available on GitHub (https://adpg.link/net8-appendix).

In this form, the difference between the Operation method returning a bool and an instance of OperationResult is small, but it exists nonetheless. By returning an OperationResult object, you can extend the return value over time, adding properties and methods to it, which you cannot do with a bool without updating all consumers.

Next, we add an error message to the result.

A single error message

Now that we know whether the operation succeeded or not, when an operation fails, we want to know what went wrong. To do that, we add an ErrorMessage property to the OperationResult record class.

With that in place, we no longer need to set whether the operation succeeded or not; we can compute that using the ErrorMessage property instead. The logic behind this improvement goes as follows:

- When there is no error message, the operation succeeded.
- When there is an error message, the operation failed.

The OperationResult record class implementing this logic looks like the following:

```
namespace OperationResult.SingleError
public record class OperationResult
{
    public bool Succeeded => string.IsNullOrWhiteSpace(ErrorMessage);
```

```
    public string? ErrorMessage { get; init; }
}
```

In the preceding code, we have these properties:

- The `Succeeded` property checks for an error message.
- The `ErrorMessage` property contains an error message that is settable when instantiating the object.

The executor of that operation looks similar but uses the new constructor, setting an error message instead of directly setting the success indicator:

```
namespace OperationResult.SingleError
public class Executor
{
    public OperationResult Operation()
    {
        // Randomize the success indicator
        // This should be real logic
        var randomNumber = Random.Shared.Next(100);
        var success = randomNumber % 2 == 0;
        // Return the operation result
        return success
            ? new()
            : new() { ErrorMessage = $"Something went wrong with the number
'{randomNumber}'." };
    }
}
```

The consuming code does the same as in the previous sample but writes the error message in the response output instead of a generic failure string:

```
app.MapGet(
    "/single-error",
    (OperationResult.SingleError.Executor executor) =>
    {
        var result = executor.Operation();
        if (result.Succeeded)
        {
            // Handle the success
            return "Operation succeeded";
        }
        else
        {
            // Handle the failure
```

```
                return result.ErrorMessage;
            }
        }
    );
```

When looking at this example, we can begin to comprehend the Operation Result pattern's usefulness. It takes us from the simple success indicator that looked like an overcomplicated Boolean and moves us toward using a data structure that conveys information about the operation to its callers.

Next, we add the possibility of setting a value when the operation succeeds.

Adding a return value

Now that the operation returns a reason for failures, we may want it to return a value for successes. To achieve this, let's build over the previous example and add a `Value` property to the `OperationResult` class:

```
namespace OperationResult.SingleErrorWithValue;
public record class OperationResult
{
    public bool Succeeded => string.IsNullOrWhiteSpace(ErrorMessage);
    public string? ErrorMessage { get; init; }
    public int? Value { get; init; }
}
```

By adding a second `init`-only property, we can set the `Value` property when the operation succeeds and fails.

In a real-world scenario, that `Value` property could be `null` in the case of an error, hence the nullable `int` property.

The operation is also very similar, but we are setting the `Value` property as well as using the object initializer in both cases (highlighted lines):

```
namespace OperationResult.SingleErrorWithValue;
public class Executor
{
    public OperationResult Operation()
    {
        // Randomize the success indicator
        // This should be real logic
        var randomNumber = Random.Shared.Next(100);
        var success = randomNumber % 2 == 0;
        // Return the operation result
```

```
        return success
            ? new() { Value = randomNumber }
            : new()
            {
                ErrorMessage = $"Something went wrong with the number
'{randomNumber}'.",
                Value = randomNumber,
            };
    }
}
```

With that in place, the consumer can use the `Value` property. In our case, the program displays it when the operation succeeds:

```
app.MapGet(
    "/single-error-with-value",
    (OperationResult.SingleErrorWithValue.Executor executor) =>
    {
        var result = executor.Operation();
        if (result.Succeeded)
        {
            // Handle the success
            return $"Operation succeeded with a value of '{result.Value}'.";
        }
        else
        {
            // Handle the failure
            return result.ErrorMessage;
        }
    }
);
```

The preceding code displays the `ErrorMessage` property when the operation fails or uses the `Value` property when it succeeds. With this, the power of the Operation Result pattern continues to emerge.

But we are not done yet, so let's jump into the next evolution.

Multiple error messages

Now we are at the point where we can transfer a `Value` and an `ErrorMessage` to the operation consumers; what about transferring multiple errors, such as validation errors? To achieve this, we can convert our `ErrorMessage` property from a `string` to an `IEnumerable<string>` or another type of collection that fits your needs better.

Here, I chose the `IReadOnlyCollection<string>` interface and the `ImmutableList<string>` class, so we know that external actors can't mutate the results:

```
namespace OperationResult.MultipleErrorsWithValue;
public record class OperationResult
{
    public OperationResult()
    {
        Errors = ImmutableList<string>.Empty;
    }
    public OperationResult(params string[] errors)
    {
        Errors = errors.ToImmutableList();
    }
    public bool Succeeded => !HasErrors();
    public int? Value { get; init; }
    public IReadOnlyCollection<string> Errors { get; init; }
    public bool HasErrors()
    {
        return Errors?.Count > 0;
    }
}
```

Let's look at the new pieces in the preceding code before continuing:

- The errors are now stored in the `ImmutableList<string>` object and returned as an `IReadOnlyCollection<string>`.
- The `Succeeded` property accounts for a collection instead of a single message and follows the same logic.
- The `HasErrors` method improves readability.
- The default constructor represents the successful state.
- The constructor that takes error messages as parameters represents a failed state and populates the `Errors` property.

Now that the operation result is updated, the operation itself can stay the same. The consumer stays almost the same as well, but we need to tell ASP.NET how to serialize the result (see the highlighted the code below):

```
app.MapGet(
    "/multiple-errors-with-value",
    Results<Ok<string>, BadRequest<string[]>> (OperationResult.
MultipleErrorsWithValue.Executor executor)
    => {
        var result = executor.Operation();
```

```
        if (result.Succeeded)
        {
            // Handle the success
            return TypedResults.Ok(
                $"Operation succeeded with a value of '{result.Value}'."
            );
        }
        else
        {
            // Handle the failure
            return TypedResults.BadRequest(result.Errors.ToArray());
        }
    }
);
```

In the preceding code, we specify that the method returns different results depending on the result of the operation (the highlighted code). That allows us to make ASP.NET Core understand that the return value of our delegate can be an `Ok<string>` or a `BadRequest<string[]>`. Without this, the return type could not be inferred, and the code would not compile. That makes sense since the function returns a `string` (`200 OK` status code) in one path and a `string[]` (`400 Bad Request` status code) in another. The `Results<T1, T2>` type allows us to do just that in a strongly typed way.

While executing, ASP.NET serializes the result to JSON before outputting it to the client.

Our Operation Result pattern implementation is getting better and better but still lacks a few features. One of those features is the possibility to propagate messages that are not errors, such as information messages and warnings, which we implement next.

Adding message severity

Now that our operation result structure is materializing, let's update our last iteration to support message severity.

First, we need a severity indicator. An `enum` is a good candidate for this kind of work because it provides a strongly typed and human-readable way to define a set of named constants, but it could also be something else. In our case, we leverage an `enum` that we name `OperationResultSeverity`.

Then we need a message class to encapsulate both the message and the severity level; let's name that class `OperationResultMessage`. The new code looks like this:

```
namespace OperationResult.WithSeverity;
public record class OperationResultMessage
{
    public OperationResultMessage(string message, OperationResultSeverity
severity)
```

```
    {
        Message = message ?? throw new ArgumentNullException(nameof(message));
        Severity = severity;
    }
    public string Message { get; }
    public OperationResultSeverity Severity { get; }
}
public enum OperationResultSeverity
{
    Information = 0,
    Warning = 1,
    Error = 2
}
```

The preceding code represents a simple data structure to replace our `string` messages.

To ensure the enum gets serialized as a string and make the output easier to read and consume, we must register the following converter in the `Program.cs` file:

```
builder.Services
    .Configure<JsonOptions>(o
        => o.SerializerOptions.Converters.Add(
            new JsonStringEnumConverter()))
;
```

Then we need to update the `OperationResult` class to use that new `OperationResultMessage` class instead. We also need to ensure that the operation result indicates a success only when there is no `OperationResultSeverity.Error`, allowing it to transmit the `OperationResultSeverity.Information` and `OperationResultSeverity.Warnings` messages:

```
namespace OperationResult.WithSeverity;
public record class OperationResult
{
    public OperationResult()
    {
        Messages = ImmutableList<OperationResultMessage>.Empty;
    }
    public OperationResult(params OperationResultMessage[] messages)
    {
        Messages = messages.ToImmutableList();
    }
    public bool Succeeded => !HasErrors();
    public int? Value { get; init; }
    public ImmutableList<OperationResultMessage> Messages { get; init; }
```

```
    public bool HasErrors()
    {
        return FindErrors().Any();
    }
    private IEnumerable<OperationResultMessage> FindErrors()
        => Messages.Where(x => x.Severity == OperationResultSeverity.Error);
}
```

The highlighted lines represent the updated logic that sets the success state of the operation. The operation is successful only when no error exists in the `Messages` list. The `FindErrors` method returns messages with an `Error` severity, while the `HasErrors` method bases its decision on that method's output.

The `HasErrors` method logic can be anything.

With that in place, the `Executor` class is also revamped. Let's have a look at those changes:

```
namespace OperationResult.WithSeverity;
public class Executor
{
    public OperationResult Operation()
    {
        // Randomize the success indicator
        // This should be real logic
        var randomNumber = Random.Shared.Next(100);
        var success = randomNumber % 2 == 0;
        // Some information message
        var information = new OperationResultMessage(
            "This should be very informative!",
            OperationResultSeverity.Information
        );
        // Return the operation result
        if (success)
        {
            var warning = new OperationResultMessage(
                "Something went wrong, but we will try again later 
automatically until it works!",
                OperationResultSeverity.Warning
            );
            return new OperationResult(information, warning) { Value = 
randomNumber };
```

```
        }
        else
        {
            var error = new OperationResultMessage(
                $"Something went wrong with the number '{randomNumber}'.",
                OperationResultSeverity.Error
            );
            return new OperationResult(information, error) { Value = 
randomNumber };
        }
    }
}
```

In the preceding code, we replaced the ternary operator of the `Operation` method with `if-else` blocks to keep the code readable as it became more complex. The `Operation` method also uses all severity levels that we introduced in this example.

You should always aim to write code that is easy to read. It is OK to use language features, but nesting statements over statements on a single line has limits and can quickly become a mess.

In that last code block, both successes and failures return two messages:

- When the operation succeeds, the method returns an information and a warning message.
- When the operation fails, the method returns an information and an error message.

From the consumer standpoint, we have a placeholder if-else block and return the operation result directly. Of course, we could handle this differently in a real application that needs to know about those messages, but in this case, all we want to see are those results, so this does it:

```
app.MapGet("/multiple-errors-with-value-and-severity", (OperationResult.
WithSeverity.Executor executor) =>
{
    var result = executor.Operation();
    if (result.Succeeded)
    {
        // Handle the success
    }
    else
    {
        // Handle the failure
    }
```

```
    return result;
});
```

As you can see, it is still as easy to use, but now with more flexibility added to it. We can do something with the different types of messages, such as displaying them to the user, retrying the operation, and more.

For now, when running the application and calling this endpoint, successful calls return a JSON string that looks like the following:

```
{
    "succeeded": true,
    "value": 56,
    "messages": [
        {
            "message": "This should be very informative!",
            "severity": "Information"
        },
        {
            "message": "Something went wrong, but we will try again later
automatically until it works!",
            "severity": "Warning"
        }
    ]
}
```

Failures return a JSON string that looks like this:

```
{
    "succeeded": false,
    "value": 19,
    "messages": [
        {
            "message": "This should be very informative!",
            "severity": "Information"
        },
        {
            "message": "Something went wrong with the number '19'.",
            "severity": "Error"
        }
    ]
}
```

Another idea to improve this design would be adding a `Status` property that returns a complex success result based on each message's severity level. To do that, we could create another `enum`:

```
public enum OperationStatus { Success, Failure, PartialSuccess }
```

Then, we could access that value through a new property named `Status`, on the `OperationResult` class. With this, a consumer could handle partial success without digging into the messages. I will leave you to play with this one on your own; for example, the `Status` property could replace the `Succeeded` property, or the `Succeeded` property could leverage the `Status` property similarly to what we did with the errors. The most important part is to define what would be a success, a partial success, and a failure. Think of a database transaction, for example; one failure could lead to the rollback of the transaction, while in another case, one failure could be acceptable.

Now that we've expanded our simple example into this, what happens if we want the `Value` to be optional? To do that, we could create multiple operation result classes holding more or less information (properties); let's try that next.

Sub-classes and factories

In this iteration, we keep all the properties but instantiate the `OperationResult` objects using static factories. Moreover, we hide certain properties in the sub-classes, so each result type only contains the data it needs. The `OperationResult` class itself only exposes the `Succeeded` property in this scenario.

A **static factory method** is nothing more than a static method that creates objects. It is handy and easy to use but less flexible than having an independent factory class.

I cannot stress this enough: be careful when designing something `static`, or it could haunt you later; `static` members are not extensible and can make their consumers harder to test.

The `OperationResultMessage` class and the `OperationResultSeverity` `enum` remain unchanged. In the following code block, we do not consider the severity when computing the operation's success or failure state. Instead, we create an abstract `OperationResult` class with two sub-classes:

- The `SuccessfulOperationResult` class represents successful operations.
- The `FailedOperationResult` class represents failed operations.

Then the next step is to force the use of the specifically designed classes by creating two static factory methods:

- The static `Success` method returns a `SuccessfulOperationResult` object.
- The static `Failure` method returns a `FailedOperationResult` object.

This technique moves the responsibility of deciding whether the operation is a success from the `OperationResult` class to the `Operation` method that explicitly creates the expected result.

The following code block shows the new `OperationResult` implementation (the static factories are highlighted):

```
namespace OperationResult.StaticFactoryMethod;
public abstract record class OperationResult
{
    private OperationResult() { }
    public abstract bool Succeeded { get; }
    public static OperationResult Success(int? value = null)
    {
        return new SuccessfulOperationResult { Value = value };
    }
    public static OperationResult Failure(params OperationResultMessage[]
errors)
    {
        return new FailedOperationResult(errors);
    }
    private record class SuccessfulOperationResult : OperationResult
    {
        public override bool Succeeded { get; } = true;
        public virtual int? Value { get; init; }
    }
    private record class FailedOperationResult : OperationResult
    {
        public FailedOperationResult(params OperationResultMessage[] errors)
        {
            Messages = errors.ToImmutableList();
        }
        public override bool Succeeded { get; } = false;
        public ImmutableList<OperationResultMessage> Messages { get; }
    }
}
```

After analyzing the code, there are a few closely related particularities:

- The `OperationResult` class has a private constructor.
- Both the `SuccessfulOperationResult` and `FailedOperationResult` classes are nested inside the `OperationResult` class, inherit from it, and are `private`.

Nested classes are the only way to inherit from the `OperationResult` class because, like other members of the class, nested classes have access to their private members, including the constructor. Otherwise, it is impossible to inherit from `OperationResult`.

Moreover, as private classes, they can only be accessed internally from the `OperationResult` class for the same reason and become inaccessible from the outside.

Since the beginning of the book, I have repeated **flexibility** many times, but you don't always want flexibility. Even if most of the book is about improving flexibility, sometimes you want control over what you expose and what you allow consumers to do, whether to protect internal mechanisms (encapsulation) or for maintainability reasons.

For example, allowing consumers to change the internal state of an object can lead to unexpected behaviors. Another example would be when managing a library; the larger the public API, the more the chances of introducing a breaking change. Nonetheless, over-hiding of elements can be detrimental to the code's consumers; if you need a class, your consumers may eventually either need it too or need to extend it.

In this case, we could have used a protected constructor instead or implemented a fancier way of instancing success and failure instances. Nonetheless, I decided to use this opportunity to show you how to lock a class in place without the sealed modifier, making extending by inheritance from the outside impossible. We could have built mechanisms in our classes to allow controlled extensibility (like the Template Method pattern), but for this one, let's keep it locked in tight!

From here, the only missing piece is the operation itself and the consumer of the operation. Let's look at the operation first:

```
namespace OperationResult.StaticFactoryMethod;
public class Executor
{
    public OperationResult Operation()
    {
        // Randomize the success indicator
        // This should be real logic
        var randomNumber = Random.Shared.Next(100);
        var success = randomNumber % 2 == 0;
        // Return the operation result
        if (success)
        {
            return OperationResult.Success(randomNumber);
        }
        else
        {
            var error = new OperationResultMessage(
                $"Something went wrong with the number '{randomNumber}'.",
                OperationResultSeverity.Error
            );
```

```
            return OperationResult.Failure(error);
        }
    }
}
```

The two highlighted lines in the preceding code block show the elegance of this new improvement. I find this code very easy to read, which was the objective. We now have two methods that clearly define our intentions when using them: `Success` or `Failure`.

The consumer uses the same code that we saw before in other examples, so I'll omit it here. However, the output is different for a successful or a failed operation. Here is a successful output:

```
{
    "succeeded": true,
    "value": 80
}
```

Here is a failed output:

```
{
    "succeeded": false,
    "messages": [
        {
            "message": "Something went wrong with the number '37'.",
            "severity": "Error"
        }
    ]
}
```

As the two preceding JSON outputs show, each object's properties are different. The only shared property of the two is the `Succeeded` property.

Beware that this type of class hierarchy is harder to consume directly since the interface (the `OperationResult` class) has a minimal API surface (it only exposes the `Succeeded` property), and each sub-class adds different properties, which are hidden from the consumers. For example, it would be hard to use the `Value` property of a successful operation directly in the endpoint handler code. Therefore, when hiding properties, as we did here, you ensure the consumers do not need to use those additional properties.

Creating small and specific interfaces is encouraged by many architectural principles, yet depending on how these are implemented, they can be harder to use.

For example, we can use this technique when sending the result to another system over HTTP (like this project does) or publish the operation result as an event (see *Chapter 19, Introduction to Microservices Architecture*, where we introduce event-driven architecture). Nevertheless, learning to manipulate classes using polymorphism will be helpful the day you need it.

Project – Registration Application

The `RegistrationApp` project incorporates notions we have studied in the chapter in a more lifelike context. Naming classes and methods `Executor`, `Operation`, and `OperationResult` was good for learning as they are directly linked to the diagrams. Yet, a more lifelike example should help you come full circle in your understanding of the Operation Result pattern.

Context: The application contains one endpoint and allows users to register for a concert. The user is simulated; he is always the same, and his name is John Doe. Users can only register for one concert (whose `Id` is equal to `1`). Other concerts yield an error.

Let's start with the data structures:

```
public record class Concert(int Id, string Name);
public record class User(string Name);
```

Those two classes are very slim as we only use them to simulate the registration process.

In a different context, we could have DTOs that are different from the domain objects. For simplicity, in this example, we are leveraging those two classes in both cases. That said, we explore this in multiple chapters of *Section 4: Application Patterns*, in other contexts than the Operation Result pattern.

Next, let's have a look at the operation result class:

```
using System.Diagnostics.CodeAnalysis;
namespace RegistrationApp;
public record class ConcertRegistrationResult
{
    [MemberNotNullWhen(false, nameof(ErrorMessage))]
    [MemberNotNullWhen(true, nameof(ConfirmationNumber))]
    public bool RegistrationSucceeded { get; init; }

    public User User { get; init; } = null!;
    public Concert Concert { get; init; } = null!;
    public string? ConfirmationNumber { get; init; }
    public string? ErrorMessage { get; init; }

    private ConcertRegistrationResult() { }
```

```
    public static ConcertRegistrationResult CreateSuccess(User user, Concert
concert, string confirmationNumber)
    {
        return new()
        {
            RegistrationSucceeded = true,
            User = user,
            Concert = concert,
            ConfirmationNumber = confirmationNumber,
        };
    }

    public static ConcertRegistrationResult CreateFailure(User user, Concert
concert, string errorMessage)
    {
        return new()
        {
            RegistrationSucceeded = false,
            User = user,
            Concert = concert,
            ErrorMessage = errorMessage,
        };
    }
}
```

The preceding class defines the `ConcertRegistrationResult` record class that represents the outcome of a concert registration process. It contains properties to indicate whether the registration was successful, the user and concert details, a confirmation number for successful registrations, and an error message for failed ones.

The class constructor's visibility is `private`, which forces consumers to use the two static factory methods, `CreateSuccess` and `CreateFailure`, that instantiate success or failure outcomes, respectively, guaranteeing that a confirmation number is provided when registration succeeds and an error message is present when it fails. The `MemberNotNullWhen` attributes allow the compiler to know that when consuming the code—I included an example in the `Program.cs` file.

Next, let's look at the `ConcertRegistrationService` class, which plays the *Executor* role:

```
namespace RegistrationApp;
public class ConcertRegistrationService
{
    public async Task<ConcertRegistrationResult> RegisterAsync(User user,
Concert concert)
```

```
    {
        var (success, confirmationNumber) = await
SimulatedRegistrationProcessAsync(user, concert);
        if (!success)
        {
            return ConcertRegistrationResult.CreateFailure(
                user,
                concert,
                "The registration to the concert failed."
            );
        }
        return ConcertRegistrationResult.CreateSuccess(
            user, concert, confirmationNumber);
    }

    private static async Task<(bool Success, string ConfirmationNumber)>
SimulatedRegistrationProcessAsync(User user, Concert concert)
    {
        // Simulate an async operation
        await Task.Delay(Random.Shared.Next(10, 100));

        // Return a simulated result
        return (concert.Id == 1, Guid.NewGuid().ToString());
    }
}
```

The preceding class exposes the `RegisterAsync` method that plays the role of the *Operation*. It simulates the concert registration process for a user. If the process is unsuccessful (the first highlighted block), the service returns a result object with an error message by leveraging the factory method `CreateFailure`. Conversely, if successful (the second highlighted block), it returns a result object with a unique confirmation number by leveraging the factory method `CreateSuccess`.

The `SimulatedRegistrationProcessAsync` method is only there to simulate accessing remote resources to convey the registration process.

Now that we have our building blocks, let's explore the consumer of that code, starting with the dependency (in the `Program.cs` file):

```
using Microsoft.AspNetCore.Http.HttpResults;
using Microsoft.AspNetCore.Http.Json;
using RegistrationApp;
using System.Text.Json.Serialization;

var builder = WebApplication.CreateBuilder(args);
```

```
builder.Services.AddSingleton<ConcertRegistrationService>();
builder.Services.Configure<JsonOptions>(o => {
    o.SerializerOptions.DefaultIgnoreCondition = JsonIgnoreCondition.
WhenWritingNull;
});
```

The preceding code tells the IoC container to always inject the same instance of the `ConcertRegistrationService` class—since it is stateless, one object can be shared and reused. Then, the code configures the `JsonOptions` class so that the ASP.NET Core serializer omits the `null` properties.

As we are about to see, setting the `DefaultIgnoreCondition` value to `JsonIgnoreCondition.WhenWritingNull` results in writing only properties that are not null (`ConfirmationNumber` or `ErrorMessage`, for example), leading to a clean output.

Now, let's look at the consumer of the *Operation*, the second part of the `Program.cs` file:

```
var app = builder.Build();
app.MapPost("/concerts/{concertId}/register",
    async Task<Results<Ok<ConcertRegistrationResult>,
BadRequest<ConcertRegistrationResult>>> (int concertId,
ConcertRegistrationService service) =>
{
    // Simulate fetching objects
    var user = GetCurrentUser();
    var concert = GetConcert(concertId);

    // Execute the operation
    var result = await service.RegisterAsync(user, concert);

    // Handle the operation result
    if (result.RegistrationSucceeded)
    {
        return TypedResults.Ok(result);
    }
    else
    {
        await LogErrorMessageAsync(result.ErrorMessage);
        return TypedResults.BadRequest(result);
    }
});
app.Run();
```

```
// Helper methods to simulate interacting with a complex system
static Concert GetConcert(int concertId) => new(concertId, $"Some amazing
concert-Part {concertId}");
static User GetCurrentUser() => new("John Doe");
static Task LogErrorMessageAsync(string message) => Task.CompletedTask;
```

The preceding code contains one endpoint and a few helper methods that simulate interacting with a complex system. The `POST` endpoint has a `concertId` parameter taken from the route and expects the IoC container to inject an instance of the `ConcertRegistrationService` class that it uses to execute the operation.

The highlighted code of the preceding block consumes the operation and handles the result. First, it calls the `RegisterAsync` method that returns an instance of `ConcertRegistrationResult`. Then, it checks whether the operation was successful or not. When successful, it returns the `result` variable with a `200 OK` status code. When the operation fails, it simulates logging the value of the `ErrorMessage` property and then returns the `result` variable with a `400 Bad Request` status code.

Have you noticed that the `LogErrorMessageAsync` method takes a `string` as a parameter, but the `ErrorMessage` property is a nullable string (`string?`)? If you look at the code in Visual Studio, you'll realize that the compiler does not complain about this, which is a result of using the `MemberNotNullWhen` attribute that I added to the `ConcertRegistrationResult` class. Without the attribute, the compiler would warn you with the following error message:

```
CS8604: Possible null reference argument for parameter 'message' in 'Task
LogErrorMessageAsync(string message)'.
```

Now, let's start the project and test it out using the HTTP request available in the `RegistrationApp.http` file:

```
@RegistrationApp_HostAddress = https://localhost:7227
POST {{RegistrationApp_HostAddress}}/concerts/1/register
###
POST {{RegistrationApp_HostAddress}}/concerts/2/register
```

The preceding file contains two requests, one that will succeed and one that will fail. When we execute the first request, we get an output like the following:

```
{
  "registrationSucceeded": true,
  "user": {
    "name": "John Doe"
  },
  "concert": {
```

```
    "id": 1,
    "name": "Some amazing concert—Part 1"
  },
  "confirmationNumber": "5c49ab31-7bcb-4c45-883c-cf2d87c2a658"
}
```

Since it is successful, we have the success indicator, the user, the concert, and the confirmation number. The highlighted lines represent the primary changes between a success and a failure. Let's look at a failed result next:

```
{
  "registrationSucceeded": false,
  "user": {
    "name": "John Doe"
  },
  "concert": {
    "id": 2,
    "name": "Some amazing concert—Part 2"
  },
  "errorMessage": "The registration to the concert failed."
}
```

This second JSON snippet represents an unsuccessful result, indicated by the first highlighted line, but instead of having a `confirmationNumber`, it has an `errorMessage` (the second highlighted line). This little detail is the reason we configured the `JsonOptions` object.

If we recap, we implemented the Operation Result pattern. The operation is consumed by a POST endpoint that simulates registering a user to a concert. The endpoint responds with a well-formatted JSON object that is slightly different for successes and failures. Internally, we leveraged static factory methods to encapsulate the creation logic of the `ConcertRegistrationResult` class and ensured that we told the compiler about that logic by leveraging `MemberNotNullWhen` attributes, which allowed us to use the `ErrorMessage` property—a nullable string—as if it was non-nullable.

Next, let's peek at some advantages and disadvantages of the Operation Result pattern.

Advantages and disadvantages

Here are a few advantages and disadvantages of the Operation Result design pattern.

Advantages

It is more explicit than throwing an `Exception` since the operation result type is specified explicitly as the method's return type. That makes it more evident than knowing what type of exceptions the operation and its dependencies can throw.

Another advantage is the execution speed; returning an object is faster than throwing an exception. Not that much faster, but faster nonetheless.

Using operation results is more flexible than exceptions and gives us design flexibility; for example, we can manage different message types like warnings and information.

Disadvantages

Using operation results is more complex than throwing exceptions because we must *manually propagate it up the call stack* (i.e., the result object is returned by the callee and handled by the caller). This is especially true if the operation result must go up multiple levels, suggesting this pattern may not be the most suitable.

It is easy to expose members not used by all scenarios, creating a bigger API surface than needed, where some parts are used only in some cases. But, between this and spending countless hours designing the perfect system, sometimes exposing an `int? Value { get; }` property is the best option. Nonetheless, always try to reduce that surface to a minimum and use your imagination and design skills to overcome those challenges!

Conclusion

At this point, we would usually explore how the **Operation Result** pattern can help us follow the SOLID principles. However, it depends too much on the implementation, so here are a few key points instead:

- The `OperationResult` class encapsulates the result, extracting that responsibility from the other system's components (SRP).
- We violated the ISP with the `Value` property in multiple examples. This infringement has a minor impact that we fixed as an example of overcoming this challenge.
- We could compare an operation result to a DTO but returned by an operation (method) instead of a REST API endpoint. From there, we could add an abstraction or stick with returning a concrete class, but sometimes, using concrete types makes the system easier to understand and maintain. Depending on the implementation, this may break different principles.

When the advantages surpass the minor impacts of those kinds of violations, it is acceptable to let them slide. Principles are ideals and are not applicable in every scenario—principles are not laws.

Most design decisions are trade-offs between two imperfect solutions, so you must choose which downsides you prefer to live with to gain the upsides.

Summary

In this chapter, we visited multiple forms of the Operation Result pattern, from an augmented Boolean to a complex data structure containing messages, values, and success indicators. We also explored static factories and private constructors to control external access. Furthermore, after all that exploration, we only scratched the surface of the almost endless possibilities surrounding how to design the resulting object returned by the operation method. Each specific use case should dictate how to make it happen. From here, I am confident you have enough information about the pattern to explore the many possibilities yourself, and I highly encourage you to.

The Operation Result pattern is perfect for crafting strongly typed return values that self-manage multiple states (error and success) or support complex states (like partial success). It is also ideal for transporting messages that are not necessarily errors, like information messages. Even in its simplest form, we can leverage the Operation Result pattern as a base for extensibility since we can add members to the result class over time, which would be impossible for a primitive type (or any type we don't control).

The `HttpResponseMessage` class returned by the methods of the `HttpClient` class is an excellent example of a concrete implementation of the Operation Result pattern. It contains a single message exposed through the `ReasonPhrase` property. It exposes a complex success state through the `StatusCode` property and a simple success indicator through its `IsSuccessStatusCode` property. It also contains more information about the request and response through other properties.

This chapter concludes *Section 3: Component Patterns,* and leads us to *Section 4: Application Patterns,* where we explore application design styles.

Questions

Let's take a look at a few practice questions:

1. Is returning an operation result when doing an asynchronous call, such as an HTTP request, a good idea?
2. What is the name of the pattern that we implemented using static methods?
3. Is it faster to return an operation result than throw an exception?
4. In what scenario might the Operation Result pattern come in handy?

Further reading

Here are some links to build on what we learned in this chapter:

- An article on my blog about exceptions (titled *A beginner guide to exceptions | The basics*): `https://adpg.link/PpEm`
- An article on my blog about Operation Result (titled *Operation result | Design Pattern*): `https://adpg.link/4o2q`

Answers

1. Yes, asynchronous operations like HTTP are great candidates for the Operation Result pattern. For example, in the **Base Class Library** (**BCL**), the `HttpResponseMessage` instance returned by the `Send` method of the `HttpClient` class is an operation result.
2. We implemented two **static factory methods**.

3. Yes, returning an object is marginally faster than throwing an exception.
4. The Operation Result pattern comes in handy when we want to return the state of the operation along with its return value as part of the main consumption flow. It is very suitable to return multiple properties describing the result of the process and is extensible.

Learn more on Discord

To join the Discord community for this book – where you can share feedback, ask questions to the author, and learn about new releases – follow the QR code below:

`https://packt.link/ArchitectingASPNETCoreApps3e`

Section 4

Application Patterns

In this section, we lay the groundwork for modern application design. Instead of focusing on smaller parts of an application, we look at it from a higher level holistically.

Chapter 14, Layering and Clean Architecture, explores layering and Clean Architecture, starting by understanding layering basics—separating concerns into distinct layers—and then discussing traditional and innovative approaches, including anemic and rich models. Finally, we introduce Clean Architecture as an advanced form of layering, guiding you toward building well-structured, maintainable, and scalable applications.

Chapter 15, Object Mappers, dives into object mappers, learning to streamline the transference of data across different layers. We also use the Aggregate Services and the Façade patterns to enhance our initial design. We finally explore open-source tools to automate and simplify mapping, focusing on generating value instead of writing boilerplate code.

Chapter 16, Mediator and CQS Patterns, focuses on the Mediator and Command Query Separation (CQS) patterns. We use them to streamline communication and to organize the application logic. We bring these concepts to life with practical examples and the MediatR library.

Chapter 17, Getting Started with Vertical Slice Architecture, explores Vertical Slice Architecture, focusing on feature-oriented design for a simpler, more maintainable codebase. We learn to organize code in independent slices and leverage several topics from previous chapters to help us do so.

Chapter 18, Request-EndPoint-Response (REPR), delves into the Request-EndPoint-Response (REPR) pattern, enhancing our applications' readability, maintainability, and testability. We build on Vertical Slice Architecture and CQS, exploring techniques to apply REPR effectively in real-world scenarios.

Chapter 19, Introduction to Microservices Architecture, introduces the essential concepts of microservices architecture, guiding you through its principles and helping you make informed decisions about adopting this architecture in your projects. We cover foundational microservices elements and delve into event-driven architecture. We also explore the Gateway, CQRS, and Microservice Adapter patterns. We then implement a Backend for Frontend (BFF) project to get hands-on practice.

This chapter equips you with the knowledge to design scalable, flexible, and resilient systems, laying the groundwork for implementing microservices in a way that aligns with your project's goals.

Chapter 20, Modular Monolith, explores Modular Monoliths, combining the classic monolith simplicity with microservices flexibility without the operational complexity. We study practical strategies for modularization, addressing challenges and providing insights into designing systems that are both easy to manage and ready for future growth. We also leverage event-driven architecture to facilitate communication between modules.

Several of these chapters could make a book themselves, so we explore some at a higher level, yet enough to help you make more informed decisions when choosing an architectural style. This section is a starting point for further reading while still being filled with helpful content, patterns, tips, and technologies to use immediately in your everyday projects.

The goal is to cover many application-level patterns with enough detail to get you started. The reason for this is that knowing enough about many techniques will help you choose the proper one for the job at hand, instead of picking the same one every time or the only one you know. Getting better at something is easier when you know where to start, but impossible if you don't know the available options.

These architectural styles offer diverse strategies for organizing codebases and applications, revealing various subsets of techniques. Understanding multiple styles enhances your ability to structure your code and comprehend others' work.

This section comprises the following chapters:

- *Chapter 14, Layering and Clean Architecture*
- *Chapter 15, Object Mappers*
- *Chapter 16, Mediator and CQS Patterns*
- *Chapter 17, Getting Started with Vertical Slice Architecture*
- *Chapter 18, Request-EndPoint-Response (REPR)*
- *Chapter 19, Introduction to Microservices Architecture*
- *Chapter 20, Modular Monolith*

The architectural styles and patterns we explore in this section help us avoid creating a "Big Ball of Mud" with our codebase. Next, we briefly explore this anti-pattern to understand what the section's content helps us avoid.

Anti-pattern – Big Ball of Mud

The Big Ball of Mud anti-pattern describes a system that ended badly or was never properly designed. Sometimes, a system starts great but evolves into a Big Ball of Mud due to pressure, volatile requirements, impossible deadlines, bad practices, or other reasons. We often refer to the Big Ball of Mud as **spaghetti code**, which means the same thing.

This anti-pattern means a very hard-to-maintain codebase, poorly written code that is difficult to read, lots of unwanted tight coupling, low cohesion, or worse: all that in the same codebase.

Applying the techniques covered in this book should help you avoid this anti-pattern. On top of that, here are a few tips to help you avoid creating a Big Ball of Mud:

- Aim at small, well-designed components that are testable.
- Enforce testability using automated testing. Remember that testing tightly coupled code is very hard, so your design might benefit from improvements if testing becomes an issue.
- Refactor and improve your codebase whenever you can, iteratively (continuous improvement). Your automated tests will help with this.
- Apply the SOLID principles.
- Define your application pattern before starting the project.
- Think of the best way to implement each component and feature with your team. When uncertain about the best approach, research the problem, develop one or more proofs of concept or prototypes, or conduct experiments. Don't shy away from abandoning ideas that do not yield the expected outcomes; it is better to fail or be wrong while experimenting than to be stuck with a Big Ball of Mud later.
- Ensure you understand the business requirements of the program you are building. You are not just writing code; you are creating business value by overcoming business problems, automating solutions, and more.
- As we study in many chapters of this section, building feature-oriented applications is one of the best ways to avoid creating a Big Ball of Mud. To lay the groundwork, we start this section with the evolution of layering to learn pitfalls to avoid and how layering can still benefit us.

14

Layering and Clean Architecture

In this chapter, we explore the inherent concepts behind layering. Layering is a popular way of organizing computer systems by encapsulating major concerns into layers. Those concerns are related to a computer vocation, such as data access, instead of a business concern, such as inventory. Understanding the concepts behind layering is essential, as many concepts and applications leverage layers.

We start this chapter by exploring the initial ideas behind layering. Then, we explore alternative ways to structure our layered applications that can help us solve different problems. We use anemic models and rich models and expose their pros and cons. Finally, we quickly explore **Clean Architecture**, an evolution of layering, and a modern way to organize layers.

This chapter lays out the evolution of layering, starting with basic, restrictive, and even flawed techniques, and then gradually moves toward more modern patterns. This journey should help you understand the concepts and practices behind layering, giving you a stronger understanding than just learning one way of doing things. The key is to understand the logic behind layering: the good, but also the bad.

In this chapter, we cover the following topics:

- Introducing layering
- Responsibilities of the common layers
- Abstract layers
- Sharing a model
- Clean Architecture
- Implementing layering in real life

Let's get started!

Introducing layering

Now that we've explored a few design patterns and played with ASP.NET Core, it is time to jump into layering. In most computer systems, there are layers. Why? Because it is an efficient way to partition and organize units of logic together. We could conceptually represent layers as horizontal software segments, each encapsulating a concern.

Classic layering model

Let's start by examining a classic three-layer application design:

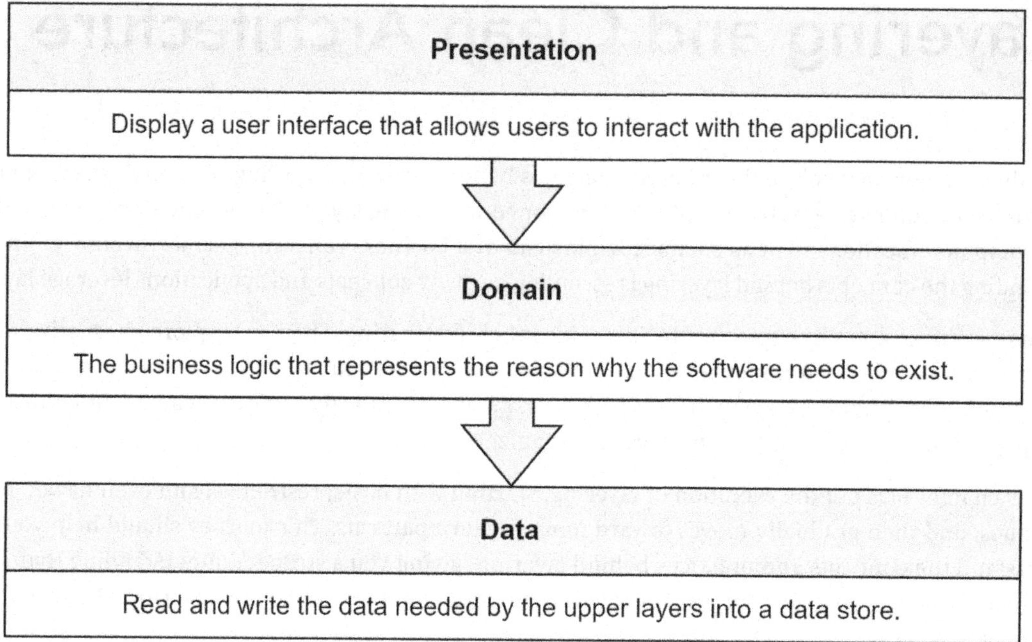

Figure 14.1: A classic three-layer application design

The **presentation layer** represents any user interface that a user can interact with to reach the domain. It could be an ASP.NET Core web application, WPF, WinForms, Android, or any other presentation layer alternative.

The **domain layer** represents the core logic driven by the business rules; this solves the application's problem. The domain layer is also called the **business logic layer** (**BLL**).

The **data layer** represents the bridge between the data and the application. The layer can store the data in a SQL Server database, a NoSQL database hosted in the cloud, a mix of many data sources, or anything else that fits the business needs. The data layer is also called the **data access layer** (**DAL**) and the **persistence layer**.

Let's jump to an example. Given that a user has been authenticated and authorized, here is what happens when they want to create a book in a bookstore application built using those three layers:

1. The user requests the page by sending a GET request to the server.
2. The server handles that GET request (the **presentation layer**) and then returns the page to the user.
3. The user fills out the form and sends a POST request to the server.
4. The server handles the POST request (the **presentation layer**) and then sends it to the **domain layer** for processing.
5. The **domain layer** executes the logic required to create a book, then tells the **data layer** to persist that data.
6. After unrolling to the presentation layer, the server returns the appropriate response to the user, most likely a page containing a list of books and a message saying the operation was successful.

Following a classic layering architecture, a layer can only talk to the next layer in the stack—the **presentation** layer talks to the **domain layer**, which talks to the **data layer**, and so on. The important part is that **each layer must be independent and isolated to limit tight coupling.**

In this classic layering structure, each layer should own its **model**. For example, the presentation layer should not send its **view models** to the **domain** layer; only **domain objects** should be used there. The opposite is also true: since the **domain** returns its own objects to the **presentation layer**, the **presentation layer** should not leak them to its consumers but organize the required information into **view models** or **DTO** instead.

Here is a visual example:

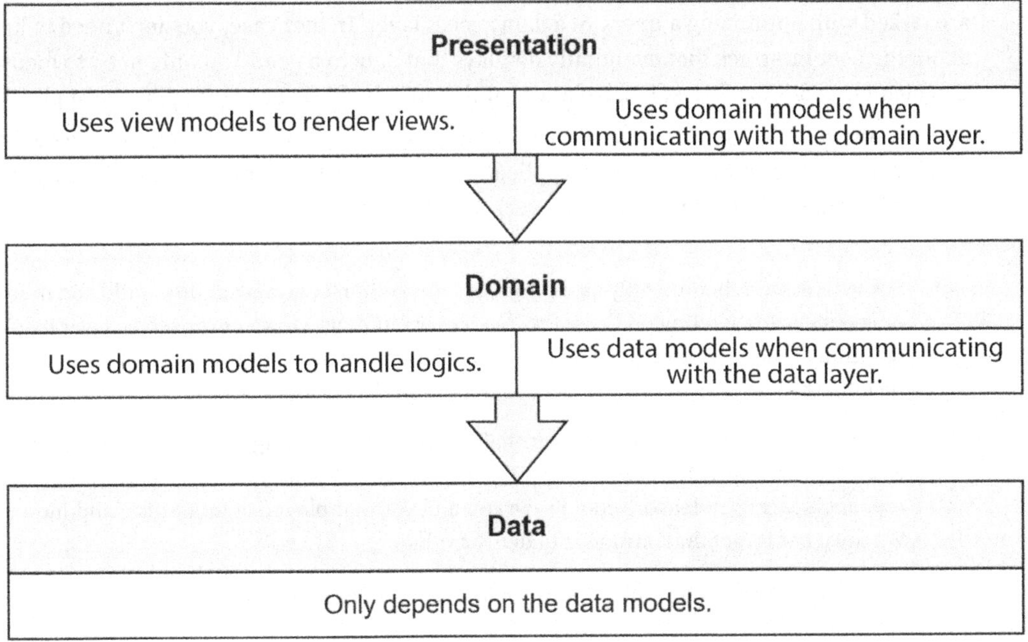

Figure 14.2: Diagram representing how the layers interact with one another

As depicted in the preceding diagram, each upper layer depends on the layer directly below it and uses its model to talk to it. For example, in a REST API application:

1. The presentation layer receives an HTTP request.
2. It then leverages the input DTO to create the appropriate domain object to send to a component in the domain layer.
3. The domain layer then converts that domain object into a data object and then uses it to communicate with a component in the data layer.
4. The data layer returns a data object to the domain layer.
5. The domain layer returns a domain object to the presentation layer.
6. The presentation layer returns a DTO to the client that initiated the request.

Even if three is probably the most popular number of layers, we can create as many as we need; we are not limited to three layers.

Let's examine the advantages and disadvantages of classic layering, starting with the advantages:

- Knowing the purpose of a layer makes it easy to understand. For example, guessing that the data layer components read or write some data somewhere is logical.
- It creates a cohesive unit built around a single concern. For example, our **data layer** should not render any user interface but stick to accessing data.
- It allows us to decouple the layer from the rest of the system (the other layers). You can isolate and work within a layer with limited to no knowledge of the others. For example, suppose you are tasked with optimizing a query in a data access layer. In that case, you don't need to know about the user interface that eventually displays that data to a user. You only need to focus on that element, optimize it, test it in isolation, and then ship the layer or redeploy the application.
- Like any other isolated unit, it should be possible to reuse a layer. For example, we could reuse our **data access layer** in another application that needs to query the same database for a different purpose (a different **domain layer**).

Some layers are theoretically easier to reuse than others, and reusability could add more or less value, depending on the software you are building. I have never seen a layer being integrally reused in practice, and I've rarely heard or read about such a situation—each instance rather ends in a not-so-reusable-after-all situation.

Based on my experience, I would strongly suggest not focusing too much on reusability when it is not a precise specification that adds value to your application. Limiting your overengineering endeavors could save you and your employers a lot of time and money. We must not forget that our job is to deliver value.

As a rule of thumb, do what needs to be done, not more, but do it well.

OK, now, let's look at the drawbacks:

- By splitting your software horizontally into layers, each feature crosses all of the layers. This often leads to cascading changes between layers. For example, if we decide to add a field to our bookstore database, we would need to update the database, the code that accesses it (**data layer**), the business logic (**domain layer**), and the user interface (**presentation layer**). With volatile specs or low-budget projects, this can become painful!
- Implementing a full-stack feature is more challenging for newcomers because it crosses all layers.
- Using layering often leads to or is caused by a separation of responsibilities between the staff. For example, DBAs manage the data layer, backend devs manage the domain layer, and frontend devs manage the presentation layer, leading to coordination and knowledge-sharing issues.
- Since a layer directly depends on the layer under it, dependency injection is impossible without introducing an **abstraction layer** or referencing lower layers from the **presentation layer**. For example, if the **domain layer** depends on the **data layer**, changing the data layer would require rewriting all of that coupling from the **domain layer** to the **data layer**.
- Since each layer owns its entities, the more layers you add, the more copies there are of the entities, leading to minor performance loss and a higher maintenance cost. For example, the **presentation layer** copies a **DTO** to a **domain object**. Then, the **domain layer** copies it to a **data object**. Finally, the **data layer** translates it into SQL to persist it into a **database** (SQL Server, for example). The opposite is also true when reading from the database.

We explore ways to combat some of those drawbacks later in this chapter.

I strongly recommend that you don't do what we just explored. It is an old, more basic way of doing layering. We look at multiple improvements to this layering system in this chapter, so keep reading before jumping to a conclusion about layering itself. I decided to explore layering from the beginning in case you have to work with that kind of application. Furthermore, studying its chronological evolution, fixing some flaws, and adding options should help you understand the concepts instead of just knowing a single way of organizing layers. Understanding the patterns is the key to software architecture, not just learning how to apply them.

Splitting the layers

Now that we've discussed layers and seen them as big horizontal slices of responsibilities, we can organize our applications more granularly by splitting those big slices vertically, creating multiple smaller layers. This can help us organize applications by features, and it could also allow us to compose various user interfaces using the same building blocks, which would be easier than reusing colossal-size layers.

Here is a conceptual representation of this idea:

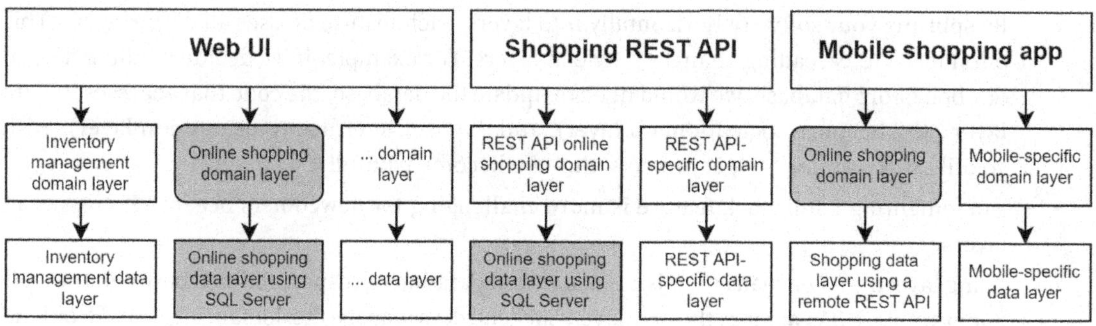

Figure 14.3: Organizing multiple applications using smaller partially shared layers

We can split an application into multiple features (vertically) and divide each into layers (horizontally). Based on the previous diagram, we named those features as follows:

- Inventory management
- Online shopping
- Others

So, we can bring in the online shopping domain and data layers to our Shopping REST API without bringing everything else with it. Moreover, we can bring the online shopping domain layer to the mobile app and swap its data layer for another that talks to the REST API.

We could also use our REST API as a plain and simple data access application with different logic attached to it while keeping the shopping data layer underneath. Doing so could yield the following recomposed programs where we replaced two smaller layers with a consolidated *REST API-specific domain layer* that uses the same data access layers as before (one of the endless possibilities):

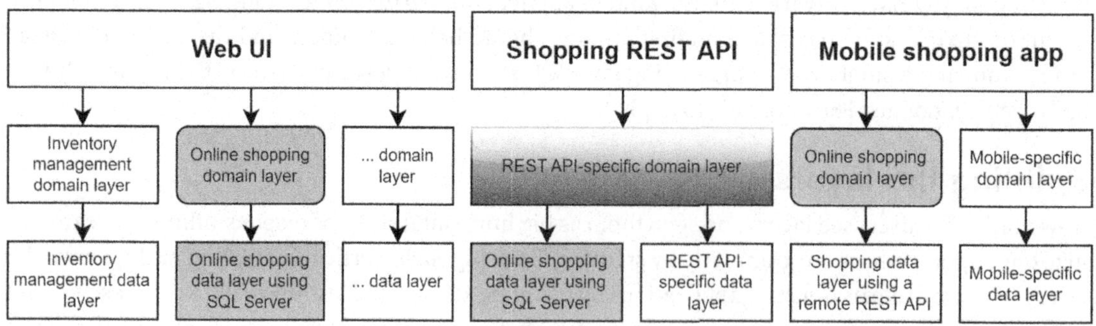

Figure 14.4: Organizing multiple applications using smaller partially shared layers

These are just examples of what we can conceptually do with layers. However, the most important thing to remember is not how the diagrams are laid out but the specifications of the applications you are building. Only those specs and good analyses can help you create the best possible design for that exact problem. I used a hypothetical shopping example here, but it could have been anything.

Splitting huge horizontal slices vertically makes each piece easier to reuse and share. This improvement can yield interesting results, especially if you have multiple frontend apps or plan to migrate away from a monolith.

A **monolithic application** (or monolith) is a program deployed as a single integrated piece with low modularity. A monolith can leverage layers or not. People often compare monolithic applications to microservices applications because they are opposites. We explore microservices in *Chapter 19, Introduction to Microservices Architecture*, and monoliths in *Chapter 20, Modular Monoliths*

Layers versus tiers versus assemblies

So far in this chapter, we have been talking about layers without talking about making them into code. Before jumping into that subject, I'd like to discuss **tiers**. You may have seen the term **3-tier architecture** somewhere before or heard people talking about **tiers** and **layers**, possibly using them interchangeably in the same context as synonyms. However, they are not the same.

In a nutshell:

- Tiers are **physical**
- Layers are **logical**

Assemblies are another concept; they are .NET compiled code used for deployment and versioning and are essential for managing and organizing your compiled code.

What is a tier?

We can deploy each **tier** on its own machine. For example, you could have a database server, a server hosting your REST API that contains the business logic (the **domain**), and another server that serves an Angular application (**presentation**); these are three tiers (three distinct machines), and each **tier** can scale independently.

We look at layers next.

What is a layer?

On the other hand, each **layer** is only the logical organization of code, with concerns organized and divided in a layered fashion. For example, you may create one or more projects in Visual Studio and organize your code into three layers. For example, a Razor Pages application depends on a business logic layer that depends on a data access layer. When you deploy that application, all these layers, including the database, are deployed together on the same server. This would be one tier and three layers. Of course, nowadays, chances are you have a cloud database somewhere, which adds a second tier to that architecture: the application tier (which still has three layers) and database tier.

Now that we've discussed **layers** and **tiers**, let's look at a **layer** versus an **assembly**.

What is an assembly?

Assemblies are consumable units of compiled code: a library or a program, and are commonly compiled into `.dll` or `.exe` files. You can compile and consume assemblies directly from other assemblies. In most cases, each project of a Visual Studio solution gets compiled into an assembly. You can also deploy them as NuGet packages and consume them from `nuget.org` or a custom NuGet repository of your choosing. That said, there is no one-to-one relationship between a layer and an assembly or a tier and an assembly.

Moreover, you do not need to split your layers into different assemblies; you can have your three layers residing in the same assembly and leverage namespaces instead to create the logical separations. It can be easier to create undesirable coupling this way, with all of the code being in the same project, but it is a viable option with some rigor, rules, and conventions. Moving each layer to an assembly does not necessarily improve the application; the code inside each layer or assembly can become mixed up and coupled with other system parts.

Don't get me wrong: you can create an assembly per layer; I even encourage you to do so in most cases, but doing so does not mean the layers are not tightly coupled. A layer is simply a logical unit of organization, so each contributor's responsibility is to ensure the layer's code stays healthy.

Furthermore, having multiple assemblies let us deploy them to one or more machines, leading to one or more tiers.

Let's now look at the responsibilities of the most common layers.

Responsibilities of the common layers

In this section, we explore the most commonly used layers in more depth. We do not dig too deep into each one, but this overview should help you understand the essential ideas behind layering.

Presentation

The **presentation layer** is probably the easiest layer to understand because it is the only one we can see: the user interface. However, the presentation layer can also be the data contracts in case of a REST, OData, GraphQL, or other types of web service. The presentation layer is what the user uses to access your program. As another example, a CLI program can be a presentation layer. You write commands in a terminal, and the CLI dispatches them to its domain layer, executing the required business logic.

The key to a maintainable presentation layer is to keep it as focused on displaying the user interface as possible with as little business logic as possible.

Next, we look at the **domain layer** to see where these calls go.

Domain

The **domain layer** is where the software's value resides and where most of the complexity lies. The **domain layer** is the home of your business logic rules.

It is easier to sell a **user interface** than a **domain layer** since users connect to the domain through the presentation. However, it is important to remember that the domain is responsible for solving the problems and automating the solutions; the **presentation layer** only links users' actions to the **domain**.

We usually build the domain layer around a domain model. There are two macro points of view on this:

- Using a **rich model**.
- Using an **anemic model**.

You can leverage **Domain-Driven Design** (**DDD**) to build that rich model and the program around it. DDD goes hand in hand with rich models, and a well-crafted model should simplify the maintenance of the program. Doing DDD is not mandatory, and you can achieve the required level of correctness without it.

Another design dilemma—on top of rich versus anemic—is persisting the domain model directly into the database or using an intermediate data model. We talk about that in more detail in the *Data* section.

Meanwhile, we look at the two primary ways to think about the domain model, starting with the rich domain model.

Rich domain model

A rich domain model is more object-oriented, in the "purest" sense of the term, and encapsulates the domain logic as part of the model inside methods. For example, the following class represents the rich version of a minimal `Product` class (part of an e-commerce application) that contains only a few properties:

```
public class Product
{
    public Product(string name, int quantityInStock, int? id = null)
    {
        Name = name ?? throw new ArgumentNullException(nameof(name));
        QuantityInStock = quantityInStock;
        Id = id;
    }
    public int? Id { get; init; }
    public string Name { get; init; }
    public int QuantityInStock { get; private set; }

    public void AddStock(int amount)
    {
        if (amount == 0) { return; }
        if (amount < 0) {
            throw new NegativeValueException(amount);
        }
```

```
            QuantityInStock += amount;
        }

        public void RemoveStock(int amount)
        {
            if (amount == 0) { return; }
            if (amount < 0) {
                throw new NegativeValueException(amount);
            }
            if (amount > QuantityInStock) {
                throw new NotEnoughStockException(
                    QuantityInStock, amount);
            }
            QuantityInStock -= amount;
        }
    }
```

The `AddStock` and `RemoveStock` methods represent the domain logic of adding and removing stock from the product inventory. Of course, we only increment and decrement a property's value in this case, but the concept would be the same in a more complex model.

The biggest advantage of this approach is that most of the logic is built into the model, making this very domain-centric with operations programmed on model entities as methods. Moreover, it reaches the basic ideas behind object-oriented design, where behaviors should be part of the objects, making them a virtual representation of their real-life counterparts.

The biggest drawback is the accumulation of responsibilities by a single class. Even if object-oriented design tells us to put logic into the objects, this does not mean it is always a good idea. If flexibility is important for your system, hardcoding logic into the domain model may hinder your ability to evolve business rules without changing the code itself (it can still be done). A rich model might be a good choice for your project if the domain is fixed and predefined.

A relative drawback of this approach is that injecting dependencies into the domain model is harder than other objects, such as services. This drawback reduces flexibility and increases the complexity of creating the models.

A rich domain model can be useful if you are building a stateful application where the domain model can live in memory longer than the time of an HTTP request. Other patterns can help you with that, such as **Model-View-View-Model** (**MVVM**), **Model-View-Presenter** (**MVP**), and **Model-View-Update** (**MVU**).

If you believe your application would benefit from keeping the data and the logic together, then a rich domain model is most likely a good idea for your project. If you are practicing DDD, I probably don't have to tell you that a rich model is the way to go. Without DDD notions, achieving a maintainable and flexible rich model is challenging.

A rich model can be a good option if your program is built around a complex domain model and persists those classes directly to your database using an **object-relational mapper** (**ORM**). Using Cosmos DB, Firebase, MongoDB, or any other document database can make storing complex models as a single document easier than a collection of tables (this applies to anemic models too).

As you may have noticed, there are a lot of "ifs" in this section because I don't think there is an absolute answer to whether a rich model is better or not, and it is more a question of whether it is better for your specific case than better overall. You also need to take your personal preferences and skills into account.

Experience is most likely your best ally here, so I'd recommend coding, coding, and coding more applications to acquire that experience.

Anemic domain model

An anemic domain model usually does not contain methods but only getters and setters. Such models must not contain business logic rules, as those rules belong to other objects, like service classes. The `Product` class we had previously would look like this:

```
public class Product
{
    public int? Id { get; set; }
    public required string Name { get; set; }
    public int QuantityInStock { get; set; }
}
```

In the preceding code, there is no method in the class anymore, only the three properties with public setters. We can also leverage a record class to add immutability to the mix. As for the logic, we must move it elsewhere, in other classes. One such pattern would be to move the logic to a **service layer**.

A **service layer** in front of such an **anemic model** would take the input, mutate the domain object, and update the database. The difference is that the service owns the logic instead of the rich model.

With the anemic model, separating the operations from the data can help us add flexibility to a system. However, enforcing the model's state at any given time can be challenging since external actors (services) are modifying the model instead of the model managing itself.

Encapsulating logic into smaller units makes it easier to manage each of them, and it is easier to inject those dependencies into the service classes than injecting them into the entities themselves. Having smaller units of code can make a system more intimidating for a newcomer as it can be more complex to understand since it has more moving parts. On the other hand, if the system is built around well-defined abstractions, it can be easier to test each unit in isolation.

However, the tests can be quite different. In the case of our rich model, we test the rules and the persistence separately. We call this **persistence ignorance**, which allows us to test business rules in isolation. Then we could create integration tests to cover the persistence aspect of the service layer and more unit and integration tests on the data and domain levels. With an anemic model, we test both the business rules and the persistence simultaneously with integration tests at the service layer level or test only the business rules in unit tests that mock the persistence part away. Since the model is just a data bag without logic, there is nothing to test there.

All in all, if the same rigorous domain analysis process is followed, the business rules of an anemic model backed by a service layer should be as complex as a rich domain model. The biggest difference should be in which classes the methods are located.

An anemic model is a good option for stateless systems, such as RESTful APIs. Since you have to recreate the model's state for every request, an anemic model can offer you a way to independently recreate a smaller portion of the model with smaller classes optimized for each use case. Stateless systems require a more procedural type of thinking than a purely object-oriented approach, leaving the anemic models as excellent candidates for that.

I personally love anemic models behind a service layer, but some people would not agree with me. I recommend choosing what you think is best for the system you are building instead of doing something based on what someone else did in another system.

Another good tip is to let the refactoring flow *top down* to the right location. For example, if you feel that a method is bound to an entity, nothing stops you from moving that piece of logic into that entity instead of a service class. If a service is more appropriate, move the logic to a service class.

Next, let's go back to the **domain layer** and explore a pattern that has emerged over the years to shield the **domain model** using a **service layer**, splitting the **domain layer** into two distinct pieces.

The Service layer

The **service layer** shields the domain model and encapsulates domain logic. The service layer orchestrates the complexity of interacting with the model or external resources such as databases. Multiple components can then use the service layer while having limited knowledge of the model:

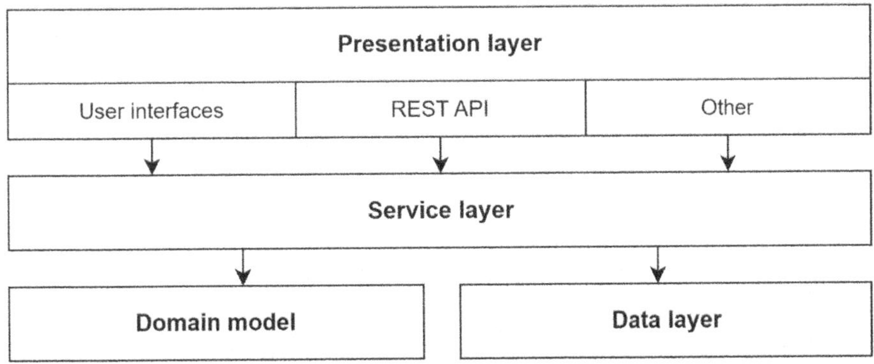

Figure 14.5: Service layer relationships with other layers

The preceding diagram shows that the presentation layer talks to the service layer, which manages the domain model and implements the business logic.

The **service layer** contains services, which are classes that interact with other **domain objects**, such as the **domain model** and the **data layer**.

We can further divide services into two categories, **domain services** and **application services**:

- **Domain services** are those services we are talking about so far. They contain domain logic and allow consumers from the presentation layer to read or write data. They access and mutate the domain model.
- **Application services** like email services are unrelated to the domain and should live elsewhere, like in a shared assembly (why rewrite an email service for every project, right?).

As with other layers, your service layer could expose its own model, shielding its consumers from domain-model (internal) changes. In other words, the service layer should only expose its contracts and interfaces. **A service layer is a form of façade.**

There are many ways to interpret this layer, and I'll try to illustrate as many as possible in a condensed manner (from simpler to more complex ones):

- The classes and interfaces of the service layer could be part of the domain layer's assembly, created in a *Services* directory, for example. This is less reusable, but it paves the way to sharing services in the future without having to manage multiple projects from the start.
- The service layer could be an assembly containing interfaces and implementation. This is a great compromise between reusability and maintenance time. Chances are you will never need two implementations (see the next point) because the services are tied to the logic; they are the domain. You could even hide the implementation, as we did with the **opaque façade** in *Chapter 11, Structural Patterns*.
- The service layer could be divided into two assemblies – one containing abstractions (referenced by consumers) and one containing implementations.
- The service layer could be an actual web service tier (such as a REST API).

When writing services code, by convention, people usually suffix a service class with `Service`, such as `ProductService` and `InventoryService`; the same goes for interfaces (`IProductService` and `IInventoryService`).

No matter which technique you choose, remember that the service layer contains the domain logic and shields the domain model from direct access.

The service layer is an amazing addition that shields and encapsulates the logic for manipulating an anemic domain model. It can defeat the purpose of a rich domain model since it already contains the domain logic but can be very useful to handle complex, non-atomic business rules that affect multiple domain objects.

The primary decider of whether or not to add a service layer is tied to the complexity of your project's domain. The more complex, the more it makes sense. The more trivial, the less it makes sense. Here are a few tips:

- Add a service layer when using an anemic model.
- Add a service layer for very complex domains.
- Do not add a service layer for low-complexity domains or *façade-over-database* applications.

A façade over a database is a simple user interface, allowing users to interact with a database without requiring technical knowledge of database systems. We dive deeper into this subject at the end of the chapter.

Now, let's look at the data layer.

Data

The **data layer** is where the persistence code goes. In most programs, we need some kind of persistence to store our application data, which is often a database. Several patterns come to mind when discussing the data layer, including the **Unit of Work** and **Repository patterns**, which are very common. We cover these two patterns very briefly at the end of this subsection.

We can persist our **domain model** as is or create a **data model** that is more suited to be stored. For example, a many-to-many relationship is not a thing in the object-oriented world, while it is from a relational database standpoint.

You can view a **data model** like a **DTO** for the data. The **data model** is how the data is stored in your data store; that is, how you modeled your data or what you have to live with.

In a classic layering project, you have no choice but to have a data model. However, we explore better solutions as we continue to explore additional options.

Modern data layers usually leverage an **object-relational mapper** (**ORM**) such as **Entity Framework Core** (**EF Core**), which does a big part of our job, making our lives easier.

In the case of **EF Core**, it allows us to choose between multiple providers, from SQL Server to Cosmos DB, including an in-memory provider. The great thing about EF Core is that it already implements the **Unit of Work** and the **Repository** patterns for us, among other things. In this book, we use the in-memory provider to cut down setup time and run integration tests.

An **ORM** is a piece of software that translates objects into a database language such as SQL. It allows mutating data, querying data, loading that data into objects, and more.

I don't want to go into too much detail about these patterns because they are not needed when you use EF Core and are hard to implement, which would divert our attention. They can also lead to bloated data access layers. However, they are important enough to deserve an overview since most Clean Architecture practitioners use a light version of the repository pattern.

If you've used EF6 before and dread Entity Framework, know that EF Core is lighter, faster, and easier to test. Feel free to give it a second shot. EF Core's performance is very high now too. However, if you want complete control over your SQL code, look for Dapper (not to be confused with **Dapr**).

Since EF Core already implements these patterns, we don't have to deal with them, but they can be very useful when used well.

I've written a multi-part article series about the Repository pattern. See the *Further reading* section.

In the meantime, let's at least study their goals to know what they are for, and if the situation arises where you need to write such components, you know where to look.

Overview of the Repository pattern

The goal of the Repository pattern is to allow consumers to query the database in an object-oriented way. It separates the logic that retrieves the data and maps it to the entity model, providing a modular and abstract approach to data access. Usually, this implies caching objects, filtering data dynamically, and translating objects into database code. EF Core represents this concept with a `DbSet<T>`, provides dynamic filtering using LINQ and the `IQueryable<T>` interface, and translates the LINQ queries into SQL.

EF Core exposes a provider model that allows consumers to access many different databases through database provider libraries. Translating to SQL is just one possibility.

People also use the term **repository** to represent the **Table Data Gateway pattern**, which is another pattern that models a class that gives us access to a single table in a database and provides access to operations such as creating, updating, deleting, and fetching entities from that database table. Both patterns are from the *Patterns of Enterprise Application Architecture* and are extensively used.

Overview of the Table Data Gateway pattern

Most homegrown custom repository implementations usually follow the Table Data Gateway pattern more than the Repository pattern because it fits most application needs and is easier to do, often wrapping EF Core behind another layer of abstraction. Building a real repository with advanced query specification capabilities is more work and implies the use of many other patterns but could benefit very complex domains.

Most repositories (Table Data Gateway) are based on an interface that looks like the following code and contains methods to create, update, delete, and read entities. They can have a base entity or not, in this case, `IEntity<TId>`. The `Id` property can also be generic or not:

```
public interface IRepository<T, TId>
    where T : class, IEntity<TId>
{
    Task<IEnumerable<T>> AllAsync(CancellationToken cancellationToken);
    Task<T?> GetByIdAsync(TId id, CancellationToken cancellationToken);
    Task<T> CreateAsync(T entity, CancellationToken cancellationToken);
    Task UpdateAsync(T entity, CancellationToken cancellationToken);
    Task DeleteAsync(TId id, CancellationToken cancellationToken);
}
public interface IEntity<TId>
{
    TId Id { get; }
}
```

One thing that often happens with those table data gateways is that people add a save method to the interface. As long as you update a single entity, it should be fine. However, that makes transactions that cross multiple repositories harder to manage or dependent on the underlying implementation (breaking abstraction). Instead of making the mistake of adding a save method to the repositories, we can leverage the Unit of Work pattern to commit or revert such transactions, moving the save method from the table data gateway there. For example, when using EF Core, we can use `DbSet<Product>` (the `db.Products` property) to add new products to the database, like this:

```
db.Products.Add(new Data.Product
{
    Id = 1,
    Name = "Banana",
    QuantityInStock = 50
});
```

For the querying part, the easiest way to find a single product is to use it like this:

```
var product = _db.Products.Find(productId);
```

However, we could use LINQ instead:

```
_db.Products.Single(x => x.Id == productId);
```

These are some of the querying capabilities that a **repository** should provide. EF Core seamlessly translates LINQ into the configured provider expectations like SQL, adding extended filtering capabilities.

Of course, with EF Core, we can query collections of items, fetching all products and projecting them as domain objects like this:

```
_db.Products.Select(p => new Domain.Product
{
    Id = p.Id,
    Name = p.Name,
    QuantityInStock = p.QuantityInStock
});
```

We can also filter further using LINQ here; for example, by querying all the products that are out of stock:

```
var outOfStockProducts = _db.Products
    .Where(p => p.QuantityInStock == 0);
```

We could also allow a margin for error, like so:

```
var mostLikelyOutOfStockProducts = _db.Products
    .Where(p => p.QuantityInStock < 3);
```

We now have briefly explored how to use the EF Core implementation of the Repository pattern, `DbSet<T>`. These few examples might seem trivial, but it would require considerable effort to implement custom repositories on par with EF Core's features.

EF Core's unit of work, the `DbContext` class, contains the save methods to persist the modifications done to all its `DbSet<T>` properties (the repositories). Homebrewed implementations often feature such methods on the repository itself, making cross-repository transactions harder to handle and leading to bloated repositories containing tons of operation-specific methods to handle such cases.

Now that we understand the concept behind the **Repository pattern**, let's jump into an overview of the **Unit of Work pattern** before going back to layering.

Overview of the Unit of Work pattern

A **unit of work** keeps track of the object representation of a transaction. In other words, it manages a registry of what objects should be created, updated, and deleted.

It allows us to combine multiple changes in a single transaction (one database call), offering multiple advantages over calling the database every time we make a change.

Assuming we are using a relational database, here are two advantages:

- First, it can speed up data access; calling a database is slow, so limiting the number of calls and connections can improve performance.
- Second, running a transaction instead of individual operations allows us to roll back all operations if one fails or commit the transaction as a whole if everything succeeds.

EF Core implements this pattern with the `DbContext` class and its underlying types, such as the `DatabaseFacade` and `ChangeTracker` classes.

Our small applications don't need transactions, but the concept remains the same. Here is an example of what happens using EF Core:

```
var product = _db.Products.Find(productId);
product.QuantityInStock += amount;
_db.SaveChanges();
```

The preceding code does the following:

1. Queries the database for a single entity.
2. Changes the value of the `QuantityInStock` property.
3. Persists the changes back into the database.

In reality, what happened is closer to the following:

1. We ask EF Core for a single entity through the `ProductContext` (a unit of work), which exposes the `DbSet<Product>` property (the product repository). Under the hood, EF Core does the following:
   a. Queries the database.
   b. Caches the entity.
   c. Tracks changes for that entity.
   d. Returns it to us.
2. We change the value of the `QuantityInStock` property; EF Core detects the change and marks the object as *dirty*—changed but not persisted to the database.
3. We tell the unit of work to persist the changes that it tracked, saving the *dirty product* back to the database.

In a more complex scenario, we could have written the following code:

```
_db.Products.Add(newProduct);
_db.Products.Remove(productToDelete);
```

```
product.Name = "New product name";
_db.SaveChanges();
```

Here, the `SaveChanges()` method triggers saving the three operations instead of sending them individually. You can control database transactions using the `Database` property of `DbContext` (see the *Further reading* section for more information).

Now that we've explored the **Unit of Work** pattern, we could implement one by ourselves. Would that add value to our application? Probably not. If you want to build a custom **unit of work** or a wrapper over EF Core, there are plenty of existing resources to guide you. Unless you want to experiment or need a custom **unit of work** and **repository** (which is possible), I recommend staying away from doing that. Remember: *do only what needs to be done for your program to be correct.*

Don't get me wrong when I say *do only what needs to be done*; wild engineering endeavors and experimentations are a great way to explore, and I encourage you to do so. However, I recommend doing so in parallel so that you can innovate, learn, and possibly even migrate that knowledge to your application later instead of wasting time and breaking things. If you are using Git, creating an experimental branch is a good way of doing this. You can then delete it when your experimentation does not work, merge the branch if it yields positive results, or leave it there as a reference (depending on the policies the team has in place).

Now that we explored a high-level view of the Repository and Unit of Work patterns, and what those common layers are for, we can continue our journey of using layers.

Abstract layers

This section looks at abstract layers using an abstract data layer implementation. This type of abstraction can be very useful and is another step closer to **Clean Architecture**. Moreover, you can abstract almost anything this way, which is nothing more than applying the **Dependency Inversion Principle** (**DIP**).

Let's start with some context and the problem:

- The **domain layer** is where the logic lies.
- The **UI** links the user to the **domain**, exposing the features built into that **domain**.
- The **data layer** should be an implementation detail that the **domain** blindly uses.
- The **data layer** contains the code that knows where the data is stored, which should be irrelevant to the **domain**, but the **domain** directly depends on it.

The solution to **break the tight coupling** between the **domain** and the **data** persistence implementations is to create an additional abstract layer, as shown in the following diagram:

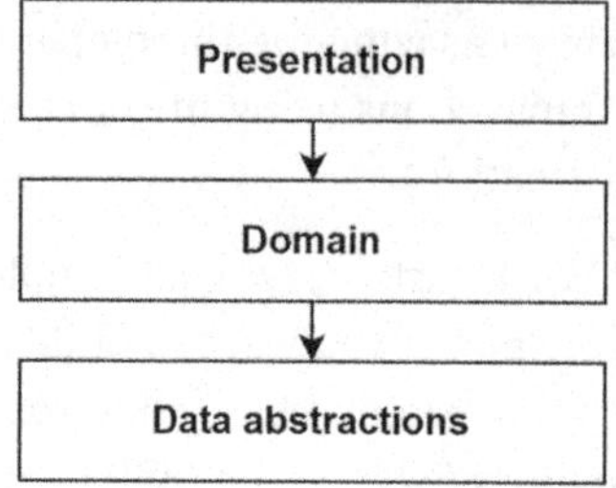

Figure 14.6: Replacing the data (persistence) layer with a data abstraction layer

Only interfaces and data model classes go into the data abstractions layer. This new layer now defines our data access API and does nothing but expose a set of interfaces—the contract.

Then, we can create one or more data implementations based on that abstract layer contract, like using EF Core. The link between the abstractions and implementations is done with dependency injection. The bindings defined in the **composition root** explain the indirect connection between the presentation and the data implementation.

The new dependency tree looks like this:

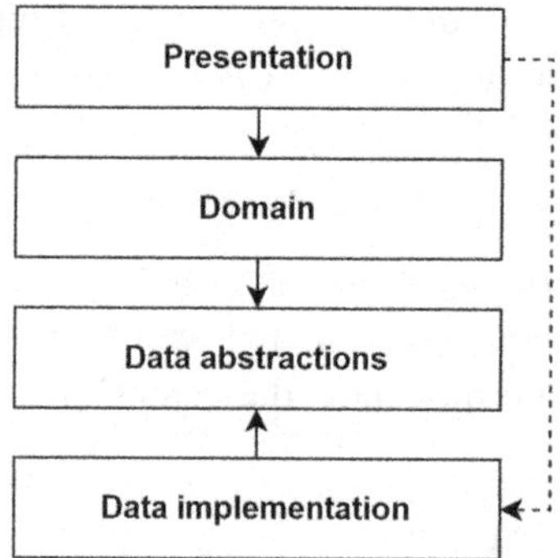

Figure 14.7: The relationships between layers

The **presentation layer** references a **data implementation layer** for the sole purpose of creating the DI bindings. We need those bindings to inject the correct implementation when creating **domain** classes. Besides, the presentation layer must not use the data layer's abstractions or implementations; it should only interact with the domain, like before.

I created a sample project that showcases the relationships between the projects (layers) and the classes. However, that project would have added pages of code, so I decided not to include it in the book. The most important thing about abstract layers is the dependency flow between the layers, not the code itself.

The project is available on GitHub (https://adpg.link/s9HX).

In that project, the program injects an instance of the EF.ProductRepository class when a consumer asks for an object that implements the IProductRepository interface. In that case, the consuming class is ProductService and only depends on the IProductRepository interface. The ProductService class is unaware of the implementation itself: it leverages only the interface. The same goes for the program that loads a ProductService class but knows only about the IProductService interface. Here is a visual representation of that dependency tree:

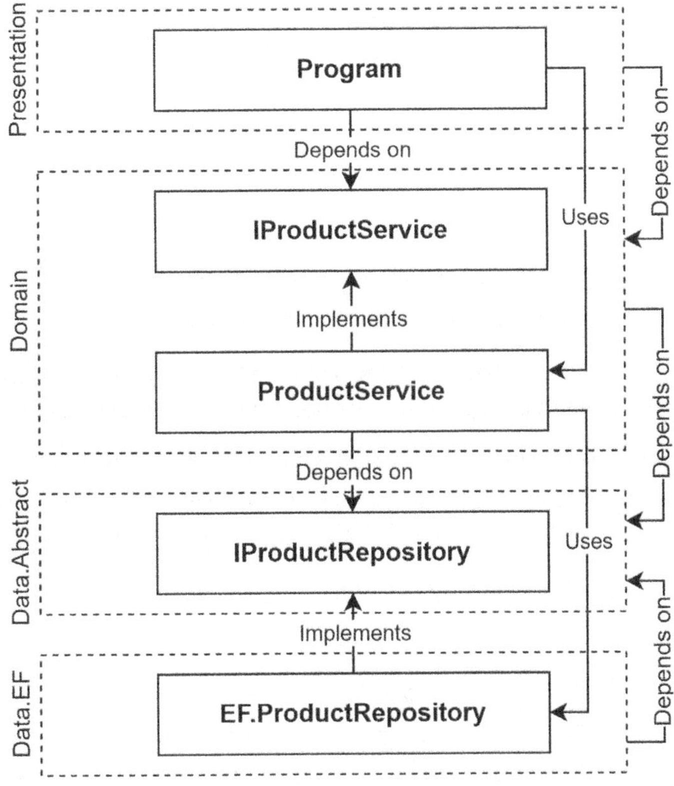

Figure 14.8: The dependency flow between layers, classes, and interfaces

In the preceding diagram, look at how dependencies converge on the Data.Abstract layer. The dependency tree ends up on that abstract data layer.

With this applied piece of architectural theory, we are inverting the flow of dependencies on the data layer by following the **DIP**. We also cut out the direct dependency on EF Core, allowing us to implement a new data layer and swap it without impacting the rest of the application or update the implementation without affecting the domain.

As I mentioned previously, swapping layers should not happen very often, if ever. Nonetheless, this is an important part of the evolution of layering, and more importantly, we can apply this technique to any layer or project, not just the data layer, so it is imperative to understand how to invert the dependency flow.

Next, let's explore sharing and persisting a rich domain model.

Sharing the model

We have explored strict layering and how to apply the DIP, but we still have multiple models. An alternative to copying models from one layer to another is to share a model between multiple layers, generally as an assembly. Visually, it looks like this:

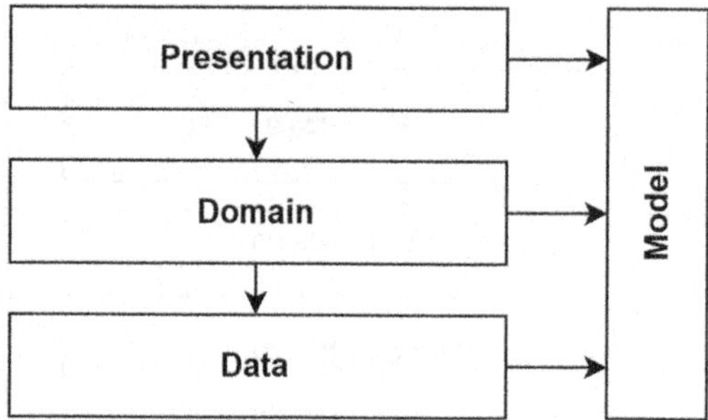

Figure 14.9: Sharing a model between all three layers

Everything has pros and cons, so no matter how much time this might save you at first, it will come back to haunt you and become a pain point later as the project advances and becomes more complex.

Suppose you feel that sharing a model is worth it for your application. In that case, I recommend using **view models** or **DTOs** at the presentation level to control and keep the input and output of your application loosely coupled from your model. This way of shielding your lower layers can be represented as follows:

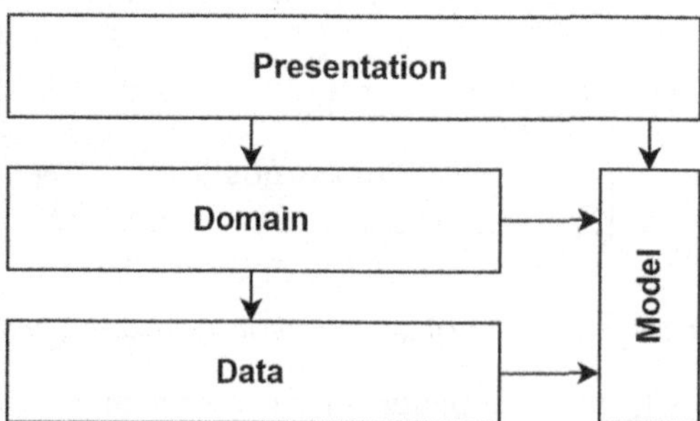

Figure 14.10: Sharing a model between the domain and data layers

By doing that, you will save some time initially by sharing your model between your domain and data layers. By hiding that shared model under the presentation layer, you should dodge many problems in the long run, making this a good compromise between quality and development time.

Moreover, since your presentation layer shields your application from the outside world, you can refactor your other layers without impacting your consumers.

This is pretty much how Clean Architecture does it but represented differently. With Clean Architecture, the model is at the center of the application and is manipulated and persisted. While the layers have different names, the concept remains very similar. More on that later.

View models and **DTOs** are key elements to successful programs and developers' sanity; they should save you many headaches in long-running projects. We revisit and explore the concepts of controlling the input and output later in *Chapter 16, Mediator and CQS Patterns*, where inputs become **commands** and **queries**.

Meanwhile, let's merge that concept with an abstraction layer. In the previous project, the **data abstraction layer** owned the **data model**, and the **domain layer** owned the **domain model**.

In this architectural alternative, we are sharing the model between the two layers. The presentation layer can indirectly use that shared model to communicate with the domain layer without exposing it externally. The objective is to directly persist the **domain model** and skip the copy from the **domain** to the **data layer** while having that data abstraction layer that breaks the tight coupling between the domain logic and the persistence.

Here is a visual representation of that:

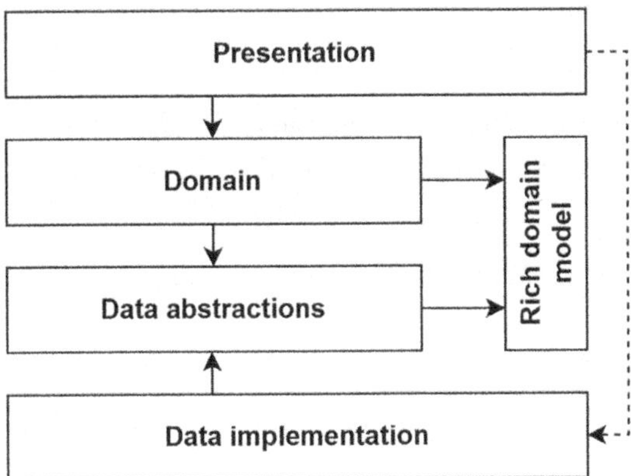

Figure 14.11: Diagram representing a shared rich model

It is well suited for **rich models**, but we can also do this for anemic models. With a **rich domain model**, you delegate the job of reconstructing the model to the ORM and immediately start calling its methods.

The ORM also recreates the anemic model, but those classes just contain data, so you need to call other pieces of the software that contain the logic to manipulate those objects.

In the code we are about to explore, the **data abstraction layer** contains only the data access abstractions, such as the repositories, and it references the new `Model` project that is now the persisted model.

Conceptually, it cleans up a few things:

- The data abstraction layer's only responsibility is to contain data access abstractions.
- The domain layer's only responsibility is implementing the domain services and the logic that is not part of that rich model. In the case of an anemic model, the domain layer's responsibility would be to encapsulate all the domain logic.
- The `Model` project contains the entities.

Once again, I skip publishing most of the code here as it is irrelevant to the overall concept. If you think reading the code would help, you can consult and explore the sample on GitHub (`https://adpg.link/9F5C`). Using an IDE to browse the code should help you understand the flow, and as with the abstract layer, the dependencies between the projects, classes, and interfaces are the key to this.

Nevertheless, here is the `StockService` class that uses that shared model so you can peek at some code that directly relates to the explanations:

```
namespace Domain.Services;
public class StockService : IStockService
{
    private readonly IProductRepository _repository;
    public StockService(IProductRepository repository)
    {
        _repository = repository ?? throw new
ArgumentNullException(nameof(repository));
    }
```

In the preceding code, we are injecting an implementation of the `IProductRepository` interface we use in the next two methods. Next, we look at the `AddStockAsync` method:

```
    public async Task<int> AddStockAsync(int productId, int amount,
CancellationToken cancellationToken)
    {
        var product = await _repository.FindByIdAsync(productId,
cancellationToken);
        if (product == null)
        {
            throw new ProductNotFoundException(productId);
        }
        product.AddStock(amount);
        await _repository.UpdateAsync(product, cancellationToken);
        return product.QuantityInStock;
    }
```

The preceding code does the following:

- The repository recreates the product (model) that contains the logic.
- It validates that the product exists.
- It uses that model and calls the `AddStock` method (encapsulated domain logic).
- It tells the repository to update the product.
- It returns the updated product's `QuantityInStock` to the consumer of the service.

The `StockService` class gates the access to the domain model (the product), fetching and updating the model through the abstract data layer, manipulating the model by calling its methods, and returning domain data (an `int` in this case, but it could be an object).

This type of design can be either very helpful or undesirable. Too many projects depending on and exposing a shared model can lead to leaking part of that model to consumers, for example exposing properties that shouldn't be exposed, exposing the whole domain model as output, or the very worst, exposing it as an input and opening exploitable holes and unexpected bugs.

Be careful not to expose your shared model to the presentation layer consumers.

Pushing logic into the model is not always possible or desirable, which is why we are exploring multiple types of domain models and ways to share them. Making a good design is often about options and deciding what option to use for each scenario. There are also tradeoffs to make between flexibility and robustness.

The rest of the code is similar to the abstract layer project. Feel free to explore the source code (`https://adpg.link/9F5C`) and compare it with the other projects. The best way to learn is to practice, so play with the samples, add features, update the current features, remove stuff, or even build your own project. Understanding these concepts will help you apply them to different scenarios, sometimes creating unexpected but efficient constructs.

Now, let's look at the final evolution of layering: Clean Architecture.

Clean Architecture

Now that we've covered many layering approaches, it is time to combine them into **Clean Architecture**. Clean Architecture is an evolution of layering, a way of organizing the relationships between the layers, similar to what we just built.

Instead of presentation, domain, and data (or persistence), Clean Architecture suggests **UI**, **Core**, and **Infrastructure**.

As we saw previously, we can design a layer containing abstractions or implementations. When implementations depend only on abstractions, that inverts dependency flow. Clean Architecture emphasizes such layers but with its own guidance about organizing them.

We also explored the theoretical concept of breaking layers into smaller ones (or multiple projects), thus creating "fractured layers" that are easier to port and reuse. Clean Architecture leverages that concept at the infrastructure layer level.

There are probably as many points of view and variants of this as there are names for it, so I'll try to be as general as possible while keeping the essence. By doing this, if you are interested in this type of architecture, you can pick a resource and dig deeper into it, following the style you prefer.

Let's take a look at a diagram that resembles a standard depiction of Clean Architecture:

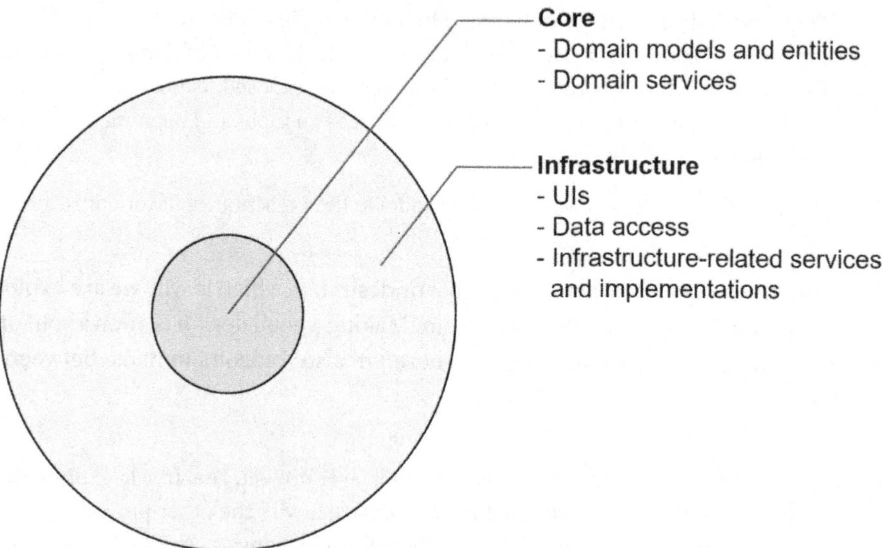

Figure 14.12: A diagram representing the most basic Clean Architecture layout

From a layering diagram-like standpoint, the preceding diagram could look like this:

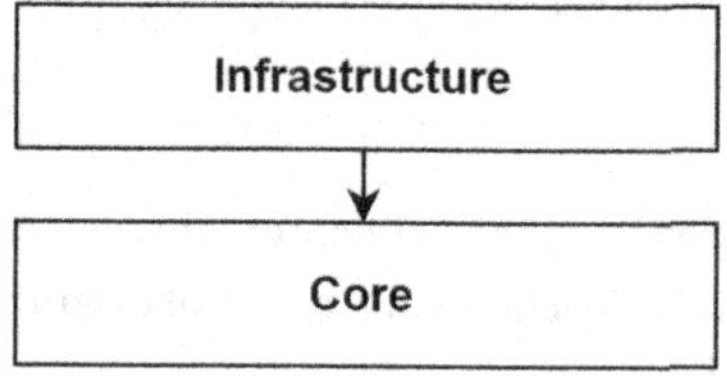

Figure 14.13: A two-layer view of the previous Clean Architecture diagram

Depending on your chosen method, you can split those layers into multiple other sublayers. One thing that we often see is dividing the **Core** layer into **Entities** and **Use cases**, like this:

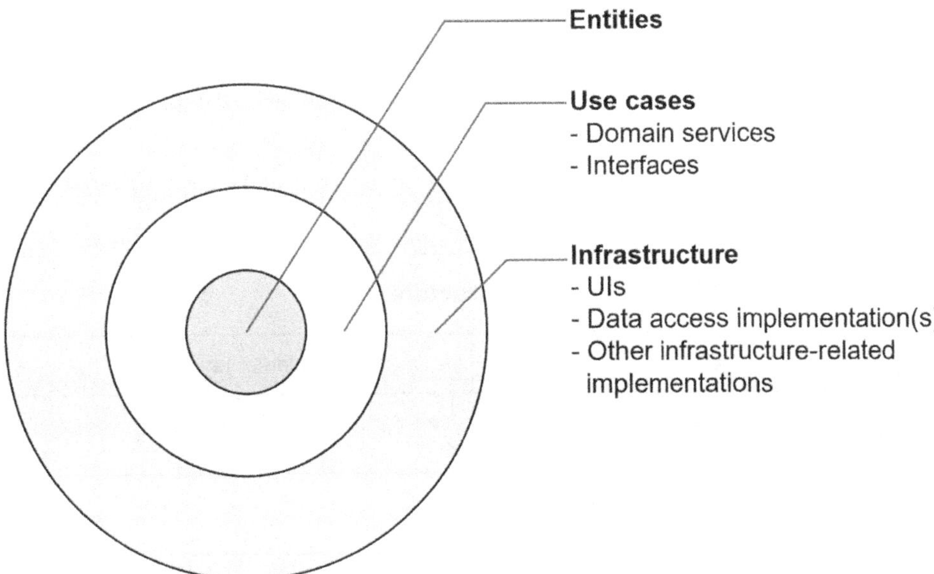

Figure 14.14: Widespread Clean Architecture layout diagram

Since people in the tech industry are creative, there are many names for many things, but the concepts remain the same. For example, giving the name "entities" to the domain model does not change its purpose. From a layering diagram-like standpoint, that diagram could be presented like this:

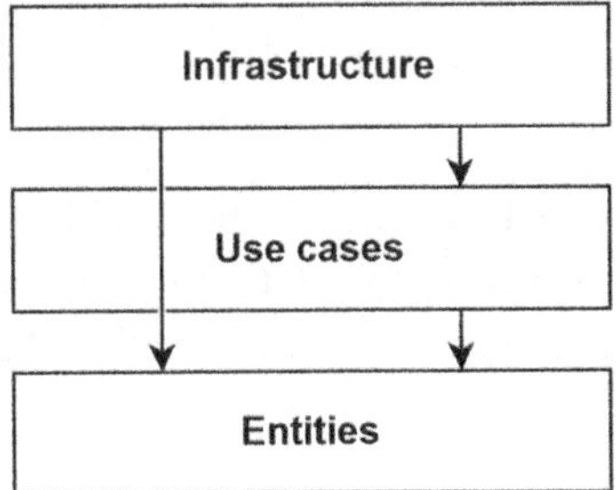

Figure 14.15: A layer-like view of the previous Clean Architecture diagram

The Infrastructure layer is conceptual and can represent multiple projects, such as an infrastructure assembly containing EF Core implementations and a website project representing the web UI. We could also add more projects to the infrastructure layer.

The dependency rule of Clean Architecture states that dependencies can only point inward, from the outer layers to the inner layers. This means abstractions like interfaces and entities—the domain model—lie inside, while concretions like interface implementations and user interfaces—the presentation—lie outside. Based on the preceding layer-like diagram, inside translates to downward while outside translates to upward. That means a layer can use any direct or transitive dependencies, which means that infrastructure can depend on use cases and entities.

Clean Architecture follows all the principles that we've been discussing since the beginning of this book, such as decoupling our implementations using abstractions, dependency inversion, and separation of concerns. These implementations are glued over abstractions using dependency injection (this is not mandatory, but it helps).

I've always found those circle diagrams a bit confusing, so here is my take on an updated, more linear diagram:

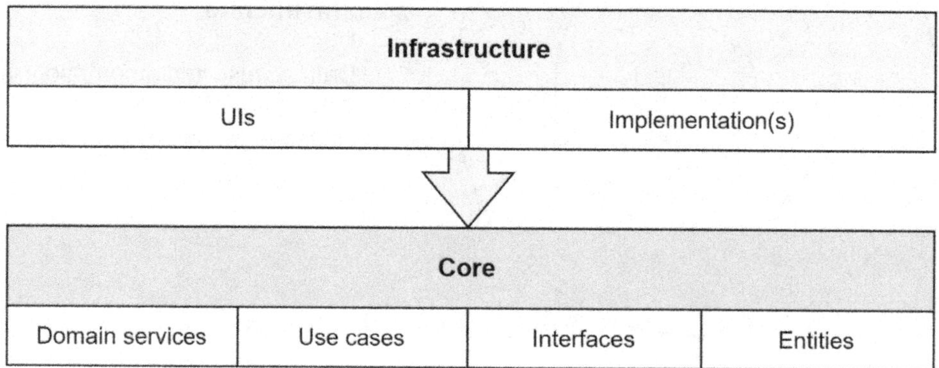

Figure 14.16: A two-layer view of Clean Architecture's common elements

Now, let's revisit our layered application using Clean Architecture, starting with the **Core layer**. The core project contains the domain model, the use cases (services), and the interfaces needed to fulfill those use cases. We must not access external resources in this layer: no database calls, disk access, or HTTP requests. This layer contains the interfaces that expose such interaction, but the implementations live in the **Infrastructure layer**.

The presentation layer was renamed **Web** and lives in the outer layer with the EF Core implementation. The **Web** project depends only on the **Core** project. Once again, since the composition root is in this project, it must load the EF Core implementation project to configure the IoC container.

Here is a diagram representing the relation between the shared model and the new Clean Architecture project structure:

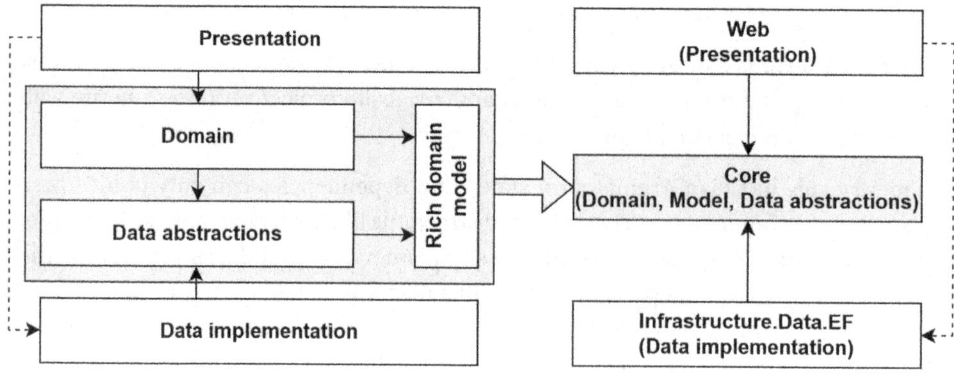

Figure 14.17: From shared project to the Clean Architecture project structure

In the preceding diagram, we took the center of the classic layered solution and merged the layers into a single **Core** project.

Here's the link to this project on GitHub: `https://adpg.link/rT1P`.

Most of the code is not that relevant since, once again, the most significant aspect is the dependency flow and relationships between projects. Nonetheless, here is a list of changes that I made aside from moving the pieces to different projects:

- I removed the `ProductService` class and `IProductService` interface and used the `IProductRepository` interface directly from the `StockService` class (`Core` project) and the `/products` endpoint (`Web` project: `Program.cs`).
- I removed the `IStockService` interface, and now both the add and remove stocks endpoints (`Web` project: `Program.cs`) depend directly on the `StockService` class.

Why use the `IProductRepository` interface directly, you might wonder? Since the **Web** project (**Infrastructure layer**) depends on the **Core layer**, we can leverage the inward dependency flow. It is acceptable to use a repository directly as long as the feature has no business logic. Programming empty shells and pass-through services adds useless complexity. However, when business logic starts to be involved, create a service or any other domain entity you deem necessary for that scenario. Don't pack business logic into your controllers or minimal API delegates.

I removed the `IStockService` interface since the `StockService` class contains concrete business rules that can be consumed as is from the infrastructure layer. I know we have emphasized using interfaces since the beginning of the book, but I also often said that principles are not laws. All in all, there is nothing to abstract away: if the business rules change, the old ones won't be needed anymore. We could have kept the interface for different reasons, but I wanted to make a point.

To wrap this up, Clean Architecture is a proven pattern for building applications that is fundamentally an evolution of layering. Many variants can help you manage use cases, entities, and infrastructure; however, we do not cover them here. There are many open-source projects that you could use to start with Clean Architecture if you seek organizational guidance.

I left a few links in the *Further reading* section.

If you think this is a great fit for you, your team, your project, or your organization, feel free to dig deeper and adopt this pattern. In subsequent chapters, we explore some patterns, such as CQRS, Publish-Subscribe, and feature-based design, which we can combine with Clean Architecture to add flexibility and robustness. These become particularly useful as your system grows in size and complexity.

Implementing layering in real life

Now that we covered all of this, it is important to note that on the one hand, there is the theory, and on the other, life is hitting you in the face. Suppose you are working in a big enterprise. In that case, chances are your employer can pour hundreds of thousands or even millions of dollars into a feature to run experiments, spend months designing every little piece, and ensure everything is perfect. Even then, is achieving perfection even possible? Probably not.

For companies that don't have that type of capital, you must build entire products for a few thousand dollars sometimes because they are not trying to resell them but just need that tool built. That is where your architectural skills come in handy. How do you design the least bad product in a maintainable fashion while meeting stakeholders' expectations? The most important part of the answer is to set expectations upfront. Moreover, never forget that someone needs to maintain and change the software over time; software does not evolve on its own; there's always something to be updated.

If you are in a position where you must evaluate the feasibility of products and features in this context, setting expectations lower can be a good way to plan for the unplannable. It is easier to overdeliver than justify why you underdelivered.

Let's dig deeper into this and look at a few tricks to help you out. Even if you are working for a larger enterprise, you should get something out of it.

To be or not to be a purist?

In your day-to-day work, you may not always need the rigidity of a **domain layer** to create a wall in front of your data. Maybe you just don't have the time or the money, or it's just not worth doing.

Taking and presenting the data can often work well enough, especially for simple data-driven applications that are only a user interface over a database, as is the case for many internal tools.

The answer to the *"To be or not to be a purist?"* question is: it depends!

What do I mean by purist? I mean respecting every single rule and principle out there to design and build the best possible software every time without considering what you are building, like the business context, the audience, the lifespan of the application, the budget constraints, the available technology stack, your team's size, and the skills of your team.

An architect or developer must assess each project's unique requirements and constraints to determine which rules and principles to prioritize. It's crucial to focus on delivering the right level of quality and functionality that fits the application's intended usage and aligns with the project's goals, timeframes, and resources. This pragmatic approach ensures that the software meets current needs and is adaptable to future changes, balancing idealism with reality.

This section covers layering, but we explore other patterns that are feature-oriented, so I suggest you continue reading and explore using the techniques from *Chapter 17, Getting Started with Vertical Slice Architecture, Chapter 18, Request-EndPoint-Response (REPR),* and *Chapter 20, Modular Monolith,* to improve your design while keeping the design overhead low.

Here are a few examples of things that the answer depends on, to help you out:

- The project; for example:
    - **Domain-heavy or logic-intensive projects** will benefit from a domain layer, helping you centralize logic for an augmented level of reusability and maintainability.
    - **Data management projects** tend to have less or no logic in them. We can often build them without adding a domain layer as the **domain** is often only a tunnel from the **presentation** to the **data**—a pass-through layer. We can often simplify those systems by dividing them into two layers: **data** and **presentation.**
- Your team; for example, a highly skilled team may tend to use advanced concepts and patterns more efficiently, and the learning curve for newcomers should be easier due to the number of seasoned engineers that can support them on the team. This does not mean that less skilled teams should aim lower; on the contrary, it may just be harder or take longer to start. Analyze each project individually and find the best patterns to drive them accordingly.
- Your boss; if the company you work for puts pressure on you and your team to deliver complex applications in record time and nobody tells your boss that it is impossible, you may need to cut corners a lot and enjoy many maintenance headaches with crashing systems, painful deployments, and more. That being said, if it is inevitable for these types of projects, I'd go with a very simple design that does not aim at reusability—aim at low-to-average testability and code stuff that just works.
- Your budget; once again, this often depends on the people selling the application and the features. I saw promises that were impossible to keep but delivered anyway with a lot of effort, extra hours, and corner-cutting. The thing to remember when going down that path is that at some point, there is no return from the accumulated **technical debt**, and it will just get worse (this applies to all budgets).
- The audience; the people who use the software can make a big difference to how you build it: ask them. For example, suppose you are building a tool for your fellow developers. In that case, you can cut corners that you would not for less technically skilled users (like delivering a CLI tool instead of a full-blown user interface). On the other hand, if you're aiming your application at multiple clients (web, mobile, and so on), isolating your application's components and focusing on reusability could be a winning design.
- The expected quality; you should not tackle the problem in the same way for building a prototype and a SaaS application. It is acceptable, even encouraged, for a prototype to have no tests and not follow best practices, but I'd recommend the opposite for a production-quality application.

- Any other things that life throws at you; yes, life is unpredictable, and no one can cover every possible scenario in a book, so just keep the following in mind when building your next piece of software:
    - Do not over-engineer your applications.
    - Only implement features that you need, not more, as per the **you aren't gonna need it** (**YAGNI**) principle.
    - Use your judgment and take the less-worst options; there is no perfect solution.

I hope you found this guidance helpful and that it will serve you in your career.

Building a façade over a database

Data-driven programs are a type of software that I have often seen in smaller enterprises. Those companies need to support their day-to-day operations with computers, not the other way around. Every company needs internal tools, and many needed them yesterday.

The reason is simple; every company is unique. Because a company is unique, due to its business model, leadership, or employees, it also needs unique tools to help with its day-to-day operations. Those small tools are often simple user interfaces over a database, controlling access to that data. In these cases, you don't need over-engineered solutions, as long as everyone is informed that the tool will not evolve beyond what it is: a small tool.

In real life, this one is tough to explain to non-programmers because they tend to see complex use cases as easy to implement and simple use cases as hard to implement. It's normal; they just don't know, and we all don't know something. In these scenarios, a big part of our job is also to educate people: advising decision-makers about the differences in quality between a small tool and a large business application. Educating and working with stakeholders makes them aware of the situation and able to make decisions with you, leading to higher project quality that meets everyone's expectations. This can also reduce the "*it's not my fault*" syndrome from both sides.

I've found that immersing customers and decision-makers in the decision process and having them follow the development cycle helps them understand the reality behind the programs and helps both sides stay happy and grow more satisfied. Stakeholders not getting what they want is no better than you being super stressed over unreachable deadlines.

That said, our educational role does not end with decision-makers. Teaching new tools and techniques to your peers is also a major way to improve your team, peers, and yourself. Explaining concepts is more challenging than it sounds and can help your own development.

Nevertheless, data-driven programs may be hard to avoid, especially if you are working for SMEs, so try to get the best out of it. Nowadays, with low-code and no-code solutions and all the open-source libraries, you might be able to save yourself a lot of this kind of trouble, but maybe not all.

Remember that someday, someone must maintain those small tools. Think of that person as you, and think about how you'd like some guidelines or documentation to help you. I'm not saying to over-document projects, as documentation often gets out of sync with the code and becomes more of a problem than a solution. However, a simple `README.md` file at the project's root explaining how to build and run the program and some general guidelines could be beneficial. Always think about documentation as if you were the one reading it. Most people don't like to spend hours reading documentation to understand something simple, so keep it simple.

When building a *façade over a database*, you want to keep it simple. Also, you should make it clear that it should not evolve past that role. One way to build this would be to use EF Core as your data layer and scaffold an MVC application as your presentation layer, shielding your database. You can use the built-in ASP.NET Core authentication and authorization mechanism if you need access control. You can then choose role-based or policy-based access control or any other option that makes sense for your tool and allows you to control access to the data the way you need to.

Keeping it simple should help you build more tools in less time, making everyone happy.

From a layering standpoint, using my previous example, you will end up having two layers sharing the data model:

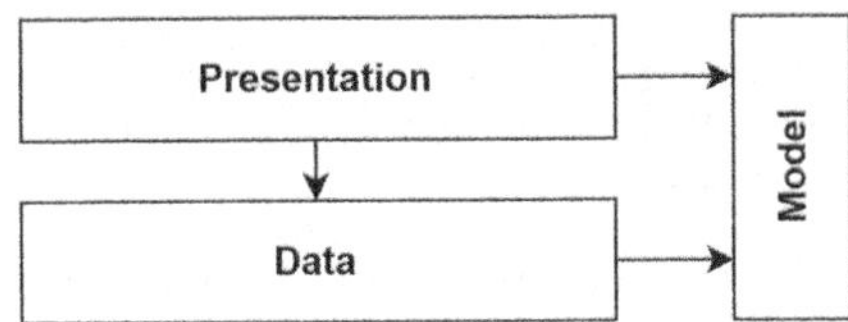

Figure 14.18: A façade-like presentation layer over a database application's design

Nothing stops you from creating a **view model** here and there for more complex views, but the key is to keep the logic's complexity to a minimum. Otherwise, you may discover the hard way that sometimes, rewriting a program from scratch takes less time than trying to fix it. Moreover, nothing stops you from using any other presentation tools and components available to you.

Using this data-driven architecture as a temporary application while the main application is in development is also a good solution. It takes a fraction of the time to build, and the users have access to it immediately. You can even get feedback from it, which allows you to fix any mistakes before they are implemented in the real (future) application, working like a living prototype.

A good database design in these sorts of applications can go a long way.

Not all projects are that simple, but still, many are; the key is to make the program good enough while ensuring you cut the right corners.

Summary

Layering is one of the most used architectural techniques when it comes to designing applications. An application is often split into multiple different layers, each managing a single responsibility. The three most popular layers are **presentation**, **domain**, and **data**. You are not limited to three layers; you can split each into smaller layers (or smaller pieces inside the same conceptual layer), leading to composable, manageable, and maintainable applications.

Moreover, you can create abstraction layers to invert the flow of dependency and separate interfaces from implementations, as we saw in the *Abstract layers* section. You can persist the domain entities directly or create an independent model for the data layer. You can also use an anemic model (no logic or method) or a rich model (packed with entity-related logic). You can share that model between multiple layers or have each layer possess its own.

Out of layering was born Clean Architecture, which guides the organization of your application into concentric layers, often dividing the application into use cases.

Let's see how this approach can help us move toward the **SOLID** principles at app scale:

- S: Layering leads us toward splitting responsibilities horizontally, with each layer oriented around a single macro-concern. The main goal of layering is responsibility segregation.
- O: Abstract layers enable consumers to act differently (change behaviors) based on the provided implementation (concrete layer).
- L: N/A
- I: Splitting layers based on features (or cohesive groups of features) is a way of segregating a system into smaller blocks (interfaces).
- D: Abstraction layers lead directly to the dependency flow's inversion, while classic layering leads in the opposite direction.

In the next chapter, we learn how to centralize the logic of copying objects (models) using object mappers and an open-source tool to help us skip the implementation, also known as productive laziness.

Questions

Let's take a look at a few practice questions:

1. When creating a layered application, is it true that we must have presentation, domain, and data layers?
2. Is a rich domain model better than an anemic domain model?
3. Does EF Core implement the Repository and Unit of Work patterns?
4. Do we need to use an ORM in the data layer?
5. Can a layer in Clean Architecture access any inward layers?

Further reading

Here are a few links to help you build on what we learned in this chapter:

- **Dapper** is a simple yet powerful ORM for .NET, made by the people of Stack Overflow. If you like writing SQL, but don't like mapping data to objects, this ORM might be for you: `https://adpg.link/pTYs`.
- An article that I wrote in 2017 about the Repository pattern; that is, Design Patterns: ASP.NET Core Web API, services, and repositories | Part 5: Repositories, the ClanRepository, and integration testing : `https://adpg.link/D53Z`.
- Entity Framework Core – Using Transactions: `https://adpg.link/gxwD`.

Here are resources about Clean Architecture:

- Common web application architectures (Microsoft Learn): `https://adpg.link/Pnpn`
- Microsoft eShopOnWeb ASP.NET Core Reference Application: `https://adpg.link/dsw1`
- GitHub—Clean Architecture by Ardalis/Steve Smith—Solution templates: `https://adpg.link/tpPi`
- GitHub—Clean Architecture by Jason Taylor—Solution templates: `https://adpg.link/jxX2`

Answers

1. No, you can have as many layers as you need and name and organize them as you want.
2. No, both have their place, their pros, and their cons.
3. Yes. A `DbContext` is an implementation of the Unit of Work pattern. `DbSet<T>` is an implementation of the Repository pattern.
4. No, you can query any system in any way you want. For example, you could use ADO.NET to query a relational database manually and create the objects using data from a `DataReader`, track changes using a `DataSet`, or do anything else that fits your needs. Nonetheless, ORMs can be very convenient.
5. Yes. A layer can never access outward layers, only inward ones.

Learn more on Discord

To join the Discord community for this book – where you can share feedback, ask questions to the author, and learn about new releases – follow the QR code below:

`https://packt.link/ArchitectingASPNETCoreApps3e`

15

Object Mappers

In this chapter, we explore object mapping. As we saw in the previous chapter, working with layers often leads to copying models from one layer to another. Object mappers solve that problem.

We first look at manually implementing an object mapper, because understanding the basics is very important to progress further. Then, we improve our design by regrouping the mappers under a mapper service, exploring the Aggregate Services pattern, and creating a mapping façade along the way, reusing the Façade pattern once more.

Finally, we replace that manual work with two open-source tools that help us generate business value instead of writing mapping code.

In this chapter, we cover the following topics:

- The Object Mapper pattern
- Code smell – too many dependencies
- Overview of the Aggregate Services pattern
- Implementing a mapping façade
- Implementing a mapping service
- Exploring AutoMapper
- Exploring Mapperly

The Object Mapper pattern

What is object mapping? In a nutshell, it is the action of copying the value of an object's properties into the properties of another object. But sometimes, properties' names do not match; an object hierarchy may need to be flattened and transformed.

As we saw in the previous chapter, each layer can own its own model, which can be a good thing, but that comes at the price of copying objects from one layer to another. We can also share models between layers, but even then, we usually need to map one object onto another. Even if it's just to map your models to **Data Transfer Objects** (**DTOs**), object mapping is almost inevitable.

Remember that DTOs define our API's contract. Independent contract classes help maintain the system, making us choose when to modify them. If you skip using DTOs, each time you change your domain model, it automatically updates your endpoint's contract, possibly breaking some clients. Moreover, if you input your model directly, a malicious user could try to bind the values of properties that they should not, leading to potential security issues (known as **over-posting** or **over-posting attacks**). Having good data exchange contracts is one of the keys to designing robust systems.

In the previous projects, the mapping logic was hardcoded, sometimes duplicated and adding additional responsibilities to the class doing the mapping. In this chapter, we extract the mapping logic into object mappers to fix that issue.

Goal

The object mapper's goal is to copy the value of an object's properties into the properties of another object. It encapsulates the mapping logic away from where the mapping takes place. The mapper is also responsible for transforming the values from the original format to the destination format when both objects do not follow the same structure.

Design

We can design object mappers in many ways. Here is the most basic object mapper design:

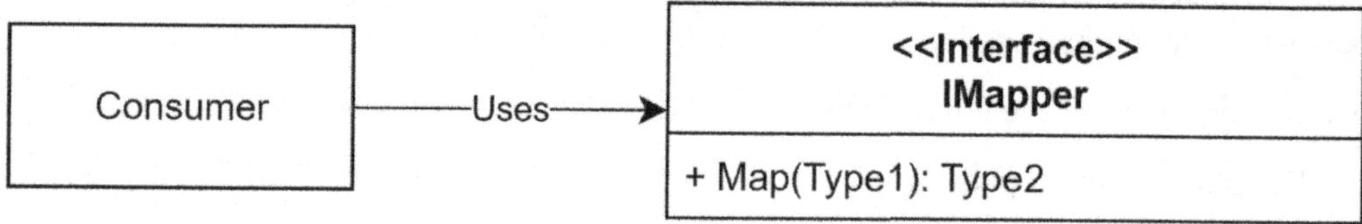

Figure 15.1: Basic design of the object mapper

In the diagram, the **Consumer** uses the `IMapper` interface to map an object of `Type1` to an object of `Type2`. That's not very reusable, but it illustrates the concept. By using the power of **generics**, we can upgrade that simple design to this more reusable version:

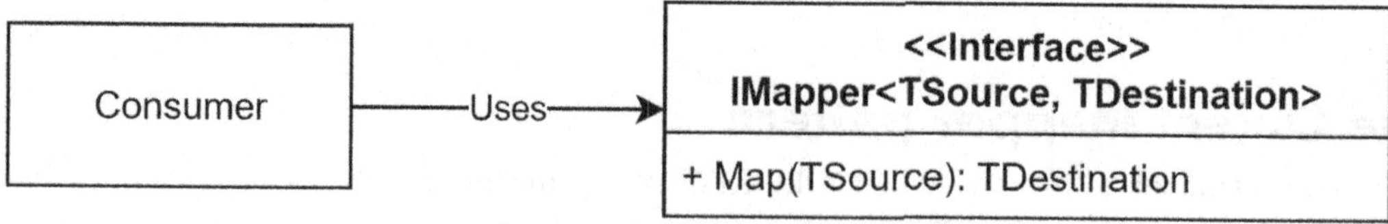

Figure 15.2: Generic object mapper design

This design lets us map any `TSource` to any `TDestination` by implementing the `IMapper<TSource, TDestination>` interface once per mapping rule. One class could also implement multiple mapping rules. For example, we could implement the mapping of `Type1` to `Type2` and `Type2` to `Type1` in the same class (a bidirectional mapper).

Another way would be to use the following design and create an `IMapper` interface with a single method that handles all of the application's mapping:

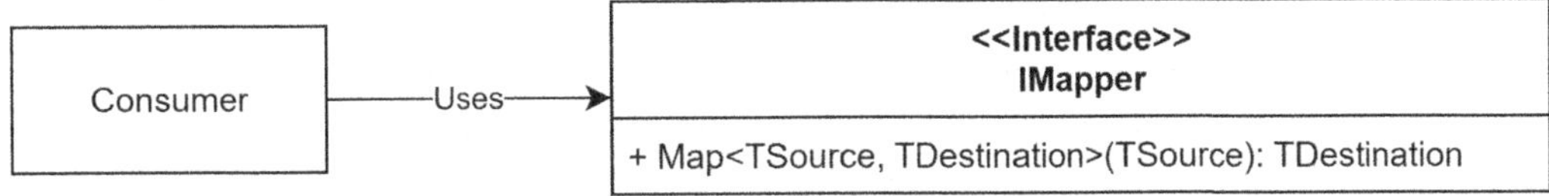

Figure 15.3: Object mapping using a single IMapper as the entry point

The biggest advantage of this last design is the ease of use. We always inject a single `IMapper` instead of one `IMapper<TSource, TDestination>` per type of mapping, which reduces the number of dependencies and the complexity of consuming such a mapper.

You can implement object mapping in any way your imagination allows, but the critical part is that the mapper is responsible for mapping an object to another. A mapper should avoid complex processes, such as loading data from a database and whatnot. It should copy the values of one object into another: that's it. Think about the **Single Responsibility Principle** (**SRP**) here: the class must have a single reason to change, and since it's an object mapper, that reason should be object mapping.

In its most basic form, we could hardcode the mapping code like this (from the `Program.cs` file in the *ManualMapping* project):

```
// Getting data/domain objects
var product = new Product(1, "Habanero pepper");
var inventories = new[] {
    new Inventory(1, "Warehouse West", 10),
    new Inventory(1, "Warehouse North", 15)
};

// Computing model into expected result
var quantityInStock = inventories.Sum(x => x.Quantity);

// Mapping to DTO
var dto = new ProductDetailsDto(product.Id, product.Name, quantityInStock);

// Using the DTO
Console.WriteLine($"ProductId: {dto.ProductId}");
Console.WriteLine($"ProductName: {dto.ProductName}");
Console.WriteLine($"ProductQuantityInStock: {dto.ProductQuantityInStock}");

// Data/domain model
public record class Product(int Id, string Name);
public record class Inventory(int ProductId, string Warehouse, int Quantity);
```

```
// DTO
public record class ProductDetailsDto(int ProductId, string ProductName, int
ProductQuantityInStock);
```

In the previous code snippet, we manually created the model using the `Product` and `Inventory` classes, simulating fetching data from a database. Then, we computed the quantity in stock based on the inventory data. We then assigned those values to the target object, a new instance of the `ProductDetailsDto` class. That code manually maps different types of objects to a new type, the DTO. Afterward, we can use that DTO through its own properties, with names that differ from the original objects, and use the computed `ProductQuantityInStock` value.

In the rest of the chapter, we explore many ways to move away from manually writing mapping code like this and how to organize those mappers to be more maintainable. This knowledge is foundational for the other chapters where we use mappers. Let's now jump into some more code to explore the design in more depth. We explore several projects and a few tools to learn ways to organize mappers and more.

Project – Mapper

This project is an updated version of the Clean Architecture code from the previous chapter, which is a REST API that allows us to view the list of products and, for each product, enables us to add and remove stocks. The project aims to demonstrate the design's versatility of encapsulating entity mapping logic into mapper classes, moving that logic away from the consumers. Of course, the project is again focused on the use case at hand, making learning the topics easier.

First, we need an interface that resides in the `Core` project so the other projects can implement the mapping they need. Let's adopt the second design that we saw:

```
namespace Core.Mappers;
public interface IMapper<TSource, TDestination>
{
    TDestination Map(TSource entity);
}
```

With this interface, we can start creating the data mappers. But first, let's create record classes instead of anonymous types to name the DTOs returned by the endpoints. Here are all the DTOs (from the `Program.cs` file):

```
// Input stock DTOs
public record class AddStocksCommand(int Amount);
public record class RemoveStocksCommand(int Amount);

// Output stock DTO
public record class StockLevel(int QuantityInStock);

// Output "read all products" DTO
```

```
public record class ProductDetails(int Id, string Name, int QuantityInStock);

// Output Exceptions DTO
public record class ProductNotFound(int ProductId, string Message);
public record class NotEnoughStock(int AmountToRemove, int QuantityInStock,
string Message);
```

Three of the four output DTOs need mapping:

- `Product` to `ProductDetails`
- `ProductNotFoundException` to `ProductNotFound`
- `NotEnoughStockException` to `NotEnoughStock`

Why not map the `StockLevel` DTO? In our case, the `StockService` returns an `int` when we add or remove stocks, so converting a primitive value like an `int` into a `StockLevel` object does not require an object mapper. Moreover, creating such an object mapper adds no value and makes the code more complex. If the service had returned an object, creating a mapper that maps an object to `StockLevel` would have brought more value.

Let's start with the product mapper (from the `Program.cs` file):

```
public class ProductMapper : IMapper<Product, ProductDetails>
{
    public ProductDetails Map(Product entity)
        => new(entity.Id ?? default, entity.Name, entity.QuantityInStock);
}
```

The preceding code is straightforward; the `ProductMapper` class implements the `IMapper<Product, ProductDetails>` interface. The `Map` method returns a `ProductDetails` instance. The highlighted code ensures the `Id` property is not `null`, which should not happen.

We could also add a guard clause to ensure the `Id` property is not `null`.

All in all, the `Map` method takes a `Product` as input and outputs a `ProductDetails` instance containing the same values.

Then let's continue with the exception mappers (from the `Program.cs` file):

```
public class ExceptionsMapper : IMapper<ProductNotFoundException,
ProductNotFound>, IMapper<NotEnoughStockException, NotEnoughStock>
{
    public ProductNotFound Map(ProductNotFoundException exception)
```

```
        => new(exception.ProductId, exception.Message);
    public NotEnoughStock Map(NotEnoughStockException exception)
        => new(exception.AmountToRemove, exception.QuantityInStock, exception.
Message);
}
```

Compared to the ProductMapper class, the ExceptionsMapper class implements the two remaining use cases by implementing the IMapper interface twice. The two Map methods handle mapping an exception to its DTO, leading to one class being responsible for mapping exceptions to DTOs.

Why map exceptions to DTOs? Doing so ensures the program is not leaking unwanted information to the client, which could be a malicious actor. Moreover, trying to serialize an exception will yield the following exception:

```
NotSupportedException: Serialization and deserialization of
'System.Reflection.MethodBase' instances is not supported.
```

Furthermore, we could use a similar technique to ensure all exceptions are mapped to a standard structure to deliver a linear error-handling experience to the API consumers. The best way to do this is to centralize this process. The code of *Chapters 18, 19,* and *20* uses that type of approach.

Let's look at the products endpoint (original value from the clean-architecture project of *Chapter 14, Layering and Clean Architecture*):

```
app.MapGet("/products", async (
    IProductRepository productRepository,
    CancellationToken cancellationToken) =>
{
    var products = await productRepository.AllAsync(cancellationToken);
    return products.Select(p => new
    {
        p.Id,
        p.Name,
        p.QuantityInStock
    });
});
```

Before analyzing the code, let's look at the updated version (from the Program.cs file):

```
app.MapGet("/products", async (
    IProductRepository productRepository,
    IMapper<Product, ProductDetails> mapper,
```

```
    CancellationToken cancellationToken) =>
{
    var products = await productRepository.AllAsync(cancellationToken);
    return products.Select(p => mapper.Map(p));
});
```

In the preceding code, the request delegate uses the mapper to replace the copy logic (the highlighted lines of the original code). That simplifies the handler, moving the mapping responsibility into mapper objects instead (highlighted in the preceding code)—one more step toward the SRP.

Let's focus on the remove stocks endpoint as it is more complex than the add stocks endpoint and skip the latter, starting with the original value from the `clean-architecture` project of *Chapter 14, Layering and Clean Architecture*:

```
app.MapPost("/products/{productId:int}/remove-stocks", async (
    int productId,
    RemoveStocksCommand command,
    StockService stockService,
    CancellationToken cancellationToken) =>
{
    try
    {
        var quantityInStock = await stockService.RemoveStockAsync(productId,
command.Amount, cancellationToken);
        var stockLevel = new StockLevel(quantityInStock);
        return Results.Ok(stockLevel);
    }
    catch (NotEnoughStockException ex)
    {
        return Results.Conflict(new
        {
            ex.Message,
            ex.AmountToRemove,
            ex.QuantityInStock
        });
    }
    catch (ProductNotFoundException ex)
    {
        return Results.NotFound(new
        {
            ex.Message,
            productId,
        });
```

```
    }
});
```

Once again, before analyzing the code, let's look at the updated version (from the `Program.cs` file):

```
app.MapPost("/products/{productId:int}/remove-stocks", async (
    int productId,
    RemoveStocksCommand command,
    StockService stockService,
    IMapper<ProductNotFoundException, ProductNotFound> notFoundMapper,
    IMapper<NotEnoughStockException, NotEnoughStock> notEnoughStockMapper,
    CancellationToken cancellationToken) =>
{
    try
    {
        var quantityInStock = await stockService.RemoveStockAsync(productId,
command.Amount, cancellationToken);
        var stockLevel = new StockLevel(quantityInStock);
        return Results.Ok(stockLevel);
    }
    catch (NotEnoughStockException ex)
    {
        return Results.Conflict(notEnoughStockMapper.Map(ex));
    }
    catch (ProductNotFoundException ex)
    {
        return Results.NotFound(notFoundMapper.Map(ex));
    }
});
```

The same thing happened for this request delegate, but we injected two mappers instead of just one. We moved the mapping logic from inline using an anonymous type to the mapper objects. Nevertheless, a code smell is emerging here; have you noticed it? We investigate this after we are done with this project; meanwhile, keep thinking about the number of injected dependencies.

Now that the delegates depend on interfaces with object mappers encapsulating the mapping responsibility, we must configure the composition root and bind the mapper implementations to the `IMapper<TSource, TDestination>` interface. The service bindings look like this:

```
.AddSingleton<IMapper<Product, ProductDetails>, ProductMapper>()
.AddSingleton<IMapper<ProductNotFoundException, ProductNotFound>,
ExceptionsMapper>()
.AddSingleton<IMapper<NotEnoughStockException, NotEnoughStock>,
ExceptionsMapper>()
```

Since `ExceptionsMapper` implements two interfaces, we bind both to that class. That is one of the beauties of abstractions; the remove stocks delegate asks for two mappers but receives an instance of `ExceptionsMapper` twice without even knowing it.

We could also register the classes so the same instance is injected twice, like this:

```
.AddSingleton<ExceptionsMapper>()
.AddSingleton<IMapper<ProductNotFoundException, ProductNotFound>,
ExceptionsMapper>(sp => sp.GetRequiredService<ExceptionsMapper>())
.AddSingleton<IMapper<NotEnoughStockException, NotEnoughStock>,
ExceptionsMapper>(sp => sp.GetRequiredService<ExceptionsMapper>())
```

Yes, I did that double registration of the same class on purpose. That proves we can compose an application as we want without impacting the **consumers**. That is done by depending on abstractions instead of implementations, as per the **Dependency Inversion Principle** (**DIP**—the "D" in SOLID). Moreover, the division into small interfaces, as per the **Interface Segregation Principle** (**ISP**—the "I" in SOLID), makes that kind of scenario possible. Finally, we can glue all those pieces together using the power of **Dependency Injection** (**DI**).

Conclusion

Object mapping is a key technique for translating data across different layers and models, such as converting domain models into **Data Transfer Objects** (**DTOs**). Object Mappers adhere to the Separation of Concerns and the **Single Responsibility Principle** (**SRP**) by encapsulating mapping logic into dedicated object mappers and streamlining the transformation process. In a nutshell, the idea is simple: create an object that knows how to copy the data of one object into another.

Before exploring more alternatives, let's see how object mapping can help us follow the **SOLID** principles:

- **S**: Using mapper objects helps to separate the responsibility of mapping types from the consumers, making it easier to maintain and refactor the mapping logic
- **O**: By injecting mappers, we can change the mapping logic without changing the code of their consumers
- **L**: N/A.
- **I**: We explored different designs that provide a small mapper interface that reduces the dependencies between the components
- **D**: The consumers depend only on abstractions, moving the implementation's binding to the composition root and inverting the dependency flow

Now that we've explored how to extract and use mappers, let's look at the code smell that emerged.

Code smell – too many dependencies

Using this kind of mapping could become tedious in the long run, and we would rapidly see scenarios such as injecting three or more mappers into a single request delegate or controller. The consumer would likely already have other dependencies, leading to four or more injected dependencies.

That should raise the following question:

- Does the class do too much and have too many responsibilities?

In this case, the fine-grained `IMapper` interface pollutes our request delegates with tons of dependencies on mappers, which suggests that the class may be doing more than it should, likely violating the Single Responsibility Principle by carrying an excessive number of responsibilities. This can lead to several downsides, such as:

- **Reduced readability**: A class with too many dependencies becomes complex and harder to understand
- **Decreased maintainability**: Changes in one part of the code may have unexpected effects on dependent classes, making maintenance more challenging
- **Mock heavy tests**: Classes with numerous dependencies are harder to unit test due to the requirement of mocking all dependencies
- **Inflated scope**: With an increased number of dependencies, the scope of the class inflates, making it less cohesive and harder to manage or refactor

The preferred solution would be to move the exception-handling responsibility away from the delegates or controllers, leveraging a middleware or an exception filter, for example. This tactic would move boilerplate code away from the endpoints. We leverage this in the code of *Chapters 18*, *19*, and *20*.

As a rule of thumb, you want to **limit the number of dependencies to three or less**. Over that number, ask yourself if there is a problem with that class; does it have too many responsibilities? Having more than three dependencies is not inherently wrong; it just indicates that you should investigate the design. If nothing is wrong, keep it at 4, 5, or 10; it does not matter. If you find a way to reduce the number of dependencies or that the class actually does too many things, refactor the code.

If you don't like having that many dependencies, you could extract service aggregates that encapsulate two or more dependencies and inject that aggregate instead. Be aware that moving your dependencies around does not fix anything; it just moves the problem elsewhere if there was a problem in the first place. Using aggregates could increase the readability of the code, though.

Instead of blindly moving dependencies around, analyze the problem to see if you could create classes with actual logic that could do something useful to reduce the number of dependencies.

Next, let's have a quick look at aggregating services, as an alternative to injecting too many dependencies.

Overview of the Aggregate Services pattern

Even if the Aggregate Services pattern is not a magic problem-solving pattern, it is a viable alternative to injecting too many dependencies into another class. It can be used in other contexts too; its goal is to aggregate many dependencies in a class to reduce the number of injected services in other classes, grouping dependencies together.

The way to manage aggregates would be to group them by concern or responsibility. Putting a bunch of services in another service just for the sake of it is rarely the way to go; aim for cohesion.

Creating one or more aggregation services that expose other services can be a way to implement service discovery in a project. As always with code smells, first analyze if there is a problem, and if there is one, ensure the problem does not lie elsewhere before moving to an aggregate services class.

Loading a service that exposes other services can be handy. However, this can create issues like reducing the possibility of constructing independent services because they all depend on one or more aggregate services classes—moving halfway between Inversion of Control and the Control Freak anti-pattern. So, don't put everything into an aggregate straight away without thinking about the specifics of what you are trying to achieve.

Let's look at an example of a mapping aggregate to reduce the number of dependencies in a console application. The aggregate supports only mapping some DTOs to a `Product` and a `Product` to a DTO.

Let's start with the model, a simple product:

```
namespace Shared.Models;
public record class Product
{
    public Product(string name, int quantityInStock, int? id = null)
    {
        Name = name ?? throw new ArgumentNullException(nameof(name));
        QuantityInStock = quantityInStock;
        Id = id;
    }
```

```
    public int? Id { get; init; }
    public string Name { get; init; }
    public int QuantityInStock { get; private set; }

    public void AddStock(int amount) { ... }
    public void RemoveStock(int amount) { ... }
}
```

Next, we look at the mapper interface and the three mapper classes that convert one object to another each. One mapper throws an `EntityValidationException`, which is also included in the following code:

```
namespace Shared.Mappers;
public interface IMapper<TSource, TDestination>
{
    TDestination Map(Tsource entity);
}

public class InsertProductToProductMapper : IMapper<InsertProduct, Product>
{
    public Product Map(InsertProduct entity)
    {
        return new(entity.Name, quantityInStock: 0);
    }
}

public class ProductToProductSummaryMapper : IMapper<Product, ProductSummary>
{
    public ProductSummary Map(Product entity)
    {
        if (entity.Id == null)
        {
            throw new EntityValidationException("Id cannot be null.");
        }
        return new(entity.Id.Value, entity.Name);
    }
}

public class UpdateProductToProductMapper : IMapper<UpdateProduct, Product>
{
    public Product Map(UpdateProduct entity)
```

```
    {
        return new(entity.Name, entity.quantityInStock, entity.Id);
    }
}

public class EntityValidationException : Exception
{
    public EntityValidationException(string message) : base(message)
    {
    }
}
```

The preceding code is quite straightforward; each class manually maps one type to another. Now that we have explored the building blocks, here's the aggregate service code and a usage example:

```
using Shared.Contracts;
using Shared.Mappers;
using Shared.Models;

namespace AggregateServices;
public interface IProductMappers
{
    IMapper<Product, ProductSummary> EntityToDto { get; }
    IMapper<InsertProduct, Product> InsertDtoToEntity { get; }
    IMapper<UpdateProduct, Product> UpdateDtoToEntity { get; }
}

public class ProductMappers : IProductMappers
{
    public ProductMappers(IMapper<Product, ProductSummary> entityToDto,
IMapper<InsertProduct, Product> insertDtoToEntity, IMapper<UpdateProduct,
Product> updateDtoToEntity)
    {
        EntityToDto = entityToDto ?? throw new
ArgumentNullException(nameof(entityToDto));
        InsertDtoToEntity = insertDtoToEntity ?? throw new
ArgumentNullException(nameof(insertDtoToEntity));
        UpdateDtoToEntity = updateDtoToEntity ?? throw new
ArgumentNullException(nameof(updateDtoToEntity));
    }

    public IMapper<Product, ProductSummary> EntityToDto { get; }
```

```
    public IMapper<InsertProduct, Product> InsertDtoToEntity { get; }
    public IMapper<UpdateProduct, Product> UpdateDtoToEntity { get; }
}
```

The preceding code regroups our three mappers under a single interface, allowing consumers to access each mapper through a property. This is the implementation of the pattern, moving dependencies from one class to the properties of another.

Now, let's have a look at the bindings (`Program.cs` file):

```
using AggregateServices;
using Microsoft.Extensions.DependencyInjection;
using Shared.Mappers;
using Shared.Contracts;
using Shared.Models;

var services = new ServiceCollection();
services
    // Register the mapper bindings
    .AddSingleton<IMapper<InsertProduct, Product>,
InsertProductToProductMapper>()
    .AddSingleton<IMapper<Product, ProductSummary>,
ProductToProductSummaryMapper>()
    .AddSingleton<IMapper<UpdateProduct, Product>,
UpdateProductToProductMapper>()

    // Register aggregate services binding
    .AddSingleton<IProductMappers, ProductMappers>()
;

var serviceProvider = services.BuildServiceProvider();
var mapper = serviceProvider.GetRequiredService<IProductMappers>();
```

The preceding code creates a `ServiceCollection`, which we normally access through the `builder.Services` property, then registers all bindings as a singleton. Each mapper is added once and the `ProductMappers` class is bound to the `IProductMappers` interface. Finally, we manually create the `ServiceProvider` from our `ServiceCollection` object and ask the container to create an implementation of the `IProductMappers` interface for us. The use of the Service Locator simulates injecting dependency in a constructor; we covered the Service Locator in *Chapter 8, Dependency Injection*. ASP.NET Core usually handles this for us, but we are in a console application, so we must manage it ourselves.

At the end of the `Program.cs` file, I added the following helper method to format the output to the console and allow us to better visualize the processes:

```
static void Write(string title, object input, object output)
{
    Console.WriteLine("===[{0}]===", title);
    Console.WriteLine("Input: {0}", input);
    Console.WriteLine("Output: {0}", output);
    Console.WriteLine();
}
```

Now, let's explore how to consume our mappers through the aggregate services (`ProductMappers`):

```
// EntityToDto
var smartphone = new Product("Smartphone", 10, id: 1);
var smartphoneSummary = mapper.EntityToDto.Map(smartphone);
Write("EntityToDto", smartphone, smartphoneSummary);

// InsertDtoToEntity
var insertProductDto = new InsertProduct("Laptop");
var laptop = mapper.InsertDtoToEntity.Map(insertProductDto);
Write("InsertDtoToEntity", insertProductDto, laptop);

// UpdateDtoToEntity
var updateProductDto = new UpdateProduct(Id: 3, Name: "Smartwatch",
quantityInStock: 5);
var smartwatch = mapper.UpdateDtoToEntity.Map(updateProductDto);
Write("UpdateDtoToEntity", updateProductDto, smartwatch);
```

The preceding code creates the input objects and then leverages the mappers to convert them into other objects. The highlighted code exposes how we use the mappers through the object properties; each mapper has its own property.

Here's a representation of the **EntityToDto** mapping block from the preceding code:

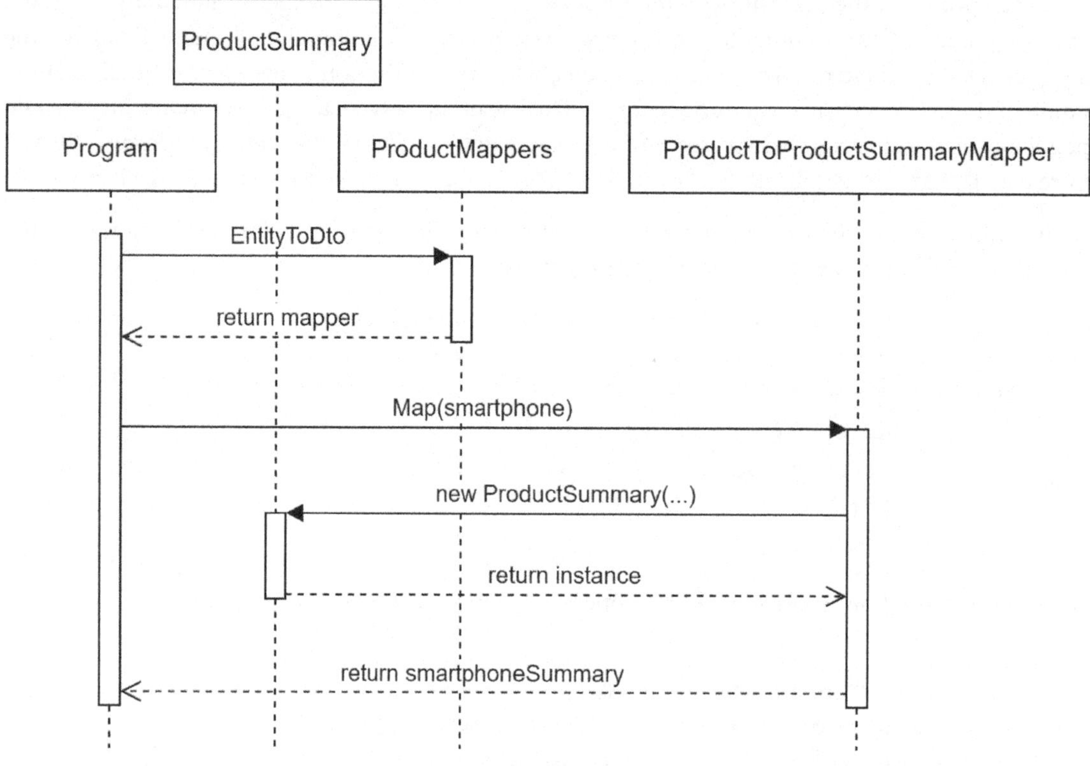

Figure 15.4: The sequence diagram of the EntityToDto mapping of a Product (smartphone) to a ProductSummary (smartphoneSummary)

Now, running the code yields the following:

```
===[EntityToDto]===
Input: Product { Id = 1, Name = Smartphone, QuantityInStock = 10 }
Output: ProductSummary { Id = 1, Name = Smartphone }

===[InsertDtoToEntity]===
Input: InsertProduct { Name = Laptop }
Output: Product { Id = , Name = Laptop, QuantityInStock = 0 }

===[UpdateDtoToEntity]===
Input: UpdateProduct { Id = 3, Name = Smartwatch, quantityInStock = 5 }
Output: Product { Id = 3, Name = Smartwatch, QuantityInStock = 5 }
```

As we can see from the preceding console, the values are copied as expected by the mappers.

If we were using a controller, we could use the aggregate like this:

```
public class ProductsController : ControllerBase
```

```
{
    private readonly IProductMappers _mapper;
    public ProductsController(IProductMappers mapper)
    {
        _mapper = mapper;
    }
    // Other methods, routing attributes, ...
    public ProductSummary GetProductById(int id)
    {
        Product product = ...; // Fetch a product by id
        ProductSummary dto = _mapper.EntityToDto.Map(product);
        return dto;
    }
}
```

In this example, the `IProductMappers` aggregate logically groups the mappers used by the `ProductsController` class under its umbrella. It is responsible for mapping `ProductsController`-related domain objects to DTOs and vice versa while the controller gives up this responsibility.

You can create aggregate services with anything, not just mappers. That's a fairly common pattern in DI-heavy applications (which can also point to some design flaws).

Now that we've explored the Aggregate Services pattern, let's explore how to make a mapping façade instead.

Implementing a mapping façade

We studied façades already; here, we explore another way to organize our many mappers by leveraging that design pattern.

Instead of what we just did, we create a mapping façade to replace our aggregate services. The code consuming the façade is more elegant because it uses the `Map` methods directly instead of the properties. The responsibility of the façade is the same as the aggregate, but it implements the interfaces instead of exposing them as properties.

This example shares a lot of the same code as the aggregate services example we just explored, so we start to look at the new code that replaces the `IProductMappers` interface and the `ProductMappers` class:

```
using Shared.Contracts;
using Shared.Mappers;
using Shared.Models;

namespace MappingFacade;
public interface IProductMapperService :
    IMapper<Product, ProductSummary>,
    IMapper<InsertProduct, Product>,
```

```
    IMapper<UpdateProduct, Product>
{
}

public class ProductMapperService : IProductMapperService
{
    private readonly IMapper<Product, ProductSummary> _entityToDto;
    private readonly IMapper<InsertProduct, Product> _insertDtoToEntity;
    private readonly IMapper<UpdateProduct, Product> _updateDtoToEntity;
    // Omitted constructor injection code
    public ProductSummary Map(Product entity)
    {
        return _entityToDto.Map(entity);
    }
    public Product Map(InsertProduct dto)
    {
        return _insertDtoToEntity.Map(dto);
    }
    public Product Map(UpdateProduct dto)
    {
        return _updateDtoToEntity.Map(dto);
    }
}
```

In the preceding code, the `ProductMapperService` class implements the `IMapper` interfaces through the `IProductMapperService` interface and delegates the mapping logic to each injected mapper: a façade wrapping multiple individual mappers.

This example also leverages a console application to make it easier to see how it works. Let's start with the dependency bindings (`Program.cs`):

```
using MappingFacade;
using Microsoft.Extensions.DependencyInjection;
using Shared.Contracts;
using Shared.Mappers;
using Shared.Models;

var services = new ServiceCollection();
services
    // Register the mapper bindings
    .AddSingleton<IMapper<InsertProduct, Product>,
InsertProductToProductMapper>()
```

```
    .AddSingleton<IMapper<Product, ProductSummary>,
ProductToProductSummaryMapper>()
    .AddSingleton<IMapper<UpdateProduct, Product>,
UpdateProductToProductMapper>()

    // Register aggregate services binding
    .AddSingleton<IProductMapperService, ProductMapperService>()
;
var serviceProvider = services.BuildServiceProvider();
var mapper = serviceProvider.GetRequiredService<IProductMapperService>();
```

The preceding code is very similar to what we did in the previous example, where only the highlighted line changed, registering our new service instead of the aggregate.

We use the same helper method to format the output to the console, so I'll skip it here. Here's how to consume this service:

```
// EntityToDto
var smartphone = new Product("Smartphone", 10, id: 1);
var smartphoneSummary = mapper.Map(smartphone);
Write("EntityToDto", smartphone, smartphoneSummary);

// InsertDtoToEntity
var insertProductDto = new InsertProduct("Laptop");
var laptop = mapper.Map(insertProductDto);
Write("InsertDtoToEntity", insertProductDto, laptop);

// UpdateDtoToEntity
var updateProductDto = new UpdateProduct(Id: 3, Name: "Smartwatch",
quantityInStock: 5);
var smartwatch = mapper.Map(updateProductDto);
Write("UpdateDtoToEntity", updateProductDto, smartwatch);
```

The preceding code uses the service and its map methods directly to execute the mapping. Next is the difference between the two examples (the first line of each block is the aggregate and the second is the service):

```
// EntityToDto
var smartphoneSummary = mapper.EntityToDto.Map(smartphone);
var smartphoneSummary = mapper.Map(smartphone);

// InsertDtoToEntity
var laptop = mapper.InsertDtoToEntity.Map(insertProductDto);
var laptop = mapper.Map(insertProductDto);
```

```
// UpdateDtoToEntity
var smartwatch = mapper.UpdateDtoToEntity.Map(updateProductDto);
var smartwatch = mapper.Map(updateProductDto);
```

The preceding code clearly shows the difference between the two techniques. Which one do you prefer? When talking about mappers, I tend toward the façade we just explored since the consumer should not know what class or property is doing what. However, in other scenarios where the services that are aggregated have different roles or more than one method, or when we want the consumer to explicitly know what property it is calling, the Aggregate Services pattern can be useful.

Now, before moving on to the next project, let's look at how a `ProductsController` class would consume the façade:

```
public class ProductsController : ControllerBase
{
    private readonly IProductMapperService _mapper;
    // Omitted constructor injection, other methods, routing attributes, ...
    public ProductSummary GetProductById(int id)
    {
        Product product = ...; // Fetch a product by id
        ProductSummary dto = _mapper.Map(product);
        return dto;
    }
}
```

As stated before, from the consumer standpoint (the `ProductsController` class), I find it cleaner to write `_mapper.Map(...)` instead of `_mapper.SomeMapper.Map(...)`. The consumer does not want to know what mapper is doing the mapping; it only wants to map what needs mapping. If we compare the mapping façade with the Aggregate Services of the previous example, the façade takes the responsibility of choosing the mapper and moves it away from the consumer. This design distributes the responsibilities between the classes better.

This was an excellent opportunity to review the Façade design pattern. Nonetheless, now that we've gone through multiple mapping options and examined the issue of having too many dependencies, it's time to move forward on our object mapping adventure with an enhanced version of our mapping façade.

Implementing a mapping service

This section explores another way to organize objects. We will end up with a similar interface to the previous example but a completely different implementation.

This example aims to simplify the implementation of the mapper façade with a universal interface. To achieve this, we are implementing the diagram shown in *Figure 13.3*. Here's a reminder:

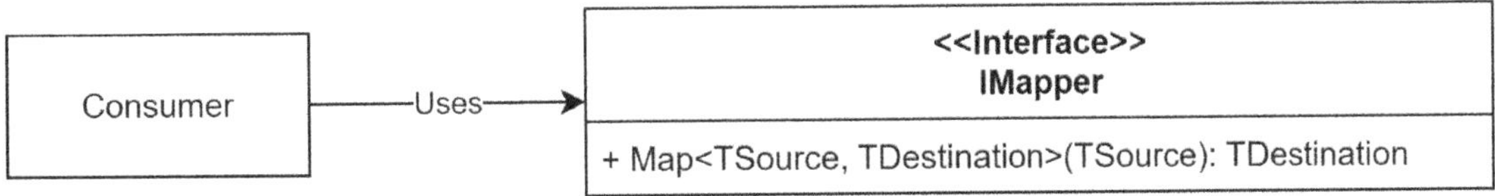

Figure 15.5: Object mapping using a single IMapper interface

Instead of naming the interface `IMapper`, we use the name `IMappingService`. This name is more suitable because it is not mapping anything; it is a dispatcher servicing the mapping request to the right mapper. Let's take a look:

```
namespace Core.Mappers;
public interface IMappingService
{
    TDestination Map<TSource, TDestination>(TSource entity);
}
```

That interface is self-explanatory; it maps any `TSource` to any `TDestination`.

On the implementation side, we are leveraging the **Service Locator** pattern, so I called the class `ServiceLocatorMappingService`:

```
using Microsoft.Extensions.DependencyInjection;

namespace Core.Mappers;
public class ServiceLocatorMappingService : IMappingService
{
    private readonly IServiceProvider _serviceProvider;
    public ServiceLocatorMappingService(IServiceProvider serviceProvider)
    {
        _serviceProvider = serviceProvider ?? throw new
ArgumentNullException(nameof(serviceProvider));
    }
    public TDestination Map<TSource, TDestination>(TSource entity)
    {
        var mapper = _serviceProvider.GetService<IMapper<TSource,
TDestination>>();
        if (mapper == null)
        {
            throw new MapperNotFoundException(typeof(TSource),
typeof(TDestination));
        }
        return mapper.Map(entity);
    }
}
```

```
public class MapperNotFoundException : Exception
{
    public MapperNotFoundException(Type source, Type destination)
        : base($"No Mapper from '{source}' to '{destination}' was found.")
    {
    }
}
```

The logic is simple:

- Find the appropriate `IMapper<TSource, TDestination>` service, then map the entity with it
- If you don't find any, throw a `MapperNotFoundException`

The key to this design is to register the mappers with the IoC container instead of the service itself. Then we use the mappers without knowing every single one of them, like in the previous example. The `ServiceLocatorMappingService` class doesn't know any mappers; it just dynamically asks for one whenever needed.

The Service Locator pattern should not be part of the application's code. However, it can be helpful at times. For example, we are not trying to cheat DI in this case. On the contrary, we are leveraging its power.

Using a service locator is wrong when acquiring dependencies in a way that removes the possibility of controlling the program's composition from the composition root, which breaks the IoC principle.

In this case, we load mappers dynamically from the IoC container, limiting the container's ability to control what to inject, which is acceptable since it has little to no negative impact on the program's maintainability, flexibility, and reliability. For example, we can replace the `ServiceLocatorMappingService` implementation with another class without affecting the `IMappingService` interface consumers.

Now, we can inject that service everywhere we need mapping and use it directly. We already registered the mappers, so we only need to bind the `IMappingService` to its `ServiceLocatorMappingService` implementation and update the consumers. Here's the DI binding:

```
.AddSingleton<IMappingService, ServiceLocatorMappingService>();
```

If we look at the new implementation of the remove stocks endpoint, we can see we reduced the number of mapper dependencies to one:

```
app.MapPost("/products/{productId:int}/remove-stocks", async (
    int productId,
    RemoveStocksCommand command,
    StockService stockService,
```

```
    IMappingService mapper,
    CancellationToken cancellationToken) => {
    try
    {
        var quantityInStock = await stockService.RemoveStockAsync(productId,
command.Amount, cancellationToken);
        var stockLevel = new StockLevel(quantityInStock);
        return Results.Ok(stockLevel);
    }
    catch (NotEnoughStockException ex)
    {
        return Results.Conflict(mapper.Map<NotEnoughStockException,
NotEnoughStock>(ex));
    }
    catch (ProductNotFoundException ex)
    {
        return Results.NotFound(mapper.Map<ProductNotFoundException,
ProductNotFound>(ex));
    }
});
```

The preceding code is similar to the previous sample, but we replaced the mappers with the new service (the highlighted lines).

And that's it; we now have a universal mapping service that delegates the mapping to any mapper we register with the IoC container.

Even if you are not likely to implement object mappers manually often, exploring and re-visiting those patterns and a code smell is very good and will help you craft better software.

This is not the end of our object mapping exploration. We have two tools to explore, starting with AutoMapper, which does all the object mapping work for us.

Exploring AutoMapper

We just covered different ways to implement object mapping, but here we leverage an open-source tool named AutoMapper that does it for us instead of implementing our own.

Why bother learning all of that if a tool already does it? There are a few reasons to do so:

- It is important to understand the concepts; you don't always need a full-fledged tool like Auto-Mapper. Moreover, if you work in a regulated enterprise, you don't have the luxury of loading every NuGet package you want and must go through a vetting process for each one.

- It allowed us to cover multiple patterns that we can use in other contexts and apply them to components with different responsibilities. So, all in all, you should have learned multiple new techniques during this object mapping progression.
- Lastly, we dug deeper into applying the SOLID principles to write better programs.

Project – AutoMapper

The AutoMapper project is also a copy of the Clean Architecture sample. The biggest difference between this project and the others is that we don't need to define any interface because AutoMapper exposes an `IMapper` interface with all the methods we need and more.

To install AutoMapper, you can install the `AutoMapper` NuGet package using the CLI (`dotnet add package AutoMapper`) or Visual Studio's NuGet package manager, or by updating your `.csproj` manually.

The best way to define our mappers is by using AutoMapper's profile mechanism. A profile is a simple class that inherits from `AutoMapper.Profile` and contains maps from one object to another. We use profiles to group mappers together cohesively like we did in the Aggregate Services and mapping façade projects, but in our case, with only three maps, I decided to create a single `WebProfile` class. To an extent, this is a cohesive group based on our limited codebase. Follow the architectural principles that you have learned in the book to help you identify the right grouping, and base your decision on the domain you are implementing.

Finally, instead of manually registering our profiles, we can scan one or more assemblies to load all of the profiles into AutoMapper by using the `AutoMapper.Extensions.Microsoft.DependencyInjection` package. When installing the `AutoMapper.Extensions.Microsoft.DependencyInjection` package, you don't have to load the `AutoMapper` package. If you don't want the dependency injection bits, you can load the `AutoMapper` package directly and handle the bindings yourself.

There is more to AutoMapper than what we cover here, but it has enough resources online, including the official documentation, to help you dig deeper into the tool. The goal of this project is to do basic object mapping.

In the *Web* project, we must create the following maps:

- Map `Product` to `ProductDetails`
- Map `NotEnoughStockException` to `NotEnoughStock`
- Map `ProductNotFoundException` to `ProductNotFound`

To do that, we create the following `WebProfile` class (in the `Program.cs` file, but it could live anywhere):

```
using AutoMapper;
public class WebProfile : Profile
{
    public WebProfile()
    {
```

```
            CreateMap<Product, ProductDetails>();
            CreateMap<NotEnoughStockException, NotEnoughStock>();
            CreateMap<ProductNotFoundException, ProductNotFound>();
        }
    }
```

A profile in AutoMapper is nothing more than a class where you create maps in the constructor. The `Profile` class adds the required methods for you to do that, such as the `CreateMap` method. What does that do?

Invoking the method `CreateMap<Product, ProductDetails>()` tells AutoMapper to register a mapper that maps `Product` to `ProductDetails`. The other two `CreateMap` calls are doing the same for the other two maps. That's all we need for now because AutoMapper maps properties using conventions, and both our model and DTO classes have the same sets of properties with the same names.

In the preceding examples, we defined some mappers in the `Core` layer. In this example, we rely on a library, so it is even more important to consider the dependency flow. We are mapping objects only in the `Web` layer, so there is no need to put the dependency on AutoMapper in the `Core` layer. Remember that all layers depend directly or indirectly on `Core`, so having a dependency on AutoMapper in that layer means all layers would also depend on it.

Therefore, in this example, we created the `WebProfile` class in the `Web` layer instead, limiting the dependency on AutoMapper to only that layer. Having only the `Web` layer depend on AutoMapper allows all outer layers (if we were to add more) to control how they do object mapping, giving more independence to each layer. It is also a best practice to limit object mapping as much as possible.

I've added a link to *AutoMapper Usage Guidelines* in the *Further reading* section at the end of the chapter.

Now that we have one profile, we need to register it with the IoC container, but we don't have to do this by hand; we can scan for profiles from the composition root by using one of the `AddAutoMapper` extension methods to scan one or more assemblies:

```
builder.Services.AddAutoMapper(typeof(WebProfile).Assembly);
```

The preceding method accepts a `params Assembly[] assemblies` argument, meaning we can pass multiple `Assembly` instances to it.

That `AddAutoMapper` extension method comes from the `AutoMapper.Extensions.Microsoft.DependencyInjection` package.

Since we have only one profile in one assembly, we leverage that class to access the assembly by passing the `typeof(WebProfile).Assembly` argument to the `AddAutoMapper` method. From there, AutoMapper scans for profiles in that assembly and finds the `WebProfile` class. If there were more than one, it would register all it finds.

The beauty of scanning for types like this is that once you register AutoMapper with the IoC container, you can add profiles in any registered assemblies, and they get loaded automatically; there's no need to do anything else afterward but to write useful code. Scanning assemblies also encourages composition by convention, making it easier to maintain in the long run. The downside of assembly scanning is that debugging can be hard when something is not registered because the registration process is less explicit.

Now that we've created and registered the profiles with the IoC container, it is time to use AutoMapper. Let's look at the three endpoints we created initially:

```
app.MapGet("/products", async (
    IProductRepository productRepository,
    IMapper mapper,
    CancellationToken cancellationToken) =>
{
    var products = await productRepository.AllAsync(cancellationToken);
    return products.Select(p => mapper.Map<Product, ProductDetails>(p));
});
app.MapPost("/products/{productId:int}/add-stocks", async (
    int productId,
    AddStocksCommand command,
    StockService stockService,
    IMapper mapper,
    CancellationToken cancellationToken) =>
{
    try
    {
        var quantityInStock = await stockService.AddStockAsync(productId,
command.Amount, cancellationToken);
        var stockLevel = new StockLevel(quantityInStock);
        return Results.Ok(stockLevel);
    }
    catch (ProductNotFoundException ex)
    {
        return Results.NotFound(mapper.Map<ProductNotFound>(ex));
    }
});
```

```
app.MapPost("/products/{productId:int}/remove-stocks", async (
    int productId,
    RemoveStocksCommand command,
    StockService stockService,
    IMapper mapper,
    CancellationToken cancellationToken) =>
{
    try
    {
        var quantityInStock = await stockService.RemoveStockAsync(productId,
command.Amount, cancellationToken);
        var stockLevel = new StockLevel(quantityInStock);
        return Results.Ok(stockLevel);
    }
    catch (NotEnoughStockException ex)
    {
        return Results.Conflict(mapper.Map<NotEnoughStock>(ex));
    }
    catch (ProductNotFoundException ex)
    {
        return Results.NotFound(mapper.Map<ProductNotFound>(ex));
    }
});
```

The preceding code shows how similar it is to use AutoMapper to the other options. We inject an `IMapper` interface, then use it to map the entities. Instead of explicitly specifying both `TSource` and `TDestination` like in the previous example, when using AutoMapper, we must specify only the `TDestination` generic parameter, reducing the code's complexity.

Suppose you are using AutoMapper on an `IQueryable` collection returned by EF Core. In that case, you should use the `ProjectTo` method, which limits the number of fields that EF will query to those you need. In our case, that changes nothing because we need the whole entity.

Here is an example that fetches all products from EF Core and projects them to `ProductDto` instances:

```
public IEnumerable<ProductDto> GetAllProducts()
{
    return _mapper.ProjectTo<ProductDto>(_db.Products);
}
```

Performance-wise, this is the recommended way to use AutoMapper with EF Core.

One last significant detail is that we can assert whether our mapper configurations are valid when the application starts. This does not identify missing mappers but validates that the registered ones are configured correctly. The recommended way of doing this is in a unit test. To make this happen, I made the autogenerated `Program` class public by adding the following line at the end of the `Program.cs` file:

```
public partial class Program { }
```

Then I created a test project named `Web.Tests` that contains the following code:

```
namespace Web;
public class StartupTest
{
    [Fact]
    public async Task AutoMapper_configuration_is_valid()
    {
        // Arrange
        await using var application = new AutoMapperAppWebApplication();
        var mapper = application.Services.GetRequiredService<IMapper>();
        mapper.ConfigurationProvider.AssertConfigurationIsValid();
    }
}
internal class AutoMapperAppWebApplication : WebApplicationFactory<Program>{}
```

In the preceding code, we validate that all the AutoMapper maps are valid. To make the test fail and validate what happens when the `AutoMapper AssertConfigurationIsValid` is not successful, you can uncomment the following line of the `WebProfile` class:

```
CreateMap<NotEnoughStockException, Product>();
```

The `AutoMapperAppWebApplication` class is there to centralize the initialization of the test cases when there is more than one.

In the test project, I created a second test case ensuring the `products` endpoint is reachable. For both tests to work together, we must change the database name to avoid seeding conflicts so each test runs on its own database. This has to do with how we seed the database in the `Program.cs` file, which is not something we usually do except for in the development or proofs of concept. Nonetheless, testing against multiple databases can come in handy to isolate tests.

Here's that second test case and updated `AutoMapperAppWebApplication` class to give you an idea:

```
public class StartupTest
{
    [Fact]
    public async Task The_products_endpoint_should_be_reachable()
```

```
    {
        await using var application = new AutoMapperAppWebApplication();
        using var client = application.CreateClient();
        using var response = await client.GetAsync("/products");
        response.EnsureSuccessStatusCode();
    }
    // Omitted AutoMapper_configuration_is_valid method
}
internal class AutoMapperAppWebApplication : WebApplicationFactory<Program>
{
    private readonly string _databaseName;
    public AutoMapperAppWebApplication([CallerMemberName]string? databaseName =
default)
    {
        _databaseName = databaseName ?? nameof(AutoMapperAppWebApplication);
    }
    protected override IHost CreateHost(IHostBuilder builder)
    {
        builder.ConfigureServices(services =>
        {
            services.AddScoped(sp =>
            {
                return new DbContextOptionsBuilder<ProductContext>()
                    .UseInMemoryDatabase(_databaseName)
                    .UseApplicationServiceProvider(sp)
                    .Options;
            });
        });
        return base.CreateHost(builder);
    }
}
```

Running the tests ensures that the mapping in our application works and that one of the endpoints is reachable. We could add more tests, but those two cover about 50% of our code.

The `CallerMemberNameAttribute` used in the preceding code is part of the `System.Runtime.CompilerServices` namespace and allows its decorated member to access the name of the method that called it. In this case, the `databaseName` parameter receives the test method name.

And this closes the AutoMapper project. At this point, you should be starting to get familiar with object mapping. I'd recommend you evaluate whether AutoMapper is the right tool for the job whenever a project needs object mapping. You can always load another tool or implement your own mapping logic if AutoMapper does not suit your needs. If too much mapping is done at too many levels, maybe another application architecture pattern would be better, or some rethinking is in order.

AutoMapper is convention-based and does a lot on its own without any configuration from us. It is also caching the conversions to improve performance. We can also create **type converters, value resolvers, value converters**, and more that work with AutoMapper. AutoMapper keeps us away from writing that boring mapping code.

AutoMapper is established, feature complete, and almost unavoidable due to the number of projects that use it. However, it is not the fastest, which is why we are exploring Mapperly next.

Exploring Mapperly

Mapperly is a newer object mapper library that leverages source generation to make it lightning-fast. There are many ways to create object mappers with Mapperly and many options to adjust the mapping process. The following project is similar to the others but using Mapperly.

We cover the following ways to use Mapperly:

- Injecting a mapper class
- Using a static method
- Using an extension method

Source generators were introduced with .NET 5, enabling developers to generate C# code automatically during the compilation process. These powerful tools serve as an advanced feature that taps into the Roslyn compiler pipeline, allowing for the creation and injection of source code into a project before it is compiled. Source generators help eliminate boilerplate code, ensure type safety, and improve performance by pre-calculating complex or static values. Unlike traditional code generation tools that create additional files, source generators do not add extra files to the project. Instead, they enhance the existing code dynamically at compile time, leading to cleaner projects and a streamlined development experience.

Project – Mapperly

To get started, we must add a dependency on the `Riok.Mapperly` NuGet package. With that done, let's explore the injected mapper. First, the class must be `partial` for the source generator to extend it (that is how source generators work). Decorate the class with the `[Mapper]` attribute (highlighted). Then, in that partial class, we must create one or more `partial` methods that have the signature of the mappers we want to create (like the `MapToProductDetails` method), like this:

```
[Mapper]
public partial class ProductMapper
```

```
{
    public partial ProductDetails MapToProductDetails(Product product);
}
```

Upon compilation, the code generator creates the following class (I formatted the code to make it easier to read):

```
public partial class ProductMapper
{
    public partial ProductDetails MapToProductDetails(Product product)
    {
        var target = new ProductDetails(
            product.Id ?? throw new ArgumentNullException(nameof(product.Id)),
            product.Name,
            product.QuantityInStock
        );
        return target;
    }
}
```

Mapperly writes the boilerplate code for us in a generated `partial` class, which is why it is so fast.

To inspect the generated code, you can add the `EmitCompilerGeneratedFiles` property in a `PropertyGroup` tag inside your project file and set its value to `true` like this:

```
<PropertyGroup>
    <EmitCompilerGeneratedFiles>true</EmitCompilerGeneratedFiles>
</PropertyGroup>
```

Then the generated C# files will be available under the `obj\Debug\net8.0\generated` directory. Change the `net8.0` subdirectory to the SDK version and `Debug` by the configuration you are using to compile the project.

To use the mapper, we must register it with the IoC container and inject it into our endpoint. Let's make it a singleton once again:

```
builder.Services.AddSingleton<ProductMapper>();
```

Then, we can inject and use it like this:

```
app.MapGet("/products", async (
    IProductRepository productRepository,
```

```
    ProductMapper mapper,
    CancellationToken cancellationToken) =>
{
    var products = await productRepository.AllAsync(cancellationToken);
    return products.Select(p => mapper.MapToProductDetails(p));
});
```

The highlighted code in the preceding block shows we can use our mapper like any other class. The biggest drawback is that we may end up injecting many mappers into a single class or endpoint if we do not consider how we create them wisely.

Moreover, we must register all of our mappers with the IoC container, which creates a lot of boilerplate code but makes the process explicit. On the other hand, we could scan the assembly for all classes decorated with the `[Mapper]` attribute.

If you want an abstraction layer like an interface for your mapper, you must design that yourself because Mapperly only generates the mappers. Here is an example:

```
public interface IMapper
{
    NotEnoughStock MapToDto(NotEnoughStockException source);
    ProductNotFound MapToDto(ProductNotFoundException source);
    ProductDetails MapToProductDetails(Product product);
}
[Mapper]
public partial class Mapper : IMapper
{
    public partial NotEnoughStock MapToDto(NotEnoughStockException source);
    public partial ProductNotFound MapToDto(ProductNotFoundException source);
    public partial ProductDetails MapToProductDetails(Product product);
}
```

The preceding code centralizes all the mapper methods under the same class and interface, allowing you to inject an interface similar to AutoMapper. In subsequent chapters, we explore ways to organize mappers and app code that does not involve creating a central mapper class.

For now, we explore how to make a static mapper, which follows a very similar process, but we must make both the class and the method `static` like this:

```
[Mapper]
public static partial class ExceptionMapper
{
    public static partial ProductNotFound Map(ProductNotFoundException
exception);
}
```

Mapperly takes the preceding code and generates the following (formatted for improved readability):

```
public static partial class ExceptionMapper
{
    public static partial ProductNotFound Map(ProductNotFoundException
exception)
    {
        var target = new ProductNotFound(
            exception.ProductId,
            exception.Message
        );
        return target;
    }
}
```

Once again, the code generator writes the boilerplate code. The difference is that we don't have to inject any dependency since it is a static method. We can use it this way (I only included the catch block, the rest of the code is unchanged):

```
catch (ProductNotFoundException ex)
{
    return Results.NotFound(ExceptionMapper.Map(ex));
}
```

It is pretty straightforward but creates a strong bond between the generated class and its consumers. You can use those static methods if having a hard dependency on a static class is acceptable for your project.

The last way to map objects we explore is very similar, but we create an extension method in the same class instead of just a static method. Here's the new method:

```
public static partial NotEnoughStock ToDto(this NotEnoughStockException
exception);
```

The generated code for that method looks like the following (formatted):

```
public static partial NotEnoughStock ToDto(this NotEnoughStockException
exception)
{
    var target = new NotEnoughStock(
        exception.AmountToRemove,
        exception.QuantityInStock,
        exception.Message
    );
    return target;
}
```

The only difference is the addition of the `this` keyword, making a regular static method into an extension method that we can use like this:

```
catch (NotEnoughStockException ex)
{
    return Results.Conflict(ex.ToDto());
}
```

An extension method is more elegant than a static method, yet it creates a bond similar to the static method. Once again, choosing how you want to proceed with your mapping is up to you.

One noteworthy thing about Mapperly is that its analyzers yield information, warnings, or errors when the mapping code is incorrect or potentially incorrect. The severity of the messages is configurable. For example, if we add the following method in the `ExceptionMapper` class, Mapperly yields the `RMG013` error:

```
public static partial Product NotEnoughStockExceptionToProduct(
    NotEnoughStockException exception
);
```

Error message:

```
RMG013 Core.Models.Product has no accessible constructor with
mappable arguments
```

Moreover, the two exception mapper methods yield messages about properties that do not exist on the target class as information. Here's an example of such a message:

```
RMG020 The member TargetSite on the mapping source type Core.
ProductNotFoundException is not mapped to any member on the
mapping target type ProductNotFound
```

With those in place, we know when something is or can be wrong, which safeguards us from misconfigurations.

Let's wrap this chapter up.

Summary

Object mapping is an unavoidable reality in many cases. However, as we saw in this chapter, there are several ways of implementing object mapping, taking that responsibility away from the other components of our applications or simply coding it inline manually.

At the same time, we took the opportunity to explore the Aggregate Services pattern, which gives us a way to centralize multiple dependencies into one, lowering the number of dependencies needed in other classes. That pattern can help with the too-many-dependencies code smell, which, as a rule of thumb, states that we should investigate objects with more than three dependencies for design flaws.

When moving dependencies into an aggregate, ensure there is cohesion within the aggregate to avoid adding unnecessary complexity to your program and just moving the dependencies around.

We also explored leveraging the Façade pattern to implement a mapping façade, which led to a more readable and elegant mapper.

Afterward, we implemented a mapper service that mimicked the façade. Despite being less elegant in its usage, it was more flexible.

We finally explored AutoMapper and Mapperly, two open-source tools that do object mapping for us, offering us many options to configure the mapping of our objects. For example, just using the default convention of AutoMapper allowed us to eliminate all of our mapping code. On Mapperly's side, we had to define the mapper contracts using partial classes and methods to let its code generator implement the mapping code for us. You can choose from many existing object mapper libraries, AutoMapper being one of the oldest, most famous, and most hated at the same time, while Mapperly is one of the newest and fastest but yet in its infancy.

Hopefully, as we are putting more and more pieces together, you are starting to see what I had in mind at the beginning of this book when stating this was an architectural journey.

Now that we are done with object mapping, we'll explore the Mediator and CQS patterns in the next chapter.

Questions

Let's take a look at a few practice questions:

1. Is it true that injecting an Aggregate Service instead of multiple services improves our system?
2. Is it true that using mappers helps us extract responsibilities from consumers to mapper classes?
3. Is it true that you should always use AutoMapper?
4. When using AutoMapper, should you encapsulate your mapping code into profiles?
5. How many dependencies should start to raise a flag telling you that you are injecting too many dependencies into a single class?

Further reading

Here are some links to build upon what we learned in the chapter:

- If you want more information on object mapping, I wrote an article about that in 2017, titled *Design Patterns: ASP.NET Core Web API, Services, and Repositories | Part 9: the NinjaMappingService and the Façade Pattern*: `https://adpg.link/hxYf`
- AutoMapper official website: `https://adpg.link/5AUZ`
- *AutoMapper's Design Philosophy is an excellent article that explains why the tool was created and what use case it is good at*, written by the library's author: `https://adpg.link/mK2W`
- *AutoMapper Usage Guidelines* is an excellent do/don't list to help you do the right thing with AutoMapper, written by the library's author: `https://adpg.link/tTKg`
- Mapperly (GitHub): `https://adpg.link/Dwcj`

Answers

1. Yes, an Aggregate Service can improve a system, but not necessarily. Moving dependencies around does not fix design flaws; it just moves those flaws elsewhere.
2. Yes, mappers help us follow the SRP. However, they are not always needed.
3. No, it is not suitable for every scenario. For example, when the mapping logic becomes complex, consider not using AutoMapper. Too many mappers may also mean a flaw in the application design itself.
4. Yes, use profiles to organize your mapping rules cohesively.
5. Four or more dependencies should start to raise a flag. Once again, this is just a guideline; injecting four or more services into a class can be acceptable.

Learn more on Discord

To join the Discord community for this book – where you can share feedback, ask questions to the author, and learn about new releases – follow the QR code below:

`https://packt.link/ArchitectingASPNETCoreApps3e`

16

Mediator and CQS Patterns

This chapter explores the **Mediator** design pattern, which plays the role of the middleman between the components of our application.

That leads us to the **Command-Query Separation** (**CQS**) pattern, which describes how to divide our logic into commands and queries.

Finally, we consolidate our learning by exploring MediatR, an open source implementation of the Mediator design pattern, and send queries and commands through it to demonstrate how the concepts we have studied so far come to life in real-world application development.

In this chapter, we cover the following topics:

- A high-level overview of Vertical Slice Architecture
- Implementing the Mediator pattern
- Implementing the CQS pattern
- Code smell – Marker Interfaces
- Using MediatR as a mediator

Moreover, this chapter covers the building blocks of the next chapter, which is about **Vertical Slice Architecture**. Let's begin with a quick overview of Vertical Slice Architecture to give you an idea of the end goal.

A high-level overview of Vertical Slice Architecture

Before starting, let's look at the end goal of this chapter and the next. This way, it should be easier to follow the progress toward that goal throughout the chapter.

As we covered in *Chapter 14, Layering and Clean Architecture*, a layer groups classes together based on shared responsibilities. For example, classes containing data access code are part of the data access layer (or infrastructure).

As explored before, we represent layers using horizontal slices in diagrams like this:

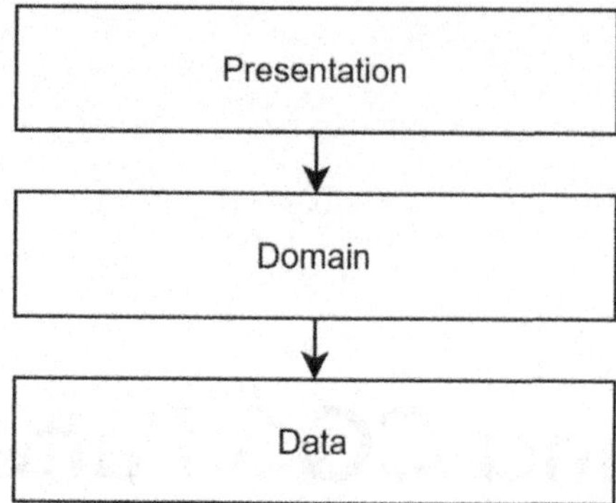

Figure 16.1: Diagram representing layers as horizontal slices

The "vertical slice" in "Vertical Slice Architecture" comes from this: a vertical slice represents the part of each layer that creates a specific feature. So, instead of dividing the application into layers, we divide it into features. A feature manages its data access code, domain logic, and possibly even presentation code. The key is to loosely couple the features from one another and keep each feature's components close together.

In a layered application, when we add, update, or remove a feature, we must change one or more layers, which too often translates to "all layers."

On the other hand, with vertical slices, we keep features isolated, allowing us to design them independently. From a layering perspective, this is like flipping your way of thinking about software to a 90° angle:

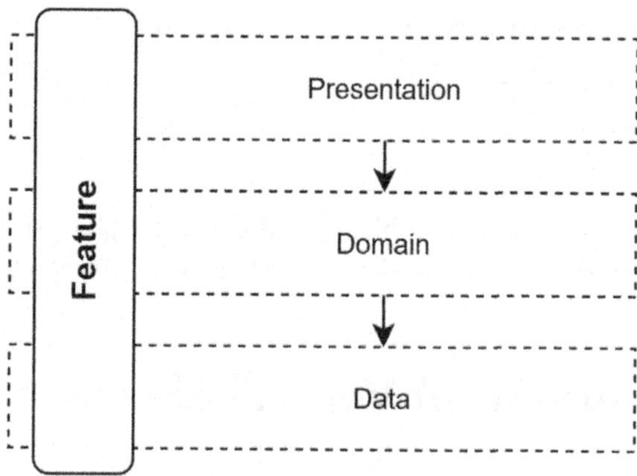

Figure 16.2: Diagram representing a vertical slice crossing all layers

Vertical Slice Architecture does not dictate the use of **CQS**, the **Mediator** pattern, or **MediatR**, which we cover in this chapter, but these tools and patterns flow very well together, as we see in the next chapter.

We explore additional ways of building feature-oriented applications in *Chapter 18, Request-EndPoint-Response (REPR)*, and *Chapter 20, Modular Monolith.*

The goal of Vertical Slice Architecture is to encapsulate features together, use CQS to divide the application into requests (commands and queries), and use MediatR as the mediator of that CQS pipeline, decoupling the pieces from one another.

You now know the plan; we explore Vertical Slice Architecture later. Meanwhile, let's begin with the Mediator design pattern.

The Mediator pattern

The **Mediator** pattern is another GoF design pattern that controls how objects interact with one another (making it a behavioral pattern). It helps break tight coupling between components of a system by mediating the communication between them.

Goal

The mediator's role is to manage the communication between objects (colleagues). Those colleagues should not communicate together directly but use the mediator instead.

A mediator is a middleman who relays messages between colleagues.

Design

Let's start with some UML diagrams. From a very high level, the Mediator pattern is composed of a mediator and colleagues:

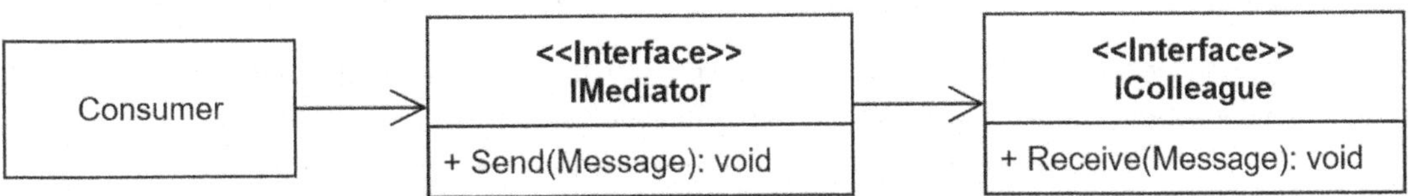

Figure 16.3: Class diagram representing the Mediator pattern

When an object in the system wants to send a message to one or more colleagues, it uses the mediator. Here is an example of how it works:

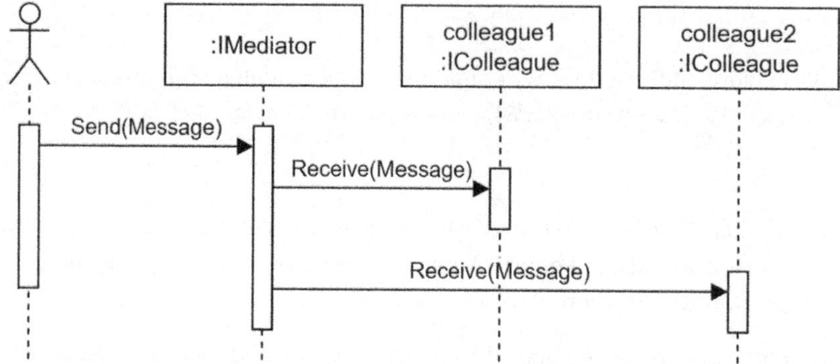

Figure 16.4: Sequence diagram of a mediator relaying messages to colleagues

That is also valid for colleagues; colleagues must also use the mediator if they need to talk to each other, as depicted in the following class diagram:

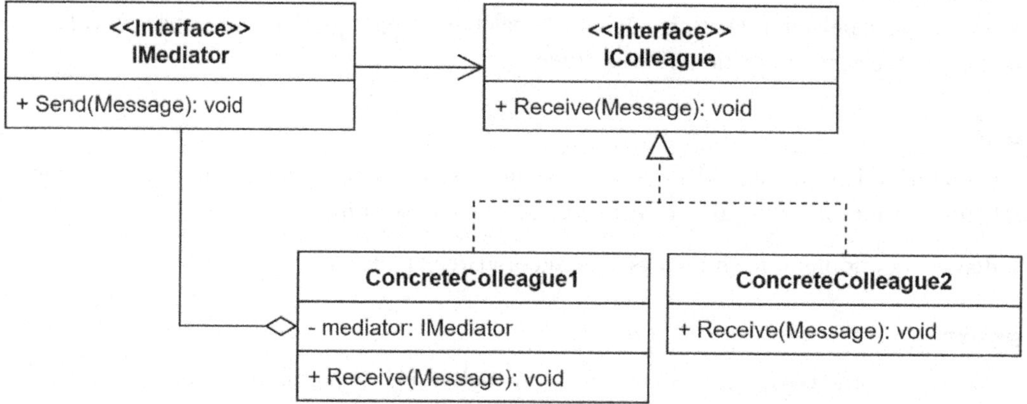

Figure 16.5: Class diagram representing the Mediator pattern including colleagues' collaboration

In this diagram, `ConcreteColleague1` is a colleague but also the consumer of the mediator. For example, that colleague could send a message to another colleague using the mediator, like this:

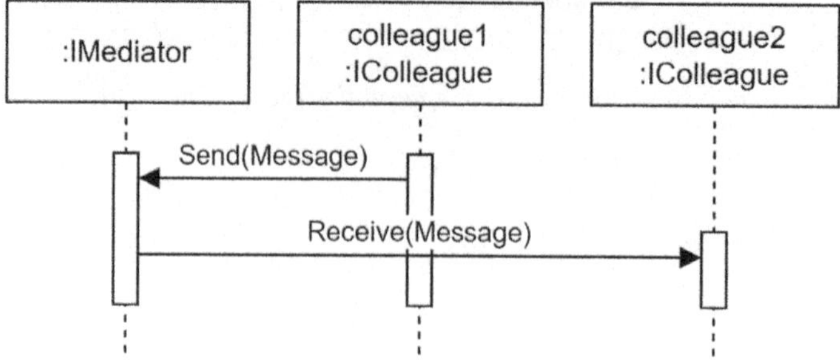

Figure 16.6: Sequence diagram representing colleague1 communicating with colleague2 through the mediator

From a mediator standpoint, its implementation most likely contains a collection of colleagues to communicate with, like this:

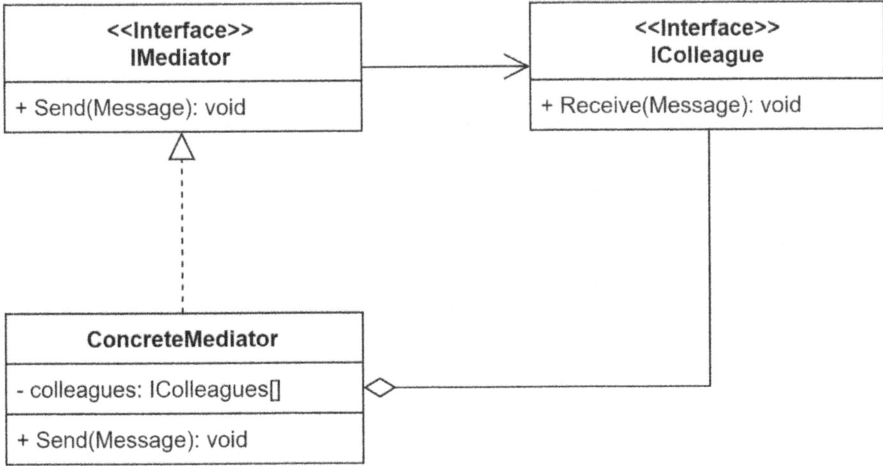

Figure 16.7: Class diagram representing a simple hypothetical concrete mediator implementation

Now that we have explored some UML diagrams, let's look at some code.

Project – Mediator (IMediator)

The Mediator project is a simplified chat system that might serve as the backend for an internal communication tool, like Discord or Teams. The system centralizes communication using the Mediator pattern, allowing various components, represented as *colleagues* in the code, to interact through a single *mediator*, preventing direct dependency between them.

To design a distributed chat system like Discord or Teams, we'd need a different design that involves multiple components and communications that run over a network. Nonetheless, a similar concept could apply.

Let's start with the interfaces:

```
namespace Mediator;
public interface IMediator
{
    void Send(Message message);
}
public interface IColleague
{
    string Name { get; }
    void ReceiveMessage(Message message);
```

```
}
public record class Message(IColleague Sender, string Content);
```

The system is composed of the following:

- The `IMediator` interface represents a mediator that can send messages to colleagues.
- The `IColleague` interface represents a colleague that can receive messages. It also has a `Name` property so we can output meaningful values.
- The `Message` class represents a message sent by an `IColleague` implementation.

Next, we implement the `IMediator` interface in the `ConcreteMediator` class, which broadcasts the messages to all `IColleague` instances:

```
public class ConcreteMediator : IMediator
{
    private readonly List<IColleague> _colleagues;
    public ConcreteMediator(params IColleague[] colleagues)
    {
        ArgumentNullException.ThrowIfNull(colleagues);
        _colleagues = new List<IColleague>(colleagues);
    }
    public void Send(Message message)
    {
        foreach (var colleague in _colleagues)
        {
            colleague.ReceiveMessage(message);
        }
    }
}
```

That mediator is simple; it forwards all the messages it receives to every colleague it knows.

The last part of the pattern is the `ConcreteColleague` class, which lets an instance of the `IMessageWriter<TMessage>` interface output the messages (we explore that interface next):

```
public class ConcreteColleague : IColleague
{
    private readonly IMessageWriter<Message> _messageWriter;
    public ConcreteColleague(string name, IMessageWriter<Message>
messageWriter)
    {
        Name = name ?? throw new ArgumentNullException(nameof(name));
        _messageWriter = messageWriter ?? throw new
ArgumentNullException(nameof(messageWriter));
    }
```

```
    public string Name { get; }
    public void ReceiveMessage(Message message)
    {
        _messageWriter.Write(message);
    }
}
```

That class could hardly be simpler: it takes a name and an `IMessageWriter<TMessage>` implementation when created, and then it stores a reference for future use.

The `IMessageWriter<TMessage>` interface serves as a presenter and controls how the messages are displayed. The `IMessageWriter<TMessage>` interface is unrelated to the Mediator pattern. Nevertheless, it is a way to manage how a `ConcreteColleague` object outputs the messages without coupling it with a specific target. Here is the code:

```
namespace Mediator;
public interface IMessageWriter<Tmessage>
{
    void Write(Tmessage message);
}
```

The consumer of the system is an integration test defined in the `MediatorTest` class. The test uses the chat system and asserts the output using a custom implementation of the `IMessageWriter` interface. Let's start by analyzing the test:

```
namespace Mediator;
public class MediatorTest
{
    [Fact]
    public void Send_a_message_to_all_colleagues()
    {
        // Arrange
        var (millerWriter, miller) = CreateConcreteColleague("Miller");
        var (orazioWriter, orazio) = CreateConcreteColleague("Orazio");
        var (fletcherWriter, fletcher) = CreateConcreteColleague("Fletcher");
```

The test starts by defining three colleagues with their own `TestMessageWriter` implementation (names were randomly generated).

```
        var mediator = new ConcreteMediator(miller, orazio, fletcher);
        var expectedOutput = @"[Miller]: Hey everyone!
[Orazio]: What's up Miller?
[Fletcher]: Hey Miller!
";
```

In the second part of the preceding `Arrange` block, we create the subject under test (`mediator`) and register the three colleagues. At the end of that `Arrange` block, we also define the expected output of our test. It is important to note that we control the output from the `TestMessageWriter` implementation (defined at the end of the `MediatorTest` class). Next is the `Act` block:

```
        // Act
        mediator.Send(new Message(
            Sender: miller,
            Content: "Hey everyone!"
        ));
        mediator.Send(new Message(
            Sender: orazio,
            Content: "What's up Miller?"
        ));
        mediator.Send(new Message(
            Sender: fletcher,
            Content: "Hey Miller!"
        ));
```

In the preceding `Act` block, we send three messages through the `mediator` instance. Next is the `Assert` block:

```
        // Assert
        Assert.Equal(expectedOutput, millerWriter.Output.ToString());
        Assert.Equal(expectedOutput, orazioWriter.Output.ToString());
        Assert.Equal(expectedOutput, fletcherWriter.Output.ToString());
    }
```

In the `Assert` block, we ensure that all colleagues receive the messages by comparing the `Output` property of each `IMessageWriter<Message>` (`millerWriter`, `orazioWriter`, and `fletcherWriter`) with what was expected (the value of the `expectedOutput` variable). Each call to the `CreateConcreteColleague` method (next code block) creates a new instance of the `TestMessageWriter` (`IMessageWriter<Message>`) and `ConcreteColleague` (`IColleague`) classes, allowing the test method to assess what each colleague received individually. Here's the code of the `CreateConcreteColleague` method:

```
    private static (TestMessageWriter, ConcreteColleague)
CreateConcreteColleague(string name)
    {
        var messageWriter = new TestMessageWriter();
        var concreateColleague = new ConcreteColleague(name, messageWriter);
        return (messageWriter, concreateColleague);
    }
```

The `CreateConcreteColleague` method is a helper method that encapsulates the creation of the colleagues, enabling us to write the one-liner declaration used in the `Arrange` section of the test.

Next, we look at the `IMessageWriter` implementation:

```
    private class TestMessageWriter : IMessageWriter<Message>
    {
        public StringBuilder Output { get; } = new StringBuilder();
        public void Write(Message message)
        {
            Output.AppendLine($"[{message.Sender.Name}]: {message.Content}");
        }
    }
} // Closing the MediatorTest class
```

Finally, the `TestMessageWriter` class writes the messages into `StringBuilder`, making it easy to assert the output. If we were to build a GUI for that, we could write an implementation of `IMessageWriter<Message>` that writes to that GUI; in the case of a web UI, it could use **SignalR** or write to the response stream directly, for example.

To summarize the sample:

1. The consumer (the unit test) sends messages to colleagues through the mediator.
2. The `TestMessageWriter` class writes those messages to a `StringBuilder` instance. Each colleague has its own instance of the `TestMessageWriter` class.
3. The code asserts that all colleagues received the expected messages.

This example illustrates that the Mediator pattern allows us to break the direct coupling between colleagues. The messages reached colleagues without them knowing about each other.

Colleagues should communicate through the mediator, so the Mediator pattern would not be complete without that. Let's implement a more advanced chat room to tackle this concept.

Project – Mediator (IChatRoom)

In the previous code sample, we named the classes after the Mediator pattern actors, as shown in *Figure 16.7*. While this example is very similar, it uses domain-specific names instead and implements a few more methods to manage the system showing a more tangible implementation. Let's start with the abstractions:

```
namespace Mediator;
public interface IChatRoom
{
    void Join(IParticipant participant);
    void Send(ChatMessage message);
}
```

The `IChatRoom` interface is the mediator, and it defines two methods instead of one:

- `Join`, which allows `IParticipant` to join `IChatRoom`

- Send, which sends a message to the others

```
public interface IParticipant
{
    string Name { get; }
    void Send(string message);
    void ReceiveMessage(ChatMessage message);
    void ChatRoomJoined(IChatRoom chatRoom);
}
```

The `IParticipant` interface is the colleague and also has a few more methods:

- Send, to send messages
- `ReceiveMessage`, to receive messages from the other `IParticipant` objects
- `ChatRoomJoined`, to confirm that the `IParticipant` object has successfully joined a chat room

```
public record class ChatMessage(IParticipant Sender, string Content);
```

The `ChatMessage` class is the same as the previous `Message` class, but it references `IParticipant` instead of `IColleague`.

Let's now look at the `IParticipant` implementation:

```
public class User : IParticipant
{
    private IChatRoom? _chatRoom;
    private readonly IMessageWriter<ChatMessage> _messageWriter;
    public User(IMessageWriter<ChatMessage> messageWriter, string name)
    {
        _messageWriter = messageWriter ?? throw new
ArgumentNullException(nameof(messageWriter));
        Name = name ?? throw new ArgumentNullException(nameof(name));
    }
    public string Name { get; }
    public void ChatRoomJoined(IChatRoom chatRoom)
    {
        _chatRoom = chatRoom;
    }
    public void ReceiveMessage(ChatMessage message)
    {
        _messageWriter.Write(message);
    }
    public void Send(string message)
    {
        if (_chatRoom == null)
```

```
        {
            throw new ChatRoomNotJoinedException();
        }
        _chatRoom.Send(new ChatMessage(this, message));
    }
}
public class ChatRoomNotJoinedException : Exception
{
    public ChatRoomNotJoinedException()
        : base("You must join a chat room before sending a message.")
    { }
}
```

The `User` class represents our default `IParticipant`. A `User` instance can chat in only one `IChatRoom`. The program can set the chat room by calling the `ChatRoomJoined` method. When it receives a message, it delegates it to its `IMessageWriter<ChatMessage>`. Finally, a `User` instance can send a message through the mediator (`IChatRoom`). The `Send` method throws a `ChatRoomNotJoinedException` to enforce that the `User` instance must join a chat room before sending messages (code-wise: the `_chatRoom` field must not be `null`).

We could create a `Moderator`, `Administrator`, `SystemAlerts`, or any other `IParticipant` implementation as we see fit. We are not done using the Mediator pattern, but I am leaving this exercise to you if you want to experiment with it.

Now let's look at the `ChatRoom` class (the mediator):

```
public class ChatRoom : IChatRoom
{
    private readonly List<IParticipant> _participants = new();
    public void Join(IParticipant participant)
    {
        _participants.Add(participant);
        participant.ChatRoomJoined(this);
        Send(new ChatMessage(participant, "Has joined the channel"));
    }
    public void Send(ChatMessage message)
    {
        _participants.ForEach(participant
            => participant.ReceiveMessage(message));
    }
}
```

The `ChatRoom` class is slimmer than the `User` class. It allows participants to join and sends chat messages to registered participants. The `ChatRoom` keeps a reference of the new `IParticipant` joining it and tells this `IParticipant` that they have successfully joined and then sends a `ChatMessage` to all participants announcing the newcomer.

With those few pieces, we have a Mediator implementation. Before moving to the next section, let's look at the `Consumer` instance of `IChatRoom`, which is another integration test. Let's start with the skeleton of the class:

```
namespace Mediator;
public class ChatRoomTest
{
    [Fact]
    public void ChatRoom_participants_should_send_and_receive_messages()
    {
        // Arrange, Act, Assert blocks here
    }

    private (TestMessageWriter, User) CreateTestUser(string name)
    {
        var writer = new TestMessageWriter();
        var user = new User(writer, name);
        return (writer, user);
    }

    private class TestMessageWriter : IMessageWriter<ChatMessage>
    {
        public StringBuilder Output { get; } = new StringBuilder();

        public void Write(ChatMessage message)
        {
            Output.AppendLine($"[{message.Sender.Name}]: {message.Content}");
        }
    }
}
```

In the preceding code, we have the following pieces:

- The test case is an empty placeholder, which we are about to look into
- The `CreateTestUser` method helps simplify the `Arrange` section of the test case, similar to before
- The `TestMessageWriter` implementation is similar to the previous example, accumulating messages in a `StringBuilder` instance

As a reference, the `IMessageWriter` interface is the same as the previous project:

```
public interface IMessageWriter<TMessage>
{
    void Write(TMessage message);
}
```

Now, let's explore the test case, starting with the `Arrange` block, where we create four users with their respective `TestMessageWriter` instances (names were also randomly generated):

```
// Arrange
var (kingChat, king) = CreateTestUser("King");
var (kelleyChat, kelley) = CreateTestUser("Kelley");
var (daveenChat, daveen) = CreateTestUser("Daveen");
var (rutterChat, _) = CreateTestUser("Rutter");
var chatroom = new ChatRoom();
```

Then, in the `Act` block, our test users join the `chatroom` instance and send messages:

```
// Act
chatroom.Join(king);
chatroom.Join(kelley);
king.Send("Hey!");
kelley.Send("What's up King?");
chatroom.Join(daveen);
king.Send("Everything is great, I joined the CrazyChatRoom!");
daveen.Send("Hey King!");
king.Send("Hey Daveen");
```

Then in the `Assert` block, since Rutter did not join the chat room, we expect no message:

```
// Assert
Assert.Empty(rutterChat.Output.ToString());
```

Since King is the first to join the channel, we expect him to receive all messages:

```
Assert.Equal(@"[King]: Has joined the channel
[Kelley]: Has joined the channel
[King]: Hey!
[Kelley]: What's up King?
[Daveen]: Has joined the channel
[King]: Everything is great, I joined the CrazyChatRoom!
[Daveen]: Hey King!
[King]: Hey Daveen
", kingChat.Output.ToString());
```

Kelley was the second user to join the chat room, so the output contains almost all messages except the line saying `[King]: Has joined the channel`:

```
Assert.Equal(@"[Kelley]: Has joined the channel
[King]: Hey!
[Kelley]: What's up King?
[Daveen]: Has joined the channel
[King]: Everything is great, I joined the CrazyChatRoom!
[Daveen]: Hey King!
[King]: Hey Daveen
", kelleyChat.Output.ToString());
```

Daveen joined after King and Kelley exchanged a few words, so we expect the conversation to be shorter:

```
Assert.Equal(@"[Daveen]: Has joined the channel
[King]: Everything is great, I joined the CrazyChatRoom!
[Daveen]: Hey King!
[King]: Hey Daveen
", daveenChat.Output.ToString());
```

To summarize the test case, we have four users. Three of them joined the same chat room at a different time and chatted a little. The output is different for everyone since the time you join matters. All participants are loosely coupled, thanks to the Mediator pattern, allowing us to extend the system without impacting the existing pieces. Leveraging the Mediator pattern helps us create maintainable systems; many small pieces are easier to manage and test than a large component handling all the logic.

Conclusion

As we explored in the two preceding projects, a **mediator** allows us to decouple the components of our system. The mediator is the middleman between colleagues, and it served us well in the small chat room samples where each colleague can talk to the others without knowing how and without knowing them.

Now let's see how the Mediator pattern can help us follow the **SOLID** principles:

- S: The mediator extracts the communication responsibility from colleagues.
- O: With a mediator relaying the messages, we can create new colleagues and change the existing colleagues' behaviors without impacting the others. If we need a new colleague, we can register one with the mediator.
- L: N/A
- I: The Mediator pattern divides the system into multiple small interfaces (`IMediator` and `IColleague`).

- **D**: All actors of the Mediator pattern solely depend on other interfaces. We can implement a new mediator and reuse the existing colleagues' implementations if we need new mediation behavior because of the dependency inversion.

Next, we explore CQRS through the CQS pattern, which allows us to separate commands and queries, leading to a more maintainable application. After all, all operations are queries or commands, no matter how we call them.

The CQS pattern

Command-Query Separation (**CQS**) is a design principle that clearly distinguishes between commands that change the state of an object or system and queries that return values without changing the state. CQS focuses on the simplicity and clarity of operations within a single system.

Command Query Responsibility Segregation (**CQRS**) extends the CQS concept to a broader architectural level. While CQRS inherits CQS's separation of commands and queries, it applies it across separate models for reading and writing, often resulting in distinct read and write data stores. This segregation facilitates scaling and optimizing the two operations independently, which can be especially beneficial in complex, high-demand, or distributed systems. However, that complexity can bring potential data synchronization challenges. CQRS is often paired with event sourcing and event-driven architectures. We explore that in *Chapter 19, Introduction to Microservices Architecture*.

In a nutshell, here's the high-level difference between the two:

- With CQS, we divide operations into commands and queries
- With CQRS, we apply the CQS concept to the system level by separating the models for reading and writing, potentially leading to a distributed system

In this chapter, we stick with CQS and tackle CQRS in a subsequent chapter.

Goal

The goal is to divide all operations (or requests) into two categories—commands and queries:

- **A command mutates the state of an application**. For example, creating, updating, and deleting an entity are commands. In theory, a command should not return a value. In practice, they often do, especially for optimization purposes.
- **A query reads the state of the application but never changes it**. For example, reading an order, reading your order history, and retrieving your user profile are queries.

Dividing operations into commands (mutator requests/writes) and queries (accessor requests/reads) creates a clear separation of concerns, leading us toward the SRP.

Design

There is no definite design for this, but for us, the flow of a command should look like the following:

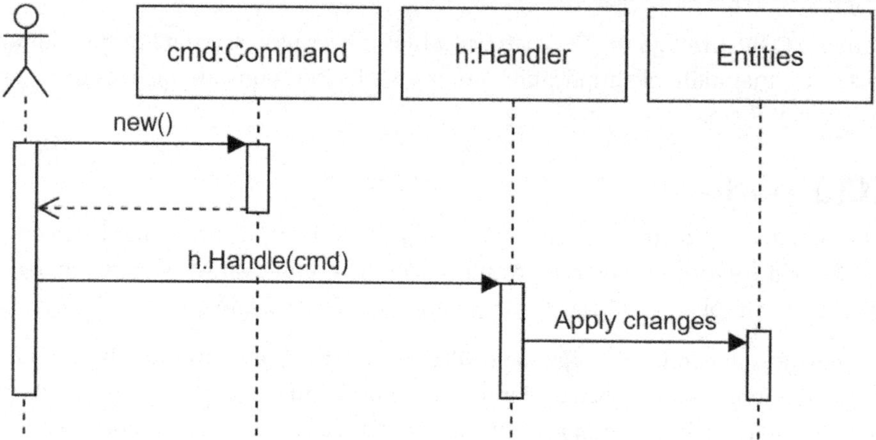

Figure 16.8: Sequence diagram representing the abstract flow of a command

The consumer creates a command object and sends it to a command handler, applying the mutation to the application. I called it `Entities` in this case, but it could have sent a SQL `UPDATE` command to a database or a web API call over HTTP; the implementation details do not matter.

The concept is the same for a query, but it returns a value instead. Very importantly, the query must not change the state of the application. A query should only read data, like this:

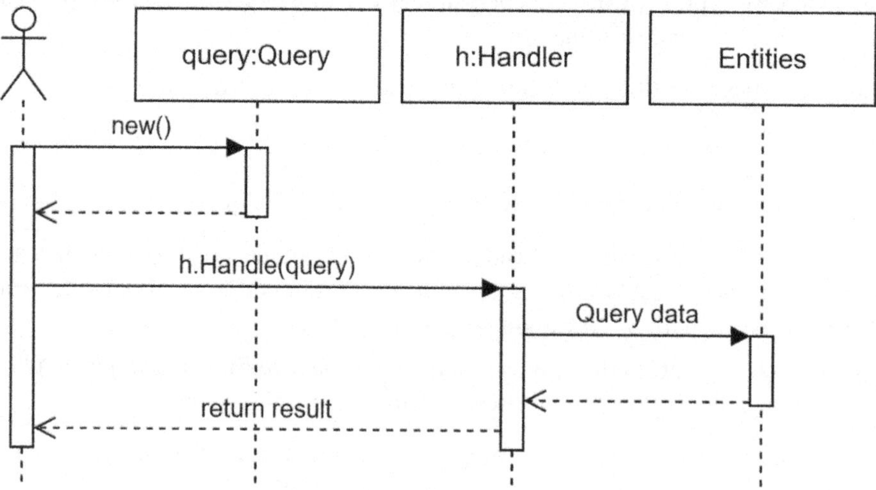

Figure 16.9: Sequence diagram representing the abstract flow of a query

Like the command, the consumer creates a query object and sends it to a handler, which then executes some logic to retrieve and return the requested data. We can replace `Entities` with anything the handler needs to query the data.

Enough talk—let's look at the CQS project.

Project – CQS

Context: We need to build an improved version of our chat system. The old system worked so well that we need to scale it up. The mediator was of help to us, so we kept that part, and we picked the CQS pattern to help us with this new, improved design. A participant was limited to a single chat room in the past, but now a participant must be able to chat in multiple rooms simultaneously.

The new system is composed of three commands and two queries:

- A participant must be able to join a chat room
- A participant must be able to leave a chat room
- A participant must be able to send a message into a chat room
- A participant must be able to obtain the list of participants that joined a chat room
- A participant must be able to retrieve the existing messages from a chat room

The first three are commands, and the last two are queries. The system is backed by the following mediator that makes heavy use of C# generics:

```
public interface IMediator
{
    TReturn Send<TQuery, TReturn>(TQuery query)
        where TQuery : IQuery<TReturn>;
    void Send<TCommand>(TCommand command)
        where TCommand : ICommand;
    void Register<TCommand>(ICommandHandler<TCommand> commandHandler)
        where TCommand : ICommand;
    void Register<TQuery, TReturn>(IQueryHandler<TQuery, TReturn>
commandHandler)
        where TQuery : IQuery<TReturn>;
}
```

If you are not familiar with generics, this might look daunting, but that code is way simpler than it looks.

You can replace the generic parameters with concrete types to help you make a mental image of generic types, transforming the abstract nature of generics into a more concrete form. For example, using the types from the code we are about to see, the query part of the `IMediator` interface would look like the following:

```
public interface IMediator
{
    IEnumerable<ChatMessage> Send(ListMessages.Query query);
    void Register(IQueryHandler<ListMessages.Query,
IEnumerable<ChatMessage>> commandHandler);
    // ...
}
```

The difference is that the generic version works for any type (`TQuery`) that implements the `IQuery<TReturn>` interface. In this case, the `ListMessages.Query` class implements the `IQuery<IEnumerable<ChatMessage>>` interface, so `TReturn` is an `IEnumerable<ChatMessage>`.

You can use this technique to design generic types as well. Start with writing one or more non-generic types or methods signatures, then extract the generic parameters from that code.

Next, the `ICommand` interface is empty, which we could have avoided, but it helps describe our intent. The `ICommandHandler` interface defines the contract that a class must implement to handle a command. That interface defines a `Handle` method that takes the command as a parameter. The generic parameter `TCommand` represents the type of command the class implementing the interface can handle. Here's the code:

```
public interface ICommand { }
public interface ICommandHandler<TCommand>
    where TCommand : ICommand
{
    void Handle(TCommand command);
}
```

The `IQuery<TReturn>` interface is similar to the `ICommand` interface but has a `TReturn` generic parameter indicating the query's return type. The `IQueryHandler` interface is also very similar, but its `Handle` method takes an object of type `TQuery` as a parameter and returns a `TReturn` type. Here's the code:

```
public interface IQuery<TReturn> { }
public interface IQueryHandler<TQuery, TReturn>
    where TQuery : IQuery<TReturn>
{
    TReturn Handle(TQuery query);
}
```

The IMediator interface allows registering command and query handlers using its Register methods. It also supports sending commands and queries through its Send methods.

Then we have the ChatMessage class, which is similar to the last two samples (with an added creation date):

```
public record class ChatMessage(IParticipant Sender, string Message)
{
    public DateTime Date { get; } = DateTime.UtcNow;
}
```

Next is the updated IParticipant interface:

```
public interface IParticipant
{
    string Name { get; }
    void Join(IChatRoom chatRoom);
    void Leave(IChatRoom chatRoom);
    void SendMessageTo(IChatRoom chatRoom, string message);
    void NewMessageReceivedFrom(IChatRoom chatRoom, ChatMessage message);
    IEnumerable<IParticipant> ListParticipantsOf(IChatRoom chatRoom);
    IEnumerable<ChatMessage> ListMessagesOf(IChatRoom chatRoom);
}
```

All methods of the IParticipant interface accept an IChatRoom parameter to support multiple chat rooms.

The updated IChatRoom interface has a name and a few basic operations to meet the requirements of a chat room, like adding and removing participants:

```
public interface IChatRoom
{
    string Name { get; }
    void Add(IParticipant participant);
    void Remove(IParticipant participant);
    IEnumerable<IParticipant> ListParticipants();
    void Add(ChatMessage message);
    IEnumerable<ChatMessage> ListMessages();
}
```

Before going into commands and the chat itself, let's take a peek at the Mediator class:

```
public class Mediator : IMediator
{
    private readonly HandlerDictionary _handlers = new();
    public void Register<TCommand>(ICommandHandler<TCommand> commandHandler)
```

```
        where TCommand : ICommand
    {
        _handlers.AddHandler(commandHandler);
    }
    public void Register<TQuery, TReturn> (IQueryHandler<TQuery, TReturn>
commandHandler)
        where TQuery : IQuery<TReturn>
    {
        _handlers.AddHandler(commandHandler);
    }
    public TReturn Send<TQuery, TReturn>(TQuery query)
        where TQuery : IQuery<TReturn>
    {
        var handler = _handlers.Find<TQuery, TReturn>();
        return handler.Handle(query);
    }
    public void Send<TCommand>(TCommand command)
        where TCommand : ICommand
    {
        var handlers = _handlers.FindAll<TCommand>();
        foreach (var handler in handlers)
        {
            handler.Handle(command);
        }
    }
}
```

The `Mediator` class supports registering commands and queries as well as sending a query to a handler or sending a command to zero or more handlers.

I omitted the implementation of `HandlerDictionary` because it does not add value to the example; it is just an implementation detail and would have added unnecessary complexity. It is available on GitHub: `https://adpg.link/2Lsm`.

Now to the commands. I grouped the commands and the handlers together to keep it organized and readable, but you could use another way to organize yours. Moreover, since this is a small project, all the commands are in the same file, which would not be viable for something bigger. Remember, we are playing LEGO® blocks; this chapter covers the CQS pieces, but you can always use them with bigger pieces like Clean Architecture or other types of architecture.

We cover ways to organize commands and queries in subsequent chapters.

Let's start with the `JoinChatRoom` feature:

```
public class JoinChatRoom
{
    public record class Command(IChatRoom ChatRoom, IParticipant Requester) :
ICommand;

    public class Handler : ICommandHandler<Command>
    {
        public void Handle(Command command)
        {
            command.ChatRoom.Add(command.Requester);
        }
    }
}
```

The `Command` class represents the command itself, a data structure that carries the command data. The `Handler` class handles that type of command. When executed, it adds the specified `IParticipant` to the specified `IChatRoom`, using the `ChatRoom` and `Requester` properties (highlighted line).

Here is the next feature:

```
public class LeaveChatRoom
{
    public record class Command(IChatRoom ChatRoom, IParticipant Requester) :
ICommand;

    public class Handler : ICommandHandler<Command>
    {
        public void Handle(Command command)
        {
            command.ChatRoom.Remove(command.Requester);
        }
    }
}
```

That code represents the exact opposite of the `JoinChatRoom` command. The `LeaveChatRoom` handler removes an `IParticipant` from the specified `IChatRoom` (highlighted line).

Nesting the classes like this allows reusing the class name `Command` and `Handler` for each feature.

Now, to the next feature:

```
public class SendChatMessage
{
    public record class Command(IChatRoom ChatRoom, ChatMessage Message) :
ICommand;

    public class Handler : ICommandHandler<Command>
    {
        public void Handle(Command command)
        {
            command.ChatRoom.Add(command.Message);
            var participants = command.ChatRoom.ListParticipants();
            foreach (var participant in participants)
            {
                participant.NewMessageReceivedFrom(
                    command.ChatRoom,
                    command.Message
                );
            }
        }
    }
}
```

This `SendChatMessage` feature, on the other hand, handles two things (highlighted lines):

- It adds the specified `Message` to `IChatRoom` (now only a data structure that keeps track of users and past messages)
- It also sends the specified `Message` to all `IParticipant` instances that joined that `IChatRoom`

We are starting to see many smaller pieces interacting with each other to create a more developed system. But we are not done; let's look at the two queries, and then the chat implementation:

```
public class ListParticipants
{
    public record class Query(IChatRoom ChatRoom, IParticipant Requester) :
IQuery<IEnumerable<IParticipant>>;

    public class Handler : IQueryHandler<Query, IEnumerable<IParticipant>>
```

```
    {
        public IEnumerable<IParticipant> Handle(Query query)
        {
            return query.ChatRoom.ListParticipants();
        }
    }
}
```

The ListParticipants handler uses the specified IChatRoom and returns its participants (highlighted line).

Now, to the last query:

```
public class ListMessages
{
    public record class Query(IChatRoom ChatRoom, IParticipant Requester) :
IQuery<IEnumerable<ChatMessage>>;

    public class Handler : IQueryHandler<Query, IEnumerable<ChatMessage>>
    {
        public IEnumerable<ChatMessage> Handle(Query query)
        {
            return query.ChatRoom.ListMessages();
        }
    }
}
```

The ListMessages handler uses the specified IChatRoom instance to return its messages.

Because all commands and queries reference IParticipant, we could enforce rules such as "IParticipant must join a channel before sending messages," for example. I decided to omit these details to keep the code simple, but feel free to add those features if you want to.

Next, let's take a look at the ChatRoom class, which is a simple data structure that holds the state of a chat room:

```
public class ChatRoom : IChatRoom
{
    private readonly List<IParticipant> _participants = new();
    private readonly List<ChatMessage> _chatMessages = new();
    public ChatRoom(string name)
    {
        Name = name ?? throw new ArgumentNullException(nameof(name));
```

```
    }
    public string Name { get; }
    public void Add(IParticipant participant)
    {
        _participants.Add(participant);
    }
    public void Add(ChatMessage message)
    {
        _chatMessages.Add(message);
    }
    public IEnumerable<ChatMessage> ListMessages()
    {
        return _chatMessages.AsReadOnly();
    }
    public IEnumerable<IParticipant> ListParticipants()
    {
        return _participants.AsReadOnly();
    }
    public void Remove(IParticipant participant)
    {
        _participants.Remove(participant);
    }
}
```

If we take a second look at the `ChatRoom` class, it has a `Name` property. It contains a list of `IParticipant` instances and a list of `ChatMessage` instances. Both `ListMessages()` and `ListParticipants()` return the list `AsReadOnly()`, so a clever programmer cannot mutate the state of `ChatRoom` from the outside. That's it; the new `ChatRoom` class is a façade over its underlying dependencies.

Finally, the `Participant` class is probably the most exciting part of this system because it is the one that makes heavy use of our mediator and CQS:

```
public class Participant : IParticipant
{
    private readonly IMediator _mediator;
    private readonly IMessageWriter _messageWriter;
    public Participant(IMediator mediator, string name, IMessageWriter
messageWriter)
    {
        _mediator = mediator ?? throw new
ArgumentNullException(nameof(mediator));
        Name = name ?? throw new ArgumentNullException(nameof(name));
```

```
        _messageWriter = messageWriter ?? throw new
ArgumentNullException(nameof(messageWriter));
    }

    public string Name { get; }

    public void Join(IChatRoom chatRoom)
    {
        _mediator.Send(new JoinChatRoom.Command(chatRoom, this));
    }
    public void Leave(IChatRoom chatRoom)
    {
        _mediator.Send(new LeaveChatRoom.Command(chatRoom, this));
    }

    public IEnumerable<ChatMessage> ListMessagesOf(IChatRoom chatRoom)
    {
        return _mediator.Send<ListMessages.Query, IEnumerable<ChatMessage>>(new
ListMessages.Query(chatRoom, this));
    }
    public IEnumerable<IParticipant> ListParticipantsOf(IChatRoom chatRoom)
    {
        return _mediator.Send<ListParticipants.Query,
IEnumerable<IParticipant>>(new ListParticipants.Query(chatRoom, this));
    }

    public void NewMessageReceivedFrom(IChatRoom chatRoom, ChatMessage message)
    {
        _messageWriter.Write(chatRoom, message);
    }
    public void SendMessageTo(IChatRoom chatRoom, string message)
    {
        _mediator.Send(new SendChatMessage.Command (chatRoom, new
ChatMessage(this, message)));
    }
}
```

Every method of the `Participant` class, apart from `NewMessageReceivedFrom`, sends a command or a query through the `IMediator` interface, breaking the tight coupling between the participants and the system's operations—the commands and queries. The `Participant` class is also a simple façade over its underlying dependencies, delegating most of the work to the mediator.

Now that we have covered the numerous tiny pieces, let's look at how everything works together. I grouped several test cases that share the following setup code:

```
public class ChatRoomTest
{
    private readonly IMediator _mediator = new Mediator();
    private readonly TestMessageWriter _reagenMessageWriter = new();
    private readonly TestMessageWriter _garnerMessageWriter = new();
    private readonly TestMessageWriter _corneliaMessageWriter = new();
    private readonly IChatRoom _room1 = new ChatRoom("Room 1");
    private readonly IChatRoom _room2 = new ChatRoom("Room 2");
    private readonly IParticipant _reagen;
    private readonly IParticipant _garner;
    private readonly IParticipant _cornelia;
    public ChatRoomTest()
    {
        _mediator.Register(new JoinChatRoom.Handler());
        _mediator.Register(new LeaveChatRoom.Handler());
        _mediator.Register(new SendChatMessage.Handler());
        _mediator.Register(new ListParticipants.Handler());
        _mediator.Register(new ListMessages.Handler());
        _reagen = new Participant(_mediator, "Reagen", _reagenMessageWriter);
        _garner = new Participant(_mediator, "Garner", _garnerMessageWriter);
        _cornelia = new Participant(_mediator, "Cornelia", _
corneliaMessageWriter);
    }
    // Omited test cases and helpers
}
```

The test program setup is composed of the following:

- One `IMediator` field initialized with a `Mediator` instance, which enables all colleagues to interact with each other.
- Two `IChatRoom` fields initialized with `ChatRoom` instances.
- Three `IParticipant` uninitialized fields, later initialized with `Participant` instances.

- Three `TestMessageWriter` instances, one per participant.
- The constructor, which registers all handlers with the `Mediator` instance so it knows how to handle commands and queries. It also creates the participants.

Once again, the names of the participants are randomly generated.

The `TestMessageWriter` implementation is a little different and accumulates the data in a list of tuples (`List<(IChatRoom, ChatMessage)>`) to assess what the participants send:

```
private class TestMessageWriter : IMessageWriter
{
    public List<(IChatRoom chatRoom, ChatMessage message)> Output { get; } =
new();
    public void Write(IChatRoom chatRoom, ChatMessage message)
    {
        Output.Add((chatRoom, message));
    }
}
```

Here is the first test case:

```
[Fact]
public void A_participant_should_be_able_to_list_the_participants_that_
joined_a_chatroom()
{
    _reagen.Join(_room1);
    _reagen.Join(_room2);
    _garner.Join(_room1);
    _cornelia.Join(_room2);
    var room1Participants = _reagen.ListParticipantsOf(_room1);
    Assert.Collection(room1Participants,
        p => Assert.Same(_reagen, p),
        p => Assert.Same(_garner, p)
    );
}
```

In the preceding test case, Reagen and Garner join Room 1, while Reagen and Cornelia join Room 2. Then Reagen requests the list of participants from Room 1, which outputs Reagen and Garner.

Under the hood, it uses commands and queries through a mediator, breaking tight coupling between colleagues. Here is a sequence diagram representing what happens when a participant joins a chat room:

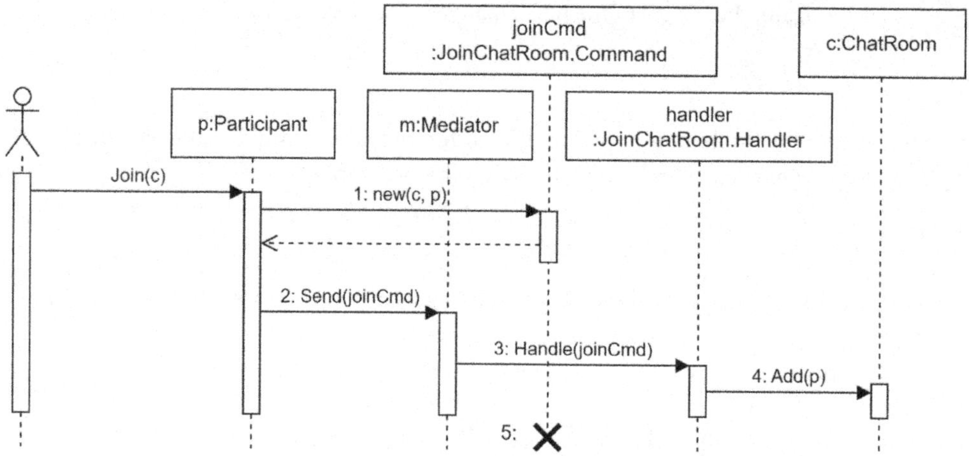

Figure 16.10: Sequence diagram representing the flow of a participant (p) joining a chatroom (c)

The preceding diagram showcases a participant (`p`) joining a chat room (`c`). Here's the explanation of this flow:

1. The participant (`p`) creates a `JoinChatRoom` command (`joinCmd`).
2. `p` sends `joinCmd` through the mediator (`m`).
3. `m` finds and dispatches `joinCmd` to its handler (`handler`).
4. `handler` executes the logic (adds `p` to the chat room).
5. `joinCmd` ceases to exist afterward; commands are ephemeral.

That means `Participant` never interacts directly with `ChatRoom` or other participants.

Then a similar workflow happens when a participant requests the list of participants of a chat room:

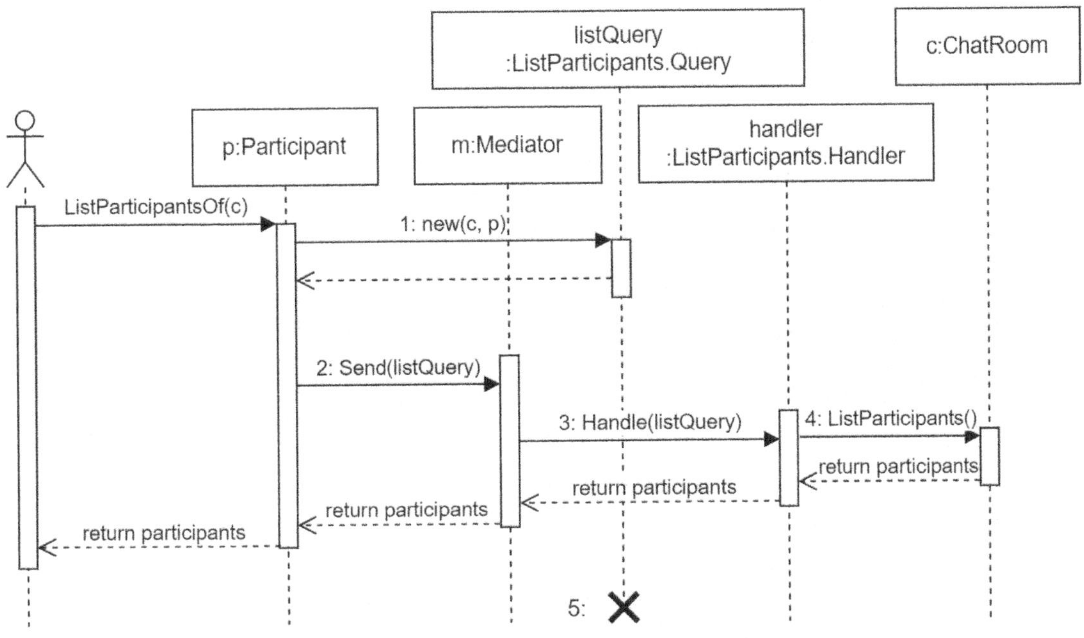

Figure 16.11: Sequence diagram representing the flow of a participant (p) requesting the list of participants of a chatroom (c)

1. `Participant` (`p`) creates a `ListParticipants` query (`listQuery`).
2. `p` sends `listQuery` through the mediator (`m`).
3. `m` finds and dispatches the query to its handler (`handler`).
4. `handler` executes the logic (lists the participants of the chat room).
5. `listQuery` ceases to exist afterward; queries are also ephemeral.

Once again, `Participant` does not interact directly with `ChatRoom`.

Here is another test case where one `Participant` sends a message to a chat room, and another `Participant` receives it:

```
[Fact]
public void A_participant_should_receive_new_messages()
{
    _reagen.Join(_room1);
```

```
        _garner.Join(_room1);
        _reagen.SendMessageTo(_room1, "Hello!");
        Assert.Collection(_garnerMessageWriter.Output,
        line =>
        {
            Assert.Equal(_room1, line.chatRoom);
            Assert.Equal(_reagen, line.message.Sender);
            Assert.Equal("Hello!", line.message.Message);
        }
    );
}
```

In the preceding test case, Reagen and Garner join Room 1, then Reagen sends a message to Room 1, and we verify that Garner receives it once.

The `SendMessageTo` workflow is very similar to the other one that we saw but with a more complex command handler:

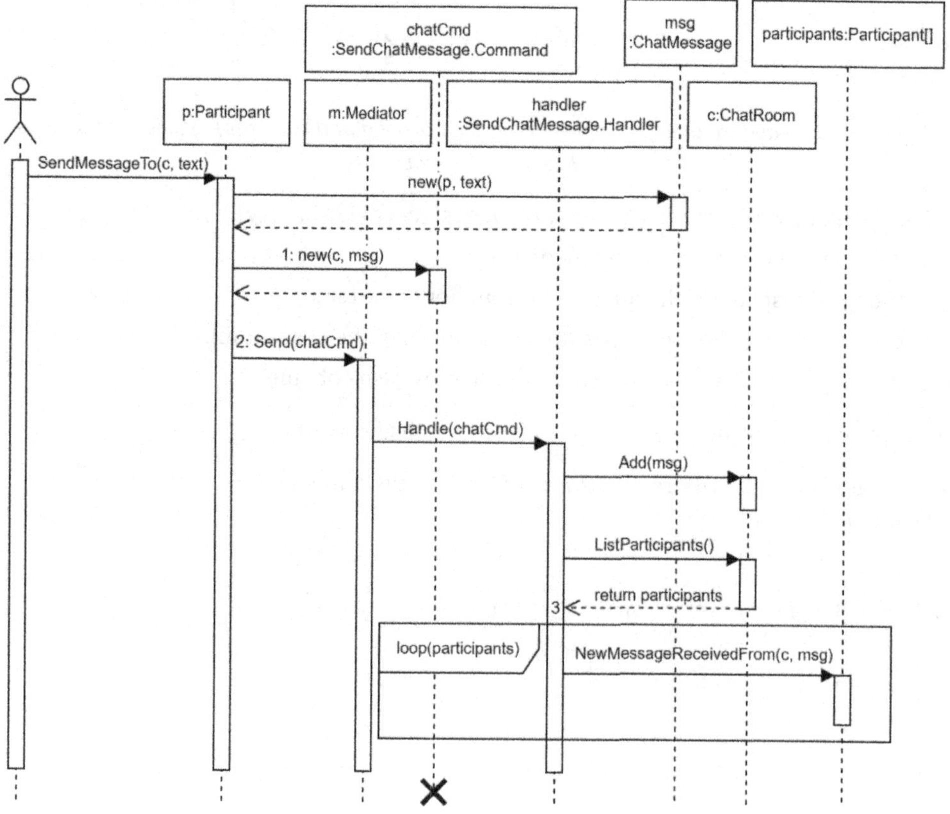

Figure 16.12: Sequence diagram representing the flow of a participant (p) sending a message (msg) to a chatroom (c)

From that diagram, we can observe that we pushed the logic to the `Handler` class of the `SendChatMessage` feature. All the other actors work together with limited to no knowledge of each other.

This demonstrates how CQS works with a mediator:

1. A consumer (the participant in this case) creates a command (or a query).
2. The consumer sends that command through the mediator.
3. The mediator sends that command to one or more handlers, each executing their piece of logic for that command.

You can explore the other test cases to familiarize yourself with the program and the concepts.

You can debug the tests in Visual Studio from the Test Explorer window. Like any code you are debugging, you can use breakpoints combined with *Step Into* (*F11*) and *Step Over* (*F10*) to explore the sample.

I also created a `ChatModerator` instance that sends a message in a "moderator chat room" when a message contains a word from the `badWords` collection. That test case executes multiple handlers for each `SendChatMessage.Command`. I'll leave you to explore these other test cases yourself so we don't wander astray from our goal.

Conclusion

The CQS and CQRS patterns suggest dividing the operations of a program into **commands** and **queries**. A command mutates data, and a query fetches data. We can apply the **Mediator** pattern to break the tight coupling between the pieces of a program using CQS, like sending commands and queries.

Dividing the program this way helps separate the different pieces and focus on the commands and queries that travel from a consumer through the mediator to one or more handlers. The data contract of commands and queries becomes the program's backbone, trimming down the coupling between objects and tying them to those thin data structures instead, leaving the central piece (the mediator) to manage the links between them.

On the other hand, you may find the codebase more intimidating when using CQS due to the multiple classes. It adds some complexity, especially for a small program like this. However, each type does less (having a single responsibility), making it easier to test than a more sizable class with many responsibilities.

Now let's see how CQS can help us follow the **SOLID** principles:

- S: Dividing an application into commands, queries, and handlers takes us toward encapsulating single responsibilities into different classes.
- O: CQS helps extend the software without modifying the existing code, such as adding handlers and creating new commands.
- L: N/A

- **I:** CQS makes it easier to create multiple small interfaces with a clear distinction between commands, queries, and their respective handlers.
- **D:** N/A

Now that we have explored CQS and the Mediator pattern, we explore the Marker Interfaces code smell.

Code smell – Marker Interfaces

We used the empty `ICommand` and `IQuery<TReturn>` interfaces in the project code samples to make the code more explicit and self-descriptive. However, empty interfaces are a sign that something may be wrong: a code smell. We call those **marker interfaces** because they mark a type for some purpose instead of defining APIs.

They may suggest an overly complicated design or misuse of object-oriented principles, reflecting an approach that favors tagging classes over more explicit or meaningful design choices. While interfaces play an integral role in defining contracts and enabling polymorphism, empty marker interfaces can obscure the purpose of a class and erode type safety by not conveying clear intentions or behaviors.

In our case, they help identify commands and queries but are empty and add nothing. We could discard them without any impact on our system. On the other hand, we are not performing magic tricks or violating any principles, so they don't harm but, rather, help define the intent. Moreover, we could leverage them to make the code more dynamic, like leveraging dependency injection to register handlers. Furthermore, I designed those interfaces this way as a bridge to the next project.

There are two types of marker interfaces that are code smells in C#:

- Metadata
- Dependency identifier

Metadata

Markers can be used to define metadata. A class "implements" the empty interface, and some consumer does something with it later. It could be an assembly scanning for specific types, a choice of strategy, or something else.

Instead of creating marker interfaces to add metadata, try to use custom attributes. The idea behind attributes is to add metadata to classes and their members. On the other hand, interfaces exist to create a contract, and they should define at least one member; empty contracts are like a blank sheet.

In a real-world scenario, you may want to consider the cost of one versus the other. Markers are very cheap to implement but can violate architectural principles. Attributes can be as cheap to implement if the mechanism is already in place or supported by the framework but can cost much more than a marker interface, depending on the scenario. Moreover, attributes are usually accessed through reflection, which brings a performance overhead and can cause issues with AOT compilation. Before deciding, I recommend you evaluate the cost of both options.

Dependency identifier

If you need markers to inject some specific dependency in a particular class, you are most likely cheating the **Inversion of Control** (**IoC**) principle. Instead, you should find a way to achieve the same goal using dependency injection, such as by contextually injecting your dependencies.

The code sample below showcases a `Consumer` class that accepts two dependencies on the `IStrategy` interface but cheats IoC by creating two sub-interfaces—`IStrategyA` and `IStrategyB`—and injecting those instead. Afterward, we explore how to fix this problem and move back control over the dependencies from the `Consumer` class to the composition root.

Let's start with the following interface:

```
public interface IStrategy
{
    string Execute();
}
```

In our program, we have two implementations and two markers, one for each implementation:

```
public interface IStrategyA : IStrategy { }
public interface IStrategyB : IStrategy { }
public class StrategyA : IStrategyA
{
    public string Execute() => "StrategyA";
}
public class StrategyB : IStrategyB
{
    public string Execute() => "StrategyB";
}
```

The code is barebones, but all the building blocks are there:

- `StrategyA` implements `IStrategyA`, which inherits from `IStrategy`.
- `StrategyB` implements `IStrategyB`, which inherits from `IStrategy`.
- Both `IStrategyA` and `IStrategyB` are empty marker interfaces.

Now, the consumer needs to use both strategies, so instead of controlling dependencies from the composition root, the consumer requests the markers:

```
public class Consumer
{
    public IStrategyA StrategyA { get; }
    public IStrategyB StrategyB { get; }
    public Consumer(IStrategyA strategyA, IStrategyB strategyB)
```

```
    {
        StrategyA = strategyA ?? throw new
ArgumentNullException(nameof(strategyA));
        StrategyB = strategyB ?? throw new
ArgumentNullException(nameof(strategyB));
    }
}
```

The Consumer class exposes the strategies through properties to assess its composition later.

Let's test that out by building a dependency tree, simulating the composition root, and then assessing the value of the consumer properties:

```
[Fact]
public void ConsumerTest()
{
    // Arrange
    var serviceProvider = new ServiceCollection()
        .AddSingleton<IStrategyA, StrategyA>()
        .AddSingleton<IStrategyB, StrategyB>()
        .AddSingleton<Consumer>()
        .BuildServiceProvider();
    // Act
    var consumer = serviceProvider.GetRequiredService<Consumer>();
    // Assert
    Assert.IsType<StrategyA>(consumer.StrategyA);
    Assert.IsType<StrategyB>(consumer.StrategyB);
}
```

Both properties are of the expected type, but that is not the problem. The Consumer class controls what dependencies to use and when to use them by injecting markers A and B instead of two IStrategy instances. Due to that, we cannot control the dependency tree from the composition root. For example, we cannot change IStrategyA to IStrategyB and IStrategyB to IStrategyA, nor inject two IStrategyB instances or two IStrategyA instances, nor even create an IStrategyC interface to replace IStrategyA or IStrategyB.

How do we fix this? Let's start by deleting our markers and injecting two IStrategy instances instead (the changes are highlighted). After doing that, we end up with the following object structure:

```
public class StrategyA : IStrategy
{
    public string Execute() => "StrategyA";
}
public class StrategyB : IStrategy
```

```
{
    public string Execute() => "StrategyB";
}
public class Consumer
{
    public IStrategy StrategyA { get; }
    public IStrategy StrategyB { get; }
    public Consumer(IStrategy strategyA, IStrategy strategyB)
    {
        StrategyA = strategyA ?? throw new
ArgumentNullException(nameof(strategyA));
        StrategyB = strategyB ?? throw new
ArgumentNullException(nameof(strategyB));
    }
}
```

The `Consumer` class no longer controls the narrative with the new implementation, and the composition responsibility falls back to the composition root.

Unfortunately, there is no way to do contextual injections using the default dependency injection container, and I don't want to get into a third-party library for this. But all is not lost yet; we can use a factory to help ASP.NET Core build the `Consumer` instance, like this:

```
// Arrange
var serviceProvider = new ServiceCollection()
    .AddSingleton<StrategyA>()
    .AddSingleton<StrategyB>()
    .AddSingleton(serviceProvider =>
    {
        var strategyA = serviceProvider.GetRequiredService<StrategyA>();
        var strategyB = serviceProvider.GetRequiredService<StrategyB>();
        return new Consumer(strategyA, strategyB);
    })
    .BuildServiceProvider();
// Act
var consumer = serviceProvider.GetRequiredService<Consumer>();
// Assert
Assert.IsType<StrategyA>(consumer.StrategyA);
Assert.IsType<StrategyB>(consumer.StrategyB);
```

From this point forward, we control the program's composition, and we can swap A with B or do anything else that we want to, as long as the implementation respects the `IStrategy` contract.

To conclude, using markers instead of doing contextual injection breaks the IoC principle, making the consumer control its dependencies. That's very close to using the `new` keyword to instantiate objects. Inverting the dependency control back is easy, even using the default container.

If you need to inject dependencies contextually, I started an open source project in 2020 that does that. Multiple other third-party libraries add features or replace the default IoC container altogether if needed. See the *Further reading* section.

The next section showcases an open source tool that can help us build CQS-oriented applications.

Using MediatR as a mediator

In this section, we are exploring MediatR, an open source mediator implementation.

What is MediatR? Let's start with its maker's description from its GitHub repository:

> *"Simple, unambitious mediator implementation in .NET"*

MediatR is a simple but very powerful tool doing in-process communication through messaging. It supports a request/response flow through commands, queries, notifications, and events, synchronously and asynchronously.

We can install the NuGet package using the .NET CLI: `dotnet add package MediatR`.

Now that I have quickly introduced the tool, we are going to explore the migration of our Clean Architecture sample but, instead, use MediatR to dispatch the `StocksController` requests to the core use cases. We use a similar pattern with MediatR to what we built in the CQS project.

Why migrate our Clean Architecture sample? The primary reason we are building the same project using different models is for ease of comparison. It is much easier to compare the changes of the same features than if we were building completely different projects.

What are the advantages of using MediatR in this case? It allows us to organize the code around use cases (vertically) instead of services (horizontally), leading to more cohesive features. We remove the service layer (the `StockService` class) and replace it with multiple use cases (features) instead (the `AddStocks` and `RemoveStock` classes).

MediatR also enables a pipeline that we can extend by programming behaviors. Those extensibility points allow us to manage cross-cutting concerns, such as request validation centrally, without impacting the consumers and use cases. We explore request validation in *Chapter 17, Getting Started with Vertical Slice Architecture.*

Let's jump into the code to see how it works.

Project – Clean Architecture with MediatR

Context: We want to break some more of the coupling in the Clean Architecture project we built in *Chapter 14, Layering and Clean Architecture*, by leveraging the **Mediator** pattern and a **CQS** approach.

The Clean Architecture solution was already solid, but MediatR will pave the way to more good things later. The only "major" change is the replacement of the `StockService` with two feature objects, `AddStocks` and `RemoveStocks`, which we explore soon.

First, we must install the `MediatR` NuGet package in the `Core` project, where the features will live. Moreover, it will transiently cascade to the `Web` project, allowing us to register MediatR with the IoC container.

In the `Program.cs` file, we can register MediatR like this:

```
builder.Services
    // Core Layer
    .AddMediatR(cfg => cfg.
RegisterServicesFromAssemblyContaining<NotEnoughStockException>())
;
```

That code scans the `Core` assembly for MediatR-compatible pieces and registers them with the IoC container. The `NotEnoughStockException` class is part of the core project.

I picked the `NotEnoughStockException` class but could have chosen any class from the `Core` assembly.

MediatR exposes the following types of messages (as of version 12):

- *Request/response* that has one handler; perfect for commands and queries
- *Notifications* that support multiple handlers; perfect for an event-based model applying the Publish-Subscribe pattern where a notification represents an event
- *Request/response streams* that are similar to request/response but stream the response through the `IAsyncEnumerable<T>` interface

We cover the Publish-Subscribe pattern in *Chapter 19, Introduction to Microservices Architecture.*

Now that everything we need related to MediatR is "magically" registered, we can look at the use cases that replace the `StockService`. Let's have a look at the updated `AddStocks` code first:

```
namespace Core.UseCases;
public class AddStocks
{
    public class Command : IRequest<int>
    {
        public int ProductId { get; set; }
        public int Amount { get; set; }
    }
    public class Handler : IRequestHandler<Command, int>
    {
        private readonly IProductRepository _productRepository;
        public Handler(IProductRepository productRepository)
        {
            _productRepository = productRepository ?? throw new
ArgumentNullException(nameof(productRepository));
        }
        public async Task<int> Handle(Command request, CancellationToken
cancellationToken)
        {
            var product = await _productRepository.FindByIdAsync(request.
ProductId, cancellationToken);
            if (product == null)
            {
                throw new ProductNotFoundException(request.ProductId);
            }
            product.AddStock(request.Amount);
            await _productRepository.UpdateAsync(product, cancellationToken);
            return product.QuantityInStock;
        }
    }
}
```

Since we covered both use cases in the previous chapters and the changes are very similar, we will analyze both together, after the `RemoveStocks` use case code:

```
namespace Core.UseCases;
public class RemoveStocks
{
    public class Command : IRequest<int>
    {
```

```
            public int ProductId { get; set; }
            public int Amount { get; set; }
        }
        public class Handler : IRequestHandler<Command, int>
        {
            private readonly IProductRepository _productRepository;
            public Handler(IProductRepository productRepository)
            {
                _productRepository = productRepository ?? throw new
    ArgumentNullException(nameof(productRepository));
            }
            public async Task<int> Handle(Command request, CancellationToken
    cancellationToken)
            {
                var product = await _productRepository.FindByIdAsync(request.
    ProductId, cancellationToken);
                if (product == null)
                {
                    throw new ProductNotFoundException(request.ProductId);
                }
                product.RemoveStock(request.Amount);
                await _productRepository.UpdateAsync(product, cancellationToken);
                return product.QuantityInStock;
            }
        }
    }
```

As you may have noticed in the code, I chose the same pattern to build the commands as I did with the CQS sample, so we have a class per use case containing two nested classes: `Command` and `Handler`. This structure makes for very clean code when you have a 1-on-1 relationship between the command class and its handler.

Using the MediatR request/response model, the command (or query) becomes a request and must implement the `IRequest<TResponse>` interface. The handlers must implement the `IRequestHandler<TRequest, TResponse>` interface.

Instead, when a command returns nothing (`void`), we must implement the `IRequest` and `IRequestHandler<TRequest>` interfaces, in which you don't specify the returned type.

More options are part of MediatR, and the documentation is complete enough to dig deeper yourself.

Let's analyze the anatomy of the AddStocks use case. Here is the old code as a reference:

```
namespace Core.Services;
public class StockService
{
    private readonly IProductRepository _repository;
    // Omitted constructor
    public async Task<int> AddStockAsync(int productId, int amount,
CancellationToken cancellationToken)
    {
        var product = await _repository.FindByIdAsync(productId,
cancellationToken);
        if (product == null)
        {
            throw new ProductNotFoundException(productId);
        }
        product.AddStock(amount);
        await _repository.UpdateAsync(product, cancellationToken);
        return product.QuantityInStock;
    }
    // Omitted RemoveStockAsync method
}
```

The first difference is that we moved the loose parameters (highlighted) into the Command class, which encapsulates the whole request:

```
public class Command : IRequest<int>
{
    public int ProductId { get; set; }
    public int Amount { get; set; }
}
```

Then the Command class specifies the handler's expected return value by implementing the IRequest<TResponse> interface, where TResponse is an int. That gives us a typed response when sending the request through MediatR. This is not "pure CQS" because the command handler returns an integer representing the updated QuantityInStock. However, we could call that optimization since executing one command and one query would be overkill for this scenario (possibly leading to two database calls instead of one).

I'll skip the RemoveStocks use case to avoid repeating myself, as it follows the same pattern. Instead, let's look at the consumption of those use cases. I omitted the exception handling to keep the code streamlined and because try/catch blocks would only add noise to the code in this case and hinder our study of the pattern:

```
app.MapPost("/products/{productId:int}/add-stocks", async (
```

```
    int productId,
    AddStocks.Command command,
    IMediator mediator,
    CancellationToken cancellationToken) =>
{
    command.ProductId = productId;
    var quantityInStock = await mediator.Send(command, cancellationToken);
    var stockLevel = new StockLevel(quantityInStock);
    return Results.Ok(stockLevel);
});
app.MapPost("/products/{productId:int}/remove-stocks", async (
    int productId,
    RemoveStocks.Command command,
    IMediator mediator,
    CancellationToken cancellationToken) =>
{
    command.ProductId = productId;
    var quantityInStock = await mediator.Send(command, cancellationToken);
    var stockLevel = new StockLevel(quantityInStock);
    return Results.Ok(stockLevel);
});
// Omitted code
public record class StockLevel(int QuantityInStock);
```

In both delegates, we inject an `IMediator` and a command object (highlighted). We also let ASP.NET Core inject a `CancellationToken`, which we pass to MediatR. The model binder loads the data from the HTTP request into the objects that we send using the `Send` method of the `IMediator` interface (highlighted). Then we map the result into the `StockLevel` DTO before returning its value with an HTTP status code of `200 OK`. The `StockLevel` record class is the same as before.

This example contains almost the same code as our CQS example, but we used MediatR instead of manually programming the pieces.

The default model binder cannot load data from multiple sources. Because of that, we must inject `productId` and assign its value to the `command.ProductId` property manually. Even if both values could be taken from the body, the resource identifier of that endpoint would become less exhaustive (no `productId` in the URI).

With MVC, we could create a custom model binder.

With minimal APIs, we could create a static `BindAsync` method to manually do the model binding, which is not very extensible and would tightly couple the `Core` assembly with the `HttpContext`. I suppose we will need to wait for .NET 9+ to get improvements into that field.

I've left a few links in the *Further reading* section relating to this.

With MediatR, we could configure more interaction between the command and the handler with `IRequestPreProcessor`, `IRequestPostProcessor`, and `IRequestExceptionHandler`. These allow us to extend the MediatR request pipeline with cross-cutting concerns like validation and error handling.

The only arguable drawback of the overall design, which has nothing to do with MediatR, is that we used the commands as the DTOs. We could create DTOs and map them to command objects. However, you will understand in the next chapter where I was heading with this transitory design.

Summary

In this chapter, we looked at the Mediator pattern, which allows us to cut the ties between collaborators, mediating the communication between them. Then we studied the CQS pattern, which advises the division of software behaviors into commands and queries. Those two patterns are tools that cut tight coupling between components.

Afterward, we packed the power of a CQS-inspired pipeline with the Mediator pattern into a Clean Architecture application that uses MediatR, an open source library. We broke the coupling between the request delegates and the use case handler (previously a service). A simple DTO, such as a command object, makes endpoints and controllers unaware of the handlers, leaving MediatR as the middleman between the commands and their handlers. Due to that, the handlers could change along the way without impacting the endpoint.

This concludes another chapter exploring techniques to break tight coupling and divide systems into smaller parts. All those building blocks lead us to the next chapter, where we piece those patterns and tools together to explore Vertical Slice Architecture.

Questions

Let's take a look at a few practice questions:

1. What does CQS stand for, and what is the purpose of this design pattern?
2. Can we use a mediator inside a colleague to call another colleague?
3. In CQS, can a command return a value?
4. How much does MediatR cost?
5. Imagine a design with a marker interface to add metadata to some classes. Do you think you should review that design?

Further reading

Here are a few links to build on what we have learned in the chapter:

- MediatR: `https://adpg.link/ZQap`
- To get rid of setting `ProductId` manually in the Clean Architecture with MediatR project, you can use the open source project `HybridModelBinding` or read the official documentation about custom model binding and implement your own:
    a. Custom Model Binding in ASP.NET Core: `https://adpg.link/65pb`
    b. Damian Edward's MinimalApis.Extensions project on GitHub: `https://adpg.link/M6zS`
- `ForEvolve.DependencyInjection` is an open source project that adds support for contextual dependency injection and more: `https://adpg.link/myW8`

Answers

1. CQS stands for Command-Query Separation. It's a software design principle that separates operations that change the state of an object (commands) from those that return data (queries). This helps in minimizing side effects and preventing unexpected changes in program behavior.
2. Yes, you can. The goal of the Mediator pattern is to mediate communication between colleagues.
3. In the original sense of CQS, no, a command can't return a value. The idea is that a query reads data while commands mutate data. A command can return a value in a looser sense of CQS. For example, nothing stops a create command from returning the created entity partially or totally. You can always trade a bit of modularity for a bit of performance.
4. MediatR is a free, open source project licensed under Apache License 2.0.
5. Yes, you should. Using marker interfaces to add metadata is generally wrong. Nevertheless, you should analyze each use case individually, considering the pros and cons before jumping to a conclusion.

Learn more on Discord

To join the Discord community for this book – where you can share feedback, ask questions to the author, and learn about new releases – follow the QR code below:

`https://packt.link/ArchitectingASPNETCoreApps3e`

Further reading

17

Getting Started with Vertical Slice Architecture

This chapter introduces Vertical Slice Architecture, an effective way to organize our ASP.NET Core applications. Vertical Slice Architecture moves elements from multiple layers to a feature-oriented design, helping us maintain a clean, simple, cohesive, loosely coupled, and manageable codebase.

Vertical Slice Architecture flips our architectural perspective toward simplified architecture. Historically, we divided the logic of a feature across various layers like UI, business logic, and data access. With Vertical Slice Architecture, we create independent slices of functionality instead. Think of your application as a rectangular cake; instead of cutting it horizontally (layers), we're cutting vertically (features), with each slice being fully functional on its own.

This style changes how we design and organize our project, testing strategies, and coding approach. We don't have to worry about bloated controllers or overly complicated "God objects"; instead, making changes becomes more manageable because of the loose coupling between features.

This chapter guides you through applying Vertical Slice Architecture to your ASP.NET Core applications, detailing how to handle commands, queries, validation, and entity mapping using CQS, MVC, MediatR, AutoMapper, and FluentValidation, which we explored in the previous chapters.

We don't have to use those tools to apply the architectural style and can replace those libraries with others or even code the whole stack ourselves. I chose this set of libraries because it is well-known and used for this type of architecture. We use a different approach in *Chapter 18, Request-EndPoint-Response (REPR)*, removing MediatR, replacing AutoMapper with Mapperly, and replacing MVC with Minimal APIs.

In this chapter, we cover Vertical Slice Architecture. By the end of the chapter, you will understand Vertical Slice Architecture and its benefits and should have the confidence to apply this style to your next project.

Let's journey through the vertical slices and piece the architecture together, one slice at a time.

Vertical Slice Architecture

Instead of separating an application horizontally (layers), a vertical slice encapsulates all horizontal concerns within a single feature scope. Here is a diagram that illustrates that:

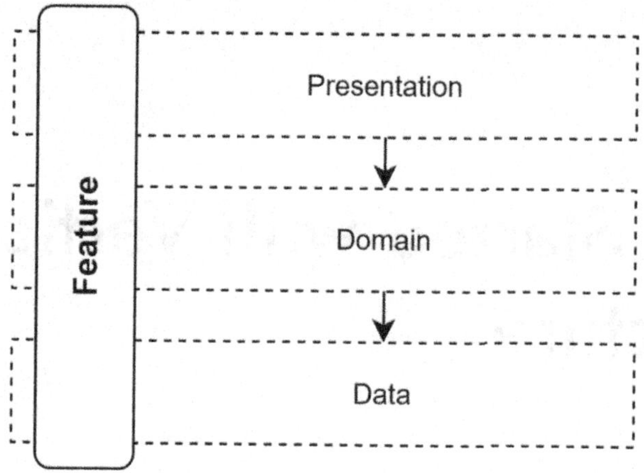

Figure 17.1: Diagram representing a vertical slice crossing all layers

Jimmy Bogard, who is a pioneer and proponent of this type of architecture, wrote the following:

> *"[The goal is to] minimize coupling between slices and maximize coupling within a slice."*

What does that mean? Let's split that sentence into two distinct points:

- "minimize coupling between slices" (improved maintainability, loose coupling)
- "maximize coupling within a slice" (cohesion)

We could see the former as saying that one vertical slice should not depend on another, so when you modify a vertical slice, you don't have to worry about the impact on the other slices because the coupling is minimal.

We could see the latter as saying that, instead of spreading code around multiple layers, with potentially superfluous abstractions along the way, let's regroup and simplify that code. That helps keep the tight coupling inside a vertical slice to create a cohesive unit of code that serves a single purpose: handling the feature end to end.

With Vertical Slice Architecture, we want to create applications for the business problem we are trying to solve instead of the developer's concerns we are used to seeing. The users have no interest in data access code, for example, but care about that new advanced search feature they are waiting for. Here's an example that showcases a few example features (slices):

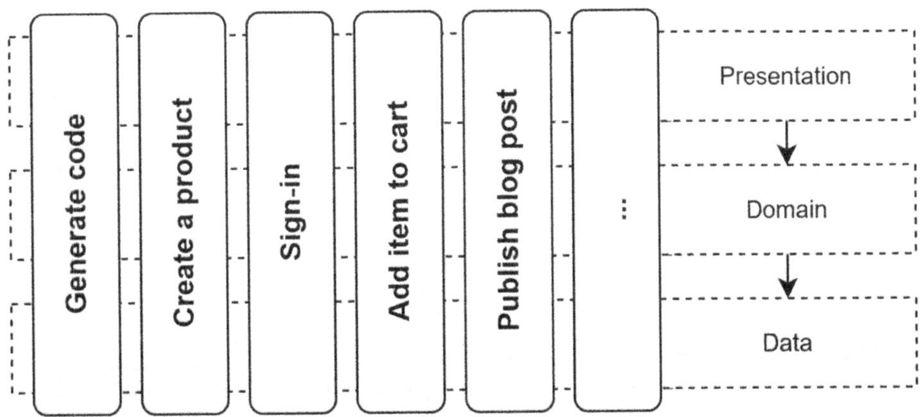

Figure 17.2: A few features (vertical slices) crossing the Presentation, Domain, and Data layers

A slice is a feature encompassing all the responsibilities it requires to operate. Yet, real life is rarely that simple, so in a more complex scenario, a slice is a feature that can be part of a hierarchy of dependencies where multiple slices can share components (coupling) from the broader feature or set of features.

Of course, the dream remains that each slice is 100% autonomous and does not depend on anything other than its own code. However, that does not often happen in the real world, so the key is to keep that dream alive by ensuring the code a slice depends on—not unique to the slice—is as close to the slice as possible; proximity can be seen as cohesion here.

To achieve that, it is best to start by writing the code for the feature (unique to the feature), then refactor that code into reusable pieces if needs emerge later, instead of creating complex abstractions or layers up front. The goal is to write business value code up front (a.k.a., working features) and deliver as much value to the users as possible, as fast as possible, while keeping the quality high by refactoring the system as it grows.

Delivering value fast does not mean skipping planning, analysis, architecture, or other phases. It means developing features one by one, including planning, analysis, and architecture. It is important to remember that we cannot ship a layer or a diagram to users, but we can ship a feature.

Let's use a shipping management program as a more complex example. The program has a multistep creation workflow, a list, and a details page. Each step of the creation flow is a slice responsible for handling its respective logic. The creation flow can be paused at any time and resumed later, so our system is more than a simple "create shipment feature."

Let's start with a diagram that represents this example:

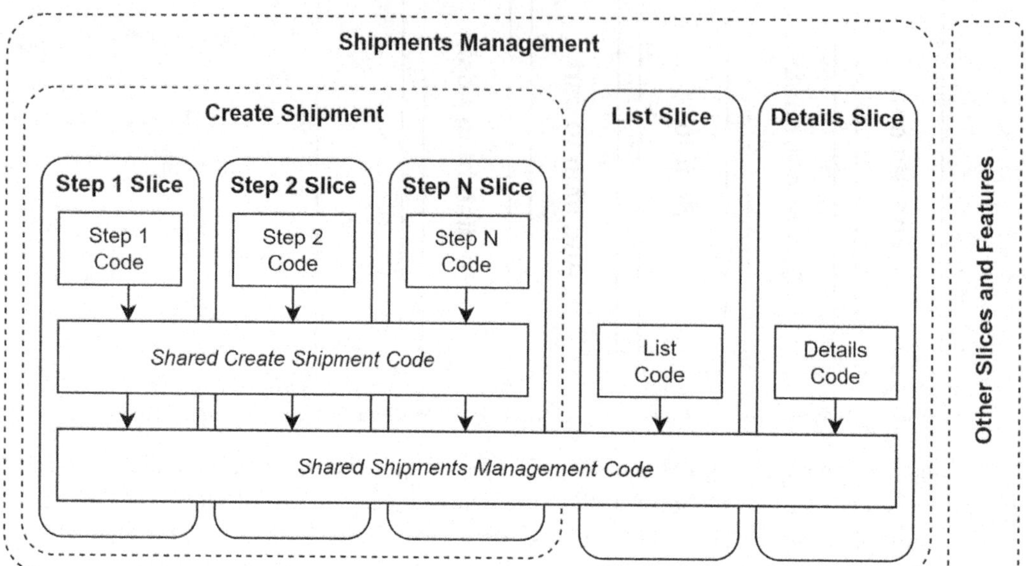

Figure 17.3: A top-down code coupling structure where smaller parts (top) depend on bigger parts (middle) of the broader feature (bottom) based on their cohesion with one another (vertically)

Based on the preceding diagram, **Step 1 Slice** is an independent feature that potentially shares some building blocks with **Step 2 Slice** and **Step N Slice**. When put together, they compose the **Create Shipment** feature, which is responsible for creating a shipment. *Shared Create Shipment Code* represents classes to orchestrate the creation flow, manage the creation process's state, and help with routing the user to the correct step. In a nutshell, it contains code that crosses each individual step's boundary or is used by more than one step. Those shared classes should be limited to use inside the **Create Shipment** flow to limit cross-feature coupling and keep cohesion high within the feature. Moreover, most of that shared code could have been coded in the steps and refactored out when the team noticed the code duplication or the opportunity to encapsulate and reuse the shared logic. Strong automated tests will tremendously help perform this exercise efficiently.

If we continue to explore the diagram in *Figure 17.3*, the **List Slice** and **Details Slice** are two other distinct features. As the diagram shows, all those features could share some building blocks—like the shipment domain model—represented by the *Shared Shipments Management Code* layer. Nevertheless, the **List Slice** should be loosely coupled with the **Create Shipment** slices and the **Details Slice**.

Let's explore the cohesion and coupling relationship of the elements of *Figure 17.3*. To start, there is strong coupling inside the *Step 1 Code*, with no coupling with the code of the other steps. The same for *Step 2 Code* and *Step N Code*. All steps share some of the *Shared Create Shipment Code*, creating coupling between the steps while keeping the cohesion high around the **Create Shipment** feature. **Create Shipment**, **List Slice**, and **Details Slice** also share some code from the *Shared Shipments Management Code*, creating some coupling between the features, while focusing the cohesion on the **Shipments Management** business capability.

For example, all slices that are part of **Shipments Management** can access or manipulate the same entities: shipments. Finally, the **Shipments Management** feature shares no code with **Other Slices and Features**.

Of course, chances are there will be shared code that crosses the entire application. The key is to have as little as possible of that kind of code and ensure the vertical slices are not tightly coupled with it. For example, creating a Minimal API or MVC filter to handle a cross-cutting concern—like error handling—does not create tight coupling with the slices because the slices are not aware of that code On the other hand, creating a class that every slice directly uses tightly couples them with that component.

The next diagram depicts what we just explored and represents the relationship between coupling, cohesion, and the quantity of code one should write for each represented category. I organized the categories as **Slices**, **Cross-slices**, and **Global**, to represent the scope of the code. Here's the diagram:

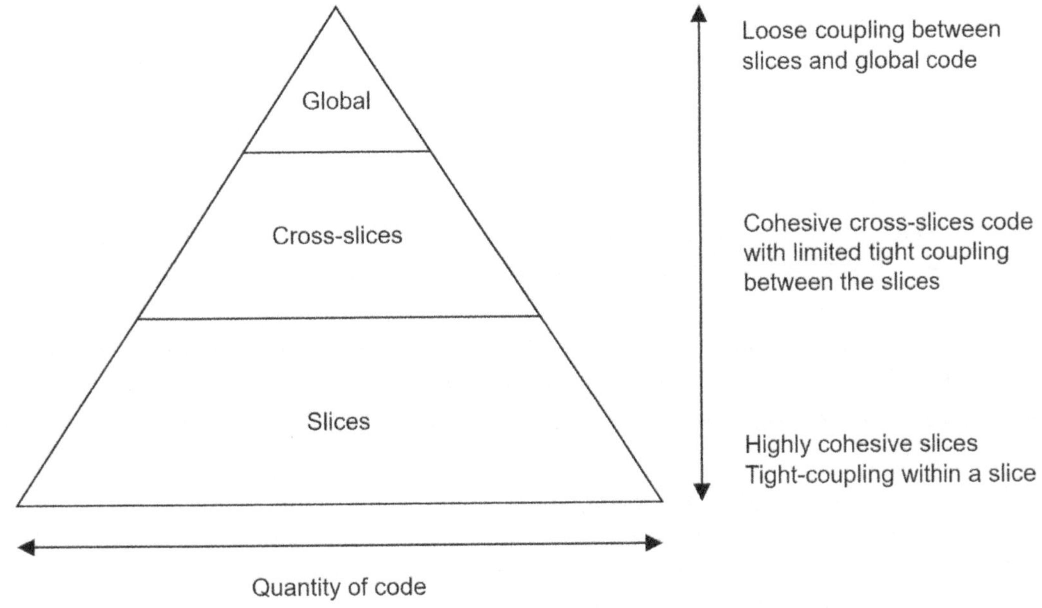

Figure 17.4: Relationships between coupling, cohesion, and the quantity of code one should write in

In real life, the preceding diagram is more like a scale than three clearly defined buckets, as represented by the vertical arrow on the right side. Basically, we want to write more slices code (features), less cross-slices code (coupling between features), and even less global code (coupling between unrelated features). Essentially, in this type of architecture, we should focus on writing more feature code to keep our features independent of one another.

When adhering to this type of architecture, we must continuously design and refactor the application, which requires stronger design skills than a predefined approach, like Clean Architecture. Moreover, you must know how to build the features end to end, limiting the division of tasks between people and centralizing them on each team member instead; each member becomes a full-stack developer. Writing automated tests that validate features' correctness will help with the refactoring. We revisit this example in the *Continuing your journey* section near the end of the chapter.

Let's now explore the advantages and disadvantages of Vertical Slice Architecture.

What are the advantages and disadvantages?

Let's explore some advantages and disadvantages of Vertical Slice Architecture.

Advantages

On the upside, we have the following:

- We reduce coupling between features, making working on such a project more manageable. We only need to think about a single vertical slice, not *N* layers, improving **maintainability** by centralizing the code around a shared concern.
- We can choose how each vertical slice interacts with the external resources it requires without considering the other slices. That adds **flexibility** since one slice can use T-SQL while another uses EF Core, for example.
- We can start small with a few lines of code (described as **Transaction Scripts** in *Patterns of Enterprise Application Architecture*, by Martin Fowler) without extravagant design or over-engineering. Then we can refactor our way to a better design when the need arises and patterns emerge, leading to a **faster time to market**.
- Each vertical slice should contain precisely the right amount of code needed to be correct—not more, not less. That leads to a **more robust** codebase (less code means less extraneous code and less code to maintain).
- It is easier for newcomers to find their way around an existing system since each feature is near-independent, leading to a **faster onboarding time**.
- All patterns and techniques you learned about in previous chapters still apply.

From my experience, features tend to start small and grow over time. Users often find out what they need while using the software, changing the requirements over time, which leads to changes in the software. After the fact, I wish many projects I worked on were built using Vertical Slice Architecture instead of layering; they would have been easier and faster to adapt to changes.

Disadvantages

Of course, nothing is perfect, so here are some downsides to Vertical Slice Architecture:

- It may take time to wrap your head around Vertical Slice Architecture if you're used to layering, leading to an adaptation period to learn a new way to think about your software
- It is a "newer" type of architecture, and people don't like change

Another thing that I learned the hard way is to embrace change. I don't think I've seen one project end as it was supposed to. Everyone identifies the missing pieces of the business processes while using the software. That leads to the following advice: release the software as fast as possible and have your customers use the software as soon as possible. That advice can be easier to achieve with Vertical Slice Architecture because you build value for your customers instead of more or less valuable abstractions and layers. Having a customer try staged software is very hard; no customer has time to do such a thing—they are busy running their business. However, releasing production-ready slices may lead to faster adoption and feedback.

At the beginning of my career, I was frustrated when specifications changed, and I thought that better planning would have fixed that. Sometimes, better planning would have helped, but sometimes, the customer just did not know how to express their business processes or needs and had to try the application to figure it out. My advice here is don't be frustrated when the specs change, even if that means rewriting a part of the software that took you days or longer to code in the first place; that will happen all the time. Learn to accept that instead, and find ways to make this process easier and faster. If you are in contact with the customers, find ways to help them figure out their needs and reduce the number of changes.

Downsides or upsides?

The following points are downsides that we can tame as upsides:

- **Full-stack skillset**: Suppose you are used to working in silos (such as the database administrators doing the data stuff while the developers are doing development). In that case, assigning tasks that touch the whole feature may be more challenging because your skillset is narrower and you are not used to doing all the tasks. On the other hand, this can become an advantage since everyone in your team has to work more closely together, leading to more learning and collaboration and possibly a future fully cross-functional team—which is excellent. Having experts on the team is great because no one is an expert in all areas, yet every member of the team can contribute to multiple areas.
- **Refactoring skillset**: Strong refactoring skills will go a long way. Over time, most systems need some refactoring, which is even more true for Vertical Slice Architecture. Refactoring may be needed due to changes in the requirements or due to technical debt. No matter the reason, you may end up with a **Big Ball of Mud** if you don't. First, writing isolated code and then refactoring to patterns is a crucial part of Vertical Slice Architecture. That's one of the best ways to keep cohesion high inside a slice and coupling as low as possible between slices. This tip applies to all types of architecture and is made easier with a robust test suite that validates your changes automatically.

A way to start refactoring that business logic would be to push the logic into the **domain model**, creating a **rich domain model**. You can also use other design patterns and techniques to fine-tune the code and make it more maintainable, such as creating services or layers. A layer does not have to cross all vertical slices; it can cross only a subset of them, as we explored in the beginning with the *Shipments Management* system.

Compared to other application-level patterns, such as layering, fewer rules lead to more choices (Vertical Slice Architecture). You can use all design patterns, principles, and best practices inside a vertical slice without exporting those choices application-wide.

How do you organize a project into Vertical Slice Architecture? Unfortunately, there is no definitive answer to that, and it depends on the engineers working on the project. We explore one way in the next project, which we build upon in the following chapters, but you can organize your project as you see fit. Then we dig deeper into refactoring and organization.

Project – Vertical Slice Architecture

Context: We are getting tired of layering, and we got asked to rebuild our small demo shop using Vertical Slice Architecture.

Here is an updated diagram that shows how we conceptually organize the project:

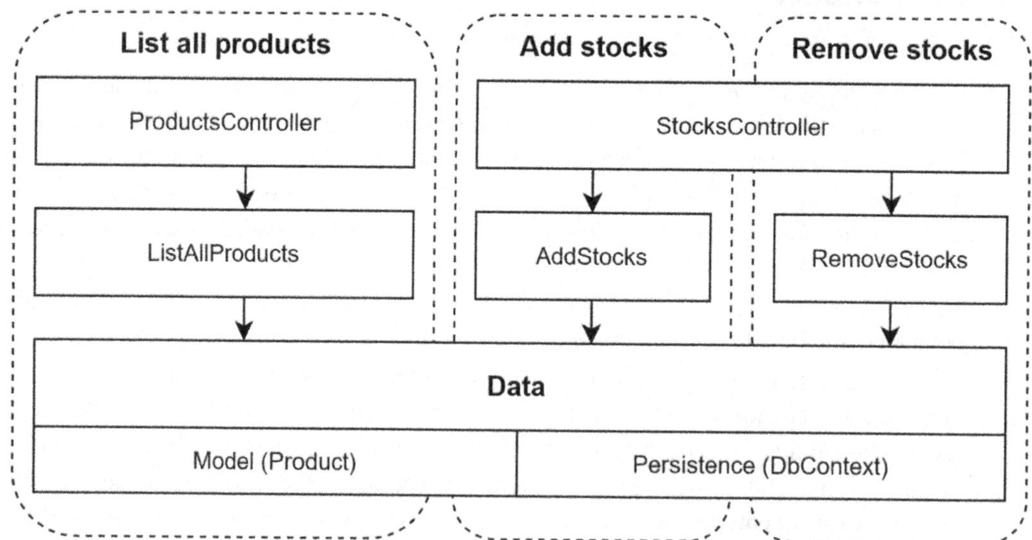

Figure 17.5: Diagram representing the organization of the demo shop project

Each vertical box is a use case (or slice), while each horizontal box is a cross-cutting concern or a shared component. This is a small project, so we share the data access code (`DbContext`) and the `Product` model between the three use cases. This sharing is unrelated to Vertical Slice Architecture, but splitting it more in a small project like this is hard and pointless.

In this project, I decided to go with web API controllers instead of Minimal APIs and an anemic model instead of a rich model. We could have used Minimal APIs, a rich model, or any combination. I chose this so you have a glimpse of using controllers, as this is something you might very well end up using. We go back to Minimal APIs in the next chapter.

Here are the actors:

- `ProductsController` is the REST API to manage products
- `StocksController` is the REST API to manage the inventory
- `AddStocks`, `RemoveStocks`, and `ListAllProducts` are the same use cases we have copied in our project since *Chapter 14, Layering and Clean Architecture*
- The persistence "layer" consists of an EF Core `DbContext` that persists the `Product` model to an in-memory database

We could add other cross-cutting concerns on top of our vertical slices, such as authorization, error management, and logging, to name a few.

Here, we focus on the "remove stock" feature to study the pattern while avoiding adding additional pages to the book with redundant code in them. The other features follow the same pattern and are available on GitHub.

Next, let's look at how we organized the project.

Project organization

Here is how we organized the project:

- The `Data` directory contains EF Core-related classes.
- The `Features` directory contains the features. Each subfolder contains its underlying features (vertical slices), including controllers, exceptions, and other support classes required to implement the feature.
- Each use case is self-contained and exposes the following classes:
    - `Command` or `Query` represents the MediatR request
    - `Result` is the return value of that request
    - `MapperProfile` instructs `AutoMapper` on how to map the use case-related objects (if any)
    - `Validator` contains the validation rules to validate the `Command` or `Query` objects (if any)
    - `Handler` contains the use case logic: how to handle the request
- The `Models` directory contains the domain model.

This project validates requests using `FluentValidation`, a third-party NuGet package, but we could have used any other validation library. FluentValidation makes it easy to keep the validation within our slices, but outside the class we want to validate. The out-of-the-box .NET validation framework, `DataAnnotations`, does the opposite, forcing us to include the validation as metadata on the entities themselves. Both have pros and cons, but FluentValidation is easier to test and extend.

The following code is the `Program.cs` file. The highlighted lines represent registering FluentValidation and scanning the assembly to find validators:

```
var currentAssembly = typeof(Program).Assembly;
var builder = WebApplication.CreateBuilder(args);
builder.Services
    // Plumbing/Dependencies
    .AddAutoMapper(currentAssembly)
    .AddMediatR(o => o.RegisterServicesFromAssembly(currentAssembly))

    // Data
    .AddDbContext<ProductContext>(options => options
        .UseInMemoryDatabase("ProductContextMemoryDB")
        .ConfigureWarnings(builder => builder.Ignore(InMemoryEventId.
TransactionIgnoredWarning))
    )

    // Web/MVC
    .AddFluentValidationAutoValidation()
    .AddValidatorsFromAssembly(currentAssembly)
    .AddControllers()
;

var app = builder.Build();
app.MapControllers();
using (var seedScope = app.Services.CreateScope())
{
    var db = seedScope.ServiceProvider.GetRequiredService<ProductContext>();
    await ProductSeeder.SeedAsync(db);
}
app.Run();
```

The preceding code adds the bindings we explored in previous chapters, FluentValidation, and the other pieces required to run the application. The highlighted lines register FluentValidation and scan the `currentAssembly` for validator classes. The validators themselves are part of each vertical slice.

Now that we've covered the organization of the project, let's look at features.

Exploring a feature

In this subsection, we explore the `RemoveStocks` feature with the same logic as in previous samples but organized differently (a.k.a., the difference between the Vertical Slice Architecture and layering styles). Since we use an anemic product model, we moved the add and remove stocks logic from the `Product` class to the `Handler` class. Let's look at the code next, as I describe each nested class.

The sample starts with the `RemoveStocks` class that contains the feature's nested classes. That helps organize the feature and saves us some headaches about naming collision. For example, we can name all command classes `Command`, and validator classes `Validator` without worrying about it. Then, we can use them using the feature class, like `RemoveStocks.Command`.

We could use namespaces instead, but tools like Visual Studio recommend adding a `using` statement and removing the inline namespace. Nowadays, it often automatically adds the `using` statement, like when pasting code, which is great for many scenarios but inconvenient for this specific one. So, using nested classes fixes this.

On the other hand, we could also name the classes `RemoveStocksCommand` and `RemoveStocksValidator`. We explore this style of code in *Chapter 20, Modular Monolith*.

Here is the `RemoveStocks` class skeleton:

```
using AutoMapper;
using FluentValidation;
using MediatR;
using VerticalApp.Data;
using VerticalApp.Models;

namespace VerticalApp.Features.Stocks;
public class RemoveStocks
{
    public class Command : IRequest<Result> {/*...*/}
    public class Result {/*...*/}
    public class MapperProfile : Profile {/*...*/}
    public class Validator : AbstractValidator<Command> {/*...*/}
    public class Handler : IRequestHandler<Command, Result> {/*...*/}
}
```

The preceding code showcases that the `RemoveStocks` class contains all the required elements it needs for its specific use case:

- `Command` is the input DTO
- `Result` is the output DTO

- `MapperProfile` is the AutoMapper profile that maps feature-specific classes to non-feature-specific classes, and vice versa
- `Validator` validates the input (the `Command` class) before an instance hits the `Handler` class
- `Handler` encapsulates the use case logic

Next, we explore those nested classes, starting with the `Command` class, which is the **input of the use case** (the request):

```
public class Command : IRequest<Result>
{
    public int ProductId { get; set; }
    public int Amount { get; set; }
}
```

The preceding request contains everything it needs to remove stock from the inventory and fulfill the operation. The `IRequest<TResult>` interface tells MediatR that the `Command` class is a request and should be routed to its handler.

The `Result` class is the return value of that handler and represents the output of the use case:

```
public record class Result(int QuantityInStock);
```

The mapper profile is optional and allows encapsulating AutoMapper *maps* related to the use case. The following `MapperProfile` class registers the mapping from a `Product` instance to a `Result` instance:

```
public class MapperProfile : Profile
{
    public MapperProfile()
    {
        CreateMap<Product, Result>();
    }
}
```

The `validator` class is also optional and allows validating the input (`Command`) before it hits the handler; in this case, it ensures the `Amount` value is greater than zero:

```
public class Validator : AbstractValidator<Command>
{
    public Validator()
    {
        RuleFor(x => x.Amount).GreaterThan(0);
    }
}
```

Finally, the most important piece is the `Handler` class, which implements the use case logic:

```
public class Handler : IRequestHandler<Command, Result>
```

```
{
    private readonly ProductContext _db;
    private readonly IMapper _mapper;

    public Handler(ProductContext db, IMapper mapper)
    {
        _db = db ?? throw new ArgumentNullException(nameof(db));
        _mapper = mapper ?? throw new ArgumentNullException(nameof(mapper));
    }

    public async Task<Result> Handle(Command request, CancellationToken
cancellationToken)
    {
        var product = await _db.Products.FindAsync(new object[] { request.
ProductId }, cancellationToken);
        if (product == null)
        {
            throw new ProductNotFoundException(request.ProductId);
        }
        if (request.Amount > product.QuantityInStock)
        {
            throw new NotEnoughStockException(product.QuantityInStock, request.
Amount);
        }

        product.QuantityInStock -= request.Amount;
        await _db.SaveChangesAsync(cancellationToken);

        return _mapper.Map<Result>(product);
    }
}
```

The `Handler` class implements the `IRequestHandler<Command, Result>` interface, which links the `Command`, the `Handler`, and the `Result` classes. The `Handle` method implements the same logic as the previous implementations from *Chapter 14, Layering and Clean Architecture*, onward.

Now that we have a fully functional use case, let's look at the skeleton of the `StocksController` class that translates the HTTP requests to the MediatR pipeline so our use case gets executed:

```
using MediatR;
using Microsoft.AspNetCore.Mvc;

namespace VerticalApp.Features.Stocks;
```

```
[ApiController]
[Route("products/{productId}/")]
public class StocksController : ControllerBase
{
    private readonly IMediator _mediator;
    public StocksController(IMediator mediator)
    {
        _mediator = mediator ?? throw new
ArgumentNullException(nameof(mediator));
    }

    [HttpPost("add-stocks")]
    public async Task<ActionResult<AddStocks.Result>> AddAsync(
        int productId,
        [FromBody] AddStocks.Command command
    ) {/*...*/}

    [HttpPost("remove-stocks")]
    public async Task<ActionResult<RemoveStocks.Result>> RemoveAsync(
        int productId,
        [FromBody] RemoveStocks.Command command
    ) {/*...*/}
}
```

In the controller, we inject an `IMediator` into the constructor. We used constructor injection because all actions of this controller use the `IMediator` interface. We have two actions, add and remove stocks.

The following code represents the remove stocks action method:

```
[HttpPost("remove-stocks")]
public async Task<ActionResult<RemoveStocks.Result>> RemoveAsync(
    int productId,
    [FromBody] RemoveStocks.Command command
)
{
    try
    {
        command.ProductId = productId;
        var result = await _mediator.Send(command);
```

```
            return Ok(result);
        }
        catch (NotEnoughStockException ex)
        {
            return Conflict(new
            {
                ex.Message,
                ex.AmountToRemove,
                ex.QuantityInStock
            });
        }
        catch (ProductNotFoundException ex)
        {
            return NotFound(new
            {
                ex.Message,
                productId,
            });
        }
    }
```

In the preceding code, we read the content of the `RemoveStocks.Command` instance from the body, the action sets the `ProductId` property from the route value, and it sends the `command` object into the MediatR pipeline. From there, MediatR routes the request to its handler before returning the result of that operation with an HTTP `200 OK` status code.

One of the differences between the preceding code and previous implementations is that we moved the DTOs to the vertical slice itself. Each vertical slice defines the input, the logic, and the output of its feature, as follows:

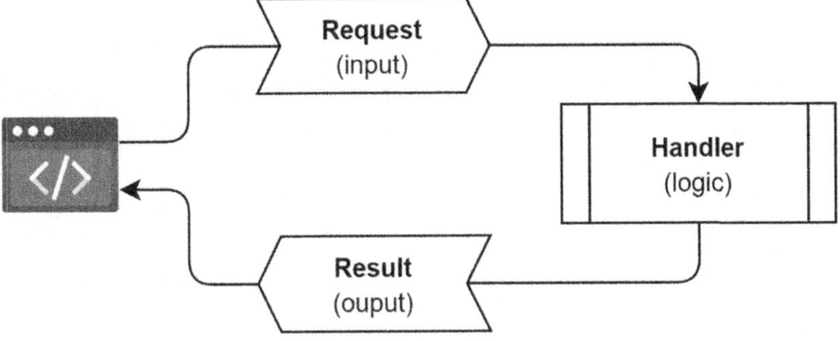

Figure 17.6: Diagram representing the three primary pieces of a vertical slice

When we add input validation, we have the following:

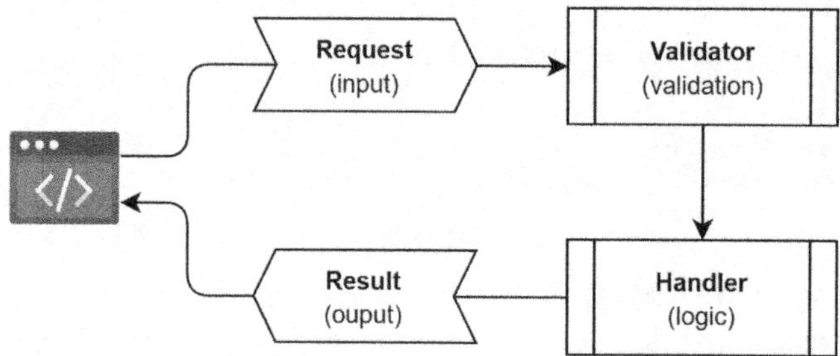

Figure 17.7: Diagram representing the three primary pieces of a vertical slice, with added validation

The controller is a tiny layer between HTTP and our domain, guiding the HTTP requests to the MediatR pipeline and the responses back to HTTP. That thin piece represents the presentation of the API and allows access to the domain logic—the features. When controllers grow, it is often a sign that part of the feature logic is in the wrong place, most likely leading to code that is harder to test because the HTTP and other logic become intertwined.

We still have the extra line for the `productId` and `try/catch` blocks in the controller's code, but we could eliminate these using custom model binders and exception filters. I included additional model-binding resources at the end of the chapter, and we dig deeper into this in the next chapter.

With that in place, it is now straightforward to add new features to the project. Visually, we end up with the following vertical slices (bold), possible vertical expansions (normal text), and shared classes (italics):

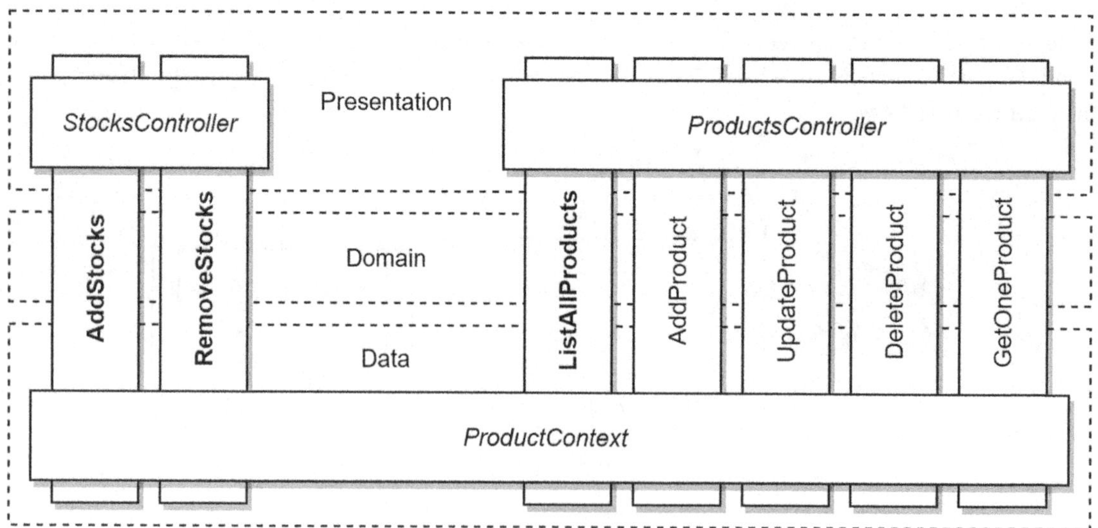

Figure 17.8: Diagram representing the project and possible extensions related to product management

The diagram shows the grouping of the two main areas: products and stocks. On the products side, I included an expansion that depicts a CRUD-like feature group to showcase a more real-life scenario where an authorized user can manage the products.

In our tiny application, it is tough to divide the data access part into more than one `DbContext`, so `ProductContext` is used by all slices, creating a shared data access layer.

In other cases, create multiple `DbContext` when possible. This has nothing to do with Vertical Slice Architecture but is a good practice to divide your domain into smaller bounded contexts.

Think about grouping features when they are cohesive and fit under the same part of the domain.

Next, let's test our application.

Testing

For this project, I wrote one integration test per use case outcome, which lowers the number of unit tests required while increasing the level of confidence in the system at the same time. Why? Because we are testing the features themselves instead of many abstracted parts independently. This is gray-box testing.

We can also add as many unit tests as we need. This approach helps us write fewer but better feature-oriented tests, diminishing the need for mock-heavy unit tests. Unit tests are practical for validating complex use cases and algorithms faster than integration tests.

Let's look at the `StocksTest` class skeleton first:

```
namespace VerticalApp.Features.Stocks;
public class StocksTest
{
    private static async Task SeederDelegate(ProductContext db)
    {
        db.Products.RemoveRange(db.Products.ToArray());
        await db.Products.AddAsync(new Product(
            id: 4,
            name: "Ghost Pepper",
            quantityInStock: 10
        ));
        await db.Products.AddAsync(new Product(
            id: 5,
            name: "Carolina Reaper",
            quantityInStock: 10
        ));
        await db.SaveChangesAsync();
```

```
    }
    public class AddStocksTest : StocksTest
    {
        // omitted test methods
    }
    public class RemoveStocksTest : StocksTest
    {
        // omitted test methods
    }
    public class StocksControllerTest : StocksTest
    {
        // omitted test methods
    }
}
```

The SeedAsync method removes all products and inserts two new ones in the in-memory test database so the test methods can run using a predictable dataset. The AddStocksTest and RemoveStocksTest classes contain the test methods for their respective use cases. StocksControllerTest tests the MVC part.

Let's explore the test that validates the happy path of the RemoveStocksTest class:

```
[Fact]
public async Task Should_decrement_QuantityInStock_by_the_specified_amount()
{
    // Arrange
    await using var application = new VerticalAppApplication();
    await application.SeedAsync(SeederDelegate);
    using var requestScope = application.Services.CreateScope();
    var mediator = requestScope.ServiceProvider.
GetRequiredService<IMediator>();

    // Act
    var result = await mediator.Send(new RemoveStocks.Command
    {
        ProductId = 5,
        Amount = 10
    });

    // Assert
    using var assertScope = application.Services.CreateScope();
    var db = assertScope.ServiceProvider.GetRequiredService<ProductContext>();
    var peppers = await db.Products.FindAsync(5);
```

```
        Assert.NotNull(peppers);
        Assert.Equal(0, peppers!.QuantityInStock);
    }
```

In the *Arrange* section of the preceding test case, we create an instance of the application, create a scope to simulate an HTTP request, access the EF Core `DbContext`, and then get an `IMediator` instance to act on.

In the *Act* block, we send a valid `RemoveStocks.Command` through the MediatR pipeline.

In the *Assert* block, we create a new scope to ensure we use a different `DbContext` instance, ensuring we are querying the data store and not the EF Core cache. Then we get the `ProductContext` out of the container using our `assertScope` scope. With that `DbContext`, we find the product, ensure it's not null, and validate that the quantity in stock is what we expect.

Using a new `ProductContext` ensures we are not dealing with any cached items from the previous operations. This is very important when testing database operations done through EF Core. In this specific case, the test code does not share the `DbContext`. However, it happens, so testing the database data from a fresh context is a good habit to ensure your tests are reliable.

To keep this short, EF Core caches the changes in memory (change tracker) until the code commits the changes to the database or rolls it back. A common error path would be to update a record and then forget to call the `SaveChanges` method. If the validity of the data is assessed using the same `DbContext`, the test will yield a positive result, while in reality, the data was never sent to the database. Why? Because the test asserted the EF Core cached value. Using a fresh `DbContext` ensures you avoid this pitfall by querying the database. Here's an example of such an error:

```
[Fact]
public async Task Erroneous_testing_methodology()
{
    // Arrange
    await using var application = new VerticalAppApplication();
    using var sharedScope = application.Services.CreateScope();
    var db = sharedScope.ServiceProvider.
GetRequiredService<ProductContext>();
    var product = db.Products.First();
    var productId = product.Id;
    // Act
    product.Name = "Never Persisted"; // Forgot to save changes

    // Assert (error)
    var p = db.Products.Find(productId);
    Assert.NotNull(p);
```

```
    Assert.Equal("Never Persisted", p.Name); // the test succeeds
but should not
}
```

The preceding test will be successful but should not be because we forgot to save the changes to the database. Here's the fixed version:

```
[Fact]
public async Task Erroneous_testing_methodology_fixed()
{
    // Arrange
    await using var application = new VerticalAppApplication();
    using var sharedScope = application.Services.CreateScope();
    var db = sharedScope.ServiceProvider.
GetRequiredService<ProductContext>();
    var product = db.Products.First();
    var productId = product.Id;

    // Act
    product.Name = "Never Persisted"; // Forgot to save changes

    // Assert (correct)
    using var assertScope = application.Services.CreateScope();
    var assertDb = assertScope.ServiceProvider.
GetRequiredService<ProductContext>();
    var p2 = assertDb.Products.Find(productId);
    Assert.NotNull(p2);
    Assert.Equal("Never Persisted", p2.Name); // The test fails
as it should
}
```

The preceding code leverages a new scope, which yields a new `DbContext`, allowing us to assess that the product changes were not persisted to the database and detect the error.

With that happy path test method, we know that if a valid command is issued to the mediator, that handler gets executed and successfully increments the stock property by the specified amount.

The `VerticalAppApplication` class inherits from `WebApplicationFactory<TEntryPoint>`, creates a new `DbContextOptionsBuilder<ProductContext>` instance that has a configurable database name, implements a `SeedAsync` method that allows seeding the database, and allows altering the application services. I omitted the code for brevity reasons, but you can consult the complete source code in the GitHub repository (https://adpg.link/mWep).

Now, we can test the MVC part to ensure the controller is configured correctly. In the `StocksControllerTest` class, the `AddAsync` class contains the following test method:

```
public class AddAsync : StocksControllerTest
{
    [Fact]
    public async Task Should_send_a_valid_AddStocks_Command_to_the_mediator()
    {
        // Arrange
        var mediatorMock = new Mock<IMediator>();
        AddStocks.Command? addStocksCommand = default;
        mediatorMock
            .Setup(x => x.Send(It.IsAny<AddStocks.Command>(),
It.IsAny<CancellationToken>()))
            .Callback((IRequest<AddStocks.Result> request, CancellationToken
cancellationToken) => addStocksCommand = request as AddStocks.Command)
        ;
        await using var application = new VerticalAppApplication(
            afterConfigureServices: services => services
                .AddSingleton(mediatorMock.Object)
        );
        var client = application.CreateClient();
        var httpContent = JsonContent.Create(
            new { amount = 1 },
            options: new JsonSerializerOptions(JsonSerializerDefaults.Web)
        );
        // Act
        var response = await client.PostAsync("/products/5/add-stocks",
httpContent);
        // Assert
        Assert.NotNull(response);
        Assert.NotNull(addStocksCommand);
```

```
        response.EnsureSuccessStatusCode();
        mediatorMock.Verify(
            x => x.Send(It.IsAny<AddStocks.Command>(),
It.IsAny<CancellationToken>()),
            Times.Once()
        );
        Assert.Equal(5, addStocksCommand!.ProductId);
        Assert.Equal(1, addStocksCommand!.Amount);
    }
}
```

The highlighted code of the preceding test case *Arrange* block mocks the `IMediator` and saves what is passed to the `Send` method in the `addStocksCommand` variable. We are using that value in the highlighted code of the *Assert* block. When creating the `VerticalAppApplication` instance, we register the mock with the container to use it instead of the MediatR one, which bypasses the default behavior.

We then create an `HttpClient` connected to our in-process application and craft a valid HTTP request to add the stocks we POST in the *Act* section.

The *Assert* block code ensures that the request was successful, verifies that the mock method was hit once, and ensures that `AddStocks.Command` was configured correctly.

From the first test, we know the MediatR piece works. With this second test in place, we know the HTTP piece works. We are now almost certain that a valid add stocks request will hit the database with those two tests.

I say "almost certain" because our tests run against an in-memory database, which is different from a real database engine (for example, it has no relational integrity and the like). In case of more complex database operations that affect more than one table or to ensure the correctness of the feature, you can run the tests against a database closer to the production database. For example, we can run the tests against a SQL Server container to spawn and tear down the databases in our CI/CD pipeline.

In the test project, I added more tests covering the removal of stocks and listing all products' features, and ensuring AutoMapper configuration correctness. Feel free to browse the code. I omitted them here as they become redundant. The objective is to explore testing a feature almost end to end with very few tests (two for the happy path in this case), and we have covered that.

Continuing your journey – a few tips and tricks

The previous project was tiny. It had a shared model that served as the data layer because it was composed of a single class. When building real-world applications, you have more than one class, so I'll give you a good starting point to tackle bigger apps. The idea is to create slices as small as possible, limit interactions with other slices as much as possible, and refactor that code into better code. We cannot remove coupling, so we need to organize it instead, and the key is to centralize that coupling inside a feature.

You want to keep all the code that makes a vertical slice as close as possible. You don't have to keep all use case classes in a single file, but I find this helps. Partial classes are a way to split classes into multiple files. If named correctly, Visual Studio will nest them under the primary file. For example, Visual Studio will nest the `MyFeature.Hander.cs` file under the `MyFeature.cs` file, and so on.

You can also create a folder hierarchy where the deeper levels share the previous levels. For example, the creation process of a workflow I implemented in an MVC application related to shipments had multiple steps, so I ended up with a hierarchy that looked like the following:

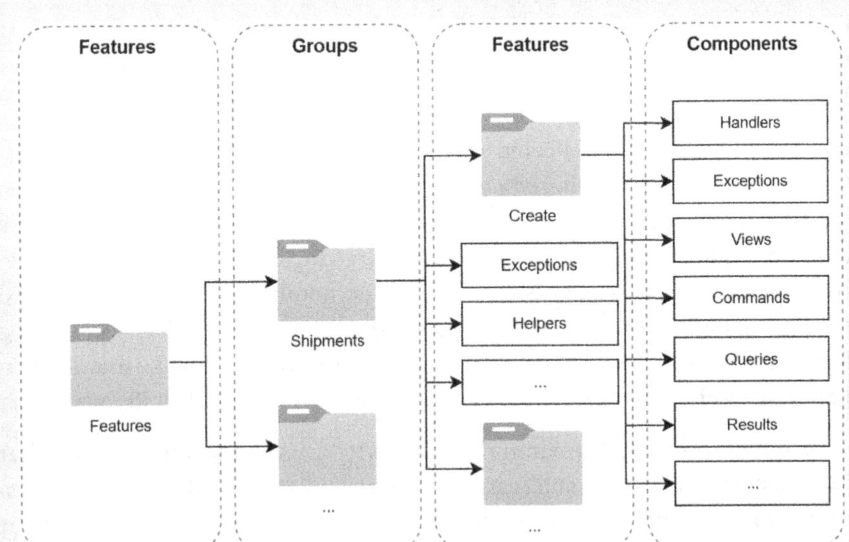

Figure 17.9: The organizational hierarchy of directories and elements

Initially, I coded all the handlers individually. Then I saw patterns emerge, so I encapsulated that shared logic into shared classes. Then I reused some upper-level exceptions, so I moved those up from the `Features/Shipments/Create` folder to the `Features/Shipments` folder. I also extracted a service class to manage shared logic between multiple use cases. Ultimately, I have only the code I need, no duplicated logic, and the collaborators (classes, interfaces) are as close as possible. The coupling between features was minimal, while parts of the system work in synergy (cohesion). Moreover, there is very little to no coupling with other parts of the system. If we compare that result to another type of architecture, such as layering, I would most likely have needed more abstractions, such as repositories, services, and whatnot; the result with Vertical Slice Architecture was cleaner and simpler.

The key point here is to code your handlers independently, organize them the best you can, keep an eye open for shared logic and emerging patterns, extract and encapsulate that logic, and try to limit interactions between use cases and slices.

Having a strong test suite will greatly help you in the long run. Here is a workflow to write such a testing suite, inspired by test-driven development (TDD), yet less rigid:

1. Write the contracts that cover your feature (input and output).
2. Write one or more integration tests covering your feature, using those contracts—the `Query` or `Command` class (`IRequest`) as input and the `Result` class as output.
3. Implement your `Handler`, `Validator`, `MapperProfile`, and any other bit that needs to be coded. At this point, the code could be a giant `Handler`; it does not matter.
4. Once your integration tests pass, refactor that code by breaking down your giant `Handle` method as needed.
5. Make sure your tests still pass.

During *step 2*, you may also test the validation rules with unit tests. It is way easier and faster to test multiple combinations and scenarios from unit tests, and you don't need to access a database for that. The same also applies to any other parts of your system that are not tied to an external resource.

During *step 4*, you may find duplicated logic between features. If that's the case, it is time to encapsulate that logic elsewhere, in a shared place. That could be creating a method in the model, a service class, or any other pattern and technique you know might solve your duplication of logic problem. Working from isolated features and extracting shared logic will help you design the application. You want to push that shared logic outside of a handler, not the other way around (of course, once you have that shared logic, you can use it as needed). Here, I want to emphasize *shared logic*, which means a business rule. When a business rule changes, all consumers of that business rule must also change their behavior. Avoid sharing *similar code* but do share business rules. Remember the DRY principle.

What is very important when designing software is to focus on the functional needs, not the technical ones. Your customers and users don't care about the technical stuff; they want results, new features, bug fixes, and improvements. Simultaneously, beware of the technical debt, so don't skip the refactoring step or your project may get in trouble. This advice applies to all types of architecture.

Agile and DevOps synergy

Vertical Slice Architecture enhances the effectiveness of Agile and DevOps methodology by promoting incremental, flexible, and value-driven development. This synergy ensures we build software that better meets user needs and adapts swiftly to changing requirements.

Harmony with the Agile principles:

- **Iterative progress**: Adhering to Agile's iterative approach, each slice is an increment of customer-centric functionality that we can deliver iteratively
- **Facilitates prioritization**: Vertical Slice Architecture makes prioritizing the backlog easier because it focuses on end-to-end features rather than broken-down components
- **Responsiveness to change**: Vertical Slice Architecture supports Agile's tenet of responding to changes by simplifying the creation, update, or deletion of features by limiting the impact on other features

- **Value-driven:** Every slice brings direct customer value, mirroring Agile's commitment to fulfilling customer needs through working increments

Fusion with the DevOps culture:

- **Cross-functional collaboration:** Vertical Slice Architecture embraces the DevOps ethos of shared responsibility and seamless cooperation between parties by prescribing teamwork across disciplines
- **Continuous Integration/Continuous Deployment (CI/CD):** Vertical Slice Architecture perfectly suits CI/CD pipelines, by enabling the integration and release of slices frequently
- **Automated testing:** Vertical Slice Architecture encourages automated testing of each feature end-to-end, enhancing DevOps goals for high-quality and frequent releases with minimal manual intervention, leading to a fast feedback loop
- **Visibility:** On top of automated tests, with working slices getting shipped rapidly, stakeholders can provide timely feedback, aligning with another critical component of Agile's and DevOps's collaborative approach

This synergy between Vertical Slice Architecture, Agile, and DevOps leads to an environment where we can deliver software that provides immediate value in increments and in a way that makes us ready to react to changes. Together, they create a robust framework for building, releasing, and maintaining quality software at a pace that matches the speed of today's business requirements. On top of that, we do not have to deal with the complexity of distributed systems like microservices architecture.

Conclusion

The vertical slice project shows how we can remove abstractions while keeping the objects loosely coupled. We also organized the project into features (verticals) instead of layers (horizontals). We leveraged the CQS, Mediator, and MVC patterns. Conceptually, the layers are still there; for example, the controllers are part of the presentation layer, but they are not organized that way, making them part of the feature. The sole dependency that crosses all our features is the `ProductContext` class, which makes sense since our model comprises a single class (`Product`). We could, for example, add a new feature that leverages Minimal APIs instead of a controller, which would be okay because each slice is independent.

We can significantly reduce the number of mocks required by testing each vertical slice with integration tests. That can also significantly lower the number of unit tests, testing features instead of mocked units of code. We should focus on producing features and business value, not the details behind querying the infrastructure or the code itself. We should not neglect the technical aspects either; performance and maintainability are also important characteristics, but reducing the number of abstractions can also make the application easier to maintain and for sure easier to understand.

Overall, we explored a modern way to design an application that aligns well with Agile and DevOps and helps generate value for our customers.

Let's see how Vertical Slice Architecture can help us follow the SOLID principles:

- **S**: Each vertical slice (feature) becomes a cohesive unit that changes as a whole, leading to the segregation of responsibilities per feature. Based on a CQS-inspired approach, each feature splits the application's complexity into commands and queries, leading to multiple small pieces. Each piece handles a part of the process. For example, we can define an input, a validator, a mapper profile, a handler, a result, an HTTP bridge (controller or endpoint), and as many more pieces as we need to craft the slice.
- **O**: We can enhance the system globally by extending the ASP.NET Core, MVC, or MediatR pipelines. We can design the features as we see fit, including respecting the OCP.
- **L**: N/A.
- **I**: By organizing features by units of domain-centric use cases, we create many client-specific components instead of general-purpose elements like layers.
- **D**: The slice pieces depend on interfaces and are tied together using dependency injection. Furthermore, by cutting the less useful abstractions out of the system, we simplify it, making it more maintainable and concise. Having that many pieces of a feature living close to each other makes the system easier to maintain and improves its discoverability.

Summary

This chapter provided an overview of Vertical Slice Architecture, which flips layers by 90°. Vertical Slice Architecture is about writing minimal code to generate maximum value by getting superfluous abstractions and rules out of the equation by relying on the developers' skills and judgment instead.

Refactoring is critical in a Vertical Slice Architecture project; success or failure will most likely depend on it. We can also use any patterns with Vertical Slice Architecture. It has lots of advantages over layering, with only a few disadvantages. Teams who work in silos (horizontal teams) may need to rethink switching to Vertical Slice Architecture and first create or aim at creating multi-functional teams instead (vertical teams).

We replaced the low-value abstraction with commands and queries (CQS-inspired). Those are then routed to their respective `Handler` using the Mediator pattern (helped by MediatR). That allows encapsulating the business logic and decoupling it from its callers. Those commands and queries ensure that each bit of domain logic is centralized in a single location.

Of course, if you start with a strong analysis of your problem, you will most likely have a head start, as with any project. Nothing stops you from building and using a robust domain model in your slices. The more requirements you have, the easier the initial project organization will be. To reiterate, all engineering practices that you know still apply.

The next chapter simplifies the concept of Vertical Slice Architecture even more by exploring the Request-EndPoint-Response (REPR) pattern using Minimal APIs.

Questions

Let's take a look at a few practice questions:

1. What design patterns can we use in a vertical slice?
2. When using Vertical Slice Architecture, is it true that you must pick a single ORM and stick with it, such as a data layer?
3. What will likely happen if you don't refactor your code and pay the technical debt in the long run?
4. What does cohesion mean?
5. What does tight coupling mean?

Further reading

Here are a few links to build upon what we learned in the chapter:

- For UI implementations, you can look at how Jimmy Bogard upgraded Contoso University:
    a. Contoso University on ASP.NET Core with .NET Core: `https://adpg.link/UXnr`
    b. Contoso University on ASP.NET Core with .NET Core and Razor Pages: `https://adpg.link/6Lbo`
- FluentValidation: `https://adpg.link/xXgp`
- AutoMapper: `https://adpg.link/5AUZ`
- MediatR: `https://adpg.link/ZQap`

Answers

1. Any pattern and technique you know that can help you implement your feature. That's the beauty of Vertical Slice Architecture; you are limited only by yourself.
2. No, you can pick the best tool for the job inside each vertical slice; you don't even need layers.
3. The application will most likely become a Big Ball of Mud and be very hard to maintain, which is not good for your stress level, the product quality, time to market of changes, and so on.
4. Cohesion means elements that should work together as a united whole.
5. Tight coupling describes elements that cannot change independently and that directly depend on one another.

Learn more on Discord

To join the Discord community for this book – where you can share feedback, ask questions to the author, and learn about new releases – follow the QR code below:

`https://packt.link/ArchitectingASPNETCoreApps3e`

18

Request-EndPoint-Response (REPR)

This chapter introduces the **Request-EndPoint-Response** (**REPR**) pattern, which we add on top of Vertical Slice Architecture and CQS. We continue to simplify our codebase to make it even more readable, maintainable, and less abstract, yet still testable.

We pronounce REPR like "reaper," which sounds way better than "rer" or "reper." I must credit Steve "Ardalis" Smith for this outstanding pattern name. I left a link to his article in the *Further reading* section.

We have leveraged this pattern already, possibly without you knowing its name. Now, it is time to formally introduce it and put a name to it, and then we assemble a technology stack to make it scalable for a real-world application.

We build that solution and then improve it during the chapter by exploring manual techniques, existing tools, and open-source libraries. The result is not perfect, but we improve this new e-commerce-inspired solution in the next few chapters.

The key to this iterative approach is learning to think about architecture and improve your design skills so that you have the tools to overcome the unique challenges the real world will throw at you. Using a larger project at this stage of the book helps you understand how to combine concepts and patterns in a scope that is a little closer to real life than a small, targeted code sample.

In this chapter, we cover the following topics:

- The Request-EndPoint-Response (REPR) pattern
- An e-commerce application—a slice of the real world

Let's explore the pattern before jumping into a more hands-on example.

The Request-EndPoint-Response (REPR) pattern

The Request-EndPoint-Response (REPR) pattern offers a simple approach, similar to what we explored in Vertical Slice Architecture, which deviates from the traditional Model-View-Controller (MVC) pattern.

As we explored in the MVC chapter, REST APIs don't have views, so we have to distort the MVC concept to make it work. REPR is more appropriate than MVC to build REST APIs in the context of HTTP, since each URL is a way to describe how to reach an endpoint (execute an operation), not a controller.

So, with REPR, a request hits an endpoint, which fulfills the request, and then the endpoint responds to the client with the result of that operation, forming a symbiotic relationship between the request, endpoint, and response: REPR.

Simple, elegant, yet very powerful.

Goal

REPR aims to align our REST APIs to HTTP and treat the inherent request-response concept behind the web as a first-class citizen in our application design. This reduces the number of new concepts we must learn and implement and streamlines the development process, making our code leaner, easier to manage, and directly aligned with client-server communication.

On top of this, the REPR pattern using Minimal APIs is well-aligned with Vertical Slice Architecture and facilitates building feature-oriented software instead of layer-heavy applications.

You could leverage the MVC framework to implement the REPR pattern as well. However, since the Minimal API model is already endpoint-oriented, it is well aligned with REPR and makes it a breeze to implement.

Design

REPR has three components:

- A request that contains the required information for the endpoint to do its work and plays the role of an input DTO
- An endpoint handler containing the business logic to execute, which is the central piece of this pattern
- A response that the endpoint returns to the client and plays the role of an output DTO

You can treat each request as a *Query* or a *Command*, as we explored in the CQS and Vertical Slice Architecture chapters.

Here's a diagram that represents this concept:

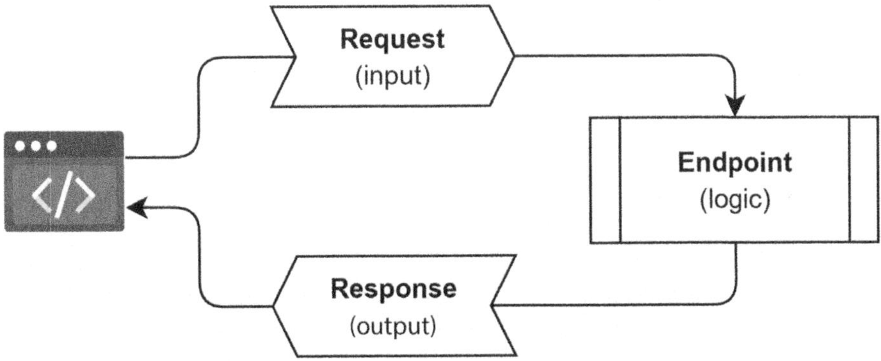

Figure 18.1: A diagram representing the logical flow and the REPR pattern

The preceding diagram should look familiar, since it resembles what we explored in the previous chapter on Vertical Slice Architecture. However, instead of Request-Handler-Result, we use Request-Endpoint-Response (a.k.a. REPR).

The bottom line is that a request can be a Query or a Command. It then hits the endpoint, which executes the logic and finally returns a response.

The server returns an HTTP response even when the response's body is empty.

Let's explore an example using a Minimal API.

Project – SimpleEndpoint

The `SimpleEndpoint` project showcases a few simple features, giving us the opportunity to explore multiple ways to organize our REPR features without dependencies on external libraries. These features are barebone implementations of the pattern and use slight naming and organizational variations.

I recommend choosing and sticking to one naming convention in a project, but in this case, the three features allow us to explore organizing our code.

Feature: ShuffleText

The first feature gets a string as input, shuffles its content, and returns it:

```
namespace SimpleEndpoint;
public class ShuffleText
```

```
{
    public record class Request(string Text);
    public record class Response(string Text);
    public class Endpoint
    {
        public Response Handle(Request request)
        {
            var chars = request.Text.ToArray();
            Random.Shared.Shuffle(chars);
            return new Response(new string(chars));
        }
    }
}
```

The preceding code leverages the `Random` API, shuffles the `request.Text` property, and then returns the results wrapped in a `Response` object.

Before executing our feature, we must create a Minimal API map and register our handler with the container. Here's the `Program.cs` class that achieves this:

```
using SimpleEndpoint;

var builder = WebApplication.CreateBuilder(args);
builder.Services.AddSingleton<ShuffleText.Endpoint>();

var app = builder.Build();
app.MapGet(
    "/shuffle-text/{text}",
    ([AsParameters] ShuffleText.Request query, ShuffleText.Endpoint endpoint)
        => endpoint.Handle(query)
);
app.Run();
```

The preceding code registers the `ShuffleText.Endpoint` as a singleton so we can inject it in the delegate. The delegate leverages the `[AsParameters]` attribute to bind the route parameter to the `ShuffleText.Request` property. Finally, the logic is straightforward; the endpoint delegate sends the request to the injected endpoint handler and returns the result, which ASP.NET Core serializes to JSON.

When we send the following HTTP request:

```
GET https://localhost:7289/shuffle-text/I love ASP.NET Core
```

We receive a randomized gibberish sentence like the following, proving that our "shuffle text" feature worked as expected:

```
{
  "text": "eo .e vNrCAT PSElIo"
}
```

This pattern is close to the simplest we can get out of the box. Next, we encapsulate the endpoint itself.

Feature: RandomNumber

This feature generates a set of random numbers between a minimum and a maximum.

The first pattern divided the code between the `Program.cs` file and the feature itself. In this implementation of the pattern, we encapsulate the endpoint delegate into the feature (the same file in this case):

```
namespace SimpleEndpoint;

public class RandomNumber
{
    public record class Request(int Amount, int Min, int Max);
    public record class Response(IEnumerable<int> Numbers);
    public class Handler
    {
        public Response Handle(Request request)
        {
            var result = new int[request.Amount];
            for (var i = 0; i < request.Amount; i++)
            {
                result[i] = Random.Shared.Next(request.Min, request.Max);
            }
            return new Response(result);
        }
    }

    public static Response Endpoint([AsParameters] Request query, Handler
handler)
        => handler.Handle(query);
}
```

The preceding code is very similar to the first feature. However, the method we named `Endpoint` is now part of the feature class (the highlighted code). The class that contains the logic is now called `Handler` instead of `Endpoint` and handles the business logic, while the `Endpoint` method is the endpoint delegate (mapped in the next code block). This change makes the full feature live closer together than the code we had in the `ShuffleText` feature.

Nonetheless, we still need to register the dependency with the container and map the endpoint to our method, like this, in the `Program.cs` file:

```
builder.Services.AddSingleton<RandomNumber.Handler>();
// ...
app.MapGet(
    "/random-number/{Amount}/{Min}/{Max}",
    RandomNumber.Endpoint
);
```

The preceding code routes the request to the `RandomNumber.Endpoint` method.

When we send the following HTTP request:

```
https://localhost:7289/random-number/5/0/100
```

We receive a result similar to the following:

```
{
  "numbers": [
    60,
    27,
    78,
    63,
    87
  ]
}
```

We moved more of our feature's code together; however, it is still divided into two files. This way of writing a feature is great if we want all parts of the feature to live together (the request and response DTOs, the logic, and the endpoint's delegate) but prefer to keep the code related to the ASP.NET Core `EndpointBuilder` elsewhere (the `app.MapGet` code, for example).

Since that is not always what we want, let's now explore a way to keep all the code together in a single feature file.

Feature: UpperCase

This feature transforms the input text to uppercase and returns the result.

Our objective is to centralize as much of the code as possible in the `UpperCase` feature class, so we control it from a single place. To achieve this, we create the following extension methods (highlighted):

```
namespace SimpleEndpoint;
public static class UpperCase
{
    public record class Request(string Text);
```

```
    public record class Response(string Text);
    public class Handler
    {
        public Response Handle(Request request)
        {
            return new Response(request.Text.ToUpper());
        }
    }

    public static IServiceCollection AddUpperCase(this IServiceCollection
services)
    {
        return services.AddSingleton<Handler>();
    }

    public static IEndpointRouteBuilder MapUpperCase(this IEndpointRouteBuilder
endpoints)
    {
        endpoints.MapGet(
            "/upper-case/{Text}",
            ([AsParameters] Request query, Handler handler)
                => handler.Handle(query)
        );
        return endpoints;
    }
}
```

In the preceding code, we changed the following:

- The `UpperCase` class is static to allow us to create extension methods. Turning the `UpperCase` class into a static class does not hinder our maintainability because we use it only as an organizer.
- We added the `AddUpperCase` method that registers the dependencies with the container.
- We added the `MapUpperCase` method that creates the endpoint itself.

In the `Program.cs` file, we can now register our feature like this:

```
builder.Services.AddUpperCase();
// ...
app.MapUpperCase();
```

The preceding code integrates the feature with ASP.NET Core by calling the `UpperCase` feature extension methods, which do the work. That showcases that all the related code is in the `UpperCase` class, thereby removing the logic from the `Program.cs` file.

I find this approach elegant and very clean for a no-dependency project. Of course, we could design this in a million different ways: use an existing library to help us, scan the assembly and auto-register our features, and more.

You can use this pattern to build a real-world application. I'd suggest creating an `AddFeatures` and a `MapFeatures` extension method that registers all the features instead of cluttering the `Program.cs` file, but besides a few final organizational touches, this is a robust enough pattern. We explore more of this in the next project.

When we send the following HTTP request:

```
GET https://localhost:7289/upper-case/I%20love%20ASP.NET%20Core
```

We receive the following response:

```
{
  "text": "I LOVE ASP.NET CORE"
}
```

Now that we have explored REPR and how to encapsulate our REPR features in several ways, we are almost ready to explore a larger project.

Conclusion

Creating a feature-based design using Minimal APIs, the REPR pattern, and no external dependencies is possible and simple. We organized our project in different ways. Each feature comprises a request, a response, and a handler attached to an endpoint.

We can combine the handler and the endpoint to make it a three-component pattern. What I like about having a distinct handler is that we can reuse the handler in a non-HTTP context; say, we could create a CLI tool in front of the application and reuse the same logic. It all depends on what we are building.

Let's see how the REPR pattern can help us follow the **SOLID** principles:

- **S**: Each piece has a single responsibility, and all pieces are centralized under a feature for ease of navigation, making this pattern a perfect SRP ally.
- **O**: Using an approach similar to what we did with the `UpperCase` feature, we can change the feature's behavior without affecting the rest of the codebase.
- **L**: N/A.
- **I**: The REPR pattern divides a feature into three smaller interfaces: the request, the endpoint, and the response.
- **D**: N/A.

Now that we have familiarized ourselves with the REPR pattern, it is time to explore a larger project, including exception handling and gray-box testing.

An e-commerce application—a slice of the real-world

This section covers parts of a larger project that extends beyond the REPR pattern, where we leverage notions we learned throughout the book and add new learning bits, while keeping the scope very narrow to ensure the project does not become too big. This learning exercise brings our journey closer to the real world. On top of this, we alter this project in the next few chapters to explore different ways to organize our code and solutions.

Context: This project slightly differs from the one we used in the previous four chapters about products and stocks. We remove the inventory from the product, add a unit price, and create a barebone shopping basket as a foundation for an e-commerce application. The inventory management became so complex that we had to extract and handle it separately (not included here).

By using the REPR pattern, Minimal APIs, and what we learned with Vertical Slice Architecture, we determine that the application contains two major areas:

- A product catalog
- A shopping cart

In this book, we focus on the shopping cart, but the code on GitHub implements parts of the product catalog as well.

For this first iteration, we keep the management of the products away from the application, supporting only the following features:

- Listing all products
- Fetching the details of a product

As for the shopping cart, we keep it to a minimum. The basket only persists the `Id` of the products in the cart and its quantity. The basket does not support any more advanced use cases. Here are the operations it supports:

- Add an item to the cart
- Fetch the items that are in the cart
- Remove an item from the cart
- Update the quantity of an item in the cart

For now, the shopping cart is not aware of the product catalog.

We improve the application in *Chapter 19, Introduction to Microservices Architecture,* and *Chapter 20, Modular Monolith.*

Let's assemble the stack we build upon next.

Assembling our stack

I want to keep the project as barebones as possible so that you learn about REPR and use Minimal APIs in the context of a larger application, without having to manually implement every single concern yourself. Here are the tools we will use to build this project:

- *ASP.NET Core Minimal API* as our backbone
- *FluentValidation* as our validation framework
- *FluentValidation.AspNetCore.Http* connects FluentValidation into Minimal API
- *Mapperly* is our mapping framework
- *ExceptionMapper* helps us handle exceptions globally, shifting our pattern to error management
- *EF Core* (InMemory) as our ORM

From a terminal window, we can use the CLI to install the packages:

```
dotnet add package FluentValidation.AspNetCore
dotnet add package ForEvolve.ExceptionMapper
dotnet add package ForEvolve.FluentValidation.AspNetCore.Http
dotnet add package Microsoft.EntityFrameworkCore.InMemory
dotnet add package Riok.Mapperly
```

We know most of those pieces and dig deeper into the new ones in time. Meanwhile, let's explore the structure of the project.

Dissecting the code structure

The directory structure is very similar to what we explored in Vertical Slice Architecture. The root of the project contains the `Program.cs` file and a `Features` directory that holds the features or slices. The following diagram represents the features:

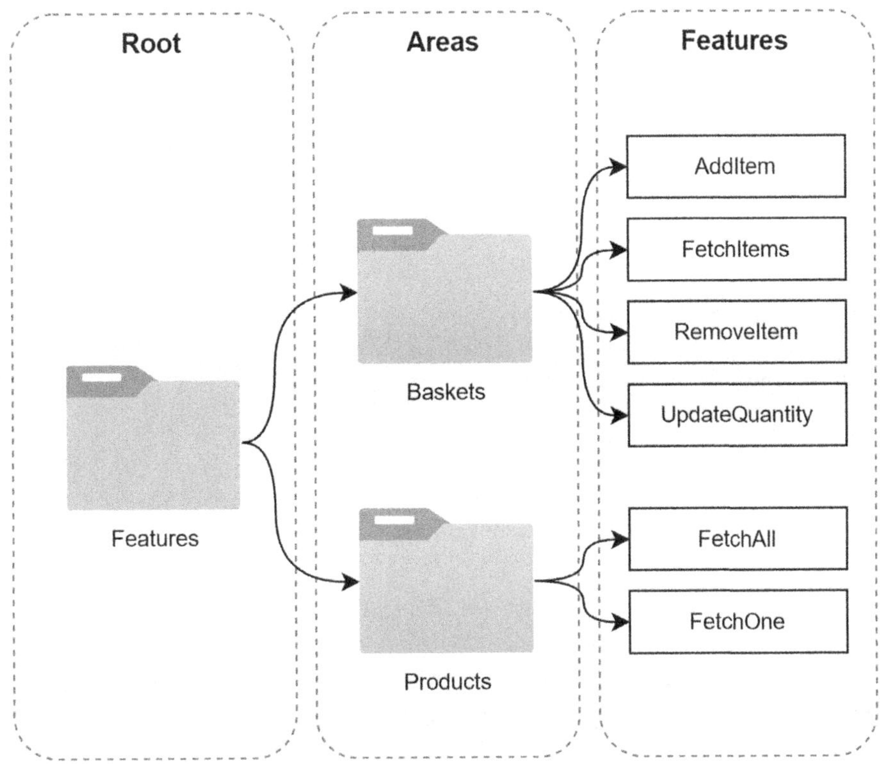

Figure 18.2: The project's directory structure, which represents the features' hierarchical relationships

The features inside each area share a cohesive bond and some pieces of code (coupling), while the two areas are entirely disconnected (loosely coupled).

The `Program.cs` file is very light and only bootstraps the application (we explore the highlighted implementation afterward):

```
using Web.Features;

var builder = WebApplication.CreateBuilder(args);
builder.AddFeatures();

var app = builder.Build();
app.MapFeatures();
await app.SeedFeaturesAsync();

app.Run();
```

The highlighted lines are extension methods defined in the `Features` class (located under the `Features` folder), which cascades the responsibility of registering the dependencies with the container, mapping the endpoints, and seeding the database to each area.

Here's the skeleton of the class that registers all the features we used in the `Program.cs` file in the preceding code block (we explore each method individually afterward):

```
using FluentValidation;
using FluentValidation.AspNetCore;
using System.Reflection;

namespace Web.Features;
public static class Features
{
    public static IServiceCollection AddFeatures(
        this WebApplicationBuilder builder){/*...*/}

    public static IEndpointRouteBuilder MapFeatures(
        this IEndpointRouteBuilder endpoints){/*...*/}

    public static async Task SeedFeaturesAsync(
        this WebApplication app){/*...*/}
}
```

Let's now explore the `AddFeatures` method:

```
public static IServiceCollection AddFeatures(this WebApplicationBuilder
builder)
{
    // Register fluent validation
    builder.AddFluentValidationEndpointFilter();
    return builder.Services
        .AddFluentValidationAutoValidation()
        .AddValidatorsFromAssembly(Assembly.GetExecutingAssembly())

        // Add features
        .AddProductsFeature()
        .AddBasketsFeature()
    ;
}
```

The `AddFeatures` method registers FluentValidation and the Minimal API filters to validate our endpoints (the highlighted line). Each slice defines its own configuration methods, like the `AddProductsFeature` and `AddBasketsFeature` methods.

We come back to those feature-specific methods. Meanwhile, let's explore the `MapFeatures` method of the `Features` class:

```
public static IEndpointRouteBuilder MapFeatures(this IEndpointRouteBuilder
endpoints)
{
    var group = endpoints
        .MapGroup("/")
        .AddFluentValidationFilter();
    ;
    group
        .MapProductsFeature()
        .MapBasketsFeature()
    ;
    return endpoints;
}
```

The `MapFeatures` method creates a root route group, adds the *FluentValidation* filter to it so the validation applies to all endpoints in this group, and then it calls the `MapProductsFeature` and `MapBasketsFeature` methods that map their features into the group.

Finally, the `SeedFeaturesAsync` method of the `Features` class seeds the database using the feature extension methods:

```
public static async Task SeedFeaturesAsync(this WebApplication app)
{
    using var scope = app.Services.CreateScope();
    await scope.SeedProductsAsync();
    await scope.SeedBasketAsync();
}
```

With those building blocks in place, the program starts, adds features, and registers endpoints. Afterward, each category of features—products and baskets—cascades the calls, letting each feature register its pieces and seed the database.

The following diagrams represent the call hierarchy from the `Program.cs` file. Let's start with the `AddFeatures` method:

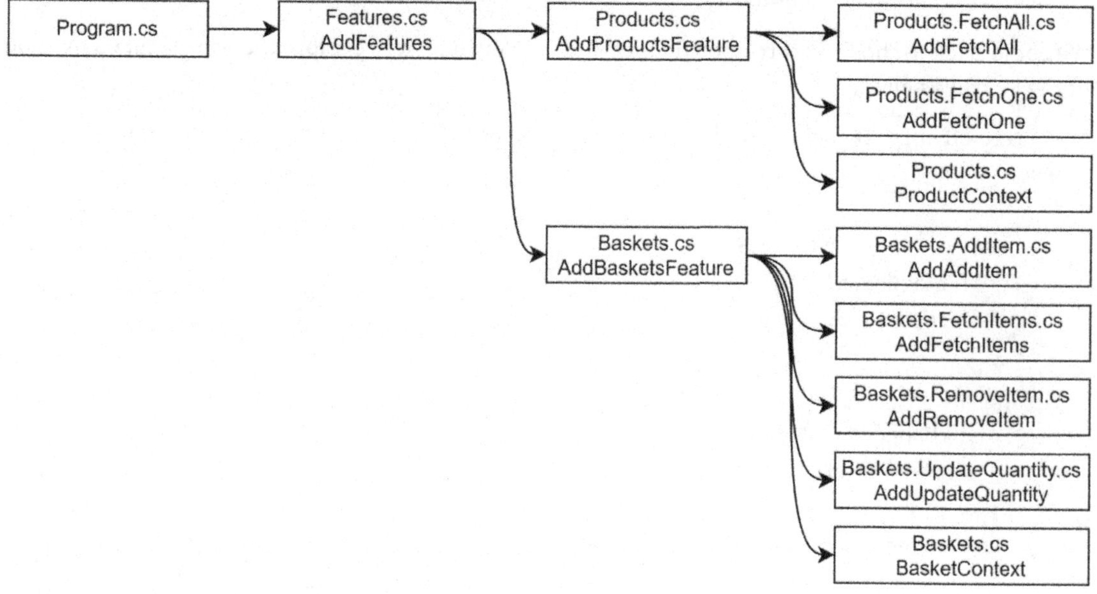

Figure 18.3: The call hierarchy of the AddFeatures method

The preceding diagram showcases the division of responsibilities where each piece aggregates its sub-parts or registers its dependencies.

A similar flow happens from the `MapFeatures` method:

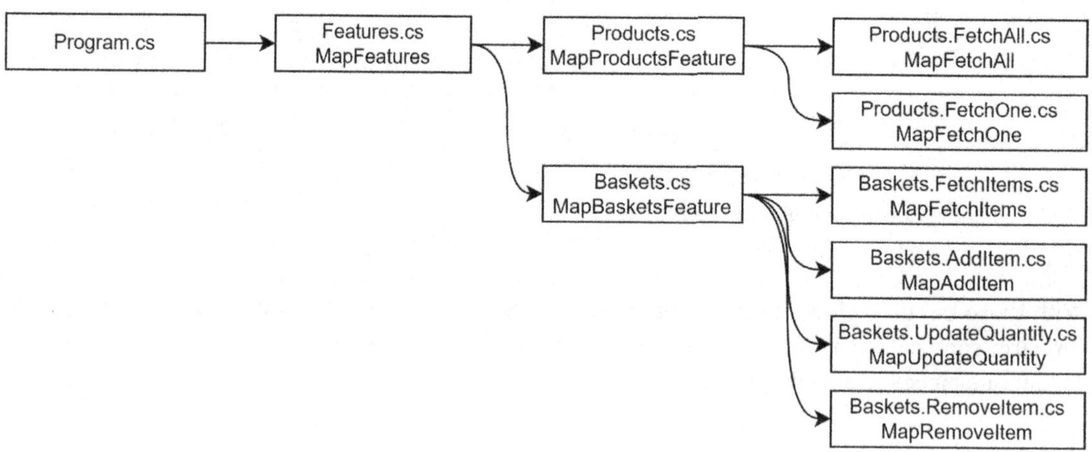

Figure 18.4: The call hierarchy of the MapFeatures method

Finally, the `SeedFeaturesAsync` method utilizes a similar approach to seed the in-memory database:

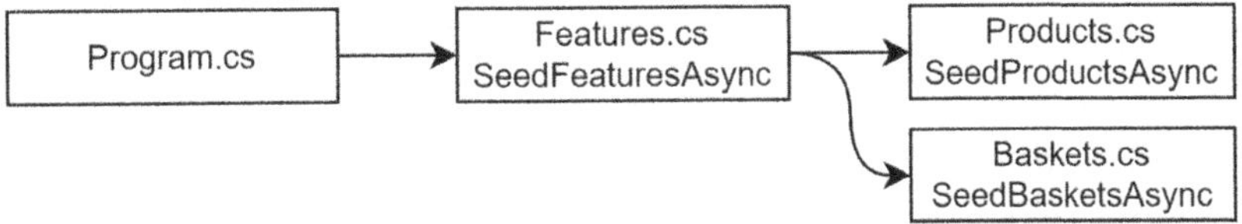

Figure 18.5: The call hierarchy of the SeedFeaturesAsync method

These diagrams showcase the entry point (`Program.cs`), cascading a call to each feature so that every piece handles itself.

In a real project using an actual database, you do not want to seed the database this way; otherwise, that code will insert a lot of duplicated data and create a mess. In this case, it works because each time we start the project, the database is empty because it only lives for the time the program runs—it lives in memory. There are numerous strategies to seed your data sources in real life, from executing a SQL script to deploying a Docker container that runs only once.

Now that we have explored the high-level view of the program, it is time to dig into a feature and explore how it works.

Exploring the shopping basket

This section explores the `AddItem` and `FetchItems` features of the shopping basket slice.

The slice is completely decoupled from the `Products` slice and does not know the products themselves. All it knows is how to accumulate product identifiers and quantities and associate those with a customer. We address this problem later.

There are no customer features and no authentication, keeping the project simple.

The code of the `Features/Baskets/Baskets.cs` file powers the shopping basket features. Here's the skeleton of that file:

```
using Microsoft.EntityFrameworkCore;
using Microsoft.EntityFrameworkCore.Diagnostics;

namespace Web.Features;

public static partial class Baskets
```

```
{
    public record class BasketItem(int CustomerId, int ProductId, int
Quantity);

    public class BasketContext : DbContext {/*...*/}

    public static IServiceCollection AddBasketsFeature(this IServiceCollection
services) {/*...*/}

    public static IEndpointRouteBuilder MapBasketsFeature(this
IEndpointRouteBuilder endpoints) {/*...*/}

    public static Task SeedBasketsAsync(this IServiceScope scope) {/*...*/}
}
```

The highlighted code of the preceding block contains the `BasketItem` data model and the `BasketContext` EF Core `DbContext`, which all basket features share. It also includes the three methods that register and make the features work (`AddBasketsFeature`, `MapBasketsFeature`, and `SeedBasketsAsync`).

I used the `partial` modifier to split the nested classes into multiple files. We explore some of those files later. I made the class `static` to create extension methods in it.

The `BasketItem` class allows us to persist a simple shopping cart to the database:

```
public record class BasketItem(
    int CustomerId,
    int ProductId,
    int Quantity
);
```

The `BasketContext` class configures the primary key of the `BasketItem` class and exposes the `Items` property (highlighted):

```
public class BasketContext : DbContext
{
    public BasketContext(DbContextOptions<BasketContext> options)
        : base(options) { }

    public DbSet<BasketItem> Items => Set<BasketItem>();

    protected override void OnModelCreating(ModelBuilder modelBuilder)
```

```
    {
        base.OnModelCreating(modelBuilder);
        modelBuilder
            .Entity<BasketItem>()
            .HasKey(x => new { x.CustomerId, x.ProductId })
        ;
    }
}
```

The AddBasketsFeature method registers each feature and the BasketContext with the IoC container:

```
public static IServiceCollection AddBasketsFeature(this IServiceCollection
services)
{
    return services
        .AddAddItem()
        .AddFetchItems()
        .AddRemoveItem()
        .AddUpdateQuantity()
        .AddDbContext<BasketContext>(options => options
            .UseInMemoryDatabase("BasketContextMemoryDB")
            .ConfigureWarnings(builder => builder.Ignore(InMemoryEventId.
TransactionIgnoredWarning))
        )
    ;
}
```

Besides the AddDbContext method, the AddBasketsFeature delegates the registration of dependencies to each feature. We explore the highlighted ones shortly. The EF Core code registers the in-memory provider that serves the BasketContext.

Next, the MapBasketsFeature method maps the endpoints:

```
public static IEndpointRouteBuilder MapBasketsFeature(this
IEndpointRouteBuilder endpoints)
{
    var group = endpoints
        .MapGroup(nameof(Baskets).ToLower())
        .WithTags(nameof(Baskets))
    ;
    group
        .MapFetchItems()
        .MapAddItem()
        .MapUpdateQuantity()
```

```
        .MapRemoveItem()
    ;
    return endpoints;
}
```

The preceding code creates a group, naming it `baskets`, and makes its endpoints accessible using the `/baskets` URL prefix. We also tag the group "Baskets" to leverage an OpenAPI generator in the future. Then, the method uses a similar pattern to the `AddBasketsFeature` method and delegates the endpoint mapping to the features.

Have you noticed that the method returns the `endpoints` object directly? This allows us to chain the feature mapping. In another scenario, we could return the group object (`RouteGroupBuilder` instance) to let the caller further configure the group. What we build should always align with the needs and technical objectives of the project.

Finally, the `SeedBasketsAsync` method does nothing; we do not create any shopping cart when starting the program, unlike the `Products` slice:

```
public static Task SeedBasketsAsync(this IServiceScope scope)
{
    return Task.CompletedTask;
}
```

We could have omitted the preceding method. I left it so we follow a linear pattern between the features. Such a linear pattern makes it easier to understand and learn. It also allows identifying the recurring pieces we could work on to automate the registration process.

Now that we have covered the shared pieces, let's add data to our shopping basket.

AddItem feature

The role of the `AddItem` feature is to create a `BasketItem` object and persist it in the database. To achieve this, we leverage the REPR pattern. Inspired by the preceding few chapters, we name the request `Command` (CQS pattern), add a mapper object using Mapperly, and leverage FluentValidation to ensure the request is valid. Here's the skeleton of the `AddItem` class:

```
using FluentValidation;
using Microsoft.EntityFrameworkCore;
using Riok.Mapperly.Abstractions;

namespace Web.Features;

public partial class Baskets
```

```
{
    public partial class AddItem
    {
        public record class Command(
            int CustomerId,
            int ProductId,
            int Quantity
        );
        public record class Response(
            int ProductId,
            int Quantity
        );
        [Mapper]
        public partial class Mapper {/*...*/}
        public class Validator : AbstractValidator<Command> {/*...*/}
        public class Handler {/*...*/}
    }
    public static IServiceCollection AddAddItem(this IServiceCollection
services) {/*...*/}
    public static IEndpointRouteBuilder MapAddItem(this IEndpointRouteBuilder
endpoints) {/*...*/}
}
```

The preceding code contains all the necessary pieces of the feature:

- The request (the `Command` class)
- The response (the `Response` class)
- A mapper object that has Mapperly generate the mapping code for us
- A validator class that ensures the input we receive is valid
- The `Handler` class containing the endpoint logic
- The `MapAddItem` method routing the requests to the `Handler` class
- The `AddAddItem` method, which registers its services with the IoC container

Let's start with the `Mapper` class that the `Handler` class uses:

```
[Mapper]
public partial class Mapper
{
    public partial BasketItem Map(Command item);
    public partial Response Map(BasketItem item);
}
```

Next, the following `Validator` class validates the `Command` object before it arrives at the `Handler.HandleAsync` method, through the `FluentValidationEndpointFilter`:

```
public class Validator : AbstractValidator<Command>
{
    public Validator()
    {
        RuleFor(x => x.CustomerId).GreaterThan(0);
        RuleFor(x => x.ProductId).GreaterThan(0);
        RuleFor(x => x.Quantity).GreaterThan(0);
    }
}
```

As a reminder, in the `Features.cs` file, we called the `AddFluentValidationFilter` method on the root route group, letting the `FluentValidationEndpointFilter` class validate the inputs for us using the `Validator` class.

Next, the `Handler` class is the core of the feature, the business logic that justifies the endpoint to exist in the first place:

```
public class Handler
{
    private readonly BasketContext _db;
    private readonly Mapper _mapper;

    public Handler(BasketContext db, Mapper mapper)
    {
        _db = db ?? throw new ArgumentNullException(nameof(db));
        _mapper = mapper ?? throw new ArgumentNullException(nameof(mapper));
    }

    public async Task<Response> HandleAsync(Command command, CancellationToken 
cancellationToken)
    {
        var itemExists = await _db.Items.AnyAsync(
            x => x.CustomerId == command.CustomerId && x.ProductId == command.
ProductId,
            cancellationToken: cancellationToken
        );
        if (itemExists)
```

```
        {
            throw new DuplicateBasketItemException(command.ProductId);
        }
        var item = _mapper.Map(command);
        _db.Add(item);
        await _db.SaveChangesAsync(cancellationToken);
        var result = _mapper.Map(item);
        return result;
    }
}
```

The preceding code contains the business logic of the feature by ensuring the item is not already in the basket. If it is, it throws a `DuplicateBasketItemException`. Otherwise, it saves the item to the database. It then returns a `Response` object.

Each customer (`CustomerId`) can have each product (`ProductId`) once in its cart (the composite primary key), which is why we test for this condition.

Next, the `MapAddItem` method routes the appropriate POST requests with a valid `Command` object in its body to the `Handler` class:

```
public static IEndpointRouteBuilder MapAddItem(
    this IEndpointRouteBuilder endpoints)
{
    endpoints.MapPost(
        "/",
        async (AddItem.Command command, AddItem.Handler handler,
CancellationToken cancellationToken) =>
        {
            var result = await handler.HandleAsync(
                command,
                cancellationToken
            );
            return TypedResults.Created(
                $"/products/{result.ProductId}",
                result
            );
        }
    );
    return endpoints;
}
```

The `Command` instance is a copy of the `BasketItem` class, while the response only returns the `ProductId` and `Quantity` properties. The highlighted lines represent the endpoint handing off the `Command` object to the use case `Handler` class.

We could write the `Handler` code in the delegate, which would make unit testing the delegate very hard.

Finally, let's look at the `AddAddItem` method that registers the feature's services with the IoC container:

```
public static IServiceCollection AddAddItem(this IServiceCollection services)
{
    return services
        .AddScoped<AddItem.Handler>()
        .AddSingleton<AddItem.Mapper>()
    ;
}
```

With all of these small pieces in place, we can send the following HTTP request:

```
POST https://localhost:7252/baskets
Content-Type: application/json

{
    "customerId": 1,
    "productId": 3,
    "quantity": 10
}
```

The endpoint responds with the following:

```
{
  "productId": 3,
  "quantity": 10
}
```

And it has the following HTTP header:

```
Location: /products/3
```

To recap, here's what happens:

1. ASP.NET Core routes the request to the delegate we registered in the `MapAddItem` method.
2. The validation middleware runs an `AddItem.Validator` object against the `AddItem.Command` sent to the endpoint. The request is valid.

3. The `HandleAsync` method of the `AddItem.Handler` class is executed.
4. Assuming the item is not already in the customer's basket, it is added to the database.
5. The `HandleAsync` method returns a `Response` object to the delegate.
6. The delegate returns a `201 Create` status code, with the `Location` header set to the URL of the product that was added.

As the preceding steps depict, the process is quite simple: a request comes in, the business logic is executed (endpoint), and then a response goes out—REPR.

There are a few more pieces, but they save us the trouble of object mapping and validation. Those pieces are optional; you can conceive your own stack with more or fewer pieces in it.

On top of the feature code, we also have a few tests to assess that the business logic remains correct over time. We cover those under the *Gray-box testing* section. Meanwhile, let's look at exception handling.

Managing exception handling

The `AddItem` feature throws a `DuplicateBasketItemException` when a product is already in the basket. However, when that happens, the server returns an error that resembles the following (partial output):

```
Web.Features.DuplicateBasketItemException: The product '3' is already in your
shopping cart.
   at Web.Features.Baskets.AddItem.Handler.HandleAsync(Command command,
CancellationToken cancellationToken) in C18\REPR\Web\Features\Baskets\Baskets.
AddItem.cs:line 57
   at Web.Features.Baskets.<>c.<<MapAddItem>b__2_0>d.MoveNext() in C18\REPR\
Web\Features\Baskets\Baskets.AddItem.cs:line 82
--- End of stack trace from previous location ---
```

That error is ugly and impractical for a client calling the API. To circumvent this, we can add a try-catch somewhere and treat each exception individually, or we can use a middleware to catch the exceptions and normalize their output.

Managing exceptions one by one is tedious and error-prone. On the other hand, centralizing exception management and treating them as a cross-cutting concern transforms the tedious mechanism into a new tool to leverage. Moreover, it ensures that the API always returns the errors in the same format, with no additional effort.

Let's program a basic middleware.

Creating an exception handler middleware

A middleware in ASP.NET Core is executed as part of the pipeline and can run before and after the execution of an endpoint.

When an exception occurs, the request is re-executed in a parallel pipeline, allowing different middleware to manage the error flow.

To create a middleware, we must implement an `InvokeAsync` method. The easiest way to do this is by implementing the `IMiddleware` interface. You can add middleware types to the default or exception-handling alternate pipelines.

The following code represents a basic exception-handling middleware:

```
using Microsoft.AspNetCore.Diagnostics;
namespace Web;
public class MyExceptionMiddleware : IMiddleware
{
    public async Task InvokeAsync(HttpContext context, RequestDelegate next)
    {
        var exceptionHandlerPathFeature = context.Features
            .Get<IExceptionHandlerFeature>() ?? throw new
NotSupportedException();

        var exception = exceptionHandlerPathFeature.Error;
        await context.Response.WriteAsJsonAsync(new
        {
            Error = exception.Message
        });
        await next(context);
    }
}
```

The middleware fetches the `IExceptionHandlerFeature` to access the error and outputs an object containing the error message (ASP.NET Core manages this feature). If the feature is unavailable, the middleware throws a `NotSupportedException`, which rethrows the original exception.

Any type of exception that a middleware of the alternate pipeline throws will rethrow the original exception.

If there is any, the highlighted code executes the next middleware in the pipeline. These pipelines are like a chain of responsibilities but with a different objective.

To register the middleware, we must first add it to the container:

```
builder.Services.AddSingleton<MyExceptionMiddleware>();
```

Then, we must register it as part of the exception-handling alternate pipeline:

```
app.UseExceptionHandler(errorApp =>
{
    errorApp.UseMiddleware<MyExceptionMiddleware>();
});
```

We could also register more middleware or create them inline, like this:

```
app.UseExceptionHandler(errorApp =>
{
    errorApp.Use(async (context, next) =>
    {
        var exceptionHandlerPathFeature = context.Features
            .Get<IExceptionHandlerFeature>() ?? throw new
NotSupportedException();
        var logger = context.RequestServices
            .GetRequiredService<ILoggerFactory>()
            .CreateLogger("ExceptionHandler");
        var exception = exceptionHandlerPathFeature.Error;
        logger.LogWarning(
            "An exception occurred: {message}",
            exception.Message
        );
        await next(context);
    });
    errorApp.UseMiddleware<MyExceptionMiddleware>();
});
```

The possibilities are vast.

Now, if we try to add a duplicated item to the basket, we get a **500 Internal Server Error** with the following body:

```
{
  "error": "The product \u00273\u0027 is already in your shopping cart."
}
```

This response is more elegant than before and easier to handle for the clients. We could also alter the status code in the middleware. However, customizing this middleware would take many pages, so we leverage an existing library instead.

Exception handling using ExceptionMapper

The `ForEvolve.ExceptionMapper` package is an ASP.NET Core middleware that allows us to map exceptions to different status codes. Out of the box, it offers many exception types to get started, handles them, and allows easy mapping between a custom exception and a status code. By default, the library serializes the exceptions to a `ProblemDetails` object (based on RFC 7807) by leveraging as many ASP.NET Core components as possible, so we can customize parts of the library by customizing ASP.NET Core.

To get started, in the `Program.cs` file, we must add the following lines:

```
// Add the dependencies to the container
builder.AddExceptionMapper();

// Register the middleware
app.UseExceptionMapper();
```

Now, if we try to add a duplicated product to the basket, we receive a response with a **409 Conflict** status code with the following body:

```
{
  "type": "https://tools.ietf.org/html/rfc9110#section-15.5.10",
  "title": "The product \u00273\u0027 is already in your shopping cart.",
  "status": 409,
  "traceId": "00-74bdbaa08064fd97ba1de31802ec6f8f-31ffd9ea8215b706-00",
  "debug": {
    "type": {
      "name": "DuplicateBasketItemException",
      "fullName": "Web.Features.DuplicateBasketItemException"
    },
    "stackTrace": "..."
  }
}
```

This output is starting to look like something!

The debug object (highlighted) only appears in development or as an opt-in option.

How can the middleware know it's a 409 Conflict and not a 500 Internal Server Error? Simple! The `DuplicateBasketItemException` inherits from the `ConflictException` that comes from the `ForEvolve.ExceptionMapper` namespace (highlighted):

```
using ForEvolve.ExceptionMapper;
namespace Web.Features;
public class DuplicateBasketItemException : ConflictException
{
    public DuplicateBasketItemException(int productId)
        : base($"The product '{productId}' is already in your shopping cart.")
    {
    }
}
```

With this setup, we can leverage exceptions to return errors with different status codes.

I have used this methodology for many years, and it simplifies the program structure and developers' lives. The idea is to harness the power and simplicity of exceptions.

For example, we may want to map EF Core errors, `DbUpdateException` and `DbUpdateConcurrencyException`, to a *409 Conflict* as well, so if we forget to catch a database error, the middleware will do it for us. To achieve this, we can customize the middleware this way:

```
builder.AddExceptionMapper(builder =>
{
    builder
        .Map<DbUpdateException>()
        .ToStatusCode(StatusCodes.Status409Conflict)
    ;
    builder
        .Map<DbUpdateConcurrencyException>()
        .ToStatusCode(StatusCodes.Status409Conflict)
    ;
});
```

With that in place, if a client hits an unhandled EF Core exception, the server will respond with something like the following (I omitted the stack trace for brevity reasons):

```
{
  "type": "https://tools.ietf.org/html/rfc9110#section-15.5.10",
  "title": "Exception of type \u0027Microsoft.EntityFrameworkCore.
DbUpdateException\u0027 was thrown.",
```

```
  "status": 409,
  "traceId": "00-74bdbaa08064fd97ba1de31802ec6f8f-a5ac17f17da8d2db-00",
  "debug": {
    "type": {
      "name": "DbUpdateException",
      "fullName": "Microsoft.EntityFrameworkCore.DbUpdateException"
    },
    "stackTrace": "..."
  },
  "entries": []
}
```

In an actual project, for security reasons, I recommend customizing the error handling further to hide the fact that we are using EF Core. We must give as little information as possible about our systems to malicious actors to keep them as secure and safe as possible. We won't cover creating custom exception handlers here because it is out of the scope of the chapter.

As we can see, it is easy to register custom exceptions and associate them with a status code. We can do this with any custom exception or inherit from an existing one to make it work with customization.

As of version 3.0.29, *ExceptionMapper* offers the following exception associations:

Exception Type	**Status Code**
`BadRequestException`	`StatusCodes.Status400BadRequest`
`ConflictException`	`StatusCodes.Status409Conflict`
`ForbiddenException`	`StatusCodes.Status403Forbidden`
`GoneException`	`StatusCodes.Status410Gone`
`NotFoundException`	`StatusCodes.Status404NotFound`
`ResourceNotFoundException`	`StatusCodes.Status404NotFound`
`UnauthorizedException`	`StatusCodes.Status401Unauthorized`
`GatewayTimeoutException`	`StatusCodes.Status504GatewayTimeout`
`InternalServerErrorException`	`StatusCodes.Status500InternalServerError`
`ServiceUnavailableException`	`StatusCodes.Status503ServiceUnavailable`

Table 18.1: ExceptionMapper custom exception associations

You can inherit from those standard exceptions, and the middleware will associate them with the correct status code, as we did with the `DuplicateBasketItemException` class.

ExceptionMapper also maps the following .NET exceptions automatically:

- `BadHttpRequestException` to `StatusCodes.Status400BadRequest`
- `NotImplementedException` to `StatusCodes.Status501NotImplemented`

In the project, there are three custom exceptions that you can find on GitHub:

- `BasketItemNotFoundException`, which inherits from `NotFoundException`
- `DuplicateBasketItemException`, which inherits from `ConflictException`
- `ProductNotFoundException`, which inherits from `NotFoundException`

Next, we explore this way of thinking about error propagation a little more.

Leveraging exceptions to propagate errors

With the middleware of *ExceptionMapper* in place, we can treat exceptions as a simple tool to propagate errors to the clients. We can throw an existing exception, like a `NotFoundException`, or create a custom reusable one with a more precise preconfigured error message.

When we want the server to return a specific error, all we must do is:

1. Create a new exception type.
2. Inherit from an existing type from *ExceptionMapper* or register our custom exception with the middleware.
3. Throw our custom exception anywhere in the REPR flow.
4. Let the middleware do its job.

Here's a simplified representation of this flow, using the `AddItem` endpoint as an example:

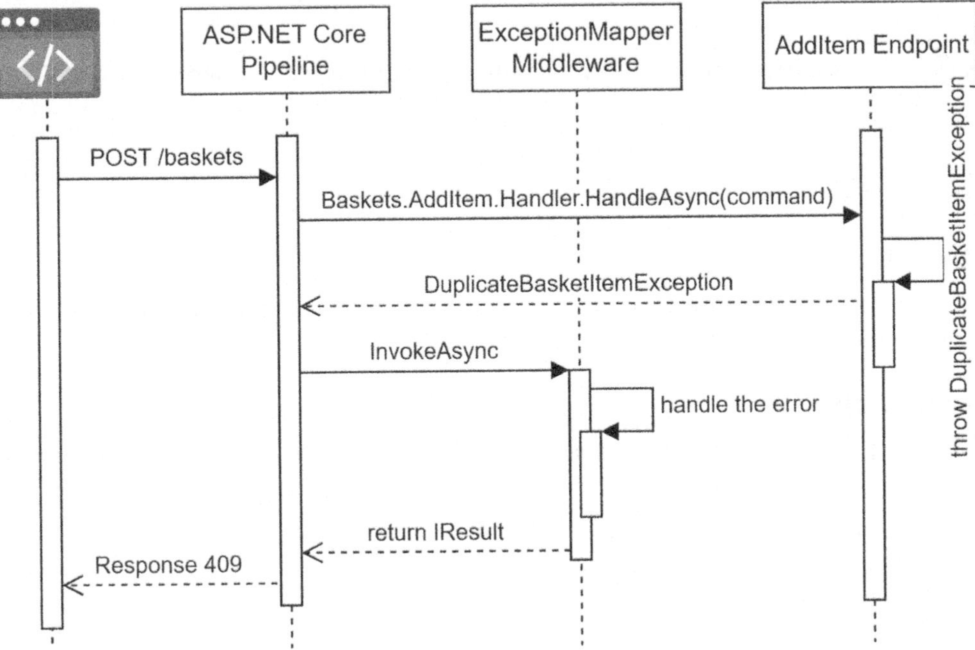

Figure 18.6: A simplified view of an exception flow using ExceptionMapper

With this in place, we have a simple way to return errors to the clients from anywhere in the REPR flow. Moreover, our errors are consistently formatted the same way.

The exception handling pattern and the `ExceptionMapper` library also work with MVC and allow us to customize error formatting.

Next, let's explore a few test cases.

Gray-box testing

Using Vertical Slice Architecture or REPR makes writing gray-box tests very convenient.

The test project mainly comprises integration tests that use the gray-box philosophy. Since we know the application under test's inner workings, we can manipulate the data from the EF Core `DbContext` objects, which allows us to write almost end-to-end tests very quickly. The confidence level we get from those tests is very high because they test the whole stack, including HTTP, not just some scattered pieces, leading to a very high level of code coverage per test case.

Of course, integration tests are slower, yet not that slow. It is up to you to create the right balance of unit and integration tests. In this case, I focused on gray-box integration testing, which led to 13 tests covering 97.2% of the lines and 63.1% of the branches. The guard clauses represent most of the branches that we do not test. We could write a few unit tests to boost the numbers if we'd like.

We explored white-, gray- and black-box testing in *Chapter 2, Automated Testing*.

Let's start by exploring the `AddItem` tests.

AddItemTest

The `AddItem` feature is the first use case we explored. We need three tests to cover all scenarios except the `Handler` class guard clauses.

First test method

The following gray-box integration test ensures an HTTP POST request adds the item to the database:

```
[Fact]
public async Task Should_add_the_new_item_to_the_basket()
{
    // Arrange
    await using var application = new C18WebApplication();
    var client = application.CreateClient();

    // Act
```

```
    var response = await client.PostAsJsonAsync(
        "/baskets",
        new AddItem.Command(4, 1, 22)
    );

    // Assert the response
    Assert.NotNull(response);
    Assert.True(response.IsSuccessStatusCode);
    var result = await response.Content
        .ReadFromJsonAsync<AddItem.Response>();
    Assert.NotNull(result);
    Assert.Equal(1, result.ProductId);
    Assert.Equal(22, result.Quantity);

    // Assert the database state
    using var seedScope = application.Services.CreateScope();
    var db = seedScope.ServiceProvider
        .GetRequiredService<BasketContext>();
    var dbItem = db.Items.FirstOrDefault(x => x.CustomerId == 4 && x.ProductId
== 1);
    Assert.NotNull(dbItem);
    Assert.Equal(22, dbItem.Quantity);
}
```

The *Arrange* block of the preceding test case creates a test application and an `HttpClient`. It then sends an `AddItem.Command` to the endpoint in its *Act* block.

Afterward, it splits the *Assert* block in two: the HTTP response and the database itself. The first part ensures that the endpoint returns the expected data. The second part ensures that the database is in the correct state.

It is a good habit to ensure the database is in the correct state, especially with EF Core or most Unit of Work implementations, because you could add an item and forget to save the changes, leading to an incorrect database state. Yet, the data returned by the endpoint would have been correct.

We could test more or fewer elements here. We could refactor the *Assert* block so that it becomes more elegant. We can and should continuously improve all types of code, including tests. However, in this case, I wanted to keep as much of the logic in the test method to make it easier to understand.

It is also a good practice to keep test methods as independent as possible. This does not mean that improving readability and encapsulating code into helper classes or methods is wrong—on the contrary.

The only opaque piece of the test method is the `C18WebApplication` class, which inherits from the `WebApplicationFactory<Program>` class and implements a few helper methods to simplify the configuration of the test application. You can treat it as an instance of the `WebApplicationFactory<Program>` class. Feel free to browse the code on GitHub and explore its inner workings.

Creating an `Application` class is a good reusability pattern. However, creating an application per test method is not the most performant method because you boot the entire program for every test.

You can use test fixtures to reuse and share an instance of the program between multiple tests. However, remember that the application's state and, potentially, the database are also shared between tests.

The second test is next.

Second test method

This test ensures that the `Location` header contains a valid URL. This test is important, since the `Baskets` and the `Products` features are loosely coupled and can change independently. Here's the code:

```
[Fact]
public async Task Should_return_a_valid_product_url()
{
    // Arrange
    await using var application = new C18WebApplication();
    await application.SeedAsync<Products.ProductContext>(async db =>
    {
        db.Products.RemoveRange(db.Products);
        db.Products.Add(new("A test product", 15.22m, 1));
        await db.SaveChangesAsync();
    });
    var client = application.CreateClient();

    // Act
    var response = await client.PostAsJsonAsync(
        "/baskets",
        new AddItem.Command(4, 1, 22)
    );

    // Assert
    Assert.NotNull(response);
    Assert.Equal(HttpStatusCode.Created, response.StatusCode);
    Assert.NotNull(response.Headers.Location);
```

```
    var productResponse = await client
        .GetAsync(response.Headers.Location);
    Assert.NotNull(productResponse);
    Assert.True(productResponse.IsSuccessStatusCode);
}
```

The preceding test method is similar to the first one.

The *Arrange* block creates an application, seeds the database, and creates an `HttpClient`. The `SeedAsync` method is one of the helper methods of the `C18WebApplication` class.

The *Act* block sends a request to create a basket item.

The *Assert* block is divided in two. The first ensures that the HTTP response contains a `Location` header and that the status code is 201. The second part (highlighted) takes the `Location` header and sends an HTTP request to validate the URL's validity. This test ensures that if we change the URL of the `Products.FetchOne` endpoint (say, we prefer `/catalog` over `/products`), this test will alert us.

We explore the third test case next.

Third test method

The last test method ensures that the endpoint responds with a 409 Conflict status when a consumer tries to add an existing item:

```
[Fact]
public async Task Should_return_a_ProblemDetails_with_a_Conflict_status_code()
{
    // Arrange
    await using var application = new C18WebApplication();
    await application.SeedAsync<BasketContext>(async db =>
    {
        db.Items.RemoveRange(db.Items);
        db.Items.Add(new(
            CustomerId: 1,
            ProductId: 1,
            Quantity: 10
        ));
        await db.SaveChangesAsync();
    });
    var client = application.CreateClient();

    // Act
    var response = await client.PostAsJsonAsync(
        "/baskets",
```

```
        new AddItem.Command(
            CustomerId: 1,
            ProductId: 1,
            Quantity: 20
        )
    );

    // Assert the response
    Assert.NotNull(response);
    Assert.False(response.IsSuccessStatusCode);
    Assert.Equal(HttpStatusCode.Conflict, response.StatusCode);
    var problem = await response.Content
        .ReadFromJsonAsync<ProblemDetails>();
    Assert.NotNull(problem);
    Assert.Equal("The product \u00271\u0027 is already in your shopping cart.",
problem.Title);

    // Assert the database state
    using var seedScope = application.Services.CreateScope();
    var db = seedScope.ServiceProvider
        .GetRequiredService<BasketContext>();
    var dbItem = db.Items.FirstOrDefault(x => x.CustomerId == 1 && x.ProductId
== 1);
    Assert.NotNull(dbItem);
    Assert.Equal(10, dbItem.Quantity);
}
```

The preceding test method is very similar to the other two.

The *Arrange* block creates a test application, seeds the database, and creates an `HttpClient`.

The *Act* block sends a request using the only item in the database, which we expect to result in a conflict.

The first part of the *Assert* block ensures that the endpoint returns the expected `ProblemDetails` object. The second part validates that the endpoint has not changed the quantity in the database.

With those three tests, we cover the relevant code of the `AddItem` feature.

The other test cases are similar, sending HTTP requests and validating the database content. Each feature has between one and three tests.

And we are done. Let's summarize what we have learned before moving on to the next chapter.

Summary

We delved into the Request-EndPoint-Response (REPR) design pattern and learned that REPR follows the most foundational pattern of the web. The client sends a request to an endpoint, which processes it and returns a response. The pattern focuses on designing the backend code around the endpoint, making it faster to develop, easier to find your way around the project, and more focused on features than MVC and layers.

We also took a CQS approach to the requests, making them queries or commands, and depicting all that can happen in a program: read or write states.

We explored ways to organize code around such a pattern, from implementing trivial to more complex features. We built a technology stack to create an e-commerce web application that leverages the REPR pattern and a feature-oriented design. We learned how to leverage middleware to handle exceptions globally and how the *ExceptionMapper* library provides us with this capability. We also used gray-box testing to cover almost all of the project's logic with just a few tests.

Next, we explore microservices architecture, which introduces numerous software engineering concepts.

Questions

Let's take a look at a few practice questions:

1. Do we need to use the *FluentValidation* and *ExceptionMapper* libraries when implementing the REPR pattern?
2. What are the three components of the REPR pattern?
3. Does the REPR pattern dictate that we use nested classes?
4. Why do gray-box integration tests provide a high degree of confidence?
5. Name an advantage of handling exceptions using middleware.

Further reading

Here are a few links to build upon what we learned in the chapter:

- FluentValidation: `https://adpg.link/xXgp`
- FluentValidation.AspNetCore.Http: `https://adpg.link/qsao`
- ExceptionMapper: `https://adpg.link/ESDb`
- Mapperly: `https://adpg.link/Dwcj`
- MVC Controllers are Dinosaurs – Embrace API Endpoints: `https://adpg.link/NGjm`

Answers

1. No. REPR does not dictate how to implement it. You can create your own stack or go with a barebones ASP.NET Core Minimal API, implementing everything by hand in the project.
2. REPR consists of a request, an endpoint, and a response.

3. No. REPR does not prescribe any implementation details.
4. Gray-box integration tests provide a lot of confidence in their outcome because they test the feature almost end to end, ensuring that all the pieces are there, from the services in the IoC container to the database.
5. Handling exceptions using middleware allows for centralizing the management of exceptions, encapsulating that responsibility in a single place. It also uniformizes the output, sending the clients a response in the same format for all errors. It removes the burden of handling each exception individually, eliminating `try-catch` boilerplate code.

Learn more on Discord

To join the Discord community for this book – where you can share feedback, ask questions to the author, and learn about new releases – follow the QR code below:

`https://packt.link/ArchitectingASPNETCoreApps3e`

19

Introduction to Microservices Architecture

The chapter covers some essential microservices architecture concepts. It is designed to get you started with those principles and to give you an overview of the concepts surrounding microservices, which should help you make informed decisions about whether to go for a microservices architecture or not.

Since microservices architecture is larger in scale than the previous application-scale patterns we visited and often involves complex components or setup, there is limited C# code in the chapter. Instead, I explain the concepts and list open-source or commercial offerings that you can leverage to apply these patterns to your applications. Moreover, you should not aim to implement many of the pieces discussed in the chapter yourself, as it can be a lot of work to get them right, and they don't add business value, so you are better off just using an existing implementation instead. There is more context about this throughout the chapter.

In this chapter, we cover the following topics:

- What are microservices?
- An introduction to event-driven architecture
- Introducing Gateway patterns
- Project – BFF (that transforms the REPR project into microservices)
- Revisiting the CQRS pattern
- The Microservices Adapter pattern

Let's get started!

What are microservices?

Microservices represent an application that is divided into multiple smaller applications. Each application, or microservice, interacts with the others to create a scalable system. Usually, but not necessarily, microservices are deployed to the cloud as containerized or serverless applications.

Before getting into too many details, these are the principles to keep in mind when building microservices:

- Each microservice should be a cohesive unit of business
- Each microservice should own its data
- Each microservice should be independent of the others

Furthermore, everything we have studied so far—the other principles of designing software—applies to microservices but on another scale. For example, you don't want tight coupling between microservices (solved by microservices independence), but coupling is inevitable (as with any code). There are numerous ways to solve this problem, such as the Publish-Subscribe pattern.

There are no hard rules about how to design microservices, how to divide them, how big they should be, and what to put where. Nevertheless, I lay down a few foundations to help you get started and orient your journey into microservices.

Beforehand, don't worry—all of the knowledge you have acquired since the beginning of this book is still worthwhile. Monolithic architecture patterns, such as Vertical Slice and Clean Architecture, are still good to know, as you can apply those to individual microservices.

Cohesive unit of business

A microservice should have a single business responsibility. Always design the system with the domain in mind, which should help you divide the application into multiple pieces. If you know **Domain-Driven Design (DDD)**, a microservice will most likely represent a **Bounded Context**, which in turn is what I call a *cohesive unit of business*. Basically, a cohesive unit of business (or bounded context) is a self-contained part of the domain with limited interactions with other parts.

Domain-Driven Design (DDD) is a software design approach focusing on understanding the business domain and its complexities to create effective domain models. It emphasizes collaboration between technical and domain experts to solve problems within a specific domain context.

Even if a **microservice** has *micro* in its name, it is more important to group logical operations under it than to aim at a micro-size. Don't get me wrong here; if your unit is tiny, that's even better. However, suppose you split a unit of business into multiple smaller parts instead of keeping it together (breaking cohesion); you are likely to introduce useless chattiness within your system (coupling between microservices). This could lead to performance degradation and to a system that is harder to debug, test, maintain, monitor, and deploy.

Moreover, it is easier to split a big microservice into smaller pieces than to assemble multiple microservices back together. To help you divide your microservices to an appropriate size, apply the SRP to your microservices; a microservice should have only one reason to change unless you have a good reason to do otherwise.

Ownership of data

Each microservice should be the source of truth of its cohesive unit of business. A microservice should share its data through an API (a web API/HTTP, for example) or another mechanism (integration events, for example). It should own that data and not share it with other microservices directly at the database level.

For instance, two different microservices should never access the same relational database table. If a second microservice needs some of the same data, it can create its own cache, duplicate the data, or query the owner of that data but not access the database table directly—**never**.

This data-ownership concept is probably the most critical part of the microservices architecture and leads to microservices independence. Failing in this will most likely lead to a tremendous number of problems. For example, if multiple microservices can read or write data in the same database table, each time something changes in that table, all of them must be updated to reflect the changes. If different teams manage the microservices, that means cross-team coordination. If that happens, each microservice is not independent anymore, which brings us to our next topic.

Microservice independence

At this point, we have microservices that are cohesive units of business and own their data. That defines **independence**.

This independence allows the systems to scale while having little to no impact on the other microservices. Each microservice can also scale independently without needing the whole system to be scaled. Additionally, when the business requirements grow, each part of that domain can evolve independently.

Furthermore, you could update one microservice without impacting the others or even have a microservice go offline without the whole system stopping.

Of course, microservices have to interact with one another, but the way they do should define how well your system runs. A little like Vertical Slice architecture, you are not limited to using one set of architectural patterns; you can independently make specific decisions for each microservice. For example, you could choose one way for how two microservices communicate with each other, while two other microservices could use a completely different way. You could even use different programming languages for each microservice.

I recommend sticking to one or a few programming languages for smaller businesses and organizations, as you most likely have fewer developers, and each has more to do. Based on my experience, you want to ensure business continuity when people leave and make sure you can replace them and not sink the ship, due to some obscure technologies used here and there (or too many technologies).

Now that we've covered the basics, let's jump into the different ways microservices can communicate using event-driven architecture.

An introduction to Event-Driven Architecture

Event-Driven Architecture (**EDA**) is a paradigm that revolves around emitting and consuming events. These events could be user actions, sensor outputs, or messages from other programs, like microservices. The core aspects of EDA include:

- **Decoupling of components:** EDA allows for the decoupling of application components or microservices
- **Asynchronous communication:** Components communicate by producing or consuming events, which allows for non-blocking interactions
- **Reactivity and adaptability:** Systems built with EDA can easily adapt to changes or new requirements by modifying how events are handled, or by introducing new events

A system modeled using EDA usually consumes streams of events instead of static states like the data stored in a relational database table. EDA systems typically rely on event stores. An event store is a specialized database system that persists the events. Such stores are usually immutable. A static state is a piece of data that is dormant and waits for actors to consume and mutate it. It is stale between every mutation. The data (a relational record, for example) represents a finite state. Conversely, events are the opposite: you consume the events in order and determine the change in state that each event brings, or what process the program should trigger in reaction to an event.

What is an event? People often interchange the words event, message, and command. Let's try to clarify this:

- A message is a piece of data that represents something, like an object, a JSON string, bytes, or anything else your system can interpret. A message usually has a payload (or body), headers (metadata), and a way to identify it (this can be through the body or headers).
- An event is a message that represents something that happened in the past.
- A command is a message sent (past tense) to inform one or more recipients to do something. It is an event acting as a targeted action trigger.
- We can use events to divide a complex system into smaller pieces or have multiple systems talk to each other, without creating tight coupling. Those systems could be subsystems or external applications, such as microservices.

Like a REST API's **Data Transfer Objects** (**DTOs**), events become the data contracts that tie the multiple systems together (coupling). It is essential to think about that carefully when designing events. Of course, we cannot foresee the future, so we can only do so much to get it perfect the first time. We can version the events to improve maintainability.

EDA is a fantastic way of breaking tight coupling between microservices but requires rewiring your brain to learn this newer paradigm. Tooling is becoming more mature, and expertise is more common, slowly closing the gap with more linear ways of thinking (like using point-to-point communication and relational databases).

Let's explore the types of events next.

Types of events

All types of events play a similar role, with different intents and scopes. Here, we categorize events into the following overlapping buckets:

- Domain events
- Integration events
- Application events
- Enterprise events

Let's get started.

Domain events

Domain events integrate pieces of domain logic together while keeping the domain logic segregated, leading to loosely coupled components that hold one domain responsibility each (the SRP).

A domain event is a term based on DDD, representing an event in the domain. This event could then trigger other pieces of logic to be executed subsequently. It allows us to divide a complex process into multiple smaller processes. Domain events work well with domain-centric designs, like Clean Architecture, as we can use them to split complex domain objects into multiple smaller pieces. Domain events are usually application events.

For example, we can use MediatR to publish domain events inside an application.

Integration events

Integration events integrate multiple systems together while keeping them independent. Integration events are like domain events but propagate messages to external systems, integrating multiple systems together while keeping them independent. For example, a microservice could send the `new user registered` event message that other microservices react to, such as saving the `user id` to enable additional capabilities or sending a greeting email to that new user.

We use a message broker or message queue to publish such events. We explore those after covering application and enterprise events.

Application events

Application events are related to a single application. An application event is an event that is internal to an application. If the event is internal to a single process, that event is also a domain event (most likely). If the event crosses microservices boundaries that your team owns (the same application), it is also an integration event. The event itself won't be different; it is the reason why it exists and its scope that defines it as an application event or not.

Enterprise events

Enterprise events are integration events that cross organizational boundaries. These are tightly coupled with your business architecture (domain). For example, a microservice sends an event that other teams, part of other divisions or departments, consume.

The governance model around those events should differ from application events that only your team consumes and should be stricter, with strong organizational oversight.

Someone must consider who can consume that data, under what circumstances, the impact of changing the event schema (data contract), schema ownership, naming conventions, data-structure conventions, and more, or risk building an unstable data highway.

I like to see EDA as a central **data highway** in the middle of applications, systems, integrations, and organizational boundaries, where the events (data) flow between systems in a loosely coupled manner.

It's like a highway where cars flow between cities (without traffic jams). The cities do not control what car goes where but are open to visitors.

Getting started with message queues

A **message queue** is nothing more than a queue we leverage to send ordered messages. A queue works on a **First In, First Out** (**FIFO**) basis. If our application runs in a single process, we could use one or more `Queue<T>` instances to send messages between our components or a `ConcurrentQueue<T>` instance to send messages between threads. Moreover, queues can be managed by an independent program to send messages in a distributed fashion (between applications or microservices).

A distributed message queue can add more features to the mix, especially for cloud programs that handle failures at more levels than a single server. One of those features is the **dead letter queue**, which stores messages that failed some criteria in another queue. For example, if the target queue is full, a message could be sent to the **dead letter queue** instead. You could requeue such messages by putting the message back at the end of the queue.

Beware that requeuing messages changes their order. If the order is important in your app, consider this.

Many messaging queue protocols exist; some are proprietary, while others are open-source. Some messaging queues are cloud-based and used *as a service*, such as Azure Service Bus and Amazon Simple Queue Service. Others are open-source and can be deployed to the cloud or on-premises, such as Apache ActiveMQ.

If you need to process messages in order and want each message to be delivered to a single recipient at a time, a **message queue** seems like the right choice. Otherwise, the **Publish-Subscribe** pattern could be a better fit for you.

Here is a basic example that illustrates what we just discussed:

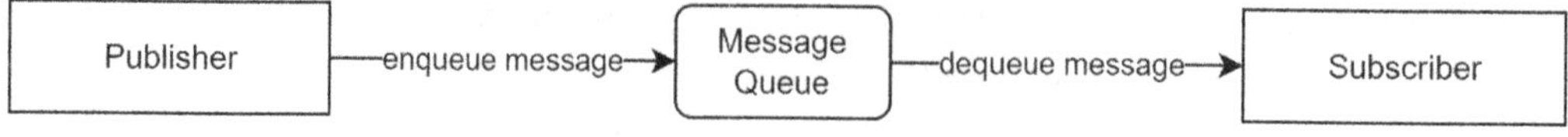

Figure 19.1: A publisher that enqueues a message with a subscriber that dequeues it

For a more concrete example, in a distributed user registration process, when a user registers, we could do the following:

- Send a confirmation email.
- Process their picture and save one or more thumbnails.
- Send an onboarding message to their in-app mailbox.

To sequentially achieve this, one operation after the other, we could do the following:

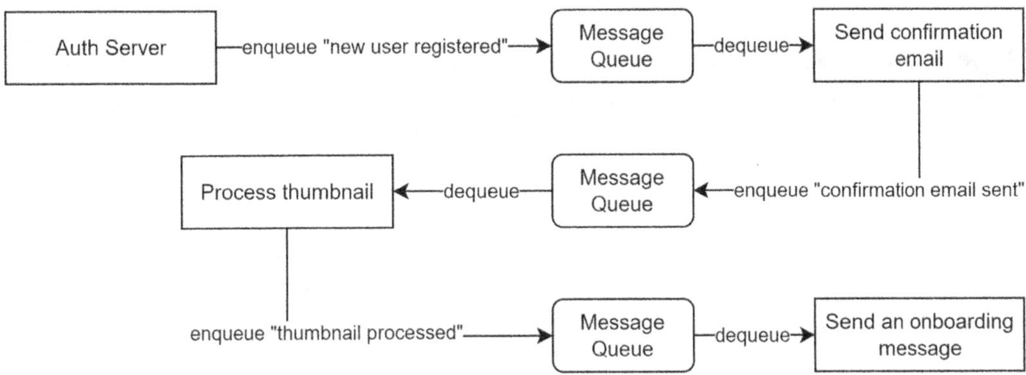

Figure 19.2: A process flow that sequentially executes three operations that happen after a user creates an account

In this case, the user would not receive the *Onboarding Message* if the process crashes during the *Process Thumbnail* operation. Another drawback would be that to insert a new operation between the *Process Thumbnail* and *Send an onboarding message* steps, we'd have to modify the *Send an onboarding message* operation (tight coupling).

If the order does not matter, we could queue all the messages from the *Auth Server* instead, right after the user's creation, like this:

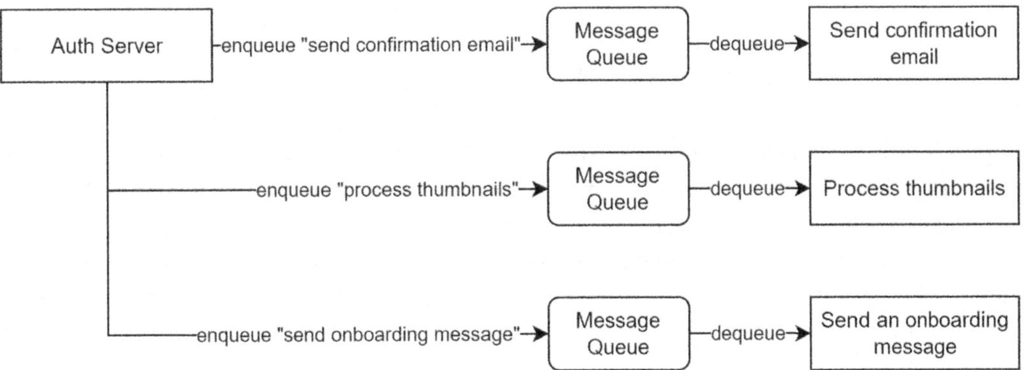

Figure 19.3: The Auth Server is queuing the operations sequentially while different processes execute them in parallel

This process is better, but the *Auth Server* now controls what should happen once a new user has been created. The *Auth Server* was queuing an event in the previous workflow that told the system that a new user registered. However, now, it has to be aware of the post-processing workflow to queue each operation sequentially to enqueue the correct commands. Doing this is not wrong in itself and is easier to follow when you dig into the code, but it creates tighter coupling between the services where the *Auth Server* is aware of the external processes. Moreover, it packs too many responsibilities into the *Auth Server*.

SRP-wise, why would an authentication/authorization server be responsible for anything other than authentication, authorization, and managing that data?

If we continue from there and want to add a new operation between two existing steps, we would only have to modify the *Auth Server*, which is less error-prone than the preceding workflow.

If we want the best of both worlds, we could use the **Publish-Subscribe** pattern instead, which we cover next, and continue building on top of this example.

Overview of the Publish-Subscribe pattern

The **Publish-Subscribe** pattern (Pub-Sub) is similar to what we did using **MediatR** and what we explored in the *Getting started with message queues* section. However, instead of sending one message to one handler (or enqueuing a message), we publish (send) a message (event) to zero or more subscribers (handlers). Moreover, the publisher is unaware of the subscribers; it only sends messages out, hoping for the best (also known as **fire and forget**).

We can use the **Pub-Sub pattern** in-process or in a distributed system through a **message broker**. The message broker is responsible for delivering the messages to the subscribers. Using a message broker is the way to go for microservices and other distributed systems, since they do not run in a single process.

This pattern has many advantages over other ways of communication. For example, we could recreate the state of a database by replaying the events that happened in the system, leading to the **event sourcing** pattern. More on that later.

The specific system design depends on the technology used to deliver the messages and the system's configuration. For example, you could use **MQTT** to deliver messages to **Internet of Things** (**IoT**) devices and configure them to retain the last message sent on each topic. That way, when a device connects to a topic, it receives the latest message. You could also configure a **Kafka** broker that keeps a long history of messages and asks for all of them when a new system connects to it. All of that depends on your needs and requirements.

MQTT and Apache Kafka

If you were wondering what MQTT is, here is a quote from their website at `https://adpg.link/mqtt`:

"MQTT is an OASIS standard messaging protocol for the Internet of Things (IoT). It is designed as an extremely lightweight publish/subscribe messaging transport [...]"

Apache Kafka's website at `https://adpg.link/kafka`:

"Apache Kafka is an open-source distributed event streaming platform [...]"

We cannot cover every single scenario of every system that follows every protocol. Therefore, I highlight some shared concepts behind the Pub-Sub design pattern so that you know how to get started. Then, you can dig into the specific technology you want (or need) to use.

One of the central pieces of the pattern is topics. A topic is a way to organize events, a channel, a place to read or write specific events so that consumers know where to find them. As you can probably imagine, sending all events to the same place is like creating a relational database with a single table: it would be suboptimal and hard to manage, use, and evolve.

To receive messages, subscribers must subscribe to topics (or the equivalent of a topic):

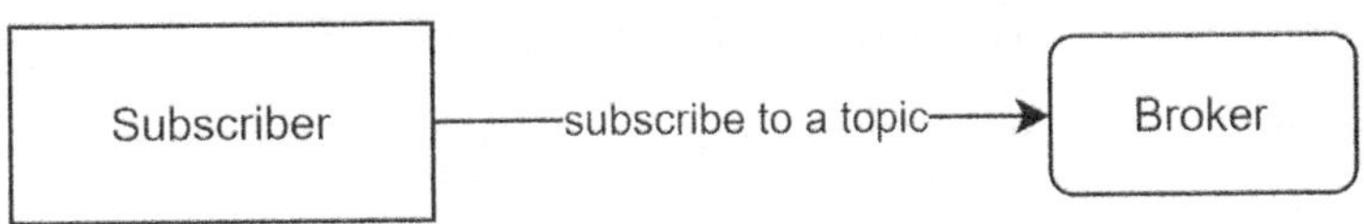

Figure 19.4: A subscriber subscribes to a Pub-Sub topic

The second part of the Pub-Sub pattern is to publish messages, like this:

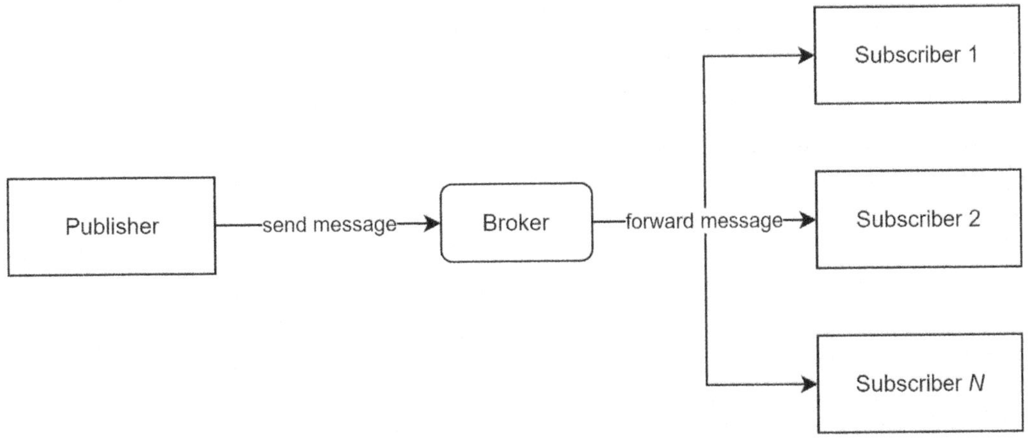

Figure 19.5: A publisher is sending a message to the message broker. The broker then forwards that message to N subscribers, where N can be zero or more

Many abstracted details here depend on the broker and the protocol. However, the following are the two primary concepts behind the Pub-Sub pattern:

- Publishers publish messages to topics.
- Subscribers subscribe to topics to receive messages when they are published.

Security is a crucial implementation detail not illustrated here. Security is mandatory in most systems; not every subsystem or device should have access to all topics.

Publishers and subscribers could be any part of any system. For example, many Microsoft Azure services are publishers (for example, Blob Storage). You can then have other Azure services (for example, Azure Functions) subscribe to those events and react to them.

You can also implement the **Pub-Sub** pattern directly inside your applications, without the need for external cloud resources, using an in-memory broker that runs within a single, standalone process, allowing components of an application to communicate with each other (we explore this in the next chapter).

The most significant advantage of the Pub-Sub pattern is breaking tight coupling between systems. One system publishes events while others consume them without the systems knowing each other.

That loose coupling leads to scalability, where each system can scale independently, and messages can be processed in parallel using the required resources. It is also easier to add new processes to a workflow, since the systems are unaware of the others. To add a new process that reacts to an event, you only have to create a new microservice, deploy it, start to listen to one or more events, and process them.

On the downside, the message broker can become the application's single point of failure and must be configured appropriately. It is also essential to consider the best delivery policies for each message type. An example of a policy could be to ensure the delivery of crucial messages while delaying less time-sensitive messages and dropping unimportant messages during load surges.

If we revisit our previous example using Pub-Sub instead of queues, we could end up with the following simplified workflow:

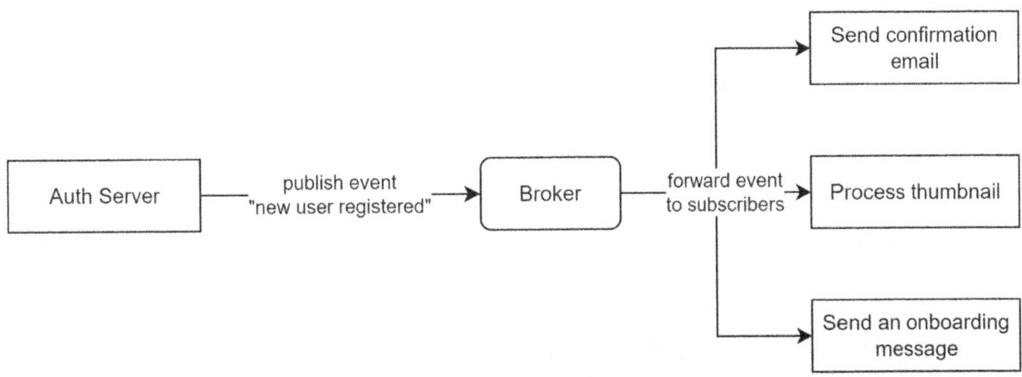

Figure 19.6: The Auth Server is publishing an event representing the creation of a new user. The broker then forwards that message to the three subscribers, who then execute their tasks in parallel

Based on this workflow, we broke the tight coupling between the *Auth Server* and the post-registration process. The *Auth Server* is unaware of the workflow, and the individual services are unaware of each other. Moreover, if we want to add a new task, we only have to create or update a microservice that subscribes to the right topic (in this case, the "**new user registered**" topic).

The current system does not support synchronization and does not handle process failures or retries, but it is a good start, since we combine the pros of the message queue examples and leave the cons behind.

Using an event broker inverts the dependency flow. The diagrams we explored show the message flow, but here's what happens on the dependency sides of things:

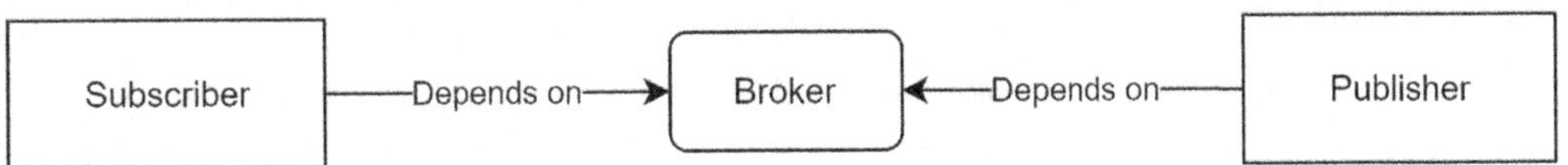

Figure 19.7: A diagram representing the inverted dependency flow of using the pub-sub pattern

Now that we have explored the Pub-Sub pattern, we look at message brokers, then dig deeper into EDA and leverage the Pub-Sub pattern to create a persistent database of events that can be replayed: the Event Sourcing pattern.

Message brokers

A message broker—or event broker—is a program that allows us to send (**publish**) and receive (**subscribe**) messages. It plays the mediator role at scale, allowing multiple applications to talk to each other without knowing each other (**loose coupling**). The message broker is usually the central piece of any event-based distributed system that implements the Pub-Sub pattern.

An application (**publisher**) publishes messages to topics, while other applications (**subscribers**) receive messages from those topics. The notion of **topics** may differ from one protocol or system to another, but all the systems I know have a topic-like concept to route messages to the right place. For example, you can publish to the `Devices` topic using Kafka, but to `devices/abc-123/do-something` using MQTT.

How you name your topics depends significantly on the system you use and the scale of your installation. For example, MQTT is a lightweight event broker recommending a path-like naming convention. On the other hand, Apache Kafka is a full-featured event broker and event streaming platform that is not opinionated about topic names, leaving you in charge of that. Depending on the scale of your implementation, you can use the entity name as the topic name or may need prefixes to identify who in the enterprise can interact with what part of the system. Due to the small scale of the examples in the chapter, we stick with simple topic names, making the examples easier to understand.

The message broker is responsible for forwarding the messages to the registered recipients. The lifetime of those messages can vary by broker or even by individual message or topic.

There are multiple message brokers out there using different protocols. Some brokers are cloud-based, such as Azure Event Grid. Other brokers are lightweight and more suited for IoT, such as Eclipse Mosquitto/MQTT. In contrast to MQTT, others are more robust and allow for high-velocity data streaming, such as Apache Kafka.

What message broker to use should be based on the requirements of the software you are building. Moreover, you are not limited to one broker. Nothing stops you from picking a message broker that handles the dialogs between your microservices and using another to handle the dialogs with external IoT devices. If you are building a system in Azure, want to go serverless, or prefer paying for SaaS components that scale without investing maintenance time, you can leverage Azure services such as Event Grid, Service Bus, and Queue Storage. If you prefer open-source software, you can choose Apache Kafka and even run a fully managed cloud instance as a service, using Confluent Cloud, if you don't want to manage your own cluster.

Next, we look at the Event Sourcing pattern.

Overview of the Event Sourcing pattern

Now that we have explored the Pub-Sub pattern, learned what an event is, and talked about event brokers, it is time to explore **how to replay the state of an application** by following the **Event Sourcing pattern**. Doing that is invaluable for debugging, auditing, and understanding the sequence of actions that led to a particular state. This approach not only enhances system resilience but also provides clear insights into the behavior of your application over time, much like having a detailed history book at your disposal.

The idea behind event sourcing is to **store a chronological list of events** instead of a single entity, where that collection of events becomes the source of truth. That way, every single operation is saved in the right order, helping with concurrency. Moreover, we could replay all of these events to generate an object's current state in a new application, allowing us to deploy new microservices more easily.

Instead of just storing the data, if the system propagates it using an event broker, other systems can cache some of it as one or more **materialized views**.

A **materialized view** is a model created and stored for a specific purpose. The data for this can come from one or more sources. A materialized view improves performance when querying that data—for example, the application returns the materialized view instead of querying multiple other systems to acquire the data. You can view the materialized view as a cached entity that a microservice stores in its own database.

One of the drawbacks of event sourcing is data consistency. There is an unavoidable delay between when a service adds an event to the store and when all the other services update their materialized views. We call this phenomenon **eventual consistency**.

Eventual consistency means that the data will be consistent at some point in the future, but not outright. The delay can be from a few milliseconds to much longer, but the goal is to keep that delay as small as possible.

Another drawback is the complexity of creating such a system compared to a single application that queries a single database. Like the microservices architecture, event sourcing is not just rainbows and unicorns. It comes at a price: **operational complexity**.

In a microservices architecture, each piece is small, but gluing them together has a cost. For example, the infrastructure to support microservices is more complex than a monolith (one app and one database). The same goes for event sourcing; all applications must subscribe to one or more events, cache data (materialized view), publish events, and more. This **operational complexity** represents the shift of complexity from the application code to the operational infrastructure. In other words, it requires more work to deploy and maintain multiple microservices and databases, and to fight the possible instability of network communication between those external systems, than it does for a single application containing all of the code. Monoliths are simpler: they work or don't; they rarely partially work.

A crucial aspect of event sourcing is appending new events to the store and never changing existing events (append-only). In a nutshell, microservices communicating using the Pub-Sub pattern publish events, subscribe to topics, and generate materialized views to serve their clients.

Example

Let's explore an example of what could happen if we combine what we just studied.

Context: We need to build a program that manages IoT devices. We begin by creating two microservices:

- The `DeviceTwin` microservice handles an IoT device's twin's data (digital representation of the device).
- The `Networking` microservice manages the networking-related information of IoT devices (how to reach a device).

As a visual reference, the final system could look as follows (we cover the `DeviceLocation` microservice later):

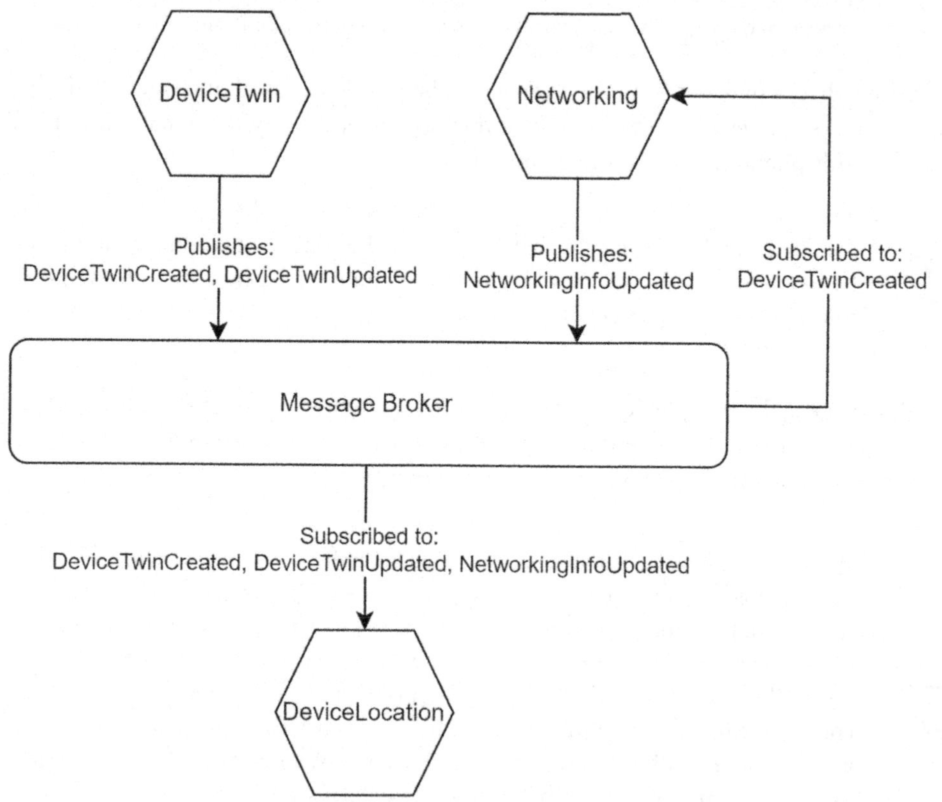

Figure 19.8: Three microservices communicating using the Pub-Sub pattern

Here are the user interactions and the published events:

1. A user creates a twin in the system named Device 1. The `DeviceTwin` microservice saves the data and publishes the `DeviceTwinCreated` event with the following payload:

```
{
    "id": "some id",
```

```
    "name": "Device 1",
    "other": "properties go here..."
}
```

In parallel, the `Networking` microservice must know when a device is created, so it subscribes to the `DeviceTwinCreated` event. When a new device is created, the `Networking` microservice creates default networking information for that device in its database; the default is `unknown`. This way, the `Networking` microservice knows what devices exist or not:

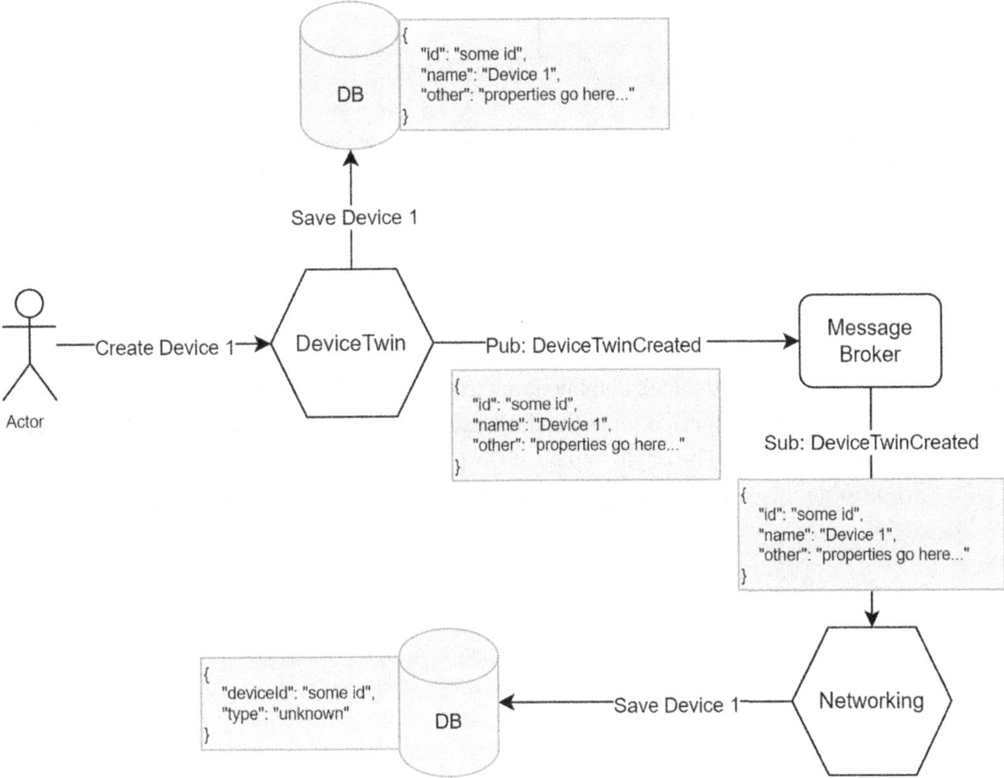

Figure 19.9: A workflow representing the creation of a device twin and its default networking information

2. A user then updates the networking information of that device and sets it to `MQTT`. The `Networking` microservice saves the data and publishes the `NetworkingInfoUpdated` event with the following payload:

```
{
    "deviceId": "some id",
    "type": "MQTT",
    "other": "networking properties..."
}
```

This is demonstrated by the following diagram:

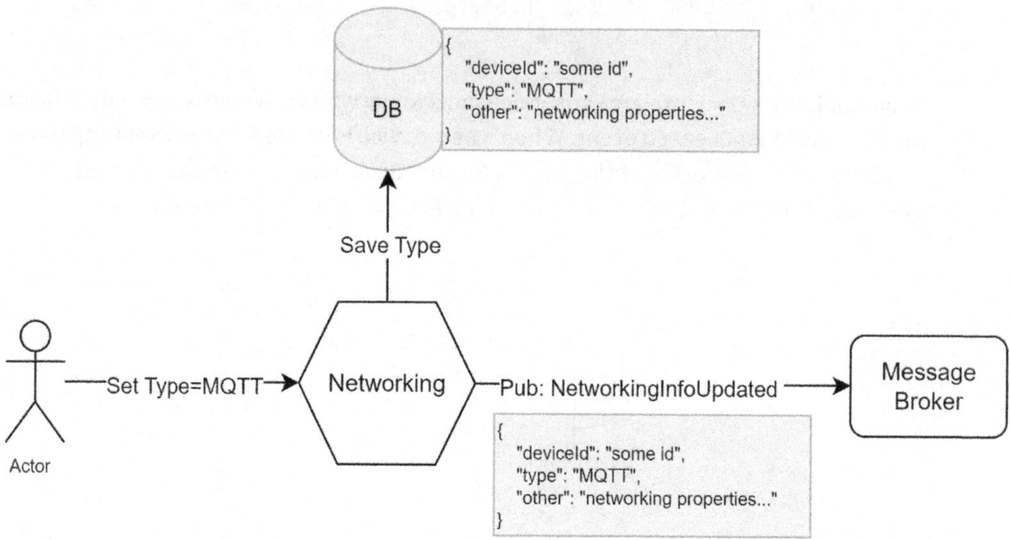

Figure 19.10: A workflow representing updating the networking type of a device

3. A user changes the device's display name to `Kitchen Thermostat`, which is more relevant. The `DeviceTwin` microservice saves the data and publishes the `DeviceTwinUpdated` event with the following payload. The payload uses **JSON patch** to publish only the differences instead of the whole object (see the *Further reading* section for more information):

```
{
    "id": "some id",
    "patches": [
        { "op": "replace", "path": "/name", "value": "Kitchen Thermostat"
},
    ]
}
```

The following diagram demonstrates this:

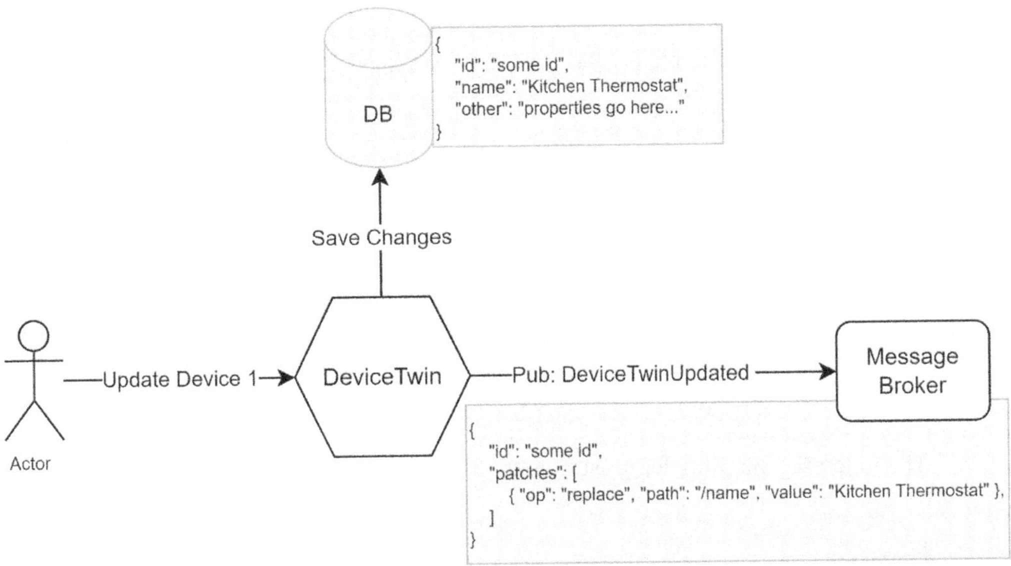

Figure 19.11: A workflow representing a user updating the name of the device to Kitchen Thermostat

From there, let's say another team designed and built a new microservice that organizes the devices at physical locations. This new `DeviceLocation` microservice allows users to visualize their devices' location on a map, such as a map of their house.

The `DeviceLocation` microservice subscribes to all three events to manage its materialized view, like this:

- When receiving a `DeviceTwinCreated` event, it saves its unique identifier and display name.
- When receiving a `NetworkingInfoUpdated` event, it saves the communication type.
- When receiving a `DeviceTwinUpdated` event, it updates the device's display name.

When the service is deployed for the first time, it replays all events from the beginning (**event sourcing**); this is what happens:

1. `DeviceLocation` receives the `DeviceTwinCreated` event and creates the following model for that object:

```
{
    "device": {
        "id": "some id",
        "name": "Device 1"
    },
    "networking": {},
    "location": {...}
}
```

   The following diagram demonstrates this:

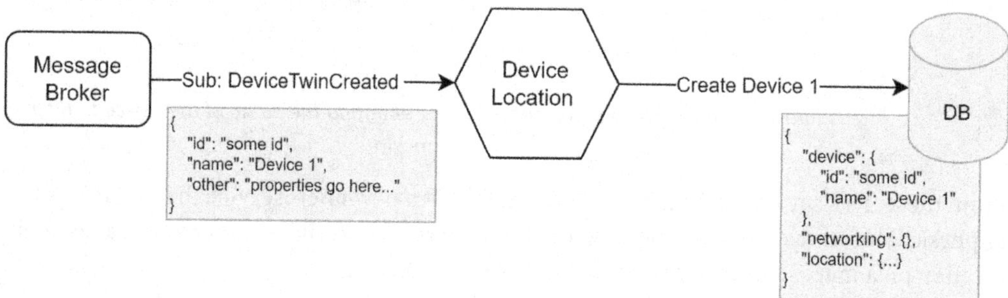

Figure 19.12: The DeviceLocation microservice replaying the DeviceTwinCreated event to create its materialized view of the device twin

2. The `DeviceLocation` microservice receives the `NetworkingInfoUpdated` event, which updates the networking type to `MQTT`, leading to the following:

```
{
    "device": {
        "id": "some id",
        "name": "Device 1"
    },
    "networking": {
        "type": "MQTT"
    },
    "location": {...}
}
```

The following diagram demonstrates this:

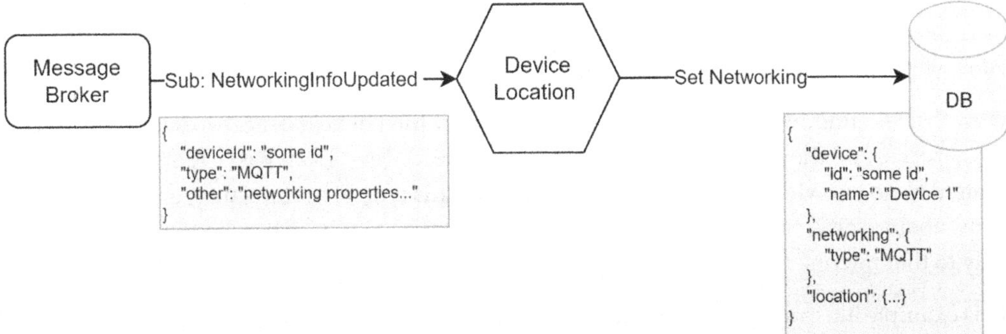

Figure 19.13: The DeviceLocation microservice replaying the NetworkingInfoUpdated event to update its materialized view of the device twin

3. The `DeviceLocation` microservice receives the `DeviceTwinUpdated` event, updating the device's name. The final model looks like this:

```
{
    "device": {
        "id": "some id",
        "name": "Kitchen Thermostat"
    },
    "networking": {
        "type": "MQTT"
    },
    "location": {...}
}
```

The following diagram demonstrates this:

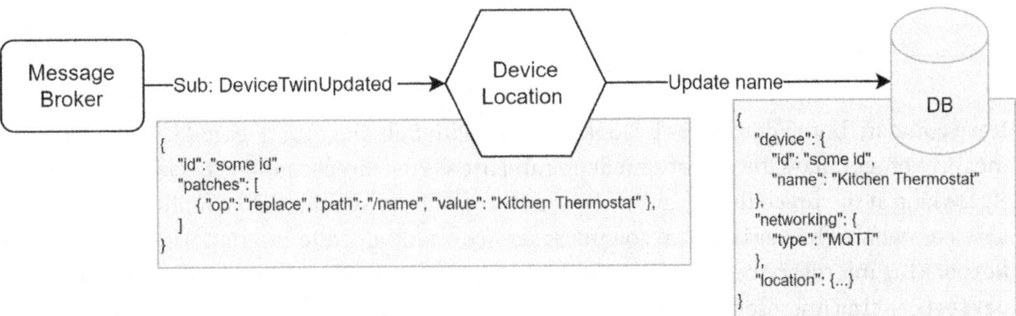

Figure 19.14: The DeviceLocation microservice replaying the DeviceTwinUpdated event to update its materialized view of the device twin

From there, the `DeviceLocation` microservice is initialized and ready. Users could set the kitchen thermostat's location on the map or continue using the other microservices. When a user queries the `DeviceLocation` microservice for information about `Kitchen Thermostat`, it displays the **materialized view**, which contains all the required information without sending external requests.

With that in mind, we could spawn new instances of the `DeviceLocation` microservice or other microservices, and they could generate their materialized views from past events—all of that with very limited to no knowledge of other microservices. In this type of architecture, a microservice can only know about events, not the other microservices. How a microservice handles events should be relevant only to that microservice, never to the others. The same applies to both publishers and subscribers.

This example illustrates the event sourcing pattern, integration events, the materialized view, the use of a message broker, and the Pub-Sub pattern.

In contrast, using direct communication (HTTP, gRPC, and so on) would look like this:

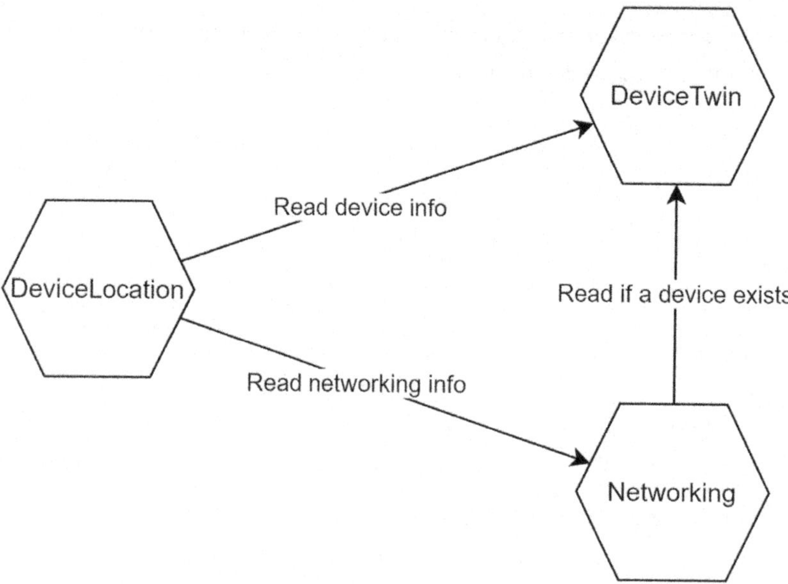

Figure 19.15: Three microservices communicating directly with one another

If we compare both approaches by looking at the Pub-Sub diagram (*Figure 19.8*), we can see that the message broker plays the role of a **mediator** and breaks the direct coupling between the microservices. By looking at the preceding diagram (*Figure 19.15*), we can see the tight coupling between the microservices, where the `DeviceLocation` microservice would need to interact with the `DeviceTwin` and `Networking` microservices directly to build the equivalent of its materialized view. Furthermore, the `DeviceLocation` microservice translates one interaction into three, since the `Networking` microservice also talks to the `DeviceTwin` microservice, leading to indirect tight coupling between microservices, which can negatively impact performance.

Suppose eventual consistency is not an option, or the Pub-Sub pattern cannot be applied or could be too hard to apply to your scenario. In this case, microservices can directly call each other. They can achieve this using HTTP, gRPC, or any other means that best suits that particular system's needs.

I won't be covering this topic in this book, but one thing to be careful of when calling microservices directly is the indirect call chain that could bubble up fast. You don't want your microservices to create a super deep call chain, or your system will likely become very slow. Here is an abstract example of what could happen to illustrate what I mean:

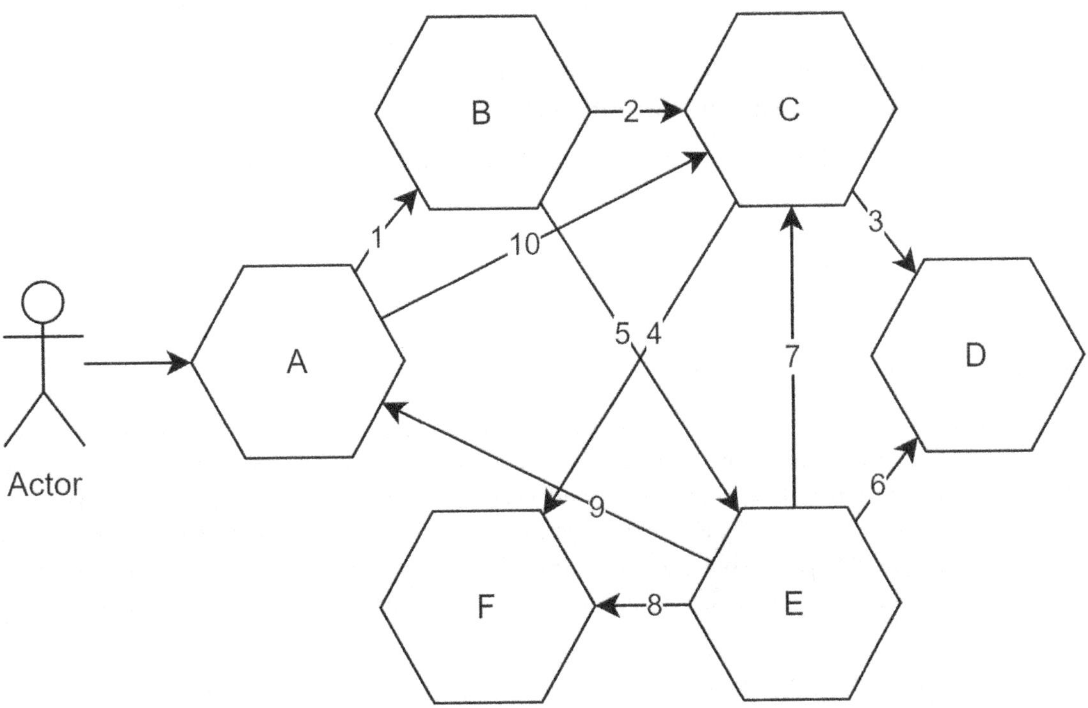

Figure 19.16: A user calling microservice A, which then triggers a chain reaction of subsequent calls, leading to disastrous performance

In terms of the preceding diagram, let's think about failures. If microservice C goes offline, the whole request ends with an error. Irrespective of the measures we put in place to mitigate the risks, if microservice C cannot recover, the system will remain down—goodbye to microservices' promise of independence. Another issue is latency: 10 calls are made for a single operation, which takes time.

Such chatty systems have most likely emerged from an incorrect domain modeling phase, leading to multiple microservices working together to handle trivial tasks. Now, think of *Figure 19.16* but with 500 microservices instead of 6. That could be catastrophic!

This type of interdependent microservices system is known as the **Death Star anti-pattern**. We can see the Death Star anti-pattern as a *distributed big ball of mud*. One way to avoid such pitfalls is to ensure that the bounded contexts are well segregated and that responsibilities are well distributed.

A good domain model should allow you to avoid building a Death Star and create the "most correct" system possible instead. Irrespective of the type of architecture you choose, if you are not building the right thing, you may end up with a Big Ball of Mud or a Death Star. Of course, the Pub-Sub pattern and EDA can help us break the tight coupling between microservices to avoid such issues.

Conclusion

EDA is a powerful design paradigm that leverages the production, consumption, and reaction to events to drive system interactions, enhance scalability, and maintain system integrity. This section has introduced EDA, emphasizing the importance of understanding event types, the role of message queues, and the Pub-Sub pattern in decoupling system components and facilitating indirect communication between microservices through a message broker.

Firstly, we defined the core concepts of events, messages, and commands, establishing that an event is a snapshot of the past, a message carries data, and a command suggests actions for other systems. We categorized events into domain, integration, application, and enterprise events, emphasizing the significance of the data contract (schema) that governs the interaction between event producers and consumers. This schema is the data contract (coupling) between the consumers of those events, which is probably the most important piece of it all: break the contract, break the system. That emphasizes the critical nature of maintaining data contracts in EDA.

Message queues are fantastic at handling traffic spikes by buffering messages, allowing applications to process messages at their own pace in high-demand scenarios. However, implementing distributed message queues can be challenging. I recommend leveraging existing systems, such as fully managed message queue systems offered by cloud providers such as AWS and Azure, or AMQP brokers such as ActiveMQ and RabbitMQ. Base your choice of message queue systems on your specific needs, skills availability, and the economic considerations of using a managed service versus local or on-premises solutions.

The Pub-Sub pattern helps break tight coupling between application parts, utilizing events (data contracts/schema) to facilitate indirect communication among microservices. With pub-sub, the different pieces are coupled with the data contract representing the events (schema) instead of each other, so changing an event's schema without warning—or versioning—risks breaking consumers. Therefore, planning for schema evolution is crucial, as schemas are vital for connecting system components.

Event sourcing leverages an event store as the source of truth, enabling historical event replay for database population, tracing, auditing, and debugging. The decision to adopt event sourcing must consider data storage requirements and retention policies, underscoring the importance of defining clear business problems and solutions.

In conclusion, EDA offers numerous advantages, including improved scalability and system flexibility, but also presents challenges, such as maintaining data contracts and managing schema evolutions. The exploration of message queues and the Pub-Sub pattern reveals the importance of choosing the right technologies and strategies based on project requirements. As we move forward, it's crucial to balance the benefits of EDA with its complexities, ensuring that the chosen architecture aligns with the specific needs and capabilities of the system and organization.

Event-driven architecture helps us follow the **SOLID** principles at cloud-scale like this:

- **S:** Systems are independent of each other by raising and responding to events. The events are the glue that ties those systems together, centralizing and dividing responsibilities without systems directly knowing each other, thereby breaking tight coupling. Each piece has a single responsibility.
- **O:** We can modify the system's behaviors by adding new consumers to a particular event and new producers without negatively impacting the other applications. This allows us to change behaviors without the others knowing about it. We can also raise new events to build a new process without affecting existing applications.
- **L:** N/A.
- **I:** Instead of building a single system, EDA allows us to create multiple smaller systems that integrate through data contracts (events), and those contracts are the messaging interfaces of the system. Each event can be as small as needed, leading to the creation of smaller, more focused communication interfaces.
- **D:** EDA enables systems to break tight coupling by depending on the events (interfaces/abstractions) instead of communicating directly with one another, inverting the dependency flow. By not knowing the other dependencies, each system relies on abstractions, enhancing flexibility and modularity.

Next, we explore some patterns that directly call other microservices by visiting a new kind of **façade**: the **Gateway**.

Introducing Gateway patterns

When building a microservices-oriented system, the number of services grows with the number of features; the bigger the system, the more microservices you have.

When you think about a user interface that has to interact with such a system, this can become tedious, complex, and inefficient (dev-wise and speed-wise). Gateways can help us achieve the following:

- Hide complexity by routing requests to the appropriate services
- Hide complexity by aggregating responses and translating one external request into many internal ones
- Hide complexity by exposing only the subset of features that a client needs
- Translate a request into another protocol

A gateway can also centralize different processes, such as logging and caching requests, authenticating and authorizing users and clients, enforcing request rate limits, and other similar policies.

You can see gateways as façades, but instead of being a class in a program, it is a program of its own, shielding other programs. There are multiple variants of the Gateway pattern, and we explore many of them here.

Regardless of the type of gateway you need, you can code it yourself or leverage existing tools to speed up the development process.

Beware that there is a strong chance that your homemade gateway version 1.0 has more flaws than a proven solution. This tip is not only applicable to gateways but to most complex systems. That being said, sometimes, no proven solution does exactly what we want, and we have to code it ourselves, which is where the real fun begins!

An open-source project that could help you out is Ocelot (`https://adpg.link/UwiY`). It is an API gateway written in C# that supports many things that we expect from a gateway. You can route requests using configuration or write custom code to create advanced routing rules. Since it is open-source, you can contribute to it, fork it, and explore the source code if necessary.

If you want a managed offering with a long list of features, you can explore Azure API Management (`https://adpg.link/8CEX`). It supports security, load-balancing, routing, and more. It also offers a service catalog where teams can consult and manage the APIs with internal teams, partners, and customers.

We can see a gateway as a **reverse proxy** that offers advanced functionalities. A gateway fetches the information that clients request, which can come from one or more resources, possibly from one or more servers. A reverse proxy usually routes a request to only one server, serving as a load balancer. Microsoft released a reverse proxy named YARP, written in C# for their internal teams, and open-sourced it (`https://adpg.link/YARP`). YARP is now part of Azure App Service (`https://adpg.link/7eu4`). If YARP does what you need, it is a product worth investing in that should evolve and be maintained over time. A significant advantage of such a service is the ability to deploy it with your application, optionally as a container, allowing us to use it locally during development.

Now, let's explore a few types of gateway patterns.

Overview of the Gateway Routing pattern

We can use the gateway Routing pattern to hide the complexity of our system by having the gateway route requests to the appropriate services.

For example, let's say we have two microservices: one that holds our device data and another that manages device locations. We want to show the latest known location of a specific device (`id=102`) and display its name and model.

To achieve that, a user requests the web page, and then the web page calls two services (see the following diagram). The `DeviceTwin` microservice is accessible from `service1.domain.com`, and the `Location` microservice is accessible from `service2.domain.com`. From there, the web application must track the two services, their domain name, and their operations. The UI has to handle more complexity as we add more microservices. Moreover, if we decide to change `service1` to `device-twins` and `service2` to `location`, we'd also need to update the web application. If there is only a UI, it is still not so bad, but if we have multiple user interfaces, each has to handle that complexity.

Furthermore, if we want to hide the microservices inside a private network, it would be impossible unless all the user interfaces are also part of that private network (which exposes it).

Here's the diagram representing the interactions mentioned previously:

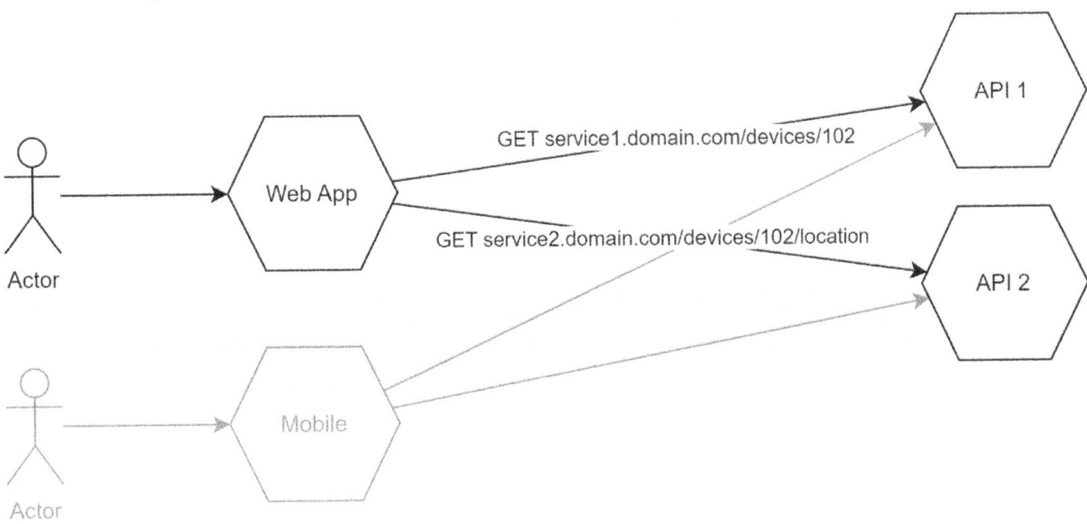

Figure 19.17: A web application and a mobile app that call two microservices directly

We can implement a gateway that does the routing for us to fix some of these issues. That way, instead of knowing what services are accessible through what sub-domain, the UI only has to know the gateway:

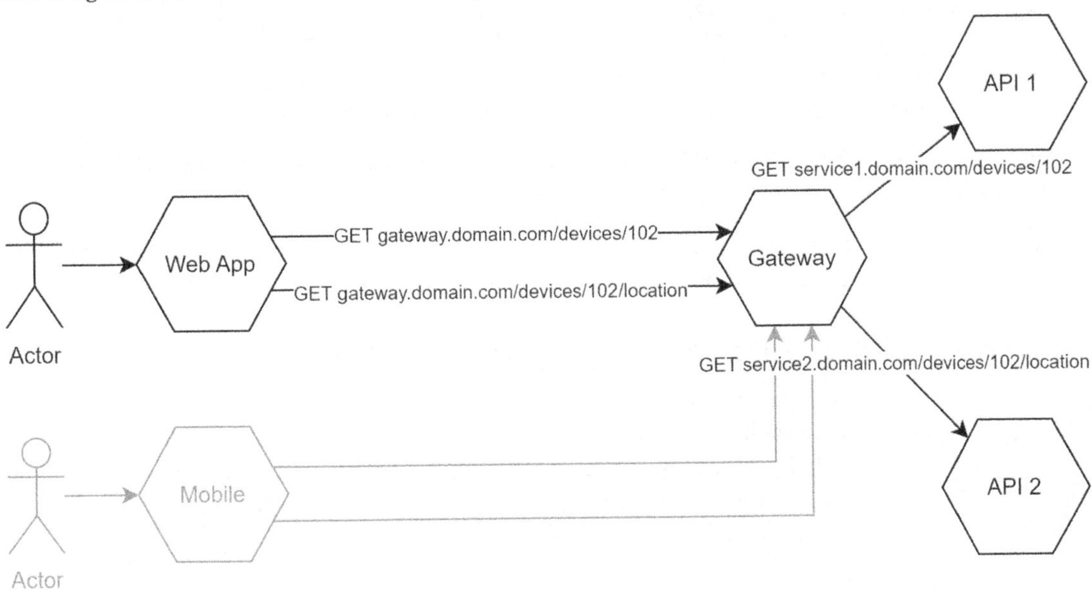

Figure 19.18: A web application and a mobile app that call two microservices through a gateway application

Of course, this brings some possible issues to the table as the gateway becomes a single point of failure. We could consider using a load balancer to ensure we have strong enough availability and fast enough performance. Since all requests pass through the gateway, we may also need to scale it up at some point.

We should also ensure the gateway supports failure by implementing different resiliency patterns, such as **Retry** and **Circuit Breaker**. The chances that an error will occur on the other side of the gateway increase with the number of microservices you deploy and the number of requests sent to those microservices.

You can also use a routing gateway to reroute the URI to create easier-to-use URI patterns. You can also reroute ports; add, update, or remove HTTP headers; and more. Let's explore the same example but using different URIs. Let's assume the following:

Microservice	URI
API 1 (get a device)	`internal.domain.com:8001/{id}`
API 2 (get a device location)	`internal.domain.com:8002/{id}`

Table 19.1: Internal microservice URI patterns

UI developers would have a harder time remembering what port leads to what microservice and what does what (and who could blame them?). Moreover, we could not transfer the requests as we did earlier (only routing the domain). We could use the gateway as a way to create memorable URI patterns for developers to consume, like these:

Gateway URI	Microservice URI
`gateway.domain.com/devices/{id}`	`internal.domain.com:8001/{id}`
`gateway.domain.com/devices/{id}/location`	`internal.domain.com:8002/{id}`

Table 19.2: Memorable URI patterns that are easier to use and semantically meaningful

As we can see, we took the ports out of the equation to create usable, meaningful, and easy-to-remember URIs.

However, we are still making two requests to the gateway to display one piece of information (the location of a device and its name/model), which leads us to our next Gateway pattern.

Overview of the Gateway Aggregation pattern

Another role we can give to a gateway is aggregating requests to hide complexity from its consumers. Aggregating multiple requests into one makes it easier for consumers of a microservices system to interact with it; clients need to know about one endpoint instead of multiple. Moreover, it moves the chattiness from the client to the gateway, which is closer to the microservices, lowering the many calls' latency, and thus making the request-response cycle faster.

Continuing with our previous example, we have two UI applications that contain a feature to show a device's location on a map before identifying it, using its name/model. To achieve this, they must call the device twin endpoint to obtain the device's name and model and the location endpoint to get its last known location. So two requests to display a small box times two UIs means four requests to maintain a simple feature. If we extrapolate, we could end up managing a huge number of HTTP requests for a handful of features.

Here is a diagram showing our feature in its current state:

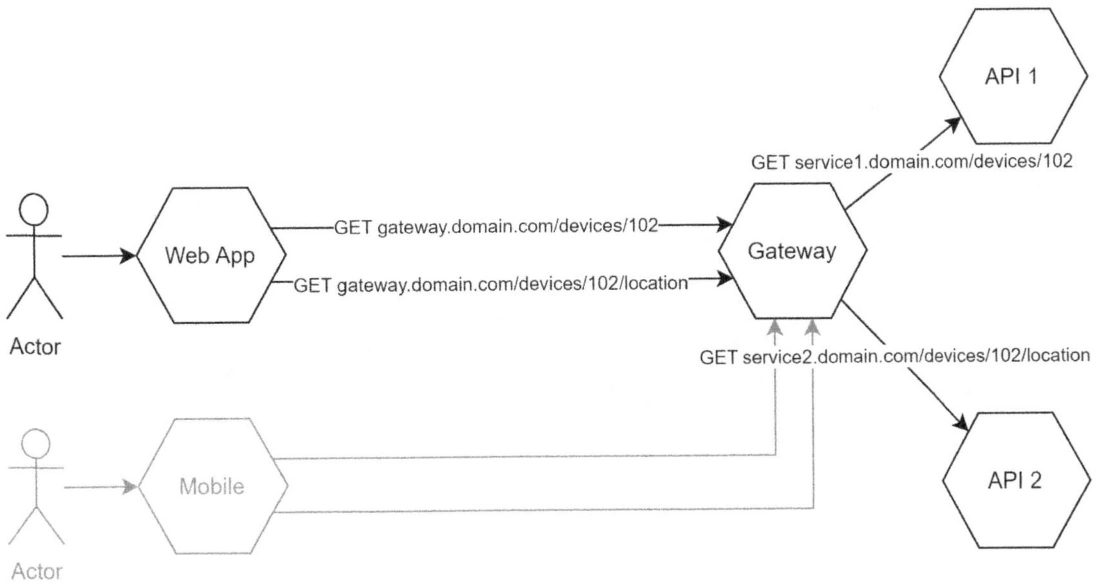

Figure 19.19: A web application and a mobile app that call two microservices through a gateway application

To remedy this problem, we can apply the Gateway Aggregation pattern to simplify our UIs and offload the responsibility of managing those details to the gateway.

By applying the Gateway Aggregation pattern, we end up with the following simplified flow:

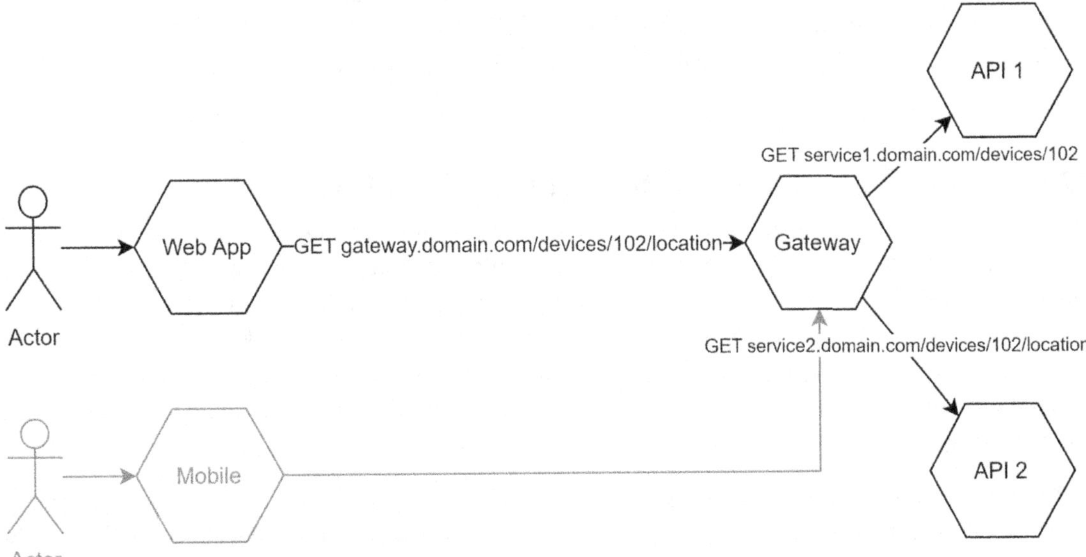

Figure 19.20: A gateway that aggregates the response of two requests to serve a single request from both a web application and a mobile app

In the previous flow, the Web App calls the Gateway that calls the two APIs, and then it crafts a response combining the two responses it got from the APIs. The Gateway then returns that response to the Web App. With that in place, the Web App is loosely coupled with the two APIs while the Gateway plays the intermediary. With only one HTTP request, the Web App has all the information it needs, aggregated by the Gateway.

Next, let's explore the steps that occurred. The following diagram shows that the Web App makes a single request (1) while the gateway makes two calls (2 and 4). In the diagram, the requests are sent in series, but we could have sent them in parallel to speed things up:

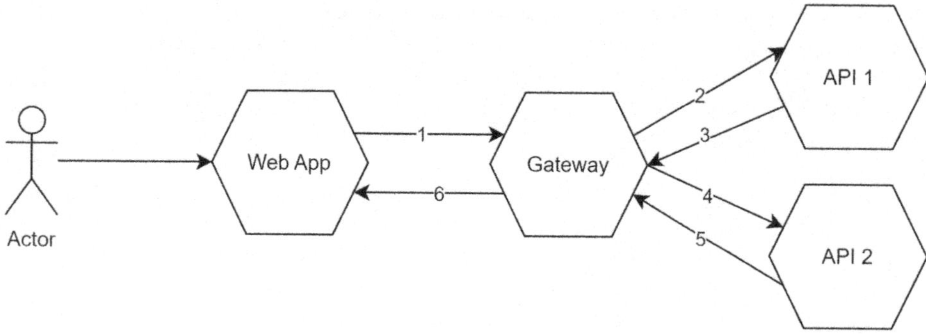

Figure 19.21: The order in which the requests take place

Like the routing gateway, an aggregation gateway can become the bottleneck of your application and a single point of failure, so beware of that.

Another important point is the latency between the gateway and the internal APIs. The clients will wait for every response if the latency is too high. So deploying the gateway close to the microservices it interacts with could become crucial for system performance. The gateway can also implement caching to improve performance further and make subsequent requests faster.

Next, we explore another type of gateway that creates specialized gateways instead of generic ones.

Overview of the Backend for Frontend pattern

The **Backend for Frontend** (**BFF**) pattern is yet another variation of the Gateway pattern. With BFF, instead of building a general-purpose gateway, we build a gateway per user interface (for each application that interacts with the system), lowering the complexity. Moreover, it allows fine-grained control of what endpoints are exposed. It removes the chances of app B breaking when changes are made to app A. Many optimizations can come out of this pattern, such as sending only the data that's required for each call instead of sending data that only a few applications use, saving some bandwidth along the way.

Let's say that our Web App needs to display more data about a device. To achieve that, we would need to change the endpoint and send that extra information to the mobile app as well. However, the mobile app doesn't need that information, since it doesn't have room on its screen to display it.

The following is an updated diagram that replaces the single gateway with two gateways, one per frontend:

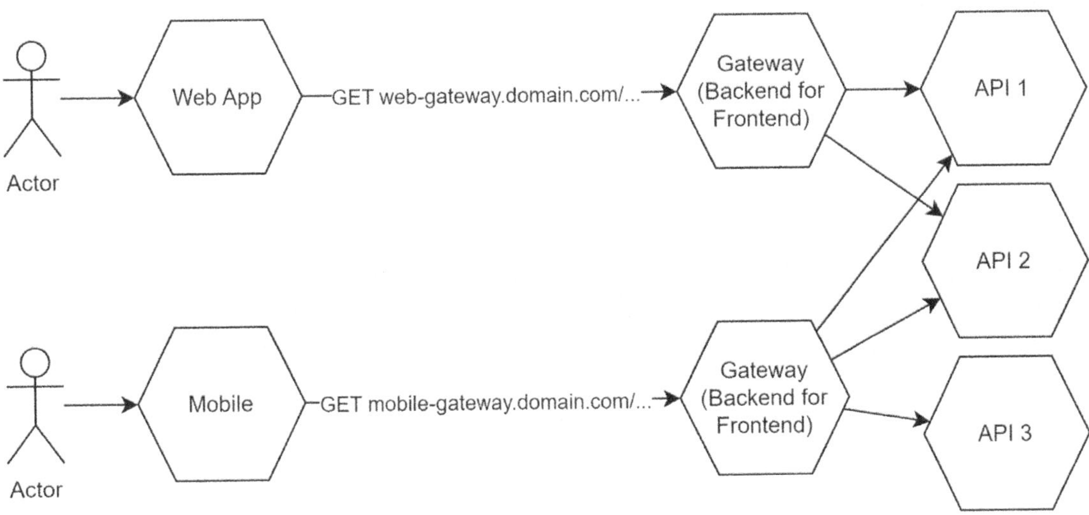

Figure 19.22: Two BFF gateways; one for a web application and one for a mobile application

Doing this allows us to develop specific features for each frontend without impacting the other. Each gateway now shields its particular frontend from the rest of the system and the other frontend. This is the most important benefit this pattern brings: client independence.

Once again, the BFF pattern is a gateway. Like other variations of the Gateway pattern, it can become the bottleneck of its frontend and its single point of failure. The good news is that the outage of one BFF gateway limits the impact to a single frontend, shielding the other frontends from that downtime.

Mixing and matching gateways

Now that we've explored three variations of the Gateway pattern, it is important to note that we can mix and match them, either at the codebase level or as multiple microservices.

For example, a gateway can be built for a single client (BFF), perform simple routing, and aggregate results.

We can also mix gateways as different applications, for example, by putting multiple BFF gateways in front of a more generic gateway to simplify their development and maintenance.

Beware that each hop has a cost. The more pieces you add between your clients and your microservices, the more time it will take for those clients to receive the response (latency). Of course, you can put mechanisms in place to lower that overhead, such as caching or non-HTTP protocols such as gRPC, but you still must consider it. That goes for everything, not just gateways.

Here is an example illustrating this:

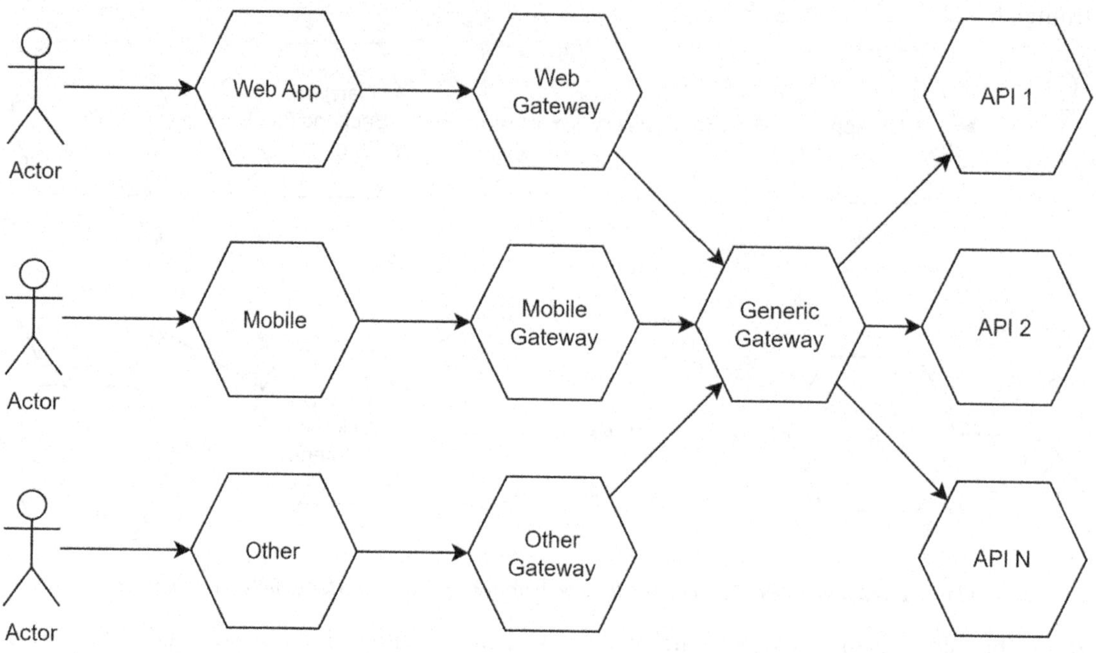

Figure 19.23: A mix of the Gateway patterns

As you've possibly guessed, the Generic Gateway is the single point of failure of all applications, while at the same time, each BFF gateway is a point of failure for its specific client.

A **service mesh** is an alternative to help microservices communicate with one another. It is a layer, outside of the application, that proxies communications between services. Those proxies are injected on top of each service and are referred to as **sidecars**. The service mesh can also help with distributed tracing, instrumentation, and system resiliency. If your system needs service-to-service communication, a service mesh would be an excellent place to look.

Conclusion

A gateway is a façade that shields or simplifies access to one or more other services. In this section, we explored the following:

- **Routing:** This forwards a request from point A to point B (a reverse proxy)
- **Aggregation:** This combines the result of multiple sub-requests into a single response
- **BFF:** This is a specialized gateway that has a one-to-one relationship with a frontend

We can use any microservices pattern, including gateways, and like any other pattern, we can mix and match them. Just consider the advantages, but also the drawbacks, that they bring to the table. If you can live with them, you've got your solution.

Gateways often become the single point of failure of the system, so that is a point to consider. On the other hand, a gateway can have multiple instances running simultaneously and be designed with resiliency in mind. Moreover, we must also consider the delay added by calling a service that calls another service, since that slows down the response time.

All in all, a gateway is a great tool to simplify consuming microservices. They also allow hiding the microservices topology behind them, possibly even isolated in a private network. They can also handle cross-cutting concerns such as security.

It is imperative to use gateways as a requests passthrough and avoid coding business logic into them; gateways are just reverse proxies. Think single responsibility principle: a gateway is a façade in front of your microservices cluster. Of course, you can unload specific tasks into your gateways like authorization, resiliency (retry policies, for example), and similar cross-cutting concerns, but the business logic must remain in the backend microservices.

The BFF's role is to simplify the UI, so moving logic from the UI to the BFF is encouraged.

In most cases, I recommend against rolling out your hand-crafted gateway and suggest leveraging existing offerings instead. There are many open-source and cloud gateways that you can use in your application. Using existing components leaves you more time to implement the business rules that solve the issues your program is trying to tackle.

Of course, cloud-based offerings exist, like Azure Application Gateway and Amazon API Gateway. Both are extendable, with cloud offerings like load balancers and **web application firewalls** (**WAF**). For example, Azure Application Gateway also supports autoscaling and zone redundancy, and it can serve as **Azure Kubernetes Service** (**AKS**) Ingress Controller (in a nutshell, it controls the traffic to your microservices cluster).

If you want more control over your gateways or to deploy them with your application, you can leverage existing options, like Ocelot, YARP, or Envoy.

Ocelot is an open-source production-ready API gateway programmed in .NET. It supports routing, request aggregation, load-balancing, authentication, authorization, rate limiting, and more. It also integrates well with Identity Server.

To quote YARP's GitHub `README.md` file: *"YARP is a reverse proxy toolkit for building fast proxy servers in .NET using the infrastructure from ASP.NET and .NET. The key differentiator for YARP is that it's been designed to be easily customized and tweaked to match the specific needs of each deployment scenario."*

Envoy is an *"open-source edge and service proxy, designed for cloud-native applications"*, written in C++. Envoy is a **Cloud Native Computing Foundation** (**CNCF**) graduated project, originally created by Lyft. Envoy was designed to run as a separate process from your application, allowing it to work with any programming language.

Which offering should you choose? If you are looking for a fully managed service, look at the cloud provider's offering of your choice. Consider YARP or Ocelot if you prefer a .NET-based implementation. Look into Envoy if YARP and Ocelot are missing some advanced capabilities. Please remember that these are just a few possibilities, not a complete list.

Now, let's see how gateways can help us follow the **SOLID** principles at cloud-scale:

- **S**: A gateway can handle routing, aggregation, and other similar logic that would otherwise be implemented in different components or applications.
- **O**: I see many ways to tackle this one, but here are two takes on this:
    a. Externally, a gateway could reroute its sub-requests to new URIs without its consumers knowing about it, as long as its contract does not change.
    b. Internally, a gateway could load its rules from configurations, allowing it to change without updating its code.
- **L**: N/A.
- **I**: Since a BFF gateway serves a single frontend system, one contract (interface) per frontend system leads to multiple smaller interfaces instead of one big general-purpose gateway.
- **D**: We could see a gateway as an abstraction, hiding the real microservices (implementations) and inverting the dependency flow.

Next, we build a BFF and evolve the e-commerce application from *Chapter 18, Request-EndPoint-Response (REPR)*.

Project – BFF

Here, we're pausing our discussion of microservices concepts and relevant patterns to work through a practical project, demonstrating how the BFF pattern works in practice. This is a long chapter, so feel free to take a break before diving into this project.

This project leverages the BFF design pattern to reduce the complexity of using the low-level API of the *REPR project* we created in *Chapter 18, Request-EndPoint-Response (REPR)*. The BFF endpoints act as the several types of gateway we have explored.

This design makes two layers of APIs, so let's start here.

Layering APIs

From a high-level architecture perspective, we can leverage multiple layers of APIs to group different levels of operation granularity. For example, in this case, we have two layers:

- Low-level APIs that offer atomic foundational operations
- High-level APIs that offer domain-specific functionalities

Here's a diagram that represents this concept (high-level APIs are BFFs in this case, but the design could be nuanced):

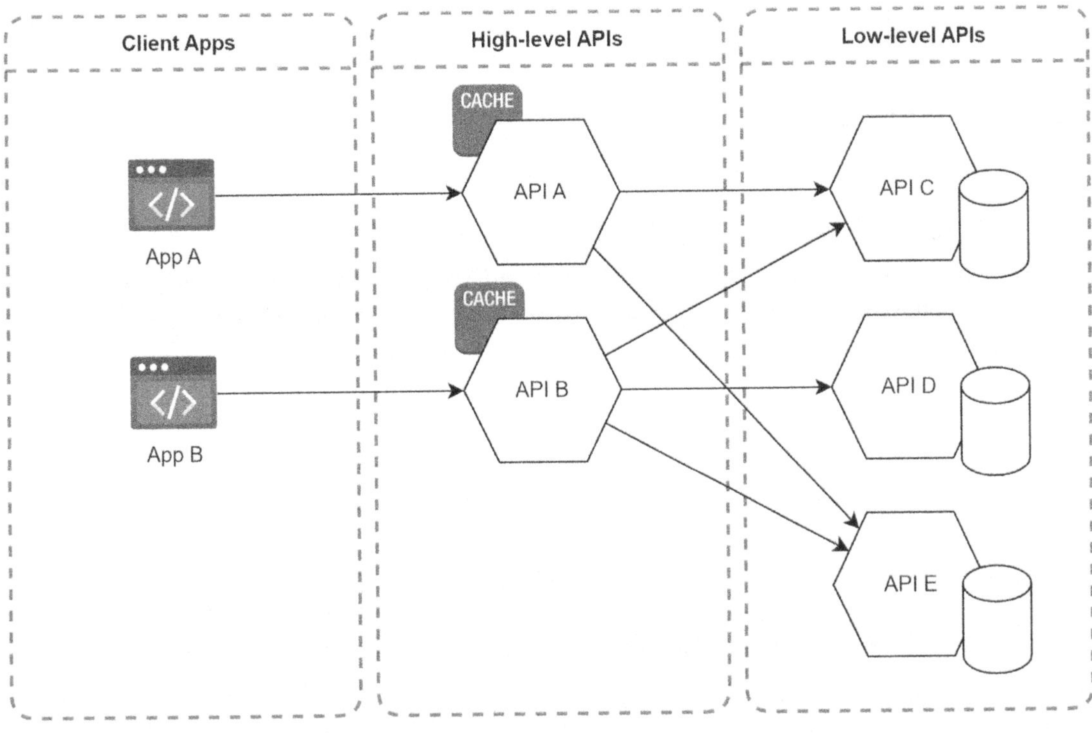

Figure 19.24: A diagram showcasing a two-layer architecture

The low-level layer showcases atomic foundational operations, like adding an item to the shopping basket and removing an item from it. Because those operations are simple, they are more complicated to use. For example, loading the products in the user's shopping cart requires multiple API calls, one to get the items and quantity, and one per item to get the product details like its name and price.

The high-level layer offers domain-specific functionalities like business capabilities, which are easier to use but can become more complex. For example, as we are about to implement, a single endpoint could handle adding, updating, and deleting items from the shopping basket, making its usage trivial for its consumer but its logic more complex to implement. Moreover, the product team might prefer a shopping cart to a shopping basket, so the endpoint's URL could reflect this.

Let's have a look at the advantages and disadvantages.

Advantages of a layered API design

- **Separation of concerns:** Separates generic from domain-specific functionalities, promoting modularity and making maintenance easier by isolating issues within specific layers.
- **Scalability and flexibility:** Allows independent scaling of each layer and reusing low-level APIs across business capabilities.

- **Efficiency:** Optimizes data fetching by aggregating responses, reducing payload sizes, and simplifying consumption.
- **Customization and security:** Facilitates tailored experiences for different client types while allowing domain-specific security measures without complicating low-level APIs.

Disadvantages of a layered API design

- **Increased complexity and development overhead:** Introducing additional layers adds complexity to deployment and monitoring and requires more effort in development, due to the need to manage and consider multiple layers, especially upfront.
- **Performance and coupling concerns:** Additional layers can introduce latency and, without careful design, lead to tight coupling between layers, affecting performance and flexibility.
- **Cross-team coordination issues:** More coordination among teams is needed to align high-level functionalities with low-level APIs, with a risk of duplicating logic across different parts of the application or delays due to conflicting priorities.
- **Risk of failures:** Adding more APIs can increase the likelihood of failures or outages. For example, an incorrectly managed cache can lead to potential issues with stale data, which then cascade to the other APIs.
- While a layered API design can offer flexibility and optimization, it also introduces additional complexities. The decision to use such an architecture should be based on the specific needs of the project, the anticipated scale, and the capabilities of the development and operations teams.

We look at booting up our two-layer API design next.

Running the microservices

Let's start by exploring the deployment topology. First, we split the *Chapter 18* REPR project into two services: *Baskets* and *Products*. Then, we add a *BFF* API that fronts the two services to simplify using the system. We do not have a UI per se, but one `http` file per project exists to simulate HTTP requests. Here's a diagram that represents the relationship between the different services:

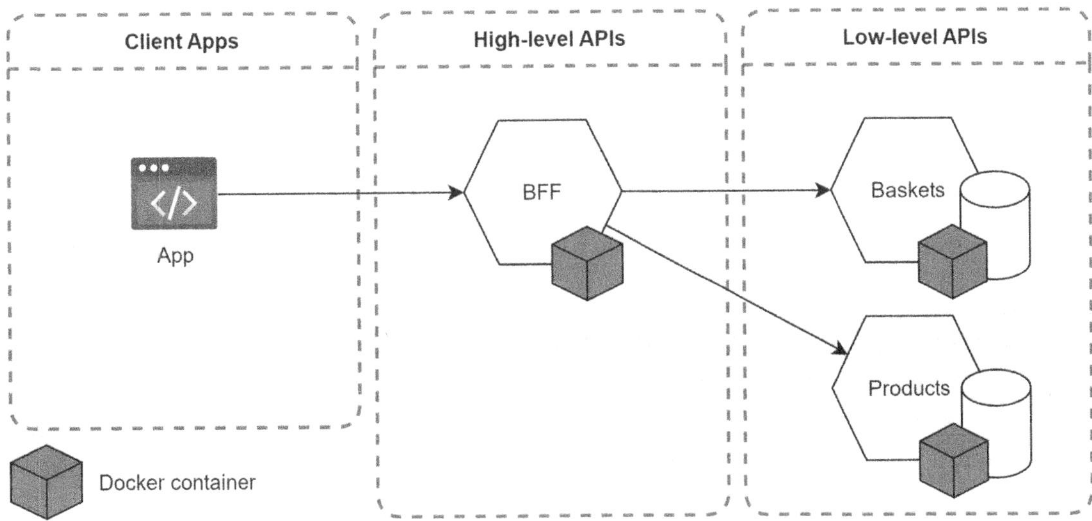

Figure 19.25: A diagram that represents the deployment topology and relationship between the different services

The easiest and most extendable way to start the projects is to use Docker, but it is optional; we can also start the three projects manually. Using Docker opens many possibilities, like using a real SQL Server to persist the data between runs and add more pieces to our puzzle, like a Redis cache or an event broker, to name a few.

Let's begin by manually starting the apps.

Manually starting the projects

We have three projects and need three terminals to start them all. From the chapter directory, you can execute the following commands, one set per terminal window, and all the projects should start:

```
# In one terminal
cd REPR.Baskets
dotnet run

# In a second terminal
cd REPR.Products
dotnet run

# In a third terminal
cd REPR.BFF
dotnet run
```

Doing this should work. You can use the PROJECT_NAME.http files to test the APIs.

Next, let's explore the second option that uses Docker.

Using Docker Compose to run the projects

At the same level as the solution file, the docker-compose.yml, docker-compose.override.yml, and various Dockerfile files are preconfigured to make the projects start in the correct order.

Here's a link to get started with Docker: https://adpg.link/1zfM

Since ASP.NET Core uses HTTPS by default, we must register a development certificate with the container, so let's start here.

Configuring HTTPS

This section quickly explores using PowerShell to set up HTTPS on Windows. If you are using a different operating system or if the instructions do not work, please consult the official documentation: https://adpg.link/o1tu

First, we must generate a development certificate. In a PowerShell terminal, run the following commands:

```
dotnet dev-certs https -ep "$env:APPDATA\ASP.NET\Https\adpg-net8-chapter-19.
pfx" -p devpassword
dotnet dev-certs https --trust
```

The preceding commands create a pfx file with the password devpassword (you must provide a password, or it won't work), and then tell .NET to trust the dev certificates.

From there, the ASPNETCORE_Kestrel__Certificates__Default__Path and ASPNETCORE_Kestrel__Certificates__Default__Password environment variables are configured in the docker-compose.override.yml file and will use the development certificate.

If you change the certificate location or the password, you must update the docker-compose.override.yml file.

Composing the application

Now that we have set up HTTPS, we can build the images using the following commands:

```
docker compose build
```

We can execute the following command to start the containers:

```
docker compose up
```

This uses the images to start the containers and feed you an aggregated log with a color per service. The beginning of the log trail should look like this:

```
[+] Running 3/0
  ✓ Container c19-repr.products-1  Created    0.0s
  ✓ Container c19-repr.baskets-1   Created    0.0s
  ✓ Container c19-repr.bff-1       Created    0.0s
Attaching to c19-repr.baskets-1, c19-repr.bff-1, c19-repr.products-1
c19-repr.baskets-1    | info: Microsoft.Hosting.Lifetime[14]
c19-repr.baskets-1    |       Now listening on: http://[::]:80
c19-repr.baskets-1    | info: Microsoft.Hosting.Lifetime[14]
c19-repr.baskets-1    |       Now listening on: https://[::]:443
...
```

To stop the services, press *Ctrl* + *C*.

When you want to destroy the running application, enter the following command:

```
docker compose down
```

Now, with `docker compose up`, our services should be running. To make sure, let's try them out.

Briefly testing the services

The project contains the following services, each containing an `http` file you can leverage to query the services, using **Visual Studio** (**VS**) or in VS Code using an extension:

Service	HTTP file	Host
`Baskets`	`Baskets.http`	`https://localhost:60280`
`BFF`	`BFF.http`	`https://localhost:7254`
`Products`	`Products.http`	`https://localhost:57362`

Table 19.3: Each service, HTTP file, and HTTPS hostname and port

We can leverage the HTTP requests from each directory to test the API. I suggest starting by trying the low-level APIs, and then the BFF, so you know if something is wrong with them directly instead of wondering what is wrong with the BFF (which calls the low-level APIs).

I use the *REST Client* extension in VS Code (`https://adpg.link/UCGv`) and the built-in support in VS 2022 version 17.6 or later.

Here's a part of the REPR.Baskets.http file:

```
@Web_HostAddress = https://localhost:60280
@ProductId = 3
@CustomerId = 1

GET {{Web_HostAddress}}/baskets/{{CustomerId}}

###

POST {{Web_HostAddress}}/baskets
Content-Type: application/json

{
    "customerId": {{CustomerId}},
    "productId": {{ProductId}},
    "quantity": 10
}
...
```

The highlighted lines are variables that the requests reuse. The ### characters act as a separator between requests. In VS or VS Code, you should see a **Send request** button on top of each request. Executing the POST request and then the GET should output the following:

```
HTTP/1.1 200 OK
Content-Type: application/json; charset=utf-8

[
  {
    "productId": 3,
    "quantity": 10
  }
]
```

If you can reach one endpoint, this means the service is running. Nonetheless, feel free to play with the requests, modify them, and add more.

I did not move the tests over from *Chapter 18*. Automating the validation of our deployment could be a good exercise for you to test your testing skills.

After you validate that the three services are running, we can continue and look at how the BFF communicates with the Baskets and Products services.

Creating typed HTTP clients using Refit

The BFF service must communicate to the Baskets and Products services. The services are REST APIs, so we must leverage HTTP. We could leverage the out-of-the-box ASP.NET Core `HttpClient` class and `IHttpClientFactory` interface, and then send raw HTTP requests to the downstream APIs. On the other hand, we could also create a typed client, which translates the HTTP calls to simple method calls with evocative names. We explore the second option, encapsulating the HTTP calls inside the typed clients.

The concept is simple: we create one interface per service and translate its operation into methods. Each interface revolves around a service. Optionally, we can aggregate the services under a master interface to inject the aggregate service and have access to all child services. Moreover, this central access point allows us to reduce the number of injected services to one and improve discoverability with IntelliSense.

Here's a diagram representing this concept:

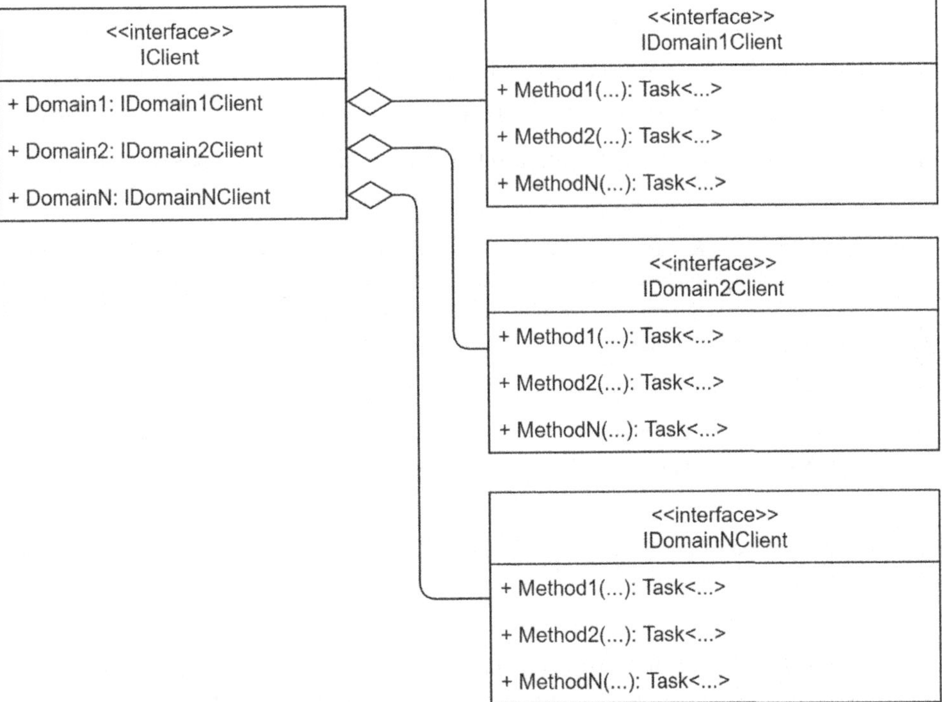

Figure 19.26: UML class diagram representing a generic typed client class hierarchy

In the preceding diagram, the `IClient` interface is composed and exposes the other typed clients, each of which queries a specific downstream API.

In our case, we have two downstream services, so our interface hierarchy looks like the following:

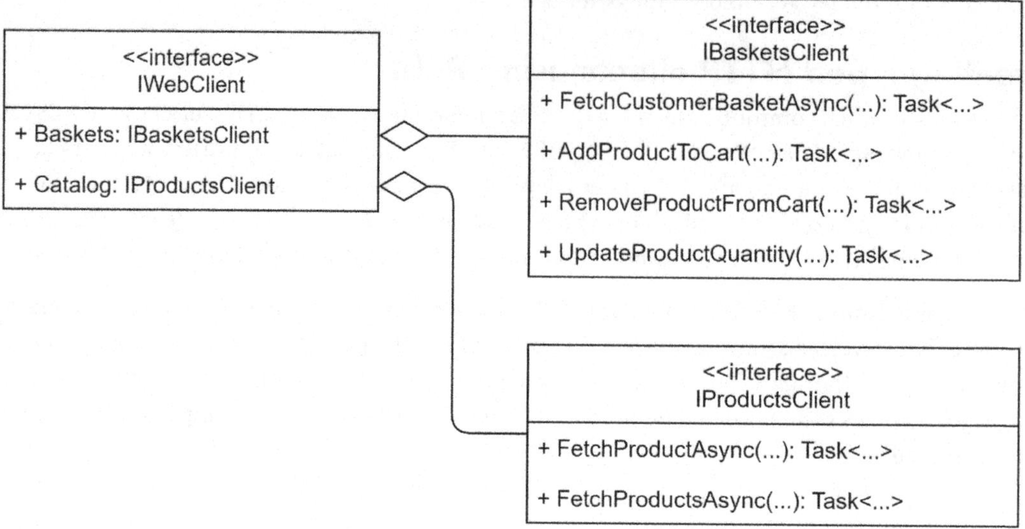

Figure 19.27: UML class diagram representing the BFF downstream typed client class hierarchy

After implementing this, we can query the downstream APIs from our code without worrying about their data contract because our client is strongly typed.

We leverage *Refit*, an open-source library, to implement the interfaces automatically.

We could use any other library or barebone ASP.NET Core `HttpClient`; it does not matter. I picked *Refit* to leverage its code generator, save myself the trouble of writing the boilerplate code, and save you the time of reading through such code. Refit on GitHub: `https://adpg.link/hneJ`

I used the out-of-the-box `IHttpClientFactory` functionalities in the past, so if you want to reduce the number of dependencies in your project, you can also use that instead. Here's a link to help you get started: `https://adpg.link/HCj7`

Refit acts like Mapperly and generates code based on attributes, so all we have to do is define our methods, and Refit writes the code.

The *BFF* project references the *Products* and *Baskets* projects to reuse their DTOs. I could have architected this in many different ways, including hosting the typed client in a library of its own so we could share it between many projects. We could also extract the DTOs from the web applications to one or more shared projects so that we don't depend on the web applications themselves. For this demo, there is no need to overengineer the solution.

Let's look at the typed client interfaces, starting with the `IBasketsClient` interface:

```
using Refit;
```

```
using Web.Features;

namespace REPR.BFF;

public interface IBasketsClient
{
    [Get("/baskets/{query.CustomerId}")]
    Task<IEnumerable<Baskets.FetchItems.Item>> FetchCustomerBasketAsync(
        Baskets.FetchItems.Query query,
        CancellationToken cancellationToken);

    [Post("/baskets")]
    Task<Baskets.AddItem.Response> AddProductToCart(
        Baskets.AddItem.Command command,
        CancellationToken cancellationToken);

    [Delete("/baskets/{command.CustomerId}/{command.ProductId}")]
    Task<Baskets.RemoveItem.Response> RemoveProductFromCart(
        Baskets.RemoveItem.Command command,
        CancellationToken cancellationToken);

    [Put("/baskets")]
    Task<Baskets.UpdateQuantity.Response> UpdateProductQuantity(
        Baskets.UpdateQuantity.Command command,
        CancellationToken cancellationToken);
}
```

The preceding interface leverages Refit's attributes (highlighted) to explain to its code generator what to write. The operations themselves are self-explanatory and carry the features' DTOs over HTTP.

Next, we look at the `IProductsClient` interface:

```
using Refit;
using Web.Features;

namespace REPR.BFF;
public interface IProductsClient
{
    [Get("/products/{query.ProductId}")]
    Task<Products.FetchOne.Response> FetchProductAsync(
        Products.FetchOne.Query query,
        CancellationToken cancellationToken);
```

```
    [Get("/products")]
    Task<Products.FetchAll.Response> FetchProductsAsync(
        CancellationToken cancellationToken);
}
```

The preceding interface is similar to `IBasketsClient` but creates a typed bridge on the *Products* API.

The generated code contains much gibberish code and would be hard to clean enough to make it relevant to study, so let's assume those interfaces have working implementations instead , forcing us to program against interfaces (a good thing).

Next, let's look at our aggregate:

```
public interface IWebClient
{
    IBasketsClient Baskets { get; }
    IProductsClient Catalog { get; }
}
```

The preceding interface exposes the two clients we had Refit generate for us. Its implementation is fairly straightforward:

```
public class DefaultWebClient : IWebClient
{
    public DefaultWebClient(IBasketsClient baskets, IProductsClient catalog)
    {
        Baskets = baskets ?? throw new ArgumentNullException(nameof(baskets));
        Catalog = catalog ?? throw new ArgumentNullException(nameof(catalog));
    }

    public IBasketsClient Baskets { get; }
    public IProductsClient Catalog { get; }
}
```

The preceding default implementation composes itself through constructor injection, exposing the two typed clients.

Of course, dependency injection means we must register services with the container. Let's start with some configuration. To make the setup code parametrizable and allow the Docker container to override those values, we extract the services' base addresses to the settings file like this (`appsettings.Development.json`):

```
{
  "Downstream": {
    "Baskets": {
```

```
        "BaseAddress": "https://localhost:60280"
      },
      "Products": {
        "BaseAddress": "https://localhost:57362"
      }
    }
  }
```

The preceding code defines two keys, one per service, which we then load individually in the `Program.cs` file, like this:

```
using Refit;
using REPR.BFF;
using System.Collections.Concurrent;
using System.Net;

var builder = WebApplication.CreateBuilder(args);
var basketsBaseAddress = builder.Configuration
    .GetValue<string>("Downstream:Baskets:BaseAddress") ?? throw new
NotSupportedException("Cannot start the program without a Baskets base
address.");
var productsBaseAddress = builder.Configuration
    .GetValue<string>("Downstream:Products:BaseAddress") ?? throw new
NotSupportedException("Cannot start the program without a Products base
address.");
```

The preceding code loads the two configurations into variables.

We can leverage all the techniques we learned in *Chapter 9, Application Configuration and the Options Pattern*, to create a more elaborate system.

Next, we register our Refit clients like this:

```
builder.Services
    .AddRefitClient<IBasketsClient>()
    .ConfigureHttpClient(c => c.BaseAddress = new Uri(basketsBaseAddress))
;
builder.Services
    .AddRefitClient<IProductsClient>()
    .ConfigureHttpClient(c => c.BaseAddress = new Uri(productsBaseAddress))
;
```

In the preceding code, calling the AddRefitClient method replaces the .NET AddHttpClient method and registers our auto-generated client with the container. Because Refit registration returns an IHttpClientBuilder interface, we can use the ConfigureHttpClient method to configure the HttpClient as we would any other typed HTTP client. In this case, we set the BaseAddress property to the values of the previously loaded settings.

Next, we must also register our aggregate:

```
builder.Services.AddTransient<IWebClient, DefaultWebClient>();
```

I picked a transient state because the service only fronts other services, so it serves the other services as they are registered, regardless of whether it is the same instance every time. Moreover, it needs a transient or scoped lifetime because the BFF must manage who is the current customer, not the client. It would be quite a security vulnerability to allow users to decide who they want to impersonate for every request.

The project does not authenticate the users, but the service we explore next is designed to make this evolve, abstracting and managing this responsibility so that we can add authentication without impacting the code we are writing.

Let's explore how we manage the current user.

Creating a service that serves the current customer

To keep the project simple, we are not using any authentication or authorization middleware, yet we want our BFF to be realistic and to handle who's querying the downstream APIs.

To achieve this, let's create the ICurrentCustomerService interface, which abstracts this away from the consuming code:

```
public interface ICurrentCustomerService
{
    int Id { get; }
}
```

The only thing that interface does is provide us with the identifier representing the current customer. Since we do not have authentication in the project, let's implement a development version that always returns the same value:

```
public class FakeCurrentCustomerService : ICurrentCustomerService
{
    public int Id => 1;
}
```

Finally, we must register it in the Program.cs class like this:

```
builder.Services.AddScoped<ICurrentCustomerService,
FakeCurrentCustomerService>();
```

With this last piece, we are ready to write some features in our BFF service.

In a project that uses authentication, you can inject the `IHttpContextAccessor` interface into a class to access the current `HttpContext` object that contains a `User` property, enabling access to the current user's `ClaimsPrincipal` object, which should include the current user's `CustomerId`. Of course, you must ensure the authentication server returns such a claim. You must register the accessor using the following method before using it: `builder.Services.AddHttpContextAccessor()`.

Features

The BFF service serves a non-existing user interface, yet we can imagine what it needs to do; it must:

- Serve the product catalog so that customers can browse the shop.
- Serve a specific product to render a product details page.
- Serve the list of items in a user's shopping cart.
- Enable users to manage their shopping cart by adding, updating, and removing items.

Of course, the list of features could go on, like allowing the users to purchase the items, which is the ultimate goal of an e-commerce website. However, we are not going that far. Let's start with the catalog.

Fetching the catalog

The catalog acts as a routing gateway and forwards the requests to the `Products` downstream service.

The first endpoint serves the whole catalog by using our typed client (highlighted):

```
app.MapGet(
    "api/catalog",
    (IWebClient client, CancellationToken cancellationToken)
        => client.Catalog.FetchProductsAsync(cancellationToken)
);
```

Sending the following requests should hit the endpoint:

```
GET https://localhost:7254/api/catalog
```

The endpoint should respond with something like the following:

```
HTTP/1.1 200 OK
Content-Type: application/json; charset=utf-8

{
  "products": [
```

```
        {
          "id": 2,
          "name": "Apple",
          "unitPrice": 0.79
        },
        {
          "id": 1,
          "name": "Banana",
          "unitPrice": 0.30
        },
        {
          "id": 3,
          "name": "Habanero Pepper",
          "unitPrice": 0.99
        }
      ]
    }
```


Here's a visual representation of what happens:

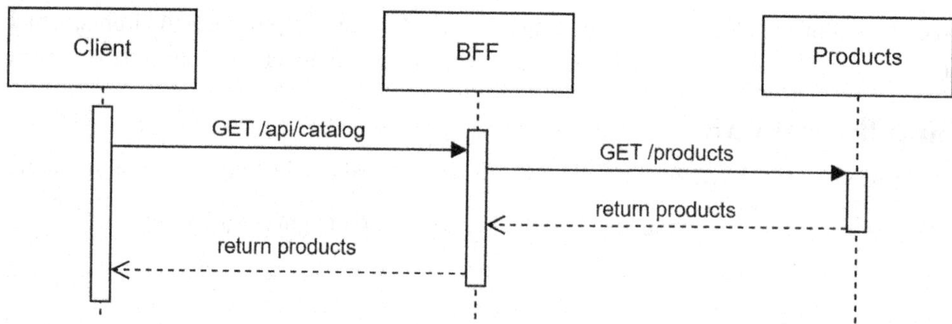

Figure 19.28: A sequence diagram representing the BFF routing the request to the Products service

The other catalog endpoint is very similar and also simply routes the request to the correct downstream service:

```
app.MapGet(
    "api/catalog/{productId}",
    (int productId, IWebClient client, CancellationToken cancellationToken)
        => client.Catalog.FetchProductAsync(new(productId), cancellationToken)
);
```

Sending an HTTP call will result in the same as calling it directly because the BFF only acts as a router.

We explore a more exciting feature next instead.

Fetching the shopping cart

The *Baskets* service only stores the `customerId`, `productId`, and `quantity` properties. However, a shopping cart page displays the product name and price, but the *Products* service manages those two properties.

To overcome this problem, the endpoint acts as an aggregation gateway. It queries the shopping cart and loads all the products from the *Products* service before returning an aggregated result, removing the burden of managing this complexity from the client/UI.

Here's the main feature code:

```
app.MapGet(
    "api/cart",
    async (IWebClient client, ICurrentCustomerService currentCustomer,
CancellationToken cancellationToken) =>
    {
        var basket = await client.Baskets.FetchCustomerBasketAsync(
            new(currentCustomer.Id),
            cancellationToken
        );
        var result = new ConcurrentBag<BasketProduct>();
        await Parallel.ForEachAsync(basket, cancellationToken, async (item,
cancellationToken) =>
        {
            var product = await client.Catalog.FetchProductAsync(
                new(item.ProductId),
                cancellationToken
            );
            result.Add(new BasketProduct(
                product.Id,
                product.Name,
                product.UnitPrice,
                item.Quantity
            ));
        });
        return result;
    }
);
```

The preceding code starts by fetching the items from the Baskets service and then loads the products using the `Parallel.ForEachAsync` method, before returning the aggregated result.

The `Parallel` class allows us to execute multiple operations in parallel, in this case, multiple HTTP calls. There are many ways of achieving a similar result using .NET, and this is one of them. When an HTTP call succeeds, it adds a `BasketProduct` item to the `result` collection. Once all operations are completed, the endpoint returns the collection of `BasketProduct` objects, which contains all the combined information required by the user interface to display the shopping cart. Here's the `BasketProduct` class:

```
public record class BasketProduct(int Id, string Name, decimal UnitPrice, int
Quantity)
{
    public decimal TotalPrice { get; } = UnitPrice * Quantity;
}
```

The sequence of this endpoint is like this (the `loop` represents the `Parallel.ForEachAsync` method):

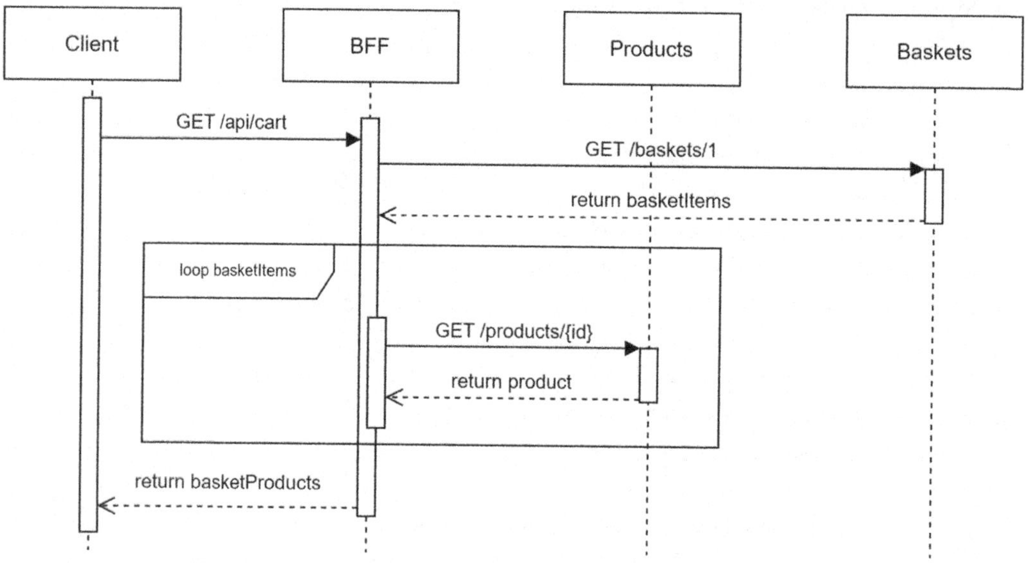

Figure 19.29: A sequence diagram representing the shopping cart endpoint interacting with the Products and the Baskets downstream services

Since the requests to the *Products* service are sent in parallel, we cannot predict the order they will complete. Here is an excerpt from the application log depicting what can happen (I omitted the logging code in the book, but it is available on GitHub):

```
trce: GetCart[0]
      Fetching product '3'.
trce: GetCart[0]
      Fetching product '2'.
trce: GetCart[0]
      Found product '2' (Apple).
```

```
trce: GetCart[0]
      Found product '3' (Habanero Pepper).
```

The preceding trace shows that we requested products 3 and 2 but received inverted responses (2 and 3). This is a possibility when running code in parallel.

When we send the following request to the BFF:

```
GET https://localhost:7254/api/cart
```

The BFF returns a response similar to the following:

```
HTTP/1.1 200 OK
Content-Type: application/json; charset=utf-8

[
  {
    "id": 3,
    "name": "Habanero Pepper",
    "unitPrice": 0.99,
    "quantity": 10,
    "totalPrice": 9.90
  },
  {
    "id": 2,
    "name": "Apple",
    "unitPrice": 0.79,
    "quantity": 5,
    "totalPrice": 3.95
  }
]
```

The preceding example showcases the aggregated result, simplifying the logic the client (UI) must implement to display the shopping cart.

Since we are not ordering the results, the items will not always be in the same order. As an exercise, you could sort the results using one of the existing properties, or add a property that saves when a customer adds the item to the cart and sort the items using this new property; the first item added is displayed first, and so on.

Let's move to the last endpoint and explore how the BFF manages the shopping cart items.

Managing the shopping cart

One of the primary goals of our BFF is to reduce the frontend's complexity. When examining the *Baskets* service, we realized it would add a bit of avoidable complexity if we were only to serve the raw operation, so instead, we decided to encapsulate all of the shopping cart logic behind a single endpoint. When a client sends a POST request to the `api/cart` endpoint, it:

- Adds the item when it is not yet in the shopping cart.
- Updates the item's quantity when it is already in the shopping cart.
- Removes an item that has a quantity equal to 0 or less.

With this endpoint, the clients don't have to worry about adding or updating. Here's a simplified sequence diagram that represents this logic:

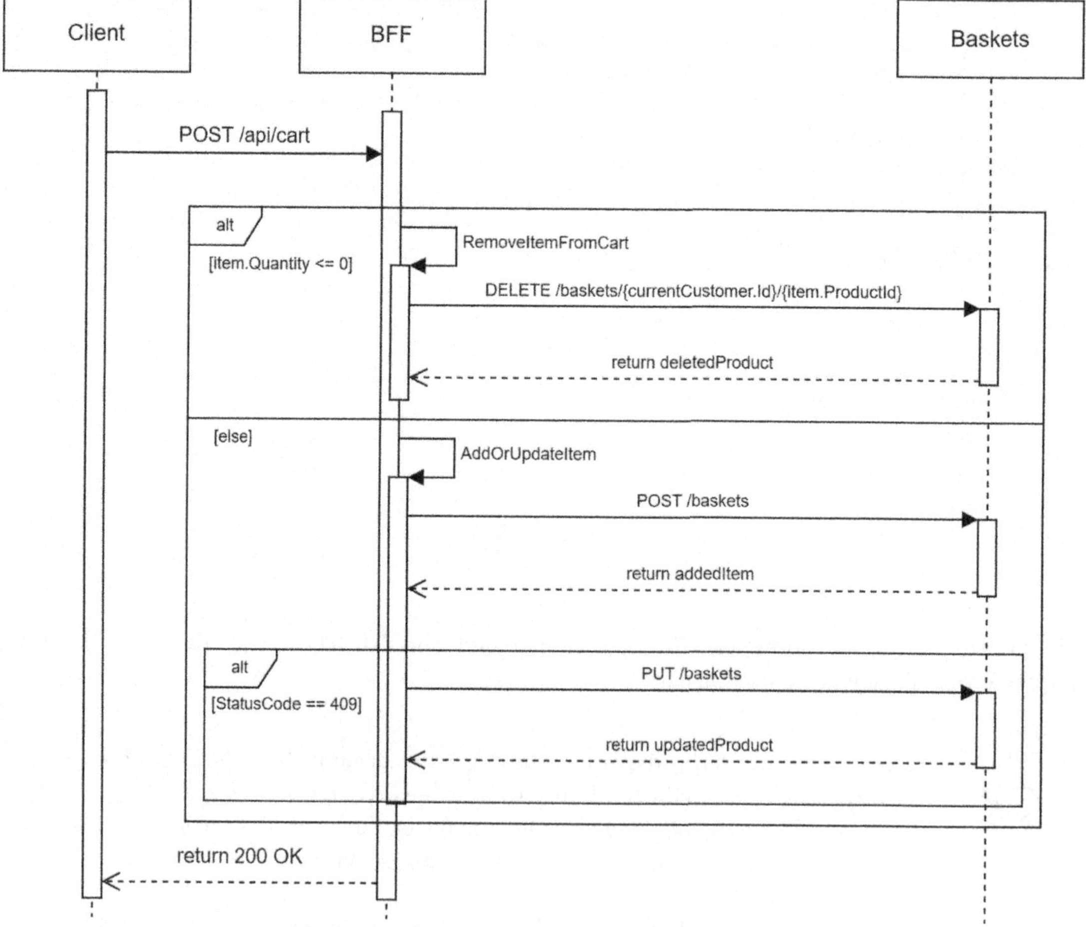

Figure 19.30: A sequence diagram that displays the high-level algorithm of the cart endpoint

As the diagram depicts, we call the remove endpoint if the quantity is inferior or equal to zero. Otherwise, we try to add the item to the basket. If the endpoint returns a `409 Conflict`, we try to update the quantity. Here's the code:

```
app.MapPost(
    "api/cart",
    async (UpdateCartItem item, IWebClient client, ICurrentCustomerService
currentCustomer, CancellationToken cancellationToken) =>
    {
        if (item.Quantity <= 0)
        {
            await RemoveItemFromCart(
                item,
                client,
                currentCustomer,
                cancellationToken
            );
        }
        else
        {
            await AddOrUpdateItem(
                item,
                client,
                currentCustomer,
                cancellationToken
            );
        }
        return Results.Ok();
    }
);
```

The preceding code follows the same pattern but contains the previously explained logic. We explore the two highlighted methods next, starting with the `RemoveItemFromCart` method:

```
static async Task RemoveItemFromCart(UpdateCartItem item, IWebClient client,
ICurrentCustomerService currentCustomer, CancellationToken cancellationToken)
{
    try
    {
        var result = await client.Baskets.RemoveProductFromCart(
            new Web.Features.Baskets.RemoveItem.Command(
                currentCustomer.Id,
                item.ProductId
            ),
            cancellationToken
        );
```

```
        }
        catch (ValidationApiException ex)
        {
            if (ex.StatusCode != HttpStatusCode.NotFound)
            {
                throw;
            }
        }
    }
```

The highlighted code of the preceding block leverages the typed HTTP client and sends a remove item command to the *Baskets* service. If the item is not in the cart, the code ignores the error and continues. Why? Because it does not affect the business logic or the end-user experience. Maybe the customer clicked the remove or update button twice. However, the code propagates to the client any other error.

Let's explore the `AddOrUpdateItem` method's code:

```
static async Task AddOrUpdateItem(UpdateCartItem item, IWebClient client,
ICurrentCustomerService currentCustomer, CancellationToken cancellationToken)
{
    try
    {
        // Add the product to the cart
        var result = await client.Baskets.AddProductToCart(
            new Web.Features.Baskets.AddItem.Command(
                currentCustomer.Id,
                item.ProductId,
                item.Quantity
            ),
            cancellationToken
        );
    }
    catch (ValidationApiException ex)
    {
        if (ex.StatusCode != HttpStatusCode.Conflict)
        {
            throw;
        }

        // Update the cart
        var result = await client.Baskets.UpdateProductQuantity(
            new Web.Features.Baskets.UpdateQuantity.Command(
                currentCustomer.Id,
```

```
                item.ProductId,
                item.Quantity
            ),
            cancellationToken
        );
    }
}
```

The preceding logic is very similar to the other method. It starts by adding the item to the cart. If it receives a `409 Conflict`, it tries to update its quantity. Otherwise, it lets the exception bubble up the stack to let the exception middleware catch it later to uniformize the error messages.

With that code in place, we can send `POST` requests to the `api/cart` endpoint for adding, updating, and removing an item from the cart. The three operations return an empty `200 OK` response.

Assuming we have an empty shopping cart, the following request adds *10 Habanero Peppers* (`id=3`) to the shopping cart:

```
POST https://localhost:7254/api/cart
Content-Type: application/json

{
    "productId": 3,
    "quantity": 10
}
```

The following request adds *5 Apples* (`id=2`) to the cart:

```
POST https://localhost:7254/api/cart
Content-Type: application/json

{
    "productId": 2,
    "quantity": 5
}
```

The following request updates the quantity to *20 Habanero Peppers* (`id=3`):

```
POST https://localhost:7254/api/cart
Content-Type: application/json

{
    "productId": 3,
    "quantity": 20
}
```

The following request removes the *Apples* (`id=2`) from the cart:

```
POST https://localhost:7254/api/cart
Content-Type: application/json

{
    "productId": 2,
    "quantity": 0
}
```

Leaving us with *20 Habanero Peppers* in our shopping cart (`GET https://localhost:7254/api/cart`):

```
[
  {
    "id": 3,
    "name": "Habanero Pepper",
    "unitPrice": 0.99,
    "quantity": 20,
    "totalPrice": 19.80
  }
]
```

The requests of the previous sequence are all in the same format, reaching the same endpoint but doing different things, which makes it very easy for the frontend client to manage.

If you prefer having the UI to manage the operations individually or want to implement a batch update feature, you can; this is only an example of what you can leverage a BFF for.

We are now done with the BFF service.

Conclusion

In this section, we learned about using the BFF design pattern to front a micro e-commerce web application. We discussed layering APIs and the advantages and disadvantages of a two-layer design. We autogenerated strongly typed HTTP clients using Refit, managed a shopping cart, and fetched the catalog from the BFF. We learned how to use a BFF to reduce complexity by moving domain logic from the frontend to the backend by implementing multiple Gateway patterns.

Here are a few benefits that we explored:

- The BFF pattern can significantly simplify the interaction between frontend and backend systems. It provides a layer of abstraction that can reduce the complexity of using low-level atomic APIs. It separates generic and domain-specific functionalities and promotes cleaner, more modular code.

- A BFF can act as a gateway that routes specific requests to relevant services, reducing the work the frontend has to perform. It can also serve as an aggregation gateway, gathering data from various services into a unified response. This process can simplify frontend development by reducing the complexity of the frontend and the number of separate calls the frontend must make. It can also reduce the payload size transported between the frontend and backend.
- Each BFF is tailored to a specific client, optimizing the frontend interaction.
- A BFF can handle issues in one domain without affecting the low-level APIs or the other applications, thus providing easier maintenance.
- A BFF can implement security logic, such as specific domain-aligned authentication and authorization rules.

Despite these benefits, using a BFF may also increase complexity and introduce potential performance overhead. Using a BFF is no different than any other pattern and must be counter-balanced and adapted to the specific needs of a project.

Next, we revisit CQRS on a distributed scale.

Revisiting the CQRS pattern

Command Query Responsibility Segregation (CQRS) applies the **Command Query Separation** (CQS) principle. Compared to what we saw in *Chapter 16, Mediator and CQS Patterns,* we can push CQRS further using microservices or serverless computing. Instead of simply creating a clear separation between commands and queries, we can divide them even more using multiple microservices and data sources to enhance scalability and flexibility. This approach allows each component to be scaled independently based on demand, improving system performance and resource efficiency.

CQS is a principle stating that a method should either return data or mutate data, but not both. On the other hand, **CQRS** suggests using one model to read the data and one model to mutate the data.

Serverless computing is a cloud execution model where the cloud provider manages the servers and allocates the resources on-demand, based on usage and configuration. Serverless resources fall into the **platform as a service** (PaaS) offering.

Let's come back to our IoT example again. We queried the last known location of a device in the previous examples, but what about the device updating that location? This can mean pushing many updates every minute. To solve this issue, we are going to use CQRS and focus on two operations:

- Updating the device location
- Reading the last known location of a device

Simply put, we have a `Read Location` microservice, a `Write Location` microservice, and two databases. Remember that each microservice should own its data. This way, a user can access the last known device location through the read microservice (query model), while a device can punctually send its current position to the write microservice (command model).

By doing this, we split the load from reading and writing the data, as both occur at different frequencies:

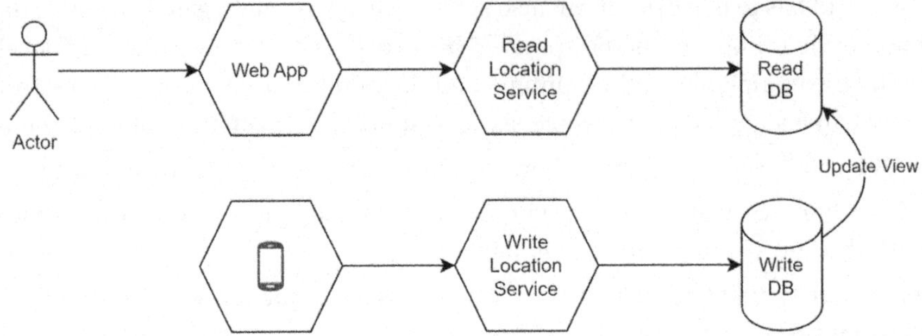

Figure 19.31: Microservices that apply CQRS to divide the reads and writes of a device's location

In the preceding schema that illustrates the concept, the reads are queries, and the writes are commands. How to update the Read DB once a new value is added to the Write DB depends on the technology at play. One essential point in this type of architecture is that, per the CQRS pattern, a command should not return a value, enabling a "fire and forget" scenario. With that rule in place, consumers don't have to wait for the command to complete before doing something else.

Fire and forget does not apply to every scenario; sometimes, we need synchronization. Implementing the Saga pattern is one way to solve coordination issues. The Saga pattern manages transactions across multiple microservices by breaking them into a series of local transactions, each with its own compensation action in case of failure, ensuring overall data consistency. See *Further reading* for more information.

Conceptually, we can implement this example by leveraging serverless cloud infrastructures, such as Azure Functions. Let's revisit this example using a high-level conceptual serverless design:

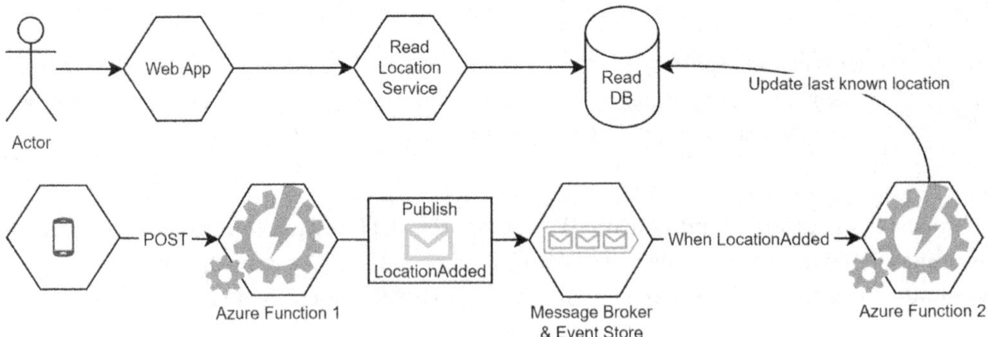

Figure 19.32: Using Azure services to manage a CQRS implementation

The previous diagram illustrates the following:

1. The device sends its location regularly by posting it to *Azure Function 1*.
2. *Azure Function 1* then publishes the `LocationAdded` event to the event broker, which is also an event store (the Write DB).
3. All subscribers to the `LocationAdded` event can now handle the event appropriately, in this case, *Azure Function 2*.
4. *Azure Function 2* updates the device's last known location in the *Read DB*.
5. Any subsequent queries should result in reading the new location.

The message broker is also the event store in the preceding diagram, but we could store events elsewhere, such as in an Azure Storage Table, a time-series database, or an Apache Kafka cluster. Azure-wise, the data store could also be CosmosDB. Moreover, I abstracted this component for multiple reasons, including the fact that there are multiple "as-a-service" offerings to publish events in Azure and multiple ways of using third-party components (both open-source and proprietary).

Time-series databases are optimized for temporally querying and storing data, where you always append new records without updating old ones. This kind of NoSQL database can be useful for temporal-intensive usage, like metrics.

Furthermore, the example demonstrates **eventual consistency** well. All the last known location reads between *steps 1* and *4* get the old value while the system processes the new location updates (commands). If the command processing slows down for some reason, a longer delay could occur before the next read DB updates. The commands could also be processed in batches, leading to another kind of delay. No matter what happens with the command processing, the read database is available all that time, whether it serves the latest data or not and whether the write system is overloaded or not. This is the beauty of this type of design, but it is more complex to implement and maintain.

Once again, we used the Pub-Sub pattern to get another scenario going. Assuming that events are persisted forever, the previous example could also support event sourcing. Furthermore, new services could subscribe to the `LocationAdded` event without impacting the code that has already been deployed.

For example, we could create a SignalR microservice that pushes the updates to its clients, extending our microservices system even more.

SignalR is a library that adds real-time web functionality to applications, enabling server-side code to push content to clients instantly. It supports WebSockets and other compatible technologies, facilitating bidirectional communication between the server and clients.

Extending our microservices system like this flows well with everything that we've explored so far, leveraging pub-sub on top of CQRS to enhance the system. Here is an updated conceptual diagram:

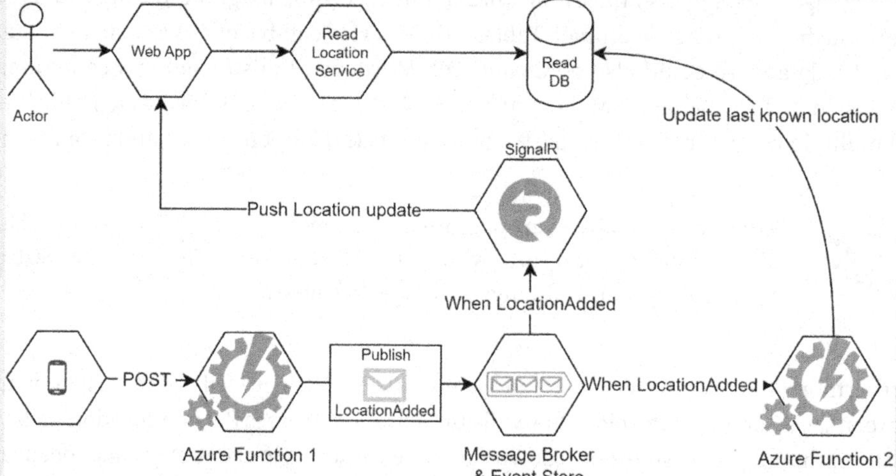

Figure 19.33: Adding a SignalR service as a new subscriber without impacting the other part of the system

The SignalR microservice could be custom code or an Azure SignalR Service (backed by another Azure Function); it doesn't matter. With this design, the Web App will know that a change occurred before the Read DB gets updated, removing the need to send a query altogether.

With this design, I wanted to illustrate that dropping new services into the mix is easier when using a Pub-Sub model than with point-to-point communication.

As you can see, a microservices system adds more and more small pieces that indirectly interconnect with each other over one or more message brokers. Maintaining, diagnosing, and debugging such systems is harder than with a single application; that's the **operational complexity** we discussed earlier. However, containers can help deploy and maintain such systems.

Starting in ASP.NET Core 3.0, the ASP.NET Core team improved **distributed tracing**. Distributed tracing is necessary to find failures and bottlenecks related to an event that flows from one program to another (such as microservices). If something bugs out, it is important to trace what the user did to isolate the error, reproduce it, and then fix it. The more independent pieces there are, the harder it can become to make that trace possible. This is outside the scope of this book, but it is something to consider if you plan to leverage microservices.

Advantages and potential risks

This section explores some advantages and risks of separating a data store's read and write operations using the CQRS pattern.

Benefits of the CQRS pattern

- **Scalability**: Given that read and write workloads can be scaled independently, CQRS can lead to much higher scalability in distributed cloud- or microservices-based applications.
- **Simplified and optimized models**: It separates the read model (query responsibility) and write model (command responsibility), which simplifies application development and can optimize performance.
- **Flexibility**: Different models increase the number of choices one can make, increasing flexibility.
- **Enhanced performance**: CQRS can prevent unnecessary data fetching and allows choosing an optimized database for each job, improving the performance of both read and write operations.
- **Increased efficiency**: It enables parallel development on complex applications, as developers can work independently on the separate read and write sides of the application.

Potential risks of using the CQRS pattern

- **Complexity**: CQRS adds complexity to the system. It is overkill for simple CRUD apps and could over-complicate the application unnecessarily. Therefore, using CQRS only in complex systems and when the advantages outweigh the cons is advisable.
- **Data consistency**: It can introduce eventual consistency issues between the read and write sides because the read model's updates are asynchronous, which does not fit every business requirement.
- **Increased development effort**: CQRS could mean increased development, testing, and maintenance efforts due to handling two separate models and more pieces.
- **Learning curve**: The pattern has its own learning curve. Team members unfamiliar with the CQRS pattern will require training and need to gain some experience.
- **Synchronization challenges**: Maintaining synchronization between the read and write models can be challenging, especially in high data volume cases.

Conclusion

CQRS helps divide queries and commands and helps encapsulate and isolate each block of logic independently. Mixing that concept with serverless computing or microservices architecture allows us to scale reads and writes independently. We can also use different databases, empowering us with the tools we need for the transfer rate required by each part of that system (for example, frequent writes and occasional reads or vice versa).

Major cloud providers like Azure and AWS provide serverless offerings to help support such scenarios. Each cloud provider's documentation should help you get started. Meanwhile, for Azure, we have Azure Functions, Event Grid, Event Hubs, Service Bus, Cosmos DB, and more. Azure also offers bindings between the different services that are triggered or react to events for you, removing a part of the complexity yet locking you in with that vendor.

Now, let's see how CQRS can help us follow the **SOLID** principles at cloud-scale:

- S: Dividing an application into smaller read and write applications (or functions) leans toward encapsulating single responsibilities into different programs.
- O: When integrated with serverless computing or microservices, CQRS enables extension without altering existing code. It achieves this by introducing new commands or queries or changing their implementation without altering the existing handling mechanisms.
- L: N/A.
- I: CQRS set us up to create multiple small interfaces (or programs) with a clear distinction between commands and queries.
- D: N/A.

Overview of the Microservice Adapter pattern

The Microservice Adapter pattern allows us to add missing features, adapt one system to another, or migrate an existing application to an event-driven architecture model, to name a few possibilities. The Microservice Adapter pattern is similar to the Adapter pattern we covered in *Chapter 11, Structural Patterns*, but applied to a microservices system that uses event-driven architecture, instead of creating a class to adapt an object to another signature.

In the scenarios we cover in this section, the microservices system represented by the following diagram can be replaced by a standalone application as well; this pattern applies to all sorts of programs, not just microservices, which is why I abstracted away the details:

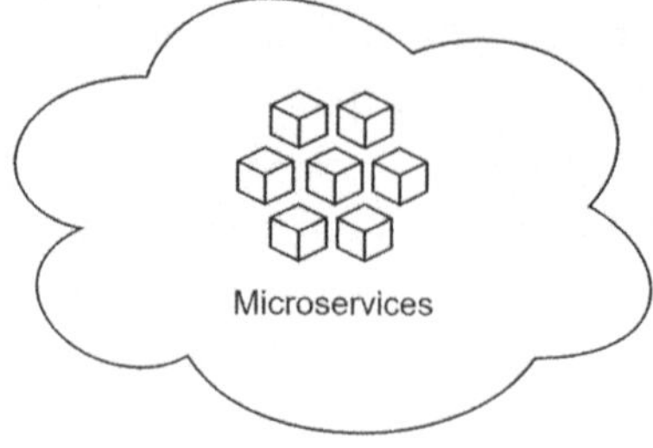

Figure 19.34: Microservices system representation used in the subsequent examples

Here are the examples we cover next and the possible usages of this pattern:

- Adapting an existing system to another
- Decommissioning a legacy application
- Adapting an event broker to another

Let's start by connecting a standalone system to an event-driven one.

Adapting an existing system to another

In this scenario, we have an existing system in which we don't control the source code or don't want to change it, and we have a microservices system built around an event-driven architecture model. We don't have to control the source code of the microservices system either if we have access to the event broker. We want to connect the existing system to the microservices system without changing the code of either.

Here is a diagram that represents this scenario:

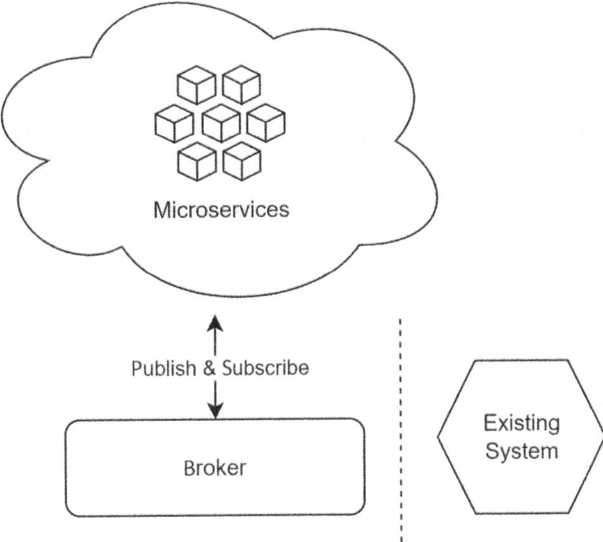

Figure 19.35: A microservices system that interacts with an event broker and an existing system that is disconnected from the microservices

As we can see from the preceding diagram, the existing system is disconnected from the microservices and the broker. To adapt the existing system to the microservices system, we must subscribe or publish certain events. Let's see how to read data from the microservices (subscribe to the broker) and then update that data in the existing system.

When we control the existing system's code, we can open the source code, subscribe to one or more topics, and change the behaviors from there.

In our case, we don't want to do that or can't, so we can't directly subscribe to topics, as demonstrated by the following diagram:

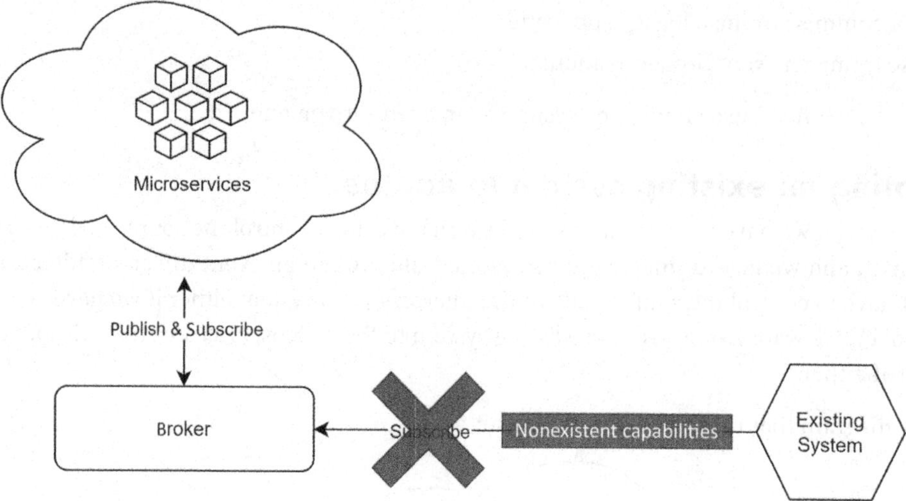

Figure 19.36: Missing capabilities to connect an existing system to an event-driven one

This is where the microservice adapter comes into play and allows us to fill the capability gap of our existing system. To add the missing link, we create a microservice that subscribes to the appropriate events and then apply the changes in the existing system, like this:

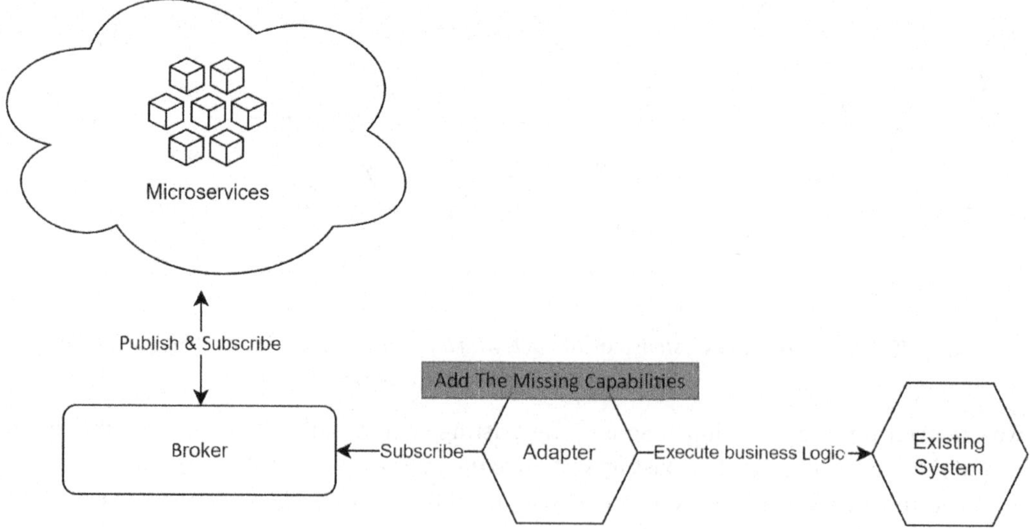

Figure 19.37: An adapter microservice adding missing capabilities to an existing system

As we can see in the preceding diagram, the `Adapter` microservice gets the events (subscribes to one or more topics) and then uses that data from the microservices system to execute some business logic on the existing system.

In this design, the new `Adapter` microservice allowed us to add missing capabilities to a system we had no control over, with little to no disruption to users' day-to-day activities.

The example assumes the existing system had some form of extensibility mechanism like an API. If the system does not, we would have to be more creative to interface with it.

For example, the microservices system could be an e-commerce website, and the existing system could be a legacy inventory management system. The adapter could update the legacy system with new order data.

The existing system could also be an old **customer relationship management** (**CRM**) system that you want to update when users of the microservices application execute some actions, like changing their phone number or address.

The possibilities are almost endless; you create a link between an event-driven system and an existing system you don't control or don't want to change. In this case, the microservice adapter allows us to follow the **Open-Closed principle** by extending the system without changing the existing pieces. The primary drawback is that we are deploying another microservice that has direct coupling with the existing system, which may be best for temporary solutions. On that same line of thought, next, we replace a legacy application with a new one, with limited to no downtime.

Decommissioning a legacy application

In this scenario, we have a legacy application to decommission and a microservices system to which we want to connect some existing capabilities. To achieve this, we can create one or more adapters to migrate all features and dependencies to the new model.

Here is a representation of the current state of our system:

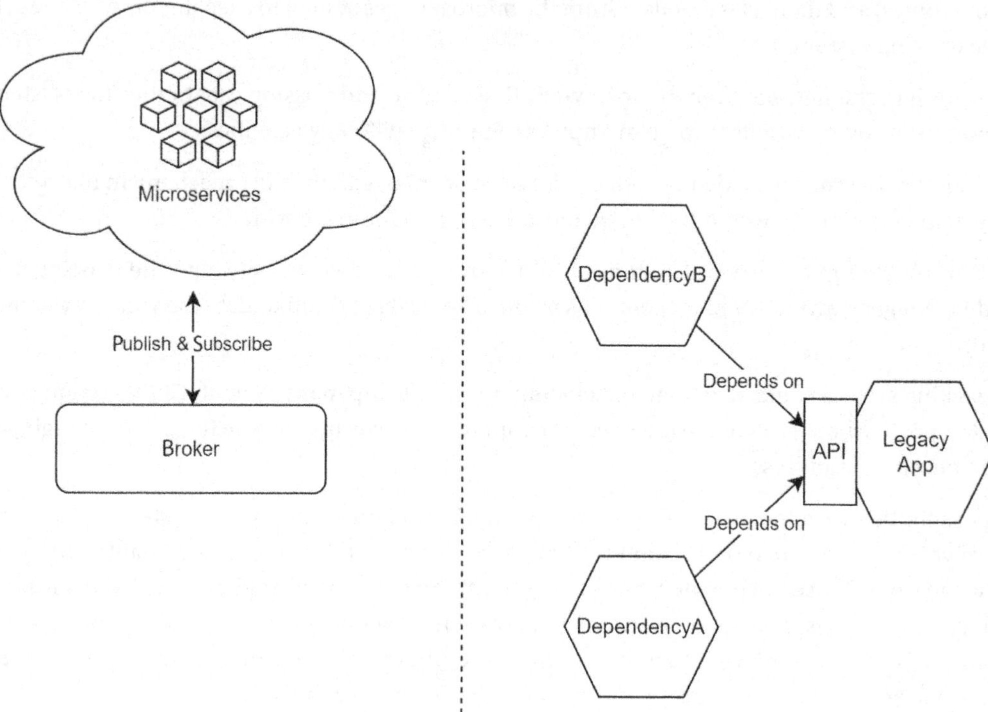

Figure 19.38: The original legacy application and its dependencies

The preceding diagram shows the two distinct systems, including the legacy application we want to decommission. Two other applications, dependency A and B, directly depend on the legacy application. The exact migration flow is strongly dependent on your use case. If you want to keep the dependencies, we want to migrate them first. To do that, we can create an event-driven `Adapter` microservice that breaks the tight coupling between the dependencies and the legacy application, like this:

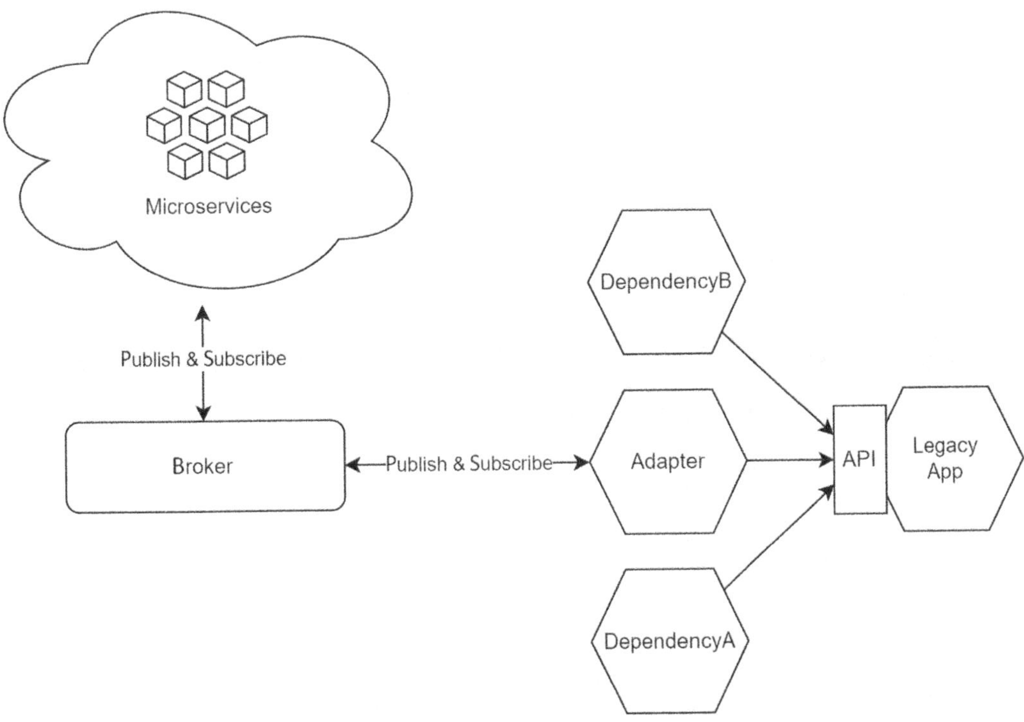

Figure 19.39: Adding a microservice adapter that implements the event-driven flow required to break tight coupling between the dependencies and the legacy application

The preceding diagram shows an `Adapter` microservice and the rest of a microservices system that communicates using an event broker. As we explored in the previous example, the adapter was placed there to connect the legacy application to the microservices. Our scenario focuses on removing the legacy application and migrating its two dependencies. Here, we carved out the required capabilities using the adapter, allowing us to migrate the dependencies to an event-driven model and break tight coupling with the legacy application. Such migration could be done in multiple steps, migrating each dependency one by one, and we could even create one adapter per dependency. For the sake of simplicity, I chose to draw only one adapter. You may want to revisit this choice if your dependencies are large or complex.

Once we are done migrating the dependencies, our systems look like the following:

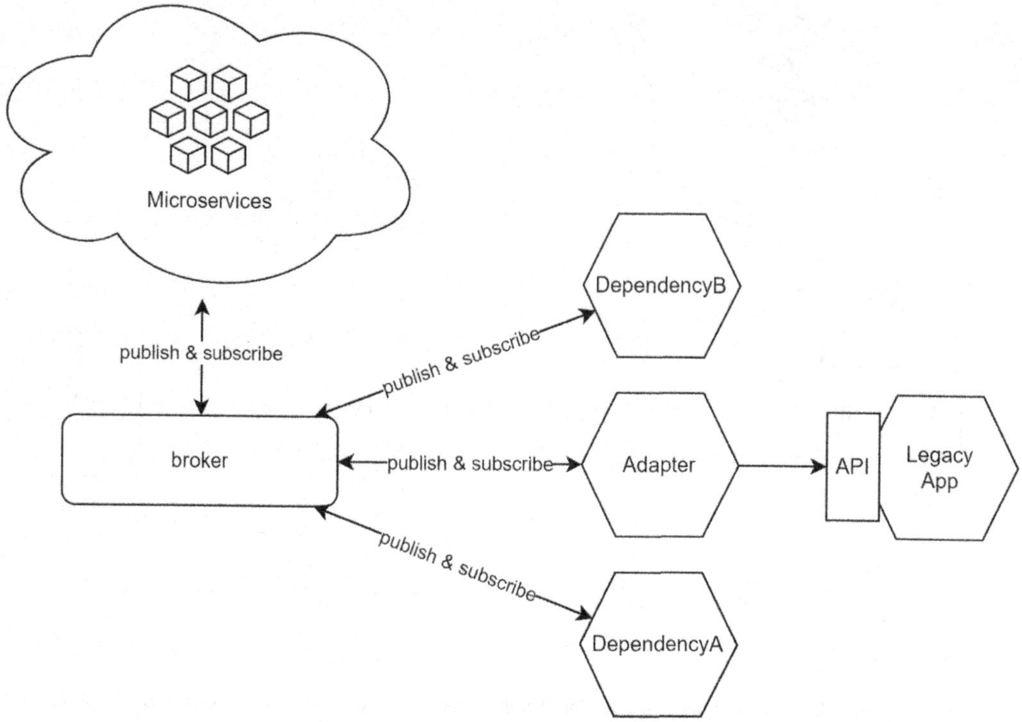

Figure 19.40: The dependencies are now using an event-driven architecture, and the adapter microservice bridges the gap between the events and the legacy system

In the preceding diagram, the Adapter microservice executes the operations against the legacy application API that the two dependencies did before. The dependencies now publish events instead of using the API. For example, when an operation happens in `DependencyB`, it publishes an event to the broker. The Adapter microservice picks up that event and executes the original operation against the API. Doing this creates more complexity and is a temporary state.

With this new architecture in place, we can start migrating existing features away from the legacy application into the new application without impacting the dependencies; we broke tight coupling.

From this point forward, we are applying the **Strangler Fig** pattern to migrate the legacy system piece by piece to our new architecture. For the sake of simplicity, think of the Strangler Fig pattern as migrating features from one application to another, one by one. In this case, we replaced one application with another, but we could also use the same patterns to split an application into multiple smaller applications (like microservices).

I left a few links in the *Further reading* section if migrating legacy systems is something you do or you simply want to know more about that pattern.

The following diagram is a visual representation that adds the modern application we are building to replace the legacy application. That new modern application could also be a purchased product you are putting in place instead; the concepts we are exploring apply to both use cases, but the exact steps are directly related to the technology at play.

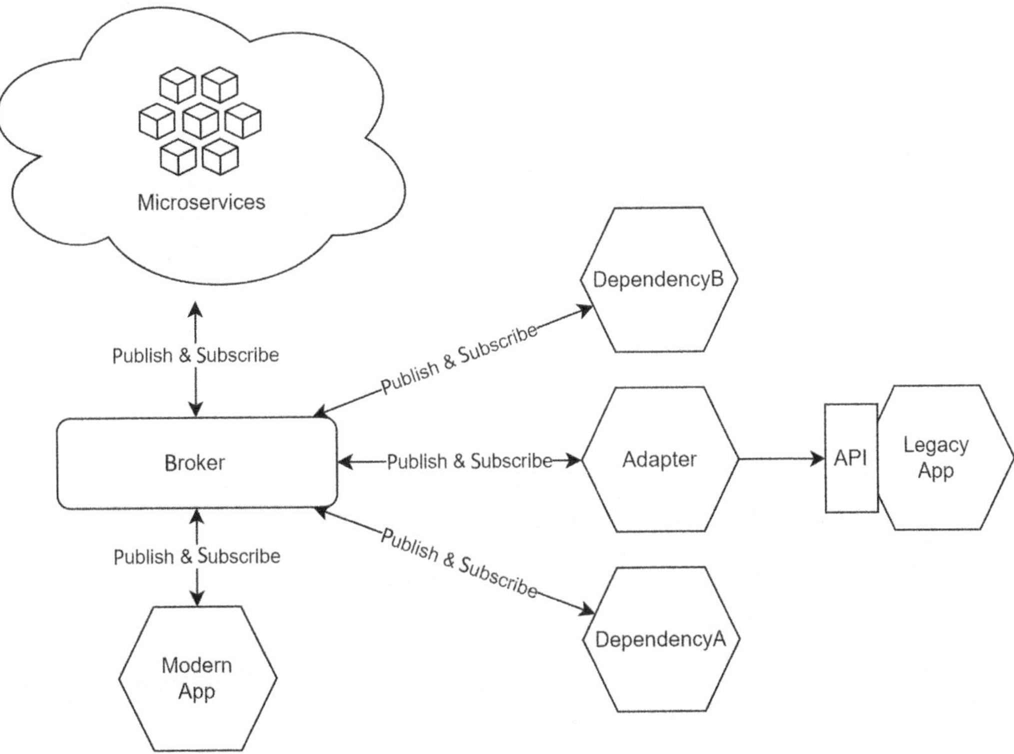

Figure 19.41: The modern application to replace the legacy application is starting to emerge by migrating capabilities to that new application

In the preceding diagram, we can see that the new modern application has appeared. Each time we deploy a new feature to the new application, we can remove it from the adapter, leading to a graceful transition between the two models. At the same time, we are keeping the legacy application in place to continue to provide the capabilities that are not yet migrated.

Once all the features we want to keep are migrated, we can remove the adapter and decommission the legacy application, leading to the following system:

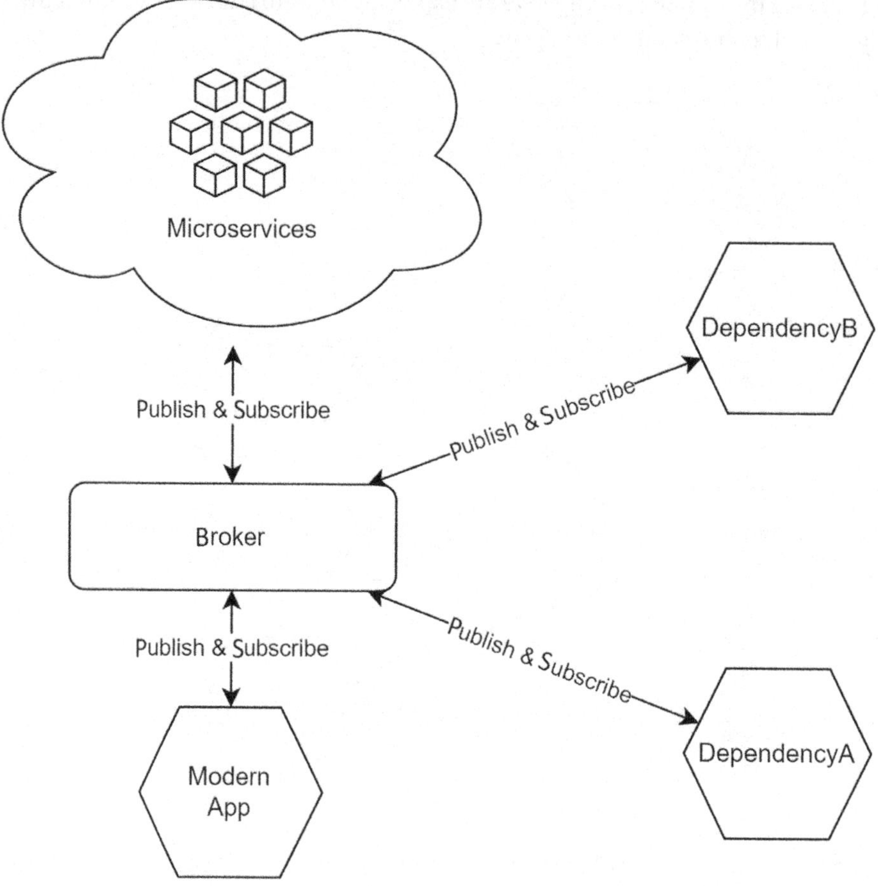

Figure 19.42: The new system topology after the retirement of the legacy application, showing the new modern application and its two loosely coupled dependencies

The preceding diagram shows the new system topology encompassing a new modern application and the two original dependencies, which are now loosely coupled through event-driven architecture. Of course, the bigger the migration, the more complex it will be and the longer it will take, but the Adapter Microservice pattern is one way to help do a partial or complete migration from one system to another.

Like the preceding example, the main advantage is adding or removing capabilities without impacting the other systems, which allows us to migrate and break the tight coupling between the different dependencies. The downside is the added complexity of this temporary solution. Moreover, during the migration step, you will most likely need to deploy both the modern application and the adapter in the correct sequence, ensuring that both systems do not handle the same events twice, leading to duplicate changes. For example, updating the phone number to the same value twice should be all right because it leads to the same final dataset. However, creating two records instead of one is more important to avoid, as it may lead to integrity errors in the dataset.

For example, creating an online order twice instead of once could create customer dissatisfaction or internal issues.

And voilà, we decommissioned a system using the Microservice Adapter pattern without breaking its dependencies. Next, we look at an **Internet of Things** (**IoT**) example.

Adapting an event broker to another

In this scenario, we are adapting an event broker to another. In the following diagram, we look at two use cases: one that translates events from broker B to broker A (left) and the other that translates events from broker A to broker B (right). Afterwards, we explore a more concrete example:

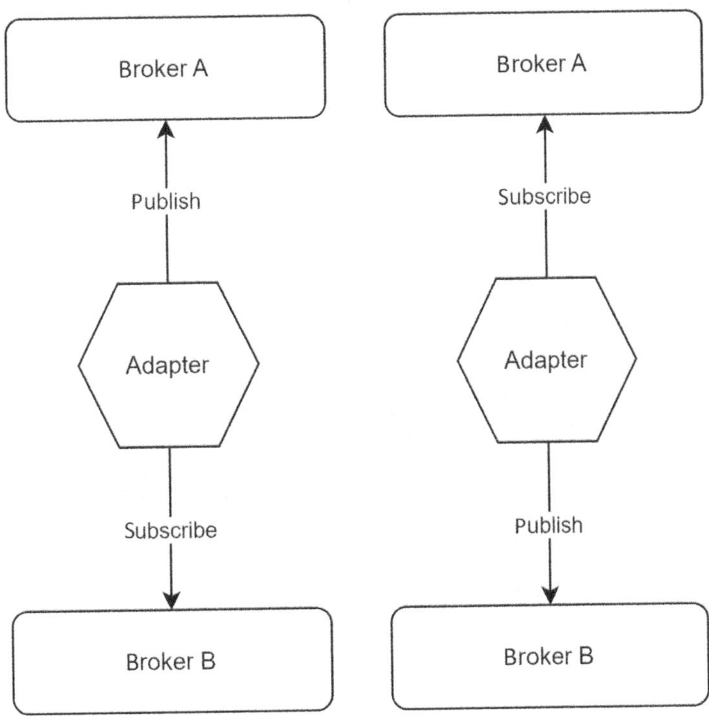

Figure 19.43: An adapter microservice that translates events from broker B to broker A (left) and from broker A to broker B (right)

We can see the two possible flows in the preceding diagram. The first flow, on the left, allows the adapter to read events from broker B and publish them to broker A. The second flow, on the right, enables the adapter to read events from broker A and publish them to broker B. Those flows allow us to translate or copy events from one broker to another by leveraging the Microservice Adapter pattern.

In *Figure 19.43*, there is one adapter per flow. I did that to make the two flows as independent as possible, but the adapters could be a single microservice.

This pattern can be very useful for an IoT system where your microservices leverage Apache Kafka internally for its full-featured suite of event-streaming capabilities, but they use MQTT to communicate with the low-powered IoT devices that connect to the system. An adapter can solve this problem by translating the messages from one protocol to the other. Here is a diagram that represents the complete flows, including a device and the microservices:

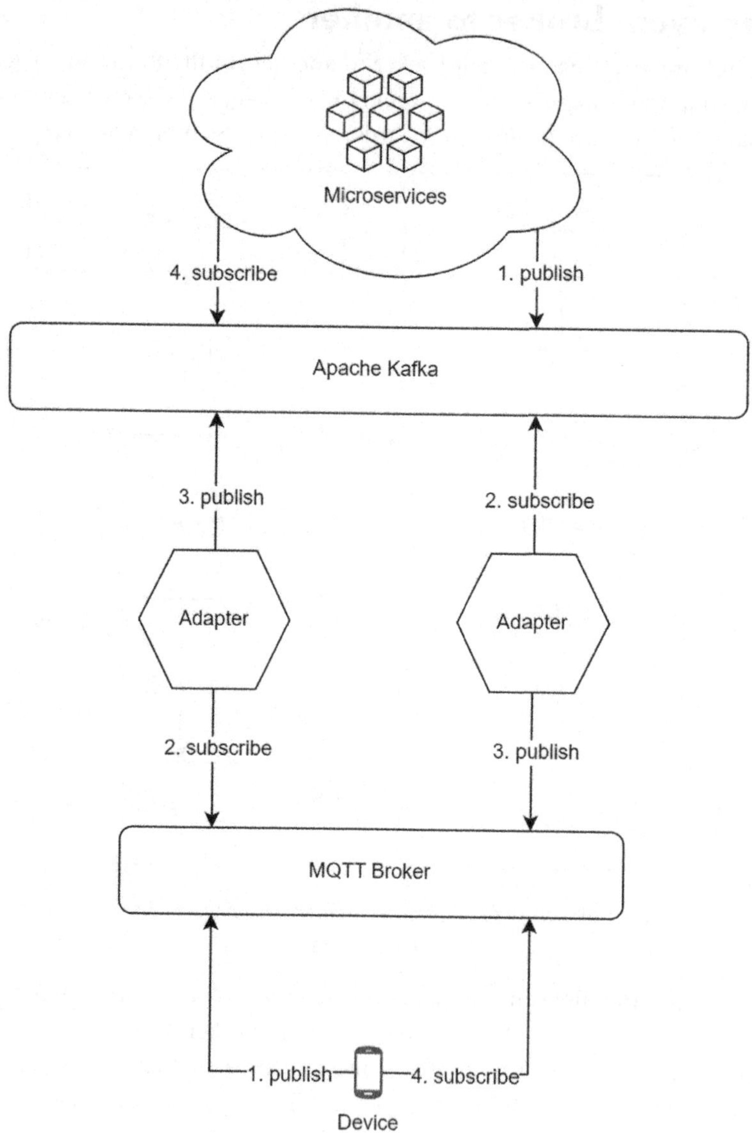

Figure 19.44: Complete protocol adapter flows, including a device and microservices

Before we explore what the events could be, let's explore both flows step by step. The left flow allows us to get events inside the system from the devices through the following sequence:

1. A device publishes an event to the MQTT broker.

2. The adapter reads that event.
3. The adapter publishes a similar or different event to the Kafka broker.
4. Zero or more microservices subscribed to the event act on it.

On the other hand, the right flow allows us to get events out of the system to the devices through the following sequence:

1. A microservice publishes an event to the Kafka broker.
2. The adapter reads the event.
3. The adapter publishes a similar or different event to the MQTT broker.
4. Zero or more devices subscribed to the event act on it.

You don't have to implement both flows; the adapter could be bidirectional (supporting both flows), we could have two unidirectional adapters that support one of the flows, or we could allow the communication to flow only one way (in or out but not both). The choice relates to your specific use cases.

Concrete examples of sending a message from a device to a microservice (left flow) could be sending its GPS position, a status update (the light is now on), or a message indicating a sensor failure.

Concrete examples of sending a message to a device (right flow) could be to remotely control a speaker's volume, flip a light on, or send a confirmation that a message has been acknowledged.

In this case, the adapter is not a temporary solution but a permanent capability. We could leverage such adapters to create additional capabilities with minimal impact on the rest of the system. The primary downside is deploying one or more other microservices, but your system and processes are probably robust enough to handle that added complexity when leveraging such capabilities.

This third scenario that leverages the Microservice Adapter is our last. Hopefully, I sparked your imagination enough to leverage this simple yet powerful design pattern.

Conclusion

We have explored the Microservice Adapter pattern, which allows us to connect two elements of a system by adapting one to the other. We explored how to push information from an event broker into an existing system that does not support such capabilities. We also explored how to leverage an adapter to break tight coupling, migrate features into a newer system, and decommission a legacy application seamlessly. We finally connected two event brokers through an adapter microservice, allowing a low-powered IoT device to communicate with a microservices system without draining its battery, and without the complexity it would incur to use a more complex communication protocol.

This pattern is very powerful and can be implemented in many ways, but it all depends on the exact use cases. You can write an adapter using a serverless offering like an Azure function, no-code/low-code offerings like Power Automate, or C#. Of course, these are just a few examples. The key to designing the correct system is to nail down the problem statement because once you know what you are trying to fix, the solution becomes clearer.

Now, let's see how the Microservice Adapter pattern can help us follow the **SOLID** principles at cloud-scale:

- S: The microservice adapter helps manage long- or short-term responsibilities. For example, adding an adapter that translates between two protocols or creating a temporary adapter to decommission a legacy system.
- O: You can leverage microservice adapters to dynamically add or remove features without impacting or with limited impact on the rest of the system. For example, in the IoT scenario, we could add support for a new protocol like AMQP without changing the rest of the system.
- L: N/A
- I: Adding smaller adapters can make changes easier and less risky than updating large legacy applications. As we saw in the legacy system decommissioning scenario, we could also leverage temporary adapters to split large applications into smaller pieces.
- D: A microservice adapter inverts the dependency flow between the system it adapts. For example, in the legacy system decommissioning scenario, the adapter reversed the flow from the two dependencies to the legacy system by leveraging an event broker.

Summary

The microservices architecture is different from everything we've covered in this book and how we build monoliths. Instead of one big application, we split it into multiple smaller ones called microservices. Microservices must be independent of one another; otherwise, we will face the same problems associated with tightly coupled classes but at the cloud scale.

We can leverage the Pub-Sub design pattern to loosely couple microservices while keeping them connected through events. Message brokers are programs that dispatch those messages. We can use event sourcing to recreate the application's state at any point in time, including when spawning new containers. We can use application gateways to shield clients from the microservices cluster's complexity and publicly expose only a subset of services.

We also looked at how we can build upon the CQRS design pattern to decouple reads and writes of the same entities, allowing us to scale queries and commands independently. We also looked at using serverless resources to create that kind of system.

Finally, we explored the Microservice Adapter pattern, which allowed us to adapt two systems together, decommission a legacy application, and connect two event brokers. This pattern is simple but powerful at inverting the dependency flow between two dependencies in a loosely coupled manner. The use of the pattern can be temporary, as we saw in the legacy application decommissioning scenario, or permanent, as we saw in the IoT scenario.

On the other hand, microservices come at a cost and are not intended to replace all that exists. Building a monolith is still a good idea for many projects. Starting with a monolith and migrating it to microservices when scaling is most likely the best solution. This allows us to develop the application faster (monolith). It is also easier to add new features to a monolith than it can be to add them to a microservice application. Most of the time, mistakes cost less in a monolith than in a microservices application.

You can also plan your future migration toward microservices, which leads to the best of both worlds while keeping operational complexity low. For example, you could leverage the Pub-Sub pattern through MediatR notifications in your monolith and migrate the event-dispatching responsibility to a message broker later, when migrating your system to microservices architecture (if the need ever arises). We explore ways to organize our monolith in *Chapter 20, Modular Monolith*.

I don't want you to discard the microservices architecture, but I want to ensure you weigh up the pros and cons of such a system before blindly jumping in. Your team's skill level and ability to learn new technologies may also impact the cost of jumping into the microservices boat.

DevOps (development [Dev] and IT operations [Ops]) or **DevSecOps** (adding security [Sec] to the DevOps mix) is essential when building microservices. It brings deployment automation, automated quality checks, auto-composition, and more. Your microservices cluster will be very hard to deploy and maintain without that.

Microservices are great when you need scaling, want to go serverless, or split responsibilities between multiple teams, but keep the operational costs in mind.

In the next chapter, we combine the microservices and monolith worlds.

Questions

Let's take a look at a few practice questions:

1. What is the most significant difference between a **message queue** and a **Pub-Sub** model?
2. What is **event sourcing**?
3. Can an **application gateway** be both a **routing gateway** and an **aggregation gateway**?
4. Is it true that real CQRS requires a serverless cloud infrastructure?
5. What is a significant advantage of using the BFF design pattern?

Further reading

Here are a few links that will help you build on what you learned in this chapter:

- Event Sourcing pattern by Martin Fowler: `https://adpg.link/oY5H`
- Event Sourcing pattern by Microsoft: `https://adpg.link/ofG2`
- Publisher-Subscriber pattern by Microsoft: `https://adpg.link/amcZ`
- Event-driven architecture by Microsoft: `https://adpg.link/rnck`
- Saga pattern by Microsoft: `https://adpg.link/3FD7`
- Microservices architecture and patterns on microservices.io: `https://adpg.link/41vP`
- Microservices architecture and patterns by Martin Fowler: `https://adpg.link/Mw97`
- Microservices architecture and patterns by Microsoft: `https://adpg.link/s2Uq`
- RFC 6902 (JSON Patch): `https://adpg.link/bGGn`
- JSON Patch in ASP.NET Core web API: `https://adpg.link/u6dw`

- Strangler Fig Application pattern:
    - Martin Fowler: `https://adpg.link/Zi9G`
    - Microsoft: `https://adpg.link/erg2`

Answers

1. The message queue gets a message and has a single subscriber dequeue it. If nothing dequeues a message, it stays in the queue indefinitely (the FIFO model). The Pub-Sub model gets a message and sends it to zero or more subscribers.
2. Event sourcing is the process of chronologically accumulating events that happened in a system instead of persisting in the current state of an entity. It allows you to recreate the entity's state by replaying those events.
3. Yes, you can mix Gateway patterns.
4. No, you can deploy micro-applications (microservices) on-premises if you want to.
5. It separates generic functionalities from app-specific ones, promoting cleaner code and modularization. It also helps simplify the frontend.

Learn more on Discord

To join the Discord community for this book – where you can share feedback, ask questions to the author, and learn about new releases – follow the QR code below:

`https://packt.link/ArchitectingASPNETCoreApps3e`

20

Modular Monolith

In the ever-evolving software development landscape, choosing the right architecture is like laying the foundation for a building. The architecture dictates how the software is structured, impacting its scalability, maintainability, and overall success. Traditional monolithic architecture and microservices have long been the dominant paradigms, each with advantages and challenges.

However, a new architectural style has been gaining traction—Modular Monoliths. This approach aims to offer the best of both worlds by combining the simplicity of monoliths with the flexibility of microservices. It serves as a middle ground that addresses some of the complexities associated with microservices, making it particularly appealing for small to medium-sized projects or teams transitioning from a traditional monolithic architecture.

I wrote an article about this in 2017 entitled *Microservices Aggregation*, but nowadays, the name *Modular Monolith* is gaining traction. The Modular Monolith architectural style is a way to modularize and organize an application, lowering our chances of creating a Big Ball of Mud.

This chapter aims to provide a comprehensive understanding of Modular Monoliths. We delve into its core principles, advantages, and key components and explore when and how to implement this architecture. We build upon our nano e-commerce application to get hands-on insights into Modular Monoliths' practical applications. Additionally, we discuss how they compare with other architectural styles to help you make informed decisions for your next projects.

By the end of this chapter, you should have a solid grasp of Modular Monoliths, why they might be the right choice for your project, and how to implement them.

In this chapter, we cover the following topics:

- What is a Modular Monolith?
- Implementing a Modular Monolith
- Project—Modular Monolith

- Transitioning to microservices
- Challenges and pitfalls

Let's start by exploring what a Modular Monolith is.

What is a Modular Monolith?

A Modular Monolith is an architectural style that aims to combine the best aspects of traditional monolithic architectures and microservices. It organizes the software application into well-defined, loosely coupled modules. Each module is responsible for a specific business capability. However, unlike microservices, all these modules are deployed as a single unit like a monolith.

The core principles of a Modular Monolith are:

- Treat each module as a microservice
- Deploy the application as a single unit

Here are the fundamental principles of a successful microservice as studied in *Chapter 19, Introduction to Microservices Architecture*:

- Each microservice should be a cohesive unit of business
- Each microservice should own its data
- Each microservice should be independent of the others

In a nutshell, we get the best of both worlds. Yet, understanding how a Modular Monolith compares with the microservices architectural style is crucial to make informed decisions.

What about Clean Architecture, Vertical Slice Architecture, and REPR? We can leverage those patterns to organize our Modular Monolith. How to build the monolith is not prescriptive, yet I find that REPR and Vertical Slice Architecture fit the role very well, so REPR is the pattern we use in this chapter.

What are traditional monoliths?

In a traditional monolithic architecture, we build the application as a single, indivisible unit. This leads to the functionalities being tightly coupled together, making it difficult to make changes or scale specific features. This approach makes creating a Big Ball of Mud easier, particularly when the team invests little effort in domain modeling and analysis before and during development.

On top of that, while this approach is simple and straightforward, it lacks the flexibility and scalability of more modern architectures.

A monolith does not have to be indivisible, yet most end up this way because it is easy to create tight coupling in a single application.

Let's look at microservices next.

What are microservices?

Microservices architecture, on the other hand, takes modularity to the extreme. Each service is a completely independent unit, running in its own environment. Microservices architecture allows for high scalability and flexibility but comes at the cost of increased operational complexity.

Chapter 19, Introduction to Microservices Architecture, covers this topic in more depth.

The following sections delve deeper into this emerging architectural style, starting with its advantages.

Advantages of Modular Monoliths

One of the best things about Modular Monoliths is that they are easy to manage. You don't have to worry about many moving parts like with microservices. Everything is in one place but still separated into modules. This makes it easier for us to keep track of things and to work with them.

With Modular Monoliths, each module is like its own small project. We can test, fix, or improve a module without affecting the others. This is great because it lets us focus on one thing at a time, which improves productivity by lowering the cognitive load required to work on that feature.

When it's time to release the software, we only have one application to deploy. Even though it has many modules, we treat them like one deployable unit. This makes managing deployments much more straightforward as we don't have to juggle multiple services like we would with microservices.

Modular Monoliths can save us money because we don't need as many resources since we deploy a single monolith. Because of that, we don't need a team to manage and run complicated infrastructure. We don't need to worry about distributed tracing between our services, which can reduce the upfront monitoring cost. This deployment style is highly beneficial when starting a project with a small team or if the team is not proficient with microservices architecture.

Modular Monoliths can still be valuable even if you are part of a large team, part of a larger organization, or have experience with microservices architecture. It is not a one or the other kind of scenario.

Next, we will look at what makes up a Modular Monolith.

Key components of a Modular Monolith

Modular Monoliths are composed of different parts called **modules**. Each module is like a mini-app that performs a specific job. This job is related to a particular business capability. A business capability comes from the business domain and covers a cohesive group of scenarios.

Such a group is called a bounded context in **domain-driven design (DDD)**. Think of each module as a microservice or a well-defined chunk of the domain.

That separation means everything we need to complete a specific task is in one module, which makes it easier for us to understand and work on the software because we don't have to jump from one place to another to get things done. So, if one module needs an update or has a problem, we can fix it without touching the others. This segregation is also perfect for testing since we can test each module in isolation to ensure it works well. For example, one module might handle a shopping cart while another takes care of the shipping, but we piece all modules together in a final aggregated application.

We can create the Modular Monolith as a single project. However, in a .NET-specific environment, when each module comprises one or more assemblies, it is harder to create unwanted coupling between modules. We explore this in the project we are about to build.

The **module aggregator**—the assembled monolith—is responsible for loading and serving the modules as if they were just one application. Another name for the module aggregator is a bootstrapper since it bootstraps the application.

Even though each module is independent, they still need to talk to each other sometimes. For example, the product catalog module might need to tell the shopping cart module that an employee has added a new product to the catalog. There are many ways to make this communication happen. One of the best ways to keep a low coupling level between the modules is to leverage event-driven architecture. On top of loose coupling, this opens doors like scaling the Modular Monolith by migrating one or more modules to a microservices architecture; more on that later.

Here's a diagram that represents these relationships:

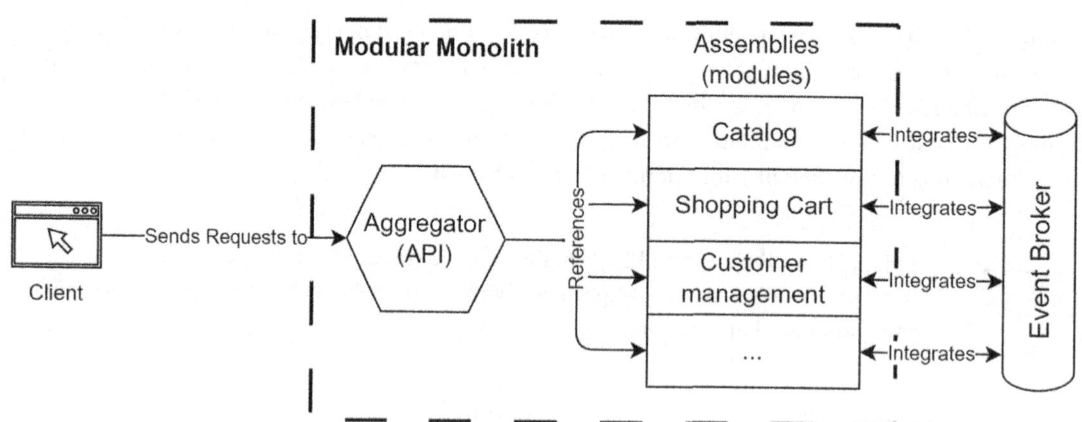

Figure 20.1: Diagram representing the relationships between the module aggregator, the modules, and an event broker

Now that we have explored the key components of a Modular Monolith, the next section discusses planning and implementing one.

Implementing a Modular Monolith

Planning is essential before building a Modular Monolith. We must consider what each module does and how modules work together. A good plan helps us avoid problems later on.

Choosing the right tools to create a lean stack is also essential. The good news is that we don't need to define a large shared stack since each module is independent. Like a slice in Vertical Slice Architecture, each module can determine its patterns and data sources. Yet, we must define a few common elements to assemble a Modular Monolith successfully. Here are a few items to consider to improve the chances of success of a Modular Monolith:

- The modules share the URL space
- The modules share the configuration infrastructure
- The modules share a single dependency injection object graph (one container)
- The modules share the inter-module communication infrastructure (event broker)

We can address the first two elements using the module name as a discriminator. For example, using the `/{module name}/{module space}` URI space would yield the following results (`products`, `baskets`, and `customers` are modules):

- `/products`
- `/products/123`
- `/baskets`
- `/customers`

Using the module name as the top-level key of the configuration also makes it easy to avoid conflicts, like `{module name}:{key}`. For example, the following JSON snippet depicts that in an `appsettings.json` file format:

```
"{module name}": {
    "{key}": "Module configs"
}
```

We can address the last two elements by managing the shared code in a certain way. For example, limiting the amount of shared code reduces the chances of conflict between the modules. Yet, multiple modules globally configuring ASP.NET Core or a third-party library can result in conflicts; centralizing those configurations into the aggregator instead and treating them as a convention helps mitigate most issues. Cross-cutting concerns like exception handling, JSON serialization, logging, and security are great candidates for this.

Here is an example of the composition of a Modular Monolith:

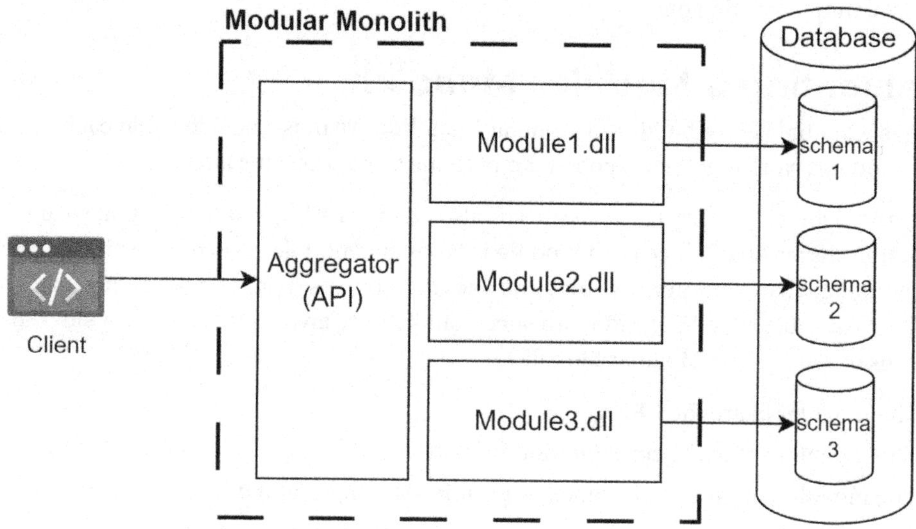

Figure 20.2: A Modular Monolith, an aggregator, and three modules, each owning its own database schema

The preceding diagram shows the aggregator—the ASP.NET Core REST API project—and three modules, each compiled into a DLL—class library projects. On top of that, each module owns its data by isolating its schema, making them completely independent. To work, the aggregator references the three projects—project references. From there, the shared IoC container provided by ASP.NET Core can load module dependencies, and we can register shared dependencies in it as well, from the aggregator `Program.cs` file for example.

In case you need to share dependencies between modules but can't centralize the configuration in the aggregator, you can create a class library shared between multiple modules. This is the same concept that we explored in *Chapter 14, Layering and Clean Architecture*.

Lastly, sharing a single way to communicate between modules and configuring it in the aggregator helps address the communication concern and lower the risk of creating tight coupling between modules.

Let's start planning the new version of our e-commerce project next.

Planning the project

Planning is a crucial part of any software. Without a plan, you increase your chances of building the wrong thing. A plan does not guarantee success, but it improves your chances. Overplanning is the other side of this coin. It can lead to **analysis paralysis**, which means you may never even deliver your project or that it will take you so long to deliver it that it will be the wrong product because the needs changed along the way and you did not adapt. Always be ready to adapt your plan to changes.

Here's a high-level way to accomplish planning a Modular Monolith:

1. Analyze and model the domain.
2. Identify and design the modules.
3. Identify the interactions between modules and design the integration events that cover those interactions.

You don't have to execute all the steps in order. You can perform many of them iteratively, or multiple people or teams can even work on them in parallel.

Once we are done planning, we can develop and operate the application. Here are a few high-level steps:

1. Build and test the modules in isolation.
2. Build and test the module aggregator application that integrates one or more modules.
3. Deploy, operate, and monitor the monolith.

Implementing a Modular Monolith, like any program, is a step-by-step process. We plan, build, test, and then deploy it. Each part is simple enough on its own, and when we piece all of them together, we get an easy-to-maintain system.

Even if continuously improving the application and refining the analysis and the model over time should yield the best results, having a good idea of the high-level domain—the modules—and at least a vague view of their interactions before starting will help avoid mistakes and potentially significant refactoring further down the road.

Here's a general representation of this process:

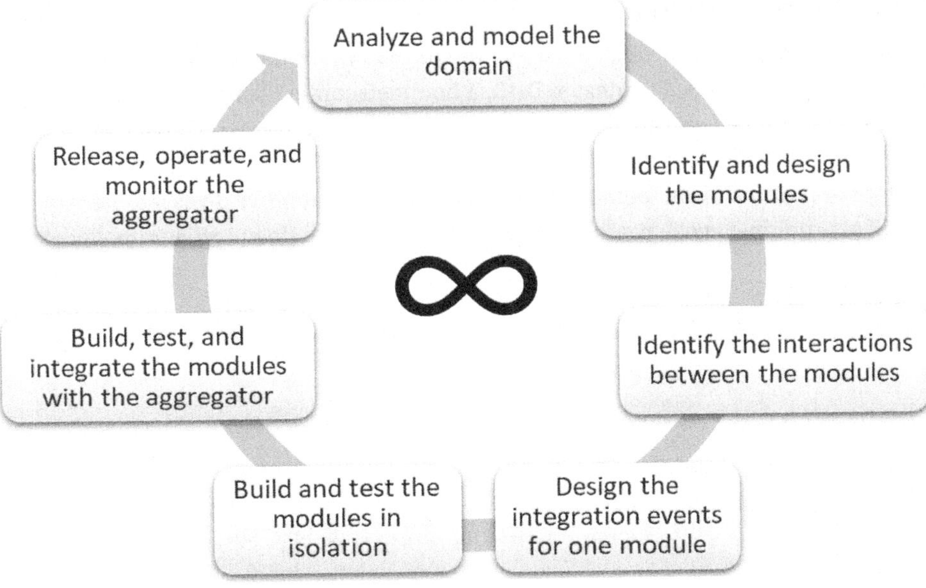

Figure 20.3: A partial Agile and DevOps view of the Modular Monolith phases

Next, we plan our nano e-commerce application.

Analyzing the domain

As we continue to iterate over the nano e-commerce application we built in *Chapter 18* and *Chapter 19*, the domain analysis is very short. Moreover, we are not expanding the application further than products and baskets because the application is already too large to fit in a single chapter. Of course, this time, we are making it a Modular Monolith. Here are the high-level entities and their relationships:

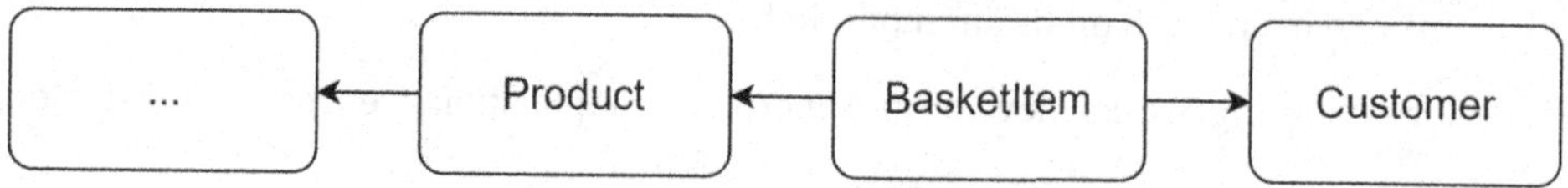

Figure 20.4: The high-level entities of our nano e-commerce app and their relationships

As the diagram shows, we have a `Product` entity that could benefit from more details like categories, hence the `...` box. We also have the `BasketItem` entity we use for people to save their shopping baskets to the database. Finally, a `Customer` entity represents the person to whom a shopping basket belongs.

We did not implement a `Customer` class, yet the customer is conceptually present through the `CustomerId` property.

Next, we split this subset of the domain into modules.

Identifying the modules

Now that we have identified the entities, it is time to map them into modules. To achieve that, we borrow the concept of bounded context to DDD. A bounded context defines the limits within which a particular model is defined and applicable. Each bounded context owns its model and does not share it with other contexts. However, multiple contexts may need the same entity. In that case, one context owns a subset of properties and behaviors of that entity while another owns another subset. That is why you will see multiple `Product` and `Customer` entities in the following diagram—let's start there:

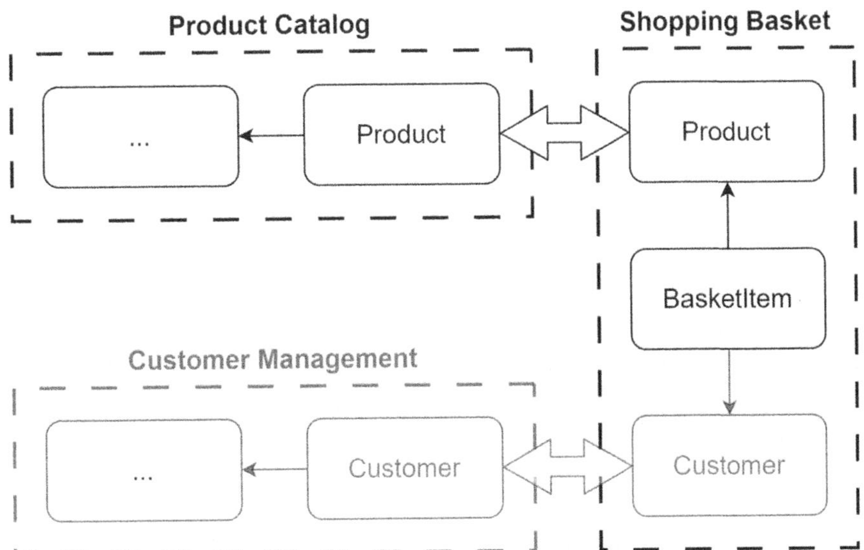

Figure 20.5: Modules (bounded context) separation and entities relationships

As expected, we have a product catalog, a shopping basket, and a customer management modules. What's new here is the relationships between the entities. The catalog mainly manages the `Product` entity, yet the shopping basket needs to know about it to operate. The same logic applies to the `Customer` entity. In this case, the shopping basket only needs to know the unique identifier of each entity, but another module could need more information.

Based on that high-level view, we need to create three modules. In our case, we continue with only two modules because the third one would be redundant and add unwanted complexity to this already large project. In an actual application, we'd have more than three modules since we'd have to manage the purchases, the shipping, the inventory, and more.

Let's look at the interactions between the modules.

Identifying the interactions between modules

Based on our analysis and limited to the two modules we are building, the shopping basket module needs to know about the products. Here's our `BasketItem` class:

```
public record class BasketItem(int CustomerId, int ProductId, int Quantity);
```

The preceding class shows that we only need to know about the unique product identifier. So, with an event-driven mindset, the shopping basket module wants to be notified when:

- A product is created
- A product is deleted

With those two events, the basket module can manage its cache of products and only allow customers to add existing items to their shopping basket. It can also remove items from customers' shopping baskets when unavailable. Here's a diagram representing these flows:

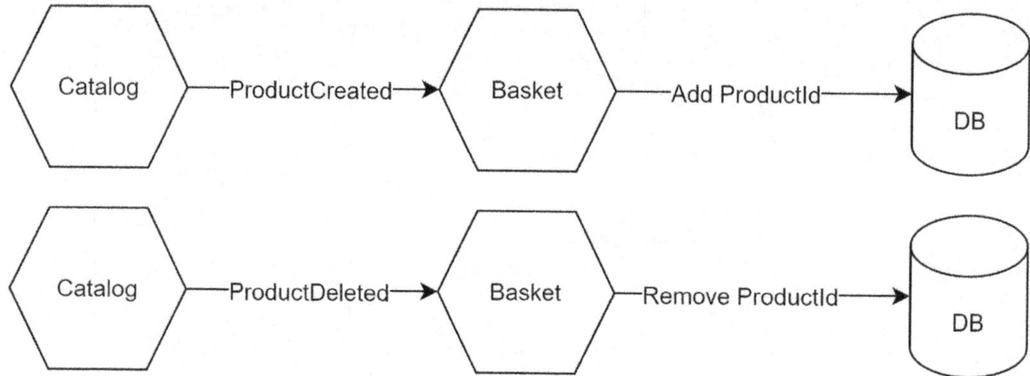

Figure 20.6: The integration event flows between the catalog and the basket modules

Now that we have analyzed the domain and the modules, before building anything, let's define our stack.

Defining our stack

We know we are using ASP.NET Core and C#. We continue leveraging minimal APIs, yet MVC could achieve the same. We also continue to leverage *EF Core*, *ExceptionMapper*, *FluentValidation*, and *Mapperly*. But what about the modules and the other shared aspects of the project? Let's have a look.

The module structure

For this project, we use a flexible yet straightforward module structure, inspired by Vertical Slice Architecture, microservices architecture, and the REPR pattern.

You can organize your projects however you like; this is not a prescriptive approach. For example, you can get inspired by other architectural styles, like Clean Architecture, or adopt your own based on your own experience, context, and work environment.

I opted for the following directory structure:

- The `applications` directory contains the deployable applications, like the aggregator. We could add **user interfaces (UIs)** in this directory or other deployable applications, like the BFF we built in *Chapter 19*. Each application is contained within its own subdirectory.
- The `modules` directory contains the modules, each within its own subdirectory.
- The `shared` directory contains the shared projects.

In real-world software, we could extend this setup and add `infrastructure`, `docs`, and `pipelines` directories to store our **Infrastructure as Code (IaC)**, documentation, and CI/CD pipelines next to our code.

What I like about this mono-repo-inspired structure is that each module and application is self-contained. For example, the aggregator's API, contracts, and tests are next to each other:

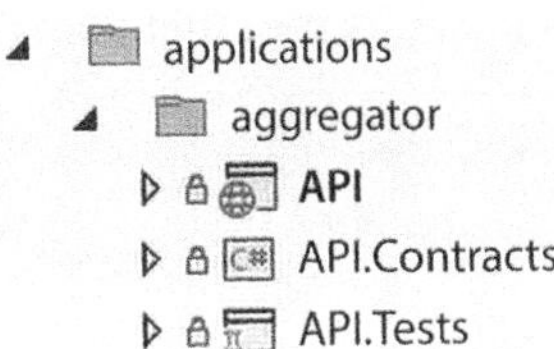

Figure 20.7: The aggregator's directory and project hierarchy

The modules are organized similarly:

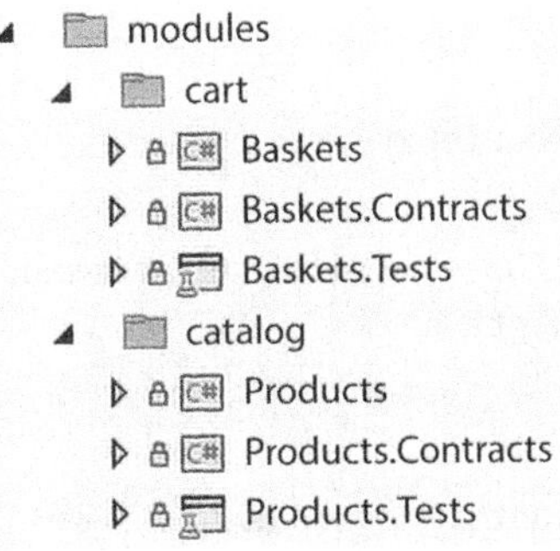

Figure 20.8: The modules' subdirectories and projects hierarchy

I changed the code structure in this version as compared to the REPR code. I got rid of the nested classes and created one class per file. This follows a more classic .NET convention and allows us to extract the API contracts to another assembly. If you remember, in *Chapter 19*, the BFF project referenced the two APIs to reuse their `Query`, `Command`, and `Response` contracts. We fix this problem through the `Contracts` class library projects in this solution.

Why is it a problem? The BFF depends on all the microservices, including their logic and dependencies. This is a recipe to introduce unwanted coupling. Moreover, since it inherits all the dependencies transitively, it increases its deployment size and vulnerability surface; more dependencies and more code means more possibilities for a malicious actor to find an exploitable hole.

On top of the API contracts, the `Contracts` projects also contain the integration events. We could have separated the API contracts and the integration events if the application was larger; in this case, we only have two integration events. Design choices must be taken relative to the current project and context.

Let's explore the URI space next.

The URI space

The modules of this application follow the previously discussed URI space: `/{module name}/{module space}`. Each module has a `Constants` file at its root that looks like this:

```
namespace Baskets;
public sealed class Constants
{
    public const string ModuleName = nameof(Baskets);
}
```

We use the `ModuleName` constant in the `{module name}ModuleExtensions.cs` files to set the URI prefix and tag the endpoints like this:

```
namespace Baskets;
public static class BasketModuleExtensions
{
    public static IEndpointRouteBuilder MapBasketModule(this
IEndpointRouteBuilder endpoints)
    {
        _ = endpoints
            .MapGroup(Constants.ModuleName.ToLower())
            .WithTags(Constants.ModuleName)
            .AddFluentValidationFilter()

            // Map endpoints
            .MapFetchItems()
            .MapAddItem()
            .MapUpdateQuantity()
            .MapRemoveItem()
        ;
        return endpoints;
    }
}
```

With this in place, both modules self-register themselves in the correct URI space.

We can apply these types of conventions in many different ways. In this case, I opted for simplicity, which is the most error-prone, leaving the responsibility to the mercy of each module. With a more framework-oriented mindset, we could create a strongly typed module contract that gets loaded automatically, like an `IModule` interface. The aggregator could also create the root groups and enforce the URI space.

Next, we explore the data space.

The data space

Since we are following the microservices architecture tenets and each module should own its data, we must find a way to ensure our data contexts do not conflict.

The project uses the EF Core in-memory provider to develop locally. For production, we plan on using SQL Server. One excellent way to ensure our `DbContext` classes do not conflict with each other is to create one database schema per context. Each module has one context, so one schema per module. We don't have to overthink this; we can reuse the same idea as the URI and leverage the module name. So, each module groups its tables under the `{module name}` schema instead of `dbo` (the default SQL Server schema).

We can apply different security rules and permissions to each schema in SQL Server, so we could craft a very secure database model by expanding this. For instance, we could employ multiple users possessing minimal privileges, utilize different connection strings within the modules, and so on.

In code, doing this is reflected by setting the default schema name in the `OnModelCreating` method of each `DbContext`. Here's the `ProductContext` class:

```
namespace REPR.Products.Data;
public class ProductContext : DbContext
{
    public ProductContext(DbContextOptions<ProductContext> options)
        : base(options) { }

    protected override void OnModelCreating(ModelBuilder modelBuilder)
    {
        base.OnModelCreating(modelBuilder);
        modelBuilder.HasDefaultSchema(Constants.ModuleName.ToLower());
    }
    public DbSet<Product> Products => Set<Product>();
}
```

The preceding code makes all ProductContext's tables part of the products schema.

We then apply the same for the basket module:

```
namespace REPR.Baskets.Data;
public class BasketContext : DbContext
{
    public BasketContext(DbContextOptions<BasketContext> options)
        : base(options) { }

    public DbSet<BasketItem> Items => Set<BasketItem>();
    public DbSet<Product> Products => Set<Product>();

    protected override void OnModelCreating(ModelBuilder modelBuilder)
    {
        base.OnModelCreating(modelBuilder);
        modelBuilder.HasDefaultSchema(Constants.ModuleName.ToLower());
        modelBuilder
            .Entity<BasketItem>()
            .HasKey(x => new { x.CustomerId, x.ProductId })
        ;
    }
}
```

The preceding code makes all BasketContext's tables part of the baskets schema.

Due to the schema, both contexts are safe from hindering the other. But wait! Both contexts have a Products table; what happens then? The catalog module uses the products.products table, while the basket module uses the baskets.products table. Different schema, different tables, case closed!

We can apply these notions to more than Modular Monoliths as it is general SQL Server and EF Core knowledge.

If you are using another relational database engine that does not offer schema or a NoSQL database, you must also think about this. Each NoSQL database has different ways to think about the data, and it would be impossible to cover them all here. The important piece is to find a discriminator that segregates the data of your modules. At the limit, it can even be one different database per module; however, this increases the operational complexity of the application.

Next, we explore the message broker.

The message broker

To handle the integration events between the catalog and the basket modules, I decided to pick MassTransit. To quote their GitHub project:

> *MassTransit is a free, open-source distributed application framework for .NET. MassTransit makes it easy to create applications and services that leverage message-based, loosely-coupled asynchronous communication for higher availability, reliability, and scalability.*

I picked MassTransit because it is a popular project with 6,400 GitHub stars as of Q1 2024 and counting. It supports many providers, including in-memory, and offers many features that meet and exceed our needs.

Once again, we could have used anything. For example, MediatR could have also done the job.

The `API` project—the aggregator—and the modules depend on the following NuGet package to use MassTransit:

```
<PackageReference Include="MassTransit" Version="8.1.0" />
```

Our usage is very simple; the aggregator registers and configures MassTransit like this:

```
builder.Services.AddMassTransit(x =>
{
    x.SetKebabCaseEndpointNameFormatter();
    x.UsingInMemory((context, cfg) =>
    {
        cfg.ConfigureEndpoints(context);
    });

    x.AddBasketModuleConsumers();
});
```

The highlighted line delegates the registration of event consumers to the basket module. The `AddBasketModuleConsumers` method is part of the `BasketModuleExtensions` class and contains the following code:

```
public static void AddBasketModuleConsumers(this IRegistrationConfigurator
configurator)
{
    configurator.AddConsumers(typeof(ProductEventsConsumers));
}
```

The `ProductEventsConsumers` class manages the two events. The `AddConsumers` method is part of MassTransit. We explore the `ProductEventsConsumers` class in the project section.

We would register the event consumers of other modules here if we had more. Yet the delegation of that registration to each module makes it modular.

Next, we write some C# code to transform our microservices application into a Modular Monolith.

Project – Modular Monolith

This project has the same building block as *Chapter 18* and *Chapter 19*, but we use the Modular Monolith approach. On top of the previous versions, we leverage events to enable the shopping basket to validate the existence of a product before allowing customers to add it to their shopping basket.

The complete source code is available on GitHub: `https://adpg.link/gyds`.

The test projects in the solution are empty. They only exist for the organizational aspect of the solution. As an exercise, you can migrate the tests from *Chapter 18* and adapt them to this new architectural style.

Let's start with the communication piece.

Sending events from the catalog module

For the catalog to communicate the events that the basket module needs, it must define the following new operations:

- Create products
- Delete products

Here are the API contracts we must create in the `Products.Contracts` project to support those two operations:

```
namespace Products.Contracts;
public record class CreateProductCommand(string Name, decimal UnitPrice);
public record class CreateProductResponse(int Id, string Name, decimal
UnitPrice);
public record class DeleteProductCommand(int ProductId);
public record class DeleteProductResponse(int Id, string Name, decimal
UnitPrice);
```

The API contracts should look very familiar by now and are similar to those from previous chapters. We then need the following two event contracts:

```
namespace Products.Contracts;
```

```
public record class ProductCreated(int Id, string Name, decimal UnitPrice);
public record class ProductDeleted(int Id);
```

The two event classes are also very straightforward, but their name is in the past tense because an event happened in the past. When the module creates the product, it notifies its subscribers that a product was created (in the past). Exactly like we studied in *Chapter 19, Introduction to Microservices Architecture*. Moreover, the events are simple data containers, like an API contract—a DTO—is.

How do we send those events? Let's have a look at the `CreateProductHandler` class:

```
namespace Products.Features;
public class CreateProductHandler
{
    private readonly ProductContext _db;
    private readonly CreateProductMapper _mapper;
    private readonly IBus _bus;

    public CreateProductHandler(ProductContext db, CreateProductMapper mapper,
IBus bus)
    {
        _db = db ?? throw new ArgumentNullException(nameof(db));
        _mapper = mapper ?? throw new ArgumentNullException(nameof(mapper));
        _bus = bus ?? throw new ArgumentNullException(nameof(bus));
    }

    public async Task<CreateProductResponse> HandleAsync(CreateProductCommand
command, CancellationToken cancellationToken)
    {
        var product = _mapper.Map(command);
        var entry = _db.Products.Add(product);
        await _db.SaveChangesAsync(cancellationToken);

        var productCreated = _mapper.MapToIntegrationEvent(entry.Entity);
        await _bus.Publish(productCreated, CancellationToken.None);

        var response = _mapper.MapToResponse(entry.Entity);
        return response;
    }
}
```

In the preceding code, we inject an `IBus` interface from MassTransit in the `CreateProductHandler` class. We also inject an object mapper and an EF Core `ProductContext`.

The `HandleAsync` method does the following:

1. Creates the product and saves it to the database.
2. Publishes a `ProductCreated` event (highlighted code).
3. Returns a `CreateProductResponse` instance based on the new product.

The `Publish` method sends the event to the configured pipe, which is in memory in our case. The code passes a `CancellationToken.None` argument here because we don't want this operation to be canceled by any external force because the change is already saved in the database.

Because of the mapping code, the publishing code may be hard to understand in a book. The `MapToIntegrationEvent` method converts a `Product` object to a `ProductCreated` instance, so the `productCreated` variable is of type `ProductCreated`. Here's the *Mapperly* mapper class with that method highlighted:

```
namespace Products.Features;
[Mapper]
public partial class CreateProductMapper
{
    public partial Product Map(CreateProductCommand product);
    public partial ProductCreated MapToIntegrationEvent(Product product);
    public partial CreateProductResponse MapToResponse(Product product);
}
```

The `DeleteProductHandler` class follows a similar pattern but publishes the `ProductDeleted` event instead.

Now, let's explore how the basket module consumes those events.

Consuming the events from the basket module

The basket module wants to cache existing products. We can achieve this in different ways. In this case, we create the following `Product` class that we persist in the database:

```
namespace Baskets.Data;
public record class Product(int Id);
```

To make use of it, we must expose the following property from the `BasketContext` class:

```
public DbSet<Product> Products => Set<Product>();
```

Then, we can start to leverage this cache.

Firstly, we must populate it when the catalog module creates a product and remove that product when deleted. The `ProductEventsConsumers` class handles both events. Here's the skeleton of this class:

```
using Products.Contracts;
namespace Baskets.Features;
```

```
public class ProductEventsConsumers : IConsumer<ProductCreated>,
IConsumer<ProductDeleted>
{
    private readonly BasketContext _db;
    private readonly ILogger _logger;
    public ProductEventsConsumers(BasketContext db,
ILogger<ProductEventsConsumers> logger)
    {
        _db = db ?? throw new ArgumentNullException(nameof(db));
        _logger = logger ?? throw new ArgumentNullException(nameof(logger));
    }

    public async Task Consume(ConsumeContext<ProductCreated> context)
    {...}
    public async Task Consume(ConsumeContext<ProductDeleted> context)
    {...}
}
```

The highlighted code represents the two event handlers. The `IConsumer<TMessage>` interface contains the `Consume` method. Implementing the interface twice with a different `TMessage` generic parameter prescribes implementing the two `Consume` methods in the `ProductEventsConsumers` class. Each method handles its own event.

When a product is created in the product module, the following method is executed in the basket module (I removed the logging code for brevity):

```
public async Task Consume(ConsumeContext<ProductCreated> context)
{
    var product = await _db.Products.FirstOrDefaultAsync(
        x => x.Id == context.Message.Id,
        cancellationToken: context.CancellationToken
    );
    if (product is not null)
    {
        return;
    }
    _db.Products.Add(new(context.Message.Id));
    await _db.SaveChangesAsync();
}
```

The preceding code adds a new product to the database if it does not exist. If it does exist, it does nothing.

We could add telemetry here to log the conflict. For example, the module could log that it received the event more than once. That could allow us to identify if there is an issue in the system or with the broker configuration.

Here's the flow of what happens when an employee creates a new product:

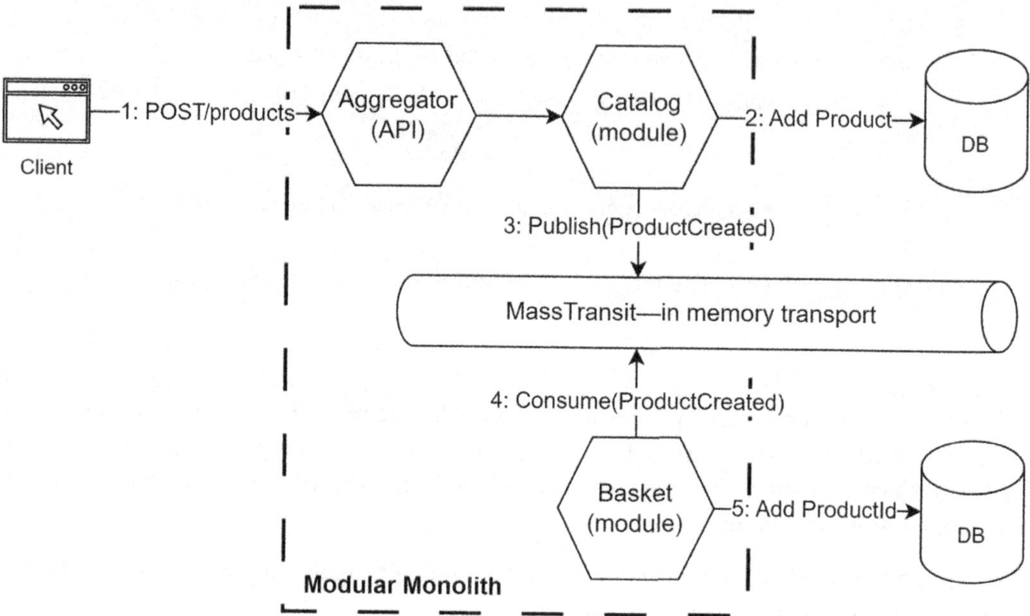

Figure 20.9: A diagram showcasing the sequence of operations when someone adds a product to the system

Let's review the operations:

1. A client sends a POST request to the API (the aggregator application). The catalog module receives the request.
2. The catalog creates the product and adds it to the database.
3. The catalog then publishes the `ProductCreated` event using MassTransit.
4. In the basket module, the `Consume` method of the `ProductEventsConsumers` class gets called by MassTransit in reaction to the `ProductCreated` event.
5. The basket module adds the product's identifier to the database; its materialized view.

Now that we know how the `ProductEventsConsumers` class handles the `ProductCreated` events, let's explore how to handle the `ProductDeleted` events (logging code omitted for brevity):

```
public async Task Consume(ConsumeContext<ProductDeleted> context)
{
    var item = await _db.Products.FirstOrDefaultAsync(
        x => x.Id == context.Message.Id,
```

```
            cancellationToken: context.CancellationToken
        );
        if (item is null)
        {
            return;
        }

        // Remove the products from existing baskets
        var existingItemInCarts = _db.Items
            .Where(x => x.ProductId == context.Message.Id);
        var count = existingItemInCarts.Count();
        _db.Items.RemoveRange(existingItemInCarts);

        // Remove the product from the internal cache
        _db.Products.Remove(item);

        // Save the changes
        await _db.SaveChangesAsync();
    }
```

The preceding `Consume` method removes the products from people's shopping baskets and the materialized view. If the product does not exist, the method does nothing because there's nothing to handle.

A similar flow happens when an employee deletes a product from the catalog and publishes a `ProductDeleted` event. The basket module then reacts to the event and updates its cache (materialized view).

Now that we have explored this exciting part of the project, let's look at the aggregator.

Inside the aggregator

The aggregator application is like an empty shell that loads the other assemblies and configures the cross-cutting concerns. It references the modules, then assembles and boots the application. Here's the first part of the `Program.cs` file:

```
using FluentValidation;
using FluentValidation.AspNetCore;
using MassTransit;
using API.HttpClient;
using Baskets;
using Products;
using System.Reflection;

var builder = WebApplication.CreateBuilder(args);
```

```
// Register fluent validation
builder.AddFluentValidationEndpointFilter();
builder.Services
    .AddFluentValidationAutoValidation()
    .AddValidatorsFromAssemblies(new[] {
        Assembly.GetExecutingAssembly(),
        Assembly.GetAssembly(typeof(BasketModuleExtensions)),
        Assembly.GetAssembly(typeof(ProductsModuleExtensions)),
    })
;

builder.AddApiHttpClient();
builder.AddExceptionMapper();
builder
    .AddBasketModule()
    .AddProductsModule()
;
builder.Services.AddMassTransit(x =>
{
    x.SetKebabCaseEndpointNameFormatter();
    x.UsingInMemory((context, cfg) =>
    {
        cfg.ConfigureEndpoints(context);
    });

    x.AddBasketModuleConsumers();
});
```

The preceding code registers the following:

- *FluentValidation*; it also scans the assemblies for validators
- The `IWebClient` interface that we use to seed the database next (the `AddApiHttpClient` method).
- *ExceptionMapper*
- The modules' dependencies (highlighted), which we add to the aggregator's IoC container so it is the one that manages the object graph for the whole application, including when injecting dependencies in the modules
- *MassTransit*; it also registers the consumers from the basket module (highlighted)

The container we register those dependencies into is also used for and by the modules because the aggregator is the host, the `WebApplication`. Those dependencies are shared across the modules.

The second part of the Program.cs file is the following:

```
var app = builder.Build();
app.UseExceptionMapper();
app
    .MapBasketModule()
    .MapProductsModule()
;

// Convenience endpoint, seeding the catalog
app.MapGet("/", async (IWebClient client, CancellationToken cancellationToken)
=>
{
    await client.Catalog.CreateProductAsync(new("Banana", 0.30m),
cancellationToken);
    await client.Catalog.CreateProductAsync(new("Apple", 0.79m),
cancellationToken);
    await client.Catalog.CreateProductAsync(new("Habanero Pepper", 0.99m),
cancellationToken);
    return new
    {
        Message = "Application started and catalog seeded. Do not refresh this
page, or it will reseed the catalog."
    };
});

app.Run();
```

The preceding code registers the ExceptionMapper middleware, then the modules. It also adds a seeding endpoint (highlighted). If you remember, we were seeding the database using the DbContext in the previous versions. However, since the basket module needs to receive the events from the catalog to build a materialized view, it is more convenient to seed the database through the catalog module. In this version, the program seeds the database when a client hits the / endpoint. By default, when starting the application, Visual Studio should open a browser at that URL, which will seed the database.

Seeding the database by sending a GET request to the / endpoint is very convenient for an academic scenario where we use in-memory databases. However, this could be disastrous in a production environment because it would reseed the database whenever someone hits that endpoint.

Let's explore the IWebClient next.

Exploring the REST API HttpClient

In the shared directory, the API.HttpClient project contains the REST API client code. The code is very similar to the previous project, but the IProductsClient now exposes a create and delete method (highlighted):

```
using Refit;
using Products.Contracts;

namespace API.HttpClient;

public interface IProductsClient
{
    [Get("/products/{query.ProductId}")]
    Task<FetchOneProductResponse> FetchProductAsync(
        FetchOneProductQuery query,
        CancellationToken cancellationToken);

    [Get("/products")]
    Task<FetchAllProductsResponse> FetchProductsAsync(
        CancellationToken cancellationToken);

    [Post("/products")]
    Task<CreateProductResponse> CreateProductAsync(
        CreateProductCommand command,
        CancellationToken cancellationToken);

    [Delete("/products/{command.ProductId}")]
    Task<DeleteProductResponse> DeleteProductAsync(
        DeleteProductCommand command,
        CancellationToken cancellationToken);
}
```

On top of this, the project only references the Contracts projects, limiting its dependencies to the classes it needs. It does not reference the complete modules anymore. This makes this project easy to reuse. For example, we could build another project, like a UI, then reference and use this typed client to query the API (Modular Monolith) from that .NET UI.

Since we created this client for a microservices application, we have two base downstream service URLs—one for the product microservice and one for the basket microservice. This nuance suits us well since we may want to migrate our monolith to microservices later.

In the meantime, all we have to do is set the two keys to the same host, like the following `appsettings.json` file from the aggregator:

```
{
  "Downstream": {
    "Baskets": {
      "BaseAddress": "https://localhost:7164/"
    },
    "Products": {
      "BaseAddress": "https://localhost:7164/"
    }
  }
}
```

With these configurations, the `AddApiHttpClient` method configures two `HttpClient` instances with the same `BaseAddress` value.

We use Refit here, like we did in *Chapter 19, Introduction to Microservices Architecture.*

Here's the code that registers the `HttpClient`:

```
using Microsoft.AspNetCore.Builder;
using Microsoft.Extensions.Configuration;
using Microsoft.Extensions.DependencyInjection;
using Refit;

namespace API.HttpClient;
public static class ApiHttpClientExtensions
{
    public static WebApplicationBuilder AddApiHttpClient(this
WebApplicationBuilder builder)
    {
        const string basketsBaseAddressKey = "Downstream:Baskets:BaseAddress";
        const string productsBaseAddressKey = "Downstream:Products:BaseAddress";
        var basketsBaseAddress = builder.Configuration
            .GetValue<string>(basketsBaseAddressKey) ?? throw new
BaseAddressNotFoundException(basketsBaseAddressKey);
        var productsBaseAddress = builder.Configuration
            .GetValue<string>(productsBaseAddressKey) ?? throw new
BaseAddressNotFoundException(productsBaseAddressKey);
```

```
        builder.Services
            .AddRefitClient<IBasketsClient>()
            .ConfigureHttpClient(c => c.BaseAddress = new
Uri(basketsBaseAddress))
        ;
        builder.Services
            .AddRefitClient<IProductsClient>()
            .ConfigureHttpClient(c => c.BaseAddress = new
Uri(productsBaseAddress))
        ;
        builder.Services.AddTransient<IWebClient, DefaultWebClient>();

        return builder;
    }
}
```

And voilà, we have a functional typed client we can reuse and a working Modular Monolith. Let's test this out next.

Sending HTTP requests to the API

Now that we have a working Modular Monolith, we can reuse similar HTTP requests to the previous versions.

At the root of the API project, we can use the following:

- The `API-Products.http` file contains requests to the product module
- The `API-Baskets.http` file contains requests to the basket module

A new outcome in this API compared to the previous versions is when we try to add a product that does not exist in the catalog to our basket, like the following request:

```
POST https://localhost:7164/baskets
Content-Type: application/json

{
    "customerId": 1,
    "productId": 5,
    "quantity": 99
}
```

The API returns the following (since the product 5 does not exist):

```
HTTP/1.1 400 Bad Request
Content-Type: application/problem+json
```

```
{
  "type": "https://tools.ietf.org/html/rfc9110#section-15.5.1",
  "title": "One or more validation errors occurred.",
  "status": 400,
  "errors": {
    "productId": [
      "The Product does not exist."
    ]
  }
}
```

That error confirms that the validation works as expected. But how are we validating this?

Validating the existence of a product

In the *add item* feature, the `AddItemValidator` class ensures the product exists while validating the `AddItemCommand` object. To achieve this, we leverage the `MustAsync` and `WithMessage` methods from `FluentValidation`. Here's the code:

```
namespace REPR.Baskets.Features;
public class AddItemValidator : AbstractValidator<AddItemCommand>
{
    private readonly BasketContext _db;
    public AddItemValidator(BasketContext db)
    {
        _db = db ?? throw new ArgumentNullException(nameof(db));

        RuleFor(x => x.CustomerId).GreaterThan(0);
        RuleFor(x => x.ProductId)
            .GreaterThan(0)
            .MustAsync(ProductExistsAsync)
            .WithMessage("The Product does not exist.")
        ;
        RuleFor(x => x.Quantity).GreaterThan(0);
    }

    private async Task<bool> ProductExistsAsync(int productId,
CancellationToken cancellationToken)
    {
        var product = await _db.Products
            .FirstOrDefaultAsync(x => x.Id == productId, cancellationToken);
```

```
            return product is not null;
        }
}
```

The preceding code implements the same rules as the previous versions but also calls the `ProductExistsAsync` method that fetches the requested product from the cache. If the result is `false`, the validation fails with the message *"The Product does not exist."*

Here's the resulting flow of this change:

1. The client calls the API.
2. The validation middleware calls the validator.
3. The validator fetches the record from the database and validates its existence.
4. If the product does not exist, the request is short-circuited here and returned to the client. Otherwise, it continues to the `AddItemHandler` class.

With this in place, we covered all new scenarios from this project. We also explored how the aggregator connects the modules together and how easy it is to keep our modules independent.

Next, we get the BFF back into the project and explore how to transition our Modular Monolith to a microservices architecture.

Transitioning to microservices

You don't have to transition your monolith to microservices; deploying a monolith is fine if it fits your needs. However, if ever you need to, you could shield your aggregator with a gateway or a reverse proxy so you can extract modules into their own microservices and reroute the requests without impacting the clients. This would also allow you to gradually transfer the traffic to the new service while keeping the monolith intact in case of an unexpected failure.

In a Modular Monolith, the aggregator registers most dependencies, so when migrating, you must also migrate this shared setup. One way to not duplicate code would be to create and reference a shared assembly containing those registrations. This makes it easier to manage the dependencies and shared configurations, but it is also coupling between the microservices and the aggregator. Leveraging the code of this shared assembly is even easier when the microservices are part of the same mono-repo; you can reference the project directly without managing a NuGet package. Yet, when you update the library, it updates all microservices and the monolith, voiding the deployment independence of each application, so be careful what code you share.

Once again, consider keeping the monolith intact versus the operational complexity that deploying microservices would bring.

In the solution, the Modular Monolith project is a migration of *Chapter 19*'s code and includes the BFF implementation. The code and the logic are almost the same. The BFF project leverages the `API.HttpClient` project and configures the downstream base addresses in its `appsettings.Development.json` file. The `BFF.http` file at the root of the project contains a few requests to test the application.

The code is available on GitHub. I suggest playing with the live application, which will yield a better result than copying the code in the book a second time. The relationships between the projects are also more evident in Visual Studio than written in a book. Feel free to refactor the projects, add tests, or add features. The best way to learn is to practice!

Next, let's have a look at the challenges and pitfalls of Modular Monoliths.

Challenges and pitfalls

It is a misconception that monoliths are only suitable for small projects or small teams. A well-built monolith can go a long way, which is what a modular structure and a good analysis bring. Modular Monoliths can be very powerful and work well for different sizes of projects.

It is essential to consider the pros and cons of each approach when selecting the application pattern for a project. Maybe a cloud-native, serverless, microservices application is what your next project needs, but perhaps a well-designed Modular Monolith would achieve the same performance at a tremendously lower cost. As a rule of thumb, start with the simplest approach.

To help you decide if a Modular Monolith is the way to go, here are some potential challenges and how to avoid or mitigate them:

Challenges and pitfalls	Mitigating actions
Too much complexity within a module: One risk is making the modules too complex. Like any piece of code, it becomes harder to manage a module if it does too many things. Moreover, the bigger the software, the more chance the shiny initial design starts to bleed into a Big Ball of Mud.	We can avoid this by keeping each module focused on a specific part of the domain and by applying the SRP. Don't be scared of refactoring the problematic module before it's too late.
Poorly defined module boundaries: If the boundaries between modules are unclear, it can create problems. For example, if two modules do similar things, it can confuse developers and lead to one part of the system depending on the wrong module. Another example is when two modules that should be part of the same bounded context are separated. In that case, the chances are that the two modules will interact a lot with each other, creating chattiness and significantly increasing the coupling between them.	We avoid this with good planning, domain analysis, and ensuring each module has only one specific job (SRP). If you spot such an issue, refactor the system as soon as possible so the technical debt does not linger. Technical debt will increase the number of problems the system will face over time and will decrease your ability to refactor those modules—more tight coupling means harder refactoring.

Scaling: Even though Modular Monoliths are easier to manage, they carry the monolith issues when they must scale up. We must deploy the whole application, so we can't scale modules independently. Moreover, even if modules own their data, they probably share one database, which must also be scaled as a whole.	If scaling the whole system is impossible, we can migrate specific modules to microservices. We can also extract in-memory services to distributed ones, like using a distributed cache or a cloud-based event broker. We can have compute- and data-intensive modules use a separate database to partially scale independently. However, these solutions make the deployment and the infrastructure more complex, which defeats the monolith's benefits.
Eventual consistency: Keeping data in sync between modules can be challenging. A drawback of using event-driven architecture and asynchronous communication.	To mitigate that, we can use an in-memory message broker that is low-latency and high-fidelity (no network involved), which is an excellent first step towards learning and dealing with eventual consistency and breaking the monolith into microservices (if the transition is ever needed). However, a more resilient broker is recommended for production so the system resists failures.
Transition to microservices: Moving an application to microservices architecture after the fact can be a significant undertaking.	Starting with an event-powered Modular Monolith should make the journey less painful.

Table 20.1: Modular Monolith challenges and mitigating actions

While Modular Monoliths offer many benefits, they can also pose challenges. The key is to plan well, keep things simple, and be ready to adapt as the program evolves.

Summary

In this chapter, we learned about the Modular Monolith architectural style, which blends the simplicity of monolithic architectures with the flexibility of microservices. This architectural style organizes software applications into distinct, loosely coupled modules, each responsible for a specific business capability. Unlike microservices, we deploy these modules as a single unit, like a monolith.

We discussed the benefits of Modular Monoliths, including easier overall management, development, and testing experiences, as well as improved cost-effectiveness and a simplified deployment model.

We saw that a Modular Monolith comprises modules, a module aggregator, and an inter-module communication infrastructure—event-driven in this case.

We learned that analyzing the domain, designing the modules, and identifying the interactions between modules before starting the development improves the chances of success of the product.

We touched on transitioning from a Modular Monolith to a microservices architecture, which involves extracting modules into separate microservices and rerouting requests.

We also highlighted the importance of knowing potential challenges and pitfalls. These include module complexity, poorly defined module boundaries, scaling limitations, and eventual consistency caused by an asynchronous communication model.

Questions

Let's take a look at a few practice questions:

1. What are the core principles of a Modular Monolith?
2. What are the advantages of Modular Monoliths?
3. What are traditional Monoliths?
4. Are poorly defined module boundaries beneficial to a Modular Monolith?
5. Is it true that transitioning an application to microservices architecture can be a significant undertaking?

Further reading

Here is a link to build upon what we learned in the chapter:

- Microservices Aggregation (Modular Monolith): `https://adpg.link/zznM`
- When (modular) monolith is the better way to build software: `https://adpg.link/KBGB`
- Source code: `https://adpg.link/gyds`

Answers

1. We must treat each module as a microservice and deploy the application as a single unit—a monolith.
2. A few moving parts make the application simpler. Each module is independent, making modules loosely coupled. Its simple deployment model leads to ease of deployment.
3. Traditional monolithic architectures built the application as a single, indivisible unit, often resulting in tightly coupled functionalities. These were usually built using layers.
4. False. Poorly defined module boundaries hinder the health of the application.
5. True. Even if a well-conceived Modular Monolith can help, the transition will be a journey.

An end is simply a new beginning

This may be the end of the book, but it is also the continuation of your journey into software architecture and design. I hope you found this to be a refreshing view of design patterns and how to design SOLID apps.

Depending on your goals and current situation, you may want to explore one or more application-scale design patterns in more depth, start your next personal project, start a business, apply for a new job, or all of those. No matter your goals, keep in mind that designing software is technical but also an art. There is rarely one way to implement a feature but multiple acceptable ways. Every decision has trade-offs, and experience is your best friend, so keep programming, learn from your mistakes, become better, and continue. The path to mastery is a continuous learning loop. Remember that we are all born knowing next to nothing, so not knowing something is expected; we need to learn. Please ask questions, read, experiment, learn, and share your knowledge with others. Explaining a concept to someone is extremely rewarding and reinforces your own learning and knowledge.

Now that this book is complete, you may find interesting articles on my blog (`https://adpg.link/blog`). Feel free to reach out on Discord, X `@CarlHugoM` (`https://adpg.link/twit`), or LinkedIn (`https://adpg.link/edin`). I hope you found the book educational and approachable and that you learned many things. I wish you success in your career.

Learn more on Discord

To join the Discord community for this book – where you can share feedback, ask questions to the author, and learn about new releases – follow the QR code below:

`https://packt.link/ArchitectingASPNETCoreApps3e`

Other Books You May Enjoy

If you enjoyed this book, you may be interested in these other books by Packt:

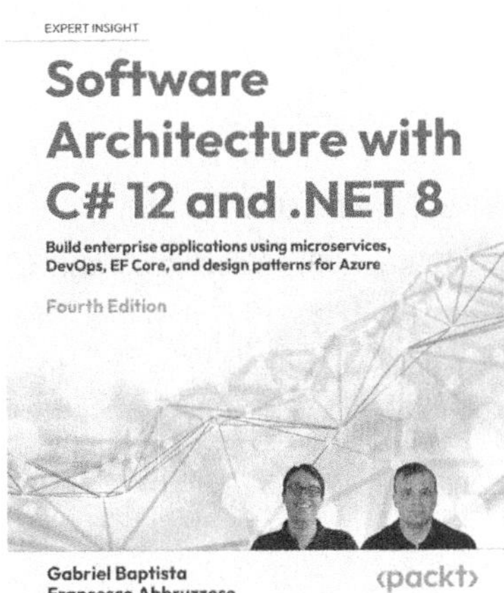

Software Architecture with C# 12 and .NET 8, Fourth Edition

Gabriel Baptista

Francesco Abbruzzese

ISBN: 9781805127659

- Program and maintain Azure DevOps and explore GitHub Projects
- Manage software requirements to design functional and non-functional needs
- Apply architectural approaches such as layered architecture and domain-driven design
- Make effective choices between cloud-based and data storage solutions
- Implement resilient frontend microservices, worker microservices, and distributed transactions
- Understand when to use test-driven development (TDD) and alternative approaches
- Choose the best option for cloud development, from IaaS to Serverless

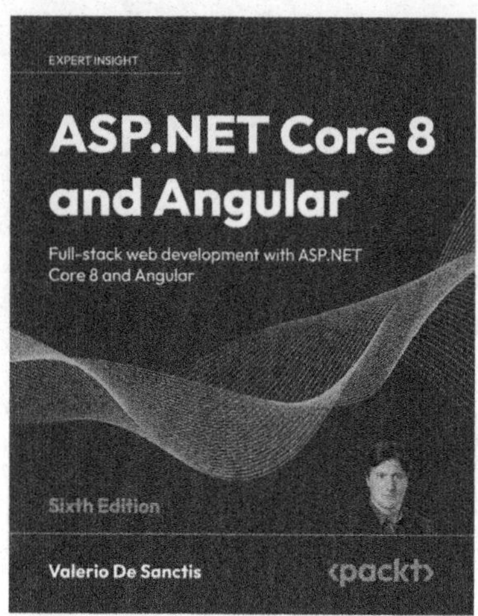

ASP.NET Core 8 and Angular, Sixth Edition

Valerio De Sanctis

ISBN: 9781805129936

- Explore the new Angular and ASP.NET Core template with Visual Studio 2022
- Use modern interfaces and patterns such as the HTML5 pushState API, webhooks, and UI data bindings
- Add real-time capabilities to Angular apps with SignalR and gRPC
- Implement authentication and authorization using JWTs
- Perform DBMS structured logging using providers such as SeriLog
- Convert a standard web application to a progressive web application (PWA)
- Deploy an Angular app to Azure Static Web Apps
- Add GraphQL support to back-end and front-end using HotChocolate and Apollo Angular

C# 12 and .NET 8 – Modern Cross-Platform Development Fundamentals, Eighth Edition

Mark Price

ISBN: 9781837635870

- Discover C# 12's new features, including aliasing any type and primary constructors
- Try out the native AOT publish capability for ASP.NET Core 8 Minimal APIs web services
- Build rich web experiences using Blazor Full Stack, Razor Pages, and other ASP.NET Core features
- Integrate and update databases in your apps using Entity Framework Core models
- Query and manipulate data using LINQ
- Build and consume powerful services using Web API and Minimal API

Packt is searching for authors like you

If you're interested in becoming an author for Packt, please visit `authors.packtpub.com` and apply today. We have worked with thousands of developers and tech professionals, just like you, to help them share their insight with the global tech community. You can make a general application, apply for a specific hot topic that we are recruiting an author for, or submit your own idea.

Share your thoughts

Now you've finished *Architecting ASP.NET Core Applications, Third Edition*, we'd love to hear your thoughts! Scan the QR code below to go straight to the Amazon review page for this book and share your feedback or leave a review on the site that you purchased it from.

https://packt.link/r/1805123386

Your review is important to us and the tech community and will help us make sure we're delivering excellent quality content.

Index

Symbols

A

D

E

N

O

Download a free PDF copy of this book

Thanks for purchasing this book!

Do you like to read on the go but are unable to carry your print books everywhere?

Is your eBook purchase not compatible with the device of your choice?

Don't worry, now with every Packt book you get a DRM-free PDF version of that book at no cost.

Read anywhere, any place, on any device. Search, copy, and paste code from your favorite technical books directly into your application.

The perks don't stop there, you can get exclusive access to discounts, newsletters, and great free content in your inbox daily

Follow these simple steps to get the benefits:

1. Scan the QR code or visit the link below

`https://packt.link/free-ebook/9781805123385`

2. Submit your proof of purchase
3. That's it! We'll send your free PDF and other benefits to your email directly

Made in the USA
Las Vegas, NV
26 August 2024